MATHEMATICS METHODS FOR ELEMENTARY AND MIDDLE SCHOOL TEACHERS

MATHEMATICS METHODS FOR ELEMENTARY AND MIDDLE SCHOOL TEACHERS

Fourth Edition

Mary M. Hatfield
Professor Emeritus, Arizona State University

Nancy Tanner Edwards
Missouri Western State College

Gary G. Bitter
Arizona State University

Jean Morrow
Emporia State University

John Wiley & Sons, Inc.
New York / Chichester / Weinheim / Brisbane / Singapore / Toronto

Acquisitions Editor: Marian Provenzano
Marketing Manager: Catherine Beckham
Production Editor: Patricia McFadden

This book was set in 10/12 Palatino by Omegatype Typography, Inc. and printed and bound by Courier Companies, Inc. The cover was printed by Phoenix Color.

This book is printed on acid-free paper. ∞

Library of Congress Cataloging-in-Publication Data

Mathematics methods for elementary and middle school teachers. — 4th ed. / Mary M. Hatfield...[et al.]
p. cm.
Includes bibliographical references and index.
ISBN 0-471-36544-0
1. Mathematics—Study and teaching (Elementary) 2. Mathematics—Study and teaching (Middle school) I. Hatfield, Mary M.
QA135.5.M36955 2000
372.7—dc21 99–40457
CIP

Credits appear on page 429, which constitutes a continuation of the copyright page.

ISBN 0-471-36544-0

Printed in the United States of America

10 9 8 7 6 5 4 3 2 1

We dedicate this edition and the CD-ROM to these teachers in the video vignettes with warm thanks for sharing their expertise and classrooms with us: Charles Addcox, Brenda Arroyos, Edie Bennett, Judy Boch, Nora Castenda, Vivian Cordoba, Dan Dillon, Valerie Jones, Linda Scheppe, Janice Shanks, Cheryl Thomas, and Olga Torres.

Contents

List of Text Activities

Calculators

Computers

Internet Searches

Cultural Relevance

Cultural Contributions

ESTIMATION

Estimation

Manipulatives

Mathematical Connections

MENTAL MATH

Mental Math

PORTFOLIO

Portfolio Assessment

PROBLEM SOLVING Problem Solving

List of CD-ROM Activities

Calculators

Check Your Mathematics Knowledge

Computers

Computer Graphing

Computer Spreadsheet/Database

Computer Software Resources

Cultural Relevance

Estimation

Manipulatives

Mathematical Connections

Mental Math

Portfolio Assessments

Position Papers

Problem Solving

Video Vignettes

[in order of appearance in book]

Activities with Video Vignettes

Preface

ABOUT THE BOOK

Mathematics Methods for Elementary and Middle School Teachers, Fourth Edition, provides preservice and in-service kindergarten through grade-eight teachers with ideas, techniques, and approaches to teaching mathematics appropriate for the twenty-first century. The book emphasizes manipulatives, problem solving, mathematical connections, estimation, mental math, portfolio and journal assessment, cultural diversity, calculators, and computers with Internet searches and CD-ROM video vignettes of actual teaching in a variety of exemplary classrooms. All are an integral part of teaching mathematics. These topics are not addressed as separate issues. As is appropriate, throughout the entire book they are treated as part of the developmental learning process.

A CD-ROM disk is provided for each reader. It includes extended learning activities, 18 video vignettes of classroom teaching, database and spreadsheet templates, and additional exercises and bibliographies for each chapter. Internet searches and commercial software programs are given as additional resources. Pertinent to today's world, a companion web site has been developed at www.wiley.com/college/hatfield. This site updates the book material continually to make it a vital resource for teachers in a quickly changing information society, and provides additional resources to enhance students' preparedness.

The book models the approach of concrete-to-abstract developmental learning. Manipulatives are emphasized throughout the book. Base 10 blocks, geoboards, attribute blocks, Cuisenaire rods, and pattern blocks are a few of the concrete materials emphasized. In addition, paper models of many of the manipulatives are shown in reduced size in the Appendix and are found in full size on the CD-ROM for readers' personal use. The CD-ROM permits readers to print additional models for their classrooms.

SPECIAL FEATURES

Journal and portfolio assessment techniques are included in each chapter where appropriate. Actual children's work is provided for preservice and in-service teachers to review and evaluate. Included in each discussion are the needs of different types of special needs learners and methods of correcting common student errors. Teachers who work with special needs students will find these materials helpful, with direct application for classroom use.

Exercises for preservice and in-service teachers are provided at three levels in each chapter, building to the higher-order thinking skills required of today's teachers. **Extended exercises** and **bibliographies** are provided on the CD-ROM. The instructor can select those most appropriate. This option makes it possible to match student work to unique situations.

The National Council of Teachers of Mathematics (NCTM) *Principles and Standards for School Mathematics* (2000) and the *Curriculum and Evaluation Standards for School Mathematics* (1989) are provided in each chapter to help relate topics in the elementary mathematics curriculum to these standards. They are integrated into the development of the mathematics concepts of selected activities clearly showing the relationships to the standards.

Activities are provided throughout the book for the following categories:

Problem Solving—emphasizes strategies and higher-order thinking

Manipulatives—uses concrete experiences for developing concepts

Calculators—emphasizes problem solving and de-emphasizes tedious computations

Mental Math—builds methods of doing computation mentally

Cultural Relevance—emphasizes activities to illustrate historical cultural contributions to mathematics along with activities promoting equity in mathematics

Computers, *spreadsheets, databases, and graphing*—uses exploration in problem solving

Estimation—emphasizes techniques to determine reasonable answers

Mathematical Connections—encourages interdisciplinary approaches to learning mathematics

Computers, *Internet*—emphasizes exploration to find current resources in mathematics for the continually changing needs of students

Children's Literature—emphasizes the interconnectedness of mathematics with the thoughts and experiences of language in the child's world

Portfolio and Journal Assessment—uses actual children's work and explanations to help teachers analyze the development of children's mathematical thinking and explore rubric scoring guides for classroom use

Video Vignettes—emphasizes the power of modeling good teaching practices for quality mathematical understanding

The following pictures will be used to alert the reader to the emphasis of each category when it appears throughout the text.

CALCULATORS

COMPUTERS

ESTIMATION

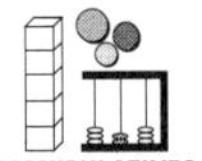
MANIPULATIVES

PROBLEM SOLVING

MATHEMATICAL CONNECTIONS

MENTAL MATH

CULTURAL RELEVANCE

PORTFOLIO

INTERNET SEARCHES

VIDEO VIGNETTE

ORGANIZATION

- The book has 15 chapters. Chapter 1 includes the past, present, and future of elementary mathematics. The philosophy is explored for emphasizing problem solving, manipulatives, the computer, the calculator, estimation, and mental math.
- Chapter 2 discusses culturally relevant mathematics with the acknowledgement that all cultures of our world have contributed to the discoveries of mathematics. The book attempts to bring students' cultural heritage to various teaching situations. Culture-relevant assessment materials are included throughout the book. Equity for all students to learn quality mathematics is modeled.
- Chapter 3 discusses how children learn mathematics. Learning theories are briefly reviewed in relation to effective teaching models and lesson plan development, including brain research studies as applied to the learning of mathematics. The chapter emphasizes the importance of good lesson planning in effective teaching.
- Chapter 4 discusses assessment of children's mathematical understandings. The chapter includes the history of assessment, types of alternative assessment, the NCTM *Assessment Standards for School Mathematics,* and international, national, and state reform efforts to change the focus of assessment. The use of rubrics or scoring guides for assessing children's work is introduced here and will be put into practice throughout the book.
- Chapter 5 offers problem-solving strategies and activities. Characteristics of good problem solvers are outlined and related to lesson planning. The NCTM *Standards* form the underpinnings of this chapter.
- Chapter 6 discusses geometry. Its perhaps unusual placement in the beginning of the book is to encourage teachers to include geometric ideas in their teaching. Concrete experiences are the key to developing informal, plane, and solid geometry. Hands-on exploration is the theme of the chapter and is emphasized throughout the remainder of the book.
- Chapter 7, on measurement, follows geometry and emphasizes the metric and customary systems. The topics of linearity, area, volume, capacity, temperature, mass, and time are carefully developed, including their related units of measurement. Activities are provided for each topic. Many of the activities encourage exploration to develop frames of reference for various units of measurement.
- Chapter 8 discusses number readiness and the beginning of the numerical aspects of mathematics. Number readiness is the initial introduction of numbers, including one-to-one correspondence, counting, and the general concept of number.
- Chapter 9 covers numeration and the development of counting systems. The base 10 numeration system is discussed in the context of the more general idea of numeration as it applies to any base system. Base 10 blocks and chip trading activities are developed as examples of proportional and nonproportional materials to use with children.
- Chapter 10 discusses operation sense of the whole number system in relation to the basic facts of addition, subtraction, multiplication, and division. Concrete materials and mental arithmetic are emphasized in the development process.
- Chapter 11 discusses the algorithms for addition, subtraction, multiplication, and division using base 10 blocks followed by chip trading activities. The calculator and computer are an integral part of the development. Alternative algorithms are discussed and illustrated by examples.

- Chapter 12 covers decimals and rational numbers, specifically common fractions, using concrete materials. The operations are explored with several models. The approach emphasizes understanding the algorithm rather than memorized procedures.
- Chapter 13 discusses ratio, proportion, percent, and rate. Pattern blocks are used to develop an understanding of percent. The calculator, estimation, and mental math are stressed in relation to ratio, proportion, percent, and rate.
- Chapter 14 develops patterns, functions, algebra, and number theory with various divisibility rules and numerical explorations. The middle school curriculum will find the topics extremely useful in developing number "sense."
- Chapter 15 explores data analysis, statistics, and probability. Types of graphs and their interpretation are discussed and illustrated with examples, including graphing calculators. Statistics and probability theory are highlighted. Real-world examples are provided, and activities to motivate students are presented. Mathematical connections are emphasized throughout the chapter.

HOW TO USE THIS BOOK

This book is a resource for teaching mathematics in the elementary and middle school. Problem solving, cooperative learning, and manipulatives are emphasized at all levels. Different learning styles are emphasized, and concrete-to-abstract materials are a prerequisite for each development.

Throughout the book, preservice and in-service teachers will be referred to as *the teacher.* The book has been class tested in college courses, and teachers have successfully used the activities with children. Using the computer as a tool offers many learning experiences for teachers as well as elementary and middle school children. We hope this careful, realistic presentation makes mathematics meaningful to elementary and middle school teachers and their students.

This book and the accompanying CD-ROM are to be used with classes that emphasize the teaching of elementary and middle school mathematics. Field experiences in relation to learning from the book are encouraged. Generally, the book is organized into seven sections per chapter—introduction, teaching strategies, assessment, summary, exercises, bibliography, and integrating technology.

Each chapter begins with a brief preview of the contents of the chapter to prepare the reader. If additional review of the mathematics that may have been covered in prerequisite college content courses is desired, you may refer to Check Your Mathematics Knowledge on the CD-ROM. This is especially true in Chapters 6 through 13, where teachers need to see the mathematical understandings to which children will be exposed from an "adult" viewpoint. The mathematical content is presented in a more symbolic, formal structure. Definitions of mathematical terms have been checked with James and James *Mathematics Dictionary,* 4th edition, 1976, and with West, Griesbch, Taylor, and Taylor, *The Prentice-Hall Encyclopedia of Mathematics,* 1982, as appropriate.

The *teaching strategies* present developmental activities that can be used with elementary and middle school students. These emphasize a variety of techniques in concrete/pictorial experiences, problem solving, cooperative learning, and computer/calculator technologies. Additional activities are available on the CD-ROM, many of which may be printed and copied as activity pages to use with your students. In order to get a feel for the mathematics classroom in which manipulatives are used, the CD-ROM contains eighteen video vignettes that exemplify the mathematics teaching advocated by the National Council of Teachers of Mathematics *Standards.*

The *assessment* sections present techniques for evaluating what the student actually knows and for correcting common error patterns and other frequently occurring difficulties of elementary and middle school students. Sample student work is included and analyzed for error patterns, a practice that we encourage in all teachers. Portfolio assessments are included in the text as well as on the CD-ROM to develop your own Professional Portfolio.

Integrating technology contains computer software resources, Internet searchers related to the topic, and a variety of computer activities. The computer activities are to be integrated into the curriculum as tools to understand and teach mathematics. Please note that a spreadsheet and a database program are needed to do the spreadsheets and databases. The computer activities can be done as explorations in an individual setting or in cooperative learning (small, noncompetitive) groups where work is shared among students to draw conclusions.

The *exercises* in the text and CD-ROM are written on three levels of difficulty. There are many exercises so that course instructors can choose which assignments are most appropriate for their course objectives. It is not our intent that everyone complete every exercise. The exercises are to encourage understanding of the content covered in the text as well as to prepare a preservice teacher for classroom instruction and to strengthen the in-service teacher's mathematics presentations. Many of the exercises can be used in future teaching, so teachers are encouraged to save them.

The *bibliographies* are references cited in the chapter. Extended bibliographies are on the CD-ROM for teachers interested in further information on a topic. Readers who are asked to search professional journals for assignments will find the bibliography a good starting point.

SUPPLEMENTS

The Instructor's Manual consists of additional worksheets for further evaluation of common errors; tips for using the CD, suggestions to the professor for using the text for: early childhood and middle school preservice methods, quarter versus semester courses, and graduate versus undergraduate courses; suggestions at the beginning of each chapter for activities, either from the text or the CD, that can be used at the very beginning of the chapter as an "anticipatory set"; an updated testbank; solutions to exercises in both the text and the CD; additional spreadsheet activities for various chapters.

The companion web site at www.wiley.com/college/hatfield consists of:

- An online study guide that can be accessed either by category (sample exercises and solutions, annotated web sites, test questions, CD update) or by chapter (1–15). Each chapter will offer the same four category selections mentioned previously, with links to the appropriate category.
- Sample exercises, consisting of 20 percent of exercises from the text and additional new, similar exercises with an emphasis on creating student activities, additional samples of student work with a rating scale (rubric), and technology-related activities.
- Annotated web sites—two or three web sites that relate specifically to the chapter at hand with either lesson plans and activities or sites that expand the students' knowledge of the particular concept.
- Additional test questions, with answers, to be used for practice, for feedback, or as an online quiz option, with the student submitting answers by e-mail.
- CD update that provides updated links (e.g., when Standards 2000 are released) to any web sites given on the CD.

The CD-ROM included with each book includes patterns for several of the manipulatives, observation forms, lesson formats, and teacher resources, which may be printed and copied. We suggest using and integrating the book and CD-ROM as shown in the diagram on the following page.

ACKNOWLEDGMENTS

Our special gratitude goes to the professors and students of Arizona State University and Missouri Western State College who participated in the two-year pilot study and to the professors and students who have given valuable suggestions for improvement as we have updated the Fourth Edition to meet the challenges of the twenty-first century. We also thank those who reviewed this edition for their thoughtful comments and suggestions: Georgia Cobbs, The University of Montana; Gilbert Cuevas, University of Miami; Steve Gregorich, California State University, Sacramento; Barbara Kinach, University of Maryland, Baltimore County; Shirley A. Leali, Weber State University; and Dr. Martha Poole Simmons, Alabama State University.

We wish to thank the following people for their help in the production of the Fourth Edition of the text: Jay Albright for his musical talent in the creation of the Fibonacci number sequence set to music; Jean Morrow for her expertise in writing the Instructor's Manual; Anne Adams for her photographic talents used in Chapter 2; Monique Mesa for sharing her personal experiences with culturally relevant mathematics; and Christa Johnson for sharing her life-saving career and its mathematics for young people to model. A special thanks to David P. Edwards, Clinical Research Director of the Richmond Ambulance Authority, for sharing real-world mathematics in the workplace.

We wish to acknowledge our former students whose actual work appears as illustrations in the book. We thank Dorothy S. Strong, Gwendolyn Long, and Telkia Rutherford of the Chicago Public Schools Mathematics Bureau and the Board of Education of the Chicago Public Schools for their willingness to share their instructional form and the student results. At Allyn & Bacon, we thank Nancy Forsyth, Kate Wagstaff, Frances Helland, and Linda Knowles. Our thanks are also extended to the staffs at John Wiley & Sons and Omegatype Typography, Inc.

A very special thanks goes out to the elementary and middle school students who were willing to share their work for the portfolio assessments: Matthew Alden, Janel Campbell, Mark Campbell, Shaun Campbell, Gregory Tanner Edwards, Travis Edwards, Andrew Kent Kirkwood, Katelyn Elaine Kirkwood, Gerald Kenzy, Rebecca Kenzy, Justin

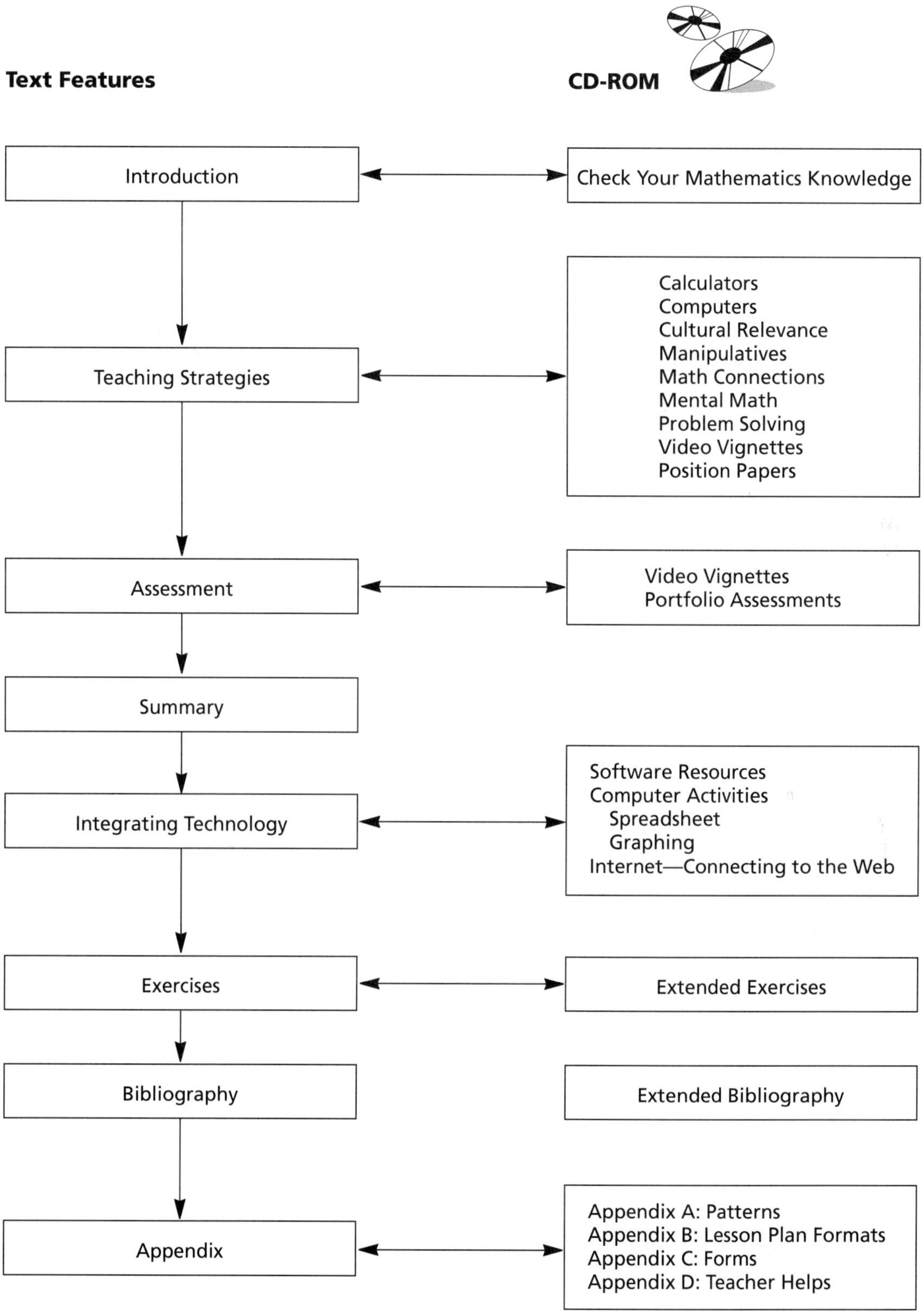

Talley, the students at Pershing Elementary-MWSC Professional Development School in St. Joseph, Missouri, and middle school students in Midlothian, Virginia. A debt of gratitude goes to Kathy Seifner, a pioneer student teacher using the TIMSS format in creative math lessons. We thank Tanya Habrock and Sheryl George's fifth-grade class at Humboldt Elementary School, St. Joseph, Missouri, for sharing their work in mathematical problem solving. Special friends, Paul Corcoran of Lawrence, Kansas, and Janice Shanks, of Glendale, Arizona, were always ready to lend their students' work for the portfolio assessments. We thank the Elwood, Kansas USD#486 Middle School Collaboration Team of Missie Orozco, Murla Leahy, Jette Wolfe, Judy Hoffman, and David Hart for sharing their Black History Month Quilt Project on the CD-ROM. We also thank Valeri Jones and her students from East Buchanan Middle School, Easton, Missouri, for the production of their classroom musical math video vignette. We thank the master teachers using the TIMSS format for sharing their performance assessment lessons on the CD-ROM. They are Earl Sharp, Stacy Sharp, Holly Flinn, Lori Keith, Jody Ide, Lynette Lower, Paula Greene, Shannon Small, Lynda Curran, Monica Turner, Kelly Owen, Stacey Vestal, Michelle Miller, Willa Thacker, Marni Ourth, Denise Hiserote, Becky Holden, and Rosemary Marsten.

The book is strengthened and enhanced by the accompanying CD-ROM. Illustrations of children learning mathematics in active, engaged environments exemplify the written text. The CD-ROM is the product of one valuable person, Paul Skiera, Director of Technology, Technology Based Learning and Research, at Arizona State University. Without Paul there would be no feasible way to have this product. The authors are deeply indebted to him and to his capable assistant, Jeff Appleton.

Another talented person who spent endless hours sharing his loving concern for the video editing of videotape is Jeff Bisbiglia. His perfection is reflected in the wonderful video vignettes he produced, and we owe him much gratitude. Last, but not least, thanks go to the participating teachers who allowed us windows into their classrooms, sharing their mathematics teaching with others to improve the teaching and learning of mathematics.

MATHEMATICS METHODS FOR ELEMENTARY AND MIDDLE SCHOOL TEACHERS

1

The Past, Present, and Future of Mathematics Education

Activities Index

IN THE TEXT

ON CD-ROM

Welcome to the world of mathematics education! It is a world with a rich heritage in the past, an exciting and sometimes overwhelming present, and a challenging future in the twenty-first century. As this book is published, knowledge is *doubling every one and a half months.* By the year 2005, it is projected that knowledge *will double every ten days!* It is exponential growth. What do you teach in a world that doubles its knowledge every ten days? You were taught mathematics that may not be appropriate for children living most of their lives in the twenty-first century. As mathematics educators, you must help prepare children for an ever-changing world by being aware of the expanding field of knowledge in mathematics.

This text has three main goals: to build on the strengths of past mathematics education, to model the successful techniques of the present, and to prepare for changes in the future. Mathematics education has always been and will continue to be an expanding field of knowledge. As human beings grow in understanding and in awareness of new possibilities, mathematics education changes. It is not the stagnant body of knowledge that many people assume. Some basic mathematical principles, such as the commutative and associative properties,

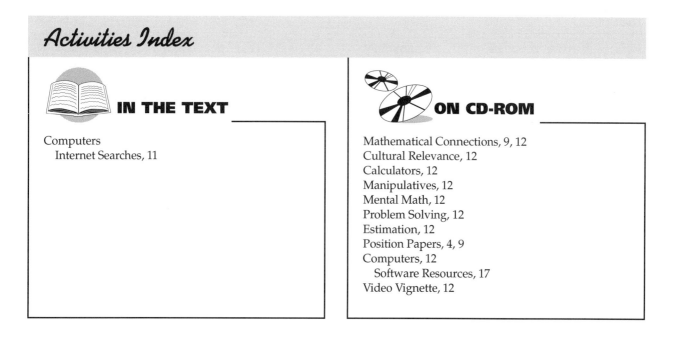

Subscripts© . . . *little thoughts below the bottom line*

have remained the same for generations, but others, such as fact strategies, are emerging as new insights. The ways to teach both the old and the new principles will change as more effective methods and new technologies develop.

What are the constants, the universals, that everyone must know in light of such dramatic growth? What are the things from the past that we can continue to use? What must be changed if we are to live successfully in such a dramatically changing world? How do we prepare elementary-school children and middle schoolers for mathematical experiences we have never had ourselves?

Our world is in the technological age. As the authors of this text, we believe in practicing what we preach. That's why this book has an accompanying CD-ROM with material to extend your learning. You will see video vignettes appear on your computer screen with actual teachers in real classrooms using the methods and materials explained in the book. You will be able to place yourself in each classroom and see the preparation required to do an outstanding job of teaching. You can then reflect on the lesson and see what you would do to extend the lesson if you were the teacher.

You will see actual student work with a version of the Logo computer language, called *Turtle Math,* as it is used by elementary-school children and middle schoolers. You will learn how to use the Internet for computer searches on newsbreaking items of interest to mathematics teachers. It is today's way of keeping up with the mushrooming growth of knowledge.

This chapter presents an overview of the pertinent course topics and the philosophy of the text. The ideas that are briefly presented here will be studied in greater detail in subsequent chapters.

PAST

What are the constants, the universals, that everyone must know from the past? What are the things from the past that we can continue to use?

From Thousands of Years Ago

All evolving cultures developed a knowledge of mathematical relationships in the ancient world, even when many cultures did not know of each other's existence. This lets us know that all human beings are mathematical creatures whether we think of ourselves that way or not. Civilizations counted items for barter and kept track with pebbles, then tally marks. They developed numeration systems to keep track of increasingly larger amounts of things. They all discovered that there is no one last number; the concept of infinity was understood. Symbols for such things gradually evolved: for example, ∞ shows no end or beginning for infinity; $\cup$ for union of sets; $\cap$ for intersection of sets; $\angle$ for angle designations.

The mathematicians of ancient China, India, South America, and Egypt discovered amazing things about number patterns, triangles, and measurement. That knowledge produced such wonders as the temples of South America and the Great Pyramids of Egypt on the African continent. Mathematical discoveries from different cultures are noted in their appropriate chapters. Chapter 2 explains the importance of children understanding the cultural relevance of mathematics. It binds all of us to the past and allows us to see that the future will continue to bring new discoveries in mathematics. Witness what we have done in the past fifteen years with fractals. Mathematics is not static; it is alive and changing.

Mathematics is nothing to be afraid of; it is our human heritage from all cultures. This is a powerful message for children. It is a constant we bring to children from the past to prepare them for their future.

From One Hundred and Fifty Years Ago

Mathematics education began as a discipline in the mid-1800s. The textbook for children and the manual for teachers were one and the same in those days. Teacher training in mathematics typically consisted of a one-page introduction to the student book (Ray, 1850). Interestingly the big ideas found on such pages sound very much like the big issues of today. A detailed look from the 1850s book is available on the CD-ROM. To summarize, the ideas were as follows.

- Teachers should use short, lively periods for oral recitation (now called oral discourse).
- Students have a range of abilities; various accomplishments need to be recognized (not un-

like Gardner's multiple intelligences, found in Chapter 3).

- The primary focus was on how well a child could analyze and reason behind answers (an emphasis of the new standards in mathematics—featured later in the next section of this chapter) rather than on memorization of facts.
- Students were expected to explain the methods they chose to arrive at the answers (a *must* according to current research—explained later in this chapter).

No matter what new mathematics and technologies we may have now or in the future, we still must teach children to reason out their own answers and to analyze the relationships presented in the models. The models will change, but the process of good mathematical thinking will always be needed. A mathematics teacher in the 1800s would have been astonished to see today's students learning mathematics with a computer, creating their own mathematical equations, and checking to see if their answers are correct—all within a few seconds. The process, however, by which children can do it *would have been understood* in schools 150 years ago.

From Our Most Recent Past

There are an abundance of noteworthy contributions made by many great mathematics educators in the twentieth century. Those contributions are noted by decades on the CD-ROM. Although there were many attempts to reform mathematics teaching in the 1900s, teachers still tended to teach the way they themselves were taught. There was more emphasis on teaching procedures, especially computation procedures, and less on how conceptual ideas were developed (Hiebert, 1999). The Third International Science and Mathematics Study (TIMSS) and the National Assessment of Educational Progress (NAEP) showed U.S. students scoring low and doing very little to solve challenging problems requiring conceptual understandings. Those countries whose students scored high did just the opposite.

In this text, the authors refer to the National Assessment of Educational Progress (NAEP) when giving results of how well students were judged on meeting the standards at the end of the twentieth century. NAEP is the only test given nationally to representative samples of students over a period of years in which scores can be compared and contrasted. The test itself has evolved as the standards have changed. The NAEP information is analyzed in many different ways using the latest statistical methods available at each testing period since its inception in 1973. In the 1990s, the results of the NAEP scores in mathematics were promising. When students had instruction aligned more with the recent mathematics standard movement stressing conceptual development, they had better scores on the National Assessment of Educational Progress (NAEP, 1996). This is an encouraging trend that shows the standard movement of the 1990s had positive effects on mathematics instruction and holds promise for more growth in the twenty-first century.

PRESENT

The present seems more overwhelming than the past because it is in the present that we have to live by the decisions we make. The future may look scary at times but at least we don't have to live there yet. As some astute philosophers have pointed out, we never get to the future. By the time we get there, it's always the present. Therefore, it's understandable why this section of the chapter is the lengthiest. It is where our decisions about children and mathematics learning are made. Here we discuss the key issues in mathematics education today as a preamble for the chapters that follow.

The key issues are (1) the new insights gained from brain research that inform our views about how students learn mathematics; (2) the emergence of the standards movement in mathematics education; and (3) the current trends in mathematics learning created by the presence of brain research and the standards movement.

Brain Research Enlarges Our View

In today's educational system Piaget's early constructivist view has been refined by continuing research. Adding to its credibility are the new findings in brain research. This research is one of the focal points of Chapter 3, How Children Learn Mathematics. Research (Sylwester, 1995; Dehaene, 1997; Diamond and Hopson, 1998) suggests that young children invent or construct much of their own mathematical knowledge. Although their thinking is immature, they enter school with some well-developed ways of using mathematics. Some educators feel that using a child's own conceptions of mathematics in programs of teaching and instruction reduces a child's tendency to develop anxiety toward mathematics later. Very often it is the view that educators hold about the importance of mathematics in the classroom that affects the anxiety that students develop toward it.

Learning associated with problem solving is strengthened, according to research, by the student's heightened awareness of metacognitive elements of the problem-solving process. *Metacognition* is one's knowledge of how one's own cognitive processes work. Evidence implies that metacognitive skills may be the reason for the difference between expert and novice problem solvers (Biehler and Snowman, 1997).

Teaching and learning mathematics is a life-long process. Technological change outdates old skills and increases the importance of others. Slide rules, log and trig tables, and mechanical calculators have given way to programmable and graphing calculators and sophisticated electronic computers. All these changes require continued construction of knowledge on the part of children and adults alike.

The Standards Movement in Mathematics Education

Remember the questions asked at the beginning of this chapter: What do you teach in a world that doubles its knowledge every ten days? How do we prepare elementary-school children and middle schoolers for mathematical experiences we have never had ourselves? It is the "big picture" that people need to know about, because the little facts, figures, and specifics change too quickly to spend any major time learning them. Learning the *process of thinking* and how to approach solving problems is more important than memorizing one way or method to get an answer. The method and the answer may change before one has a chance to use them. How could educators actually write a curriculum that would support change itself? That was the challenge for educators during the final decade of the twentieth century. It followed that educators needed to go on record to state what really mattered in mathematics learning. Hence, the standards movement was born.

Mathematics educators were the first group to take on the challenge of creating new academic standards to prepare people for a rapidly changing world. Under the auspices of the National Council of Teachers of Mathematics (NCTM) three sets of standards were written—*Curriculum and Evaluation Standards* (1989), *Professional Standards for Teaching Mathematics* (1991), and *Assessment Standards* (1995). Together they form a trilogy that covers all the bases of *who, what, when, where, why, how,* and *how much* in mathematics teaching.

The overall vision of these mathematics standards deals with the "big picture" of mathematics, how to solve problems, reason out answers, and communicate mathematically. Each set of standards will remain a classic because of the impact on public and teacher awareness engendered over the last ten years. The trilogy of standards are found on the CD-ROM for those who wish to reference the original work. Specific descriptions of each standard appear throughout the book where appropriate for each of the concepts studied. Chapter activities and CD-ROM activities also show which segment of the NCTM *Standards* is being emphasized as you work on some of the activities. Not all activities are marked in the interest of brevity. All activities *do support* the standards.

EXTENDED ACTIVITIES

Name of Activity

- Mathematics Book from 1850
- Mathematics Contributions by the Decades
- The Original Standards (1989, 1991, 1995)
- *Curriculum and Evaluation Standards*
- *Professional Standards for Teaching Mathematics*
- *Assessment Standards*

POSITION PAPER

The NCTM Standards (2000). The new *National Council of Teachers of Mathematics Standards, 2000: Principles and Standards for School Mathematics* (NCTM, 2000) combines the work of the original three manuscripts into one document. At this writing the *Principles and Standards* are still in their draft form and changes in detailed descriptions will be forthcoming. The Internet, however, makes it possible to view the latest thinking of the writing group, and you are encouraged to view the entire *Principles and Standards* document at the NCTM Internet site, **http://nctm.org.**

A summary of the *Principles and Standards* is presented here. There are four main changes in the document: (1) the professional teaching standards and the assessment standards have been condensed and renamed "guiding principles"; (2) a new curriculum process standard called "representation" has been added; (3) the number of curriculum standards have been condensed from thirteen to ten; and (4) grade levels have been further subdivided into smaller grade-level clusters in the early years of child development.

1. **The Guiding Principles.** The original *Standards* (1989, 1991, 1995) and the *Principles and Standards* (2000) were never meant to prescribe specific mathematics objectives and/or performances, but rather to guide persons in the broad beliefs of what needs to be valued as the nation works with students in the twenty-first century. The word *principles* was chosen to convey the idea of broad tenets from which to guide quality mathematics instruction. Think about the set of classroom teaching hints from the 1850s as you review these six guiding principles. How do they differ and how are they similar across the centuries?

   - *Equity Principle:* Mathematics instructional programs should promote the learning of mathematics by all students. Striving for equity also implies striving for excellence in mathematics instruction. To achieve this goal, teachers must believe and actively work for high expectations and provide strong support to students if inequities are to be successfully overcome.

   - *Mathematics Curriculum Principle:* Mathematics instructional programs should emphasize important and meaningful mathematics through curricula that are coherent and comprehensive. This implies fewer topics and deeper understanding of mathematical ideas through a well-chosen curriculum, organized and integrated in a meaningful manner. Studies should emphasize the interconnectedness among mathematics topics and between other disciplines. What students know and are able to do should become progressively deeper and broader as a system of mathematical understanding.

   - *Teaching Principle:* Mathematics instructional programs depend on competent and caring teachers who teach all students to understand and use mathematics. This implies that teachers plan the use of worthwhile mathematics tasks with analysis and reflection of student learning. The learning environment should promote positive mathematics dispositions, encouraging oral and written student discourse among individual students and the teacher in both small group and large class settings. Students need experiences to read, write, and orally communicate their mathematical ideas so that mathematics becomes natural when speaking with others.

   - *Learning Principle:* Mathematics instructional programs should enable all students to understand and use mathematics. This implies that students need to build on prior experiences by using the five processes of problem solving, reasoning, representing, communicating, and making connections. Students need to grapple with complex and interesting tasks that are not immediately solved, enjoying the disposition to use their minds so that they become confident in their own abilities. No matter what they face in the world, they will have the sense of mathematical power needed to solve new sets of problems. They know they have within them what it takes.

   - The use of many problem forms is advocated so that students become competent mathematical problem solvers. Some problems should be open-ended with no right answer, whereas others may have models to follow with predictable formulas. The time allotted for solving problems should approximate the real world, in which problems can take days or months to solve or be short daily problems that can be done more quickly.

     People need to value mathematics. Students should have a variety of experiences in the cultural, historical, and scientific evolution of mathematics so that they can see the importance mathematics will play in their lifetimes and in the lifetimes of their children.

   - *Assessment Principle:* Mathematics instructional programs should include assessment to monitor, enhance, and evaluate the mathematics learning of all students and to inform teaching. Assessment is a cyclic process of (1) setting clear goals in the planning stage, (2) gathering evidence using various methods, (3) interpreting evidence through valid inferences enabled by teacher expertise, (4) using the inferences to make decisions and/or take action, and (5) repeating the process. One never really finishes assessment; it is ongoing. Even when teachers use summative assessment at the end of a semester, it is added to the ongoing evaluation of students as they progress through the education system, as evidenced by the all-too-familiar piece of paper called a school transcript.

   - *Technology Principle:* Mathematics instructional programs should use technology to help all students understand mathematics and should prepare them to use mathematics in an increasingly technological world. Technology is a tool that enhances mathematical thought. It should free students to concentrate on the big ideas of mathematics by giving students procedural fluency from the complex and numerous calculations that hinder mathematical development. When calculations are few and easy, technology is not an appropriate tool. Mental math and quick paper calculations are more appropriate in these situations. Technology should help prepare students for the increasing demands of a competitive society if they understand its purposes, strengths, and limitations. As always, students need the guidance from knowledgeable teachers to discern when the use of technology is appropriate.

2. **The New Curriculum Process Standard Called "Representation."** Representation joins the original process standards of problem solving, reasoning, communication, and connections as one of the five processes that permeate all mathematical thinking. Representations enable physical, social, and mathematical phenomena to be modeled and interpreted in meaningful ways that enhance mathematical understanding. Numerous learning theories stress that children learn mathematics by concrete representations, moving to pictorial representations and finally to symbolic representations. It has become apparent through numerous research studies that good teaching involves continual representations in mathematics. These studies appear where appropriate throughout the text. In summary, representation belongs as a process standard based on research and observation of good teaching procedures.
3. **The Number of Curriculum Standards Condensed.** The number of curriculum standards have been condensed from the original thirteen to ten (NCTM, 2000):

   Five standards describe the mathematical content that students should learn:

   - Number and operation
   - Patterns, functions, and algebra
   - Geometry and spatial sense
   - Measurement
   - Data analysis, statistics, and probability

   The other five standards describe the mathematical processes through which students should acquire and use their mathematical knowledge:

   - Problem solving
   - Reasoning and proof
   - Communication
   - Connections
   - Representation

   The content standard of number and operation now takes in the 1989 curriculum standards of estimation, number sense and numeration, concepts of whole number operations, and whole number computations. Each of these is a natural subset of number and operation. This text divides the number and operation concepts into chapters representing the subsets of number readiness; numeration; operation sense; operation with whole numbers, common fractions and decimals; and percent, ratio, proportion, and rate. The chapters mirror the way the concepts are divided in school mathematics curriculum.

   Box 1.1 shows the curriculum standards and a brief description of each one (NCTM, 2000, pp. 48–50).
4. **Grade Levels Divided into Smaller Grade Clusters.** Grade levels have been divided into Pre-K–2, grades 3–5, grades 6–8, and grades 9–12. The division at the earlier grade levels reflects the current research in early child development, which states that preschool children and primary children have thought structures different from those of third and fourth graders. More middle schools start at grade six than grade five. Sixth graders can hold their own much better with eighth graders than can fifth graders. The new grade-level divisions allow for more developmentally appropriate materials to be created for each group. Because NCTM materials to support the new *Standards* were not available at this writing, grade divisions in the following chapters reflect 1989 *Standards.*

Support for Teaching the NCTM Standards. Programs as well as students must be evaluated. Concerns include a judgment on appropriate resources for support of the mathematics goals. Concrete manipulatives (physical objects to be handled) should be used to help children actively construct their world mathematically. On the CD-ROM, look for some suggestions for using hands-on materials, entitled "Tips for Using Manipulatives for Teaching Mathematics."

Equity for *all* students is also a program goal. If all students are to experience the exhilaration that mathematical power brings to people, then procedures must be in place so that everyone can be a part of the program.

More and more excellent resources are being produced to help teachers plan activities to teach

BOX 1.1 Mathematics Curriculum Standards: Pre-K–12

Standard 1: Number and Operation

Mathematics instructional programs should foster the development of number and operation sense so that all students—

- Understand numbers, ways of representing numbers, relationships among numbers, and number systems.
- Understand the meaning of operations and how they relate to each other.
- Use computational tools and strategies fluently and estimate appropriately.

Standard 2: Patterns, Functions, and Algebra

Mathematics instructional programs should include attention to patterns, functions, symbols, and models so that all students—

- Understand various types of patterns and functional relationships.
- Use symbolic forms to represent and analyze mathematical situations and structures.
- Use mathematical models and analyze change in both real and abstract contexts.

Standard 3: Geometry and Spatial Sense

Mathematics instructional programs should include attention to geometry and spatial sense so that all students—

- Analyze characteristics and properties of two- and three-dimensional geometric objects.
- Select and use different representational systems, including coordinate geometry and graph theory.
- Recognize the usefulness of transformations and symmetry in analyzing mathematical situations.
- Use visualization and spatial reasoning to solve problems both within and outside of mathematics.

Standard 4: Measurement

Mathematics instructional programs should include attention to measurement so that all students—

- Understand attributes, units, and systems of measurement.
- Apply a variety of techniques, tools, and formulas for determining measurements.

Standard 5: Data Analysis, Statistics, and Probability

Mathematics instructional programs should include attention to data analysis, statistics, and probability so that all students—

- Pose questions and collect, organize, and represent data to answer those questions.
- Interpret data using methods of exploratory data analysis.
- Develop and evaluate inferences, predictions, and arguments that are based on data.
- Understand and apply basic notions of chance and probability.

Standard 6: Problem Solving

Mathematics instructional programs should focus on solving problems as part of understanding mathematics so that all students—

- Build new mathematical knowledge through their work with problems.
- Develop a disposition to formulate, represent, abstract, and generalize in situations within and outside mathematics.
- Apply a wide variety of strategies to solve problems and adapt the strategies to new situations.
- Monitor and reflect on their mathematical thinking in solving problems.

Standard 7: Reasoning and Proof

Mathematics instructional programs should focus on learning to reason and construct proofs as part of understanding mathematics so that all students—

- Recognize reasoning and proof as essential and powerful parts of mathematics.
- Make and investigate mathematical conjectures.
- Develop and evaluate mathematical arguments and proofs.
- Select and use various types of reasoning and methods of proof as appropriate.

Standard 8: Communication

Mathematics instructional programs should use communication to foster understanding of mathematics so that all students—

- Organize and consolidate their mathematical thinking to communicate with others.
- Express mathematical ideas coherently and clearly to peers, teachers, and others.

(continued)

BOX 1.1 Mathematics Curriculum Standards: Pre-K–12 *(Continued)*

- Extend their mathematical knowledge by considering the thinking and strategies of others.
- Use the language of mathematics as a precise means of mathematical expression.

Standard 9: Connections

Mathematics instructional programs should emphasize connections to foster understanding of mathematics so that all students—

- Recognize and use connections among different mathematical ideas.
- Understand how mathematical ideas build on one another to produce a coherent whole.
- Recognize, use, and learn about mathematics in contexts outside of mathematics.

Standard 10: Representation

Mathematics instructional programs should emphasize mathematical representations to foster understanding of mathematics so that all students—

- Create and use representations to organize, record, and communicate mathematical ideas.
- Develop a repertoire of mathematical representations that can be used purposefully, flexibly, and appropriately.
- Use representations to model and interpret physical, social, and mathematical phenomena.

Source: National Council of Teachers of Mathematics, 2000 (draft): 48–50.

concepts in line with the *Standards.* The NCTM *Addenda Series* (Leiva, 1993; Curcio, 1994) can help a novice teacher see what some of those concepts might be and how to structure classroom activities to get the job done. The *Addenda Series* will be referenced in this book where appropriate. NCTM journals, as well as other leading journals in elementary and middle school curriculum, have featured the ideas to teach the NCTM *Standards.* As shown in early childhood journals, the NCTM *Standards* can relate equally well to children ages two through five (Waite-Stupiansky and Stupiansky, 1995).

Curricula Projects. The National Science Foundation (NSF) has funded eight ongoing programs to develop curricula in line with the NCTM *Standards.* To date, there are three elementary programs and five middle school programs scattered around the nation. The National Centers for Implementation of Standards-Based Mathematics Curricula (1999) have the charge to disseminate the curricula to interested people working with elementary and middle school students. The centers maintain web sites where teachers can explore activities and dialogue with other teachers as they try the activities with students. The elementary web site http://www.arccenter.comap.com and the middle school web site http://www.showme-center.missouri.edu may be of interest to you as you think of activities to use with students yourself.

Learning the concerns and triumphs of practicing teachers can be enlightening. You can be a part of the network that is forging new mentors for teachers of all levels as they use the Internet to learn to talk and listen to colleagues across the country. The list of NSF programs follows.

Elementary Programs	Middle School Programs
UCSMP Elementary: *Everyday Mathematics* Chicago, IL	*Connected Mathematics* (6–8) East Lansing, MI
Investigations in Number, Data, & Space (K–5) Cambridge, MA	*Mathematics in Context* (5–8) Madison, WI
Math Trailblazers: A Mathematical Journey Using Science and Language Arts (K–5) Chicago, IL	*MathScape* (6–8) Newton, MA
	Middle School Mathematics Through Applications Project (6–8) Menlo Park, CA
	Middle Grades Math Thematics (STEM, 6–8) Missoula, MT

Look to this text's web site at http://www.wiley.com/college/hatfield for an updated list of new programs as they are developed. It is anticipated that Pre-K–2 program sites will be added as the new NCTM *Principles and Standards* gain a foothold across the country.

Opposing Views of the Standards Movement. The *Standards* movement has had its critics, who have lashed out at the *Standards* in particular and mathematics education reform in general. Some critics have felt the *Standards* were not specific enough concerning the "facts" that needed to be studied in mathematics. Others resented one body of people telling them what they needed to do. Still others did not want anything changed for them, no matter what the changes were to be.

When things seem to move faster than we can comprehend, it is tempting to simply switch the subject, to pretend that change is not happening. When some people hear a strange sound in their car's engine, they simply turn up the car radio to drown out the sound. That works for awhile, but as anyone can tell you, the engine has a way of getting the attention it needs. It eventually stops a person cold. That analogy fits what has happened to some people as they have viewed the NCTM *Standards* movement.

This rapid escalation of mathematics knowledge will occur with or without our consent. There is no escaping it. A concentration on teaching mathematics by memorization and long tedious calculations will stop a person's ability to teach mathematics effectively. A concentration on the *processes* of mathematics as application in the real world seems to be the wisest solution to adjust quickly to a rapidly changing body of knowledge.

Other Expert Positions on Standards for Mathematics Learning

Other professional academic groups have also seen the need to adjust to a rapidly changing world. They, too, have presented position papers on the needs in mathematics learning. Those having a definite effect on your role as a teacher of mathematics have been chosen for presentation here.

National Council for the Accreditation of Teacher Education (NCATE). NCATE is a national group that accredits colleges of education. To receive national accreditation from NCATE, colleges must meet certain standards in their preparation of teachers. There are specific mathematics guidelines for the preparation of elementary and middle school teachers (NCATE, 1998; NCATE, 1999). These standards were written in conjunction with the NCTM to ensure that teachers can instruct the way the new student standards require. Check the CD-ROM for these standards and what they mean for elementary education candidates.

Included in the general elementary sections of the NCATE standards is the requirement that teachers know and can teach the contributions made by many cultures in the development of each academic area. Chapter 2 of this text prepares you to teach the cultural contributions made in the field of mathematics. A second requirement is the acknowledgment that all students can learn each subject area. Chapter 3 of this text and subsequent content chapters describe ways you can teach mathematics to special needs students. The NCATE middle school standards and the standards for elementary mathematics specialists follow the same lines.

Research from the National Commission on Teaching and America's Future found that the number of institutions that were NCATE-accredited in a state is the strongest predictor of well-qualified teachers. All three states that required NCATE accreditation for their colleges in the 1980s experienced higher than average score gains on national student testing in the 1990s (Darling-Hammond and Berry, 1998). That may be one reason why knowing both the teacher and student standards has become important when interviewing for a teaching position. For example, interviews with school administrators (Gillespie, 1998; Edwards, 1999) from the East coast to the Midwest verify that those hired first for teaching positions in many districts are those who know and can use the current student and teacher mathematics standards in actual classroom experiences.

National Directives. Recommendations for curricula, for professional development of teachers, and for national goals for education have been proposed from a number of perspectives. Commissions, national boards, and presidential proclamations have all prepared responses to the standards movement.

EXTENDED ACTIVITIES

Name of Activity

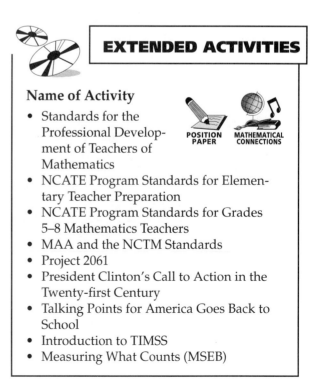

- Standards for the Professional Development of Teachers of Mathematics
- NCATE Program Standards for Elementary Teacher Preparation
- NCATE Program Standards for Grades 5–8 Mathematics Teachers
- MAA and the NCTM Standards
- Project 2061
- President Clinton's Call to Action in the Twenty-first Century
- Talking Points for America Goes Back to School
- Introduction to TIMSS
- Measuring What Counts (MSEB)

Explanations of each of these directives can be found on the CD-ROM.

TIMSS. Despite the increasing importance of mathematics in a world that is both highly technological and highly competitive, the United States lags behind other developed nations in student mathematics achievement (Forgione, 1997; Reese et al., 1997). The Third International Math and Science Study found that average Japanese high school students performed better in mathematics than all but the top 5 percent of U.S. high school students. TIMSS has spurred new teaching methods in America's classrooms. Chapter 4 of this text on assessment explores the changes in detail. The new methods will also be shared in subsequent chapters when appropriate to specific content areas. A general introduction to TIMSS is found on the CD-ROM as released by the U.S. Department of Education. Those who are interested in comparing the United States standards with those standards expected of students across the world might enjoy visiting the TIMSS web site, http://www.ustimss.msu.edu, or reading the book, *What Students Abroad Are Expected to Know about Mathematics: Defining World Class Standards* (American Federation of Teachers, 1997).

Current Trends in Mathematics Learning

A General Overview. The new brain research and the standards movement have influenced mathematics educators to look at new alternatives for teaching mathematics, which can be taught to different groups of students through different curricula, which differ in style and content as well as in different ways of studying. Teachers who can teach mathematics by targeting a particular student's learning style are able to expand that student's future prospects. Brain research has shown that educators need to eliminate the assumption that their students have no mathematical knowledge before they enter the classroom and bring the out-of-class mathematics into the classroom. Educators should identify and reinforce out-of-school mathematical experiences and knowledge. In a strictly utilitarian sense, pupils filter through their senses all kinds of mathematical activities. As an example, architecture acquaints students with two-dimensional representations of three-dimensional objects. There are many other applications of mathematics in everyday life.

The vision of the NCTM's *Principles and Standards* (2000) is that mathematical reasoning, representation, problem solving, communication, and connections are to be the focal point of learning and teaching mathematics in active learning settings.

Active Learning with Real-World Applications for All Students. Research (Neyland, 1996; Teppo, 1998) shows that students learn best when they are actively engaged in the experience, with new learning connected to things they already know. This also applies to students with special needs (Thornton and Bley, 1994). Connections can grow increasingly more complex by the middle school years, when students begin to decide what their real-world occupations may be. An NCTM focus issue on middle school connections (NCTM, 1999; Christ, 1995) may prove helpful to read if you are planning to work with middle school students.

Another connection for active learning is children's literature. Many stories can have mathematics themes or can be used to teach special mathematics concepts. Thiessen, Matthias, and Smith (1998) have gathered over 550 works of children's literature with annotated notes on how each can be used with mathematics. Their book is an excellent resource for any teacher. A selected set of children's literature that can be used with various mathematics content is listed at the end of each of this text's content chapter.

Because students need to reflect on and record their mathematical knowledge and behaviors through oral and written discourse, the current emphasis is on communications, especially journal writing and oral reporting in mathematics. This text also presents ideas for mathematics communication in the content chapters.

The integration of passive and active learning can be most effectively accomplished by the teacher when the students' experiences are brought into the classroom and used to illustrate the learning experience. Unfortunately, heretofore the instruction of mathematics has not been designed toward the usefulness of mathematics, but instead has sought to validate it. As students increase their educational level, they decrease their study of mathematics unless they are entering fields in which a mathematics background is essential. Mathematics, then, is often received only by an elite mathematical group.

Current trends show that many programs and curriculum studies are being put into place that emphasize mathematics for *all* students (Apple, 1995; Kloosterman and Cougan, 1994; Leder, 1995). Mathematics is not an elitist endeavor.

Technology. Technology has made it possible for people to keep up with the rapidly changing knowledge in all fields. The authors of this text advocate the use of technology to enhance mathematics learning and want to model how technology can be effective in the many areas of mathematics education, such as interactive multimedia, digital media, the Internet, and mathematical programming in various computer languages, including Logo with *Turtle Math* (Clements, 1994) and LEGO MINDSTORMS (LEGO Group, 1998).

Digital Media—The Internet. Although the Internet may be a relatively new name to many readers, it is actually thirty years old! This international network was set up in the name of defense—to be prepared and ready—for quick communication in emergencies. It has no direct line of command to anything or anybody in the sense that we normally think. It has no beginning point or place of origin and no place or entity where things stop. It was purposely set up so that the communication could be open.

There is no end of the many things one can find and do on the Internet. New things are added daily. Richard De A'Morelli said that "nearly all the knowledge that our civilization has gathered since the dawn of history is accessible on the Internet if you know where to look for it" (Spectrum, 1995).

World Wide Web. The World Wide Web (WWW), was created in 1993. The Web (as it is called) makes things more accessible at greater speeds. People can create, and transport, and download pictures, games, and interactive activities on the Web. At the end of each chapter we have placed web addresses with ideas that may help you search more efficiently. The Internet is a very fluid place, constantly changing. It is likely that you will find more things on the Internet and the World Wide Web than the authors could imagine at the time this text was printed. The following web sites demonstrate the power of the Internet. The authors cannot guarantee that any of these Internet sources will still be in operation by the time you read this text, however.

Activity 1.1

INTERNET SEARCHES

EXPLORING WEB SITES

DIRECTIONS

Visit these web sites for interactive activities. From this list which three did you enjoy the most? Why?

http://neptune.galaxy.gmu.edu/~drsuper/
http://discoveryschool.com/schrockguide/math.html

- AskERIC
  http://ericir.syr.edu/Virtual/Lessons/Mathematics/index.html
- Swarthmore forum
  http://forum.swarthmore.edu/math.topics.html
  http://forum.swarthmore.edu/~steve/

Activity Continues

- New Hampshire Public Television
  http://www.nhptv.org/kn/vs/mathlab.sht
- Columbia Education Center
  http://www.col-ed.org/cur/#math3/
- Busy Teachers
  http://www.ceismc.gatech.edu/busyt/homepg.htm
- Girls Tech
  http://www.crpc.rice.edu/CRPC/Women/GirlTECH/Lessons/
- Eisenhower National Clearing House
  http://www.enc.org/classroom/index.htm
- Teachers for Teachers
  http://www.pacific.net/~mandel/Math.html
- Teachers
  http://www.teachers.net/curriculum/mathematics.html

Supporting the NCTM *Principles and Standards* (2000):

- Mathematics as Problem Solving; Communication
- Worthwhile Mathematical Tasks—The Learning Principle
- The Technology Principle

The Internet Keeps This Text Current. Technology via the Internet can help keep this book a vital, current entity. A book is much like a car in today's society. A new car will depreciate by half its new car price just driving it off the lot. With knowledge doubling almost every month, a book is quickly obsolete by the time the ink has dried on its pages.

The authors of this text have enabled a World Wide Web page on the Internet to keep you, the reader, updated on new, emerging topics and issues in mathematics teaching. You can reach us, the authors, by typing the following command:

www.wiley.com/college/hatfield

We look forward to hearing from you. We have a registry page so that we can know who you are, and you can see that we are real, live human beings too. Also look for the online study guide.

Computer Technology. Note that "technology" does not just mean computers; it also includes calculators of all types. Middle school students are using more sophisticated calculators with pictures of graphs plotted in seconds that took long steps of tedious computations to do in the past. The graphing calculators help students quickly observe reactions to variable

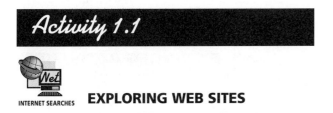

Video Vignette

Teacher's Reflections on Mathematics Teaching

Activity #1

- Play the video vignette called "Teacher's Reflections on Mathematics Teaching." The teacher, Mrs. Torres, discusses her vision of how a mathematics classroom should look.
- Think about these questions as you watch the video and be ready to discuss them with your colleagues:
  - What points does Mrs. Torres stress about the mathematics classroom? How does this vision relate to what you have read in this chapter about the standards?
  - What beliefs about children's learning are evidenced in the video? How are they similar or different from your feelings about mathematics instruction?

Activity #2—Observations of Good Teaching with the Standards

- View the following series of video clips. Don't worry about the mathematics content seen in the videos. You will have the chance to view each one of these in light of the content in Chapters 6–15. The video clips are short and can be seen quickly:
  - Chapter 7: Pizza Perimeter
  - Chapter 9: Whale Math
  - Chapter 9: Numeration Games [Note a clip of a college class in on it too]
  - Chapter 10: Dinosaur Legs
  - Chapter 15: Graphing Probability
- Think about these questions as you watch the video and be ready to discuss them with your colleagues:
  - How you would feel if you were in an elementary or middle school classroom like the ones you see here? Compare these classrooms to your learning experiences.
  - Describe what you see going on in terms of learning environment, student actions, teacher actions, questions asked.
  - How might these classrooms need to change in the future?

changes in equations and problem solve new possibilities. Research supports the positive impact of calculator use on the development of problem-solving strategies (Heid et al., 1998). The technology principle in the *Principles and Standards* (NCTM, 2000) calls for all students to have access to calculator technology. All students should be able to determine when and where calculator use is appropriate.

There is a motivational power to technology that draws in students and teachers alike. Views on how and why this works are seen in the ASCD Yearbook, *Learning with Technology* (ASCD, 1998). The current issues continue to change as new inventions in technology literally appear on the scene daily.

You will see firsthand how several of the applications work as you use the CD-ROM provided with this text. You will have the opportunity to view experienced elementary and middle school teachers as they teach mathematics lessons in their classrooms. The power of the CD-ROM format enables you to rerun the videos as many times as you want. You have the capability to stop the video at any time and work on the critical thought questions that accompany each video. You will be able to view the videos from multiple perspectives as you look for how teachers handle different aspects of a mathematics lesson. Interactive multimedia combines audio, text, animation, music, graphics, photos, print materials, and full-motion video to produce a learning and teaching environment with the user actively engaged in the process.

Other Current Trends. The list in Figure 1.1 constitutes the current trends and issues receiving the most attention as measured by mathematics research and professional journal articles. Scan the titles and think about how many examples you saw in the Video Vignette.

After reading this section, it is easy to see why people may regard present-day mathematics teaching as overwhelming at times. Professional organi-

EXTENDED ACTIVITIES

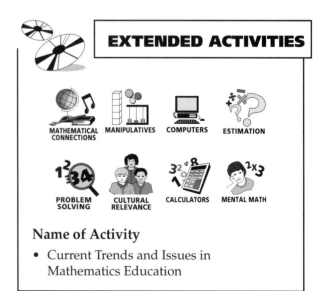

Name of Activity

- Current Trends and Issues in Mathematics Education

FIGURE 1.1

Current Trends in Mathematics Learning

Trends in Problem Solving
Trends in Estimation and Mental Math
Trends in Communication
  Issue: Cooperative Learning
  Issue: Journal Writing
Trends in Mathematical Connections
  Issue: Links to Literature
Trends in Mathematical Reasoning
Trends in Early Childhood Mathematics
Trends in Equity: Mathematics for ALL Students
  Issue: Culturally Relevant Mathematics
  Issue: Math Anxiety
  Issue: Women in Mathematics
Trends in Assessment
  Portfolio Assessment for Students and Teachers
Trends in the Use of Manipulatives
Trends in Technology
  Calculators
  Microcomputers
  Computer-Assisted Instruction
    Drill and Practice Programs
    Problem-Solving Programs
    Application Programs
      Databases
      Spreadsheets
      Graphics
  Computer-Managed Instruction

Current trends and issues on the CD-ROM.

zations such as the National Council of Teachers of Mathematics issue position papers on many current trends. Visit the NCTM web site (**www.nctm.org**) to read the council's position on topics such as The "Every Child" Statement, Calculators and the Education of Youth, Early Childhood Mathematics Education, Teaching Mathematics in Middle School, and The Use of Technology in the Learning and Teaching of Mathematics.

FUTURE

It is exhilarating to project into the future. The idea has fascinated people for generations. Think of the books of prophesy in many religions dating back thousands of years and the sustaining interest in *Star Trek* for the television generation. Although some of the projections made in this section may seem outlandish, each projection is based on ideas and research specifications that are now on the drawing boards, or should we say on computer boards. The profession of teaching may have a change in focus, but there will still be plenty for a teacher to do.

Mathematics in the Twenty-First Century School

The school will still be divided into its physical plant and its curriculum, but not all lessons will need to be taught there. Students will be able to call up lessons from their homes via computer Internet links around the world. The teacher will communicate last-minute assignments or ideas to students in their homes via the Internet hookup. Still, human beings are social creatures who need to come together to express what they have learned and listen to others. There will still be a need for a gathering place—*the school.*

A New Vision of School. Just think...no more heavy book bags! "Books" will be thin, round CD-ROMs, like the one that comes with this book. They will contain 600,000 bits or more of information and video filled with all sorts of knowledge. One laptop will replace the weight of many books.

Video as a part of CD-ROM technology will bring mathematics studies into the "real world" with students able to see mathematics at work. Students will problem solve along with the professionals on the scene through Internet hookups and downlinks to schools. Chapter 5 of this text discusses the problem-solving strategies necessary to do this type of mathematical thinking.

Technology is changing our physical world. As Burrill (1998) points out, technology will make some of the things we have done in the past unnecessary or even impossible to do. For example, manual adjustments of traffic lights will be unnecessary and even detrimental. Intelligent transportation systems will adjust the traffic lights blocks ahead to enable emergency vehicles to move swiftly to their destinations. Richmond, Virginia, has the "state of the art" system already begun. The CD-ROM activity in Chapter 15 in this text shows you the control room and the bank of computers that maintain the system. Students will not need to know how to do any one math procedure but rather to know about algorithms, and will practice for the real twenty-first century world of work by creating new algorithms themselves. The Richmond system depends on people who can keep creating new procedures as adjustments to the system. Learning only one procedure would throw the system into chaos!

A New Vision of Teachers. Teachers must know more than one way to get a solution before they can feel comfortable or even know how to ask the right questions when young people are trying to find different solutions. Teachers must know what is reasonable when students give solutions that have no corresponding answer in the teacher's manual

(Steen, 1997; Carl, 1995). The activities in the text and on the CD-ROM are geared to get you thinking on your own about mathematics. Sometimes there is one correct answer, but many ways to get to it. Other times there will be many answers but one way to get to them. A teacher must be able to know when and how to switch from one thought pattern to another to optimize the solution to the problem. This is not an easy task, but an essential one if we are to be ready for twenty-first century students.

Burrill (1998) states the challenges that will face all mathematics teachers in the future:

> *Connect the mathematics that you teach with the curriculum that you are supposed to teach. Find out what mathematics is taught in your grade cluster. Think hard about technology and how it can be used. Design your lessons carefully, and choose tasks that matter. Bring closure to the lessons that you teach. Help your students see the mathematics in what they do. Keep families informed about the mathematics as you are teaching and why. (p. 593)*

We are all in this together—parents, teachers, administrators, students. No one must be left out of the loop when planning for mathematics in the future.

SUMMARY

We have seen that the most important mathematical values of the ancient world are still the elements that are the most important in the present and will be in the future. How we decide to place the valuable old truths in the new package of constant change is a formidable task. We are challenged to remain focused and informed on the current trends in mathematics learning as knowledge doubles at geometric rates all around us.

Our hope is to use the technology of the present and future to preserve the importance of mathematics through the ages. As Professor Ray expressed it in the 1850s in *Ray's Intellectual Arithmetic,* the importance of mathematics is unequaled:

> *When properly taught, it is one of the most useful and interesting studies in which pupils can engage, and should be omitted by no one.*
>
> *By its study, learners are taught to reason, to analyze, to think for themselves; while it imparts confidence in their own reasoning powers, and strengthens the mental faculties. (p. 7)*

This book is dedicated to help you "impart confidence in their own reasoning powers" to every student you teach.

EXERCISES

For extended exercises, see the CD-ROM.

A. Memorization and Comprehension Exercises
Low-Level Thought Activities

1. Describe how your mathematics training was different from that of your parents and grandparents.
2. Pick a futurist and outline that person's prediction for education in the next century.
3. Identify several commercial software products for each of the following software types:
   - **a.** Drill and practice
   - **b.** Tutorial
   - **c.** Problem solving
   - **d.** Simulations
   - **e.** Spreadsheets
   - **f.** Graphics
   - **g.** Databases
   - **h.** Interactive multimedia
   - **i.** Shareware on the Internet

B. Application and Analysis Exercises
Middle-Level Thought Activities

1. Search professional journals to see how mathematics education has changed over the

years. Find the earliest journal in your library with articles about the teaching of mathematics. Compare it with journals from:

a. The late 1960s through the early 1970s
b. The mid to late 1970s
c. The 1980s
d. The present

What patterns or trends do you see? What do they tell you about mathematics education? How can they help you predict what might happen in the future? Use the following format to report on the pertinent findings:

Journal Reviewed: ______________________________

Publication Date: ____________ Grade Level: ____________

Subject Area: ______________________________

Author(s): ______________________________

____

Major Findings: ______________________________

____

Study or Teaching Procedure Outlined: ______________

____

Reviewed by: ______________________________

____

Some journals of note are listed here to help you get started, but there are many more. Search your library to discover what is available. Other chapters have similar assignments, so learning the journals now will pay off later.

Journal for Research in Mathematics Education
Mathematics Teacher
School Science and Mathematics
Teaching Children Mathematics
Mathematics Teaching in the Middle School

2. Review at least two articles on the teaching of calculators and two articles on the teaching of computers in elementary and middle school classrooms. Computer applications for classroom use are found in the journals in the following list. This is by no means an exhaustive list. Search the periodicals section of your library for more.

Learning and Leading with Technology
Technology and Learning
The Journal of Computers in Mathematics and Science Teaching
Computers in the Schools
T.H.E. Journal

C. **Synthesis and Evaluation Exercises**
High-Level Thought Activities

1. Speculate what you perceive the elementary or middle school classroom will be like in fifty years.
2. Write a letter to your students' parents explaining why you will be using a calculator and/or computer in your mathematics class all year.
3. Using the software evaluation form on the CD-ROM, evaluate a simulation, a problem-solving, a tutorial, and a drill-and-practice piece of software.
4. Reflect on the goals for students in the NCTM *Standards* document. Write a descriptive paragraph on each goal as to its importance in the students' future and how classroom instruction can help achieve those goals.
5. What additional insights other than those mentioned in this chapter must teachers have to survive the present and prepare for the future in mathematics education?

BIBLIOGRAPHY

For an extended bibliography, see the CD-ROM.

American Federation of Teachers and National Center for Improving Science Education, ed. *What Students Abroad Are Expected to Know about Mathematics: Defining World Class Standards.* Vol. 4. Reston, VA: National Council of Teachers of Mathematics, 1997.

Apple, Michael W. "Taking Power Seriously: New Directions in Equity in Mathematics Education and Beyond." Ed. Walter G. Secada, Elizabeth Fennema, and Lisa Byrd Adajian. *New Directions for Equity in Mathematics Education.* Cambridge, Eng.: Cambridge University Press, 1995: 329–348.

Association for Supervision and Curriculum Development, *Learning with Technology: 1998 Yearbook.* Ed. Chris Dede. Alexandria, VA: ASCD, 1998.

———, ed. "The Motivational Power of Technology," Focus Issue. *Curriculum/Technology Quarterly* 8 (Winter 1998).

Biehler, Robert F., and Jack Snowman. *Psychology Applied to Teaching.* 8th ed. Boston: Houghton Mifflin, 1997.

Brough, Judith A. "Changing Conditions for Young Adolescents: Reminiscences and Realities." *Educational Horizons* 68 (Winter 1990): 78–81.

Burrill, Gail. "The President's Report: Changes in Your Classroom: From the Past to the Present to the Future." *Journal for Research in Mathematics Education* 29 (November 1998): 583–593.

Calcari, Susan. *Scout Report.* Online posting. http://rs.internic.net/scout_report-index.html World Wide Web. 9 January 1999.

Carl, Iris M., ed. *Seventy-Five Years of Progress: Prospects for School Mathematics.* Reston, VA: National Council of Teachers of Mathematics, 1995.

Christ, George M. "Curriculums with Real-World Connections." *Educational Leadership* 52 (May 1995): 32–35.

Clements, Douglas H. *Turtle Math* Rev. Vers. 1.01. Diskette. Montreal: Logo Computer Systems, Inc., 1994.

Clinton, William J. *President Clinton's Call to Action for American Education in the 21st Century.* Washington, DC: U.S. Department of Education, 1998.

Curcio, Frances R., ed. *Grades 5–8 Addenda Series* (6 books). Reston, VA: National Council of Teachers of Mathematics, 1994.

Darling-Hammond, Linda, and Barnett Berry. *Reforming Teaching: Another View of Why and How.* Washington, DC: National Commission on Teaching and America's Future, 1998.

Dede, Chris, ed. *Learning with Technology.* 1998 ASCD Yearbook. Alexandria, VA: Association for Supervision and Curriculum Development, 1998.

Dehaene, Stanislas. *The Number Sense: How the Mind Creates Mathematics.* New York: Oxford, 1997.

Diamond, Marian, and Janet Hopson. *Magic Trees of the Mind: How to Nurture Your Child's Intelligence, Creativity, and Healthy Emotions from Birth Through Adolescence.* New York: Dutton, 1998.

Edwards, Nancy Tanner. Interview with Margaret Bangerter, Mathematics Curriculum Coordinator, St. Joseph, MO. January 7, 1999.

Forgione, Pascal D., Jr., ed. *Introduction to TIMSS: The Third International Mathematics and Science Study.* Washington, DC: U.S. Department of Education, 1997.

Gillespie, Linda. "How to Use Writing across the Curriculum." Workshop presented to New Teachers of Chesterfield County, VA. October 1, 1998.

Heid, M. Kathleen, Charlene Sheets, Mary Ann Matras, and James Menasian. "Classroom and Computer Lab Interaction in a Computer-Intensive Algebra Curriculum." Paper presented at the annual meeting of the American Educational Research Association, San Diego. April 1998.

Hiebert. James. "Relationships between Research and the NCTM Standards." *Journal for Research in Mathematics Education* 30 (January 1999): 3–19.

Kloosterman, Peter, and Monica Clapp Cougan. "Students' Beliefs about Learning School Mathematics." *The Elementary School Journal* 94 (March 1994): 375–388.

Leder, Gilah C. "Equity Inside the Mathematics Classroom: Fact or Artifact?" Ed. Walter G. Secada, Elizabeth Fennema, and Lisa Byrd Adajian. *New Directions for Equity in Mathematics Education.* Cambridge, Eng.: Cambridge University Press, 1995.

LEGO Group. *LEGO MINDSTORMS: Robotics Invention System.* Billund, Denmark: Lego Corp., 1998.

Milne, William J. *Standard Arithmetic.* New York: American Book Co., 1892.

Morehouse, Pam. "The Building of an Airplane (with a little help from friends)." *Educational Leadership* 52 (May 1995): 56–57.

National Assessment of Educational Progress. *Mathematics Framework for the 1996 National Assessment of Educational Progress.* Washington, DC: National Assessment Governing Board, U.S. Department of Education, 1996.

National Centers for Implementation of Standards-Based Mathematics Curricula. *Services of the Centers and Satellites.* Under Grant ESI-9729328, ESI-9714999, and ESI-961968. Washington, DC: National Science Foundation, 1999.

National Council for the Accreditation of Colleges of Teacher Education. *Elementary Education Program Review Standards: Draft Document.* Washington, DC: NCATE, 1999.

———. *Mathematics Program Review Standards.* Washington, DC: NCATE, 1998.

National Council of Teachers of Mathematics. *Assessment Standards for School Mathematics.* Reston, VA: NCTM, 1995.

———. *Curriculum and Evaluation Standards for School Mathematics.* Reston, VA: NCTM, 1989.

———. *Mathematics Teaching in the Middle School* 4 (January 1999): 213–276.

———. *Principles and Standards for School Mathematics.* Reston, VA: NCTM, 2000 (to be published).

———. *Professional Standards for Teaching Mathematics.* Reston, VA: NCTM, 1991.

National Research Council. *Everybody Counts: A Report to the Nation on the Future of Mathematics Education.* Washington, DC: National Academy Press, 1989.

Neyland, Jim, ed. *Mathematics Education: A Handbook for Teachers.* Vol. 2. Reston, VA: National Council of Teachers of Mathematics, 1996.

Ray, Joseph. *Intellectual Arithmetic.* New York: Van Antwerp, Bragg, 1850.

Reese, Clyde M., Karen E. Miller, John Mazzeo, and John A. Dossey. NAEP 1996 Mathematics Report Card for the Nation and the States. Washington, DC: National Center for Educational Statistics, 1997.

Spectrum. Online posting. Spectrum@pacificnet.net. Spectrum Universal. (14 August 1995).

Steen, Lynn Arthur, ed. *Why Numbers Count—Quantitative Literacy for Tomorrow's America.* Reston, VA: National Council of Teachers of Mathematics, 1997.

Sylwester, Robert. *A Celebration of Neurons: An Educator's Guide to the Brain.* Alexandria, VA: Association for Supervision and Curriculum Development, 1995.

Teppo, Anne R., ed. *Qualitative Research Methods in Mathematics Education.* Reston, VA: National Council of Teachers of Mathematics, 1998.

Thiessen, Diane, Margaret Matthias, and Jacquelin Smith. *The Wonderful World of Mathematics: A Critically Annotated List of Children's Books in Mathematics.* 2nd Ed. Reston, VA: National Council of Teachers of Mathematics, 1998.

Thornton, Carol A., and Nancy S. Bley, ed. *Windows of Opportunity: Mathematics for Students with Special Needs.* Reston, VA: National Council of Teachers of Mathematics, 1994.

Waite-Stupiansky, Sandra, and Nicholas G. Stupiansky. "Think Math." *Scholastic Early Childhood Today* (March 1995): 38–45.

Integrating Technology

Video Vignettes: Lesson Plans in Action

- Chapter 1: *Teacher's Reflections on Mathematics Teaching*
- Chapter 7: *Pizza Perimeters*
- Chapter 9: *Whale Math*
- Chapter 10: *Dinosaur Legs*
- Chapter 15: *Graphing Probability*

Computer Software Resources

...for Topics on the Past, Present, and Future of Mathematics Education

Internet Searches

Surfing the Internet for Topics on the Past, Present, and Future of Mathematics Education

Use the World Wide Web (WWW) and navigate through the system, searching for new information under major headings, and subheadings similar to the following:

Mathematics Education
  Discussion Groups on Lesson Plans, Current Research, etc.
  Interactive Bulletin Boards
NCTM
  Hot Topics
  Research Studies
  Updates on the *Standards*
  Curriculum and Evaluation Standards address http://www.enc.org/
Children's Sources on the Internet
  See those mentioned in the chapter to start your search.

Surfing the Internet for Freeware Logo Programs

Use any Internet connection that can put you in touch with shareware programs. Many groups exist and more are coming into existence daily. Navigate through the system, searching for shareware programs.

You are looking for programs that have Logo in the title.

Several shareware groups on the Internet have made Logo startup systems to share. Individual commands may differ slightly from one kind of Logo to another. You may need to experiment.

The right-hand panel of each Logo screen will show you the commands that run that particular program in Logo. Those are the commands you may need to convert to a new Logo system.

(continued)

Integrating Technology (continued)

Surfing the Internet for Children's LEGO MINDSTORM Homepages

The LEGO-Logo MINDSTORMS system permits children to link their Lego programs to the Lego Systems Homepage.

You can view their creations at http://www.LEGOMINDSTORMS.com.

- *Remember*... the Web is fluid... new topics and ways to search for topics change daily.
- Be adventurous... think of some new things you could try.

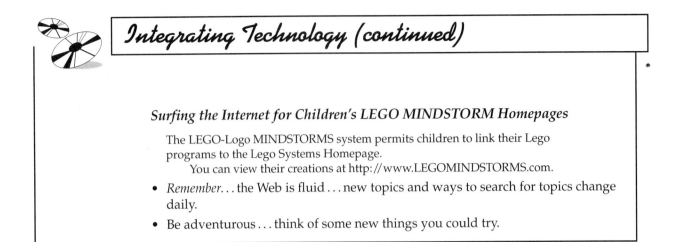

2

Culturally Relevant Mathematics

Activities Index

IN THE TEXT

ON CD-ROM

Culturally relevant mathematics is a term that shows awareness on the part of educators that all subjects, including mathematics, exist within a cultural environment that must not be ignored. A richness of mathematical understanding has evolved from diverse cultures of the past and the present. All students deserve the right to know, appreciate, and benefit from the mathematical contributions of these cultures.

The term *culturally relevant mathematics* has a two-prong definition:

1. The recognition that mathematics has been present in every culture since societies have had recorded histories to document its use by people; the giftedness of many cultures in mathematics, that is, *multiculturalism.*
2. The effect of mathematics on any culture and its people; the right for *all* people to acquire the mathematical power for success in today's world, that is, *equity.*

We discuss both aspects of cultural relevance in this chapter. Mathematics is affected by the diverse cultures in which it finds itself—where mathematics must play out its daily role; and it is affected by the cultural pluralism of the students who come to learn mathematics. Where students are coming from and where they need to go to use mathematics effectively in today's global society may be worlds apart.

The National Council of Teachers of Mathematics (NCTM) has produced several position papers reaffirming the importance of mathematics education for all people in underrepresented groups and second language learners. They are found in Chapter 1 on the CD-ROM.

The overriding challenge for teachers, mathematics teachers included, is to help all students find a place in our pluralistic world where they can exercise their human rights to the pursuit of mathematical success (Ravitch, 1991/92; Nelson, Joseph, and Williams, 1993; Campbell and Rowan, 1997; Michael-Bardele, 1998). The issue centers on several key questions for mathematics teachers: How can we take students from culturally diverse backgrounds and give them the mathematical understanding needed to be full participants in society? How much of a part do diverse cultural backgrounds and beliefs play in the acquisition of mathematics understanding? This chapter explores some of the research being done to help answer these questions. We also examine some of the exemplary teaching practices that show the most promise to help achieve equal access to mathematics power for all students.

THE GIFTEDNESS OF MANY CULTURES IN MATHEMATICS

Cultural Contributions: A Sense of Pride

Many qualities from diverse cultures can be used to help, not hinder, mathematics equity for all students. Zaslavsky (1998) states that the discipline of mathematics can no longer be viewed as culture-free. *Ethnomathematics* is one term used to describe the awareness that different ethnic groups, national societies, and so on bring their unique sociocultural understandings to the performance of mathematics. The International Study Group on Ethnomathematics was organized in 1985 as an affiliate group of the National Council of Teachers of Mathematics. Information on the group is available at the NCTM web site listed in the Internet resources at the end of this chapter. Membership is open to all interested persons and many countries are represented in its list of members.

Respect for one's own culture and the respect for the culture of others is essential as we strive for quality of life. The 1990 mathematics goals for each grade level in the Chicago public schools, for example, include the contributions that have been made by diverse cultures in the field of mathematics. Students have the opportunity to see the contributions mentioned as they study each strand. When this approach is followed consistently each year, children begin to believe that their culture and other cultures *really did* make contributions to the things they are studying. Pride and a sense of hope, rather than learned helplessness, are education's goals for students who previously would never have considered mathematics as a viable option in their lives.

The following testimony best explains why an emphasis on multiculturalism in mathematics is of the utmost importance. Monique Mesa (Figure 2.1) from Kansas City, Missouri, is a 1995 teacher education graduate:

> *Coming from a bi-cultural family, I feel that multicultural education is very important. Whenever we talked about Hispanics or other cultures in school, I felt a sense of pride. I think it is important for all children to experience that feeling of pride in their cultural background. It does wonders for their self-esteem.*

FIGURE 2.1

Monique Mesa. (Photo taken by Anne Adams.)

The list of contributions as they relate to all grade levels is presented so that each reader can take advantage of the opportunity to learn about other cultures and to share the information with students in the future (see Box 2.1). This is a summary of the culturally relevant facts appearing in current curriculum materials. Much greater detail is presented in each chapter as various mathematics concepts are discussed.

Sample mathematics activities celebrating different cultures follow in the content chapters where appropriate for elementary and middle school students. The range of possible mathematics activities is great, so the authors have picked cultural activities they feel are especially appropriate to teach stu-

BOX 2.1 Mathematics Objectives That Reflect Multiculturalism

Multiculturalism is summarized in a statement following each of the seven strands related to the State Goals for Learning in Mathematics. A multicultural statement precedes the list of objectives for each strand at each grade level K–12.

Arithmetic: Many peoples contributed to the development of the modern system of numerals. (Africans were the first to use numerals. Ancient Egyptians in Africa invented a symbol for ten that replaced 10 tally marks and a symbol for one hundred that replaced 100 tally marks. The Chinese invented negative numbers. Native Americans were the first to use a symbol for zero. Ancient Egyptians invented unit fractions.)

Quantitative Relationships: Students should know that the ancient Egyptians invented proportional scale drawing. They enlarged figures proportionally by transferring drawings from grids of small squares to grids of large squares.

Measurement: Students should be able to relate the origin of geometry to real-life situations. (Examples: The annual flooding of the Nile River in Africa created a need to measure the area of triangles, rectangles, and circles. The building of the pyramids created a need to develop formulas for the volume of pyramids. The unit of measurement was the cubit, the length of the pharaoh's forearm. The 24-hour day—12 hours of day and 12 hours of night—originated in Egypt.)

Algebraic Concepts: Students should know that Africans invented rectangular coordinates by 2650 B.C. and used them to make scale drawings and starclocks. The students should examine the Egyptian use of the distributive property in multiplication. (Example: Ancient Egyptians multiplied 21×34 by selecting $(1 + 4 + 16) \times 34$ from successive doublings of 1×34.) They should explore patterns to find the next term in the sequence *1, 7, 49, 343,* which was taken from an ancient Egyptian papyrus. Students should know that the word *algebra* is Arabic in origin and that Europe received algebra as a gift from Asia and Africa.

Geometric Concepts: Students should know that the first concepts of congruence were developed in Africa and Asia and that cotangents and similar triangle principles were used in the building of the African pyramids. The students should examine the contributions to geometry made by people all over the world. (Examples: Eskimos built igloos in the shape of a catenary. Mozambicans built rectangular houses by using equal-length ropes as the diagonals. The Babylonians used the right triangle theorem 1500 years before Pythagoras was born. The term *Pythagorean theorem* is a misnomer.)

Data Analysis: Students should know that many peoples used and contributed to statistics and probability. (Examples: The Mayan people learned to predict eclipses by analyzing astronomical tables that they had made over the centuries. The peoples of Egypt and Mesopotamia developed geometric formulas through experimentation and data analysis.) Students should explore methods for collecting statistics and predicting outcomes related to real-life problems. (Examples: In Africa, ancient Egyptian governments prepared budgets and levied taxes based on data analysis. Measurements of the annual flood, made with a Nilometer, were used to predict the size of the harvest.)

Applications: Students should explore methods for collecting statistics and predicting outcomes related to real-life problems. (Examples: In Africa, ancient Egyptian governments prepared budgets and levied taxes based on data analysis. Measurements of the annual flood, made with a Nilometer, were used to predict the size of the harvest. The modern method of using the so-called Pascal's triangle was actually invented in Asia by the Chinese and the Persians 500 years before Pascal was born.)

Source: Strong, 1991c, p. 38.

dents at strategic skill levels. Activities that promote cultural relevance in mathematics are denoted with the cultural relevance icon.

General activities are presented in this chapter to give the reader a sense of the diversity of mathematics lessons for use in classrooms. Those chosen are from the most prominent cultures of today's schools in the United States and Canada, namely African American, Native American, Hispanic American, Asian American, and European American. Since the European American perspective has been the one largely appearing in textbooks over the years, only the more unusual and unknown mathematical facts are discussed. This includes the accomplishments of woman mathematicians from various countries whose contributions have been largely ignored in textbooks over the years. Many multicultural resources in mathematics are beginning to appear in print (Caduto and Bruchac, 1989; 1991; Kunjufu, 1987a, 1987b, 1987c; Akoto, 1990; Reimer and Reimer, 1992, 1995; Spence, 1996; Strong, 1990, 1991a, 1991b; Secada, Fennema, and Adajian, 1995; Voolich, 1993; Taylor, 1997; Mingo 1997 to name only a few). The chapter Bibliography attempts to list some of the best resources available to the classroom teacher. Readers are encouraged to start making a list of resources as they find them. With more and more mathematics resources in print, the classroom teacher has the opportunity to provide exciting mathematics lessons with cultural perspectives for elementary and middle school students.

African American Heritage

From the Great Pyramids of Egypt to the irrigation of desert into farmlands along the Nile River, Africans have been creating mathematical formulas in geometry, measurement, algebra, and statistics (data analysis) for generations. The tradition of using many kinds of unique mathematics continues in African societies of today.

The African American heritage values extended family and encourages resilience seen in a positive sense of self, reflected in "positive self-talk" (Malloy, 1997). Life, the very act of living, is considered more valuable than time. The here and now is important. Time implies something in the future and is less valued than what is occurring at the present. A meeting scheduled for 10:00 A.M. may get under way at 10:20 A.M. Since time is relative, arriving "around" the time a meeting or school event is due to start is *not* considered rude or unorganized. The African American heritage includes the quality of speaking in proverbs, with holistic thought patterns seen as desirable to view the whole picture or system of events. This ability proved valuable over many centuries when creating many of the mathematical systems on which our modern mathematical structures are built.

Unique Systems of Mathematics Today. In the spirit of positive cultural contributions, Zaslavsky (1991) prepared lessons for sixth and ninth graders on the mathematics used by African societies. She reports that the students were fascinated to see Tanzanian round houses achieving the greatest floor area for a given amount of building material. The students discovered this principle for themselves after a difficult hands-on experience involving surface areas of circles and squares. The students were equally fascinated to find that the Bakuha children of Zaire can do graphing in network theory that adult Belgian ethnographers could not do. The students were given lessons on the points of graphing or network theory showing the intelligence of the Chokwe elders of Angola. Zaslavsky reports that many students went looking for traceable networks in other designs after they experienced the lessons for themselves. Several African American students expressed delight to know that children from the African country of Zaire could perform mathematics that adults in the white culture could not do. Davidson and Kramer (1997) describe the same effect during similar units of study.

African Mathematics from the Ancient World. You will see African teaching ideas throughout the text and on the CD-ROM. Sample activities are shown here for the elementary and middle school.

African Ideas in Elementary Mathematics. This activity comes from the use of the numeration system in ancient Africa. Bohan and Bohan (1993) started elementary lessons by having children problem solve the similarities between the system of ancient times and our system today. Children were asked to write large numbers in the ancient system. They found that the string of numerals seemed very long and tedious to write. Bohan and Bohan then encouraged students to problem solve ways they could make the ancient system less cumbersome. The journal article shows the work of several students.

After reading the journal article, a student teacher decided to motivate her class by telling them that other children across the country had done the activity too. She said she would let her students compare their number systems with those she had found in the Bohan and Bohan article after her class had finished the work. The following reflection became part of the student teacher's professional portfolio. *Important—Notice that the students are always told which cultural group is being celebrated in the mathematics activity.* That is vital if we ever hope to have students understanding the giftedness of all cultures. The student teacher's words are modeled in the activity.

Activity 2.1

CREATING YOUR OWN NUMERATION SYSTEM WITH ANCIENT AFRICA AS AN EXAMPLE

MATERIALS

- Pictures shown to children from the Bohan and Bohan (1993) article
- Pencil and paper to make their own systems

DIRECTIONS

1. Show how to write a large number in the Egyptian system from Africa as presented in the article.
2. Use these words to start the activity: "The ancestors of our African Americans invented a great numeral system in a country called Egypt. The African numerals in the activity are much too long to write every time. What way could you invent to make the number shorter to write? Write out how you would explain your system to a first grader."
3. Figure 2.2 shows Teisha's work and explanation.
4. Teisha took a ruler and measured her numeral to the one in the journal each time. This was her own idea; no one had told her to do this.
5. Then Mary's King Tut system from the journal article was shown to Teisha. Figure 2.3 shows Teisha's response.

Activity Continues

FIGURE 2.3

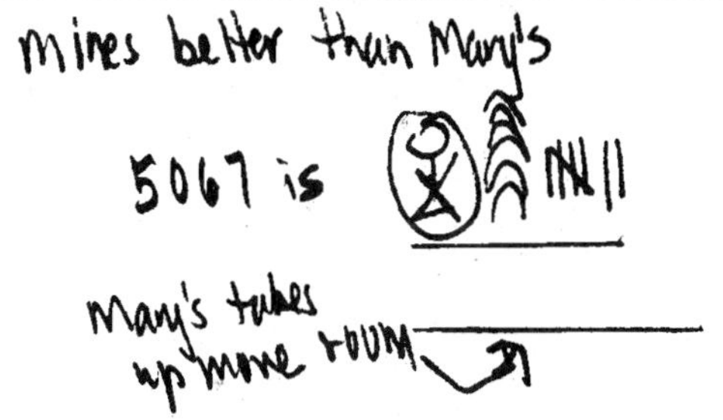

Teisha compares her work to Mary's.

Teisha meticulously measured her numeral and Mary's numeral with the ruler. She demonstrated that her numeral took up less space. She was quite proud of this discovery.

6. Then Teisha was shown that Mary's numeral for 9642 would be shorter than hers. Mary's 9642 was not shown in the book, so the student teacher drew it like this:

FIGURE 2.4

Student teacher's drawing of 9642 as Mary's system would show it.

FIGURE 2.2

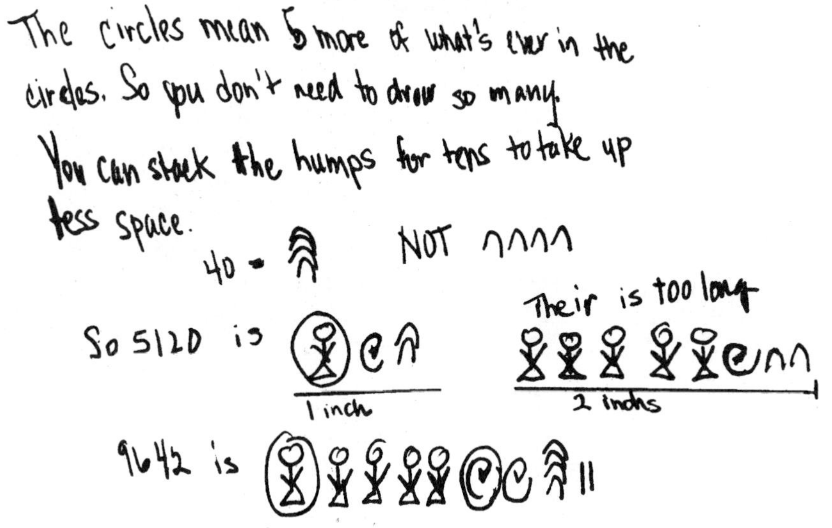

Teisha's numeration system.

Activity Continues

7. Teisha's response: She looked very disappointed and insisted on measuring hers and Mary's with a ruler although it was easy to see that Mary's was shorter. Then she said, "Mary's is okay, but I still like mine better. You just don't have to use really big numbers. I will only write numbers up to 6000 and then it would be shorter than hers."

Your Portfolio Reflection:

What understandings did Teisha bring to the task that she chose 6000 as the significant numeral to use here? How would you rate her understanding of mathematical concepts for an elementary school student?

Supporting the NCTM *Principals and Standards* (2000):

- Mathematics as Problem Solving; Mathematics as Communication
- Worthwhile Mathematical Tasks; Mathematics as Oral and Written Discourse—The Teaching Principle
- Evaluating Students' Achievement—The Assessment Principle
- The Equity Principle . . . assessment should promote equity

In this example the student teacher learned a clever way to use professional journals in teaching. There are many new assessments in which children's actual work is shown in journal articles. It is often easier to motivate a class with the promise that they can see the work of others doing the same activity. Students are fascinated that others across the country are asked to do the same things they are. Classroom management improves when your class asks the familiar question:

Students: "Do we have to do this?"

Teacher: "I can't imagine that you want that class in Missouri to look better than we do. I want you to be the kings and queens of the mountain, the top dogs in math. You are such a super class of thinkers!"

The preceding discourse is quick and works wonders to stop the whining of students by providing a challenge to do good problem solving. If the students' answers are not as good as the journal group at first, encourage them by saying that the journal group has been doing it a lot longer than they have. That is assuredly true, since authors practice a strategy or skill with a class before publishing the first work of most students.

Internet services are wonderful sources for students talking to students. Look on the book's web site for an updated list to share with you elementary students. Plan some problems like the ones shown in the Bohan and Bohan article and go online for student-to-student written discourse. There will be more Internet links in the future for children and teens. Keep your eyes open for the new technologies coming out. The possibilities are endless!

African Ideas in Middle School Mathematics. The following activities are ones that have been used with middle school students. The first one is actually a unit of activities. The students experience the tremendous size of the Great Pyramids in Egypt by using ratio and proportion measurements on the athletic field and in the classroom. This set of mathematics lessons gives students an appreciation for what it took to make the pyramids. The superior mathematical knowledge of the Egyptians in the African culture should be stressed. What would a people have to know to construct a pyramid 13 acres square at its base? Yes, you read it correctly—13 acres square at the base!

EXTENDED ACTIVITIES

Name of Activity

- Black History Connections—A Middle School Unit
- Pyramid Measurements
- Babylonian Logo Activity Created by African American Middle School Students

A third activity shows the work of middle school students, eighth graders, who had been studying the early Babylonian numeration system. In the early Babylonian numeration system, the size of the numeral was significant. The bigger the numeral, the larger the number it represented. The students had been working with the Logo computer language since early elementary school. They invented their own Babylonian system on the computer. The program is presented on the CD-ROM so you can see how students can integrate mathematics, computer technology, and cultural awareness all in the same mathematics project. This activity was done in cooperative groups. It shows how the students programmed the keystrokes to make each numeral.

Resources for Contributions of African Americans Who Used Mathematics. Jawanza Kunjufu has written several books to help teachers and students learn more about the contributions of African Americans to our lives. The books are in both elementary and junior–senior high editions and come with a teacher's guide (Kunjufu, 1987a, 1987b, 1987c). Students can use the bibliographies in these books to find more interesting facts about the scientists and inventors who used mathematics in their work. Some facts you will learn include many "firsts" invented by African Americans; for example, first traffic light, first book on electricity, first parallel circuitry, first machine to mass produce shoes, first tires on moon buggy, first surgeon to operate on human heart in United States, first to develop blood plasma, first drafted plans of telephone for Alexander Graham Bell, first railroad car coupler; the list goes on and on.

The first African American mathematician, Benjamin Banneker (1731–1806), deserves special note. Some of his accomplishments were:

- Made the first clock in America
- Surveyed and designed layout of Washington, D.C. (with five others)
- Reconstructed the whole plan from memory when original was stolen
- Wrote *Almanac* in 1792, which received international acclaim
- Wrote first science book by an African American

Teachers interested in the work of African American mathematicians and the education of African American children in mathematics are welcome to join the Benjamin Banneker Mathematics Association. It is an affiliated group of the National Council of Teachers of Mathematics. Information about the group can be found by contacting NCTM. It is easy to see why the group chose the name of Benjamin Banneker.

Other resources that add cultural interest to African mathematics lessons are briefly reviewed here. Of course, these are only a few of the many books that are available. They have been chosen because the authors have used them in classrooms and know they have been enjoyed by students, regardless of their heritage. One book is by Atlantis Tye Browder (1991), an eight-year-old who visits Africa for the first time and discovers the mathematical insights of her ancestors. Children love her discoveries and find it fascinating that an eight-year-old can be published. Her obvious pride in her discoveries and what she learns about cities in North America makes delightful reading. The 27 photos, 15 illustrations, and 3 maps help children and adults understand the region and contributions of Africa to our world.

A book by Ellis (1989) contains beautiful pictures of the art, textile designs, sculpture, and architecture of Africa for beginning readers. The geometric designs fit well with an introduction to shapes in early geometry lessons. Those ideas are seen in Chapter 6. The book features the Afro-Bets Kids, an adventuresome group of children known to many students in grade school.

Another book, called *Shaka: King of the Zulus* (Stanley and Vennema, 1988), shows how a young boy used logic and reasoning, the essence of mathematics, to change the methods of battle and took the Zulu people from a small tribe to a great nation. Today there are more Zulus in South Africa than any other group. There are monuments erected and many historical accounts written about this great chief. Many of the accounts were written by admiring Englishmen who studied Shaka's ability to analyze and invent new battle strategies. Middle school students find such biographies fascinating.

Another book, called *My First Kwanzaa Book* (Chocolate, 1992) can be used with beginning counting activities. Kwanzaa is a nonreligious holiday celebrating the seven principles of African life—unity (helping each other), self-determination (deciding things for ourselves), collaboration and responsibility (working together to make life better), cooperative economics (supporting our own businesses), purpose (a reason for living), creativity (using our minds and hands to create things), and faith (belief in self, ancestors, and the future). Each day from December 26 to January 1 a candle is lit in remembrance of one of the seven principles. Children of all cultures can do the counting activities listed in Chapter 10. A teacher can feature the number 7 in honor of Kwanzaa. Certainly, the seven virtues are desirable ones for all peoples. Jacobs and Becker (1997) describe the mathematical pattern used in the lighting of the Kwanzaa candles:

> *There is one black candle, three red candles, and three green candles. On the first night the black candle is lit in the middle position. The second night the black candle and a red candle are lit. The third night the black, the red, and a green candle are lit. This pattern continues with each night having an additional candle lit, alternating red and green as the additional candle. On the seventh night, all candles are lit, with three red, then a black candle, and then three green. If each night's candles are burned completely in a single night, what is the total number of candles used and how many of each color are used over the seven days? (p. 109)*

Jacobs and Becker (1997) also point out that the similarity to the structure of the menorah candlestick holder for the Chanukah lighting can be shown to students, with similar math problems created to figure out how many candles would be needed for the eight-night celebration of Chanukah. Students from one culture are often surprised to see that students from another culture may celebrate with similar rituals while commemorating different events and thoughts. Activities like those described here make for a rich environment in which to explore mathematics.

Native American Heritage

The Native American heritage is *one with nature.* All things are seen as having a soul; they are celebrated just for "being." No one needs any other reason to focus on their existence. The Native American culture is one of cooperation and deep value of the extended family. Nature speaks and teaches the worth of cooperation and deep care for others. Native American stories may be seen by other cultures as always ending with a moral, but it should *not* be taken as a means of preaching morality. It is merely restating the worth of the soul from which the story had its being.

Native American Culture in Mathematics Lessons. Native Americans celebrate their oneness with nature in art, music, dance, and in the language of wholeness. Mathematics may be seen: (1) in the blending of stories with the resulting actions of reasoning and problem solving, and (2) as symmetry of nature in its designs and proportions, a harmony in all things.

Native American Ideas in Stories of Reasoning and Problem Solving. Mathematics lessons can focus on the use of Native American stories to start an activity in mathematics. Two beautiful books have received high praise for their use of Native American stories, *Keepers of the Earth, Keepers of the Animals,* and *Keepers of Life* (Caduto and Bruchac, 1989, 1991, 1994). Teacher's guides are also available. See the activity called, "Creating Proportions with Native American Stories" in Chapter 13 as an example of how the stories can be used to start a mathematics lesson that leads to problem solving and reasoning answers to mathematics problems.

Notice that each story comes from a different tribal nation. *It is important to tell the name of the tribal nation during the telling of the story.* It is a form of deep respect to acknowledge the tribe for its contribution to the wisdom of the Native American peoples. It is much like European Americans who are proud to be French, Italian, or British. Each tribal nation has its own language, customs, and stories. It is a mistake to put all Native Americans in one "basket," just as it is a mistake to do the same to any group who has given much to preserve its identity and contributions.

Other story starters are modeled throughout the text and on the CD-ROM along with teaching ideas for mathematics lessons.

EXTENDED ACTIVITIES

Name of Activity

- Native American Story Starters with Mathematics Concepts

CULTURAL RELEVANCE

PROBLEM SOLVING

Native American Ideas in Symmetry and Harmony of Nature. Mathematics is seen as a symmetry of nature in its designs and proportions. Taylor and her associates (1991) found that tesselations with attribute pieces (seen in Chapter 6) bear a strong resemblance to Native American patterns as seen on many beautiful art objects and in cloth designs. Students enjoyed the lessons prepared for use with hands-on attribute pieces to create their own tesselations. The designs could be transferred to paper to create an ink pattern that could be duplicated for others to see. Taylor and associates (1991) give many examples of the creative tesselations along with the Native American designs.

Elementary and Middle School Lessons. The activity on the CD-ROM, Finding Native American Designs with Mirror Puzzles, starts with a simple design of the sun, recalling the brightness and warmth of life. Young children can do this one. Middle school students can do the more intricate designs shown at the end of the activity. At first students merely try to place a mirror on the boxed design to make the same designs shown on the paper. After they see how the process works, older children can make a Native American design and duplicate it on a copy machine several times. Then they can cut, flip, or rotate the image to make various figures. Other students can use the activity as a mirror match. The activity is modeled after the format of mirror images seen in *The Mirror Puzzle Book* by Marion Walter (1988). The Native American designs are sketched from various pictures (U.S. Bureau of Indian Affairs, 1993; Arnold, 1982) with many coming from Pueblo pottery designs.

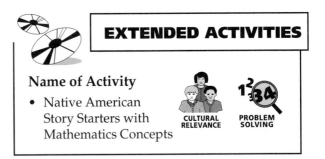

Match the design in the box. The detailed lesson plan is on the CD-ROM.

The Logo computer language is especially good for making repeated designs created by students at many grade levels. Look through books of Native American art and make stylized versions of the Native American symbols, much as the Native American artists do (Bradley 1992, 1993). Children's literature books such as *The Flute Player* (Lacapa, 1990) and *Antelope Women* (Lacapa, 1992) show patterns that can be replicated or used as a basis for students to create their own patterns. These books provide an excellent connection with art across the curriculum.

Clo Mingo (1997) has created several middle school activities for the TI-82 graphing calculator using ideas from the Anasazi tribe. These include ways to show the Sun Dagger spiral petroglyph found near the top of Fajada Butte in Chaco Culture National Historical Park, placed there by the ancient Anasazi to record equinoxes, solstices, and phases of the moon in a nineteen-year cycle. Mingo's innovative ideas appear on the CD-ROM.

EXTENDED ACTIVITIES

CALCULATORS | MATHEMATICAL CONNECTIONS | CULTURAL RELEVANCE

Name of Activity

- Finding Native American Designs with Mirror Puzzles
- Wild Animal Math: A Native American Lesson
- Graphing Calculator with Anasazi Math

Mathematics Resources from Native American Educators. Each year the U.S. Bureau of Indian Affairs sponsors a week-long workshop at Haskell Indian University in Lawrence, Kansas, where Native American elementary and secondary teachers come together to write mathematics and science lessons from a cultural perspective. The lessons are bound into books and are available through the Bureau of Indian Affairs. Some of the lessons are featured in this text and on the CD-ROM. Editor Joyce Haines (1992) wrote:

> *This book may be used in part or whole for educational purposes.*
>
> *The developers of individual lesson units in this curriculum guide are solely responsible for citing any materials borrowed from other authors. The editor and workshop consultants disclaim any liability for violation of publication rights or copyright laws.*

It is in the spirit of education and respect for the Native American traditions that we give you a sampling of the lessons available through the Bureau of Indian Affairs.

Lessons for the Early and Middle School Grades. A grade-2 mathematics lesson, Wild Animal Math, is shown on the CD-ROM (Henley, 1992, pp. 163–166). There are many more like this one in the Native American curriculum books for science and mathematics (see Haines, 1992).

Starting in 1993, Native American mathematics teachers have met at the annual meeting of the National Council of Teachers of Mathematics. The group wants to conduct a contest in reservation schools for a Native American mathematics design for the group. The group will be named after a Native American symbol common to all tribes. The decisions on the logo and the name of the group have not been made as of this printing. As with all affiliated groups of NCTM, membership is open to all. Information about the group will be available from NCTM through the mail and on the Internet.

Hispanic American Heritage

The work ethic and extended family are two strong images in Hispanic culture. The father is revered as the head of the family. Family activities are valued and a sense of celebration prevails when the extended family is together. Feast days, marriages, and special holidays are cause for celebration and may last over several days. Children are the responsibility of the whole extended family, not just the mother and father (Morales-Jones, 1998). Time versus life issues are much the same as they are in the African American community.

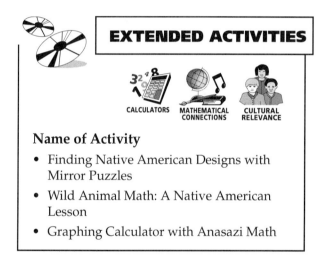

Hispanic American Culture in Mathematics Lessons. Beane (1990) points to the positive cultural values of "extended family" seen in both the African American and Hispanic American culture. A goal of the project Say YES was to have children bring parents, grandparents, aunts, and uncles to school on Saturday to explore family math projects. Beane reports a significant rise in test scores, student attitudes, and self-esteem among the students who participated in the project. Many books and articles have been written under the topic, "Family Math." Homework gets the family involved to ask questions that involve reasoning and patterning. When the directions are clear and the expectations communicated by the teacher, the teacher can count on a Hispanic family being a part of the mathematics homework. Hispanic culture has much to teach all families of the beauty of doing mathematics together.

Hispanic Teaching Ideas from the Ancient World. The Mayan society of Central America is a prime example of the power of the mind to create efficiency in mathematics. Cut off from the rest of the world, they invented the most remarkable number system of all the ancient civilizations. They needed only three symbols to write any number they wished—a dot, a line, and an oval eye. Just as a 0 is a place holder in our system that makes things ten times larger, the oval eye meant that things were twenty times larger. The following activity can be used with young children or expanded to teach middle school students. It is adapted from a similar exercise seen in Mitchell (1978). The activities stress the reasoning and patterning skills first used by the Mayans.

Activity 2.2

CULTURAL RELEVANCE
MATHEMATICAL CONNECTIONS

FINDING THE NEXT MAYAN NUMBER

MATERIALS

- Each child copies the numbers with the blank spaces along the way.

DIRECTIONS

Elementary Students (see Figure 2.5):

1. Use these words to start the activity:
   "This lesson shows the smart thinking of the Mayan people. They are the ancestors of the Hispanic Americans today. Study the numerals of the Mayan system. Fill in the blanks for the next number."

FIGURE 2.5

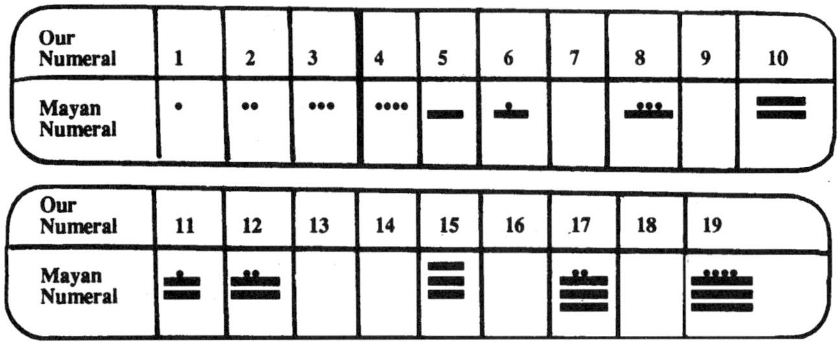
Our Numeral
1
2
3
4
5
6
7
8
9
10
Mayan Numeral
Our Numeral
11
12
13
14
15
16
17
18
19
Mayan Numeral

Mayan numeral chart for early grades to do.

FIGURE 2.6

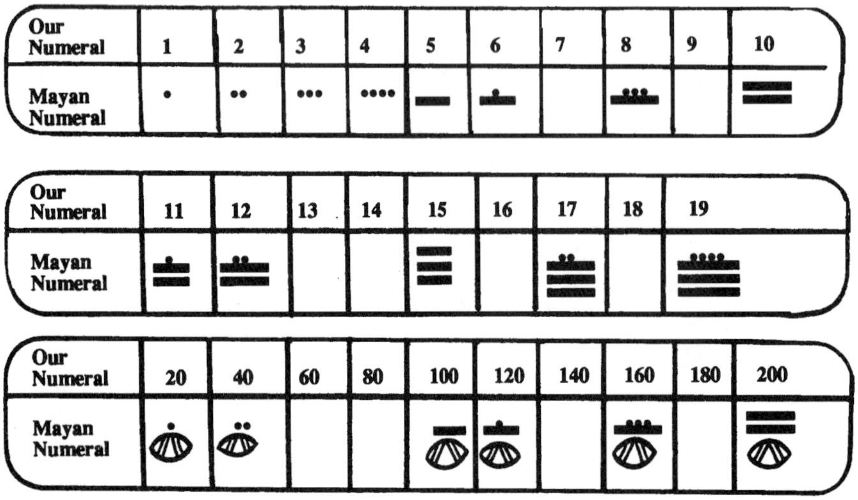
Our Numeral
1
2
3
4
5
6
7
8
9
10
Mayan Numeral
Our Numeral
11
12
13
14
15
16
17
18
19
Mayan Numeral
Our Numeral
20
40
60
80
100
120
140
160
180
200
Mayan Numeral

Mayan numeral chart for middle school.

Activity Continues

2. Explain how you figured it out by writing in your journal. Then tell a friend.

Middle School Students (see Figure 2.6):

1. Use these words to start the activity:
   "This lesson shows the smart thinking of the Mayan people. They are the ancestors of the Hispanic Americans today. Study the numerals of the Mayan system. Fill in the blanks for the next number. Think what is happening with the oval eye. How many times larger are things becoming?"
2. Explain how you figured it out by writing in your journal. Then tell a friend.
3. Think of several new numerals you could write following the system. Show your choices to a friend. Decide together if the numeral follows the Mayan pattern.

Supporting the NCTM *Principles and Standards* (2000):

- Mathematics as Reasoning/Patterning; Mathematics as Communication
- Worthwhile Mathematical Tasks; Mathematics as Oral and Written Discourse—The Teaching Principle
- Monitoring Students' Progress and Achievement—The Assessment Principle

Other creative lessons using the mathematics of the Mayan culture (Lara-Alecio, Irby, and Morales-Aldana, 1998) stress the relationship between numeral and number, geometry, and mathematical calculations in astronomy. These lessons appear in the NCTM journal geared for grades three to five, but teachers may find the lessons work equally well with older students.

Hispanic Teaching Ideas from Today's World. If you were to ask children to name one thing from the Hispanic American culture, they would echo the word, "Taco!" Hispanic cuisine is a large favorite among young people. It can be used to teach measurement ideas in both the English measurement system and the metric system. One such idea is to find simple Hispanic American recipes that require a minimal amount of cooking and a large amount of measuring. The following activity showcases a recipe from the book *Make a World of Difference: Creative Activities for Global Learning* (Office on Global Education, 1990). It is adapted here for a mathematics lesson using metric measurement for young children and middle school students.

Our students in Canada have had more experience with the metric system than students in the United States. However, both groups tend to cook with recipes still in the standard English measurement system. This lesson is an attempt to give students hands-on experiences with manipulatives in measuring liquids in the metric system.

Activity 2.3

COOKING UP METRICS WITH HISPANIC AMERICAN RECIPES

MATERIALS

- A standard set of measuring spoons
- An indelible magic marker and adhesive tape (it won't come off in the dishwasher)

DIRECTIONS

Label the measuring spoons in milliliters (mL) with the tape as follows:

Tablespoon measure = 15 mL
Teaspoon measure = 5 mL
½ teaspoon measure = 2.5 mL
¼ teaspoon measure = 1.25 mL

Elementary Students:

Read the recipe (Figure 2.7) and measure with the new measurement tools.

FIGURE 2.7

Pinto Bean Cake (makes 1 large cake)

2 cups all-purpose flour
5 mL baking powder
2 1/2 mL baking soda and salt
1/2 cup butter, softened
1 cup each of sugar, warm water, diced apples, raisins, chopped nuts
2 eggs, beaten
1 cup cooked pinto beans, mashed
5 mL vanilla extract

Sift together flour, baking powder, baking soda, and salt. Cream butter, sugar, and eggs together. Add water and flour alternately. Stir in pinto beans, apples, raisins, nuts, and vanilla. Bake in greased pan at 350° for 45 minutes. Cool and frost, if desired.

A toaster oven can be used for classroom cooking.

Hispanic American recipe à la metric.

Activity Continues

Middle School Students (grades 5–8):

Research favorite Hispanic American recipes and change them to be expressed in metric measurement. This can be fun for everyone. Remember we all love to eat!

Hispanic stories in children's literature (Soto, 1995, 1996, 1998) can be used to show patterning and logic in mathematics for the elementary grades. *The Old Man and His Door* and *Chato's Kitchen* delight children with Hispanic story characters that prove to be very clever and outwit those who do not use logic in problem solving.

Contributions from Hispanic Americans in Mathematics. Did you ever wonder when the first mathematics book was written in the Americas and who wrote it? The honor goes to an early Hispanic American, Juan Diez. His book was published in 1556 in Mexico City. Its topic was the most needed mathematics of the time. With the Europeans coming to Central America in large numbers, the Old World people and the New World people needed to communicate with each other in business transactions. Diez wrote about business mathematics so people could use money to trade with one another fairly.

On a more modern note, Hispanic American mathematics teachers are in the process of organizing a group to be affiliated with the National Council of Teachers of Mathematics. The group is still in the early planning stages. Look on the Internet under NCTM or mail an inquiry to NCTM about the group.

Asian American Heritage

The Asian culture is one that shows respect for its cultural heritage and respect for its people. This respect is a way of life. It permeates how people communicate with one another. The ideas of the elders are revered because wisdom comes with living a long life of honor in the face of many trials and hardships over time. Respect for another person's ideas are considered before one's own. An Asian person who finds that his or her idea differs from other people's thoughts on the same subject would never say, "I disagree with you. Let's look at this again." Instead the person would say something like this: "There are those who may have thought of another answer. I believe that it has been expressed this way."

Interestingly, teachers who have used this approach in classroom discipline have found less behavior problems that escalate to violent disruptions when students work together (Kansas City, Missouri Public Schools Police Division, 1993). If we are to use student-to-student discourse as advised in the NCTM *Standards* (1989, 1991, 2000), we need to take a valuable lesson from Asian culture. Try wording "I statements" into third person statements and watch the positive effect it has on others as you work in cooperative settings.

Asian American Culture in Mathematics Lessons. There are many mathematical discoveries and theorems studied throughout elementary and secondary education that have their roots in Asian culture. Box 2.1 on page 21 includes the more common ones.

Asian Teaching Ideas from the Ancient World. Some of the most interesting ideas in number theory come directly from the Chinese heritage. They are covered in detail in Chapter 14. Origami, the art of Asian paper folding, can be the focus of fascinating geometric investigations (Pappas, 1993). Chapter 6 features the legend about tangrams. It is a delightful story to introduce many activities using tangrams and points to the ingenuity of the Asian people. You are encouraged to consult the chapter bibliography for other resources to include in your lessons. We show a few ideas on the CD-ROM that are not covered in specific content chapters. The activities present elementary and middle school teaching ideas.

An ancient problem-solving activity comes from the Indian people on the subcontinent of India (not to be confused by the name "Indian" given incorrectly to the Native Americans). This activity comes from these Asian Indian people and one of the earliest mathematics activity books stressing cultural heritage (Mitchell, 1978). Similar stories and children's games are found in Krause (1993), Orlando (1993), Vogt (1994), and Zaslavsky (1994, 1995). Some student game activities from around the world are particularly well suited for the middle school.

Activity 2.4

HINDU PROBLEM SOLVING FROM INDIA

MATERIALS

- Paper with copies of the figures in Figure 2.8

DIRECTIONS

Elementary Students:

1. Use these words with Figure 2.8 to start the activity:
   "This lesson shows the smart thinking a man named

Activity Continues

Bhaskara from India did long ago. He is one of the ancestors of the Asian Americans today. He used a number system invented by his people. It looks like this":

FIGURE 2.8

Hindu numerals from ancient times.

2. "Does it look familiar? From where do you think we got our numbers?"
3. "Bhaskara wrote a math book to make his daughter happy when she was very sad. He told number stories about bees and animals using big numbers in the tens and hundreds. Write some stories about bees using the numbers the way Bhaskara would have written them."
4. Do other examples you think up yourself. Tell a classmate your stories and show your Hindu numerals. Decide together if the numeral fits the correct pattern.

Middle School Students:

1. Use these words to start the activity:

   "This lesson shows the smart thinking a man named Bhaskara from India did long ago. He is one of the ancestors of the Asian Americans today. He told many math stories about Hindu gods. Here is one of them" (from Mitchell, 1978, p. 39):

   Bhaskara had a problem about Hari, a god who had four hands. He wanted to pick up a hammer, a shell, a flower, and a discus. . . . Hari wonders in how many ways he can pick up these four things. Can you figure it out? (Hint: Make a chart like this and finish it. The total number of ways may surprise you.)

	First Hand	Second Hand	Third Hand	Fourth Hand
1st way	Hammer	Shell	Flower	Discus
2nd way	Hammer	Shell	Discus	Flower
3rd way	Hammer	Flower	Shell	Discus

2. Do other examples to finish the chart. Show your problem-solving chart to a classmate. Decide together if the answers fit the correct pattern.

Asian Ideas in Today's Mathematics. The abacus can be used for an example of a faster calculator than our Western one. If you have Asian American students in your class who know how to use the abacus, ask them to demonstrate or bring in a family member who can demonstrate the abacus. One activity that some classes have enjoyed is a challenge race between the abacus and the electronic calculator. Have the class predict who will win. Let the class choose the most proficient class member on the calculator. If the Asian guest uses the abacus daily, he or she will win the competition hands down. Students are fascinated and in real admiration of the person's ability to work so fast with the abacus. Finish the lesson by asking, "Why do you suppose Asian Americans still use the abacus today?" The class knows that answer for sure!

Another idea blends literature and mathematics. Mitsumasa Anno's beautiful counting book, appropriately called *Anno's Counting Book* (1977), is wonderful for young children just learning to count. He uses connecting cubes to show each number right alongside the beautiful scene on each page. It is a means to connect concrete experiences with the pictorial level. With each number from 1 to 12, he adds more and more scenic elements to match the number featured on that page. People are challenged to see how many things of that number are included in the scene. The scene also changes with the seasons from January to December. Here are some activities that integrate computer knowledge with counting.

Activity 2.5

CREATING A NEW COUNTING BOOK LIKE ANNO DID

MATERIALS

- *Anno's Counting Book*
- Logo program or other computer program with picture capability

DIRECTIONS

1. Read *Anno's Counting Book* to start the activity.

Elementary Students:

1. Think of a way to do a book like Anno's but make it different from his.
2. Some ideas from elementary students in the past:

   Do a scene from our town and count to 12.

   Do higher numbers from where Anno left off . . . like 13 to 20.

   "Do one big picture on big paper and don't tell anyone what the number is so they will have to really count all the things" (actual words of one student).

   Do holidays instead of seasons.

   Do an inside scene of a house at different times instead of outside.

Activity Continues

3. Suggest that one easy way to keep the basic scene the same is to add to it from picture to picture in the computer. The students save each picture as frame 1, frame 2, etc.
4. Students can color the pictures after they are printed or use a color printer if one is available in the school.

Middle School Students (grades 5–8):

1. Do the same basic activity but decide to share it with a lower grade student who needs help in counting.
2. One group did graph coordinates with algebra equations building more detail with each picture. Think of the game *Battleship* to understand how they started.

A sample of pictures created with the computer language Logo for the early grades and the algebra equation book are also on the CD-ROM. You can use the books to get your own students started to think about ways they create a book to show what they are learning in mathematics.

EXTENDED ACTIVITIES

MATHEMATICAL CONNECTIONS   COMPUTERS

Name of Activity

- Greg's Halloween Counting Book
- Algebra Coordinates Add-on Book
- Abacus Fun

Other wonderful mathematics books for children by Mitsumasa Anno include *Anno's Counting House* (1981), *Anno's Math Games* (1982), *Anno's Magic Seeds* (1995), and with Masaichiro Anno, *Anno's Mysterious Multiplying Jar* (1983). Some of these books have special teacher's pages in some editions while other editions of the same books were written for the general reading audience and contain no teacher suggestions.

Contributions from Asian Americans in Mathematics. Asians and Asian Americans are known for their high scholarship. Many people have distinguished themselves in the field of science and mathematics. The best known of modern times may be Srinivasa Ramanujan. His bibliography appears in middle school mathematics books and in journal presentations (Perl and Manning, 1982; Reimer and Reimer, 1992, 1995; Voolich, 1993). Perl and Manning's book (1982) also features Native Americans, Hispanics, and African American mathematicians. Voolich (1993) points out that there are very few Chinese mathematicians that can be cited or studied because the historical writings did not include the names of the individuals making mathematics discoveries at various points in the Chinese political system.

European American Heritage

As stated at the beginning of the chapter, history, literature, and mathematics texts are replete with examples of the superior work of European and European American contributions to mathematics. Only the unusual stories and least known mathematicians, that is, women, are featured here.

A Most Unusual Story for Elementary-Age Children and Middle Schoolers. Mathematics in ancient times had its set of interesting characters. Mathematicians were not the dull lot that students often think they were. The most unusual story from an elementary and middle school perspective is the story of Archimedes. Archimedes, a Sicilian, is considered one of the greatest mathematicians who ever lived. However, it was his thrill of discovering one particular mathematical insight that captures the interest of elementary-age children and middle schoolers. The story goes something like this:

> *Archimedes was always thinking of math problems to solve. Archimedes was sure that there could be a mathematical way to figure out when a crown was made of pure gold and when it was not. Then dishonest people could not fool the king, which unfortunately had already happened. One day while he was in a public bathhouse (taking a bath, of course), Archimedes found a solution to the problem. He was so excited, that he actually ran out of the bathhouse and down the street NAKED, shouting that he had solved the problem!*

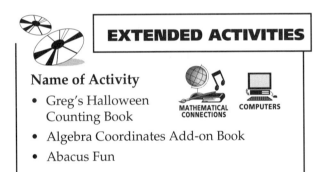

The humor of youth being what it is this true story fascinates students. They cannot imagine anyone getting that excited about solving math problems. This is one of those stories that clever teachers can use to their advantage. When students give the old, familiar saying, "Do we *have* to do these math problems?" a teacher can say, "Hey, Archimedes ran through the streets *naked* for math problems. I'm just asking you to write a few answers fully clothed. Consider yourselves lucky." A wink and a good-natured laugh at just the right time has kept many a math teacher popular when a mathematics concept was less than scintillating in and of itself. Use interesting mathematical history to put some pizzazz in your lessons.

Women in the Culture of Mathematics Lessons. Students need to know that there are women who have succeeded in mathematics—*women of all cultures.* Women and Mathematics Education (WME) has been an affiliated group of the National Council of Teacher of Mathematics since 1983. Its purpose is to promote mathematics education of girls and women. The position paper for Women and Mathematics (1997) is available on the CD-ROM. It is listed with the other position papers in an Extended Activities box later in this chapter. The organization publishes a yearly bibliography of pertinent articles and research findings (Mark, 1998). The book has over one thousand listings since its first compilation in 1990. As with all NCTM affiliated groups, the organization is open to all interested persons and now lists nearly 700 members. Updated information on the group may be found on the NCTM web site.

Women as mathematicians is not a new idea. The Greek woman, Hypatia (circa 415 B.C. to 370 B.C.) traveled to Alexandria, Egypt, to study mathematics (Nichols, 1996). This is further proof that the African continent was recognized by ancient civilizations as the place to go if one wished to be on the forefront of mathematical thought. Hypatia explored conic sections and diophantine equations. She was killed because of the kinds of things she was teaching. Interestingly, those mathematical ideas are part of the high school curriculum in today's schools. An activity showing hyperbola cuts in conic sections, honoring Hypatia, was published for student use over 20 years ago (Perl, 1978). New resources (Morrow, 1996; Morrow and Perl, 1997) similar to the original are available for middle school teachers who want to show young women that a career in mathematics in a very real possibility.

Middle school is the time when girls decide what math courses they will pursue in high school. It may be the last time a teacher has the opportunity to effectively influence math choices. The opportunity to see how other women have used mathematics in successful careers is a needed example for young girls who may have no idea how mathematics is used in the real world. A series of videotapes (Riley, 1999) showing successful women using math at work have won several prestigious awards, including the Gold Medal from the International Film and Video Festival in New York and Young Adults Award from the American Library Association. Women tell in their own words what mathematics has done for them in the world of work. Each video is no longer than 15 minutes, allowing teachers time to discuss the video in an average class period. Resource guides are available to aid middle school teachers as they plan the post-video discussions. The video entitled, *Math at Work: Women in Nontraditional Careers,* may be shown separately if teachers feel they cannot allot class time for all eight videotapes.

It is suggested that students study famous women mathematicians and find examples of their mathematical work when it is available. The study sheet in Activity 2.6 is presented to motivate students to learn the role, importance and national heritage of each woman mathematician.

Activity 2.6

WOMEN IN MATHEMATICS

MATERIALS

- Names are given on a sheet.

DIRECTIONS

1. Use these words with Figure 2.9 to start the activity: "This lesson shows the smart thinking of the women from many cultures, starting long ago. Some examples are shown here. Find out more about these women. Come ready to tell others what you discovered."

FIGURE 2.9

Find Out What They Did

Maria Angesi (Italian)	Evelyn Boyd Granville (African American)
Emmy Noether (Jewish from Germany)	Edna Paisano (Hispanic American)
Mary Fairfax Somerville (Scottish)	Marjorie Lee Brown (African American)
Sophie Germain (French)	
Grace Hopper (American)	

Find Out Which One of the Above

Shared ideas with Einstein
Was called a witch—and why
Made patterns of sand on a drum (inventing many unique number patterns)
Invented COBOL computer language

Famous women mathematicians.

2. Students follow the names on the sheet, going to the library to look up more information to make a correct match.

Activity Continues

3. Find other examples. Explain how you found out the contribution of each woman mathematician by writing in your journal. Show your choices to a friend.

Supporting the NCTM *Principles and Standards* (2000):

- Mathematics as Connections; Mathematics as Communication
- Mathematics as Oral and Written Discourse—The Teaching Principle
- Monitoring Students' Progress—The Equity Principle

IN CELEBRATION OF ALL MATHEMATICIANS

Voolich (1993) includes a wonderful list of mathematicians' birthdays along with clever ideas for writing biographies. The list includes many nationalities and both genders. An innovative teacher can use the list in several ways. One way is to have students look at the list to see whether they share a birthday with a famous mathematician. With 121 names, students can always find a mathematician close to their birthday. The students can learn more about the person and try to find out what contribution he or she made to the field of mathematics.

Assignments like this are especially important in the middle school years when students are making decisions that affect their choice of high school courses in mathematics and science. Those options mushroom into career choices before students realize what has happened to them. As teachers, all of us must let students know that they can be anything they want to be. Mathematics is power of thought in the great achievements of humankind. Students don't have to leave their dreams behind in fear of mathematics. We offer this thought in the spirit of our Native American sisters and brothers.

You, Too, Can Feel the Wind

Do not be afraid
to walk in the footprints of time.
The wind will hold you uplifted
in your flight to the eagle's eye.
See the earth below
all is clear as you fly to the circle of life.
The eagle goes before you
keeping the promise. . . . you, too, can feel the wind.

—*NTE*

EQUITY IN MATHEMATICS: THE RIGHT OF ALL PEOPLE TO ACQUIRE MATHEMATICAL POWER

Every student has the right to acquire the mathematical power for success in today's world. However, equity in mathematics has not always been forthcoming. There are many forces that influence equity in mathematics education. Research points to three areas in particular: (1) the impact of technology, (2) the development of problem solving and critical thinking, and (3) the use of cultural qualities needed to help, not hinder, mathematics equity for all students.

The Impact of Technology

It seems that all persons have, at one time or another, felt powerless to understand technology. Such feelings may afflict readers of this book when looking at the new problem-solving tasks and emerging technologies. Research shows that certain groups of students have not received the exposure to technology that would allow them to grow accustomed to its full use, notably the use of computer technology in the schools. Four classes of people have emerged: (1) those who do not have exposure to the active use of technology, (2) those who have limited use of technology for low-level minimal tasks, (3) those who use a technological advancement to its fullest potential, and (4) the "power brokers" who invent the technology itself.

Students who find themselves the farthest away from the mainstream culture of white America will find less and less opportunity to be active participants in the use of technology. The Office of Technology Assessment (1988) found that low-socioeconomic-status urban schools have fewer computers per student than do affluent urban, suburban, and rural schools, effectively limiting the availability of computer training. Other studies have shown that, even when there are enough computers available, Hispanic American students (Ingle, 1988), Native Americans (Cheek, 1984), and African American students (Ingle, 1988) are assigned computer time to do drill and practice of minimal mathematics skills without the opportunity to use the computer to discover their potential to apply logical and critical reasoning skills in programming. Unfortunately, updated reports by Silver, Smith, and Nelson (1995), Leder (1995), and Tate (1995) have shown that these conditions have not improved much since the 1980s, when Cheek and Ingle did their original studies.

Equity with Computer Technology. The mathematical reasoning power of Logo (Papert, 1980) and LEGO Group's MINDSTORMS Robotics (1998) is the purpose for their inclusion in this text and on the CD-ROM. Therefore, persons working with children can help them unlock for themselves the power of mathematical reasoning through the use of applied computer technology. Naturally, if Hispanic Americans, African Americans, and Native Americans are excluded from the second and third groups, it goes without saying that the educational system is denying them the right of access to the fourth group as the real power brokers who can develop the next advancements of technology.

Think of the sense of power and accomplishment a student would have when creating his or her own robot with the LEGO computer system. The Logo computer activities shown in this chapter are typical of what second- and third-grade students can do with one to two 20-minute periods per week to explore Logo possibilities. The authors of this text have seen students of varying socioeconomic levels, in white and nonwhite populations, create such Logo procedures in the early grades.

Equity with Calculator Technology. The calculator is becoming more and more accessible to all children. It may very well be the "technology of choice" because its cost is minimal compared to the purchase price of classroom computers. Virtually all students participating in the 1996 National Assessment of Educational Progress reported that they or their family owned a calculator. Access to school-owned calculators was greater at each level than computer accessibility in schools. (Reese et al., 1997).

Scores on the 1990, 1992, and 1996 National Assessment of Educational Progress (NAEP) also showed that there was a clear relationship between calculator use and performance on the assessment, with the more problems answered correctly when the calculator was used (Kouba et al., 1997). No such relationship was seen for students with or without exposure to computers. This result presents further evidence that time spent on the appropriate use of calculators in mathematics classrooms will pay off with higher scores in mathematics assessments.

The calculator gives students an efficient way to see the "whole" pattern and movement of a mathematical principle without tedious calculations getting in the way of understanding. This efficiency is of particular benefit to students who process information simultaneously as field-dependent learners. Research cited later in this chapter discusses the evidence that many nonwhite cultures analyze learning tasks from the field-dependent point of view, making the calculator an appropriate device to use. The following is a typical example of a calculator activity that can be used with students even as young as the primary age.

Activity 2.7

NUMBER PATTERNS

MATERIALS

1. Calculator with a repeat key. The activity can be done without the repeat key, but it will require more pressing of keys.
2. Number chart similar to Figure 2.10.

DIRECTIONS

1. The teacher pairs students to work in teams of two with one student working with the calculator while the other student shades in the appropriate number box.

   Alternative approach: A student can work alone, doing both jobs at one time.

2. The teacher uses the following terminology to help the students begin the calculator work:

   "What happens when you repeatedly add 2 starting at 11? Press the number 11. Watch it appear on the calculator. Now press "+ 2 =" and shade in the number you see on the number chart. Press "+ 2 =" again and record the next number. Keep shading in the numbers on the chart for two more rows. Look for a pattern. Predict what numbers will be shaded in the next row before you put the numbers in the calculator. Were you correct?"

3. Can you predict what would happen if you started with the number 12 in the calculator and added 2 to that number?

FIGURE 2.10

10	11	12	13	14	15	16	17	18	19
20	21	22	23	24	25	26	27	28	29
30	31	32	33	34	35	36	37	38	39
40	41	42	43	44	45	46	47	48	49

(The shaded areas show the answers given by the child.)

Number patterns.

4. Teachers can provide a chart with 100 numbers on it and let the children explore with various patterns.

Schlelack (1991) reports success using the same basic technique as shown in the preceding activity with the subtraction of numbers as ("– 2 ="). Preservice and in-service teachers should take every opportunity to do the calculator activities appearing throughout this text. Readers are encouraged to use these activities with all children, being careful not to neglect children from diverse cultures when planning calculator activities. The more knowledgeable the teacher, the more frequently calculators will be used by children.

Equity with Other Emerging Technologies. Ingle (1988) challenges educators to create "opportunities for using the new information technologies not merely as entertainment media outlets, but also as tools for exchanging communication, knowledge, and information across long-standing barriers of ignorance, geography, language, cultural and economic diversity" (p. 3).

Tate (1995) calls on the entire education community to face the financial commitment to equity. If the NCTM *Standards* are to be met, all students must have equitable access to the financial resources available. This is especially true in areas such as the Internet and multimedia technologies, which require initially expensive equipment such as modems and video-compatible power computers. If white affluent children are the only ones using the Internet, we have created a devastating situation that pulls people further and further apart.

Ultimately, it is classroom teachers, who know what technologies are available, who must push for access in all buildings for all students. Teachers of mathematics are in a unique position to accept Ingle's challenge as the frontline instructors who can teach young people the uses of computers and calculators to stimulate their own minds and reasoning powers.

The Development of Problem Solving and Critical Thinking

The development of problem solving and critical thinking in mathematics is the second theme emerging in culturally relevant mathematics. Students from all cultures must become independent problem solvers if they are to experience a sense of freedom from individuals who would take advantage of them. Think of the first time you went to buy a car. It became apparent very quickly that the car dealer knew something about the manipulation of interest payments that was extremely hard for a novice to follow. Imagine the disappointed look of the car dealer who realizes that you know something about how to compute interest and when it applies to a larger payment over too long a period to make it an economically feasible transaction. Now that's when mathematics becomes culturally relevant in the real world! All of us have the right to develop these skills.

NAEP results (1990, 1992, 1996) show that all ethnic groups made statistically significant gains in scores over the last decade; however, the differences among ethnic groups remained stable, with Asian Americans receiving the highest scores, followed by whites, Native Americans, Hispanic Americans, and African Americans, respectively, in grade four and grade eight. In grade twelve, Hispanic Americans scored higher than Native Americans and African Americans. Reese et al. (1997) caution that the findings by ethnic group do not account for the other factors of socioeconomics of home and school and the encouragement to take higher mathematics courses. When those factors were considered, studies have shown nonwhite populations who took more mathematics courses showed greater gains in test scores than their white counterparts who took the same kind and number of math courses (Lubienski, 1997; Rechin, 1994; Powell, 1990). Reports show that early intervention before the high school years is definitely time well spent when encouraging nonwhite students to have greater exposure to mathematics applications (Campbell and Rowan, 1997; Walker and McCoy, 1997; Khisty, 1997; Beane, 1990). These findings indicate that critical thinking and problem solving are possible for all cultural groups with early and consistent exposure to mathematics. The remainder of this chapter discusses proven ways to aid students of diverse cultures on the journey to mathematical power.

The Role of Language in Problem Solving and Critical Thinking. A statement about the rights of students with limited English proficiency as second language learners was drafted in 1998 by the National Council of Teachers of Mathematics. It is available on the CD-ROM. See the goals for Native American Education also.

Numerous studies reported by Cummins (1992), Khisty (1995), and Warren and Rosebery (1995) document the important role that language plays in problem solving when one goes beyond rudimentary skills in basic mathematics. Even children as young as age four experience a semantic sensitivity when presented with word problems. It becomes even more important when limited English proficient (LEP) students are placed in mathematics classrooms.

EXTENDED ACTIVITIES

Name of Activity

CULTURAL RELEVANCE POSITION PAPER

- Position Paper on Mathematics for Second-Language Learners
- Mathematics Education of Underrepresented Groups
- Goals for Native American Education
- Women and Mathematics Education Aims

Projections for the year 2000 have 3.4 million students classified as LEP students. Of this group, 77 percent are Hispanic American (Khisty, 1995). Frequently LEP students are mainstreamed into mathematics classrooms because it is thought that mathematics involves minimal language skills; yet that assumption is not true when a student does problem solving, logic, and real-world applications. This practice leads to student failure and a sense of hopelessness when dealing with mathematics.

Modeling and Scaffolding. Khisty (1995; 1997) talks of the need to develop teachers who use modeling and scaffolding as a process in oral discourse. A teacher modeling the mathematical language is not a new idea, but the idea of scaffolding may be new to many teachers. *Scaffolding* is the process of providing support for students' answers by asking more probing questions and giving cues as the students construct their responses. It is similar to the elaborating technique shown in Chapter 3. The difference is the emphasis on the support structure; the scaffold does not come down until the answers are secure and firmly grounded.

A Language within a Language. Teachers need to know that mathematics is a language within a language. How mathematical concepts are expressed in Spanish is not just a word-for-word translation from English—or any other language. Khisty (1995) points to the word *left* as an example. It is taught as a direction in language translations, not as a mathematical concept for remainder (that which remains, or is left, after subtraction). The tragedy is that less than 4 percent of the nation's teachers are prepared to teach LEP students.

How students interpret the syntax of sentence structure within a word problem also affects the number of correct answers that will be given (Thomas, 1997; Casteel and Rider, 1994; Mestre and Gerace, 1986). Even what looks like a simple question has hidden complexities. Thomas (1997, pp. 40–41) asks us to consider the differences in these two questions:

- If a man takes 3 minutes to run 500 meters, how long will it take him to run a kilometer?
- A man took 3 minutes to run 500 meters. He kept running at the same speed. How long did it take him to run a kilometer?

Thomas points out that the implied logical connectives (*if...then*) are difficult for young people to understand even without syntax problems of other languages. Some cultures would not use an *if* statement unless one was looking for the exception. Therefore students may spend their time thinking the speed varies instead of seeing the implied constant speed as important information. Thomas also points out that the word *long* means time duration rather than length, but this may not be apparent to many second-language speakers. The second sentence would help all learners and still enable teachers and test writers to judge the students' mathematical ability.

Mestre and Gerace (1986) report on the problems turning simple algebraic statements into acceptable equations. The most common mistake occurred in what has come to be called the variable-reversal error. The error may be seen in problems such as the following:

Write an equation using the variables S and P to represent the following statement:

> *"There are six times as many students as professors at a certain university." Use* S *for the number of students and* P *for the number of professors. (Mestre and Gerace, 1986, p. 143)*

The answer $6S = P$ was given by approximately 35 percent of white American engineering undergraduates, whereas 54 percent of the Hispanic Americans gave the "variable-reversal" answer. During student interviews, it was discovered that the common misconception was to use the S and P as if they were labels instead of representing them correctly as mathematical variables to stand for the *number* of students and the *number* of professors. Students apparently used a sequential left-to-right literal translation of the problem:

six times as many students as professors

$$6 \times S = P$$

or $6S = P$

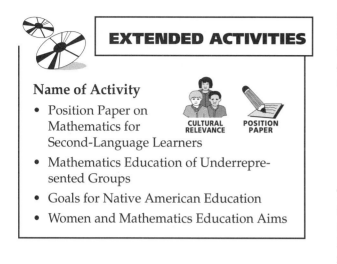

rather than allowing their critical thinking processes to analyze what the problem was really saying about the *number* of people in one group compared to the *number* of people in the other group, leading to the correct answer of $S = 6P$. Mestre and Gerace (1986) gave Hispanic American students problems worded as follows:

> *Write an expression with variables for the following statements:*
> *Six times the length of a stick is 24 feet.*
> *If a certain chain were four times as long it would be 36 feet.* (p. 144)

All of the 14 students interviewed answered the problems correctly. These examples point out the need emphasized in Chapter 3 that student interviews and assessments must be done to see what the students really understand. More than a pencil-and-paper test must be used by teachers, especially when working with students with limited English proficiency.

Teachers need to restructure difficult sentences like those seen in the previous studies. However, this still will not help students at standardized test time unless test writers change the sentence structure of word problems to eliminate as many language inconsistencies as possible. The education community must band together to make classroom instruction *and* test evaluations fair for all students.

The Role of Conceptual Thinking in Other Cultures. Mestre and Gerace (1986) and Beane (1990) have documented that students tend to think of higher mathematical thinking as rule generated rather than concept based. This disposition may be caused by teachers who tend to teach a concept in a step-by-step formation that overemphasizes a patterned way of looking for a solution. Of course, it works when dealing with only one type of problem per assignment, but it hardly helps when given many problems with different thrusts, presented in sentence structures with varying syntax.

Generalized Procedures More Important Than Step-by-Step Rules. When African American and Hispanic American students were presented various problem-solving tasks and taught general procedures to approach any word problem (similar to those seen in Chapter 5) rather than step-by-step techniques, the students scored higher on the standardized achievement tests at the end of the year (Carey et al., 1995). Carey and associates tell of a program to build on the knowledge that children bring to school. It has been funded with good results by the National Science Foundation for ten years to date. The program is called Cognitively Guided Instruction (CGI). Key word approaches to problem solving are eliminated in favor of general processing strategies. Three questions are stressed: (1) What do you think? (2) How did you get that? and (3) Did anyone solve the problem another way? You will read more about CGI in other chapters in this text.

The Techniques of Storytelling. If Warren and Rosebery (1995) were to use the scaffolding metaphor, they would suggest that the scaffold must not just support an old structure or way of teaching. It must support a new way of learning that goes beyond the language and study of middle-class European tradition in science and mathematics. They advocate the use of techniques akin to storytelling rather than the discovery approach. They are called *theory building* and *criticism.* Both approaches are in keeping with the storytelling model seen most frequently in non-white cultures. As emphasized in the first part of this chapter, many cultures tell fascinating folktales that weave a message around the story. Warren and Rosebery (1995) suggest that mathematical and scientific ideas be constructed the same way. The following example contrasts the discovery approach and the storytelling approach.

Activity 2.8

CULTURAL RELEVANCE   PROBLEM SOLVING

THE DISCOVERY APPROACH AND THE STORYTELLING APPROACH

MATERIALS

- Use the Native American mirror activity for symmetry found on the CD-ROM.

CONTRAST THE DIFFERENCE IN APPROACHES

The Discovery Approach

Find all the possible ways to move the mirror around the symbol of the sun to match each drawing. How many did you find? Did you find all of them? Which ones were difficult to find? How could you do the activity again to find more matches next time? Can you discover another way to do the activity? Come up with another way. See how many ways you can find.

The Storytelling Approach (Theory Building and Criticism)

Theory Building: There is a way to place the mirror that will reflect each of the drawings you see before you. Let's place the mirror at a straight angle to the paper and look in the mirror to see what will be reflecting back at us. Now let's move the mirror slowly around a center point of the design and look for another pattern. Let's do this again. What direction would be wise for us to continue to move the mirror? Are there any other directions you would like to choose that would follow the same ideas we have seen here?

Activity Continues

Criticism: Is this the only way we could have done the activity? What variations could we use if we were to follow the same general concept but still look for another way to do the same activity?

Supporting the NCTM *Principles and Standards* (2000):

- Mathematics as Problem Solving; Mathematics as Communication
- Worthwhile Mathematical Tasks; Mathematics as Oral and Written Discourse—The Teaching Principle
- Monitoring Students' Progress—The Equity Principle

Did you notice the subtle differences between the approaches? Either approach culminates with students understanding the same things about the activity. It's the means to the end that is important. To a person from a noncompetitive culture, *how many* ways one can discover to do something is not important. Finding the message or theory behind the activity is the important thing. The first way implies everyone is alone discovering what they can, but the storytelling way involves the teacher and students together, walking through the parts of the problem like an adventuresome story. This is one way to make problem solving more relevant for nonwhite cultures.

More Techniques to Make Problem Solving Relevant. In an attempt to make problem solving more relevant, some texts have chosen problems from real-world experiences. Unfortunately, many of the examples appear ludicrous to those who work with nonwhite populations. Large numbers of these children are not privy to the economic world from which many examples are taken. Here is a sample of such a problem:

Example

On a revolving charge account, Mrs. Dallins purchased $27.50 worth of clothing and $120.60 worth of furniture. She then made two monthly payments of $32.00 each. If the interest charges for the period of two months were $3.25, what did Mrs. Dallins then owe on the account? (Mestre and Gerace, 1986, p. 157)

It goes without saying that many students do not understand what a "revolving charge account" is, nor do they have mathematical understanding of it. Many students in the study did not understand the terms "monthly payments" and "interest."

Another problem is mathematics assignments from well-meaning but uninformed teachers who are unaware of the deep cultural implications of the word problems they assign. On one such assignment the classroom teacher had cut several food coupons from a local paper and asked the children to find the best buy for their money if they had only seven dollars to spend. The teacher evaluated one child's responses to the assignment as unsatisfactory when the student chose only the lettuce and green beans, leaving out the obvious bargain on two selections of beef coupons. The teacher did not realize that the child's Hindu culture did not permit the choice of beef. The student, who received a failing grade on the paper, was left thinking that something was wrong mathematically.

Another example comes from Ladson-Billings (1995), involving African American students working with a problem in a different social context than their white, middle-class counterparts. She shares the following (pp. 131–132):

> *It costs $1.50 to travel each way on the city bus. A transit system "fast pass" costs $65 a month. Which is the more economical way to get to work, the daily fare or the fast pass?*
>
> *The white, middle-class, suburban youngsters who read this problem suggested that the daily fare was cheaper. At $1.50 each way, a worker would pay $3 a day on approximately 20 work days a month, for a total of $60, five dollars cheaper than the "fast pass." By contrast, many of the inner-city youngsters felt that there was not enough information provided for them to solve the problems. One of their questions was, "How many jobs are we talking about?" Their own experiences were that people often held several low-paying part-time jobs to make a living wage. Thus, it is conceivable that a worker would need to ride the bus several times a day (and pay several fares) to get to different jobs. The students further suggested that most people they know ride the bus because they do not own a car and would be using the bus for reasons other than commuting. Going to stores, church, visiting, and to the movies might all involve using the bus. The 20 days the nine-to-five suburban commuter might use the bus is not the same as the 30 or 31 days a month an inner-city person without a car might require public transportation. Finally, the inner-city students asked, "If the fast pass is not cheaper, why do they constantly advertise them on the TV as the best way to go?" Their question addressed the ethics of business and advertising to which they are subjected.*

All of the preceding experiences stand as warning signals to teachers. We all need to constantly evaluate the kind of problems we give students to solve. This is also a good reason to use oral and written discourse in authentic assessment. When teachers give students the opportunity to tell why they chose their answers to real-life problems, the test scores improve. Teachers often realize how bright students really are. The educational community can be proud of its choice to use authentic assessment in testing programs by states and provinces. It shows real promise for equity in mathematics.

There Are Ways That Help. In an attempt to override syntax problems and inappropriate real-world experiences, some programs use students' own self-generated preferences for word problems. Students fill out an interest inventory from which examples are written. To be successful the word problems must be written in language that children understand at the time of instruction (Flores, 1997; Campbell and Rowan, 1997). Textbook examples are rewritten, as in the following example from Lopez and Sullivan (1991, p. 96):

Typical Textbook Version: *Janice* expects 30 friends to come to a *party.* If each friend will get a 9-ounce serving of *soda,* how many 15-ounce cans of *soda* are needed?

Personalized Version: *Alberto* expects 30 friends to come to *his birthday party* on *February 3.* If each friend will get a 9-ounce serving of *Dr. Pepper,* how many 15-ounce cans of *Dr. Pepper* are needed?

The authors encourage teachers to try the interest inventory approach in their own classrooms to determine whether it makes a difference with children from various cultures. If some of the students get better mathematics scores when word problems are presented this way, teachers will know they have helped those students who find cultural barriers in regular textbook problems.

The most ideal situation for LEP students is to have a mathematics teacher who is proficient in both English and the student's primary language. The Video Vignette on the CD-ROM from "Chapter 12: Rectangles and Fractions," is an excellent classroom example. The teacher quickly switches from one language to another, so much so that you may need to watch the video more than once to see it. She also encourages students to share orally with one another and to write journal entries about their mathematics discoveries. Not all teachers are capable of handling the language barrier, but all teachers can participate in the other things that research shows culturally diverse students need in order to be successful learners. The innovative mathematics program called Project IMPACT (Campbell and Rowan, 1997, p. 65) sets guidelines in accord with the TIMSS recommendations seen in Chapter 1. The list of guidelines for success are seen in Figure 2.11.

FIGURE 2.11

Project IMPACT

- Use mixed-ability groups as often as possible to promote the language growth of students who are less facile.
- Have students write in journals about the mathematics they are learning.
- Have students share their ideas in small groups or pairs before sharing with the entire class.
- Have students write their own story problems using personal experiences, and then expect students to share their problems with the rest of the class.
- Have students explain the information in a word problem or restate the problem in their own words using whole-class sharing before expecting students to work on the problems individually, in pairs, or in groups.
- During class discussions, first call on students with language difficulties or with fewer experiences. Doing so allows these children to share the ideas that are more apparent and challenges those with more experience or language to stretch for ideas.
- Allow students to adjust the numbers in, or the circumstances of, a problem if they are having difficulty understanding the problem or using the numbers given. Always ask the students to explain why they made the adjustments.
- When students with no English fluency come to the classroom, assign them a buddy who can help with translation. If that is not possible, use concrete materials or diagrams and connect them to words so that the students can understand the problem as much as possible without necessarily understanding all the language.

Approaches to Support the Effective Use of Language.

Minority Students Can Problem Solve in Authentic Ways. Students in the MAC-mathics Program in the Chicago Public Schools created the student book, *MAC-mathics: Mathematics Applications in Chicago, Grades 3–8* (Strong, 1991a). Students must be considered "at risk" in their understanding of mathematics in order to qualify for the program, which has sections for the primary, intermediate, and upper

Video Vignette

Math in the Bilingual Classroom

Using Ms. Torres' classroom vignette, consider the approaches of Project IMPACT for helping culturally diverse learners.

- Analyze the approaches (Figure 2.11) that you see evidence of in this bilingual classroom.

grades. The students are paid to create word problems with real-world applications from their experiences. Each year the three groups publish a book of problems for other students to use, and there is an autograph-signing party for the young authors at the end of each summer. The examples included on the CD-ROM show the same theme chosen by the primary and the upper-grade groups. Notice how the word problems offer a graduated level of difficulty from the primary age to the upper-grade age. The topics, experiences, names, and written examples were created solely by students for students.

The authors applaud the children of the MAC-mathics program for their hard work and proven ability to write and answer difficult mathematics problems from real-life situations. The authors encourage readers of this text to try the same approach with children in their schools. When mathematics has real meaning coming from young people's own experiences, students of all cultures tackle mathematics as real achievers.

The Use of Cultural Qualities to Help Mathematics Equity

Other studies also point to the positive qualities students bring from their cultural background that can be used to benefit mathematics instruction. Learning style and speed (Malloy, 1997; Webb, 1998; Mestre, 1986; Mestre and Gerace, 1986; personal communication, Dorothy S. Strong, January 17, 1992; Carey et al., 1995; Cheek, 1984; Hale-Benson, 1986; and Keynes, 1995) have been consistently mentioned in recent years.

Learning Style. Malloy (1997), Guild (1994), Wilson (1992), Cheek (1984), and Hale-Benson (1986) believe that Native Americans, African Americans and Hispanic Americans tend to assimilate learning tasks from a field-dependent view as opposed to the field-independent approach. A field-dependent view sees a learning task as a whole experiential base. Learning facts is seen as an integrated part of the whole picture. A detailed analysis of mathematics tasks presented from a field-dependent view is presented in Chapter 3. Another term associated with this learning style is *simultaneous synthesis,* which refers to the way the brain processes the information; whereas *field-dependent* refers to the actual way the material is viewed in the environment. Some of the researchers feel more people in the white population tend to see tasks from a field-independent approach, using *successive synthesis* as the way to process the information. The field-independent approach focuses on details and features within a task without the need to see its placement as an integrated part of a whole. Brain research (Jensen, 1998) indicates that people may prefer a whole-to-part, simultaneous view of material when it is seen for the first time. Mathematics textbook approaches have tended to reinforce the part-to-whole, successive view of learning when introducing concepts for the first time.

The authors stress that generally mathematics educators have been slow to adopt the idea of field-dependent and field-independent learning processing styles and multiple intelligences (Carey et al., 1995; Hiebert and Carpenter, 1992; Secada, 1991; Tiedemann, 1989). They point to research that shows children solve most mathematical concepts with similar strategies rather than different ones. They feel each person must be allowed to follow his or her own way without stereotypes of any kind.

As stated before, the authors are in agreement with the real-world approach. However, it does make sense to start the learning of any new concept using the strengths of each child, whatever the learning processing strategy or modality may be. Then children can be switched to other strategies that simulate the real world more closely once they have found success and initial understanding of a new concept. If there are children of minority groups that could profit from a learning style approach, teachers would be remiss not to try simultaneous and successive processing with new mathematics concepts. The authors present both approaches in the assessment part of Chapters 6 through 15.

Teachers need to be aware of how to change mathematics tasks presented in textbooks and worksheets from one learning style to the other, as presented in Chapter 3. Students can achieve mathematical competence through the use of either learning style, and it makes sense to present new concepts in the easiest style for each child. The student's chance for success is greater!

EXTENDED ACTIVITIES

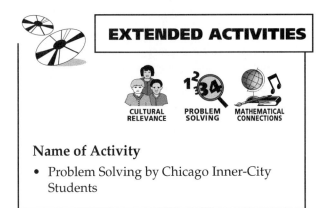

Name of Activity

- Problem Solving by Chicago Inner-City Students

Speed of Performance. Speed of performance is not viewed as an important quality in many nonwhite cultures. If mathematics programs and tests stress speed as an important variable, nonwhite students in classrooms are at risk for failure. The problem-solving discussion in Chapter 5 points out that good problem solving may require a slow pace where time is taken to consider all options before the best solution is obtained. The great mathematics problems took years, sometimes generations, to be solved. Teaching children to race through life making quick decisions about all types of subject matter may not be in the best interests of any student. The NCTM *Principles and Standards* (2000) stress less effort on speed and more effort on critical thinking. The new ways to do student assessments concentrate on the thought processes of students as they work through one problem on a test, as advocated by TIMSS. These efforts should be encouraged as ways to help students from diverse cultures have a better chance for mathematics achievement.

Noncompetitive Settings. Many students from nonwhite cultures do better in noncompetitive settings. Cooperative learning strategies are most important in such settings (Bush, 1990). Little Soldier (1989) found that cooperative grouping, stressing noncompetitive situations, best matches the group-oriented values of Native Americans. Khisty (1995), Stanic and Hart (1995), and Warren and Rosebery (1995) point to greater mathematical successes in noncompetitive classroom environments for Hispanic Americans and females. Cooperative learning appears to have merit for many groups of students.

SUMMARY

As teachers, all of us must let students know that they can be anything they want to be. Mathematics is the stepping-stone to success in a world of many careers. Each child's culture can be a strength, not a detriment. It is up to us to find the way to get through to each student. We must help students see the richness of mathematics from other cultures as well as their own. We must work with the institutions and agencies that can assist in mathematics equity. As we move forward to the twenty-first century, the Swahili admonition, *Harambee!* fits our time. Let's all pull together. We cannot hope to make a world of peace unless we all build a sense of pride in its people. *Mwalimu, Baki na heri!* (Teacher, remain in peace!—from Kiswahili, the most widely spoken African language).

EXERCISES

For extended exercises, see the CD-ROM.

A. **Memorization and Comprehension Exercises**
Low-Level Thought Activities

1. Name the three areas in which current research is taking place in culturally relevant mathematics.
2. Look at a unit of instruction from a current elementary or middle school math textbook. Classify how many pages are presented as field-dependent or field-independent tasks. Does the textbook favor any one processing strategy over another? If so, what implications does this emphasis have for students from other cultures?

B. **Application and Analysis Exercises**
Middle-Level Thought Activities

1. Using the material gathered in exercise A2, find the pages that are presented in the field-independent learning style and restructure the activity page as a field-dependent activity.
2. Search for culturally relevant topics that you could use in your teaching of mathematics. Look at current textbook series, professional journals, history of mathematics texts, and children's books.
3. Find a book featuring the history of mathematics and list the influences on the history of mathematics by the following noted people in the last 200 years:
   a. An African American
   b. A Hispanic American

c. A Native American
d. An Asian American
e. A woman mathematician
f. A European American

C. **Synthesis and Evaluation Exercises**
High-Level Thought Activities

1. Using the materials you found under section B, design a culturally relevant lesson using a mathematical concept of your choice. Remember to include cooperative grouping, field-dependent tasks, calculator and computer activities, and hands-on applications to the real world.
2. Visit a classroom at math time where the majority of students are from nonwhite cultures. Observe the learning styles of the students related to the types of task structure required in the math lesson. List those parts of the lesson that were particularly relevant to culturally diverse populations. If some materials might be better changed to a different approach, suggest what changes you would recommend. Justify your answer based on current research in the field.
3. Volunteer your time to tutor in an after-school program in which you can have the opportunity to work with students from cultures other than your own. Prepare materials to help them in mathematics for their grade level. You can use the culturally relevant charts throughout this text to help you start tutoring with meaningful materials.
4. What are the techniques effective teachers use to integrate important mathematical contributions by different cultures into the curriculum? How can a teacher integrate these ideas into the learning and understanding of mathematics?

BIBLIOGRAPHY

For an extended bibliography, see the CD-ROM.

Akoto, Agyei, ed. *Positive Afrikan Images for Children.* Trenton, NJ: The Red Sea Press, 1990.

Anno, Mitsumasa. *Anno's Counting Book.* New York: Thomas Y. Crowell Company, 1977.

———. *Anno's Counting House.* New York: Philomel Books, 1981.

———. *Anno's Math Games.* New York: Philomel Books, 1982.

———. *Anno's Magic Seeds.* New York: Philomel Books, 1995.

Anno, Masaichiro, and Mitsumasa Anno. *Anno's Mysterious Multiplying Jar.* New York: Philomel Books, 1983.

Arnold, David L. "Pueblo Pottery: 2,000 Years of Artistry." *National Geographic* 162 (November 1982): 593–605.

Beane, DeAnna Banks. "Say YES to a Youngster's Future." *Journal of Negro Education* (Summer 1990): 360–374.

Bohan, Harry, and Susan Bohan. "Extending the Regular Curriculum through Creative Problem Solving." *Arithmetic Teacher* 41 (October 1993): 83–87.

Bradley, Claudette. "Teaching Mathematics with Technology: Making a Navajo Blanket Design with Logo." *Arithmetic Teacher* 40 (May 1993): 520–523.

Bradley, Claudette. "Teaching Mathematics with Technology: The Four Directions Indian Beadwork Design with Logo." *Arithmetic Teacher* 39 (May 1992): 46–49.

Browder, Atlantis Tye, with Anthony T. Browder. *My First Trip to Africa.* Washington, DC: The Institute of Karmic Guidance, 1991.

Bush, William S. "Factors Related to Changes in Elementary Students' Mathematics Anxiety." *Focus on Learning Problems in Mathematics* 13 (Spring 1990): 33–44.

Caduto, Michael J., and Joseph Bruchac. *Teacher's Guide to Keepers of the Earth: Native American Stories and Environmental Activities for Children.* Golden, CO: Fulcrum Publishing, 1988.

Caduto, Michael J., and Joseph Bruchac. *Keepers of the Earth: Native American Stories and Environmental Activities for Children.* Golden, CO: Fulcrum Publishing, 1989.

Caduto, Michael J., and Joseph Bruchac. *Keepers of the Animals: Native American Stories and Wildlife Activities for Children.* Golden, CO: Fulcrum Publishing, 1991.

Campbell, Patricia F., and Thomas E. Rowan. "Teacher Questions + Student Language + Diversity = Mathematical Power." Ed. Janet Trentacosta and Margaret J. Kenney. *Multicultural and Gender Equity in the Mathematics Classroom: The Gift of Diversity. 1997 Yearbook.* Reston, VA: National Council of Teachers of Mathematics, 1997.

Carey, Deborah A., Elizabeth Fennema, Thomas P. Carpenter, and Megan L. Franke. "Equity and Mathematics Education." Ed. Walter G. Secada, Elizabeth Fennema, and Lisa Byrd Adajian. *New Directions for Equity in Mathematics Education.* Cambridge, Eng.: Cambridge University Press, 1995: 93–125.

Casteel, Clifton A., and David P. Rider. "Reading Comprehension in Caucasian Middle School Students: Effects of the Race of the Protagonists." *British Journal of Educational Psychology* 64 (February 1994): 19–27.

Cheek, Helen Neely. "Increasing the Participation of Native Americans in Mathematics." *Journal for Research in Mathematics Education* 15 (March 1984): 107–113.

Chocolate, Deborah M. Newton. *My First Kwanzaa Book.* New York: Scholastic, 1992.

Clements, Douglas H., and Julie Sarama Meredith. *Turtle Math: Teacher's Resource Exploring Math Through Measurement and Geometry.* Highgate Springs, VT: Logo Computer Systems, 1994.

Cuevas, Gilberto J. "Mathematics Learning in English as a Second Language." *Journal for Research in Mathematics Education* 15 (March 1984): 134–144.

Cummins, James. "Bilingualism and Second Language Learning." *Annual Review of Applied Linguistics* 13 (February 1992): 51–70.

Davidson, Ellen, and Leslie Kramer. "Integrating with Integrity: Curriculum, Instruction, and Culture in the Mathematics Classroom." Ed. Janet Trentacosta and Margaret J. Kenney. *Multicultural and Gender Equity in the Mathematics Classroom: The Gift of Diversity. 1997 Yearbook.* Reston, VA: National Council of Teachers of Mathematics, 1997.

Dossey, John A., Ina V. S. Mullis, and Chancey O. Jones. *Can Students Do Mathematical Problem Solving? Results from Constructed-Response Questions in NAEP's 1992 Mathematics Assessment.* (Report No. 23-FR01) U.S. Department of Education (August) 1993.

Ellis, Veronica Feeman. *Afro-Bets First Book About Africa: An Introduction for Young Readers.* Orange, NJ: Just Us Books, 1989.

Flores, Alfinio. "*Si Se Puede,* 'It Can Be Done': Quality Mathematics in More than One Language." Ed. Janet Trentacosta and Margaret J. Kenney. *Multicultural and Gender Equity in the Mathematics Classroom: The Gift of Diversity. 1997 Yearbook.* Reston, VA: National Council of Teachers of Mathematics, 1997.

Guild, Pat. "The Culture/Learning Style Connection." *Educational Leadership* 51 (May 1994): 16–21.

Haines, Joyce E., ed. *Culturally-Based Mathematics and Science Curriculum 1992.* Washington, DC: U.S. Bureau of Indian Affairs, 1992.

Hale-Benson, Janice E. *Black Children: Their Roots, Culture, and Learning Styles.* Baltimore: John Hopkins University Press, 1986.

Hiebert, J., and Thomas P. Carpenter. "Learning and Teaching with Understanding." Ed. Douglas A. Grouws. *Handbook of Research on Mathematics Teaching.* New York: Macmillan, 1992.

Henley, Cynthia. "Math—Grade 2 'Wild Animal Math'." Ed. Joyce E. Haines. *Culturally-Based Mathematics and Science Curriculum 1992.* Washington, DC: U.S. Bureau of Indian Affairs, 1992.

Ingle, Henry. *Sharpening the Issues and Shaping the Policies: The Role of the New Information Media and Technology.* Claremont, CA: Tomas Rivera Center, National Institute for Policy Studies, 1988.

Jacobs, Judith E., and Joanne Rossi Becker. "Creating a Gender-Equitable Multicultural Classroom Using Feminist Pedagogy." Ed. Janet Trentacosta and Margaret J. Kenney. *Multicultural and Gender Equity in the Mathematics Classroom: The Gift of Diversity. 1997 Yearbook.* Reston, VA: National Council of Teachers of Mathematics, 1997.

Jensen, Eric. *Teaching with the Brain in Mind.* Alexandria, VA: Association for Supervision and Curriculum Development, 1998.

Kansas City, Missouri Public Schools Police Division. *10 Tips for Crisis Prevention* [handout], Missouri Western State College Workshop, October 10, 1993. St. Joseph, MO: Author, 1993.

Keynes, Harvey B. "Can Equity Thrive in a Culture of Mathematical Excellence?" Ed. Walter G. Secada, Elizabeth Fennema, and Lisa Byrd Adajian. *New Directions for Equity in Mathematics Education.* Cambridge, Eng.: Cambridge University Press, 1995: 57–92.

Khisty, Lena Licón. "Making Inequality: Issues of Language and Meanings in Mathematics Teaching with Hispanic Students." Ed. Walter G. Secada, Elizabeth Fennema, and Lisa Byrd Adajian. *New Directions for Equity in Mathematics Education.* Cambridge, Eng.: Cambridge University Press, 1995: 279–297.

Khisty, Lena Licón. "Making Mathematics Accessible to Latino Students: Rethinking Instructional Practice." Ed. Janet Trentacosta and Margaret J. Kenney. *Multicultural and Gender Equity in the Mathematics Classroom: The Gift of Diversity. 1997 Yearbook.* Reston, VA: National Council of Teachers of Mathematics, 1997.

KidsConnect. Online posting. IConnect@ala.org. E-mail. 10 January 1996.

Kouba, Vicky L., Judith Zawojewski, and Marilyn E. Strutchens. "What Do Students Know About Numbers and Operations?" Ed. Patricia Ann Kenney and Edward A. Silver. *Results from the Sixth Mathematics Assessment of the National Assessment of Education Progress.* Reston, VA: National Council of Teachers of Mathematics, 1997.

Krause, Marina. *Multicultural Mathematics Materials.* Reston, VA: National Council of Teachers of Mathematics, 1993.

Kunjufu, Jawanza. *Lessons from History: A Celebration in Blackness.* Elementary Ed. Chicago: African American Images, 1987a.

———. *Lessons from History: A Celebration in Blackness.* Jr.-Sr. High Ed. Chicago: African American Images, 1987b.

Ladson-Billings, Gloria. "Making Mathematics Meaningful in Multicultural Contexts." Ed. Walter G. Secada, Elizabeth Fennema, and Lisa Byrd Adajian. *New Directions for Equity in Mathematics Education.* Cambridge, Eng.: Cambridge University Press, 1995: 126–145.

Lara-Alecio, Rafael, Beverly J. Irby, and Leonel Morales-Aldana. "A Mathematics Lesson from the Mayan Civilization." *Teaching Children Mathematics* 5 (3) (November 1998): 154–159.

Leder, Gilah C. "Equity Inside the Mathematics Classroom: Fact or Artifact?" Ed. Walter G. Secada, Elizabeth Fennema, and Lisa Byrd Adajian. *New Directions for Equity in Mathematics Education.* Cambridge, Eng.: Cambridge University Press, 1995: 209–224.

LEGO Group. *MINDSTORMS Robotics Invention System.* CITE: Europress, Interactive Factory, & SRI International, 1998.

Little Soldier, Lee. "Cooperative Learning and the Native American Student." *Phi Delta Kappa* 71 (October 1989): 161–163.

Lopez, Cecilia L., and Howard J. Sullivan. "Brief Research Report: Effects of Personalized Math Instruction for Hispanic Students." *Contemporary Education Psychology* 16 (1991): 95–100.

Lubienski, Sarah Theule. "Class Matters: A Preliminary Excursion." Ed. Janet Trentacosta and Margaret J. Kenney. *Multicultural and Gender Equity in the Mathematics Classroom: The Gift of Diversity. 1997 Yearbook.* Reston, VA: National Council of Teachers of Mathematics, 1997.

Malloy, Carol E. "Including African American Students in the Mathematics Community." Ed. Janet Trentacosta and Margaret J. Kenney. *Multicultural and Gender Equity in the Mathematics Classroom: The Gift of Diversity. 1997 Yearbook.* Reston, VA: National Council of Teachers of Mathematics, 1997.

Mark, June, ed. *Selected Bibliography for Gender Equity in Mathematics and Technology Resources Published in 1990–1997.* South Hadley, MA: Women and Mathematics Education (WME), 1998.

Mestre, Jose P. "Teaching Problem-Solving Strategies to Bilingual Students: What Do Research Results Tell Us? *Journal of Mathematics Education, Science, and Technology* 17(4) (1986): 393–401.

Mestre, Jose P., and William J. Gerace. "A Study of the Algebra Acquisition of Hispanic and Anglo Ninth Graders: Research Findings Relevant to Teacher Training and Classroom Practice." *NABE Journal* (Winter 1986): 137–165.

Michael-Bandele, Mwangaza. "The African Advantage: Using African Culture to Enhance Culturally Responsive Comprehensive Teacher Education." Ed. Mary E. Dilworth. *Being Responsive to Cultural Differences: How Teachers Learn.* Thousand Oaks, CA: Corwin Press, 1998.

Mingo, Clo. "Grounded Practice: Lessons in Anasazi Mathematics Emerging from the Multicultural Classroom." Ed. Janet Trentacosta and Margaret J. Kenney. *Multicultural and Gender Equity in the Mathematics Classroom: The Gift of Diversity. 1997 Yearbook.* Reston, VA: National Council of Teachers of Mathematics, 1997.

Morales-Jones, Carmen A. "Understanding Hispanic Culture: From Tolerance to Acceptance." The Delta Kappa Gamma Bulletin (Summer 1998): 13–17.

Morrow, Charlene. "Women and Mathematics: Avenues of Connection." Ed. Lyn Taylor. *Learning Problems in Mathematics* 18 (1, 2, 3; 1996): 4–18.

Morrow, Charlene, and Teri Perl, eds. *Notable Women in Mathematics: A Biographic Dictionary.* Westport, CT: Greenwood Press, 1997.

Morrow, Jean, and Ruth Harbin-Miles. *Walkway to the Future: Implementing the NCTM Standards in K–4 Grades.* Needham, MA: Janson Publications, 1996.

National Assessment of Educational Progress. *Mathematics Framework for the 1996 National Assessment of Educational Progress.* Washington, DC: National Assessment Governing Board, U.S. Department of Education, 1990.

———. *Mathematics Framework for the 1996 National Assessment of Educational Progress.* Washington, DC: National Assessment Governing Board, U.S. Department of Education, 1992.

———. *Mathematics Framework for the 1996 National Assessment of Educational Progress.* Washington, DC: National Assessment Governing Board, U.S. Department of Education, 1996.

National Council of Teachers of Mathematics. *Assessment Standards for School Mathematics.* Reston, VA: NCTM, 1995.

———. *Curriculum and Evaluation Standards for School Mathematics.* Reston, VA: NCTM, 1989.

———. *Principles and Standards for School Mathematics.* Reston, VA: NCTM, 2000 (to be published).

———. *Professional Standards for Teaching Mathematics.* Reston, VA: NCTM, 1991.

Nelson, David, George Gheverghese Joseph, and Julian Williams. *Multicultural Mathematics: Teaching Mathematics from a Global Perspective.* New York: Oxford University Press, 1993.

Nichols, Beverly W. "Calculating Women: 1600 Years of Beating the Odds, Classroom Activities and Interdisciplinary Ideas." National Council of Teachers of Mathematics Annual Meeting. San Diego, CA: April 1996.

Office of Technology Assessment. *Power On! New Tools for Teaching and Learning.* Washington, DC: U.S. Government Printing Office, 1988.

Papert, Seymour. *Mindstorms: Children, Computers, and Powerful Ideas.* New York: Basic Books, 1980.

Pappas, Theoni. *The Children's Mathematics Calendar 1993.* San Carlos, CA: Wide World Publishing/Tetra House, 1993.

Perl, Teri. Math Equals: *Biographies of Women Mathematicians + Related Activities.* Menlo Park, CA: Addison-Wesley, 1978.

Perl, Teri Hock, and Joan M. Manning. *Women, Numbers and Dreams.* Santa Rosa, CA: National Women's History Project, 1982.

Powell, Lois. "Factors Associated with the Underrepresentation of African Americans in Mathematics and Science." *Journal of Negro Education* 59 (1990): 292–298.

Ravitch, Diane. "A Culture in Common." *Educational Leadership* 49 (December 1991/January 1992): 8–11.

Rechin, Kevin. "Test Gap Widening between Rich and Poor." *Lansing Star Journal* 4 (December 1994): 9A.

Reese, Clyde M., Karen E. Miller, John Mazzeo, and John A. Dossey. *NAEP 1996 Mathematics Report Card for the Nation and the States: Findings from the National Assessment of Educational Progress.* Washington, DC: Office of Educational Research and Improvement, U.S. Department of Education, 1997.

Reimer, Wilbert, and Luetta Reimer. *Historical Connections in Mathematics: Resources for Using History of Mathematics in the Classroom.* Fresno, CA: AIMS Education Foundation [P.O. Box 8120], 1992.

Reimer, Wilbert, and Luetta Reimer. *Historical Connections in Mathematics: Resources for Using History of Mathematics in the Classroom.* Fresno, CA: AIMS Education Foundation [P.O. Box 8120], 1995.

Riley, Jocelyn, Producer. *Math at Work: Women in Nontraditional Careers.* Madison, WI: Videotaped by Her Own Words, 1999.

Schlelack, Jane F. "Reaching Young Pupils with Technology." *Arithmetic Teacher* 38 (February 1991): 51–55.

Secada, Walter G. "Degree of Bilingualism and Arithmetic Problem Solving in Hispanic First Graders." *Elementary School Journal* 92 (1991): 213–231.

Secada, Walter G., Elizabeth Fennema, and Lisa Byrd Adajian, Eds. *New Directions for Equity in Mathematics Education.* Cambridge, Eng.: Cambridge University Press, 1995.

Silver, Edward A., Margaret Schwan Smith, and Barbara Scott Nelson. "The QUASAR Project: Equity Concerns Meet Mathematics Education Reform in the Middle School." Ed. Walter G. Secada, Elizabeth Fennema, and Lisa Byrd Adajian. *New Directions for Equity in Mathematics Education.* Cambridge, Eng.: Cambridge University Press, 1995: 9–56.

Sofaer, Anna. *The Sun Dagger.* Bethesda, MD: Atlas Video, Videotaped by Bullfrog Films, 1993.

Spence, Bunnie S. "The Arcs of Archaelogy." *Mathematics Teaching in the Middle School* 1 (March–April 1996): 688–693.

Stanic, George M. A., and Laurie E. Hart. "Attitudes, Persistence, and Mathematics Achievement: Qualifying Race and Sex Differences." Ed. Walter G. Secada, Elizabeth Fennema, and Lisa Byrd Adajian. *New Directions for Eq-*

uity in Mathematics Education. Cambridge, Eng.: Cambridge University Press, 1995: 258–276.

Strong, Dorothy S. (Mathematics Ed.). *Systemwide Objectives and Standards.* Vol. 1–3. Chicago: Board of Education of the City of Chicago, 1990.

———. (Mathematics Ed.). *Mathematics Instruction Planning Manual.* Chicago: Board of Education of the City of Chicago, 1991a.

———. (Mathematics Ed.). *Mathematics Tutor Training Manual.* Chicago: Board of Education of the City of Chicago, 1991b.

———. (Mathematics Ed.). *Mathematics Tutor Training Manual.* Chicago: Board of Education of the City of Chicago, 1991c.

Tate, William. "Economics, Equity, and the National Mathematics Assessment: Are We Creating a National Toll Road?" Ed. Walter G. Secada, Elizabeth Fennema, and Lisa Byrd Adajian. *New Directions for Equity in Mathematics Education.* Cambridge, Eng.: Cambridge University Press, 1995: 191–206.

Taylor, Lyn. "Integrating Mathematics and American Indian Cultures." Ed. Janet Trentacosta and Margaret J. Kenney. *Multicultural and Gender Equity in the Mathematics Classroom: The Gift of Diversity. 1997 Yearbook.* Reston, VA: National Council of Teachers of Mathematics, 1997.

Taylor, Lyn, Ellen Stevens, John J. Peregoy, and Barbara Bath. "American Indians, Mathematical Abilities, and the *Standards.*" *Arithmetic Teacher* 38 (February 1991): 14–21.

Thomas, Jan. "Teaching Mathematics in a Multicultural Classroom: Lessons from Australia." Ed. Janet Trentacosta and Margaret J. Kenney. *Multicultural and Gender Equity in the Mathematics Classroom: The Gift of Diversity. 1997 Yearbook.* Reston, VA: National Council of Teachers of Mathematics, 1997.

Tiedemann, J. "Measures of Cognitive Style: A Critical Review." *Educational Psychologist* 24 (1989): 261–275.

United States Bureau of Indian Affairs. *National Resources in Mathematics and Science: Summer 1993.* Washington, DC: Bureau of Indian Affairs, 1993.

Vogt, Sharon. *Multicultural Math.* Greensboro, NC: Carson-Dellosa, 1994.

Voolich, Erica Dakin. "Using Biographies to 'Humanize' the Mathematics Class." *Arithmetic Teacher* 41 (September 1993): 16–19.

Walker, Erica N. and Leah P. McCoy. "Students' Voices: African Americans and Mathematics." Ed. Janet Trentacosta and Margaret J. Kenney. *Multicultural and Gender Equity in the Mathematics Classroom: The Gift of Diversity. 1997 Yearbook.* Reston, VA: National Council of Teachers of Mathematics, 1997.

Warren, Beth, and Ann S. Rosebery. "Equity in the Future Tense: Redefining Relationships Among Teachers, Students, and Science in Linguistic Minority Classrooms." Ed. Walter G. Secada, Elizabeth Fennema, and Lisa Byrd Adajian. *New Directions for Equity in Mathematics Education.* Cambridge, Eng.: Cambridge University Press, 1995: 298–328.

Webb, Michael. "Culture: A View toward the Unexplored Frontier." Ed. Mary E. Dilworth. 61–77. *Being Responsive to Cultural Differences: How Teachers Learn.* Thousand Oaks, CA: Corwin Press, 1998.

Wilson, Amos N. *Awakening the Natural Genius of Black Children.* New York: Afrikan World InfoSystems, 1992.

Zaslavsky, Claudia. *Multicultural Math: Hands-On Math Activities from Around the World.* New York: Scholastic, 1994.

———. *The Multicultural Math Classroom: Bringing in the World.* Portsmouth, NH: Heinemann, 1995.

———. "Multicultural Mathematics for the Middle Grades." *Arithmetic Teacher* 38 (February 1991): 8–13.

———. "Ethnomathematics and Multicultural Mathematics Education." *Teaching Children Mathematics* 4 (May 1998): 502–503.

CHILDREN'S LITERATURE

Caduto, Michael J., and Joseph Bruchac. *Keepers of Life: Native American Stories and Environmental Activities for Children.* Golden, CO: Fulcrum Publishing, 1994.

Cohlene, Terri. *Turquoise Boy, a Navajo Legend.* Mahwah, NJ: Watermill Press, 1990.

de Poala, Tomie. *The Legend of the Indian Paintbush.* New York: G. P. Putnam's Sons, 1988.

———. *The Popcorn Book.* New York: Scholastic Book Services, 1978.

Goble, Paul. *Iktomi and the Boulder, a Plains Indian Story.* New York: Orchard Books, 1988.

Krensky, Stephen. *Children of the Earth and Sky.* New York: Scholastic, 1991.

Kunjufu, Jawanza. *Teacher's Guide to Lessons from History: A Celebration in Blackness.* Elementary and Jr.-Sr. High Ed. Chicago: African American Images, 1987c.

Lacapa, Michael. *The Flute Player: An Apache Folktale.* Flagstaff, AZ: Northland Publishing, 1990.

———. *The Antelope Women.* Flagstaff, AZ: Northland Publishing, 1992.

Mitchell, Merle. *Mathematical History: Activities, Puzzles, Stories, and Games.* Reston, VA: National Council of Teachers of Mathematics, 1978.

Office on Global Education. *Make a World of Difference: Creative Activities for Global Learning.* Rev. ed. New York: Friendship Press, 1990.

Orlando, Louise. *The Multicultural Game Book.* New York: Scholastic, 1993.

Soto, Gary. *Chato's Kitchen.* New York: G. P. Putnam & Sons, 1995.

———. *The Old Man and His Door.* New York: G. P. Putnam & Sons, 1996.

———. *The Old Man and His Door.* [Spanish Edition]. New York: G. P. Putnam & Sons, 1998.

Stanley, Diane, and Peter Vennema. *Shaka: King of the Zulus.* New York: Mulberry Paperback Book, 1988.

Walter, Marion. *The Mirror Puzzle Book.* Ipswich, Eng.: Ancient House Press, 1988.

Integrating Technology

Video Vignettes: Lesson Plans in Action

- *Math in the Bilingual Classroom*

Computer Software Resources

. . . for Culturally Relevant Mathematics

Internet Searches

Surfing the Internet for Topics on Culturally Relevant Mathematics

Use the World Wide Web (WWW) and navigate through the system, searching for new information under major headings and subheadings similar to the following:

Mathematics Education
- Discussion Groups on Equity Issues
- Interactive Bulletin Boards
- Moses Algebra Project
- Multicultural Mathematics

NCTM
- Benjamin Banneker Association
- Native American Mathematics Educators
- Hispanic American Mathematics Educators
- Equity Issues
- New Position Papers on Equity, Limited English Proficiency (LEP)
- Multicultural Mathematics
- Women and Mathematics Education

Sources (by ethnic group)
- Latino books for children on the World Wide Web at:
  http://latino.sscnet.ucla.edu/Latino_Bibliography.html

- *Remember. . .* the Web is fluid . . . new topics and ways to search for topics change daily.
- Be adventurous . . . think of some new things you could try.

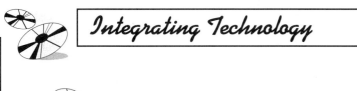

3

How Children Learn Mathematics

Activities Index

Children learn mathematical concepts from both the informal, unstructured experiences in their environment and the more formal, structured educational setting known as school. The objective of this chapter is to help teachers understand how children learn mathematics and solve problems so they can plan competent mathematics instruction.

The knowledge of how human beings learn is expanding daily. New discoveries being made in the scientific and educational communities are exploding onto the popular scene as well. Research studies of the brain continue to add growing insights across many disciplines. This research challenges our previous knowledge of how things are supposed to work. New research with implications for mathematics learning come from the three major schools of learning theory—the Cognitive/Constructivists, the Behaviorists, and information processing. Although there are many theories of learning, only those with the most impact on mathematics education have been included for study. The effective use of these theories in structuring mathematics activities is presented and coordinated with the NCTM *Principles and Standards for School Mathematics* (2000).

THE CHANGING SCENE OF HOW PEOPLE LEARN: THE BRAIN CONNECTION

Research studies of the brain (Jensen, 1998; Dehaene, 1997; Wolfe, 1998; Gorman, 1995; Lemonick, 1995; Nash, Park, and Willwerth, 1995; Swerdlow, 1995; and Sylwester, 1995) are proving the brain to be marvelously resilient and flexible, a quality known as *plasticity*. We are learning that one part of the brain is capable of taking over the actions normally

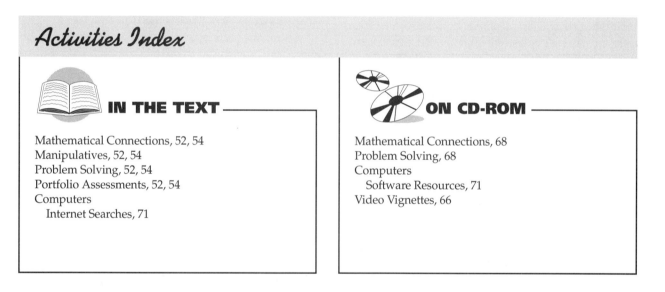

Subscripts© . . . *little thoughts below the bottom line*

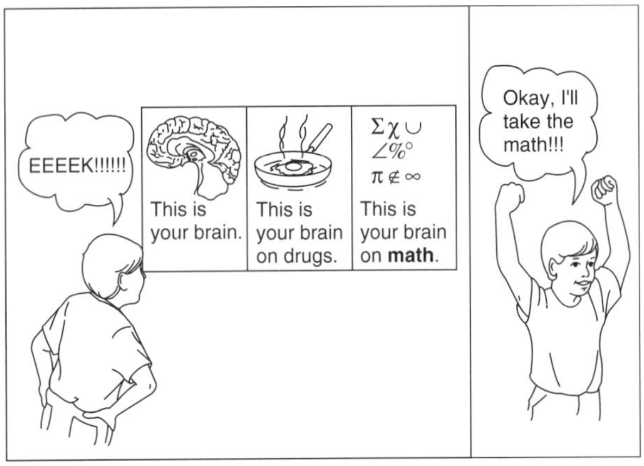

done by another part if the need arises as a result of some unforeseen malfunction or impairment. It appears that the brain is "wired" with trillions of *neurons,* nerve cells so small that 30,000 can fit on a pinhead. These neurons make connections with other neurons through *synapses,* the point at which electric impulses pass from one neuron to another. It is a very active process; one neuronal connection spurs the connections of other neurons.

The more stimulation children receive in their environment, the more they can interact with the things around them. Research shows that the more interaction a person has with the environment, the more neuronal connections are made. These connections form *networks.* These growing networks of more and more complex neuronal connections are how we learn and remember. Neuronal networks virtually control everything that keeps us going. Neuronal connections can organize the brain continually. Although neurons can create more and more intricate network connections, they cannot create themselves. Once neurons have died, they are gone forever. Alcohol, drugs, and some injuries to the brain destroy the neurons within brain cells, causing those neutronal connections to be lost permanently. Robert Sylwester (1995) and Eric Jensen (1998) have written understandable, engaging accounts about the intricate workings of the brain; the books are especially relevant for educators. Anyone interested in a more in-depth knowledge of brain research is encouraged to read the Sylwester and Jensen books. Another "must read" for math educators is Stansislas Dehaene's book (1997) on how the mind creates mathematics.

Use It or Lose It

We know that if a person decides not to use a perfectly good arm, over time he or she loses the ability to use the arm altogether. It appears that this is true for the brain as well. If the neuronal connections are not continually activated, knowledge governed by that network connection will be lost. Researchers point to the ability that infants have to vocalize all sorts of sounds. Children in any culture can trill an *r* sound or place a click in-between their babbling. If the children come from a culture where they do not use the trilled *r* sound, as in Spanish, or the fast click between syllables of words, as in several African tribal languages, the ability to use those sounds will be lost.

Linguists point to the fact that adults who learn another language later in life will never become native speakers of the language as if they had learned it in infancy. They can learn to make the sounds, but they are never natural or quick in their productions. Brain research supports the idea that neuronal connections must be used if they are to remain vital in the life of human beings.

Implications for Mathematics Teachers. The environment you provide your students must be one that allows them to have interaction with highly stimulating materials and ideas. (There are those concrete manipulatives and higher-order thinking ideas showing up again!) To do anything less means you have stopped the possibilities of knowledge that cannot be created as efficiently or as effectively later in life. It is interesting to note that the original NCTM *Curriculum and Evaluation Standards* (1989) and the NCTM *Professional Standards for Teaching Mathematics* (1991) appeared to be right on target with the results of brain research, although they were published before the surge of brain research in the mid- to later 1990s.

The Sooner, the Better

Brain researchers have found that the process of forming new neuronal connections is most intense during childhood. For example, children who have had exposure to playing a musical instrument at earlier ages, notably before the age of seven, actually have a larger brain capacity (that is, more neuronal networks) in the area of the brain that governs music (Jensen, 1998; Schlaug 1994). People who learn to play a musical instrument later in life do not show the size differences that those who started when they were younger have.

Children who have undergone surgery to remove either hemisphere of the brain have shown surprising resiliency and transfer of brain functions. Swerdlow (1995) reports that one young boy with no left hemisphere (the hemisphere normally credited with handling music, poetry, and mathematics) enjoyed playing the piano and found mathematics to be his strongest subject in school. Although older stroke victims also show evidence of transfer of brain functions, the transfer is slow and often takes arduous, repeated actions for even the simplest of tasks. If transfer has to occur, the sooner it happens, the better.

Armstrong (1994) believes that logical-mathematical intelligence must peak early in young adulthood. He points out that most of the great mathematical discoveries have been made by mathematicians in their early adult years, before the age of forty. He notes that Blaise Pascal and Karl Friedrich Gauss were just teenagers when they developed their most notable mathematical ideas in projective geometry and hyperbolic geometry, respectively.

Implications for Mathematics Teachers. If you are a teacher of preschool and elementary-age children, you are teaching at a person's most critical time of brain development. While it may be tempting to leave all the hard work of planning lessons with concrete manipulatives, interactive technologies, and higher-order thinking questions to another teacher a year or two down the road, it appears that children cannot afford to let precious time slip away. Every day in the classroom must be a day of active participation for each child.

Brain research will continue to grow as scientists find better ways to focus on brain activity. For up-to-date research you are encouraged to do the Internet Searches at the end of this chapter using topic names. Recent brain research showing the most promise gives two pictures of brain activity: (1) magnetic resonance imaging (MRI) and (2) positron-emission tomography (PET). MRI and PET pictures allow researchers to observe brain activity as a person performs a learning task. The image of the brain's activity shows on a computer monitor. As the machines become more affordable, it is conceivable that school districts will be able to purchase the equipment. If so, teachers would be able to watch students' actions as they performed mathematics tasks in their classrooms. Such technology would allow major transformations in a teacher's ability to plan lessons appropriate for each learner. Searching the Internet using MRI or PET terms may prove helpful for those who want to keep current in this exciting dimension of learning.

LEARNING THEORIES APPLIED TO MATHEMATICS

This chapter shows various theories as they coexist in the development of students' understandings of mathematics. Table 3.1 shows the key points of the three major schools of learning theory and some examples of the theories of each. Key points of each theory have been included also. Some readers may find the table beneficial as a means for comparison. However, each theory and its mathematical implications are explained in more detail in the following paragraphs.

The Constructivists

Just as brain research adds new implications for mathematics learning, it also reaffirms other theories of learning long thought to be pertinent to mathematics education. Most notable is the Constructivist learning theory. The works of Jean Piaget, Lev Vygotsky, and Jerome Bruner have had a great impact on the study of how children learn mathematics.

TABLE 3.1 Learning Theories with Implications for Mathematics Instruction

Learning Is Action	*Learning Is Reaction*	*Learning Is Process*
Cognitive/Constructivist	**Behaviorist**	**Information Processing**
Bruner	**Reinforcement Theory**	**Thought Processing**
Modes of reality	Immediate feedback	Field-dependent
Enactive	Programmed learning	Field-independent
Iconic		**Learning Styles**
Symbolic		Perceptual factors
Vygotsky		Visual
Zone of proximal development		Auditory
Piaget		Tactile
Stages of development		**Gardner**
Sensorimotor		Multiple intelligences
Preoperations		
Concrete operations		
Formal operations		

Constructivists believe that children must be allowed to experiment physically with the things around them if they are to learn. They believe active learning builds mental structures—theories that appear to coincide well with the developments of brain research.

Jean Piaget. Jean Piaget, a Swiss philosopher-epistemologist, conducted extensive research for over sixty years (1920s to 1980) on the development of children's cognitive abilities. Piaget and his coworkers devised ingenious learning tasks, some of which tested children's understanding of mathematics. These tasks and their results are presented throughout the book where appropriate. Special attention to Piagetian research as it relates to number readiness is found in Chapter 8. The focus in this chapter is Piaget's theory insofar as it applies to the general learning of mathematics.

Piaget's theory is age and stage related, which means that people go through definite developmental stages in their lives. Each stage must be completed before a person can attain the next stage. Interestingly, Piaget found that the development of mathematics proceeds through the same stages in a collective sense (taking many generations) that each person goes through individually in a relatively short amount of time. People must act on their environment at each stage until bits of knowledge form schemes (interlocking the bits of knowledge together to perform meaningful actions) which, in turn, form changed mental structures. These changed mental structures thrust a person into the next developmental stage. In a literal sense, the person no longer sees the world the same way. Notice that through the approximate age of twelve, every stage requires action on the environment. In mathematics, this means that elementary-age children must learn the operations of addition, subtraction, multiplication, and division through the use of hands-on materials that allow them to physically examine what is happening when an arithmetic operation is performed.

When students enter the formal operational stage, Piagetians believe that mental transformations can take place without the need of concrete materials. Students are then capable of understanding abstract concepts that cannot be easily proved in the physical world. An example would be the existence of irrational numbers having no repeating decimal pattern that can be keyed back to a basic building unit in our numeration system. Some studies have shown that not all people may attain formal operational thought, and still others may attain it far beyond the age of twelve. For this reason, some eighth graders have trouble understanding irrational numbers.

Piagetian Theory in Practice. Nothing helps a person understand a complex, intricate theory like Piaget's better than conducting one's own experiments with children in the various stages of cognitive development. Activity 3.1 on Piagetian developmental stages is presented to help you begin to place yourself in the role of a keen observer, much like Piaget did during his sixty years of research. It is hoped that the basic outline in Table 3.2 has more meaning after doing the activity in its entirety.

TABLE 3.2 Developmental Stages of Piagetian Theory

Name of Stage	Permits
Sensorimotor	Actions on objects
Preoperational	Actions on reality
Concrete operational	Actions on operations
Formal operational	Operations on operations

Activity 3.1

MATHEMATICAL CONNECTIONS · PROBLEM SOLVING · PORTFOLIO · MANIPULATIVES

ASSESSMENT OF PIAGET'S DEVELOPMENTAL STAGES WITH CHILDREN

MATERIALS

1. Pan of sand, salt, or paper filler.
2. Several containers in various shapes, to include those pictured in Figure 3.1. Each should be hollow.

FIGURE 3.1

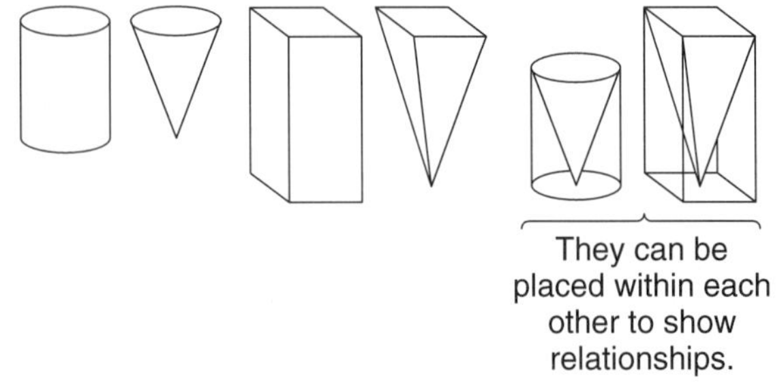

They can be placed within each other to show relationships.

Cylinders, cones, prisms, and pyramids.

Activity Continues

DIRECTIONS

1. Select a child in each of the following age groups:
   - Toddler to two years old
   - Two- to six-year-old
   - Six- to twelve-year-old
   - Over twelve years old
2. Try the activities listed below and allow each person to explore with the containers.
3. Record what each child does. This becomes a good *professional portfolio item,* documenting your ability as a keen observer of student actions.
4. Check with the responses Piaget found in each of these age groups as seen below. Reflect on the responses of your child. See how well they match Piaget's explanations.
5. WHAT PIAGET FOUND:

Sensorimotor Stage (toddler to two years old)

Do not use filler with young child. This is the "oral" time; children will eat the filler! They truly "act" on everything.

Teacher says: "Here are some objects just for you."

Actions on Objects

Children will touch, taste, squeeze, pinch, drop, and bang (to hear noise), roll, throw, stack, pretend to drink from can, and so on.

Children see the objects as extensions of themselves. Out of sight, out of mind describes this time of action.

Toward the end of this stage, children will use two-word oral language to describe what they are doing.

Expect language such as: "can go" "me drink" "see box," and so on.

Preoperational Stage (two- to six-year-old)

Teacher says: "Here are some objects and some filler. Show me what you can do with them."

Actions on Reality

Children know that objects exist outside of themselves (have their own reality), recognize that objects have properties, will use words to tell you so.

Children will scoop up filler in containers and dump it all over surfaces; may fill one container from another; may hide containers in filler, and so on.

Children say that objects are "pointed, square, flat, pointed, round," and so on.

Concrete Operational Stage (six- to twelve-year-old)

Teacher says: "Here are some objects and some filler. Explore and find out what you can do with them. Tell me what you have discovered."

Activity Continues

Actions on Operations

Children will "operate" on objects by systematically filling containers back and forth; will make statements that acknowledge the interrelatedness of the objects; will show that they understand how to reverse actions by filling and unfilling containers.

Children will figure out which containers hold the most, the least, equivalent amounts, and so on. They will predict before they do the actions.

If they do not think about predicting things on their own, teacher says: "Can you predict what will happen before you pour the filler in the containers?"

Children's oral discourse will include such descriptions as the following: "the rounded and square cans hold three times as much filler as the 'pointed' cans." They can also express it as "the pointed cans hold one-third as much as the ones with all sides flat."

Formal Operational Stage (over 12 years)

Teacher says: "Tell me what you know about these objects from using other objects like these in the past. Explore to check out any predictions you make."

Operations on Operations

Children no longer need the objects to work on the relationships; can generalize a simple volume formula for the operations on pyramids and cylinders, not just the ones shown to them. They can symbolize the formula as well.

For cylinders	For pyramids
$V = \pi r^2 h$	$V = \frac{1}{3}(l \times w \times h)$

Supporting the NCTM *Principles and Standards* (2000):

- Mathematics as Reasoning, Communication, Problem Solving, and Representation
- Student's Role in Discourse; Teacher's Role in Discourse; Analysis of Teaching and Learning—The Teaching Principle
- Monitoring Student Progress; Judging Progress toward Mathematical Power—The Learning Principle

We explore more of Piaget's theory in later chapters. Piaget's ideas concerning conservation of quantity, liquid, weight, and volume are noted throughout the text where appropriate. Piagetian theory has helped teachers have a more realistic view of what children can be expected to do at the appropriate developmental times. Brooks and Brooks (1993) assert that Piaget himself did not adhere to a strict age and stage theory in the last ten years of his research. He continued to stress the progression from one set of mental structures to another as seen in the preceding activity, but he did not link concepts to a strict age as he did in the early years. The Piagetian approach of asking questions and building on the answers of children helped inform educators of the need for oral discourse as seen in the original and subsequent NCTM *Standards*.

Lev Vygotsky. Other learning theorists, along with Piaget, believe that people are continually constructing and restructuring knowledge. One such theorist is Vygotsky. His work also delineates stages of development. At first, names of things, including beginning mathematical concepts, are not arbitrary; instead, names are assigned to objects and used intentionally. Children experience an urgency to assign each object a unique name from 18 months of age. The name fuses together with the covert action on the object, and children will not decenter from it until five to six years of age (Vygotsky, 1962; Miller and Eller-Miller, 1989). Covert actions and the disposition to perform the same action with the same-named object are called mapping. Eventually children come to accept that a name may represent a variety of meanings, enlarging that which is included in the mapping. When people can produce and analyze a complex skill on their own, Vygotsky says it is internalized in the *zone of proximal development* (Vygotsky, 1978).

Vygotsky's work has appeal to today's Constructivists because his research gives credence to the idea that children can be guided to better mathematical understandings as they progressively analyze complex skills on their own (Biehler and Snowman, 1997). Vygotsky's research showed that children could internalize actions involving complex knowledge more quickly with the guidance of good analyzing questions (discourse) from a teacher. Vygotsky called the place where such concepts are internalized the zone of proximal development. Concepts approximate real understanding, action by action, construct by construct. Therefore, no two people will have the same understanding of the concepts. Each builds (constructs) his or her own reality depending on the kinds of discourse and experience each has. Teacher intervention and quality instruction become very important in Vygotsky's view of Constructivism.

Vygotsky's Theory in Practice. The next activity explores the differences in two children's construction of concepts in geometry. The activity uses Vygotsky's ideas to help each internalize the experience. Both were in the same class and both were exposed to the same initial instruction. Use this as a starting point to do your own observation and assessment of children's work for your professional portfolio.

Activity 3.2

ASSESSMENT OF VYGOTSKY'S CONSTRUCTIVISM

MATERIALS

1. Three 10-cm squares cut from paper
2. Scissors, pencil, and a straight edge

DIRECTIONS

1. Read the experience of the two fourth-graders described here.
2. Then pick a student from an elementary grade of your choice and follow the same activity, checking to see at which point your student may approximate the same understandings of these children.
3. *Teacher:* "Here are three squares. Do they cover the same amount of area? How do you know?"

   Both children place all three squares on top of each other, proving congruency.

   Teacher: "Place a straight edge diagonally from one corner to its opposite corner on one of the squares. Mark the line with a pencil and cut the square into two pieces." (Teacher models the placement of the straight edge.)

   Both children follow the directions.

   Teacher: "Find other ways to put the two pieces together."

   Both children perform the following actions:

FIGURE 3.2

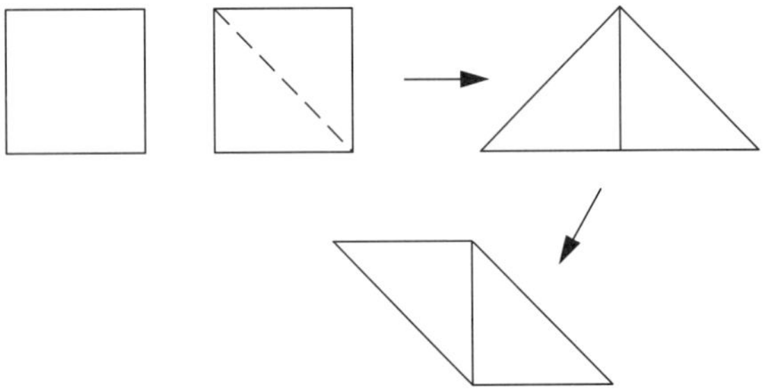

Square with first cut and two of the earliest transformations.

Teacher: "Now take the next square and mark it with two diagonals and cut it apart. Can you arrange the pieces to match the triangle and the parallelogram you made first?"

Child 1: "Yes, I can do it if I can use the first two I made to put these pieces on." (Teacher nods and child makes the figures seen below on top of the first two pieces.)

Activity Continues

FIGURE 3.3

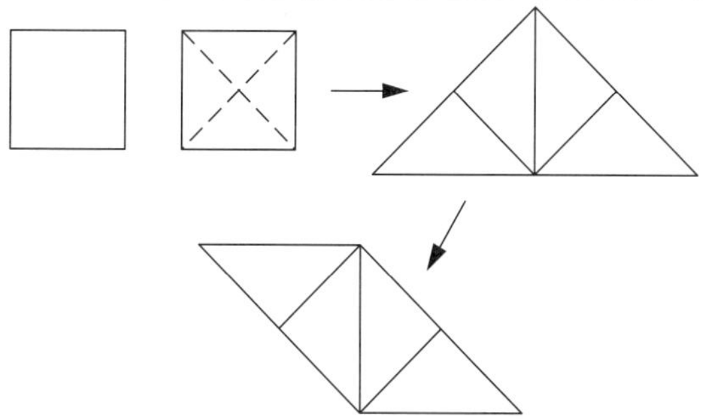

Square with two cuts and same transformations.

Child 2: Makes no verbal commitment, but moves quickly to make the following arrangement *without* using the first two pieces to match. Then child 2 says: "The parallelogram is getting longer and thinner."

FIGURE 3.4

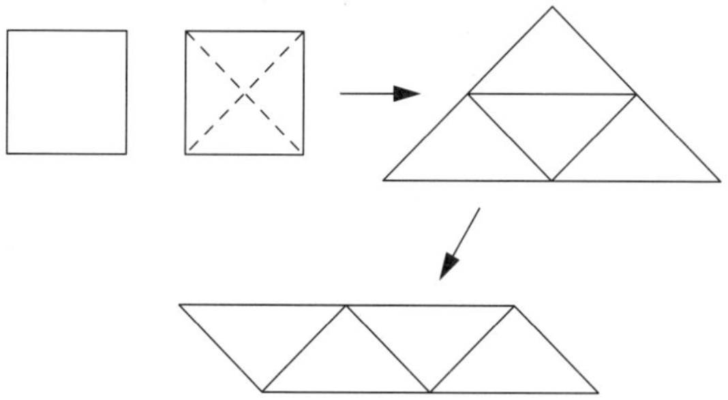

Square with two cuts and resulting new transformations.

Teacher asks: "Does the longer parallelogram cover the same area as the wider parallelogram you made before?"
Child 2: "Yes it does. See." (Child places longer, thinner parallelogram on the other one.)
Child 1: Watches what is going on but when asked, he states that "it is different because it changes to be longer and thinner. It's the same when it's like the first one but it is different when it is here like the long and thin one."
Teacher to Child 1: "Did you take anything away or add anything to change the area?"
Child 1: "No, nothing's gone but it is still different. Its area can't be the same because it is different. Its area is the same only when I match it up."

The teacher then gives a third square to both children and asks them to cut it into eight pieces like the one shown in Figure 3.5.

Activity Continues

FIGURE 3.5

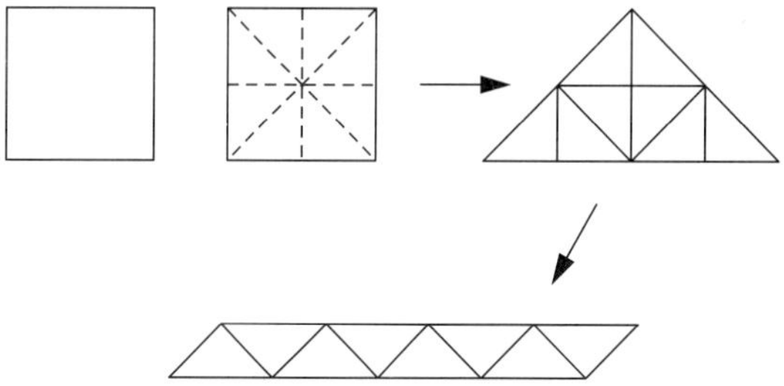

Square with four cuts and resulting eight triangles in new forms.

Child 1: Cuts the eight triangles but says, "They are too little to do anything with them, to make the big triangle or anything else. There are just too many pieces."
Child 2: "I know I can make an even longer parallelogram. See." (Child places pieces as seen at the bottom of Figure 3.5.)
Teacher to Child 2: "What do you think will happen if I kept giving you more and more squares to cut?"
Child 2: "I would keep making longer and thinner parallelograms with the same area."
Teacher: "How do you know that?"
Child 2: "I know because you started me out matching them all up from the same square so I know it all has the same area."

TEACHER REFLECTION

1. What do you know about each child as a learner from this experience?
2. Which child pushes his or her zone of proximal development further during the lesson?
3. Was the teacher wise in not asking Child 1 the last question? Why or why not?
4. What do you expect would have happened if the teacher had asked Child 1 the last question?
5. Could the teacher have worded any questions differently to help children arrive at an understanding without telling the answer?
6. What activity(s) should be planned next for Child 1? for Child 2?

Supporting the NCTM *Principles and Standards* (2000):

- Mathematics as Reasoning, Communication, Problem Solving, and Representation
- Student's and Teacher's Role in Discourse; Analysis of Teaching and Learning—The Teaching and Learning Principles
- Monitoring Student Progress; Judging Progress Toward Mathematical Power—The Assessment Principle

Vygotsky's theory would state that the teacher took each child to his or her own zone of proximal development based on the variety of meanings that each child was able to use in mapping the activity at that point in time. Each constructed his or her own reality of the events. A teacher believing in Constructivism would continue to work with both children, providing activities to stimulate the mapping of their own events within their own mental structures. The teacher would use each child's reasoning ability and suppositions as a starting place to help the child grow to more complex understandings. As you can see from the teacher reflection questions in the Vygotsky activity, it takes an alert teacher to do the job required using the Constructivist teaching technique.

Jerome Bruner. Another cognitive theorist is Jerome Bruner, a Harvard psychologist, who studied how people select, retain, and transform knowledge. Bruner (1966, 1983) believed that learning is an active process that permits people to go beyond the information given to them to create new possibilities on their own. His theory is not age or stage related. According to Bruner, there are three modes of representing reality that occur in the same order but interact throughout a person's life (Table 3.3).

When new or additional knowledge is to be learned, people must progress through one mode to the next for learning to occur. Mathematics educators frequently refer to the three modes as *concrete, pictorial,* and *symbolic.* Every elementary mathematics textbook starts with the pictorial and progresses to the symbolic. However, every series stresses the need for the teacher to present each new concept with concrete materials first.

Other Theorists. Mathematics educators have expanded on the initial three-phase model of Bruner. They desire the middle level to encompass more than just the pictorial or iconic representations of Bruner. Mary Baratta-Lorton (1976) emphasized the importance of the child's active explorations with mathematics and encouraged delaying the symbolic level. There is no pressure to ever abandon the concrete or pictorial in this model (Labinowicz, 1980). Their early work has been the foundation for many mathematics learning activities today.

TABLE 3.3 Three Modes of Reality in Bruner's Theory

Mode	Definition
Enactive	Action on reality in concrete ways without the need for imagery, inference, or words
Iconic	Pictorial need to represent reality; internal imagery that stands for a concept
Symbolic	Abstract, arbitrary systems of thought

Baratta-Lorton Model

1. *Intuitive concept level*—Logical relations among objects; manipulatives; free to explore; free from calculation.
2. *Connecting level*—Familiar activities now done with math symbols; higher level of abstraction.
3. *Symbolic level*—May still use concrete objects or pictorial representations of the concrete but emphasis is on symbols and what can be learned from them.

Another theorist whose writings apply to mathematics is Heddens. The Heddens model (1986) emphasizes that fine-line changes are occurring in the middle transitional positions. Figure 3.6 shows the model a child might use to discover the meaning of $2 + 1 = 3$.

The Heddens model is important when working with special needs students who may need more gradual changes during the middle transition period from the pictorial to the abstract. All of the models that we have discussed presuppose that students are doing the active hands-on exploration by themselves. This issue has implications for computer software as well. The best software may be programs in which students can directly affect the image on the screen. Logo is an excellent computer language because of its interactive ability. This text shows student work with the Logo programming language in various content chapters.

Today's Constructivists in the Classroom. There are many theorists who are advocating the Constructivist viewpoint today. Many education articles have been written for the classroom teacher, showing ways to structure the classroom environment for the enhancement of cognitive development in mathematics (Brooks and Brooks, 1993; Clement, 1991; Davis, Maher, and Noddings, 1990; Forman, 1989; Kamii and Dominick, 1998) to name only a few. Their ideas blend nicely with the NCTM *Standards* (1989, 1991, 1995, 2000).

FIGURE 3.6

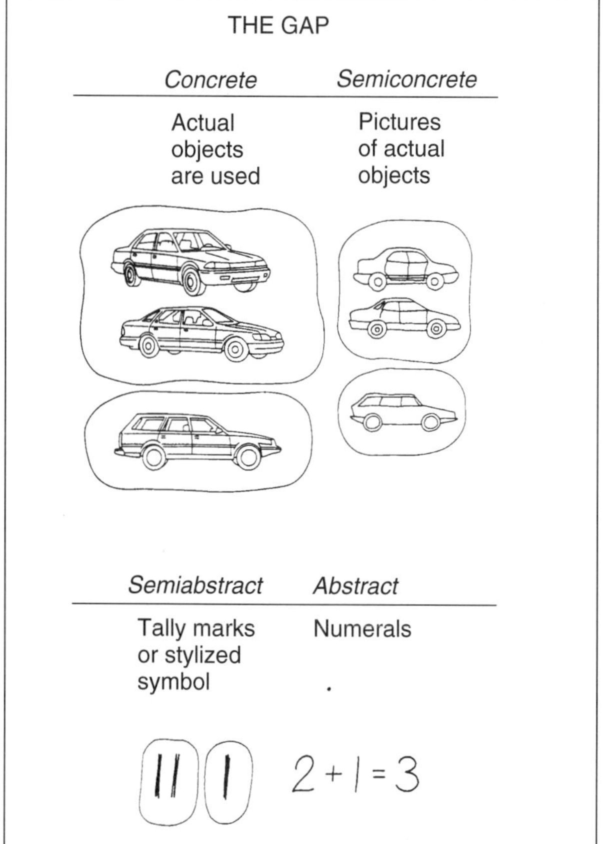

James Heddens's model.

In fact, a scene from a Constructivist classroom and a scene from an NCTM *Standards* classroom would look very similar. This close association has led critics of the *Standards* movement to question which movement is leading and which movement is following. Geary (1994) believes that what is taught in mathematics education is largely governed by educational fads and political ideology of the moment rather than by research in how students learn. For a lively philosophical discussion, see Orton (1995) and Cobb (1995). Both the Constructivists and the *Standards* advocates point to research that supports their views. This includes the new brain research, discussed earlier.

Elaborating Techniques. Constructivists believe the teacher is a guide, not a lecturer. Therefore, effective classrooms must include time for students to think aloud. This student interaction allows time for verifying answers, which works best in cooperative groups. Students who have trouble expressing their thoughts should be taught *elaborating techniques* (ways to guide their thought structures) to reach appropriate mathematical conclusions. An example of an elaborating technique may be helpful at this point. Some readers may have had no previous experience with the Logo computer language. A procedure could be frightening the first time it is tried. Here is an elaborating technique to help students understand some of the things Logo can do with numbers. The student's words and the teacher's words should be read alternating back and forth as a dialogue (see Figure 3.7 on page 58).

Notice, in the dialogue presented in Figure 3.7, the teacher never told the answer but guided responses to (1) promote transfer of learning from that which was familiar to that which was unknown, (2) direct problem solving on the student's own, and (3) guide the encoding process so that the student would associate PR with getting that which is seen on the screen. These three points are essential steps in developing the elaborating technique with students.

Assessment of Student Work Is Ongoing and Integrated. The area of assessment may well be the most influential of all the areas to affect mathematics in the beginning of the twenty-first century as introduced in America's Goals in Chapter 1. These goals call for the assessment of student learning throughout the grades in mathematics. Education professionals are calling for the assessment to be comprehensive, blending together many of the trends already discussed in Chapters 1 and 2. The call is to move from tests made up of microdetailed items with multiple-choice answers to a variety of assessment procedures.

Some procedures would involve the ideas of writing across the curriculum by asking students to explain in writing the rationale for the choices they made, thereby gaining insight into how students are thinking about mathematics. Mathematics professionals have already recommended that multiple-choice tests be eliminated from the curriculum before grade 4 (Mathematical Sciences Education Board, 1991). They advocate the use of portfolios of student work, interviews, diaries, cooperative group projects as well as individual projects, student demonstrations, and the elaborating technique to help assess the depth of students' mathematical reasoning (NCTM Assessment Principle).

A diary is defined as a running record of how a student solves mathematics problems. Diaries may be written by the student or stated orally. Oral responses are recorded for the record by an aide or teacher. Progress is seen by comparing reasoning from project to project over an extended period of time.

FIGURE 3.7

Student's Elaborating Techniques	With Teacher's Guidance
I can't tell what this program will do.	Key words are sometimes helpful in solving any mystery. What do you see?
I see the word MAKE used more than any other word, but I don't know what the "A and "1 mean.	Create a sentence with the word MAKE in it . . . just like you do in everyday language.
I MAKE a picture with red paint.	What were the important words after MAKE in your sentence?
Picture and red paint.	So red paint told you what you would do to the picture. Now what do you think "A and "1 are doing in the Logo program? Use the same wording.
"1 tells what to do to "A. So 2 must tell what to do to B, and A + B must be 1 + 2 which is 3. But I still don't know what PR means.	You could run the program and see if it helps you find out.
The program just answered 3. So PR must mean I get some kind of answer.	Yes, anytime you see PR, it means something is going to be done that you can see or it will be PRINTED so you can see the answer.
I was right.	You were right.

Alternating dialogue between student and teacher.

A portfolio is a sample of student work performed over time. It may include a student's diary, but it can exist without the student's explanation of answers in diary form.

Diagnostic Interview Techniques. Classroom instruction must also encompass diagnostic interviews as assessment between learner and teacher. Mathematical achievement improves as teachers understand students' misconceptions about mathematics and move to remediate the problems before they become too complex. The diagnostic interview technique has proved helpful in assessing problem areas. The *diagnostic interview technique* is the teacher's observation of a student's thought process through questioning to learn the degrees of understanding or misconception of a mathematical concept or principle. Interviews may occur individually or in a group. It is recommended that teachers tape the interviews to improve their questioning technique over time. Audiotapes or videotapes work well as long as they do not distract students from sharing their thoughts. The wait time between teacher question and student responses may require adjustment to meet the individual or group needs. There is no one ideal wait time, but it is widely known that most teachers wait only a second or two between responses. This is definitely not long enough.

Teachers should ask questions as students are working with a concept or principle. Teachers must remember that they are not correcting student misconceptions at this point; they are learning what the misconceptions are. Rowan and Robles (1998) suggest strategies and extensive questions to handle an interview with competence. See Chapter 4 of the CD-ROM for the detailed list. Three of the strategies are as follows:

1. *Discouraging the "parroting" responses of students.* Students frequently give an explanation back to the teacher just as the teacher has worded it in a teaching session. To make certain that the student truly understands the concept, Labinowicz suggests that the teacher ask, "How would you explain this to a first grader who doesn't understand it?" (1985, p. 29)
2. *Asking students to justify their answers.* Students may answer an example correctly but have no idea what the reasoning is behind it, and some students can reason correctly but still come up with erroneous answers. Sometimes they have trouble with both. Students should be asked to prove that their reason or their answer is the correct one.

3. *Keeping a student elaborating on a procedure or reason.* Teachers must remain noncommittal and nonjudgmental if they are to learn what students really think. Enough encouragement should be provided without implying that the student explanation is correct or incorrect.

Use words like	*"Keep going"*
	"I'm listening"
	"Tell me more"
rather than	"Okay"
	"Good"
	"All right"

Words like okay, good, and all right imply that the answers are correct. These responses should be avoided because a teacher does not want to imply that a wrong answer is correct when it will need to be retaught later, possibly confusing the student even more.

When a teacher moves from the role of assessor to the role of teacher, it is helpful to use the pupil-teacher elaborating technique demonstrated later in this chapter in the lesson-plan presentation. It guides the student to correct responses without negating the work a student has done in the interview session.

Diaries, portfolios, elaborating techniques, and assessment interviews represent a closer approximation to what is required to solve problems in the real world. Such assessment procedures would eliminate students getting the correct answers by chance when explanations have to be made to justify their responses.

The Behaviorists

Behaviorist theories stress the stimulus–response approach to learning. Each bit of information (stimulus) can be linked to a desired response if the correct contingency is presented to students. It is likely that the Behaviorists will explain the new findings of brain research as further evidence of the stimulus–response theory. Neuron-to-neuron synapses are electric connections from which one neuron responds to another neuronal stimulus. These form a network as more and more stimulus–response connections are made. The more positive the experience, the more the individual repeats the conditions under which the original connection was made, reinforcing that connection. Learning will still be seen as reactions to stimuli.

Immediate Feedback. Behaviorists believe that the sooner individuals know that a stimulus–response connection is a desired one, the more individuals will remember and produce the response again. Jensen (1998, p. 33) explains that the brain is "...self-referencing. It decides what to do based on what has just been done." The feedback must be specific rather than general and the learner must feel in control of the process. This also validates the work of Madeline Hunter (Wolfe, 1998), who believed that effective teaching was enabling good student decision making. The Hunter Every Pupil Response (EPR) is a way to reach every child quickly, to let the child know the teacher is assessing his or her learning even in a classroom with many students. Figure 3.8 shows what it might be like for a teacher to receive many answers to the problem-solving cards written by Greenes, Schulman, and Spungin (1992). Overwhelming is a word that comes to mind! Is it any wonder then that educators are advocating the use of peer groups (cooperative learning) to respond to one another while the teacher tries to reach everyone with so many diverse answers? Clipboards and Palm Pilots are becoming more frequently held by teachers than chalk in the twenty-first century!

Reis and her colleagues (1998) state that it is not the cooperative grouping that matters; it is what happens in the group that counts. There is no substitute for students sharing their problem-solving strategies with others; quality discourse makes the difference. Such discourse can be evaluated by self, group, whole class, and teacher to enhance the growth of quality responses. McGrath (1998) presents several forms for assessing the quality of responses in a variety of settings. The problem-solving cards in Figure 3.8 could start oral or written communication during a lesson.

Notice that there are a few misconceptions in some of the responses of the children in Figure 3.8. As a teacher, can you tell which ones they are? What would you do to stop an undesirable stimulus–response connection from becoming fixed in the mind of a child?

Theorists such as William Glasser (1990) and Alfie Kohn (1993) dispute the idea that children have to receive a reward for each small task, such as the teacher's acknowledgment after every response. Glasser and Kohn feel that children should have the satisfaction that comes from knowing they can use their brains to solve problems. This also seems to be the ultimate goal of most teachers. Teachers know that receiving immediate praise for a task well done is not likely to happen for every situation in the real world. It would appear that brain research agrees with Glasser and Kohn. Neurons grow and form more connections just from the process of problem solving; it does not seem to matter to the brain whether the answer is correct or not (Jensen, 1998.) In

FIGURE 3.8

Problem-solving cards using higher-level thought activities.

summary, feedback keeps the brain self-referencing, but it is the process rather than the one correct response that matters.

People want the stimulation that immediate feedback brings. Society has sped up immediate feedback to the point that individuals are not willing to wait even a few additional seconds for a response. People who were content with the speed of computers a few years ago are now demanding faster processing chips. They feel a wait of 5 seconds is too long. Wait 5 seconds between computer commands when you are working on a computer. How did it feel to you? Even the rules of baseball changed in the summer of 1995 to speed up the playing time in an attempt to keep the fans interested in the game.

Computer games have given powerful reinforcement to immediate feedback for young people today. Teachers are in competition with modern technology to keep lesson responses novel, well-paced, and stimulating.

Programmed Learning. Immediate feedback is an important component of *programmed learning,* which is defined as a series of small steps to which a student is asked to respond with immediate feedback given. Although programmed learning has been presented on simply constructed learning machines for many years, computers have made programmed learning accessible to more and more school children in a more efficient manner.

The computer language of Logo is a good example. In the 1980s and early 1990s, Logo required that students leave the turtle action screen to write procedures in a line-by-line command setting. By 1994, *Turtle Math* had been invented (Clements and Meredith, 1994). It allows children to do the procedure right on the same screen. Students can click on a button and each path or angle will be labeled with the command that made it. Students can instantly see the results of their actions.

Information-Processing Theories

Information processing is the study of how humans encode, store, and retrieve information. The theory uses the computer as its model. Designers created computers based on what was known about how humans acquire information. This analogy appears to be breaking down as new research is done on the brain. Our minds are not comparable to computers as once thought. Dehaene (1997) points out that the human brain takes longer to process numbers or differentiate between two numbers the closer they are together. This is not true for digital computers. They perform the calculations in the same amount of time regardless of how distant or close the numbers are to each other. Interestingly, Dehaene believes this proximity effect may have something to do with the fact that humans have more trouble remembering the answer to 9 + 8, than 9 + 4. The observation of such phenomena and how it is encoded, stored, and retrieved is the work of information processing. Information processing is the newest of the three schools of thought, and it is premature to designate definitive leaders. Two aspects of information processing are thought processing and learning styles.

Thought Processing. *Thought processing* is defined as the strategies used to organize and classify new information or skills to obtain order out of a confusing series of stimulus events. Two of these strategies have a direct relationship to how children perceive mathematics. *Simultaneous thought processing* requires stimulus material to be presented all at once (simultaneously), seeing the whole before its parts. A person begins to look for patterns and relationships to break down the whole into its respective parts to arrive at appropriate solutions. Persons using this thought processing are said to be *field-dependent learners*. *Successive thought processing* requires stimulus material to be presented from one component part to the next (successively), leading from detail to detail until the whole is seen. A person begins to look for patterns and relationships between details, building the respective parts into the whole to arrive at correct solutions. Persons using this thought processing are said to be *field-independent learners.*

At the beginning of this chapter, Table 3.1 presented the three schools of thought on learning theories. Readers who are field-dependent learners may find themselves referring to the table as they read these paragraphs to see how all of the material fits together. Other readers may have profited little from it and skipped immediately to the paragraphs that outlined details of each theory. Such readers would be using successive thought processing or are field-independent learners. Material has been presented using both thought processing modes in this text. Perhaps you will be able to analyze your own processing preferences as you work in the text.

Some people may adopt processing styles depending on their perception of how difficult the material is from task to task. Figures 3.9 through 3.14 on pages 61–64 show typical mathematical problems seen in elementary and middle school books and worksheets. In each set, both problems are teaching the same concept. The problems on the top of each set require students to process the information by

1. Counting the objects one by one until the entire set is calculated, or

2. Constructing the information one part at a time to get the answers.

This is successive synthesis—the part-to-whole processing strategy used by field-independent learners.

FIGURE 3.9

Field-Independent (successive synthesis)

Shade the part to show the fraction.

$\frac{1}{2}$ $\frac{1}{4}$ $\frac{1}{3}$ $\frac{1}{2}$

Field-Dependent (simultaneous synthesis)

Mark the fraction for the shaded part.

$\frac{1}{3}$ $\frac{1}{4}$ $\frac{1}{2}$ $\frac{1}{3}$ $\frac{1}{4}$ $\frac{1}{2}$ $\frac{1}{3}$ $\frac{1}{4}$ $\frac{1}{2}$

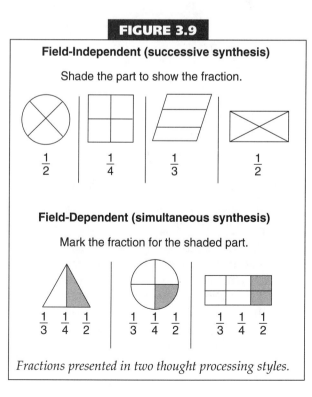

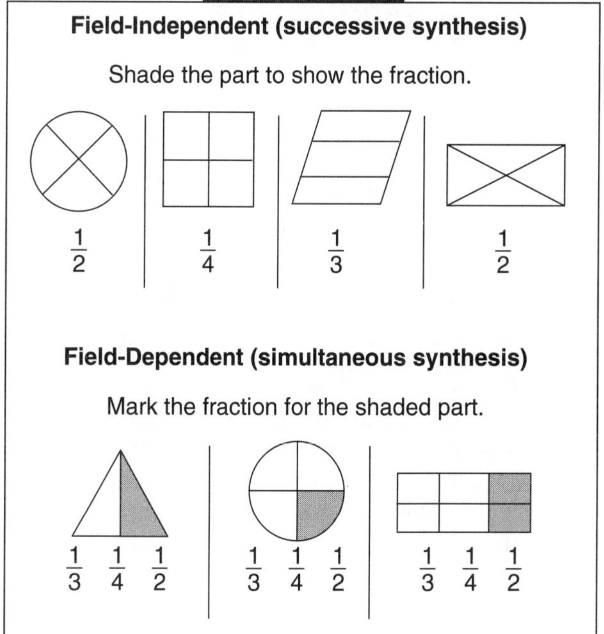

Fractions presented in two thought processing styles.

FIGURE 3.10

Find the answer to each picture.

____ + ____ = ____

flew away

____ − ____ = ____

Finish all the number combinations using all of the picture below.

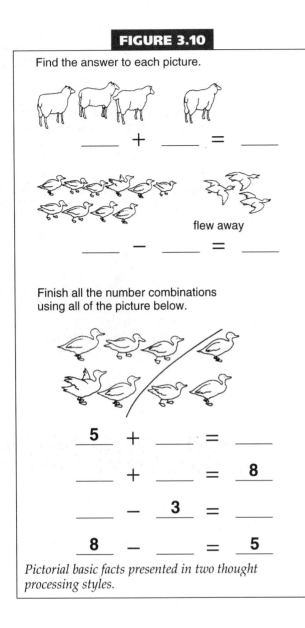

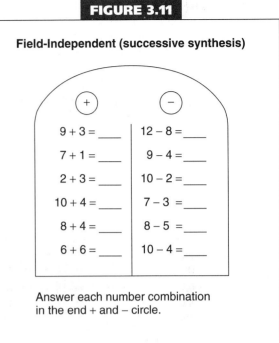

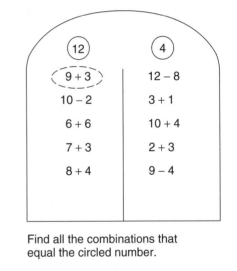

5 + ____ = ____

____ + ____ = 8

____ − 3 = ____

8 − ____ = 5

Pictorial basic facts presented in two thought processing styles.

FIGURE 3.11

Field-Independent (successive synthesis)

+	−
9 + 3 = ___	12 − 8 = ___
7 + 1 = ___	9 − 4 = ___
2 + 3 = ___	10 − 2 = ___
10 + 4 = ___	7 − 3 = ___
8 + 4 = ___	8 − 5 = ___
6 + 6 = ___	10 − 4 = ___

Answer each number combination in the end + and − circle.

Field-Dependent (simultaneous synthesis)

12	4
9 + 3	12 − 8
10 − 2	3 + 1
6 + 6	10 + 4
7 + 3	2 + 3
8 + 4	9 − 4

Find all the combinations that equal the circled number.

Symbolic basic facts presented in two thought processing styles.

The problems on the bottom of each set require students to process the information by

1. Receiving the entire set of answers all at once, deciding which sets do not belong, and partitioning them away from the whole, or
2. Seeing the entire relationship pattern that one part has to another.

This is simultaneous synthesis—the whole-to-part processing strategy used by field-dependent learners.

Some students are very confused with all the material seen at once as shown on the bottom of Figures 3.10 to 3.14. They may know the answers to the problems, but they may not be able to show what they really know because processing the information in this format is so difficult. Other students are equally confused when they are asked to determine an answer without seeing all the possible responses from which to deductively reason the answer as shown on the top of Figures 3.9 to 3.14.

The assessment section of each chapter presents ways to teach difficult mathematical concepts using simultaneous and successive processing strategies that may help students learn mathematics more effectively.

Learning Styles. The term *learning styles* is another component of information processing that can

FIGURE 3.12

Field-Independent (successive synthesis)

1							
							64

Write the numerals from 1 to 64 in the blocks going across. What patterns do you see with eights and fours?

Field-Dependent (simultaneous synthesis)

1	2	3	4	5	6	7	8
9	10	11	12	13	14	15	16
17	18	19	20	21	22	23	24
25	26	27	28	29	30	31	32
33	34	35	36	37	38	39	40
41	42	43	44	45	46	47	48
49	50	51	52	53	54	55	56
57	58	59	60	61	62	63	64

Look at the filled-in chart above. What patterns do you see with fours? With eights? What addition combinations can you see easily?

Fact strategy chart presented in two thought processing styles.

FIGURE 3.13

Field-Independent (successive synthesis)

6¢

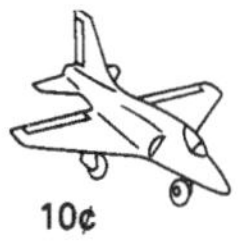

10¢

Draw the circle to show the coins you would need to buy each toy. Put a 1, 5, or 10 in the coin to show a penny, nickel, or dime.

Field-Dependent (simultaneous synthesis)

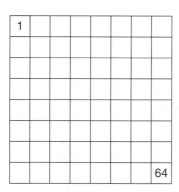

Circle the correct amount of coins needed to buy each toy.

Money presented in two thought processing styles.

mean different things depending on the author's interpretation. Learning style generally encompasses emotional, sociological, environmental, psychological, and physical factors, including perceptual data received through the senses.

It is beyond the scope of this text to include all these factors. Therefore, we have chosen to comment only on that which we feel has a salient relationship to the study of mathematics—the perceptual learning style. *Perceptual learning style* refers to a person's preference for material presented through one or more of the five senses. The visual, auditory, and tactile modalities are the ones most appropriate for the study of mathematical concepts.

Gardner's Multiple Intelligences. Howard Gardner has received much recognition in the 1990s for his theory of multiple intelligences. Gardner (1983, 1987, 1993) believes that there are at least seven different basic intelligences that human beings use to process information about the world around them. By 1995 Gardner had added an eighth, the naturalist, to the list (Kristeller, 1995). The eight intelligences as they might be applied to a mathematics lesson are represented in Figure 3.15.

The theory has appeal because all teachers know that they can reach some children better through one medium than another (Armstrong, 1994; Lazear, 1991). Gardner believes that people of all ages learn better if the material is presented through the areas of intelligence in which they are most gifted. It may be wise for elementary and middle school teachers of mathematics to present new mathematics concepts through the eight areas of intelligence. This means planning eight different approaches to the same con-

FIGURE 3.14

Field-Independent (successive synthesis)

Create your own:
- Draw a tangent. Label it *CD*.
- Draw a radius. Label it *AS*.
- Draw a diameter. Label it *RS*.
- Draw a chord. Label it *XY*.
- Draw a ray. Label it *AZ*.

Field-Dependent (simultaneous synthesis)

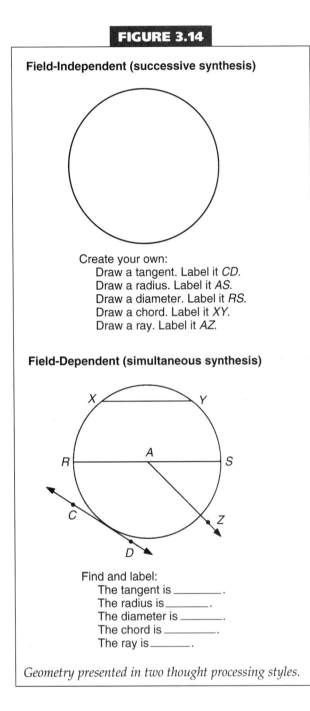

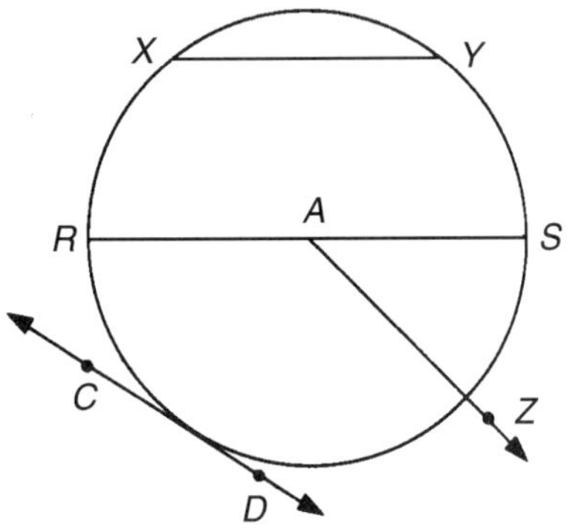

Find and label:
- The tangent is ______.
- The radius is ______.
- The diameter is ______.
- The chord is ______.
- The ray is ______.

Geometry presented in two thought processing styles.

tent. Proponents of multiple intelligences say that children's sense of well-being and willingness to grapple with hard concepts far outweigh the expanded time a teacher needs to plan multiple lessons. When students learn the material more easily, a teacher's job becomes easier as well. As you plan for effective instruction in the pages to follow, look for ways to integrate all eight intelligences in your teaching.

Many Differing Views. Many researchers differ on their beliefs about learning styles, processing strategies, and multiple intelligences. Different studies are cited in support of processing styles and learning styles. The proponents point to general classroom situations of success, more so than empirical research studies (Armstrong, 1994; Cheek, 1985; Hale-Benson, 1986; Marzano et al., 1988). Generally mathematics educators have been slow to adopt the idea of field-dependent and field-independent processing styles and multiple intelligences (Carey et al., 1995; Hiebert and Carpenter, 1992; Secada, 1991; Tiedemann, 1989). They point to research that shows children solve most mathematical concepts with similar strategies rather than different ones. They feel each person must know how to reason mathematically whichever way a concept occurs in the real world. For example, mathematics educators know it is not realistic to expect a person to handle fractions in everyday life *only* through art (a spatial intelligence), nor is it realistic to project money trends one at a time (a field-independent preference) without consideration of how the whole set of projections affect one another.

The authors are in agreement with the real-world approach. However, it does make sense to start the learning of any new concept using the strengths of each child, whatever the processing strategy or modality may be. Then children can be switched to other strategies that simulate the real world more closely once they have found success and initial understanding of a new concept. Therefore, a variety of visual, auditory, and tactile techniques and processing strategies are shared throughout the text in the hope that teachers will use a variety of learning aids to reach as many students as possible when teaching difficult mathematical concepts.

PLANNING FOR EFFECTIVE LEARNING OF MATHEMATICS

Classroom Instruction

Classroom instruction can be structured so that students attain a greater understanding of mathematics. Research in lesson plan presentations, diagnostic interview techniques, and assessment procedures add to the successful elementary and middle school experience in mathematics.

This section features several video lessons of experienced elementary and middle school teachers guiding mathematics learning in real classrooms. The videos appear on the CD-ROM for your study individually, in a small group, or as an entire class. These teachers show how it is possible to put the ideas discussed in Chapters 1, 2, and 3 together, creating quality lessons.

FIGURE 3.15

Gardner's eight multiple intelligences in a math lesson.

This section presents two types of lesson plan forms to help you structure effective learning in mathematics—the Chicago Mathematics Instructional Process and one based on international research (TIMSS).

The Chicago Mathematics Instructional Process. The Chicago model was researched in the Chicago public schools to teach the diverse population of students who attend the second largest school district in the United States. Its success as a planning tool merits your perusal for possible use in your own planning. This form purposely puts the student activities first and what the teacher will do to ready students for the activities second. This placement encourages teachers to realize that it is the students' ideas and relevant experiences that guide the instruction. You can access this lesson plan under the Chicago Mathematics Instructional Process on the CD-ROM. There is a completed lesson so you can see how teachers have planned in this format. There is also a blank form to be printed for your use in Appendix B of the CD-ROM to help you plan your own classroom instruction.

The TIMSS Lesson Plan Format. The second lesson plan format comes from the extensive research that followed the results of the Third International Mathematics and Science Study (TIMSS) (Forgione, 1997). TIMSS researchers found that Japanese classrooms are structured remarkably the same across the country of Japan. The emphasis is on reasoning, problem solving, using representations meaningfully and on communicating mathematically first by the student alone, then in a small group, and then in the total class. Table 3.4 shows the structure of the lesson.

Appendix B on the CD-ROM contains a blank copy of the TIMSS lesson plan format to help structure your thoughts as you prepare to write your own TIMSS lessons. The form includes space for you to write thought questions in the style advocated by the elaborating technique seen earlier in this chapter.

It is interesting to note that these same points have been advocated by the NCTM *Standards.* There is a thrust to have more TIMSS lessons in America's classrooms. Many of the state assessment tests require more constructed responses and journal explanations. The TIMSS format fosters the very things being tested in many of the state examinations. Interviewers are starting to ask teacher candidates how much experience they have had teaching the TIMSS way. The message is clear—*The TIMSS format is valued!* In Chapter 4 on the CD-ROM and where appropriate throughout the text, you will be shown lesson activities and portfolio assessments of actual students' work in the TIMSS format so you can sharpen your skills at trying to write and teach mathematics lessons the TIMSS way.

The TIMSS research showed that the U.S. curriculum spent more time on overpracticing procedures and focusing on little topics before students understood how and why they related to the big picture of mathematics. What little topics should we eliminate so that the big ideas are the ones remaining from the lessons we should develop? What would you give up if you had to? Look for journal articles and research studies that deal with this issue. There will be

TABLE 3.4 The TIMSS Lesson Plan Format

1. The teacher gives one rich, multistep problem to the class.
2. Each student tries to figure the problem out on his or her own for 5 to 10 minutes using concrete, pictorial, or symbolic representations as needed.
3. Students share how they are doing the task in small groups for 10 to 15 minutes.
4. Each group decides which approach of the students is the one they want to use together.
5. Each group presents what they have done and their thoughts about how they are reasoning. This is done in front of the whole class. Every group member stands with his or her group in front of the class.
6. Each solution stays on the board until all problems are done. (Japanese teachers rarely use overheads even in college because they believe that students with different learning styles need to keep looking at what has been done even after the class discussion has moved on to another solution.)
7. The whole class then decides which approach or approaches seem best. The teacher keeps asking questions if students seem to need help in making a decision. The teacher guides the students to correct reasoning patterns if all solutions prove to be incorrect.
8. As an extension to some activities, students write in individual journals what they learned from the lesson, including rationale for alternative solutions if there is more than one way to arrive at solutions.

Video Vignette

Candy Sales

Directions:

- After viewing the video, use the sample lesson plan for video vignettes in Table 3.5.
- How many ideas from this chapter can you see being used in the video?
- What evidence do you notice about these students' dispositions about mathematics?
- Analyze the classroom environment in terms of the Learning Principle (NCTM, 2000).

Name of Activity

- Looking for TIMSS

Pick five video clips that you have not seen. Analyze them for how well they use the TIMSS format in the teacher's lessons. Since the videos are short, you may have to imagine what part of the TIMSS lesson would have come before the clip and how much would come after the clip.

many opinions. As we begin the twenty-first century, what topics will remain in the curriculum at the end of this decade?

The Video Vignette: Actual Teachers in Classrooms. The lesson guide in Table 3.5 was developed for the Video Vignettes. Its detailed questions will guide you through the videos. The same format is used for all the video teaching lessons. Note its high correlation with the key concepts NCTM *Standards* and TIMSS.

Homework in Light of the New Approaches to Instruction. If classroom instruction is changing, it stands to reason that the kind of homework assignments are changing also. Rote learning is out; thinking power is in. Increased parental involvement is one of the goals for the twenty-first century (Clinton, 1998). Family math has become a major theme in some school districts. Children with their parents or guardians can work together on math projects started at school and finished with the family at home. Some districts even have Saturday family math days on which parents and children come to school on Saturday to work on math projects together.

These mathematics activities require thinking skills that go far beyond the basic-fact drill and practice associated with the homework of a decade ago. As you will see in Chapter 10, basic facts are taught more as thinking strategies rather than speed drills. So even when basic facts are sent home for practice, they do not appear in drill form. Morrow and Harbin-Miles (1996) have designed mathematics activities that give a challenge to children and permit communication between parent and child at the same time. Their book addresses classroom activities for teaching in the style of the NCTM *Standards* in grades K–4. The classroom activities are engaging and definitely model many worthwhile mathematical tasks. One example is included on the CD-ROM, the Black Hole of 3 and 6, to show how an activity started at school can become an assignment for celebration at home. At the end of the activity, the children's homework assignment is to share what they

TABLE 3.5 Lesson Plan for Video Vignettes

This is an example of a lesson plan to use for analyzing the vignettes based on the NCTM *Principles and Standards for School Mathematics* (2000).

Tasks

Tasks are the projects, problems, questions, applications, and exercises in which students are engaged. Worthwhile mathematical tasks are those that encourage students to develop their understandings, skills, and conceptual development. Such tasks have alternative solutions strategies, fuel students' curiosity, facilitate classroom discourse, and help make sense of the mathematics.

Think about the task in the vignette:

- How does the teacher encourage students to analyze important mathematical ideas?
- Do the tasks nurture mathematical thinking and make connections with past experiences?
- Do they provide for a diverse range of student learning and encourage all students to participate?
- Do the tasks fit into a coherent curriculum?

Discourse

Discourse refers to the ways of representing, thinking, talking, agreeing, or disagreeing about mathematics. The nature of discourse is to provide insight into mathematics thinking that teachers can use to make decisions about curriculum and purposeful teaching.

Think about the discourse in the vignette:

- How does the teacher use discourse to engage students in mathematical ideas?
- How does the teacher use discourse as a tool to generate legitimate mathematical reasoning?
- Does the discourse build mathematical confidence and allow for an exchange of ideas?
- In what ways does the teacher orchestrate discussions and balance knowing when to ask, tell, and redirect the discourse?

Learning Environment

The learning environment is the context in which the tasks and discourse are embedded. It represents the setting for learning and shapes the ways of knowing what is expected in the mathematics classroom.

Think about the learning environment in the vignette:

- How does the learning environment engage students to build new understanding, refine their thinking, and develop confidence in their abilities?
- How does the environment provide for alternative ways of approaching tasks?
- How does the environment promote mathematical reasoning, communicating, and representations?
- How does the teacher use tasks and tools such as technology and engagement with concrete materials to support mathematics learning?

discovered with their parents or guardians. Morrow and Harbin-Miles also include a form for a letter home to parents and a report on the activity to be filled out by the parent (1996, pp. 21–23).

EXTENDED ACTIVITIES

Name of Activity

- The Black Hole of 3 and 6
- The Chicago Mathematics Instruction Process

PROBLEM SOLVING MATHEMATICAL CONNECTIONS

You can see that it takes considerably more thought on the part of the teacher to construct such activities and letters that help lead parents or guardians as well as children into a new, exciting world of mathematics. Some teachers have found it worth their time to purchase books like *Walkway to the Future* with ready-made activities and letters. As classroom teachers become more adept at using the problem-solving approach to homework, they may write their own material.

SUMMARY

No one learning theory or method of instruction will suit every situation all the time for every person. An effective teacher uses all theories wisely, coordinating the difficulty of the task with stages of cognitive development and a student's individual learning style and thought processing preference. Although consideration of all the factors may look like an impossible task for any teacher, conscious practice of several approaches over time will help a teacher become secure and familiar with balancing many factors at once.

Brain research will continue to bring new insights to help teachers be more effective in the classroom. When we can unlock the mysteries of the mind, we will be able to respond to students' needs in ways that we can only glimpse today. It is truly an exciting time to choose mathematics education as a career.

EXERCISES

For extended exercises, see the CD-ROM.

A. Memorization and Comprehension Exercises
Low-Level Thought Activities

1. Supporting the idea of more mature thought in the use of EPRs, show three different ways to make an EPR to teach a concept like 5 + 2 = 2 + 5.

B. Application and Analysis Exercises
Middle-Level Thought Activities

1. Using a child's mathematics textbook, change a page requiring one processing strategy to the other processing strategy. Sketch how the new page would look.
2. Apply the three points needed for a successful elaborating technique to teach one of the problem-solving strategies found in Chapter 5.

C. Synthesis and Evaluation Exercises
High-Level Thought Activities

1. Create (synthesize) a model lesson plan for a mathematics concept of your choice. Choose the TIMSS or Chicago lesson plan model introduced in this chapter. Evaluate how all the components can work together. Include as many of the following components in the plan as possible:
   - **a.** Elaborating techniques for the concept.
   - **b.** Cooperative learning.
   - **c.** Every pupil response (EPR).
   - **d.** An idea for mathematical connections.
   - **e.** Concrete, pictorial, symbolic material in the correct sequence.
   - **f.** Find or make worksheets that include both simultaneous and successive thought processing strategies.
   - **g.** Plan activities for the auditory, visual, and tactile learner to include in the develop-

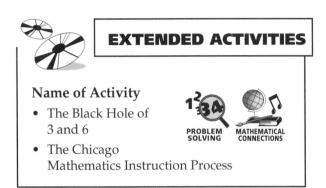

ment or controlled practice part of the lesson plan.

h. Diagnostic interview strategies to help students who may have difficulty with the concept.

i. List interactive computer software that could be used with the concept. Reviews of software programs may be found in

   i. Teaching material catalogs.

   ii. Reference section of the library.

   iii. Professional journals and magazines.

j. List three mastery learning objectives on which students will be evaluated at the end of the lesson (that is, What do you want the students to be able to do after you have taught the lesson that they could not do before?). List them as observable behaviors.

2. Pick a conversation from a teaching scene in your observation of a classroom. Write out a dialogue using the elaborating technique in the spirit of the Constructivist method of teaching.

BIBLIOGRAPHY

For an extended bibliography, see the CD-ROM.

Armstrong, Thomas. *Multiple Intelligences in the Classroom.* Alexandria, VA: Association of Supervision and Curriculum Development, 1994.

Baratta-Lorton, Mary. *Mathematics Their Way.* Menlo Park, CA: Addison-Wesley, 1976.

Biehler, Robert F., and Jack Snowman. *Psychology Applied to Teaching.* 7th ed. Boston: Houghton Mifflin, 1997.

Brooks, Jacqueline Grennon, and Martin G. Brooks. *In Search of Understanding: The Case for Constructivist Classrooms.* Alexandria, VA: Association for Supervision and Curriculum Development, 1993.

Bruer, John T. "Brain Science, Brain Fiction." *Educational Leadership* 58 (November 1998): 14–18.

Bruner, Jerome S. *Toward a Theory of Instruction.* New York: Norton, 1966.

———. *In Search of Mind: Essays in Autobiography.* New York: Harper & Row, 1983.

Burns, Marilyn. *The Math Solution: Teaching for Mastery through Problem Solving.* Sausalito, CA: Marilyn Burns Education Associates, 1984.

Carey, Deborah A., Elizabeth Fennema, Thomas P. Carpenter, and Megan L. Franke. "Equity and Mathematics Education." Ed. Walter G. Secada, Elizabeth Fennema, and Lisa Byrd Adajian. *New Directions for Equity in Mathematics Education.* Cambridge, Eng.: Cambridge University Press, 1995.

Cheek, Helen Neely. "Increasing the Participation of Native Americans in Mathematics." *Journal for Research in Mathematics Education* 15 (March 1985): 107–113.

Clement, John. "Constructivism in the Classroom—A Review of Transforming Children's Mathematic Education: International Perspectives." Ed. Leslie P. Steffe and Terry Wood. *Journal for Research in Mathematics Education* 22 (November 1991): 422–429.

Clements, Douglas H., and Julie Sarama Meredith. *Turtle Math.* [Computer Program and Teacher's Resource]. Highgate Springs, VT: Logo Computer Systems, 1994.

Clinton, William J. *President Clinton's Call to Action for American Education in the 21st Century.* Washington, DC: U.S. Department of Education, 1998.

Cobb, Paul. "The Relevance of Practice: A Response to Orton." *Journal for Research in Mathematics Education* 26 (May 1995): 230–253.

Davis, Robert B., Carolyn A. Maher, and Nel Noddings, eds. "Constructivist Views on the Teaching and Learning of Mathematics." *Journal for Research in Mathematics Education Monograph No. 4.* Reston, VA: National Council of Teachers of Mathematics, 1990.

Dehaene, Stanislas. *The Number Sense: How the Mind Creates Mathematics.* New York: Oxford University Press, 1997.

Forgione, Pascal D., Jr., ed. *Introduction to TIMSS: The Third International Mathematics and Science Study.* Washington, DC: U.S. Department of Education, 1997.

Gardner, Howard. *Frames of Mind: The Theory of Multiple Intelligences.* New York: Basic Books, 1983.

———. "Beyond IQ: Education and Human Development." *Harvard Educational Review* 57(May 1987): 187–193.

———. *Multiple Intelligences: The Theory in Practice.* New York: Basic Books, 1993.

Geary, David C. *Children's Mathematical Development: Research and Practical Applications.* Hyattsville, MD: American Psychological Association, 1994.

Glasser, William. *The Quality School: Managing Students Without Coercion.* New York: Harper Perennial, 1990.

Gorman, Christine. "How Gender May Bend Your Thinking." *Time* 17 July 1995: 51.

Greenes, Carole, Linda Schulman, and Rika Spungin. "Stimulating Communication in Mathematics." *Arithmetic Teacher* 40 (October 1992): 78–82.

Hale-Benson, Janice E. *Black Children: Their Roots, Culture, and Learning Styles.* Baltimore, MD: Johns Hopkins University Press, 1986.

Heddens, James W. "Bridging the Gap between the Concrete and the Abstract." *Arithmetic Teacher* 33 (February 1986): 14–17.

Hiebert, James, and Thomas P. Carpenter. "Learning and Teaching with Understanding." Ed. Douglas A. Grouws. *Handbook of Research on Mathematics Teaching.* New York: Macmillan, 1992.

Hunter, Madeline. Keynote address of the opening session conducted at the 40th Annual Conference of the Association for Supervision and Curriculum Development, Chicago, March 23, 1985.

Jensen, Eric. *Teaching with the Brain in Mind.* Alexandria, VA: Association for Supervision and Curriculum Development, 1998.

Kamii, Constance. "Reform in Primary Mathematics Education: A Constructivist View." *Educational Horizons* 70 (January 1991): 19–26.

Kamii, Constance, and Ann Dominick. "The Harmful Effects of Algorithms in Grades 1–4." Ed. Lorna J. Morrow and Margaret J. Kenney. *The Teaching and Learning of Algorithms in School Mathematics,* 1998: 130–140.

Kamii, Constance, Sally Jones, and Linda Joseph. "When Kids Make Their Own Math, They Can Make Math Their Own." *Power Line* 1. 2 (April 1991): 1–2.

Kirby, John R., Ed. *Cognitive Strategies and Educational Performance.* New York: Academic Press, 1984.

Kohn, Alfie. *Punished by Rewards: The Trouble with Gold Stars, Incentive Plans, A's, Praise and Other Bribes.* New York: Houghton Mifflin, 1993.

Kristeller, Julie. "A Classroom for Every Child." *Scholastic Early Childhood Today* 10 (August–September 1995): 35–40.

Labinowicz, Ed. *The Piaget Primer: Thinking, Learning, Teaching.* Menlo Park, CA: Addison-Wesley, 1980.

———. *Learning from Children: New Beginnings for Teaching Numerical Thinking, a Piagetian Approach.* Menlo Park, CA: Addison-Wesley, 1985.

Lazear, David. *Seven Ways of Teaching: The Artistry of Teaching with Multiple Intelligences.* Palatine, IL: Skylight Publishing, 1991.

Lemonick, Michael D. "Glimpses of the Mind." *Time* 17 July 1995: 44–51.

Marzano, Robert J. *A Different Kind of Classroom: Teaching with Dimensions of Learning.* Alexandria, VA: Association for Supervision and Curriculum Development, 1992.

Marzano, Robert J., Ronald S. Brandt, Carolyn Sue Hughes, Beau Fly Jones, Barbara Z. Presseisen, Stuart C. Rankin, and Charles Suhor. *Dimensions of Thinking: A Framework for Curriculum and Instruction.* Alexandria, VA: Association for Supervision and Curriculum Development, 1988.

Mathematical Sciences Education Board of the National Research Council. Paper presented for A National Summit on Mathematical Assessment, "Closing Remarks: A Summary of Group Discussions," April 24, 1991, Washington, DC, p. 3.

McGrath, Kathleen L. "What Is the Score on Scored Discussions?" *Mathematics Teaching in the Middle School* 4 (September 1998): 50–58.

Miller, Arnold, and Eileen Eller-Miller. *From Ritual to Repertoire: A Cognitive-Developmental Systems Approach with Behavior-Disordered Children.* New York: John Wiley & Sons, 1989.

Morrow, Jean, and Ruth Harbin-Miles. *Walkway to the Future: Implementing the NCTM Standards in K–4 Grades.* Dedham, MA: Janson Publications, 1996.

Nash, Madeleine, Alice Park, and James Willwerth. "'Consciousness' may be an evanescent illusion." *Time* 17 July 1995: 52.

National Council of Teachers of Mathematics. *A Year of Mathematics.* Reston, VA: NCTM, 1982.

National Council of Teachers of Mathematics. *Assessment Standards for School Mathematics.* Reston, VA: NCTM, 1995.

———. *Curriculum and Evaluation Standards for School Mathematics.* Reston, VA: NCTM, 1989.

———. *Principles and Standards for School Mathematics.* Reston, VA: NCTM, 2000 (to be published).

———. *Professional Standards for Teaching Mathematics.* Reston, VA: NCTM, 1991.

Orton, Robert E. "Ockham's Razor and Plato's Beard." *Journal for Research in Mathematics Education* 26 (May 1995): 204–209.

Reis, Sally M., Sandra N. Kaplan, Carol A. Tomlinson, Karen L. Westberg, Carolyn M. Callahan, and Carolyn R. Cooper. "A Response: Equal Does Not Mean Identical." *Educational Leadership* 58 (November 1998): 74–77.

Rowan, Thomas E., and Josepha Robles. "Using Questions to Help Children Build Mathematical Power." *Teaching Children Mathematics* 4 (May 1988): 504–509.

Secada, Walter G. "Degree of Bilingualism and Arithmetic Problem Solving in Hispanic First Graders." *Elementary School Journal* 92 (1991): 213–231.

Schlaug, Gottfried. "Brain: Music of the Hemispheres." *Discover* (March 1994): 15.

Schultz, Karen A. "Representational Models from the Learners' Perspective." *Arithmetic Teacher* 33 (February 1986): 52–55.

Slavin, Robert E. "Synthesis of Research on Cooperative Learning." *Educational Leadership* 48.5 (1991): 71–82.

Strong, Dorothy S. (Mathematics Ed.). *Systemwide Objectives and Standards.* Vols. 1–3. Chicago: Board of Education of the City of Chicago, 1990.

———. (Mathematics Ed.). *Mathematics Instruction Planning Manual.* Chicago: Board of Education of the City of Chicago, 1991a.

———. (Mathematics Ed.). *Mathematics Tutor Training Manual.* Chicago: Board of Education of the City of Chicago, 1991b.

Swerdlow, Joel L. "Quiet Miracles of the Brain," *National Geographic* 187 (June 1995): 2–41.

Sylwester, Robert. *A Celebration of Neurons: An Educator's Guide to the Brain.* Alexandria, VA: Association for Supervision and Curriculum Development, 1995.

Tiedemann, Joachim. "Measures of Cognitive Style: A Critical Review." *Educational Psychologist* 24 (1989): 261–275.

Vygotsky, Lev Semenovich. *Thought and Language.* Trans. E. Haufmann and G. Vakar. Cambridge, MA: MIT Press, 1962.

———. *Mind in Society.* Cambridge, MA: Harvard University Press, 1978.

Wolfe, Pat. "Revisiting Effective Teaching." *Educational Leadership* 58 (November 1998): 61–64.

Integrating Technology

Video Vignettes: Lesson Plans in Action

- *Candy Sales*
- Name of Activity: Looking for TIMSS

Supporting the NCTM *Standards* (2000)

- Worthwhile Mathematical Tasks; The Teacher's Role in Discourse; The Student's Role in Discourse—The Teaching Principle

Make your own lesson plan as you follow along with students in a real classroom setting. Follow the example found in this chapter—either TIMSS or the Chicago lesson plan format.

Computer Software Resources

...for How Children Learn Mathematics

Internet Searches

Surfing the Internet for Topics on How Children Learn Mathematics

Use the World Wide Web (WWW) and navigate through the system, searching for new information under major headings and subheadings similar to the following:

- Mathematics Education
  - Problem Solving
  - Constructivist
  - Cognitive Studies
  - Learning
    - NSF Projects
    - Programs
    - Multiple Intelligences
    - Cooperative Learning
  - Equity or Cultural Diversity
  - Feedback and Motivation
  - Effective Teaching Research
- Brain Research
  - Magnetic Resonance Imaging (MRI)
  - Positron-Emission Tomography (PET)
  - Mathematics
  - Logic
  - Patterns and Relationships
- NCTM
  - Problem Solving
  - Equity Issues
  - Professional Teaching Standards

- *Remember*... the Web is fluid... new topics and ways to search for topics change daily.
- Be adventurous... think of some new things you could try.

4

Assessment in Mathematics

Activities Index

IN THE TEXT

ON CD-ROM

On almost any given day, children are being assessed in school classrooms in some fashion—application of phonetic sounds for reading, comprehension of facts from a science newsletter, mastery of basic mathematics facts, ability to use small motor skills for using scissors, or detection of rhythm patterns in music. Such scenarios reveal that a variety of assessment tools are used, yet in school-based situations, classroom assessment typically signifies teacher-made or textbook-supplied tests over an instructional unit to determine mastery of content. Standardized achievement tests have become a powerful political tool in American education. Children know the importance of tests when they ask the proverbial question, "Is this going to be on the test?"

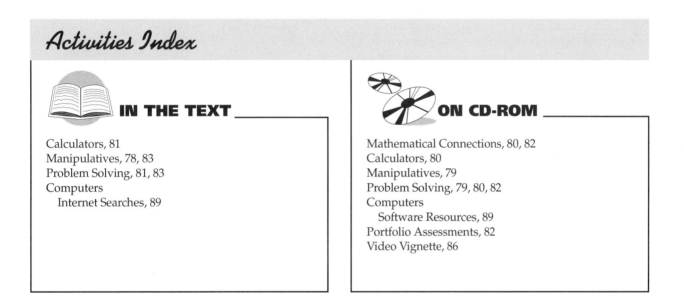

Today's curriculum reform efforts are also accompanied by assessment issues. Many teachers claim they would like to change their teaching practices, but they need to cover material that is "on the test." Teachers are well aware of the power of achievement tests as they see the local newspaper articles on published achievement results that allow district-to-district or school-to-school comparisons and know that some principals use the data for classroom-to-classroom comparisons. As educators begin to recognize the importance of a different mathematics education for American youth, improved means of measuring student learning and attitudes are needed. "We must ensure that tests measure what is of value, not just what is easy to test. What is tested is what gets taught. Tests must measure what is most important" (National Research Council, 1989, p. 8).

This chapter addresses the issues associated with the assessment of mathematics learning and examines a variety of assessment approaches and strategies for observing, collecting, and evaluating student work and student learning.

HISTORY

The United States is a nation obsessed with assessment, constant evaluation, and achievement. America's very foundation is based on hard work, striving for the unattainable goal, rags-to-riches stories, and motivation. However, Americans did not initiate the premise of assessment. The history of evaluating and testing human knowledge and capabilities dates back to the beginning of historical record. Early measurements were primarily oral examinations such as those used by Socrates to measure the understanding of his followers and examinations used by primitive cultures to determine knowledge of customs.

Standardized Testing

Educational testing in the United States did not appear until about the middle of the 1800s. Boston schools in 1845 appear to have instituted the first examinations in the United States. As a result of increased enrollments, school committees abandoned the more traditional individual oral examinations and opted for a written test that could be administered to the entire class. J. M. Rice developed a battery spelling test and set the stage for a standardized test. His test compared the knowledge and capabilities of students at different schools, in addition to evaluating the teaching methods of their instructors.

Around the beginning of the 1900s, individual intelligence scales were developed by Binet and Simon, followed by group intelligence tests for measuring army recruits during World War I. Soon thereafter, Thorndike published a series of tests in arithmetic, spelling, and English composition that became the first standardized achievement tests (Romberg, 1992).

From 1900 to the 1960s, evaluation evolved from the written exams, standard specimens, and student comparisons. Referred to as the psychometric period (the measurement of psyche), this era offered general intelligence, aptitude, and achievement tests to test and compare the knowledge of a large audience of students. The notion that everything that exists can be measured dominated the twentieth century.

Educators began to consider how these tests were related to the school curriculum. Ralph Tyler, considered by many to be the father of educational evaluation, developed a model of evaluation that compared objectives for the course with observed student behaviors. In addition to assessing the students' accomplishments, the tests revealed whether or not teachers had accomplished their instructional objectives. In the mid-1950s, Bloom organized instructional objectives into a taxonomy separated by three domains (cognitive, affective, and psychomotor). Educational behaviors could be arranged into a hierarchy from simple to complex to provide a framework for constructing tests. Several large-scale achievement tests have arrayed test items and scales in "content-by-process matrices in which the content dimension is some classification of mathematical topics and the process dimension is a version of Bloom's taxonomy" (Kilpatrick, 1993, p. 35).

Romberg, Wilson, and Khaketla's study (1989) of six commonly used standardized tests found a low match of content described in the NCTM *Standards* and content of the tests. The areas with the least amount of coverage on the tests were the process standards of mathematical problem solving, reasoning, connections, and communication. A similar study by Romberg, Wilson, and Chavarria (1990; Forgione, 1997) concluded that newly demonstrated state tests and test materials from several foreign countries reflected the objectives of the NCTM *Standards* better than the American standardized tests.

National Assessment of Educational Progress

Since the 1960s, student mathematics achievement in the United States has been measured by the National Assessment of Educational Progress (NAEP), a program of the United States Department of Education. Based on a sample size of 25,000 students at three grade levels, NAEP data are collected on trends in eleven academic areas. In recent years, data on student achievement were reported as "The Nation's Report Card" giving group comparisons by race and ethnicity, gender, type of community, and region. Interest in state-comparative information resulted in the data providing state-by-state or state-to-nation comparisons of student achievement.

A significant number of educators are concerned that federal, state, and local policymakers may misuse such data to make inappropriate comparisons and inaccurate conclusions. External assessment expectations play a powerful role in determining what curriculum is taught, particularly when student performances are compared and reported. With new emphasis on the NAEP data for state-by-state comparisons, teachers place increased importance on preparing students for the test and thus may narrow the curriculum to cover NAEP topics.

To counter this concern, the 1990 NAEP assessment established mathematical objectives based on expectations from the National Council of Teachers of Mathematics' *Curriculum and Evaluation Standards for School Mathematics* (NCTM, 1989). The items reflected a balance from five content domains (Numbers and Operations; Measurement; Geometry; Data Analysis, Statistics, and Probability; and Algebra and Functions). Items included multiple choice, open-response, and use of a calculator (Dossey and Swafford, 1993). The 1996 and 1998 assessments of fourth, eighth, and twelfth graders included performance tasks on the mathematics and science tests with constructed response items included.

International Studies

Since NAEP, other profile tests have been administered to study mathematical performance. The International Association for the Evaluation of Educational Achievement has conducted a cycle of international comparative studies since 1960. This nongovernmental organization represents thirty-five countries interested in assessment of outputs of national education systems. Data from the First International Mathematical Study, the Second International Mathematical Study, the Assessment Performance Unit in England, and the Third International Mathematics and Science Study (TIMSS) provide information for setting standards for international survey research, as well as valuable insights into aspects of the teaching and learning process (Robitaille and Donn, 1993).

A major focus of TIMSS is an analysis of the curriculum for cross-national comparisons. Another component of the TIMSS relates to the incorporation of alternative assessment methods. Participation in international studies such as TIMSS can provide information about national educational systems that become critical for policy decisions. The disappointing results of American students' scores have prompted some of the push for national assessments in the United States. Student achievement on TIMSS lessons are scored by rubrics (guides) after lessons are taught, as shown later in this chapter.

State Assessment Programs

The push to measure educational progress continued to increase. Mandated state testing programs began in 1972 and grew until by 1989, every state in the United States had a mandated testing program. Statewide testing is generally conducted at three grade levels, such as grades four, eight, and twelve. Teachers found themselves spending more instructional time on topics included on the state tests. Along with this phenomenon, there was decreased time spent on developing higher-order thinking skills and dealing with complex problems that take time to solve.

With mathematics reform efforts initiated in many states and accompanied by new state curriculum frameworks or essential skills, many individual states have instigated forms of statewide assessment in mathematics. Some states revised existing assessment programs, while other states made fundamental changes in assessment practices. Vermont and Kentucky were among the first to rely mostly on performance-based assessment. Kentucky's state assessment program, which was aligned with a new state curriculum framework, included open-response items, performance tasks, and student portfolios. Connecticut, Virginia, and Ohio have redesigned tests to reflect alternative forms of assessment on a statewide basis. Fundamental changes in state assessment introduced in California generated such public concern and political unrest that the new tests were abandoned and replaced with a more traditional assessment system.

Many of these states' new assessment systems are closely aligned with the outcomes for change in mathematics supported in the state systemic initiative programs. Systemic reform reflects broad consensus-building with an infrastructure to sustain and expand reform efforts. The variety of state objectives in mathematics and the diversity of state assessment programs limit state-to-state comparisons. States continue to seek ways of obtaining reliable data for comparing performance of schools. Many questions face educators regarding the multiple purposes and uses associated with statewide assessments.

CHANGING ASSESSMENT

American educators and society in general have embraced standardized testing as the means to determine the effectiveness of education. The public gives great attention to published standardized test scores. Indeed, many teachers teach to the test and learning goals become determined by the content of the tests. Researchers have evidence that testing shapes instruction and that test-defined instruction has the effect of driving out good teaching and "deskilling" those teachers who remain (Elliot, 1999). To restore meaning and trust to testing, we must examine the purpose of testing and who are the stakeholders in testing.

Purpose of Assessment

The purpose of assessment is to provide useful information regarding students' understanding and skills. Appropriate assessment contributes to the teacher's ability to understand students' needs in order to provide opportunities to develop children's mathematical abilities. Authentic assessment provides a maximum of information about children's learning strategies, knowledge, and abilities as they are allowed to show what they are able to do (van den Heuvel-Panhuizen and Gravemeijer, 1993). Assessment should provide information to

- Students to get information about themselves as learners of mathematics
- Teachers to make informed decisions about instruction
- Parents to obtain information about their children's mathematical competencies and abilities
- Administrators to become informed about the effectiveness of mathematics programs
- Interested public to learn about the effectiveness of a school's educational system

The Evaluation Efforts of the NCTM

In 1989 the reform efforts for mathematics were initiated by the National Council of Teachers of Mathematics *Curriculum and Evaluation Standards for School Mathematics* (NCTM, 1989). Reform efforts require a change in curriculum and instruction that must also occur in assessment. Traditional standardized testing that assesses the ability to answer multiple choice, true-false, or recall questions limits the range of student skills and knowledge that can be measured. Effective reform requires professional, political, and public consensus on the issues of how curriculum and instruction are to be measured. The original NCTM *Curriculum and Evaluation Standards* (1989) and the subsequent *Principles and Standards for School Mathematics* (NCTM, 2000) include standards for evaluating student performance and curricula programs that emphasize classroom assessment. In order for the *Standards* to become a reality, evaluation methods must change.

The *Standards* offer procedures for observing, collecting, and evaluating student work and student learning in an effort to improve the teaching and learning of mathematics. The Assessment Principle (NCTM, 2000) is a tool for implementing the *Curriculum Standards* and effecting change within the classroom. The main purpose of any evaluation is to help teachers better understand what students know and make meaningful instructional decisions based on this knowledge. The focus is on what happens in the classroom as students and teachers interact; therefore these standards call for changes beyond the mere modification of tests.

Classroom assessment envisioned in the *Standards* presents an environment that differs from many present classrooms. Such assessments are conducted in a climate of trust, without an emphasis on speed and accuracy, allow student questioning, provide a context for immediate feedback, and incorporate tasks that have instructional value. Cohen and Fowler (1998) state that good assessment should include basic learning of problem solving and critical thinking, along with mental mathematics, mathematics vocabulary, journal writing, calculator activities—all designed for mathematics understanding—and ending with assessment-designed strategies.

Assessment communicates to the public, students, and teachers what we value in mathematics. Educators must be careful that the message is appropriate. Assessment should reveal more than just what students know and can remember. In the past, it has been associated with the possession of information and memorized facts, rather than the acquisition of complex understandings.

Assessment Standards

With widespread acceptance of the original NCTM *Curriculum and Evaluation Standards* and school districts scrambling to create *Standards*-based classrooms, the NCTM *Assessment Standards for School Mathematics* (NCTM, 1995) were created. The *Assessment Standards* establish additional criteria for student and program evaluation and expand the earlier *Evaluation Standards.* Now known as the Assessment Principle, it defines assessment as "a process of gathering evidence about a student's knowledge of, ability to use, and disposition toward, mathematics and of making inferences from that evidence for a variety of purposes" (NCTM, 1995, p. 3).

The Assessment Principle (NCTM, 2000) provides a guide to direct reflection about current assessment practices and helps evaluate the quality and purpose of assessment. The six criteria for judging the quality of mathematics assessment state that mathematics assessments should:

- Reflect the mathematics that all students need to know and be able to do
- Enhance mathematics learning

- Promote equity
- Be an open process
- Promote valid inferences about mathematics learning
- Be a coherent process

Activities and ideas for assessment tools are included in the original *Assessment Standards.* Educators can assimilate the ideas provided and adapt them to better suit their needs. In the personalization of the examples each individual considers the underlying issues of alternative assessment practices. Figure 4.1 presents a performance task from the *Assessment Standards* that illustrates several of the standards. Which ones do you think could relate to the task?

FIGURE 4.1

Take an acute triangle with an interior point *P*. Consider the perpendiculars from point *P* to the sides and the triangle formed by the three feet of these perpendiculars on the three sides. This is the pedal triangle of pedal point *P*.

1. Measure
   a. The sum of the perpendicular distances to the three sides of the original triangle from *P*.
   b. The sum of the distances from *P* to the three vertices of the original triangle.
   c. The area of the pedal triangle.
   d. The perimeter of the pedal triangle.
2. Explore how these measures change for different locations of *P* inside the triangle.
3. What conjectures can you make about the sums, areas, and perimeters found in your explorations? Do you think your conjecture will apply to any triangle?

- Make a convincing argument for your answer. Your argument can be written or oral.
- Support your argument with the data you collected.
- Use tables or graphs to present your data.
- Explain a situation where someone would want to know this information.

Sum to sides = 2.55 inches
Sum to vertices = 5.67 inches
Area (Pedal triangle 1) = 0.81 square inches
Perimeter (Pedal triangle 1) = 4.50 inches

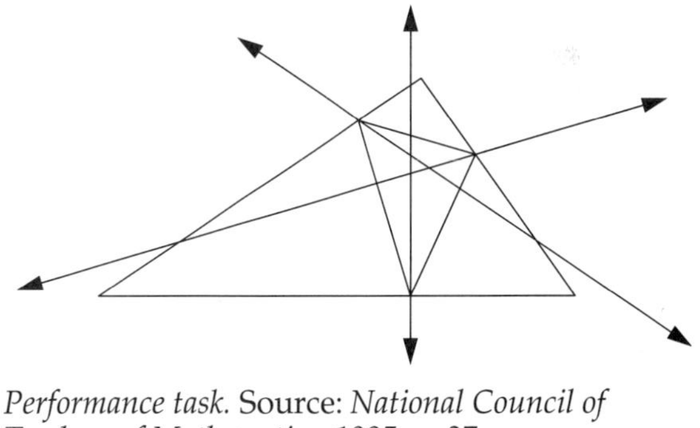

Performance task. Source: *National Council of Teachers of Mathematics, 1995, p. 37.*

Performance-Based Assessment

Concerned educators who wish to change the scope and focus of assessment have coined a number of words to describe the change from the simple close-ended, multiple choice tests to new assessment methods, such as authentic assessment, performance-based assessment, and alternative assessment. Whichever terminology applies, basically the same concept of assessment is envisioned: assessment is consistent with curriculum goals, embedded in real-world situations, and encompasses a number of procedures for observing, collecting, and evaluating student learning. The characteristics of alternative assessment are as follows:

- Students perform, create, and produce.
- Tasks require problem solving or higher-order thinking.
- Problems are contextualized.
- Tasks are often time-consuming and need days to complete.
- Scoring rubrics or scoring guides are required.

The performance-based assessment requires careful scrutiny of student work. Not all students will understand a task well enough to achieve success without well-placed guidance on a teacher's part. Since the emphasis is on the students' development of critical thinking processes, the teacher must become an expert at interviews, observations, questioning, and performance-based scoring.

Interviews

Interviews provide a source of rich information concerning what a child is thinking or feeling about mathematics. Information from interviews may provide insights into how to direct the student's learning as well as the assessment of his or her conceptual knowledge of mathematics. Interviews should not be limited to a diagnostic-prescriptive viewpoint. Information about conceptual understandings of students showing computational proficiencies can indicate the shallow understandings many academically talented students have about explaining mathematical procedures (Huinker, 1993). Questions should be prepared in advance and include probe questions to gather additional information. Encourage students to use drawings, illustrations, manipulatives, or models to explain their thinking. Many teachers use phrases to get students to verify their answers such as, "How do you know that?" "How would you explain that answer to another person?" "How would you explain your thinking to a younger brother or sister?" "Is there another way to get the answer?" (Figure 4.2).

Remember the purpose of the interview is to gather useful information about how students think and feel about mathematics. You may wish to audiotape or videotape the interview to give full attention to the student. Be sure you show positive, encouraging responses and avoid nonverbal body language. Listen carefully, practice long wait time after posing the question, and be sure to avoid giving any feedback to indicate a "right" or "wrong" response.

The learning model discussed in Chapter 9 and shown here in Activity 4.1 is a good guide for interview questions. The sequence of concrete representation, verbal explanations, and real-world situations presents a triad for assessing students' connections between various levels of representations, as shown in the activity, "Modeling Numbers."

Observations

Teachers observe students working individually and in groups every day of school. In this manner, teachers acquire a great deal of information about what students know and understand. The difficult task becomes knowing how to document students' learning from informal observations. In the past, objective data collection was preferred over subjective information, which may have caused some teachers to doubt the level of expertise they have in documenting student learning from subjective sources of data. Use the activities on the CD-ROM to gather observational data on your students' understandings.

In order to make observing and recording a reasonable task, a checklist is recommended to be used for recording information. A checklist is designed to record a number of widely based objectives over a series of days or weeks, and would require several pages to include the names of every student. Teachers use a variety of checklists, some for individuals, some for groups, some very specific, and others general, broad checklists (Figure 4.3). A specific inventory checklist may be created to assess problem solving (Figure 4.4). This checklist can be put on the

FIGURE 4.2

Interview Do's and Don'ts

- Find a quiet spot where you won't be interrupted.
- Ask some easy, interesting questions at the start.
- Accept the child's responses without judgment.
- Keep a neutral, accepting manner ("uhuh," and nodding head) rather than giving praise and feedback such as "good," "that's right," "great job."
- Keep your tone of voice the same for correct and incorrect responses.
- Probe right answers as well as incorrect ones.
- Establish a good wait time. Do not hurry to repeat the question again.
- Encourage the child to "think out loud."
- Encourage alternative solutions, verifications of answers, and asking, "how do you know that?"
- Avoid giving body clues or letting the child know when errors have been made.
- Do not interrupt the child.
- Do not begin to teach the "correct way."

Activity 4.1

MANIPULATIVES **MODELING NUMBERS**

Show me "three hundred fifty-seven"
with the materials
with numbers
with words

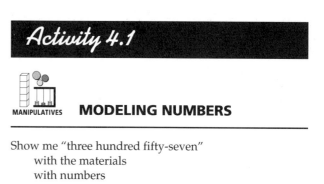

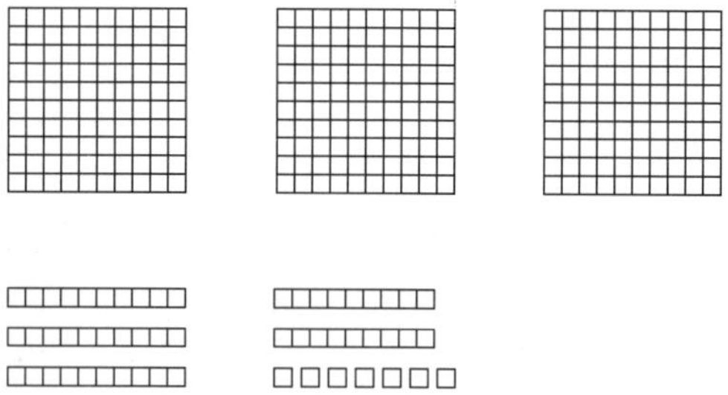

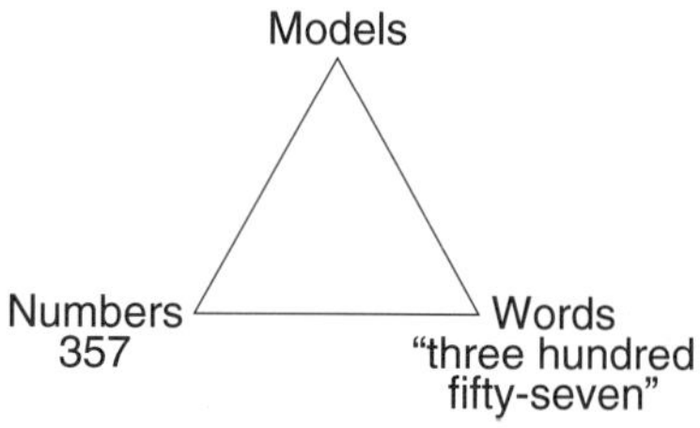

computer and quickly scored by the touch of the screen or by any hand-held computer. Total class records can be updated and printed in a few minutes.

EXTENDED ACTIVITIES

Name of Activity

- Number Sense—Using Benchmarks

PROBLEM SOLVING MANIPULATIVES

Observations may serve to obtain information about understandings as well as attitudes (Figure 4.5 on page 80) about mathematics. By using a checklist, information can be recorded in an orderly, focused fashion without interfering with instruction. Some teachers elect to focus on one group of students at a particular time with a specific list of skills; other teachers prefer a total listing of the class with broad objectives. In order to successfully use the information from observations to guide instruction, some specific plan for recording is needed. If a group checklist is used, you might want to have large sections for recording purposes. This sheet can be cut apart if you wish to place the information into the individual student's file. Be sure to record the date of the observations.

FIGURE 4.3

Week of ________________ **Tasks**	**Andy**	**Clara**	**Fernando**	**Maria**	**Nick**
Uses counting-on to find sums					
Counts by twos					
Touches objects for counting					
Uses models to show sets					
Ready for connecting level					

Checklist for observations.

FIGURE 4.4

Problem-solving strategies used:	**Juan**	**Tushan**
1. Estimation and Check	✓	
2. Drawing Pictures, Graphs, and Tables		
3. Elimination of Extraneous Data		✓
4. Simplifying the Problem		
5. Developing Formulas and Writing Equations		
6. Looking for Patterns		✓
7. Modeling		
8. Flowcharting		
9. Working Backwards	✓	
10. Acting Out the Problem		
11. Insufficient Information		

Problem-solving checklist.

Observations can also be made about individuals. An effective plan to keep information based on observations is to record the comments on small index cards. These dated cards can be placed directly into the student's assessment folder. Another efficient approach is to write comments on an address label or Post-It Notes, which can be easily transferred to the student's assessment folder.

Questioning

The issue of questioning is addressed in the original *Professional Standards for Teaching Mathematics* (NCTM, 1991) and now as the *Teaching Principle.* This document calls for teachers to limit the number of questions that can be responded to with a yes/no answer or with a short, one-word response. Mathematics is viewed as a subject with specific right answers and asking the right kind of questions will help dispel that notion.

Teachers need to develop more open-response questioning techniques and to ask students to explain their answers. Ask students to defend their answer, to think of another way to solve the problem,

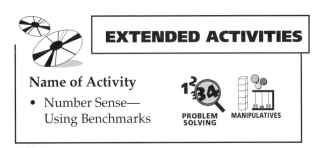

FIGURE 4.5

Behaviors	Andy	Clara	Fernando	Maria	Nick
Works well with others on problems					
Stays on task					
Takes care of materials					
Completes task within appropriate time					
Enjoys working with materials					
Enjoys working with others					
Participates in shared situation					
Shows self-confidence					
Accepts role assigned in group					
Listens to other classmates					

Checklist for attitude.

and to share their thinking with a partner. When teachers develop this kind of questioning environment, students should begin asking good questions of one another. Practice allowing children a long time to respond to an answer. Right and wrong answers should be given the same degree of respectful listening followed by probes for explaining the answer. Encourage students to use the same technique with one another.

To facilitate student-to-student discourse, have students talk to each other and verify their solutions. Direct questions like, "Amy, do you agree with Samantha?" "Explain your thinking about her answer." Many teachers serve as megaphones repeating answers given by students rather than requiring students to speak more loudly and to interact directly. The teacher should pose interesting questions, then become the facilitator for orchestrating good discourse. Rowan and Robles (1998, pp. 505–506) present a list of possible questions to be used to open avenues of thinking for students. The list is extensive. It may be printed out from the CD-ROM. The list can "save" the teacher who is just starting to develop questioning skills.

Performance Tasks

Performance tasks represent just what they say they are—a student's performance on a particular mathematical task or investigation. Assessment comes through observations, interviews, and examination of the outcome or product. Many educators view performance assessment as time-consuming and subjective. These aspects are true; however, there are many advantages.

Performance assessment provides for obtaining information about students' understandings, applications, misconceptions, and motivations. Performance assessment calls for students to demonstrate, build, create, or, in other words, to actually show they can *do* the task.

EXTENDED ACTIVITIES

CALCULATORS PROBLEM SOLVING MATHEMATICAL CONNECTIONS

Name of Activity

- Create the Graph
- Hidden Digits
- Use Questioning Skills with Student Assessments
- Purposes and Methods of Assessment

The Mysterious Money problem (in the following Activity) can be explored in many ways and teachers should devise a plan for assessing group solutions. Think about how you would solve the Mysterious Money problem, then decide the number of points your solution deserves.

In group investigations it becomes more difficult to monitor the mathematics problem solving. One approach is to use the Analytic Scoring Scale (Figure 4.6) developed by Charles, Lester, and O'Daffer (1994), the forerunner of many assessment guides used today. An advantage of this scale is that a teacher can focus on only one of the stages at a time. Problem solving requires higher-order thinking that is more difficult to measure. Students are often not able to communicate their thinking and the processes they use.

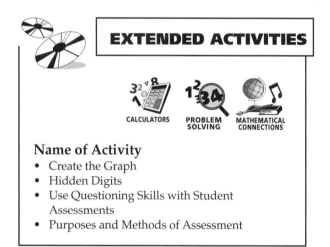

FIGURE 4.6

Understanding the problem	0: Complete misunderstanding of the problem 3: Misunderstanding or misinterpreting part of the problem 6: Complete understanding of the problem
Planning a solution	0: No attempt or totally inappropriate plan 3: Partially correct plan based on part of the problems being interpreted correctly 6: Plan that leads or could have led to a correct solution if implemented properly
Getting an answer	0: No answer or wrong answer based on an inappropriate plan 1: Copying error, computational error, or partial answer for a problem with multiple answers 2: Incorrect answer following from an incorrect plan that was implemented properly 3: Correct answer and correct label for the answer

Analytic Scoring Scale. Source: *Charles, Lester, and O'Daffer, 1994, p. 30.*

Activity 4.2

CALCULATORS PROBLEM SOLVING

MYSTERIOUS MONEY PROBLEM

An absentminded bank teller switched the dollars and cents when he cashed a check for Jana, giving her dollars instead of cents and cents instead of dollars. After buying a five-cent stamp, Jana discovered that she had exactly twice as much left as the amount of her original check. What was the amount of the check?

Here are five ways of adapting the problem:

- Change the context to switching digits on a license plate (leaving the same difficulty level).
- Change the numbers from a five-cent stamp to a twenty-three-cent stamp (making the problem harder).
- Change the number of conditions (for example, Jana finds a coin, thus making the problem harder).
- Reverse given and wanted information (making the problem easier).
- Change the combination of context, numbers, conditions, and information (given/wanted).

Source: Thompson, 1976, p. 104.

Test experts claim that performance tasks can be designed to gather information about high-level cognitive behaviors. Some educators claim such tasks are well-suited to assess collaborative learning. Students are encouraged to try various approaches, to create unique solutions, and to work with others on projects. This type of assessment replicates what happens frequently in the workplace when solutions to problems are being sought. Review some of the examples of performance tasks illustrated here that are from various projects, state assessments, or other sources. Think about how much information could be obtained about the child's level of understanding and thinking by using tasks such as the Taxman Game. The scoring guide provides characteristics for determining how to evaluate a student's response. More information on scoring is presented later in this chapter.

Activity 4.3

PROBLEM SOLVING

TAXMAN GAME

The game of Taxman is a number game played with you and the Taxman. Every time it is your turn, you can take any number in the list, as long as at least some factors of that number are also in the list. You get your number, and the Taxman gets all of the factors of that number.

Play several games of Taxman with these ten numbers.

1 2 3 4 5 6 7 8 9 10

Make a record of your best game. Be sure to show which numbers you took and the order in which you took them, not just the final score.

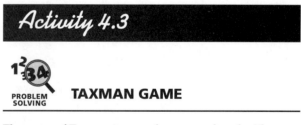

Activity Continues

Then answer the following questions:

Did you beat the Taxman? __________

What number did you choose first? __________ Why?

Do you think anyone could ever play a better game than your best game? __________. Explain why or why not.

Suppose you were going to play Taxman with whole numbers from 1 to 95.

What number would you choose first? __________

Why?

Source: Mathematical Sciences Education Board, 1993, p. 107.

Protorubric for Scoring Taxman

Characteristics of the High Response:

- The high-level response is one that demonstrates an optimal game, communicates it effectively, and generally shows an understanding of choosing the largest available prime as the best first move.

Characteristics of the Medium Response:

- A winning game is described, although it need not be an optimal one.
- The first number chosen is justified simply on the basis that it works out to be a winning first move.
- A correct answer, with some justification. (Of course, this response will have to depend on the best game that the students can find. If a less-than-optimal game is described, then an answer of yes is correct here.)

Characteristics of the Low Response:

- Some game is described, but sketchily and perhaps ambiguously (that is, it may not be possible to tell in what order the numbers were selected).
- No justification is provided for the first number chosen, or the justification does not take into account the factors of the number.

Source: Mathematical Sciences Education Board, 1993, pp. 107, 113–114.

Designing quality performance tasks is more difficult than it may first appear. The tasks should have enough structure to produce a wide range of responses. DeGraw (1999a; 1999b) presents many clever assessment tasks with actual student responses to aid a teacher's scoring ability. DeGraw follows this pattern:

- Start with an idea.
- Test the idea.
- Begin converting the idea.
- Consider response formats.
- Develop teacher notes.
- Draft an assessment approach.
- Try out the task.
- Revise where necessary.

DeGraw has written for both elementary and middle school.

The activity "Laura's Dinner" on the CD-ROM is an example of an assessment task written in the TIMSS format with a connection to children's literature (Seifner, 1998). The task allows for depth of thought and open-ended discussion in small groups before presentation of each group's chosen recipe before the class. The scoring guide and the work of three students are included. The book is one from Laura Ingles Wilder's *Little House* series. Your task is to review the assessment and then decide which score should be given to each student's work. After scoring the work, decide how you would use Rowan and Robles' questions to guide low-performing students to a better understanding.

Teachers using the TIMSS format to construct alternative performance assessments have reported a rise in the state assessment scores dealing with math problem solving after using the TIMSS approach for only half a year (Sharp and Ingram, 1998). The CD-ROM contains over 30 performance assessments constructed in the TIMSS format. Each assessment has been used successfully with students. The assessments range from kindergarten to grade eight and contain samples of actual student responses. They are labeled "Portfolio Assessments" because they make excellent teaching activities for teacher portfolios. Try several of the assessments with your own classes and include them in your professional portfolio. School officials want to hire teachers who have had experience teaching and scoring student performance assessments.

EXTENDED ACTIVITIES

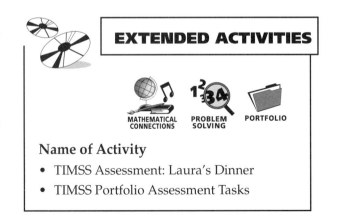

Name of Activity

- TIMSS Assessment: Laura's Dinner
- TIMSS Portfolio Assessment Tasks

Performance assessment and open-ended tasks must be relevant to the child's world in order to take on the claim of being "authentic assessments." For example, to ask children in inner-city schools to imagine going on a vacation to Disney World and calculating cost, mileage, meals and tips, amusement ride costs, and so on, may not be appropriate and meaningful tasks for these children. When constructing performance tasks, ask the question, "Is this task using a contrived context?" Issues of diversity, gender, socioeconomic levels, appropriate language and context, and interest level should be given attention. Getting students to communicate and explain their thinking requires a great deal of sensitivity on the teacher's part. Such settings may create a level of discomfort for some students. Students from diverse backgrounds do not share the same experiences and values. Researchers with the Classroom Assessment in Mathematics Network warn, "Teachers in urban classrooms using context-enriched assessment items have found that the assessment tasks fail to produce sufficient knowledge about their students' thinking and understandings because culture-rich context limits entry for many students. A culture-rich context is one that embeds experiences and values that are native to particular groups of students. Students from diverse backgrounds do not share the same type of experiences and opportunities" (Santos, Driscoll, and Briars, 1993). Puddle Questions (Westley, 1994) are excellent examples of activities all students seem to enjoy.

Activity 4.4

MANIPULATIVES PROBLEM SOLVING

SHOW YOU KNOW HOW

In a newspaper or magazine, find pictures that have examples of similarity and congruence (or rectangular solids, and so on).

Draw a picture to show how you can make regions that are partitioned equally.

Make a spinner to show that the probability of getting red is twice that of getting blue and the probability of getting yellow is half of that of getting blue.

Make a paper triangle that shows the different lines of symmetry—the medians.

With the blocks, show me the difference between addition and subtraction.

With a paper circle, show how it can be folded into a square, an octagon, and a triangle.

Calculators and Testing

One interesting aspect of the testing dilemma is the inclusion of calculators for mathematics testing. Although the inclusion of calculators into mathematics instruction has been slow and controversial, the proliferation of hand-held calculators continues. With the advent of graphing calculators and fraction calculators, materials to help teachers implement a calculator-based curriculum have significantly increased. The *Curriculum Standards* recommend that all students should have a calculator available while studying mathematics and that "tasks for assessing students' learning should be aligned with the curriculum's instructional approaches and activities, The NAEP now includes parts where students can use the calculator. The test item is followed by a question to determine whether the student used a calculator or not. NAEP results show that students consistently score higher on thought questions when they chose to use the calculator (Reese et al., 1997).

Recently the use of calculators on mathematics tests has been allowed on standardized tests such as the Standard Achievement Test, the Scholastic Aptitude Test (SAT), and the National Assessment of Educational Progress. Since 1995, graphing calculators are permitted on the SAT. Issues of the strengths and weaknesses, as well as the appropriateness, of calculators for tests will continue to be debated.

The use of calculators on mathematics tests is almost the same as the chicken and egg question. If mathematics instruction does not include the effective use of calculators, many mathematics tests will continue to disregard the use of calculators. One thing is clear, technology will continue to improve in capabilities and ease of use. As Harvey (1992) states, "Each time calculators become more capable and more responsive to mathematics instruction—and each is occurring—mathematics tests will have to be changed" (p. 168).

The widespread use of performance tasks is evident in two large-scale, respected tests. The College Board has incorporated performance assessment tasks in its Advanced Placement (AP) program for 40 years. Although the scoring entails weeks of grading the student products and open-ended responses, the Board regards the tests as appropriate and effective. As mentioned earlier, the National Assessment of Educational Progress includes performance tasks in its new mathematics and science assessments.

Student Portfolios

Portfolios are common ways to show a record of one's work in art or writing, but now are being used in many mathematics classes to show student progress. In the past teachers have kept folders of students'

FIGURE 4.7

Student's self-reflection should be part of the information.

Student should be involved in selecting the pieces to be included.

Scores on achievement data should not be included in portfolios.

Portfolio selections should reflect the rationale, intent, content, standards, and judgments of the student's activities.

Student's personal goals, interests, attitudes should be reflected.

Portfolio selections should contain information that illustrates growth and changes in skills and understandings.

Students need models of portfolios as well as feedback on how others reflected on their portfolios.

Guidelines for developing portfolios. Source: *Paulson, Paulson, and Meyer, 1991.*

work, but a portfolio represents a large collection of materials, papers, projects, pictures, copies of group reports, reports of student investigations, and math journal writings. The collection often is a year-long reflection of one's work. Student portfolios can provide evidence of performance tasks that illustrate conceptual understanding. They also can represent a record of student reflections, feelings, and self-assessments.

Portfolios offer a power tool for communicating to students and parents what is valued as important information about students' mathematical endeavors. Teachers should develop a purpose for their use that considers the function served, intended audience, and demonstrated competencies. Some guidelines to consider for developing portfolios are in Figure 4.7. Remember the portfolio should signify a vision of mathematics that goes beyond the right answer and should emphasize worthwhile mathematical tasks and a supportive learning environment.

Multimedia technology provides an effective way to collect information for portfolio assessments. Large amounts of information can be added to or retrieved easily and managed efficiently. Students can type their reflections using hypertext electronic notebooks and teachers can review the work to determine interests, understandings, and skills. The reduced paperwork and easy retrieval are important benefits. Students' work can be scanned directly into the portfolio and digitized photos and video can be included.

Portfolios have gained popularity to the point of becoming part of a school district's school improvement plan to statewide assessment programs based on portfolios. Mumme (1991) offers numerous examples of student's portfolios and reflective writings. She suggests, "We must work to make appropriate instructional materials available for teachers and provide resources such as manipulatives and technology. Most importantly, teachers must be supported with sustained, site-based professional development. Portfolios may provide the mechanism to link each of these in reforming mathematics education" (p. 26).

Self-Assessment

Although self-assessment is a common activity in which we all frequently engage, students would not list it as an aspect of mathematics assessment. However, the new focus on assessment encourages students to learn about themselves as a mathematics student. When selecting pieces for the portfolio, many teachers ask students to include a piece of work that illustrates their best work and select one that represents their worst work. Encouraging students to write about what they know about mathematics is another aspect of self-assessment.

Self-evaluation places the responsibility of learning on the student. It also involves turning a critical eye on one's mathematical knowledge, feelings of confidence, and attitudes toward mathematics. Some teachers ask students to predict the mathematics grade they should get from an assignment or on a project. According to research, self-assessment is tied to important aspects of the metacognitive process (Kenney and Silver, 1993). Student self-assessment involves being aware of one's own personal understandings of content and cognitive processes (knowing about what you know) and using self-evaluation (monitoring what you are doing while you are doing it). Therefore, both self-assessment and self-evaluation occur simultaneously. An example of a self-assessment sheet is shown in Figure 4.8.

Scoring Performance-Based Assessments

Alternative ways to grade students' work become necessary when using performance-based assessment systems. Two methods that are commonly used are analytic and holistic. In analytic scoring, specific points are identified to be addressed. Points

FIGURE 4.8

Math Journal of ______________________________

Self-Assessment of My Math Work

Student Scoring Guide
Circle where you think you are after solving the problem.

	General Criteria	Specific Criteria for this Task:
5 Mastery	• I did this perfectly. I was AWESOME!	
4 Integrating	• I was almost perfect.	
3 Nurturing	• I knew what I was doing but I forgot a few things.	
2 Developing	• I thought I knew what I was doing, but I forgot a lot of things.	
1 Starting	• I started but I got lost quickly.	

Kind of Problem

☐ Open-Ended — I made up a new problem

☐ Discovery — I found a way to solve

☐ Guided Discovery — I followed the clues

I used the following problem-solving strategies:

____ 1. Estimation and Check
____ 2. Developing Formulas and Writing Equations
____ 3. Drawing Pictures, Graphs, and Tables
____ 4. Elimination of Extraneous Data
____ 5. Modeling
____ 6. Flowcharting
____ 7. Working Backwards
____ 8. Insufficient Information
____ 9. Simplifying the Problem
____ 10. Acting out the Problem
____ 11. Looking for Patterns

The part I had most trouble with was:

The part I understood best was:

What I still need to work on is:

Student self-assessment sheet.

are given if the student's response includes that particular point. Holistic scoring means that the entire response is considered and assigned a point. This scoring method allows the teacher to make more subjective decisions about the student's thinking. The advantage of holistic scoring is that it is quicker. This technique is used in large-scale assessment when an overall judgment of performance is needed and it is easier to get consistency among assessors with holistic scoring.

The term associated with scoring of assessment tasks is "rubric" or "scoring guide." Rubrics must come from the qualities desired in the task.

A general mathematics rubric (scoring guide) is shown in Figure 4.9 on page 86. It allows the teacher to write specific criteria (analytic) for any performance-based task while being used as a holistic guide for quick assessment. These numbers may be turned into grades if teachers feel the need to do so. Clauson (1998) shows how scoring guides with children's writing can be used as grades. Such scoring guides show the degree of progress that is being made. Space for brief comments provides additional information for parents about their child's progress. Summary reports provide information for teachers about differences in student performances.

FIGURE 4.9

Level	General Criteria	Specific Criteria (Chosen by the Teacher)
4+ Advanced	• Shows understanding of concepts • Reasoning pattern is consistent and well structured • Gives clear explanations • Allows for more than one approach or solution • Performs the task with accuracy • Goes beyond the requirements of the task	
4 Proficient	• Shows understanding of concepts • Reasoning pattern is consistent and well structured • Gives clear explanations • Allows for more than one approach or solution	
3 Near Proficiency	• Shows understanding of concepts • Reasoning pattern is consistent and well structured • Gives clear explanations	
2 Progressing	• Shows understanding of concepts • Reasoning pattern is consistent	
1 Starting	• Shows some understanding of concepts • Little if any reasoning pattern	

Comments on Student Growth: ____

____

Generic scoring guide for performance-based assessments.

New Standards Project

In 1991 at a National Summit on Mathematics Assessment, recommendations were made to create new prototypes of mathematics assessment tasks that reflect the spirit of the *Standards.* Principles and goals for mathematical assessment were created to guide the expansion of the *Evaluation Standards.* As a result of the Summit, the New Standards Project evolved, as noted in Chapter 1.

The New Standards Project is creating an overall system of assessment by which districts and individual schools could develop their own tests that are aligned with national curriculum standards. This project will create new performance assessments, portfolios, and projects based on real-life tasks. See the Internet addresses for the centers given in Chapter 1.

Video Vignette

How Do I Know What My Students Understand?

Directions:

After viewing the video, answer these questions:

- In what ways did Mrs. Castenda say she assesses students?
- What ways were shown in the actual classroom with students?
- Which scoring guides in this chapter could be adapted for use in scoring the kinds of work shown by the students in Mrs. Castenda's class? Justify your choices by telling why each guide would be good to use.

SUMMARY

Standards-driven reform requires new assessments that are better aligned with the changes being sought in curriculum and pedagogy. Formidable barriers must be surmounted to implement valid assessment tools. With state, national, and international assessment models being created, the implementation of standards based on new mathematical goals for students will continue to be a focus. As Pipho (1995) remarks, "It is possible that achieving a statewide model of standards-driven instruction, supported by a high stakes testing program, might take longer and involve more changing than either the political or the educational world can handle" (p. 198).

This chapter presented the backdrop for the assessment approaches used throughout the book. In each chapter, there will be opportunities for you to practice the principles of peformance-based assessment using portfolios of your reflective thinking, samples of children's work for you to analyze, and video vignettes of children in mathematics classrooms. Our hope is to prepare you to become aware of the issues surrounding alternative assessment and to put them into practice.

EXERCISES

For extended exercises, see the CD-ROM.

A. Memorization and Comprehension Exercises
Low-Level Thought Activities

1. Explain what is meant by the term "alternative" assessment and name examples of what assessment tools are included.
2. What do the NCTM documents claim should receive less attention with respect to student assessment?
3. Discuss five or six reasons parents would oppose alternative testing.

B. Application and Analysis Exercises
Middle-Level Thought Activities

1. Explain, and provide examples, of what teachers and other educators mean when they say, "The tests drive the curriculum."
2. Discuss the differences between standardized testing and alternative assessment.
3. Peruse current mathematics textbooks and ancillary materials (teachers' resources that accompany the textbook series). Describe your reactions and concerns for using the publishers' testing materials.

C. Synthesis and Evaluation Exercises
High-Level Thought Activities

1. Collect samples of performance tasks and share with others. Develop scoring guides to be used with them.
2. Suppose you plan to give a talk to parents on a Back-to-School Night describing your classroom assessment procedures. Since you are a strong advocate of alternative assessment, what would you say in this talk? Give supporting evidence and references from the educational arena.
3. Look through this textbook and check the CD-ROM for examples of children's work. Write rubrics or "scoring guides" for each one. Share and discuss with classmates.

BIBLIOGRAPHY

For an extended bibliography, see the CD-ROM.

American Federation of Teachers, National Council on Measurement in Education, and National Education Association. *Standards for Teacher Competence in Educational Assessment of Students.* Washington, DC: Authors, 1990.

Charles, Randall I., Frank Lester, and Phares O'Daffer. *How to Evaluate Progress in Problem Solving.* Reston, VA: National Council of Teachers of Mathematics, 1994.

Clauson, Donna J. "How Rubrics Become Grades." *Mathematics Teaching in the Middle School* 4 (October 1998): 118–119.

Cohen, Ira S., and Joan V. Fowler. "Create Assessments That Do It All." *Mathematics Teaching in the Middle School* 4 (September 1998): 44–47.

DeGraw, Mishaa, ed. *Balanced Assessment for the Mathematics Curriculum: Elementary Assessment.* White Plains, NY: Dale Seymour Publications, 1999a.

———. *Balanced Assessment for the Mathematics Curriculum: Middle School Assessment.* White Plains, NY: Dale Seymour Publications, 1999b.

Dossey, John A., and Jane O. Swafford. "Issues in Mathematics Assessment in the United States." Ed. Morgens Niss. *Cases of Assessment in Mathematics Education: An ICMI Study.* Norwell, MA: Kluwer Academic Publishers, 1993. 43–57.

Elliot, Ian. "A Math Class That's 'Something Special.'" *Teaching K–8.* (January 1999): 50–54.

Forgione, Pascal D., Jr., ed. *Introduction to TIMSS: The Third International Mathematics and Science Study.* Washington, DC: U.S. Department of Education, 1997.

Harvey, John G. "Mathematics Testing with Calculators: Ransoming the Hostages." Ed. Thomas A. Romberg. *Mathematics Assessment and Evaluation: Imperatives for Mathematics Educators.* Albany: State University of New York Press, 1992. 139–168.

Herman, Joan L. "Issues in Developing Quality Alternative Assessments." Paper presented at National Council of Supervisors Annual Meeting, Seattle, WA, March 1993.

Huinker, DeAnn M. "Interviews: A Window to Students' Conceptual Knowledge of the Operations." Ed. Norman L. Webb and Arthur R. Coxford. *Assessment in the Mathematics Classroom.* Reston, VA: National Council of Teachers of Mathematics, 1993. 80–86.

Kenney, Patricia Ann, and Edward A. Silver. "Student Self-Assessment in Mathematics." Ed. Norman L. Webb and Arthur R. Coxford. *Assessment in the Mathematics Classroom.* Reston, VA: National Council of Teachers of Mathematics, 1993. 229–238.

Kilpatrick, Jeremy. "The Chain and the Arrow: From the History of Mathematics Achievement." Ed. Morgens Niss. *Investigations into Assessment in Mathematics Education.* Norwell, MA: Kluwer Academic Publishers, 1993. 31–46.

Long, Donna J. "Assessment: Alternatives for the Future." Unpublished paper, Indiana Department of Education, 1993.

Mathematical Sciences Education Board (MSEB). *Measuring Up: Prototypes for Mathematics Assessment.* Washington, DC: National Academy Press, 1993.

Mumme, Judy. *Portfolio Assessment in Mathematics.* Santa Barbara, CA: California Mathematics Project, University of California, 1991.

National Council of Teachers of Mathematics. *Assessment Standards for School Mathematics.* Reston, VA: NCTM, 1995.

———. *Curriculum and Evaluation Standards for School Mathematics.* Reston, VA: NCTM, 1989.

———. *Principles and Standards for School Mathematics.* Reston, VA: NCTM, 2000 (to be published).

———. *Professional Standards for Teaching Mathematics.* Reston, VA: NCTM, 1991.

National Research Council. *Everybody Counts: A Report to the Nation on the Future of Mathematics Education.* Washington, DC: National Academy Press, 1989.

Paulson, F. Leon, Paulson, Pearl R., and Meyer, Carol A. "What Makes a Portfolio a Portfolio?" *Educational Leadership* 48 (December 1991): 60–63.

Pipho, Chris. "The Search for a Standards-Driven Utopia." *Phi Delta Kappan* 77 (November 1995): 198–199.

Reese, Clyde M., Karen E. Miller, John Mazzeo, John A. Dossey. *NAEP 1996 Mathematics Report Card for the Nation and the States.* Washington, DC: National Center for Educational Statistics, 1997.

Robitaille, David F., and J. Stuart Donn. "TIMSS: The Third International Mathematics and Science Study." Ed. Morgens Niss. *Investigations into Assessment in Mathematics Education.* Norwell, MA: Kluwer Academic Publishers, 1993: 229–243.

Romberg, Thomas A. "Evaluation: A Coat of Many Colors." Ed. Thomas A. Romberg. *Mathematics Assessment and Evaluation: Imperatives for Mathematics Educators.* Albany: State University of New York Press, 1992. 10–36.

Romberg, Thomas A., Linda Wilson, and Mamphono Khaketla. "The Alignment of Six Standardized Tests with the NCTM Standards." Unpublished paper, University of Wisconsin-Madison, 1989.

Romberg, Thomas A., Linda Wilson, and Silvia Chavarria. "An Examination of State and Foreign Tests." Unpublished paper, Wisconsin Center for Education Research, Madison, 1990.

Rowan, Thomas E. and Josepha Robles. "Using Questions to Help Children Build Mathematical Power." *Teaching Children Mathematics* 4 (May 1998): 504–509.

Santos, Maria, Mark Driscoll, and Diane Briars. "The Classroom Assessment in Mathematics Network." Ed. Norman L. Webb and Arthur F. Coxford. *Assessment in the Mathematics Classroom.* Reston, VA: National Council of Teachers of Mathematics, 1993: 220–228.

Seifner, Kathy. "Laura's Dinner." Prepared TIMSS Performance Assessment Task. MAT 351 Student Math Teacher. Pershing Elementary Professional Development School. St. Joseph, MO, Spring 1998.

Sharp, Earl, and Rosemary Ingram. "Workshop on Problem Solving Using TIMSS Approach in Performance Assessment." Lake Contrary Accelerated School, St. Joseph, MO, October 30, 1998.

Shepard, Lorrie A. "Why We Need Better Assessments." *Educational Leadership* 46 (April 1989). 4–9.

Stenmark, Jean Kerr. *Assessment Alternatives in Mathematics.* Berkeley, CA: EQUALS, University of California, 1989.

Thompson, M. *Experiences in Problem Solving.* Reading, MA: Addison-Wesley, 1976.

van den Heuvel-Panhuizen, Marja, and Koeno Gravemeijer. "Tests Aren't All Bad: An Attempt to Change the Face of Written Tests in Primary School Mathematics Instruction." Ed. Norman L. Webb and Arthur F. Coxford. *Assessment in the Mathematics Classroom.* Reston, VA: National Council of Teachers of Mathematics, 1993. 54–64.

Westley, Joan. *Puddle Questions. Grades 1–8 Series.* Worth, IL: Creative Publications, 1994.

Wilder, Laura Ingalls. *The Long Winter.* New York: Harper, 1953.

Integrating Technology

Video Vignettes: Assessment in Action

- *How Do I Know What My Students Understand?*

Computer Software Resources

...for Assessment in Mathematics

Internet Searches

Surfing the Internet for Assessment Topics

Use the World Wide Web (WWW) and navigate through the system, searching for new information under major headings and subheadings similar to the following:

Mathematics Education
- Alternative Assessment
- Authentic Assessment
- Portfolio
- Eisenhower Clearing House for Math and Science
- Interviews
- New Standards Project
- National Education Goals
- Curriculum Frameworks

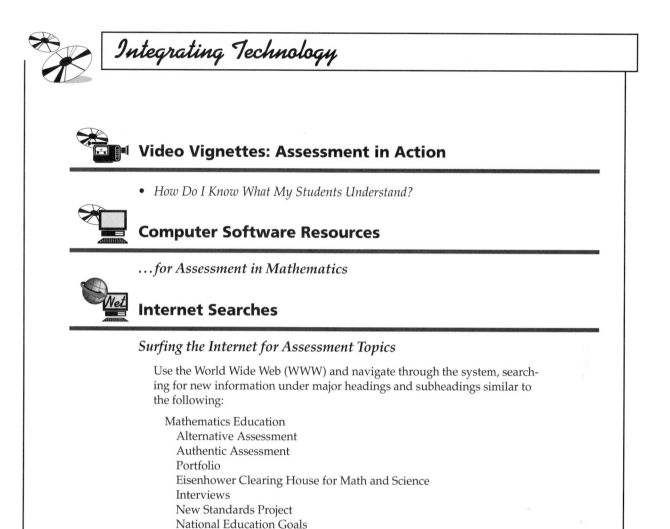

5

Problem Solving

Activities Index

IN THE TEXT

ON CD-ROM

PROBLEM SOLVING

The Magnitude of Problem Solving

Problem solving is the oldest intellectual skill known to humanity. The ability to understand a problem, relate it to a similar problem or to past experiences, speculate about the possible solution, and carry through until the problem is solved is basic to human survival. Without the ability to solve problems, human beings would have become extinct. Even prehistoric cave dwellers needed to solve problems dealing with food gathering and climate conditions.

The Complexity of Problem Solving. As writers and researchers started to work with the concept of problem solving, it became apparent that problem solving is a complex topic that can be viewed in different ways: (1) as an educational method, (2) as a broad definition, and (3) as an environment in and of itself.

As an Educational Method. Problem solving as an educational method has received a good deal of attention. Some people may remember solving mathematical problems dealing with how many hours two painters would require to paint a room if one worked twice as fast as the other. For many people, this is an unpleasant memory because they felt as though they were stumbling blindly through problems without much guidance from the teacher or the textbook. Sometimes teachers resist teaching problem-solving skills because of their own frustrating experiences with problem solving.

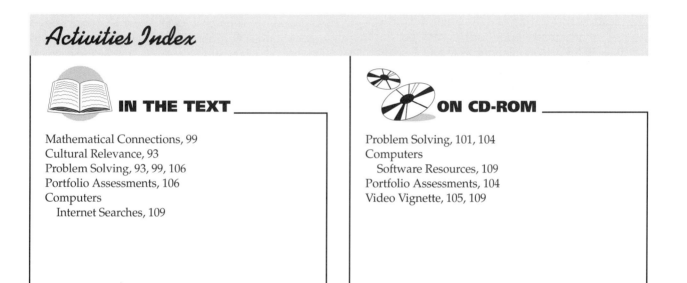

As a Broad Definition. The term *problem solving* is broad and refers to a complex of cognitive activities and skills. George Polya, a noted scholar in the area of problem-solving theory, held that solving a problem is finding the unknown means to a distinctly conceived end (Polya, 1957). To solve a problem is to find a way where no way is known, to find a way out of a difficulty, to find a way around an obstacle, to attain a desired end that is not immediately attainable, by appropriate means.

As an Environment in and of Itself. The environment of problem solving involves a problem with no immediately obvious solution and a problem solver who is capable of trying to find the solution by applying previously learned knowledge. Problem solving involves simple word problems, real-world applications, nonroutine problems and puzzles, and the creation and testing of mathematical conjectures leading to new discoveries (Branca, 1980).

It is helpful to remember that one essential aspect of problem solving is basic logic. Consider that most story problems contain words like *and, not,* and *or,* and basic logic can present a problem in the elementary classroom where it is not usually taught. Yet, in order to solve problems, students must master logical means for finding a solution. Means for solving such problems are presented later in this chapter.

The Many Facets of Problem Solving. As with any complex issue, problem solving has been broken down into digestible parts in an attempt to understand this broad topic more fully. We have constructed Table 5.1 for those among you who are field-dependent learners since you like to see the whole field and how everything fits into the big picture. Each of these facets of problem solving are considered separately in this section of the text for those field-independent learners who want to concentrate on one thing at a time.

The Methods, Kinds, and Procedures of Problem Solving

Methods of Integrating Problem Solving. There are three common methods of interpreting problem solving:

1. As a goal,
2. As a process,
3. As a skill.

As a Goal. When problem solving is interpreted as a goal, it does not rely on particular procedures and methods, specific problems, or even mathematical content. Instead it becomes an end in itself. Problem solving opens up the mind to see new possibilities performed in unique ways. If we apply the ideas of constructivism presented in Chapter 3, we would ask ourselves, "What would an effective classroom look like if the teacher were to follow the Constructivist/*Standards* approach?" The teacher would have the student actively engaged in constructing the subject matter, first concretely, then pictorially, and finally symbolically. This includes a heavy emphasis on appropriate manipulatives in mathematics. The primary concepts, the "big ideas" of all subjects (mathe-

TABLE 5.1 The Facets of Problem Solving

Methods of Interpreting	Kinds of Problem Solving	How to Structure Your Mind—the Procedures[a]	What to Do—Strategies to Use[b]	When to Apply—NCTM *Standards* on Problem Solving
1. As a goal 2. As a process 3. As a skill	1. Open-ended 2. Discovery 3. Guided discovery	1. Understand the problem. 2. Devise a plan using strategies. 3. Carry out the plan. 4. Look back to check solution to see whether correct; if not—try again.	1. Estimate and check. 2. Look for patterns. 3. Insufficient information. 4. Draw pictures, graphs, or tables. 5. Eliminate extraneous data. 6. Develop formula and write equation. 7. Model. 8. Work backward. 9. Flowchart. 10. Simplify problem. 11. Act out the problem.	*K–8 Grades:* 1. Use approaches to investigate content. 2. Formulate problems from everyday and math situations. 3. Develop and apply strategies to a wide variety of problems. 4. Verify and interpret results. 5. Generalize solutions and strategies to new problem. 6. Acquire confidence.

[a]*Source:* Polya, 1957.
[b]This is not a definitive list; more can be added.

matics included), would be presented rather than looking at separate, isolated skills (Bybee et al., 1989). The curriculum material would be presented as questions to be posed and problems to be solved rather than facts to be learned. How to structure effective problem-solving experiences is so important that we have reserved this entire chapter to problem solving and how to help students learn from it. We encourage you to read this chapter carefully as a beginning to the structure of good mathematics lessons.

As we learned in Chapter 2, the celebration of people's cultural heritage gives *all* children in the classroom a sense of pride. There are various collections of stories coming from different cultures that show how people have been clever problem solvers through the ages. One such collection tells fifteen folktales from around the world in which the heros and heroines have been clever problem solvers (Shannon, 1994). Each story is presented and then children are asked to explain how the problem was solved. The children then turn the page to see the solution as the folktale ends. This book and others are excellent resources if you are teaching problem solving as a goal to be enjoyed for the power it brings to the mind.

As a teacher you can take any folktale or story and give it the same suspense that Shannon gives in his delightful book. Just stop the story before the ending is told and ask children to think of ways to solve the problem. The following is a story coming from Africa and told around campfires over the years (Edwards and Judd, 1976):

> *An airplane had taken off from the Nairobi airport loaded with medical supplies for several remote villages far away from the African city. Approaching the landing field on a plateau above one of the villages, the pilot was alarmed to see no landing lights on the field. In the dense darkness of the night he could see no forms nor outlines to help guide him to a safe landing. It was too far to fly to the next village on the limited gas supply he had. HE HAD TO LAND! He circled several times with his mind running helplessly from one idea to another—none of which looked workable.*

Stop and let the students suggest possible ways to solve the problem. Then continue on:

How the Problem Was Solved in the African Village

> *Then he saw a very faint flicker—a little dot of yellow. It was still no help. One dot in the thick darkness gave no guidance at all. It was impossible to tell what in the world it was. Then a startling thing began to take place. As if out of nowhere the pilot began to see another flickering dot, and another, and another until there must have been over a hundred of them! Very methodically, in a well organized, unified fashion, the dots became two rows of landing lights showing the outline of the landing strip. As the pilot gradually descended onto the field, he could see the people standing on either side of the field holding their burning torches high above their heads.*
>
> *One torch just could not do the mammoth job needed. It took a well-organized, purposeful, committed people who knew that the sound of an approaching plane at dark meant action on their part as a whole village. (pp. 28–29)*

Activity 5.1

CULTURAL RELEVANCE · PROBLEM SOLVING

CREATING YOUR OWN PROBLEM-SOLVING STORY FROM CULTURAL FOLKTALES

MATERIALS

Stories you find in the library or have heard told over the years.

DIRECTIONS

1. Read over the story and decide where you want to stop and let the student problem solve a successful ending. This may be oral discourse or written discourse.
2. Then finish the story, making sure the students see the cultural group in the story as heroes and heroines for their ability to problem solve in a tough situation.

Supporting the NCTM *Principles and Standards* (2000):

- Mathematics as Connections . . . with cultures; Mathematics as Problem Solving and as Communication
- Worthwhile Mathematical Tasks for Teachers—The Teaching Principle

As a Process. As a process, problem solving is seen as an opportunity to exercise certain methods, strategies, and heuristics. *Heuristics* involves the discovery of the solution to the present problem on one's own. New assessment tasks are being developed in many states and provinces with questions that require the students to come up with a heuristic to solve a problem. The students can draw from any of life's experiences or what they have learned in school to help them. An example of such a task asks fourth-grade students to think of more than one way to solve a problem (Kansas State Board of Education, 1993):

> *If two of your classmates each have three dimes and four nickels, demonstrate and explain two different ways to determine the total amount of money the students have.* (p. 27)

By demonstration and explanation, teachers can see how well students are developing mathematical power in the process of problem solving.

As a Skill. Problem solving as a skill demands more attention to specific types of problems and methods of solution. The interpretation that the teacher brings to problem solving will determine the approach taken in the classroom.

Here is a typical task that helps children see the relationship of addition and multiplication with the number 9 in our number system:

How many different patterns can you find?

9
18
27
36
45
54
63
72
81

Teachers who want to stress the problem-solving strategy of looking for patterns would choose a task like the preceding one. It focuses on that particular skill in problem solving. There are many books that feature skill development in problem solving. One such book is *Problem Solving: Tips for Teachers* (O'Daffer, 1988). It showcases classroom activities in which one particular strategy is needed to solve a problem.

Kinds of Problem Solving. The approaches to teaching problem solving can be classified generally into three types: open-ended, discovery, and guided discovery. Earlier in Chapter 3, there was an example of three teachers asking higher-order thought questions in which children were asked to respond in three different ways. These ways are examples of the three approaches to teaching problem solving. Let's look at the activities now that we have a way to classify each type of problem.

Open-Ended Questions. The open-ended question has a number of possible solutions, so the process of solving the problem becomes more important than the answer itself. Notice in Figure 5.1 that the teacher's interest is *not* in having students solve any of the problems they write. The purpose is to see whether they understand when such a procedure would be appropriate to apply in problem solving.

FIGURE 5.1

The open-ended question in problem solving.

Discovery Questions. Discovery questions usually have a terminal solution, but there are a variety of methods the student can use to reach the solution. Figure 5.2 shows an example of a discovery situation.

There are a limited number of solutions to this problem, but the students can arrive at the answers from their understanding about numbers. As in this illustration, some students will approach the answer from an understanding of odd and even numbers; others from a knowledge of products in multiplication; and still others from a visual awareness of the difference in "look" between single- and double-digit numbers.

FIGURE 5.2

The discovery question in problem solving.

FIGURE 5.3

The open-ended question in problem solving.

Guided Discovery Questions. Guided discovery questions, by far the most common type, include clues and even directions for solving the problem so that the student does not become overly frustrated and give up. Figure 5.3 shows a typical teacher question with guided discovery. The teacher channels the students' thinking by giving clues that narrow the focus of possible solutions.

Kinds of Problems. Problems can be broadly categorized as either "word" problems or "process" problems. You may remember doing a lot of word problems during your elementary and high school years. Generally, those problems were found at the end of the section and were mostly the drill problems at the top of the page wrapped in words. In first-year algebra, those problems were often subdivided as age problems, coin problems, mixture problems, distance problems, one-step, two-step, and multistep problems. When the *Standards* were published, instructors began to realize that such artificial distinctions in the surface characteristics of problems were at least a nuisance and often a hindrance to students developing their problem-solving skills. A better approach seems to be that of using a few problems in any given lesson and discussing their similarities and differences in order to foster the students' metacognition. Such an approach encourages students to look at the mathematical structure of the problems rather than focusing on less helpful details such as the characters in the problem or the "key words." An example of three problems that could be used in this way is shown here:

1. Jose is collecting pretty stones during his vacation in the Rockies for his classmates. If he wants 4 stones for each student and there are 18 students in his class, how many stones must he collect?
2. Carla is moving 18 small blocks across the front step using a toy truck. She can only put 4 blocks on the truck at a time. How many trips will it take to move all 18 blocks?
3. Renee is bringing brownies for her Brownie troop meeting. If there are 16 brownies in the box and she gives 2 brownies to each person, how many are at the Brownie troop meeting?

Questions to be asked include: In what ways are problems 1 and 2 alike? In what ways are they different? In what ways are problems 2 and 3 alike? In what ways are they different?

Process problems are generally written in word form, but they are significantly different from the common word problem, which is usually solved through an application of known facts or algorithms. Process problems do not often yield to the simple application of basic facts and/or algorithms. Generally, process problems call for logical reasoning and the use of problem-solving strategies. An example of a process problem is the "Handshake Problem" that is described in the discussion of the "Act It Out" strategy later in this chapter (Morrow and Harbin-Miles, 1996).

How to Structure Your Mind: The Procedures. Whatever approach is taken, it is important to understand the process of solving problems. Polya (1957) identified four phases of the process:

1. The student understands the question and is motivated to answer it.
2. The student has learned facts and strategies that are useful in solving problems.
3. The student applies various strategies until the problem is solved.
4. The student checks the solution to see if it is correct. If not, another strategy must be tried.

Accepting Polya's phases as a working model, the teacher is presented with step-by-step instructions in teaching. The problem must be designed and posed in such a way that (a) the student is capable of deciphering clues and determining what information is being requested and (b) the student becomes involved in the problem and is interested in solving it. Many books and teaching aids on the market present more or less effective problem-solving exercises. A number of computer-assisted instruction programs rely on problem solving as a way of teaching organizational and decision-making skills. Other teachers can be an excellent source of advice about what types of problems are effective.

Another model for teaching problem solving is based on the research in Cognitively Guided Instruction (Peterson, Fennema, and Carpenter, 1991; Hiebert et al., 1996). The teacher poses a rich (worthwhile) mathematical task for students. After students have had an opportunity to work on the problem, the teacher asks students to begin explaining their work. Students share the process they used in solving the problem. The focus of the classroom discourse is the process. Students are encouraged to listen to and question one another. The role of the teacher in planning instruction and assessment in this approach to problem solving is critical and depends in great part on his or her ability to analyze children's thinking and on his or her knowledge of what is developmentally appropriate for these learners. A well-worded problem or task that leads to good discourse in the classroom can be more productive, mathematically speaking, than fifty isolated "drill and kill" exercises (van Zoest and Enyart, 1998).

Problem solving involves several aspects of learning and teaching—how to decode the problem (a reading skill) and how to translate the answer to a meaningful end (a writing skill). Many educators support the technique of having students write the numerical answer in a full sentence. This approach forces the students to reflect on their answer as they translate it. It may also provide an opportunity to consider the reasonableness of the answer. Asking students to verify and justify their answers in a written form often helps them clarify their thinking.

Problem-Solving Strategies

Strategies are methods by which a problem can be solved. The strategies used to solve problems are determined by two factors: (1) the skill and sophistication level of the student, and (2) the range of mathematical tools that the student has previously mastered. The degree to which the student is able to compare a problem to a familiar situation, problem, or experience tends to dictate which strategy he or she uses. The more complex the problem to be solved, the more strategies that may be required to solve the problem. Therefore, students need to learn as many strategies as possible to become effective problem solvers. Research (Carey et al., 1995) shows that students may become more proficient problem solvers by using various strategies. Eleven strategies are described here, although some educators have identified as many as sixteen (Suydam, 1982). Sample problems are given for each strategy.

Estimation and Check. Estimation is the strategy of proposing an approximate answer to determine a range within which the solution might fall. The assumed answer is checked in relation to the solution. Estimation can be done on a daily basis in the classroom. Such a strategy is effective in two types of problem solving:

1. In problems where there are too few data to allow for elimination of unlikely answers.
2. In problems that deal with very large unknown quantities.

Example 1

Your school principal has enough ribbons for the 350 science fair participants. If the following number of students from each grade level had entries in the science fair, does the principal have enough ribbons? Use front-end truncation and compensation to estimate the number of ribbons the principal needs.

Grade 3	102	Grade 5	165
Grade 4	127	Grade 6	139

Example 2

Jho-Ju held a yard sale and charged a dime for everything, but would accept a nickel if the buyer were a good bargainer. At the end of the day, she realized that she had sold all 20 items and taken in the grand total of $1.90. She had only dimes and nickels at the end of the day. How many of each did she have?

In order to make our estimation and check useful, it would be helpful to build a chart or table to help us organize our guesses. For instance, a student might begin by guessing 5 dimes. Then, since there are 20 coins, that means there would be 15 nickels. But the total must also come to $1.90. So, the student decides to create a column for the value of the dimes, the value of the nickels, and the total value. Finally, the guess is rated as "high" or "low" in relation to the answer of $1.90. Several guesses are illustrated below.

Dimes	Nickels	Value of Dimes	Value of Nickels	Total Value	Rating
5	15	$0.50	$0.75	$1.25	Low
15	5	1.50	0.25	1.75	Low
20	0	2.00	0.00	2.00	High
18	2	1.80	0.10	1.90	Just right

Source: Herr and Johnson (1994).

This problem will be revisited in Chapter 14.

Estimation can also be the content of a problem-solving situation. Consider this problem from the

TIMSS' middle school problem set. Internationally, about 50% of the students answered this item correctly (43% of seventh graders, 53% of eighth graders). Of the U.S. students participating, 32% of the seventh graders and 34% of the eighth graders responded correctly (Beaton et al., 1996).

Rounded to the nearest 10 kg the weight of a dolphin was reported to be 170 kg. Write down a weight that might have been the actual weight of the dolphin.

Solution: Any number in the range from 165–174.

Looking for Patterns. Some problems are designed in such a way that the only way to solve them is to identify patterns in the data given in order to predict the data not given. Students need to practice examining given data to see whether it reveals a predictable pattern. Once the pattern is established, the student can calculate the unknown data in order to solve the problem. Putting data into table format will help show the pattern.

Example 1

The peg puzzle can be used to create patterns to make a generalization. In the activity, the object is to exchange the black and white pegs (Figure 5.4) by moving in a prescribed order.

FIGURE 5.4

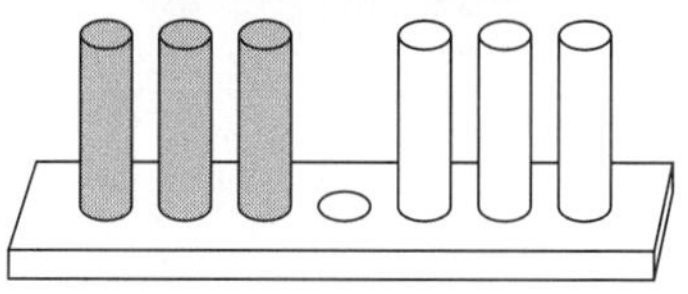

Peg puzzle.

Directions:

1. Move a peg forward one space into an empty hole, jump one peg if it is a different color. Pegs can only move forward.
2. Play with a partner—one player moves the whole time while the other partner counts the moves. Then switch positions.
3. First start with one pair (a peg of each color), find the minimum number of moves to exchange pegs from one side to the other. Record in the following table. Try again with two pairs and find the minimum number of moves. Look for a pattern in the table:

Number of Pairs (x)	Number of Moves (y)
1	3
2	8
3	15
4	?
5	?

Example 2

Students must be made aware that patterns are not always as projected from a few samplings. Figure 5.5 is an example of a time when the beginning pattern does not hold.

FIGURE 5.5

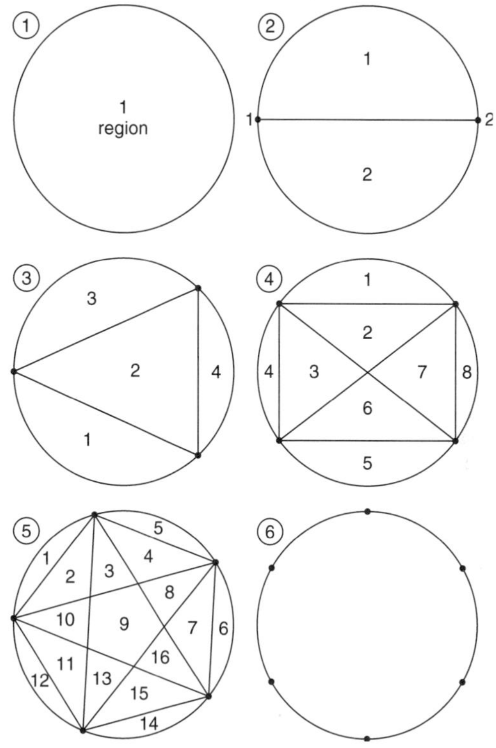

Points and regions of circles.

What is the maximum number of regions formed by connecting all the points in a circle?

Number of Points	Number of Regions
1	1
2	2
3	4
4	8
5	?
6	?

Find out what the next one would be.

Insufficient Information. Sometimes not enough information is supplied in the problem.

Example

How much will it cost to buy a 5-pound bag of dog food today if it cost \$.20 less last week?

Solution: The insufficient information is what the actual cost of the dog food was last week. Without knowing this, \$.20 cannot be added to the base price to find out this week's price.

Drawing Pictures, Graphs, and Tables. If students have difficulty grasping a problem that seems too complex or abstract, they might find it helpful to create a visual image to assist them. Aids such as drawing pictures, graphs, and tables provide a graphic means of displaying numerical data in a way that students can see. Graphs can help to demonstrate relationships among data that may not be apparent immediately. A visual image can also help students keep track of intermediate steps required to solve the problem.

Example 1

A farmer planted 8 rows of beans and put 12 beans in each row. How many beans did the farmer plant?

Solution: Drawing a sketch such as this one will quickly indicate the repeated addition or multiplication needed for solving the problem.

× × × × × × × × × × × ×
×
×
×
×
×
×
×

Example 2

Who won the bowling tournament? Who had the highest score?

Solution: Create a bowling average computer database (a computerized method of organizing and storing information that can be easily retrieved) to keep continuous, up-to-date records of bowling results each week. The information can be ordered using the database, and the table is convenient for displaying the data to solve problems. A sample database template (the outline of the records) follows:

		Bowling Average			
Name	Week	Game 1	Game 2	Game 3	Average
Bitter	1	155	185	175	172
Hatfield	1	182	175	180	179
Edwards	1	158	192	188	179
Smith	1	177	182	188	182
Bitter	2	182	189	188	186
Hatfield	2	182	178	168	176
Edwards	2	155	187	177	173
Smith	2	177	166	197	180

Elimination of Extraneous Data. Many problems are designed with information that is necessary to solve the problem as well as information that is not needed. The students' first task is to sort through the information given to determine what is necessary and what is extraneous. If students fail to do this, they may waste time trying to produce irrelevant and insignificant data. Operating on clues about relevant and extraneous data, students can narrow the range of possible solutions instead of trying to use meaningless information.

Example

Rambo is a 35-pound dog. He eats a 5-pound bag of dog food that costs $3.14 every week. How much does it cost to feed him for four weeks?

Extraneous information: Can the extra information be found?

Developing Formulas and Writing Equations. It is often useful to invent a formula into which one can plug numbers to arrive at an answer. Students learn that routine formulas often have real-world applications and that numbers stand for objects and concepts in a mathematical formula. It is helpful to give students exercises that require the translation of ideas into words and numbers.

Example

Translate "every day for six weeks" into numbers.

Solution: $6 \times 7 = 42$

Modeling. Constructing a physical representation or model of the problem is another way of helping students to conceptualize the operations necessary to solve a problem. Students may even be more interested in a problem that they can manipulate manually, as evidenced by the popularity of puzzles in teaching arithmetic and geometry. Teachers who have access to microcomputers and graphics software can make good use of the modeling strategy. Students can be given problems that ask them to construct a variety of shapes. Computer graphics can be used to motivate students to take an active interest in the problem-solving process (Oliver and Russell, 1986).

Example

Have students arrange six markers in the following triangular pattern.

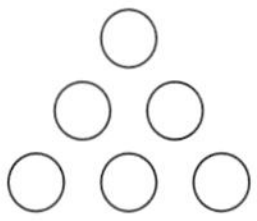

Move just two markers and turn the triangle "upside down."

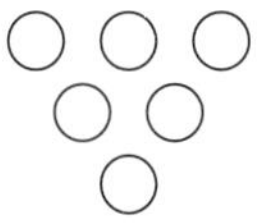

Solution: Students can try different moves. The solution is to move the outside markers in the bottom row to the top row.

Working Backward. Geometric proofs call for the strategy of working backward. More common everyday problem solving calls for this skill as well.

Example 1

Prove that angle x is 60 degrees.

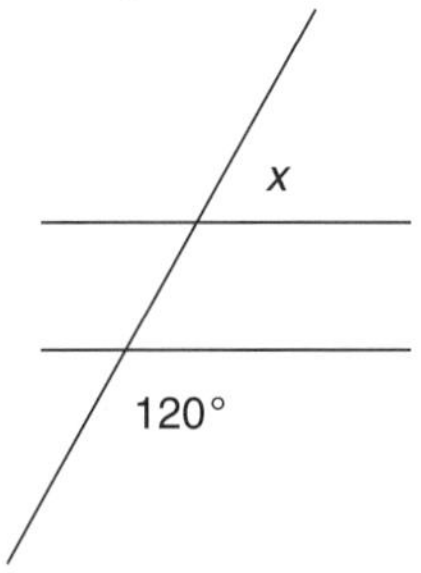

The answer is given, that $x = 60$ degrees. Now the student needs to work backward to find out how to get the answer.

Example 2

T he lumber truck left enough lumber to build three recreation rooms, but only one-half of that is needed for even the biggest recreation room. This room will be only $\frac{2}{3}$ as large as the biggest recreation room. Will I have enough if I offer to give $\frac{5}{8}$ of it back?

Flowcharting. Borrowing the concept of flowcharting from the field of computers, teachers can assist students in visualizing the process of solving a problem by using a flowchart. A *flowchart* is a detail-by-detail outline of steps that must be taken and conditions that must be met before the solution is reached. It is not necessary to use the various symbols that programmers use in flowcharting. If presented like the example in Figure 5.6, the shape of the boxes can help young children to decide where to place each decision. Children can be shown the process of problem solving by a chart with directional arrows, showing the way one step leads to another or requires testing for a certain condition.

Activity 5.2

MATHEMATICAL CONNECTIONS PROBLEM SOLVING

PROBLEM SOLVING WITH FLOWCHARTS

DIRECTIONS

Draw a flowchart that shows all of the sequential steps required to buy an ice cream cone.

Note: This kind of activity has also been featured in elementary reading texts, an area supporting mathematical connections.

FIGURE 5.6

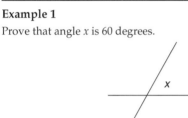

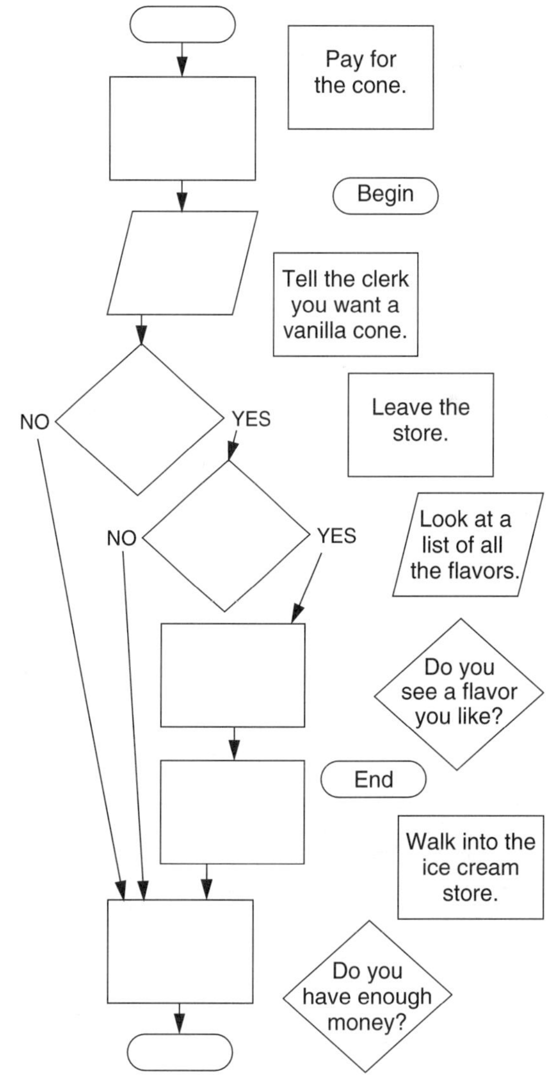

Ice cream cone flowchart.

Activity Continues

Supporting the NCTM *Principles and Standards* (2000):

- Mathematics as Problem Solving, Connections
- Worthwhile Mathematics Tasks—The Teaching Principle
- The Assessment Principle—using a variety of high-quality evidence

Acting Out the Problem. Acting out a problem is similar to the modeling strategy, although it differs in that it does not depend on physical objects or visual aids that students can manipulate. Students are more likely to view the problems as real-life situations if acting is encouraged and it will be easier for them to see the steps involved.

Example 1

If a salesperson sells $1.50 worth of groceries to one customer, $3.25 to another, and $2.75 worth of groceries to a third customer, how much has the salesperson sold altogether? What is the total dollar value if that same amount is sold every day for four days?

Solution: Students take the roles of the salesperson and the customers in the store. They may actually exchange play money to simulate earnings and expenditures, but the visual aids are not necessary for the students. They can see just by acting that the process is one of addition for the salesperson and one of subtraction for the customer.

Example 2

The sixth-grade girls' basketball team at Washington School won the district championship. All 12 members of the team congratulate each other with a handshake. How many handshakes would that be?

Solution: Have 12 students in the class represent the team members. Have the other students keep a written record of the number of handshakes. The first person shakes hands with the other 11 team members. The second person shakes hands with the remaining 10 team members. The third person shakes hands with the remaining 9 team members, and so on until the next to last person shakes hands with the 1 remaining team member. That is a total of $11 + 10 + 9 + 8 + 7 + 6 + 5 + 4 + 3 + 2 + 1$, or 66 handshakes.

Example 3

Many of today's mathematics textbooks provide lessons on problem-solving strategies. Our advice to you is to read the problems carefully or you may find one like the following. The strategy to be used is "Act It Out."

Maria can run 5 laps around the school track in the time it takes Susan to run 3 times around the track. How many laps will Maria have run when Susan has run 12 laps.

Solution: The "Act It Out" strategy would be difficult to employ here—not too many students can pace their running so exactly. A table or chart, or writing an equation using proportional reasoning would be far more effective strategies.

Simplifying the Problem. Substitute smaller numbers that can be handled with quick estimation skills so students can test the reasonableness of their answers before doing the problem with the original numbers. Have students substitute basic facts or easy number combinations so they can get a sense of the appropriateness of the operation chosen.

Example 1

A person bought a car for 25 percent less than the original price of $3495. How much was paid?

Solution:

Think: 25 percent off $100 would be $75.
Think: 25 percent off $1000 would be $750.
Think: 25 percent off $3000 would be $3 \times 750 = \$2250$.

Each answer fits into the general pattern,

$$0.25 \times \text{old price} = x$$
and
$$\text{old price} - x = \text{sale price}$$

Then the original numbers can be supplied.

Another way to approach this problem would be to substitute 10 percent of $3000. Think about how that answer is obtained, then work up to 25 percent of $3000, and finally to the actual numbers.

Example 2

A new school is set to open. There are 1000 lockers in the school, all with closed doors. On the first day of school, the students decide they must do something special to start the new year in their new school. So, they decide to enter the building one at a time. The first student to enter opens the doors of every locker. The second person closes the doors of the even-numbered lockers. The third person changes the door (from open to closed or closed to open) of every third locker. Likewise, the fourth, fifth, sixth, and on to the one-thousandth student. After all the students have changed the locker doors, which locker doors are closed?

Solution: Suppose instead of 1000 lockers, there were only 25 lockers. Now, students can either act it out using their school lockers, or they can create a chart similar to the following:

1	2	3	4	5	6	7	8	9	10	11	12	13	14	15	16	17	18	19	20	21	22	23	24	25
C	O	C	O	C	O	C	O	C	O	C	O	C	O	C	O	C	O	C	O	C	O	C	O	C
		O			C			O			C			O			C			O			C	
			C				C				O				C				C				O	
				O					C					C					O					O
					O						C						O						C	
						O							C							C				

Fill in as much more of the chart as you need to. Take time to look for a pattern as well. At this point (only 6 students completed) it is difficult to see what the pattern might be. When you have completed the chart for 10 students, you will see that lockers 1, 4, and 9 are closed; all the others are open. You may recognize these as the first three perfect squares. A pattern seems to be emerging. Continue to see if you are right. Other problems can be found on the CD.

The *Standards* in Problem Solving

The vision of the *Principles and Standards* (NCTM, 2000) is that problem solving permeates all topics of mathematics. It serves as the foundation for developing mathematical knowledge and reasoning. Problems are formulated by children from everyday situations and may extend over several days. Review the problem-solving strand in the *Curriculum and Evaluation Standards* (NCTM, 1989) on the CD-ROM and *Principles and Standards* (2000) from the NCTM website (**http://www.nctm.org**). Think of the many facets of problem solving talked about in this section of the text. Contemplate a teacher's role in weaving methods, procedures, and strategies of problem solving with the principles espoused in the NCTM *Standards* for a Pre-K–8 curriculum to benefit all children. We have a huge and exciting task to do!

EXTENDED ACTIVITIES

Name of Activity

- More Process Problems

PROBLEM SOLVING

Effective Teaching of Problem Solving

Yes, our job as teachers of problem solving does seem monumental. We must remember that "...in real life, few mathematical situations can be clearly classified as belonging to one content strand or another, and few situations require only one facet of mathematics thinking" (Reese et al., 1997). Figure 5.7 illustration from the NAEP 1996 Mathematics Report Card for the Nation and the States helps us to visualize this reality.

There are techniques to use and assessments with rubrics to evaluate ourselves and our students when we start to slip back into old, nonproductive habits. A *rubric* is a standard by which to assess one's level of ability in a topic or concept in a structured, objective manner. We explore some techniques and rubric assessments in this section.

FIGURE 5.7

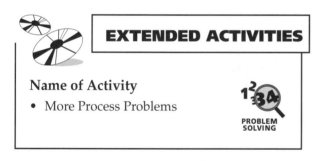

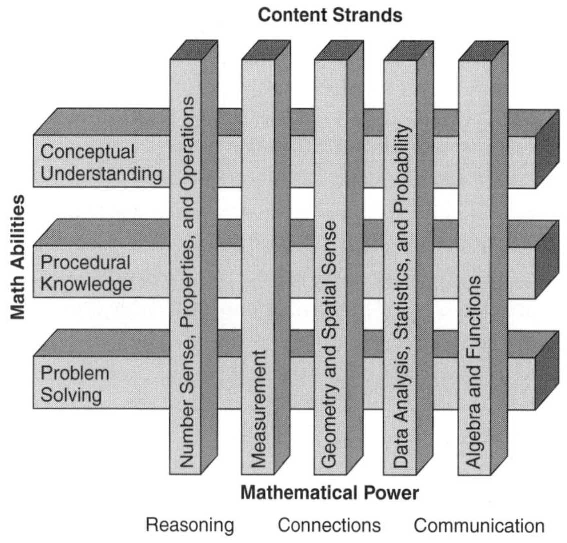

The interrelatedness of mathematical content, processes and skills. Source: National Assessment Governing Board, Mathematics Framework for the 1996 National Assessment of Educational Progress.

Effective Techniques for Teaching Problem Solving. Effective teaching of problem solving involves techniques, other than the strategies discussed, to make students feel more comfortable with the problem-solving experience (Suydam, 1982). The key principles are emphasized in the following paragraphs and may be used as a checklist for teachers:

- *Model a positive attitude for your students.* If you convey the excitement, satisfaction, and sense of accomplishment that successfully solving a problem can provide, your students will catch the spirit and be more willing to tackle problems themselves.
- *Choose problems carefully, paying special attention to interest and difficulty level.* Students are not motivated to solve problems that they find boring, irrelevant, too easy, or too difficult. Other teachers can be excellent advisors on appropriate problems to present. Collect students' work when they are asked to generate word problems, and use these settings as examples.
- *Put students in small groups and allow them to work together on problem-solving exercises.* Some teachers have found that students are more successful at problem solving when they work in pairs or

teams (Biglan and Kirkpatrick, 1986). Cooperative learning enables the exchange of ideas about which strategies to use and provides assistance in estimating and testing results. Each student needs to experience several ways of conceptualizing the problem and selecting strategies. Cooperative learning establishes an environment that supports problem solving. "A small group structure has the potential to maximize the active participation of each student and reduce individual isolation. When organized in small groups, more students have the opportunity to offer their ideas for reaction and receive immediate feedback. This provides a setting that values social interaction, a needed element of children's learning" (Burns, 1984, p. 41). In addition, combine collaborative problem solving with individual accountability. Provide a 5- to 10-minute individual "think time" before the cooperative group work begins, or have each student respond individually in a journal, perhaps justifying the process/solution the group used, or solving a similar type of problem.

- *Identify wanted, given, and needed information.* Before students can solve a problem, they must understand the three types of information that are involved in the problem itself:

  a. Wanted information—the solution.

  b. Given information—presented in the problem.

  c. Needed information—information not presented in the problem but required to solve it.

  It may be useful for students to create a list or table showing what data apply to the three categories above. Include the likely source of the needed information because students cannot solve a problem if they do not have access to the information required.
- *Pose the problem in such a way that students clearly understand what is expected of them.* No matter how motivated students are, they will not be able to solve problems unless the problem and accompanying instructions are stated clearly and simply. Ask students to repeat directions to check for understanding. Foster an environment in which they feel comfortable asking questions when they do not understand. If necessary, introduce them to vocabulary words that are used in the problems. This point also supports English as a subject for mathematical connections.
- *Present a wide range of problems.* Students may become bored if they are expected to work similar problems repeatedly. They should practice a strategy or problem type only until it is mastered. At that point, it is time to introduce a new type of problem so that students continue to feel challenged.
- *Present problems often.* Make problem solving a frequent part of class instruction so that students do not see it as an isolated skill but as an ongoing, familiar, and necessary process.
- *Provide opportunities for students to structure and analyze problems.* Discuss the makeup of a problem as well as its components. Students will develop a language for discussing strategies and patterns for analyzing problems that would not be possible otherwise.
- *Provide opportunities for students to solve different problems with the same strategy.* Such opportunities provide the practice necessary for students to master a given strategy. Students also develop an important sense that strategies are flexible and can be applied to a wide range of situations. Also encourage students to solve the same problem with different strategies. This approach makes them aware that they have choices about how to approach a problem.
- *Help students select an appropriate strategy for a particular problem.* Model problem-solving strategies for students each day. Use the "think-aloud" method to share your approach to a problem rather than just springing the strategy or answer on them. At first, students have little experience on which to base judgments about which strategies are most effective with specific types of problems. Trial and error are frustrating ways to choose a strategy. If students are assisted in selecting the best strategy and in defining the qualities that make it effective, they gain experience that will aid them later when making judgments on their own. Ask three questions of your students during any problem-solving situation. "What are you doing?" "Why are you doing that?" "How is it helping you?" These questions are not meant to be sarcastic or demeaning, nor to be asked only of those who are having difficulty with the problem at hand. Rather, these questions are intended to help students learn to be reflective about their problem-solving processes and strategies—to think about their thinking. In this way, you will help them move from novice problem solvers toward becoming expert problem solvers.
- *Help students recognize problems that are related.* Students need to be trained to see structural relatedness of problems. Teachers need to create

related problems by varying the data and condition of a single problem. Ask students to list key words and features of the problems to identify their similarities.

- *Allow students plenty of time to solve problems, discuss results, and reflect on the problem-solving process.* Students need to be able to discuss their methods and rationales as a way of organizing and processing their experience. As mentioned earlier in this book, research shows that elaborating techniques are rewarded by higher achievement in mathematics. Also, have students communicate in written and oral form daily. One school in Massachusetts credits their high performance on the state assessment to their use of this learning strategy (Gaines, 1998).
- *Demonstrate to students how they can estimate and test their answers.* This process can save students the frustration of wasted time and effort in problems in which the range of results is not immediately obvious. Students also need to be shown how they can work a problem backward or use other methods of testing their answers.
- *Discuss how the problem might have been solved differently.* With many problems, a variety of strategies will result in correct solutions. Ask students what other methods they could have used after a problem is solved successfully. Help students see that various approaches to the problem are acceptable. The selection of strategies depends, in part, on learner style and preference. Various strategies that can be used with different learning styles are mentioned where appropriate throughout this text.

Kinds of Cooperative Grouping Activities. Reflections on the above techniques reveal the possibilities for cooperative group activities in problem solving.

Problem-Solving Activities. Problem solving is one type of assignment that works well in cooperative groups. Students learn to solve problems by brainstorming many possible solutions. Current research examining behaviors that students demonstrate during group problem-solving sessions, such as monitoring their own thoughts, the thoughts of their teammates, and the problem-solving process, are similar to those exhibited by expert mathematicians when they solve problems (Artzt and Newman, 1990a, b).

1. **A grid approach.** Using a grid to structure beginning thought processes has proved helpful to some groups. A problem-solving grid from *Learning 91* (Trahanovsky-Orletsky, 1991) in Figure 5.8 could be adapted to a cooperative learning lesson. The basic parts of the grid are as follows:

   a. Finding: What are you looking for? What is the answer you want to find?
   b. Given: What does the problem tell us? What information is given?
   c. Conditions: Does the problem set any limits, or requirements?
   d. Noise: Is there information included in the problem that you do not need?
   e. Key words: Are there important words that tell you what operation to use—addition, subtraction, etc.?
   f. Hidden numbers: Are there numbers that do not look like numbers—two for 2, first for one, quarter for 0.25, etc.?
   g. Planning the solution: What are you looking for? What is given?
   h. Finding the solution: Solve the equation. What does x represent?
   i. Looking backward: Does the number make sense?

   Each cooperative group of four students may be given a problem to solve and asked to go through the problem-solving steps in order. To ensure that each member of the group has a definite role, two of the sections of the grid could be

FIGURE 5.8

Finding?	Given?	Conditions?
Noise?	Key words?	Hidden numbers?
Planning the solution	Finding the solution	Looking backward

Problem-solving grid.

the assigned responsibility of each student, with the entire group responsible for the last step.

2. **A weekly problem approach.** Another possible way of organizing problem-solving activities (Artzt and Newman, 1990a) would be assigning problems on Monday with each group asked to solve the problem by the end of the week. Some problems require more time to solve than one math session may provide. Groups can find time to meet before recess, or at the end of the day, to continue to explore solutions. Teachers report hearing children giving each other assignments to do before they meet again. The groups present their solutions and how they went about solving the problem for the whole class to hear. The teacher asks the students to keep track of how many different solutions and strategies were used to solve the problem. Over time this becomes a powerful message that there is more than one way and often multiple solutions to math problems. Weekly problems and extended projects can come from many sources.

Assessment to Rate Group Problem Solving. There will be times when you will decide to assess the class during a collaborative problem-solving activity. With this approach, students may be asked to solve a problem as a collaborative group and to submit one group solution. An analytic scoring rubric based on Polya's plan for problem solving (Figure 5.9) may be used at this time. In this situation, all the members of the group received the same score or rating. Many teachers recommend including some form of individual accountability at the same time. Thus, students might be asked to submit individual papers describing the solution process, or justifying the solution, or applying the process to a similar problem.

FIGURE 5.9

Group Members ____________________

A. ____ Understands the problem
- 3 Group thoroughly understands the problem
- 2 Group understands parts of the problem, some but not all of the constraints
- 1 Group does not understand the problem
- 0 Group does not attempt to understand the problem

B. ____ Selects a strategy
- 3 Group selects a strategy that leads to an appropriate solution
- 2 Group only partially selects a strategy that will work
- 1 Group selects an inappropriate strategy
- 0 Group does not select a strategy

C. ____ Determines a solution
- 3 Group determines a correct/appropriate solution
- 2 Group determines a solution that is partially correct
- 1 Group determines an inappropriate or incorrect solution
- 0 Group does not find any solution

D. ____ Verifies results
- 3 Group logically verifies results
- 2 Group verifies partial results
- 1 Group does not know how the solution is workable
- 0 Group cannot verify the results

Analytic scoring rubric for cooperative group problem solving.

Assessments to Rate Ourselves and Our Students. Teachers can use the assessment rubrics on the CD-ROM (see Activity box, Portfolio Assessments: A Student's Work with Problem Solving) to periodically rate themselves and their students on the necessary skills to become good problem solvers and teachers of good problem solvers.

Metacognition has been suggested as an aid for problem solving. *Metacognition* is one's knowledge of how one's own cognitive processes work. Good problem solvers can learn from observing their own actions and mental processes as they work on problems.

A checklist taken from Capper's work (1984) has been made into a rubric. It is included in the checklist assessment (see Extended Activities box).

Capper (1984) cites research to show that elementary and middle school students can improve their problem-solving skills if a teacher makes them routinely aware of their own thought processes in relation to the checklist assessment on CD-ROM just described. There is ample research to suggest that

EXTENDED ACTIVITIES

Name of Activity
- Checklist Assessment of You as a Good Problem Solver

PORTFOLIO | PROBLEM SOLVING

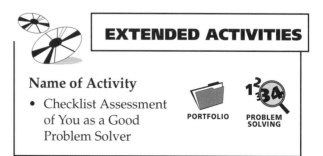

Video Vignette

Doubling

You may recognize Ms. Thomas and her class from the video vignette in Chapter 3.

- Spend some time in reflective analysis of this lesson. When you first view the video segment, stop the tape once the children have made their choice of the first ($5 per day) option. Is that the choice you would make? If it is, what would be your next step in this lesson? If not, how would you lead the class to explore the options further? After you answer these questions, continue viewing the vignette.
- Use the lesson plan for Video Vignettes (Table 3.5) to analyze Ms. Thomas's lesson in terms of tasks, discourse, and learning environment.
- What evidence in the video vignette illustrates Ms. Thomas's attempt to monitor student learning?

You may want to use your written reflective analysis for your portfolio.

people of all ages do a better job of problem solving if they are aware of how they structure and apply their own mental approaches to problem-solving tasks (Carey et al., 1995; Covey, 1990; Marzano, 1992). Therefore, it behooves all teachers who want to nurture good problem solvers to spend some time with metacognition in mathematics. Some questions that structure self-thought for children follow:

- "What did your brain tell you to do when you saw the ____________________?" (describe the task)
- "How does your brain help you remember what to tell a first grader about this problem?" (This is similar to the Labinowicz example seen earlier in the chapter.)
- "When does your mind tell you which steps you need to get the correct answer?"

Some children's answers are delightful and insightful at the same time. One very active first grader responded this way when asked:

Teacher: "What did your brain tell you to do when you saw the large and small shapes on the table to sort into sets by color?"

Child: "I said, 'Brain, I need help,' and my brain said, 'Sit down. You jump around too much. See the colors. Make color piles.' Then I said, 'Thanks,' and my brain said, 'You're welcome. Come again.'"

An example of a form for written self-reflection is shown in Figure 5.10.

FIGURE 5.10

Use the following scale to rate yourself in the problem-solving work that you are doing.

1—Almost always

2—Sometimes

3—Never

4—I need to try this

____ While problem solving, I use the Polya 4 step plan.

Do I understand the question?

What strategy should I select?

How did I work the problem out?

Does my solution make sense?

____ I use problem solving strategies such as trial and error, make it simpler, make an organized list, and use or draw a picture.

____ I like solving challenging problems.

____ Problem solving is: (you fill in the blanks below)

____

____

Self-reflection on my problem-solving work.

Putting It All Together: A Student's Work with Problem Solving. We have covered a great amount of information on problem solving in a few short pages. Let's see how well you can reflect on what you have just read. The following guided reflection can be used in your professional portfolio to document your ability to evaluate student work and journal writing. This student's class had just begun journal writing. This was one of P. J.'s first attempts to show his work. The teacher had stressed that she wanted the students to explain how they arrived at their solutions. P. J. was happy with his work. He told the teacher that his work would show he really understood the problem. What do you think?

Activity 5.3

PORTFOLIO PROBLEM SOLVING

PORTFOLIO ASSESSMENTS: A STUDENT'S WORK WITH PROBLEM SOLVING

STUDENT PROBLEM SOLVER: P.J.

The following problem is a sample of the type found in some fifth-grade textbooks:

> This is the story of five friends in the fifth-grade class, Mateo, Red Cloud, Maria, Shaloma, and Daniel. What is the order of the shortest to the tallest person in the group?
>
> Mateo is a super basketball player even though he is the next to shortest person in the class. Red Cloud is the tallest boy in the class but does not play basketball. He likes to play video games with the tallest person in the class who stands 5′6″ tall. Shaloma stands 4′6″ tall, a foot shorter than her best friend, Maria. Shaloma is taller than Mateo and shorter than Red Cloud.

P.J. solved the problem this way:

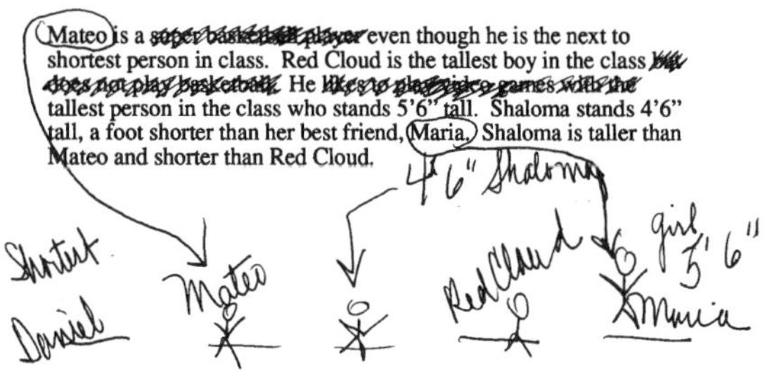

DIRECTIONS

1. Which of the strategies does P. J. seem to use? How can you tell? Justify your answer.
2. Use one of the scoring rubrics presented in Chapter 4 to score P. J.'s work.
3. Compare your score to the score given by the rubric.
4. What does that tell you about portfolio assessments with problems like these?

Supporting the NCTM *Principles and Standards* (2000):

- Mathematics as Problem Solving, Communication
- Worthwhile Mathematical Tasks for Teachers—The Teaching Principle
- The Assessment Principle

SUMMARY

Problem solving is here to stay. We have seen research from three points of view: the Constructivists, brain studies, and mathematics education. They all advocate problem solving as a "must" for the twenty-first century in schools. You will see the problem-solving icon throughout the text and on the CD-ROM when a task lends itself to a problem-solving approach. Many activities represent thought-provoking projects to use with elementary and middle school students.

The benefits of introducing students to problem-solving strategies early and consistently are many. Flexibility of thought to see more than one correct answer is one advantage. Problem solving is an effective means of making mathematics more relevant to students. Formulas into which numbers are plugged to calculate an answer may not appear to students to have much to do with their daily lives. However, if the same formula can be integrated into problems that are interesting to students, students develop a sense that mathematical principles are valuable in solving problems that arise in the real world.

Problem solving integrates all areas of the curriculum because it draws on reading, writing, social studies, economics, science, and so on when developing real-world examples. Mathematical connections help the marriage of words and numbers, both of which must be understood and processed before a problem can be solved. The subjects of problems can convey information about nearly any topic, and students can learn a variety of facts while they are applying strategies to solve problems. Perhaps most importantly, students acquire the basic problem-solving skills and methods that will serve them well throughout their lives.

EXERCISES

For extended exercises, see the CD-ROM.

A. Memorization and Comprehension Exercises
Low-Level Thought Activities

1. Name the problem-solving strategy that could be best used for each of the following examples:
   a. A train picked up passengers at the following rate: 1 at the first stop, 3 at the second stop, 5 at the third stop, and so on. How many passengers got on the train at the sixth stop?
   b. Translate "five hours at $10.00 per hour" into numbers.
   c. How many different ways can five squares be arranged so that if two squares touch, they border along a full side?

B. Application and Analysis Exercises
Middle-Level Thought Activities

1. Apply the three points needed for a successful elaborating technique to teach one of the problem-solving strategies found in this chapter.
2. Pick one grade level and analyze an elementary or middle school textbook to see what problem-solving strategies are used the most in that grade level. Find three word problems that could be solved by more than one strategy. Show the solutions using different strategies. Label each strategy as you use it.
3. Find a process problem. Show the solution using different strategies. Label each strategy as you use it.

C. Synthesis and Evaluation Exercises
High-Level Thought Activities

1. After analyzing all the information in exercise B2, above, create (synthesize) a model lesson plan for a problem-solving lesson. Choose the lesson plan model introduced in Chapter 3. Evaluate how all the components can work together. Include as many of the following components in the plan as possible:
   a. Elaborating techniques for the concept.
   b. Cooperative learning.
   c. Every pupil response (EPR).
   d. An idea for mathematical connections.
   e. Concrete, pictorial, symbolic material in the correct sequence.
   f. Find or make worksheets that include both simultaneous and successive thought processing strategies.
   g. Plan activities for the auditory, visual, and tactile learner to include in the development or controlled practice part of the lesson plan.
   h. Diagnostic interview strategies to help students who may have difficulty with problem solving.
   i. List interactive computer software that could be used with the concept. Reviews of software programs may be found in
      i. Teaching material catalogs
      ii. Reference section of the library
      iii. Professional journals and magazines
   j. List three mastery learning objectives on which students will be evaluated at the end of the lesson (that is, What do you want the students to be able to do after you have taught the lesson that they could not do before?). List them as observable behaviors.

BIBLIOGRAPHY

For an extended bibliography, see the CD-ROM.

Artzt, Alice F., and Claire Newman. "Cooperative Learning." *Mathematics Teacher* 83 (September 1990a): 448–452.

———. *How to Use Cooperative Learning in the Mathematics Classroom.* Reston, VA: National Council of Teachers of Mathematics, 1990b.

Beaton, Albert, E., Ina V. S. Smith, Michael O. Martin, Eugenio J. Gonzalez, Dana L. Kelly, and Teresa A. Smith. *Mathematics Achievement in the Middle School Years: IEA's Third International Mathematics and Science Study (TIMSS).* Chestnut Hill, MA: TIMSS International Study Center, Boston College, 1996.

Biglan, Barbara, and Susan Kirkpatrick. "Using the Computer to Enhance Problem-Solving Skills." In: *NECC 1986 Proceedings.* San Diego: National Educational Computing Conference, 1986.

Branca, Nicholas A. "Problem Solving as a Goal, Process, and Basic Skill." Ed. Stephen Krulik and Robert E. Reys. *Problem Solving in School Mathematics.* 1980 Yearbook of the National Council of Teachers of Mathematics. Reston, VA: National Council of Teachers of Mathematics, 1980. 2–7.

Burns, Marilyn. *The Math Solution: Teaching for Mastery through Problem Solving.* Sausalito, CA: Marilyn Burns Education Associates, 1984.

Bybee, Rodger, C. Edward Buchwald, Sally Crissman, David R. Heil, Paul J. Kuerbis, Carolee. Matsumoto, and Joseph D. McInerney. *Science and Technology Education for the Elementary Years: Frameworks for Curriculum and Instruction.* Andover, MA: The National Center for Improving Science Education, 1989.

Capper, Joanne. *Research into Practice Digest,* Vol. I, No. 1a, and Vol. II, No. 1b. *Thinking Skills Series: Mathematical Problem Solving: Research Review and Instructional Implications.* Washington, DC: Center for Research into Practice, 1984.

Carey, Deborah, A., Elizabeth Fennema, Thomas P. Carpenter, and Megan L. Franke. "Equity and Mathematics Education." Ed. Walter G. Secada, Elizabeth Fennema, and Lisa Byrd Adajian. *New Directions for Equity in Mathematics Education.* Cambridge, Eng.: Cambridge University Press, 1995.

Covey, Steven R. *The Seven Habits of Highly Effective People.* New York: Simon and Schuster, 1990.

Edwards, Nancy Tanner, and Peter A. Judd. *Stewardship: The Response of My People.* Independence, MO: Herald Publishing House, 1976.

Forman, G. "Helping Children Ask Good Questions." *The Wonder of It: Exploring How the World Works.* Ed. B. Neugebauer. Redmond, WA: Exchange Press, 1989.

Gaines, Judith. *School Did Its Homework on MCAS.* Boston, MA: The Boston Globe, December 30, 1998.

Geary, David. C. *Children's Mathematical Development: Research and Practical Applications.* Hyattsville, MD: American Psychological Association, 1994.

Herr, Ted, and Ken Johnson. *Problem Solving Strategies. Crossing the River with Dogs and Other Mathematical Adventures.* Berkeley, CA: Key Curriculum Press, 1994.

Hiebert, James, and Thomas P. Carpenter. "Learning and Teaching with Understanding." Ed. Douglas A. Grouws. *Handbook of Research on Mathematics Teaching.* New York: Macmillan, 1992.

Hiebert, James, Thomas P. Carpenter, Elizabeth Fennema, Karen Fuson, Piet Human, Hanlie Murray, Alwyn Olivier, and Diane Wearne. "Problem Solving as a Basis for Reform in Curriculum and Instruction." *Educational Researcher 25* (May 1996): 12–21.

Kansas State Board of Education. *Kansas Mathematics Curriculum Standards: Mathematical Power for All Kansans.* Topeka: Kansas State Printing Office, 1993.

Marzano, Robert J., *A Different Kind of Classroom: Teaching with Dimensions of Learning.* Alexandria, VA: Association for Supervision and Curriculum Development, 1992.

Morrow, Jean, and Ruth Harbin-Miles. *Walkway to the Future: Implementing the NCTM Standards in K–4 Grades.* Dedham, MA: Janson Publications, 1996.

National Council of Teachers of Mathematics. *Assessment Standards for School Mathematics.* Reston, VA: NCTM, 1995.

———. *Curriculum and Evaluation Standards for School Mathematics.* Reston, VA: NCTM, 1989.

———. *Principles and Standards for School Mathematics.* Reston, VA: NCTM, 2000 (to be published).

———. *Professional Standards for Teaching Mathematics.* Reston, VA: NCTM, 1991.

O'Daffer, Phares, ed. *Problem Solving: Tips for Teachers.* Reston, VA: National Council of Teachers of Mathematics, 1988.

Oliver, Terry A., and Rebecca Gaye Russell. "Using Low-Resolution Graphics to Develop Problem Solving Skills." *Computer Teacher* 13 (May 1986): 50–51.

Peterson, P. L., Elizabeth Fennema, and Thomas Carpenter. "Teachers Knowledge of Students' Mathematics Problem Solving Knowledge." Ed. J. Brophy. *Advances in Research on Teaching.* Vol. 2. *Teachers' Subject Matter Knowledge.* Greenwich, CT: JAI Press, 1991.

Polya, George. *How to Solve It: A New Aspect of Mathematical Method.* 2nd ed. Princeton, NJ: Princeton University Press, 1957.

Reese, Clyde M., Karen E. Miller, John Mazzeo, and John A. Dossey. *NAEP 1996 Mathematics Report Card for the Nation and the States: Findings from the National Assessment of Educational Progress.* Washington, DC: U.S. Department of Education, 1997.

Shannon, George. *More Stories to Solve: Fifteen Folktales from Around the World.* New York: Beech Tree Paperback Books, 1994.

Suydam, Marilyn N. "The Problem of Problem Solving." *Problem Solving* 4 (September 1982): 1–2, 5.

Trahanovsky-Orletsky, Ann E. "What's the Problem?" *Learning* 91 19(9) (May–June 1991): 19–22.

Trowell, Judith M. (Ed.). *Projects to Enrich School Mathematics: Level 1.* Reston, VA: National Council of Teachers of Mathematics, 1990.

Van Zoerst, Laura E. and Ann Enyart. "Discourse of Course: Encouraging Genuine Mathematical Conversations." *Mathematics Teaching in the Middle School* 4(3) (1998): 150–157.

CHILDREN'S LITERATURE

Clement, Rod. *Counting on Frank.* Milwaukee, WI: Gareth Stevens Children's Books, 1991.

Cooney, Barbara. *Miss Rumphius.* New York: Viking Penguin, 1982.

Nolan, Helen. *How Much, How Many, How Far, How Heavy, How Long, How Tall Is 1000?* Toronto: Kids Can Press, 1995.

Schwartz, David M. *If You Made a Million.* New York: Lothrop, Lee, & Shepard Books, 1989.

Scieszka, Jon and Lane Smith. *Math Curse.* New York: Penguin Books, 1995.

Integrating Technology

Video Vignettes: Lesson Plans in Action

- *Doubling*

Supporting the NCTM *Principles and Standards* (2000):

- Worthwhile Mathematical Tasks; The Teacher's Role in Discourse; The Student's Role in Discourse—The Teaching Principle

Computer Software Resources

...for Problem Solving

Internet Searches

Surfing the Internet for Topics on Problem Solving

Use the World Wide Web (WWW) and navigate through the system, searching for new information under major headings and subheadings similar to the following:

- Problem Solving
  - Constructivist
  - Cognitive Studies
  - Learning
    - NSF Projects
    - Programs
    - Multiple Intelligences
    - Cooperative Learning
  - Equity or Cultural Diversity
  - Feedback and Motivation
  - Effective Teaching Research
- Brain Research
  - Mathematics
  - Logic
  - Patterns and Relationships
- NCTM
  - Problem Solving
  - Equity Issues
  - Standards 2000

- *Remember...* the Web is fluid ... new topics and ways to search for topics change daily.
- Be adventurous ... think of some new things you could try.

6

Geometry and Spatial Reasoning

Activities Index

IN THE TEXT

ON CD-ROM

Geometry provides many concrete experiences that can be used in the teaching of mathematics. Introducing geometry early in this book may inspire teachers to use the many objects in the world around us to teach mathematics. When considering topics included in the study of mathematics, geometry may be overlooked or mentioned much later than other areas. Geometry has not always been part of the scope and sequence of an elementary mathematics program. Textbooks prior to the 1960s generally included only measures of area and volume. Geometry should be viewed as an opportunity to have lots of hands-on, interactive experiences with geometric concepts. However, there are some teachers who see mathematics as primarily "arithmetic" and would choose to skip geometry but would never skip a chapter on long division with larger numbers. Geometry is relegated to the back of many common textbooks. According to the low performance of eighth graders on the Third International Mathematics and Science Study (Beaton et al., 1996) geometry curriculum in the United States reflects a lack of focus and demanding content.

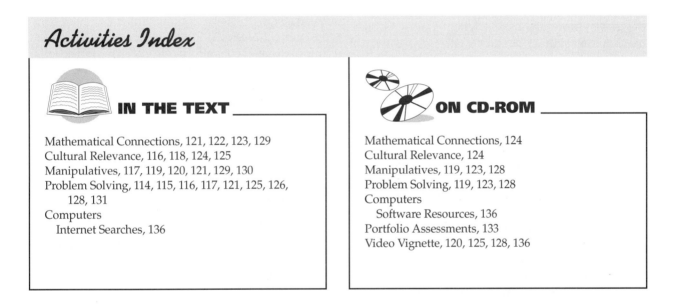

There remain many unresolved issues in the problems related to school geometry. A discussion of these and suggestions for their resolution are given by Usiskin (1987). He presents findings related to our students' continued poor performance, lack of geometry knowledge, and dimensions of geometry related to curriculum problems. "Geometry is too important in the real world and in mathematics to be a frill at the elementary school level or a province of only half of all secondary school students" (Usiskin, 1987, p. 30).

INFORMAL GEOMETRY

Many of us may think of geometry as a study of axioms, postulates, proofs of theorems, constructions, and so on. What geometry are we talking about: motion geometry, solid geometry, plane geometry, Euclidean geometry, or another type? The important issue is not the name, but rather the type of experiences we intend children to have as part of the elementary school geometry curriculum. Experiences in geometry should allow for the intuitive investigation of concepts and relationships. Activities should provide rich backgrounds and solid foundations for the generalizations about geometric relationships that come during the middle school grades. Geometry should encourage children to explore a variety of geometric concepts. This approach results in a study of "informal geometry."

Importance of Geometry. The study of geometry is important for many reasons. One of the most important reasons is to develop adequate spatial skills. During childhood, children respond to the three-dimensional world of shapes as they play, build, and explore with toys and other materials. These early geometry experiences are useful in developing spatial abilities. Spatial sense is "an intuitive feel for one's surroundings and objects in them" according to the *Curriculum Standards* (NCTM, 1989, p. 49). These abilities must be nurtured through geometric activities. Spatial skills include interpreting and making drawings, forming mental images, visualizing changes, and generalizing about perceptions in the environment.

These abilities, in turn, will promote the ability to reason, to predict, and to represent knowledge in appropriate ways. Developing spatial skills is also an important part of everyday life.

Geometry plays an important role in people's everyday lives. Many practical experiences involve problem-solving situations that require a knowledge of geometric concepts, such as making frames, determining the amount of wallpaper, paint, grass, or fertilizer to buy, and other work situations. Geometry easily integrates with other disciplines.

Many aspects of our world can be viewed from a geometric perspective. The use of geometric models, designs, pictures, or shapes helps students to analyze and make sense of problems and to illustrate and describe their mathematical thinking and ideas. For example, area models can be used to approach multiplication, decimals, fractions, and percents. Students should be given the opportunity to explore mathematical concepts and relationships from a geometric or spatial view. Another important benefit from geometry is that it provides opportunities to develop logical thinking and reasoning.

Geometry provides an opportunity to use hands-on materials and to stimulate creative visualization of mathematical ideas. Activities involve drawing, constructing, measuring, transforming, and comparing geometric figures. The *Standards* for geometry mention such action verbs. Children may approach geometry as a challenging change from the more computational component of other aspects of mathematics. Geometric concepts provide an excellent link between language and mathematics.

It is an unfortunate mistake when a teacher treats geometry as an optional branch of mathematics and chooses to skip this topic. In order to teach informal geometry effectively, teachers must be familiar with the characteristics of geometric figures and the relationships between them. Although the direction for change is away from naming geometric figures and memorizing geometric vocabulary, these terms may need to be reviewed for content in this chapter. Check the CD-ROM for geometric vocabulary and definitions.

Check Your Mathematics Knowledge

On Geometry

- Geometry Terminology Review

. . . a refresher from mathematics coursework . . . Lest you forget!

TEACHING STRATEGIES

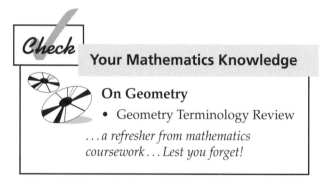

Activities for informal geometry are characterized by using manipulative materials, exploring concepts in both two- and three-dimensional space, and discovering relationships. Patterns are provided in the Appendix and on the CD for attribute blocks (pieces), geoboard, geometric recording paper, and tangrams. The focus is to provide experiences that will produce meaningful definitions and properties of geometric ideas across time. For example, after numerous experiences with materials, the child will accumulate facts and discover the properties of a square. With a teacher's guidance, the child's thinking will gradually sharpen so that when a definition is needed, it will hold meaning for the child. As you read through the rest of this chapter, examine the activities and the thinking process underlying them. Keep in mind that children need many experiences from a variety of materials to ensure the development of geometric concepts.

Van Hiele Levels. Two Dutch educators, Pierre van Hiele and Dina van Hiele-Geldof, studied children's acquisition of geometric concepts and the development of geometric thought. These findings hold many ideas that should be considered when reading this chapter. The van Hieles concluded that children pass through five levels of reasoning in geometry in much the same way that Piaget said children must proceed through the stages in cognitive development (Chapter 3). The five levels are described by Fuys and Liebov (1993) as follows:

- *Level 0—Visualization:* The student reasons about basic geometric concepts, such as simple shapes, by means of visual considerations. The student reacts to geometric figures as wholes. A square is a square because it *looks* like one.
- *Level 1—Analysis:* The student reasons about geometric concepts by means of an informal analysis of the parts and attributes and relationships among the parts of a figure. A square is a square because it has four equal sides and four right angles.
- *Level 2—Abstraction:* The student logically orders the properties of concepts, forms abstract definitions, and can distinguish between the necessity and sufficiency of a set of properties in determining a concept. A square's definition is dependent on some properties that are related to other shapes. The student sees that a square can be both a rectangle and a parallelogram.
- *Level 3—Deduction:* The student reasons formally within the context of a mathematical system, complete with undefined terms, axioms, an underlying logical system, definitions, and theorems. This is the level needed to perform well in a high school geometry class as the student has developed the ability to prove theorems.
- *Level 4—Rigor:* The student can compare systems based on different axioms and can study various geometries in the absence of concrete models.

The van Hieles proposed that progress through the five levels is more dependent on instruction than on age or maturation. They submitted five sequential phases of learning: information, directed orientation, explication, free orientation, and integration. According to the van Hieles, instruction developed according to this sequence promotes the acquisition of a level.

The first three levels (0–2) should be experiences in informal geometry during the elementary and middle school years. The van Hieles asserted that children should have a wide variety of exploratory experiences. Children should move through those levels with an understanding of geometry that will prepare them for the deductive study of geometry in high school and perhaps college where level 3 is required.

Performance of students in the National Assessment of Educational Progress (Struchens and Blume, 1997) indicate that most students at fourth and eighth grades are operating at the holistic level on van Hiele levels. These data suggest they need more spatial reasoning and use of deductive reasoning. Video segments of U.S. eighth-grade classes in the Third International Mathematics and Science Study (Forgione, 1997) illustrate that the lessons focus primarily on procedural knowledge (61 percent); students were not actively thinking and reasoning about mathematics. Although achievement in fourth-grade geometry revealed only two countries performing better than the United States, by eighth grade more than half the countries did better than the United States in geometry. Another research study of interest is the investigation of students using one of the reform-based curricula projects incorporating geometry as a regular strand since kindergarten (Carroll, 1998). With an emphasis on hands-on learning and problem-solving situations, this project reports these students showed gains in higher van Hiele levels than the comparison group.

Many students experience great difficulty handling high school geometry, and it may stem from the fact that inadequate experiences were provided in previous grades. The deductive study of geometry should be delayed until the student has developed the mental maturity required for this study. Unfortunately this practice is not often followed; so the student takes the class, receives low grades, develops a negative attitude, and may not choose to proceed further in mathematics classes.

This chapter discusses two main aspects of geometry: the study of two-dimensional objects known as plane geometry, and the study of three-dimensional objects known as solid geometry. As you read this chapter, consider how you can relate three-dimensional shapes to two-dimensional shapes, what models you can use to teach the goals of geometry in

BOX 6.1 Curriculum and Evaluation Standards

In grades K–4, the mathematics curriculum should include two- and three-dimensional geometry so that students can—

- Describe, model, draw, and classify shapes.
- Investigate and predict the results of combining, subdividing, and changing shapes.
- Develop spatial sense.
- Relate geometric ideas to number and measurement ideas.
- Recognize and appreciate geometry in their world.

In grades 5–8, the mathematics curriculum should include the study of the geometry of one, two, and three dimensions in a variety of situations so that students can—

- Identify, describe, compare, and classify geometric figures.
- Visualize and represent geometric figures with special attention to developing spatial sense.
- Explore transformations of geometric figures.
- Represent and solve problems using geometric models.
- Understand and apply geometric properties and relationships.
- Develop an appreciation of geometry as a means of describing the physical world.

Source: National Council of Teachers of Mathematics, 1989, pp. 48, 112.

an intuitive manner, and what levels of geometric thinking are involved. Review the *Curriculum Standards* (NCTM, 1989) in Box 6.1 to see the instructional goals suggested for the geometry curriculum.

Solid Geometry

Solid geometry involves three-dimensional shapes, their properties and relationships. Children's early experiences with geometry are centered around objects with three dimensions—blocks, cans, cones, balls, and boxes. Many children had building blocks at home or at preschool with which they constructed structures and patterns. Collections of empty oatmeal containers, food cans, soda cracker boxes, paper towel rolls, and other various sized boxes provide representations of solids for children to explore, compare, and construct. Shape exploration of three-dimensional figures should begin informally with shape explorations and classifications (level 0 activities).

Jensen and Spector (1986) suggest activities to involve children in experiencing solids and their properties. In these teacher-directed activities, the children pretend they are suspended inside various space figures and they describe the figure's properties. For example, "Imagine that you are in something like this round oatmeal box. This is your personal cylinder. Pretend that your fingertips are just touching the inside of your cylinder... draw the biggest circles possible by rotating your arms slowly" (Jensen and Spector, 1986, p. 14).

Activity 6.1

PROBLEM SOLVING

GUESS WHAT I AM!

MATERIALS

- Various three-dimensional shapes
- Container

PROCEDURE

Put the shapes in a container and ask different children to close their eyes, take a shape, and describe it to others who are trying to guess the shape selected. Using precise vocabulary becomes important.

In the classroom, commercial materials should be available for play and exploration. Plastic models and wooden models are needed to provide different perspectives about the figures. The transparent, plastic models help children realize that each figure has an inside and an outside. Ask children to describe and classify the shapes according to their properties.

Activity 6.2

PROBLEM SOLVING

CAN YOU BUILD IT?

PARTNERS

MATERIALS

- Interlocking cubes or wooden cubes

PROCEDURE

Have children set a barrier such as a large notebook or an encyclopedia between them. One student makes a structure from the materials and then describes it to the other student who uses materials to try to duplicate the structure. Precise vocabulary and communication skills are developed along with spatial visualization skills.

Activity 6.3

PROBLEM SOLVING

LET'S FACE IT

MATERIALS

- Soma cubes or wooden cubes
- Isometric dot paper

PROCEDURE

Have students make a structure with the cubes (or select a Soma cube). Draw the structure from the various views—front, bottom, sides on isometric dot paper. See the example in Figure 6.1.

FIGURE 6.1

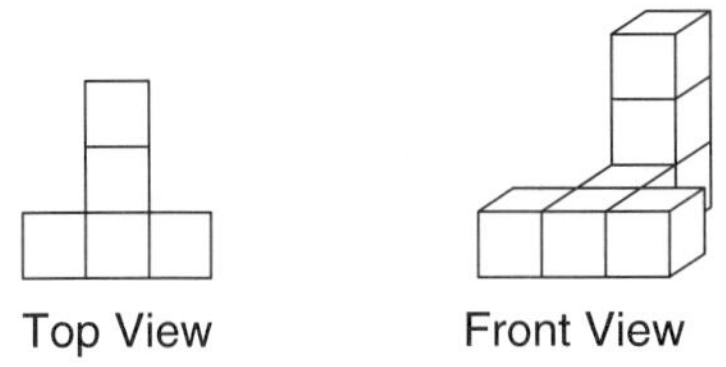

Draw the back view.

Different views of a structure.

The vocabulary associated with these activities is important. Younger children may call the shapes, "box, ball, can," but as they build greater understanding of the shapes, the proper names will become common, "prism, sphere, cylinder." As children learn to be more precise in describing and classifying solids, have them make a table of the properties:

Solid	Number of Edges	Number of Faces	Number of Vertices

Students need to relate the study of geometry to their environment by finding examples in their homes of objects that look like the solids being studied. They can create wall charts with pictures of the shapes. Have students take a can or box and cut apart all the individual faces that compose that figure. Another activity is to have students build a solid from squares. These experiences help them visualize the individual components of the figure and how a vertex is formed. Students in middle grades often have not had such experiences with informal geometry and need to work with models just as younger children do. Participation in such activities helps build the visualization necessary in working with formulas for solids.

Relating Three-Dimensional to Two-Dimensional. Once children begin to see how three-dimensional shapes are made up of various parts, they can design nets that make up the figures. A "net" is the pattern that can be made by covering ("wrapping") the figure in paper without any overlapping pieces. This activity allows children to identify the two-dimensional features of three-dimensional figures. Leeson (1994) describes many activities using Soma cubes and other three-dimensional shapes to improve spatial visualization skills. He has students find all the possible nets for a cube and record them on graph paper. Lamphere (1994) takes a drawing of a one-story house and has children draw images of doors, windows, skylights, and so on to show various views of the house. Children are asked to sketch how the building will look when folded and to explain what geometric shapes can be seen. Middle-grade students can find total surface area of the house, design two-story houses, and combine houses into apartments or townhouses and design nets for the structures. Such activities use concrete representations to improve the perception of spatial relationships. Perhaps these experiences will help us to know how much wrapping paper is needed to cover the present we need to wrap! Check the CD-ROM for additional activities on using nets.

Activity 6.4

PROBLEM SOLVING

MAKING NETS

MATERIALS

- Different-sized containers (cereal boxes, oatmeal containers, and so on)
- Graph paper

PROCEDURE

Students will identify their solid by name and discuss the properties of it. Draw a net to fold into the shape. Explain how the drawing was done by describing the faces of the solid. Verify that your net will fold into the shape. Estimate the area of each face, then use the graph paper to determine the area. How much wrapping paper will be needed to cover your container without overlaps?

Students can construct poster board or tagboard models from printed patterns. Cutting and assembling the figures help children learn about edges, corners, faces, and other parts of solid figures. With older children, these models can be used to develop understanding of the formulas. Check the CD-ROM for an activity illustrating the formula for the volume of a pyramid using cardboard models.

A number of curriculum projects and replacement units in mathematics have developed activities for spatial visualization. Much work in this area has been done in the Netherlands with accompanying assessments of visualization abilities of students (Geddes and Fortunato, 1993). Research from several studies indicate a strong correlation between spatial ability and problem-solving performance and that spatial skills can be improved through instruction. More experiences with solid geometry are available in the NCTM Addenda Series *Geometry and Spatial Sense* (Del Grande et al., 1993), which contains exercises for drawing nets of pentominoes, using Logo to draw geometric figures, and constructing three-dimensional structures.

Activity 6.5

PROBLEM SOLVING

SOLIDS EXPLORATION

1. Make nets of the pentominoes (see Activity 6.23 on page 128). Which of the shapes can be folded into a topless box (without a lid)? Prove it using your nets.
2. The Box problem:
   Someone in a factory bought cardboard that was six squares by four squares. They figured that each sheet of cardboard could be cut into four pieces so each piece would fold into a topless box. How could the sheet be cut?
3. Have four to six empty containers. Label them with alphabet letters. Which one holds the most? Which one holds the least? Which ones hold about the same amount? Test your predictions with rice, milo, salt, or another granular substance.

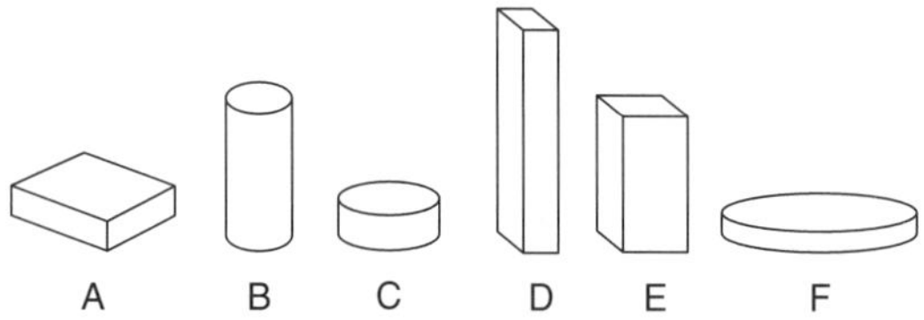

Activity 6.6

CULTURAL RELEVANCE

AFRICAN CULTURE AND MATHEMATICS

Claudia Zaslavsky has written a lot about mathematical projects that illustrate African societies. A unit on African network patterns illustrates how African children are able to carry out tasks to determine the conditions under which a network is traceable that adults find difficult to perform. Have students construct a house with the largest area for a given perimeter. Such experiences illustrate the wealth of mathematical ideas developed by African peoples and provide opportunities to appreciate other cultures. Check the chapter bibliography to obtain these journal references (Zaslavsky 1989, 1990).

Supporting the NCTM *Principles and Standards* (2000):

- Mathematics as Reasoning, Communication, Representation, Connections; Geometry and Spatial Sense

Activity Continues

- Worthwhile Mathematical Tasks—The Teaching Principle
- The Equity Principle

Plane Geometry

Plane geometry is the study of two-dimensional figures, their properties and relationships. Early activities could include classifying or sorting cut-out shapes or commercial materials such as pattern blocks or attribute blocks (also called attribute pieces). The child needs concrete models of the shapes to feel the shape and relate the name to its properties—number of edges, corners, and other attributes.

Attributes	Values
Size	Large, small
Shape	Circle, square, rectangle
Color	Red, yellow, green, blue
Thickness	Thin, thick

An important aspect of teaching geometry is to have students become familiar with the properties of shapes. A good activity is to have students find representatives of shapes in their environment. For example, the borders of the following could be selected: the file cabinet's sides are rectangles; the ceiling tiles are rectangles; the floor tiles are squares; the wastepaper basket rim is a circle; the flag is a rectangle; the traffic sign for yield is a triangle; the stop sign is an octagon. Give children a set of shapes to sort into some classifying scheme—shapes with three sides and the others; shapes with four corners and the others; shapes with no corners and the others. With attribute blocks, or cut-out shapes of different colors and sizes, many other classifying systems are possible. The following activities offer strategies to reinforce properties of shapes as well as logical reasoning skills.

Activity 6.7

PROBLEM SOLVING

CAN YOU SORT IT?

Make cards with various cutout shapes pasted on them (one shape per card). Give children a sorting rule or have another stack of cards with sorting rules on them.

Activity Continues

Have children use shape properties to describe a mystery shape. Listening to the clues, the partner or other group members guess the shape.

Activity 6.8

MANIPULATIVES

CHANGE IT AND DESCRIBE IT

MATERIALS

- Corrugated cardboard (sides of boxes)
- Push pins
- Yarn

PROCEDURE

Give each child a certain length of yarn, a piece of cardboard, and several push pins. Have them create shapes on the cardboard and write in their journals about the properties of each shape: Triangle, square, pentagon, hexagon, octagon. As each new shape is made by adding one (or two) push pins, describe the change in properties. What is the effect on the area? What is the effect on the perimeter? Explain your thinking.

Supporting the NCTM *Principles and Standards* (2000):

- Mathematics as Reasoning, Communication, Representation; Geometry and Spatial Sense
- Worthwhile Mathematical Tasks—The Teaching Principle
- Mathematics Curriculum Principle

Activity 6.9

PROBLEM SOLVING

ONE- AND TWO-DIFFERENCE TRAINS

MATERIALS

- Attribute blocks (or similar cut-outs; see Appendix and CD)

PROCEDURE

Place the attribute blocks in a pile on the floor or table. Start with one block. Have students take turns adding one

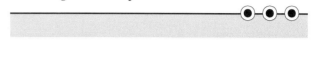

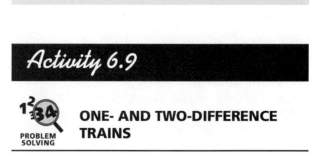

Activity Continues

block to the train so that each block is placed next to one that is different from it in just *one* way. Have the student verbalize the difference as each block is added. For example, the starting block is a green, small triangle. The first player adds a green, *large* triangle. The next player adds a *yellow* large triangle. The next player adds a yellow, large *square*. Play until all blocks are in the train. This goal may require some rearranging, which is allowed at the end of the round. Players can also see if they can get the end of the train to join to the beginning block. This objective may also require some rearranging.

VARIATION

Do the preceding activity, and have each piece differ from the others by *two* attributes. For example, start with a thick, red, large, square. The next player places a thick, *green, small* square in the train—two attributes are different (color, size). Thickness may be achieved by pasting attribute pieces on styrofoam, painted to match the color of each piece.

Cultural Contributions

CULTURAL RELEVANCE

CULTURAL CONTRIBUTIONS TO GEOMETRY

The following material developed by the Chicago Public Schools should be shared with students at each of the appropriate grade levels.

K–3

Students should examine the contributions to geometry made by peoples all over the world. For example, the peoples of Egypt and Mesopotamia studied squares, rectangles, triangles, and circles. For greater strength, the Eskimos use geometric shapes to form their igloos. Mozambicans build rectangular houses by using equal-length ropes as diagonals.

4–8

Students should know that the first concepts of congruency were developed in Africa and Asia and that cotangents and similar triangle principles were used in the building of the African pyramids. The students should examine the contributions to geometry made by peoples all over the world. For example, Eskimos build strong dome-

Activity Continues

shaped igloos. Mozambicans build rectangular houses by using equal-length ropes as diagonals (Strong, 1990).

Geoboards. Making shapes on a geoboard offers one of the best opportunities to explore the properties of shapes. A geoboard is usually a 6- × 6-inch board or plastic square with 25 nails or pegs placed into a 5 × 5 array. A geoboard pattern is provided in the Appendix and on the CD-ROM. The reader may wish to print out and plasticize or laminate the pattern in the CD Appendix or use it as a model when making a wooden geoboard. (Other arrangements of nails or pegs are possible, such as circular, isometric, or other dimensions of an array.) The most common arrangement is shown in Figure 6.2. Rubber bands can be stretched around the nails or plastic pegs to create shapes or designs. This is an invaluable teaching device for geometry as it allows children to create shapes, designs, and patterns to express ideas about geometry in a quick, accurate manner. Where it is impossible to ask a young child to make a square or octagon, the geoboard quickly provides such experiences.

FIGURE 6.2

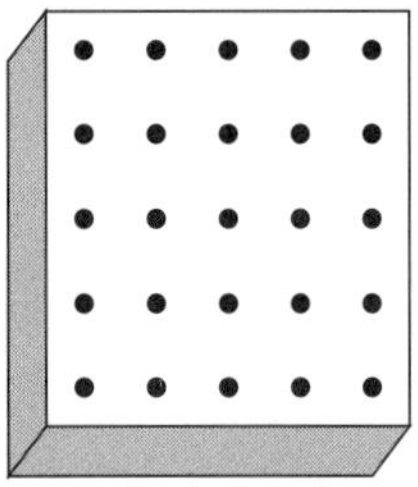

Geoboard in 5 × 5 array.

Some teachers fear that rubber bands may become projectiles and have found that using the term "geobands" helps reduce the temptation. Whatever procedure you use, provide adequate opportunities for free exploration with the geoboard. Have children copy their design or creation onto geometric dot paper (a replica of the 5 × 5 array using large dots for the nails), thereby keeping a record of their work. Both types of recording sheets are in the Appendix (reduced size) and on the CD-ROM (full size). The following activities use geoboards with children. More geoboard activities are discussed later in the chapter and on the CD-ROM.

EXTENDED ACTIVITIES

Name of Activity

- Geoboard Explorations
- Understanding Construction of a Pyramid

PROBLEM SOLVING MANIPULATIVES

Activity 6.10

MANIPULATIVES

USING A GEOBOARD

PROCEDURE

Copy This Shape

Hold up a large card with a shape on it. Have class copy the shape onto its geoboards. Discuss the name and properties of the shape. Have children copy other shapes and designs. Make a shape on an overhead geoboard and have the children copy it. Rotate the shape (Figure 6.3), and see whether the children still call it by the same name. This is a good assessment technique.

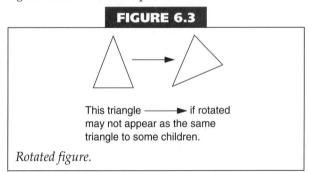

FIGURE 6.3

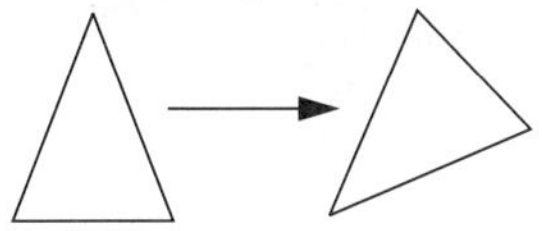

This triangle ——► if rotated
may not appear as the same
triangle to some children.

Rotated figure.

Make This Shape

Ask students to make a shape with four sides. Have them compare their shapes and discuss the names and possibilities. Ask children to make a shape with four equal sides, a figure with six sides, or a figure that touches six nails. Depending on grade level you can vary the level of difficulty, for example, make a shape with one obtuse angle. Make the largest shape possible. Make the smallest shape possible. The possibilities are endless for this activity.

Dividing Our Shapes

Have students make a shape and subdivide it into other shapes. Make the activity more difficult by giving specific directions on the shapes that are to be formed. Incorporate vocabulary and terminology.

Activity Continues

Have children make the largest square possible on their geoboards. Take another band and divide the shape into two congruent regions. What are the names of the regions formed? Divide one of the regions again. Now what shape is formed?

How Am I Classifying?

Have students make a shape on their geoboards. Then decide a way to classify them into two groups. Ask them to put their geoboard figure into the appropriate set. Line the geoboards in the chalk tray. Do with many attributes.

Another way to have children experience the properties and attributes of shapes is by making shapes with yarn and soda straws. The straws can be cut into various lengths to form other shapes such as scalene triangles, parallelograms, and trapezoids. Cut straws in half if smaller shapes are easier for students to manage. Thread six or eight straws onto the yarn. Have the children take the number of straws needed for the shape; for example, three straws will form a triangle, and push the other straws apart from them on the yarn. See Figure 6.4 for additional ideas about this device. Straws can also be used to construct three-dimensional figures.

FIGURE 6.4

Soda straw constructions.

As relationships are explored, it might help to put the properties of the geometric figures into chart form. Write the name of the polygon, the number of sides, and the number of angles. Children in upper elementary grades classify triangles by sides (equilateral, isosceles, or scalene) or by angles (acute, right, or obtuse). When classifying shapes with four sides, children should realize there are many of these figures—rectangle, square, rhombus, trapezoid, parallelogram. Additional information about their properties is needed to specifically identify the shape such as kind of angles, number of congruent sides, and number of parallel sides.

Activity 6.11

MANIPULATIVES

ROLL A TRIANGLE

MATERIALS

- Three dice
- Soda straws
- Yarn

PROCEDURE

In groups have students try to build triangles. Roll three dice. Each face stands for the length of a side of the triangle to be cut from the straws. Using yarn to thread the pieces of straw, make triangles. Record the lengths and whether a triangle was formed. Build ten triangles and study the data. Label the characteristics of the triangles and name them. Make a rule for deciding what conditions must be met with the length of the sides to make a triangle. What can be said about the angles needed?

Roll	Triangle	Characteristics
3, 3, 5	Yes—isosceles	Two sides equal, two angles unequal

Tangrams. Tangrams can provide many experiences for understanding congruent and similar figures. (*Congruent* means figures with the same size and shape. *Similar* means figures with the same shape and with all corresponding parts being proportional.) The seven pieces of the tangram puzzle are illustrated in Figure 6.5. The puzzle can be made by students through a series of folds and cuts to form the tans such as Mr. Addcox's lesson "Making Tangrams" on the CD-ROM. A discussion of how to discover the areas of the square parallelogram, triangle, and trapezoid can accompany a similar lesson for middle level students (Duke, 1998).

Designs can be made by putting a square, parallelogram, and five triangles into silhouette patterns of people, animals, objects, or geometric figures. Many aspects of these shapes lend themselves to the discovery of concepts such as shape, congruence, similarity, properties of polygons, symmetry, area, and perimeter. Additional tangram activities can incorporate other mathematical topics including fractions, decimals, percents (see Chapter 13), probability, and proportions.

FIGURE 6.5

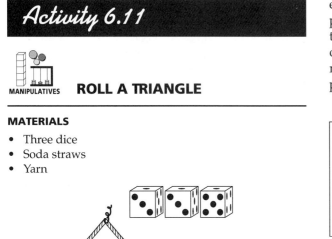

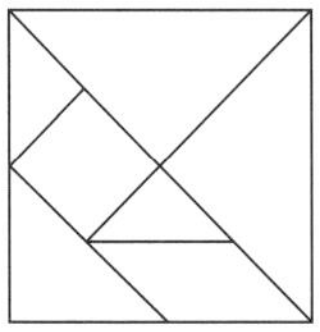

Tangram puzzle.

There are several stories about the tangram puzzle's origin and name. The following myth offers an interesting introduction to the puzzle:

A very long time ago, in the land of China, there was a man named Mr. Tan. He had a beautiful porcelain tile of which he was extremely proud. He thought of it as a treasure. When he heard that the Emperor was coming to the village where he lived, Mr. Tan wanted to present the tile to the Emperor as a gift. As he began polishing his tile, he dropped it and it broke into the seven pieces of the tangram puzzle. Mr. Tan was very unhappy. Then he thought that if he could put the pieces back together, he would have the square tile again. Mr. Tan thought it would be easy to do, but it took him a very long time. While he was trying to form the square, he discovered lots of interesting

Video Vignette

Making Tangrams

In this limited-English classroom, Mr. Addcox's students create a set of tangrams.

- What techniques does he use to have children analyze and describe the properties of shapes?
- What evidence do you see that he is incorporating components of the NCTM *Principles and Standards*? Use the Table 3.5 lesson plan to analyze the lesson.
- Listen to the number of precise geometric terms used in this lesson. How does Mr. Addcox support the mathematics learning of these bilingual students?

shapes and designs . . . over 7000 in all. Let's see if we can make some of our own designs with the tangram puzzle pieces.

The following are some activities to do with tangrams. Many commercial books are available that contain activities with tangrams. These can provide experiences in spatial relationships as well as geometric concepts.

Activity 6.12

MANIPULATIVES PROBLEM SOLVING

USING TANGRAMS

MATERIALS

- Tangram sets (see Appendix and CD-ROM)

PROCEDURE

1. Sort the pieces into similar and congruent shapes. How many shapes are the same size (congruent)? How many shapes are the same shape but differ in size?
2. Take the two small congruent triangles and see what other shapes you can create with them. Are any of these new shapes congruent to other tangram pieces? Which ones?
3. It is possible to form many squares using different combinations of tangram pieces. How many squares can be formed?
4. With the two large congruent triangles, find what other shapes you can form with them. Name these shapes. Draw the tangrams used to form each shape—*if* you can make the shape.

	Number of Tangrams Used					
Shape	2	3	4	5	6	7
Triangle						
Rectangle						
Trapezoid						
Parallelogram						
Square						

5. What alphabet letters and which numbers can be made?

Activity 6.13

MANIPULATIVES MATHEMATICAL CONNECTIONS

LITERATURE CONNECTION

PROCEDURE

1. Read the book, *Grandfather Tang's Stories: A Tale Told with Tangrams* (Tompert, 1990). Have the students make the figures from the story. Create tangram pictures to depict or "illustrate" characters from other stories.
2. Students can create their own stories and use tangram designs to "illustrate" their stories (Figure 6.6). Have the students outline their puzzle picture and keep a copy of how to put the puzzle together again. The authors/creators could put their books at a center where other students can read the story and solve the puzzles.

FIGURE 6.6

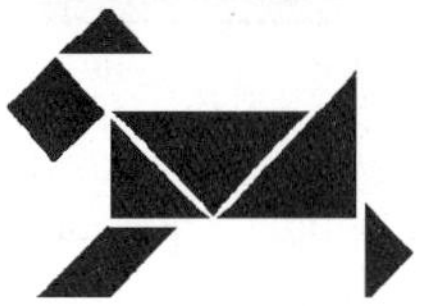

Tangram dog.

Activity 6.14

MANIPULATIVES

CAN YOU PICTURE THIS?

Have one student create a tangram picture. Working in pairs, the students should be back-to-back or they can use a manila file folder as a screen between them. One partner describes how the tangram picture is formed to the partner who has not seen the picture. The student should use precise vocabulary to describe the design so that the partner can recreate it using his or her own set of tangrams. Compare the pictures and discuss results. Trade roles and see who had clearer directions.

Symmetry

The concept of symmetry is another important aspect of informal geometry experiences in the elementary grades. Symmetry is a way to describe geometric properties of shapes. Children have an almost intuitive sense of symmetry. Children may determine symmetry by visual inspection of a design. Paper folding and art designs offer opportunities to experience symmetry. Children might make a long line of paper dolls or cut-out Valentine hearts or Christmas trees and see the many lines of symmetry.

Activity 6.15

MATHEMATICAL CONNECTIONS

SYMMETRY IN ART ACTIVITIES

DIRECTIONS

1. Fold a piece of paper in half and cut out a design or figure. Have students look at only one side of the folded paper as they cut through both parts.
(*Note:* When working with young children, stress that the folded line is to remain intact so that the figure comes out symmetrical.)
2. *A variation:* Put finger paint on a piece of paper, then fold the paper in half. Using the eraser on a pencil, have children create a design on the folded paper which, when opened to full length, will show a symmetrical design.

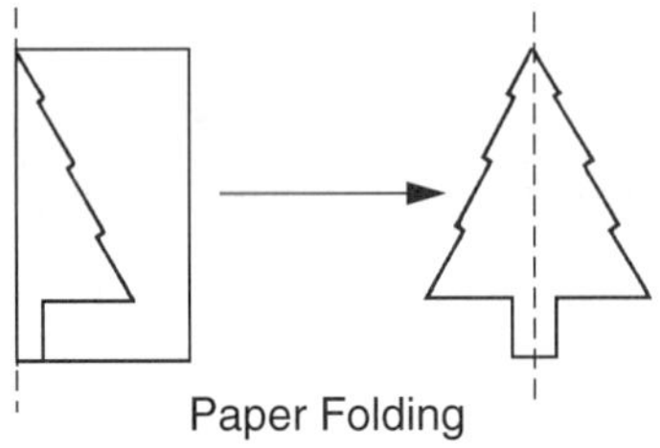

Paper Folding

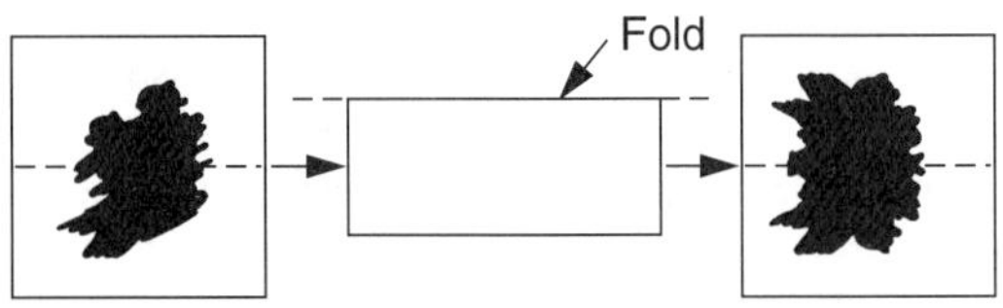

Finger Paint Folding

FIGURE 6.7

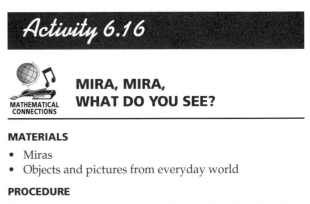

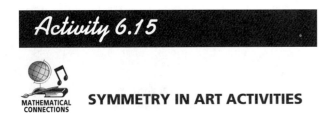

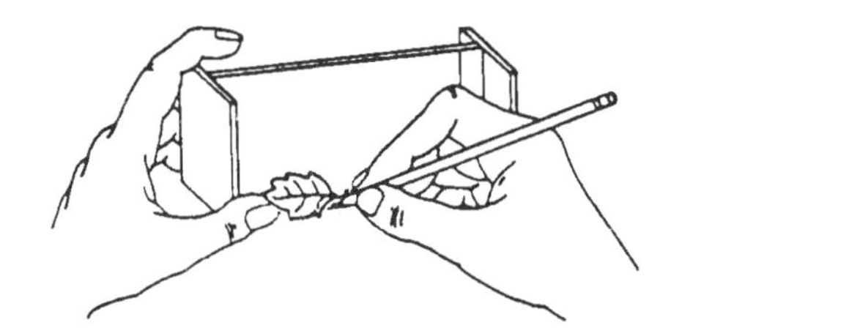

Testing for lines of symmetry with a Mira.

Line Symmetry. There are two types of symmetry—line and rotational. The activities discussed earlier are examples of line symmetry. A figure with line symmetry has a line of symmetry, which can be determined, and the exact same image appears on both sides of the line. To test for lines of symmetry, use a mirror or a Mira (a commercial device of red plexiglass), or have the figure traced and folded (Figure 6.7). To test for line(s) of symmetry using a mirror or Mira, place the mirror or Mira on the figure and move it until half the figure is reflected on the mirror or plexiglass. This portion should coincide with the portion of the figure behind the mirror.

Activity 6.16

MATHEMATICAL CONNECTIONS

MIRA, MIRA, WHAT DO YOU SEE?

MATERIALS

- Miras
- Objects and pictures from everyday world

PROCEDURE

Explore objects and pictures with the Mira. Find familiar objects such as coins, stamps, buttons, and keys. Predict about the movement of objects by turning them, sliding them, flipping them, and so on. Trace images and check for lines of symmetry and congruence.

Try folding a square to determine how many lines of symmetry you can create. A fold line is called an axis of symmetry. To test for symmetry using the folding method, have students fold the traced figure until the two halves match exactly. The tracing can also be flipped about the line of symmetry. Students can investigate familiar objects for symmetry (windows, wheels, human body) and will find that many objects have more than one line of symmetry.

EXTENDED ACTIVITIES

Name of Activity

- Working on Nets
- Mira Transformations
- Tangram Quilts

PROBLEM SOLVING MANIPULATIVES

Symmetry can also be explored using geoboards and pattern blocks with older children. The figures or designs can be tested with mirrors, and the figures can be reproduced with geometric dot paper or pattern block paper and folded to show lines of symmetry. Letters of the alphabet can be used for younger children.

Here are some additional suggestions to develop new connections for real-world experiences with symmetry. Since children (especially girls) love to cut out paper dolls using folded paper, explore designing clothing by creating patterns. Have children bring in examples from home if possible. Other examples such as leaves, snowflakes, hearts, and even humans show that regularity of form abounds in our environment.

Activity 6.17

MATHEMATICAL CONNECTIONS

GEOMETRY SURROUNDS US

PROCEDURE

1. Have students look for examples of symmetry (butterfly wings) in the world around them. Bring in the samples to class, post, and discuss the lines of symmetry.
2. Nature offers many examples (such as honeycombs) of tilings, or tessellating shapes. Have students share examples with others.
3. Explore patterns in nature that show flip, turn, and slide.
4. Look for advertisements, products, or manufactured materials that have geometric properties. Bring examples to class to discuss and share.

Rotational Symmetry. A figure that has rotational symmetry can be rotated or turned (less than a full turn) around a point until a matched figure results. An example of a figure with rotational symmetry is a square.

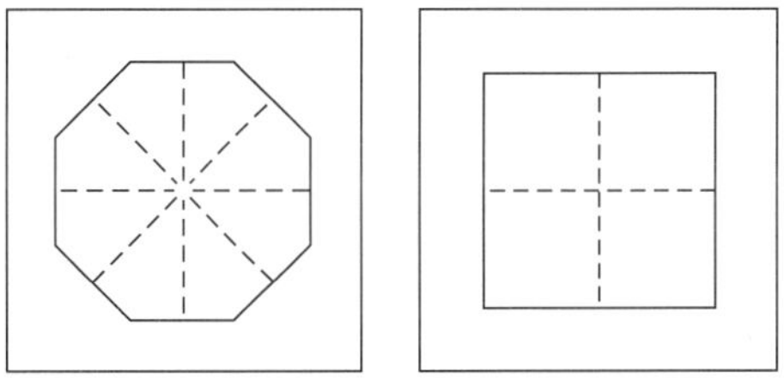

Testing for Lines of Symmetry

A quarter turn produces a square, a half turn produces a square, and a three-quarter turn produces another matched square figure. A square has four ways it can match the traced square, so it has rotational symmetry of order 4. The Chrysler Corporation trademark when tested for rotational symmetry has five turns that produce the matched figure. Examine patterns, decorations, or designs to find examples of rotational symmetry.

Rotational Symmetry in Chrysler Symbol

Activity 6.18

MATHEMATICAL CONNECTIONS

SYMMETRY IN LETTERS AND WORDS

DIRECTIONS

1. Symmetry can be found in letters of the alphabet or with some words (for example, "wow"). Use a small rectangular mirror and determine which students have names that begin with a capital letter with one line of symmetry or two lines of symmetry.

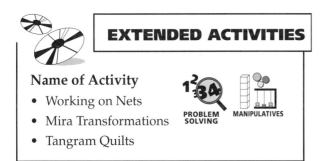

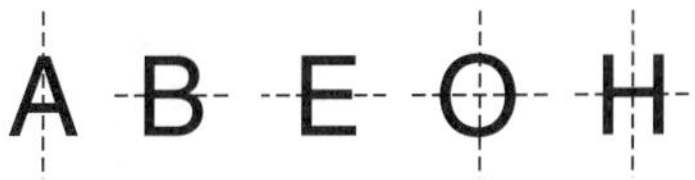

Lines of Symmetry for Letters

Activity Continues

2. Ask the following questions:
   Whose initials are symmetrical? Which letters have rotational symmetry?
   Which shapes have an infinite number of lines of symmetry?
3. Use Venn diagrams to sort the letters by types of symmetry. Have children look at things that have line symmetry—buildings, people, pictures, leaves, plants, and cars.

Activity 6.19

CULTURAL RELEVANCE

INDIAN BEADWORK WITH LOGO

American Indians in Alaska have been using a Logo program that is designed to write procedures to show American Indian beadwork designs. Read Bradley (1992) about the effectiveness for planning Logo Designs to create Sioux Indian beadwork. What do you feel are the significant features of such a project?

Even kindergarten children can develop better spatial visualization skills through rotational symmetry exercises. Kalb (1994) uses "arrow pattern" activities for children to demonstrate turns and flips with their hands. For example, to demonstrate a flip along a horizontal axis, a child would first place the palm down and then place the palm up. She asserts that such activities give a different perspective on teaching and allow assessment of spatial problem-solving strategies.

Another interesting application of symmetry can be found in arts of many cultures. Children can analyze the symmetrical patterns in quilts and rugs for line and rotational symmetry. Many connections with other subjects such as social studies, art, and history can be explored. Children can study the art of quilting through many children's books as well as design their own quilt patterns. Navajo rugs are another rich setting for examining symmetry and provide an opportunity to integrate mathematics into the study of culture. You might like to read the creative lessons for problem solving with quilts that many teachers have shared. (Carey, 1992; Zaslavsky, 1990).

EXTENDED ACTIVITIES

Name of Activity

- Making Quilts Shows Our Culture
- Geometry Tells the Story

CULTURAL RELEVANCE MATHEMATICAL CONNECTIONS

FIGURE 6.8

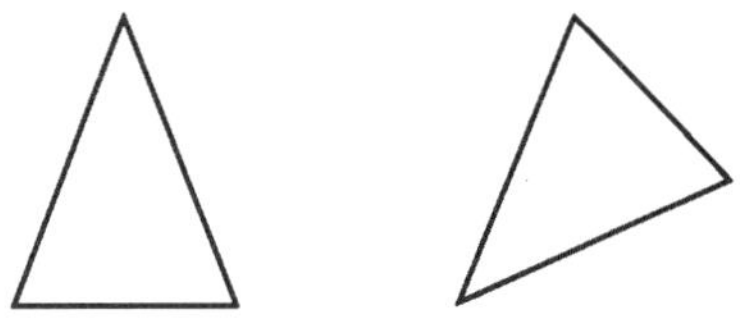

Isosceles Triangle   Rotated

Rotated figures may confuse children.

Activity 6.20

CULTURAL RELEVANCE

CULTURAL ILLUSTRATIONS

Read the book, *Less Than Half, More Than Whole* (Lacapa and Lacapa, 1994). Discuss the children's struggle with the questions raised in the book.

Why do you think the authors selected this title? What does this title mean to you? The book contains designs in the illustrations that represent many cultures. What patterns and symmetrical designs do you see? Explain your thinking. What examples of transformational geometry do you see?

Supporting the NCTM *Principles and Standards* (2000):

- Geometry and Spatial Sense; Mathematics as Reasoning, Communication, Connections, Representation
- Worthwhile Mathematical Tasks—The Teaching Principle
- The Equity Principle

The orientation of a figure may influence a child's interpretation and perception of that figure. If an isosceles triangle is usually drawn with its base horizontal, a rotation of the triangle (Figure 6.8) may cause a change in perception about that figure causing the child not to recognize the isosceles triangle. Children may have such limited experiences with shapes that they may feel the triangle is not "right-side up." Children often think that the only figures that are triangles are those that are equilateral. They are unduly influenced by the orientation of figures even though they are familiar with the geometric vocabulary. Watch the video vignette on the CD-ROM for examples.

Transformations

Transformational geometry gives children some experience with changing their orientation and perspective about figures. This area of study deals with motion geometry and three basic motions: flips, slides, and turns. The motions follow certain rules, and the figure that results may produce a transformation that is a mirror image of the original figure. A *flip* creates a reflected image of the original shape and is found frequently in our environment. A *slide* motion is when the figure moves along a plane with no changes in the position of the points. A *turn* is a rotation around a point. Children can acquire an intuitive notion of flips (reflection), slides (translation), and turns (rotation) by working with pattern cards and tessellations (Figure 6.9).

A tessellation is a design covering a flat surface without overlaps or gaps. Building a tessellation may involve motion geometry of slides, flips, and turns. Tessellations are also called tiling patterns. The study of tessellations has numerous applications to other fields with a genuine, natural multicultural connection in the context of art. Children's storybooks such as *A Clock for the Dreamer* (Friedman, 1994) present ways to investigate transformations. Geometric ideas and terms take on true meaning when students create and describe tiling patterns (Harris, 1998).

FIGURE 6.9

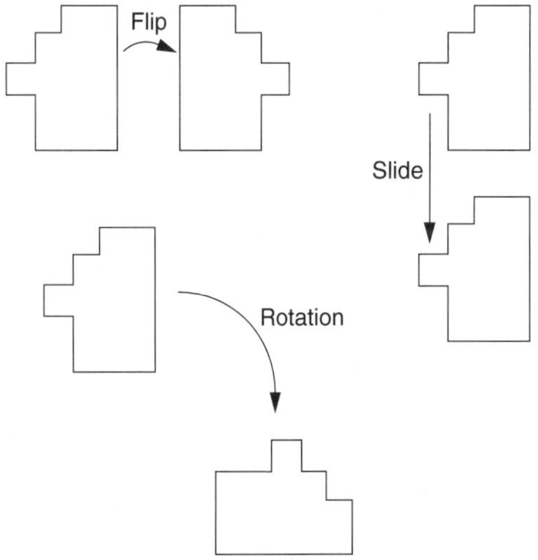

Transformational geometry.

Video Vignette

Shape Sort

View the video vignette of the first graders working on sorting poster board shapes. Watch the differences between the children's conceptualizations about triangles.

- What did you learn about the first girl's understanding of triangles?
- What can be determined about the second girl's understanding of triangles? Compare to the boy's statements about triangles.
- What follow-up assessment would you do?
- What instructional activities would you design?

Activity 6.21

CULTURAL RELEVANCE — PROBLEM SOLVING

TESSELLATION TIME

MATERIALS

- Pattern blocks
- Paper

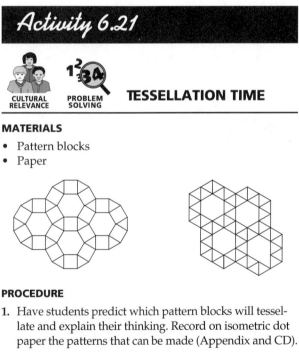

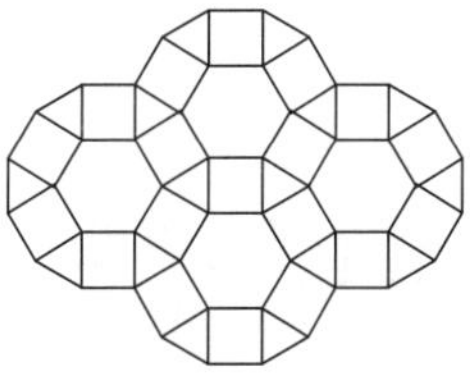

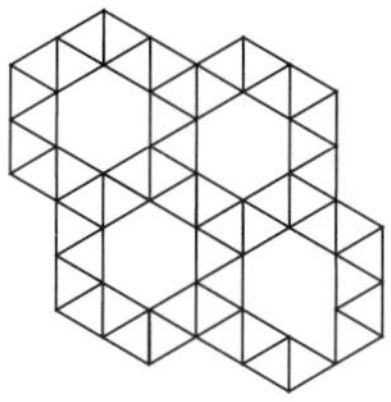

PROCEDURE

1. Have students predict which pattern blocks will tessellate and explain their thinking. Record on isometric dot paper the patterns that can be made (Appendix and CD).
2. Combine pattern blocks into designs that will tessellate. These are called semiregular tessellations.
3. Find examples of tessellations in our world.
4. Explore why shapes or designs tessellate using angle measurements. Explore shapes other than regular polygons.
5. Investigate tessellations in Chinese lattice designs or Arabic patterns (Williams, 1993).

Activity 6.22

PROBLEM SOLVING

ESCHER DESIGNS

Study the work of M. C. Escher. Use the Internet to see whether there are clubs or forums that have Escher's work. Check the Internet for projects devoted to geometry. The Geometry Forum and the Geometry Center are two funded by the National Science Foundation.

Create your own interesting Escher-type design. Start with a square. Cut a section from one side and slide this cut-away part to the opposite side of the square and attach. Cut another section from one of the other two parallel sides and slide it to the opposite side and attach. You have made a shape that tessellates. Repeat four to six more times. Place the pieces together into a design. Use your imagination about what details you can add to show what your design could represent. Try to see many different interpretations (Kaiser, 1988, p. 24).

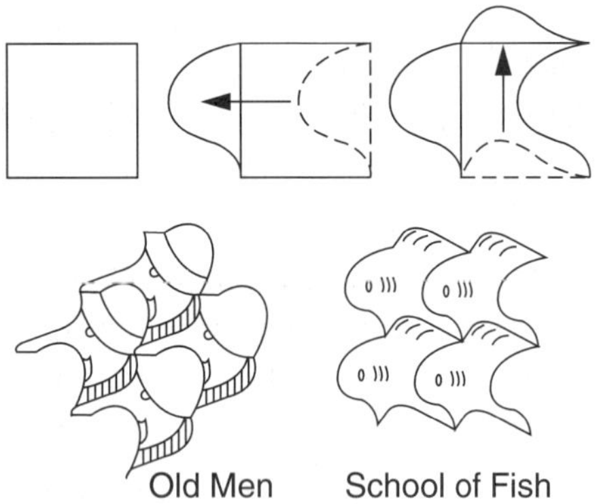

Old Men School of Fish

Make these shapes tesselate!

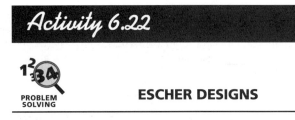

These activities involve the ability to visualize images at both a perceptual and a representational level. While the perceptual level is based on manipulation of objects and visual impressions, the representational level relies on mental manipulations, imagination, and thought. Performing a mental operation (for example, Euclidean transformation) is a more difficult task and may be limited by a child's developmental level in that it requires formal operational thought (in a Piagetian sense).

The *Principles and Standards* (NCTM, 2000) call for the development of spatial sense that includes insights and intuitions about two- and three-dimensional shapes and their characteristics, the interrelationships of shapes, and the effects of changes made on shapes. Such experiences allow children to develop a more comprehensive understanding about shapes and their properties. Rich experiences with geometry will encourage children to see uses of geometry in their lives.

To extend their knowledge of plane figures, children need to understand many properties of figures: the number of sides, the length of the sides, the size of the angles, parallel and perpendicular lines contained in the figure, the number of angles. As these concepts are encountered in the elementary mathematics program, it is important that experiences be provided to allow for guided discovery of what these concepts mean. Paper folding and origami are excellent ways to develop the visualization, precise language, and careful thinking required to understand geometric principles. Inexpensive wax paper serves as an effective material for paper folding activities because it is clear and easy to see through, and when it is creased, leaves a visible line.

Logo

One exciting potential for improving students' knowledge of geometric concepts lies in computer technology. Logo, or "turtle geometry," presents many useful possibilities to foster children's spatial reasoning in a computer microworld. In order to create shapes, the child must analyze a shape into its parts. Research (Battista and Clements, 1992) on the effectiveness of Logo indicates that such activities help children make a transition from a visual level to a descriptive-analytical level. Logo activities provide opportunities for children to study angle measurement of polygons in a problem-solving environment. Angles of rotation can also be discovered with older children using Logo. The NCTM Addenda book, *Geometry and Spatial Sense* (Del Grande et al., 1993), offers some ideas for exploring these concepts with students.

Other valuable tools for technology use are software packages such as *The Geometric Supposer*

(Sunburst Communications, 1997), *Cabri* (Texas Instruments, 1997), and *The Geometer's Sketchpad* (Jackiw, 1995).

Students using such software can construct a wide variety of figures using a toolbox including a compass, straightedge, and a point tool. After the figures are created, can be explored and transformed in almost unlimited ways. Students can make conjectures about angles and triangles, examine transformations and symmetrical features, and make mathematical connections. For a more complete explanation with lots of illustrations, read Taylor's article (1992) and Bay, Bledsoe, and Reys' (1998) unit on transforming shapes of states. Also check the Computer Software Resources on the CD-ROM.

Area and Perimeter

Area, the number of square units required to cover a surface, and *perimeter,* the distance around an area, are two components of the study of geometry. Often children reverse the two terms and their meanings.

One aspect of a child's cognitive development that Piaget studied was the child's concepts of geometry. His tasks assessed conservation of length, area, and volume and were based on the child's ability to reason that the measure was unchanged by displacement. Many twelve- to fourteen-year-olds still had trouble being convinced that the area remains unchanged with different configurations such as in Figure 6.10. Children also had difficulty believing that perimeters could change but areas remain the same, as in Figure 6.11. Watch the video vignette, "Pizza Perimeters," as fourth graders explore such geometric concepts. Try the activities on the CD-ROM, listed in the Extended Activities box on page 128 to develop better understandings of these principles.

FIGURE 6.10

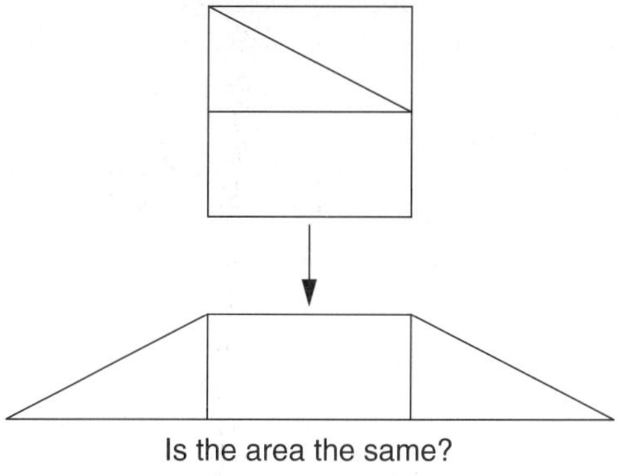

Conservation of area.

FIGURE 6.11

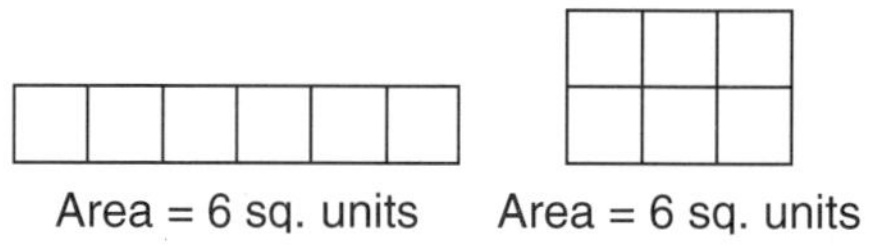

Perimeters not the same—areas are the same.

FIGURE 6.12

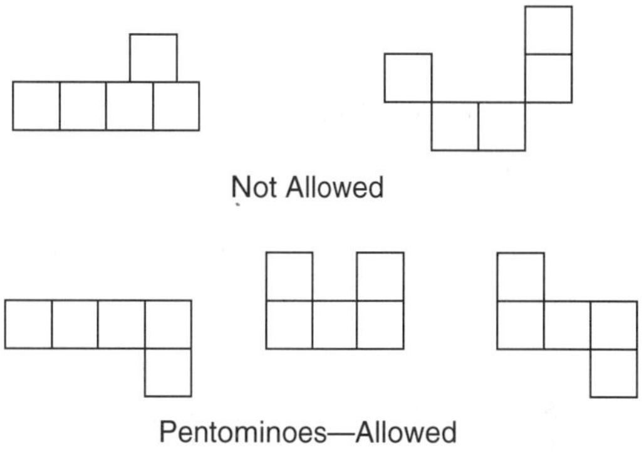

Pentominoes exercises.

Pentominoes. Pentominoes provide an exercise in perception and logical reasoning and help demonstrate some geometric principles of congruency. Pentominoes are made of five (pent-) congruent squares that must have every square touching at least one side of another square (Figure 6.12). Have children cut squares out of graph paper or use plastic tiles to form the pentominoes.

A common activity is to form the twelve different pentominoes that can be constructed. Individual squares such as mosaic tiles, which can be moved easily, work better with younger children. The shapes can then be cut from graph paper and kept as a record. Making the shapes out of paper allows children to test whether the newly formed shape is unique. The shape, when flipped or rotated, may produce a figure that has already been found. If the two shapes are congruent, they are the same shape (Figure 6.13).

FIGURE 6.13

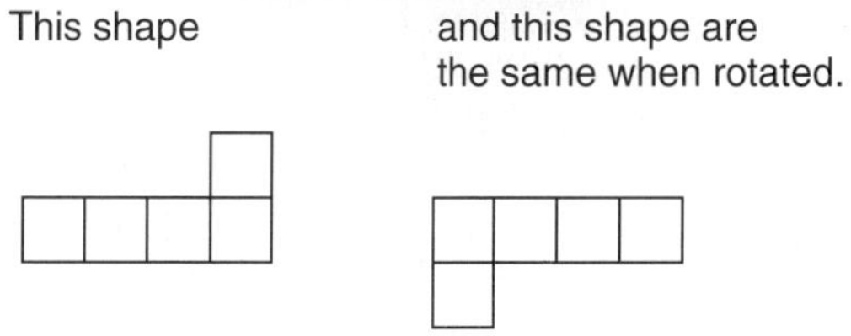

Rotating shapes.

If this task is too hard for younger children, it can be made easier by starting with three squares, for which there are only two different arrangements. Next try the different arrangements of four squares, or tetrominoes. Kaiser (1988) and Onslow (1990) offer additional activities using pentominoes.

Activity 6.23

PROBLEM SOLVING

PENTOMINOES

MATERIALS

- One cut-out set of the 12 pentominoes (use graph paper—one inch or centimeter; see Appendix and CD)

PROCEDURE

1. Find the area and perimeter of each pentominoe. Have you found all possible arrangements?
2. Which nets can be folded to make a cube without a lid? What do you notice about those that can be folded?
3. Use all 12 pentominoes and form a 6 × 10 rectangle (6 units wide and 10 units long). Form a 5 × 12 rectangle. What other rectangular arrangements can you make?
4. Use two pentominoes and make a 2 × 5 rectangle. Any others? Use three different pentominoes and make a 3 × 5 rectangle. Any others? Continue making rectangles with different numbers of pentominoes. Do you see a pattern? Write any predictions you can make.
5. Using two pentominoes, find all the tessellations that can be made. Color them using graph paper to show the tessellations.
6. Using a checkerboard, try to place all the pentominoes on the board without overlapping the pieces. As a partner game, each player draws six pieces and in turn places a pentomino on the board until no plays remain. The winner is the player with more pieces on the board.

Supporting the NCTM *Principles and Standards* (2000):

- Mathematics as Problem Solving, Representation, Reasoning
- Tools for Enhancing Discourse—The Learning Principle, The Mathematics Principle
- The Assessment Principle

Video Vignette

Pizza Perimeters

Mr. Dillon's fourth graders are presented with a problem to solve involving area and perimeter. He uses a real-life scenario to give added meaning to the problem.

- Analyze this lesson in terms of the NCTM Teaching Principle, worthwhile mathematical tasks. Describe your reactions.
- What aspects of the NCTM *Standards* do you see exemplified in this lesson?
- What follow-up activities would you suggest should happen after this lesson?

EXTENDED ACTIVITIES

PROBLEM SOLVING MANIPULATIVES

Name of Activity

- Area of 4
- Perimeter of 30
- Possible or Impossible

Tangrams and Geoboards. Area and perimeter can also be explored with tangrams and geoboards. These teaching activities help develop an intuitive understanding about how area can remain the same regardless of various transformations. Students who rely heavily on perceptual cues gain understanding about conservation of area. The geoboard is an effective device to show area formulas for parallelograms and triangles. Rather than use the formula that requires the student to visualize a line segment as the height, the strategy with geoboards is to form a rectangle around the region, determine the area of the rectangle and from there determine the area of the other figure.

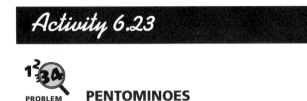

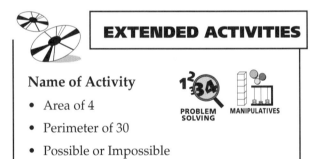

Activity 6.24

MANIPULATIVES MATHEMATICAL CONNECTIONS

DISCOVERING AREA WITH TANGRAMS

MATERIALS

- Tangram sets (see Appendix and CD-ROM)

PROCEDURE

1. Use the two smallest triangles. Make a square. This square represents a square unit of measure. What is the area of the triangle?
2. Use the two smallest triangles. Make a parallelogram. What is the area of this shape?
3. Use the three smallest triangles. Make a square. What is the area? Use the same pieces and make a triangle, rectangle, trapezoid, and parallelogram. What is the area of each shape? If one edge of the square has a value of one unit, compare their perimeters. Write about your perceptions.
4. Using the five smallest pieces (all except the two large triangles), form the same five shapes. Compare the area and perimeter of each shape.
5. Which shape do you feel has the greatest area? Why? Greatest perimeter? Why?
6. If the total area for the square made from the seven tangrams is one, what fractions, decimal, percent relationships are there? What ratios are there for area and perimeter of the different pieces?

Activity 6.25

MANIPULATIVES

EXPLORING AREA AND PERIMETER WITH GEOBOARDS

MATERIALS

- Geoboards
- Rubber bands (geobands)
- Geoboard dot paper (Appendix and CD-ROM)

PROCEDURE

1. The distance between two adjacent nails is considered a unit of length •–• (as it appears on the geoboard). What is the perimeter for the first row?

Activity Continues

2. Make a figure with a perimeter of 6, 7, 10. Figures need right angles. How many different ways can you construct figures with a perimeter of 8?
3. Make the smallest square possible. This is called one square unit of area. Can you make squares with areas of 1 through 16?
4. Make these figures on a geoboard: perimeter 12, area 9; perimeter 8, area 4; perimeter 12, area 8.
5. Make the smallest right triangle possible. What is the area of the triangle? Construct a square on each side of the triangle. What is the area of each square? What is the relationship between these areas? Can you prove the Pythagorean theorem $a^2 + b^2 = c^2$? On a 10×10 geoboard investigate more right triangles.

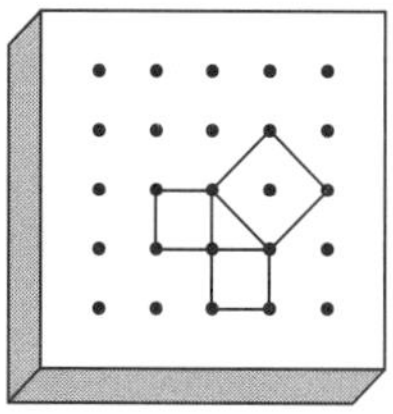

6. Consider line segment $\overline{MN}$. Can you predict the area of the square which has this line segment as one side? Can you predict the area of the right triangle that has this line segment as one side?

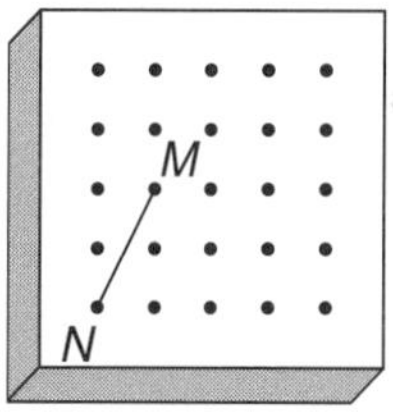

7. How many square units are in the figures below?

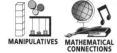

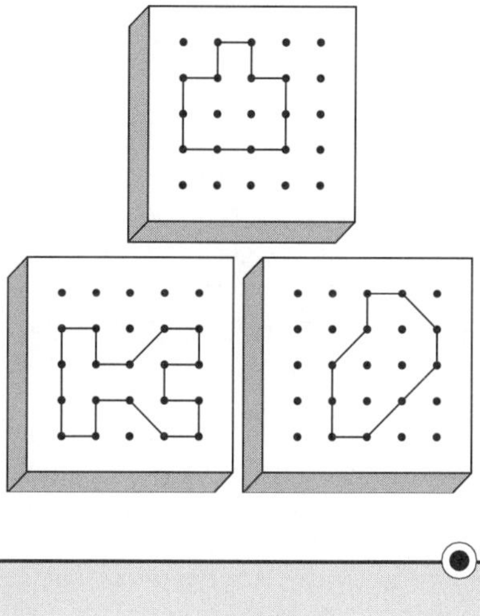

Activity 6.26

MANIPULATIVES

ADDITIONAL ACTIVITIES FOR AREA WITH GEOBOARDS

MATERIALS

- Geoboards
- Rubber bands (geobands)
- Geoboard dot paper (Appendix and CD)

PROCEDURE

1. Make the smallest square. How many nails touch the rubber band? How many nails are inside?
2. Stretch the band around five nails. What is the area of this shape? How many nails touching (*T*)? How many nails are inside (*I*)? Repeat questions with six nails. Continue in a similar manner. Develop these data into a table:

Area (*A*)	Nails Touching (*T*)	Nails Inside (*I*)

3. What patterns do you see? What can you predict?
4. Keep the number of nails inside as zero and increase the number of nails touching. What effect does this have on the area? Why? What patterns can be found?
5. Keep the number of nails touching as four and vary the number of nails inside. What effect does this have on the area? Why? What patterns can be seen?
6. If there is a relationship between these two variables, can a function be found to express that relationship?
7. Form a right triangle on the geoboard such as a base of 2 and a height of 3. Find the area by enclosing this figure with a rectangular region. Describe the area of the triangle.

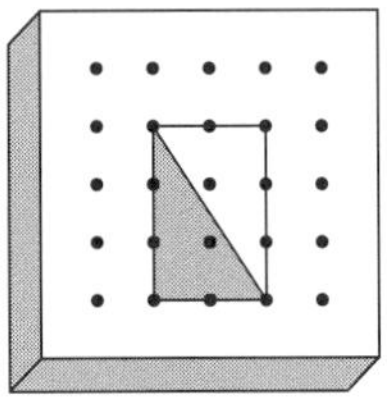

8. Form an acute triangle with a base of 3 and a height of 2. Find the area by enclosing this figure with two rectangles. Inside each rectangle is a right triangle. Since the area of a right triangle is half the area of the surrounding rectangle, add the two areas together to find the total area of the acute triangle. Check using the formula for area of triangle: $A = \frac{1}{2}bh$.

Activity Continues

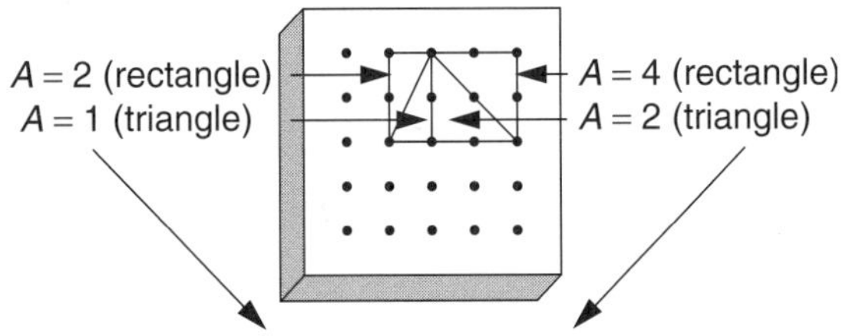

1 + 2 = 3 total area of acute triangle.

9. Form a parallelogram. Form a rectangle around it and find the area of the rectangle. Children can see the relationship between the two figures and how the area formula for a parallelogram, $A = h \times b$, is computed.

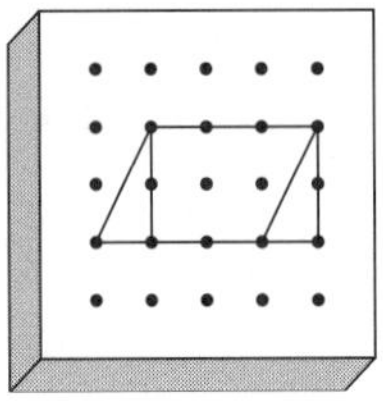

10. Write a formula to find the area of any region using the number of nails touching (*T*) and the number of nails inside (*I*). This formula is known as Pick's theorem. Check the area of the triangle in step 8. It is $T = 6$, $I = 1$, so $T/2 + I - 1$ (constant) = area, or $6/2 + 1 - 1 = 3$.

Coordinate Geometry

Geoboards can also be used to practice geometry and ordered pairs. The arrangement of nails or pegs on the geoboard can provide a grid in which each place denotes a point and each point is labeled from 0 to 4 (Figure 6.14). A strip of tape with the points labeled may help remind students of the numbers. The ordered pair notation of (1, 3) would refer to "over one

FIGURE 6.14

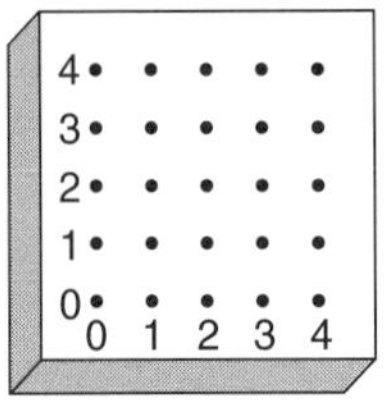

Geoboard with coordinates.

peg and up three pegs." Connecting cubes can be placed over a chosen peg or nail. Working in pairs, students guess where the cube or cubes are located on the unseen geoboard in the same way that the game Battleship is played. Another activity is to create a shape or design on the geoboard with a rubber band and, using ordered pair notation, have the child describe that shape to a partner who either makes the figure on a geoboard or on geometric dot paper. This encourages precise language and accuracy of naming the coordinates.

Activity 6.27

PROBLEM SOLVING

WHAT IS THE FIGURE?

MATERIALS

- Geoboards
- Rubber bands (geobands)
- Geoboard dot paper (Appendix and CD)

PROCEDURE

1. Connect these nails and record the figure formed:
   (1,1), (1,2), (1,3), (2,1), (2,4), (3,1), (3,2), (3,3)
2. Connect these nails and record the figure formed:
   (0,0), (1,0), (1,1), (2,1), (2,2), (3,2), (3,3), (4,3), (4,4)
3. Make a shape, record the coordinate pairs, and ask a friend to record the figure formed.

These activities only begin to illustrate the many experiences that can be provided for studying plane geometry in an informal way. Spatial visualization is an important aspect of geometric problem solving. The study of geometry should focus heavily on concrete and pictorial experiences. Students also need opportunities to explore scale drawings, illustrate tessellations, develop appropriate mathematical language, and investigate geometric properties through constructions.

Geometric Constructions

Constructions are geometric drawings of angles and figures using a protractor, compass, and straightedge (a ruler without markings). Constructions with a protractor or a compass are generally delayed until middle school grades.

A *protractor* is a tool used to measure angles. To understand measuring angles, children should have experiences with Logo where they move the turtle by degrees or turn themselves or the hands of a clock. Students can see the effect of enlarging the size of the angle and compare how far they must move their arms or the hands of a clock to get certain angles. Without such preparation, they are unsure about what an angle is, and are misled about the length of the sides. Often children say that angle *MNO* (Figure 6.15) is greater than angle *xyz* because they are comparing the length of the sides.

FIGURE 6.15

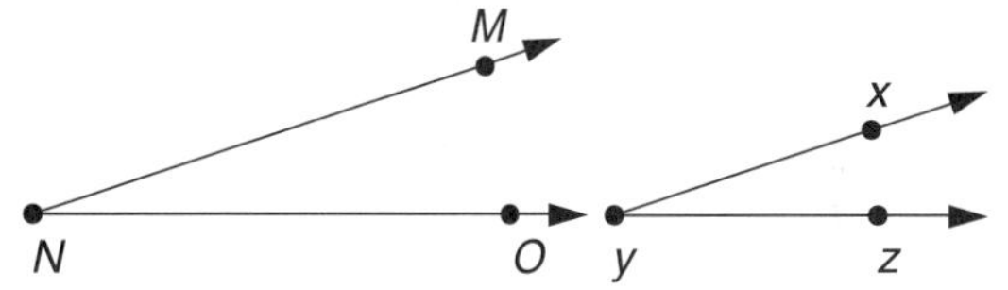

Comparing size of angles.

Students need to feel comfortable extending the length of the sides of an angle for a better measurement. Using a protractor (Figure 6.16) correctly means the child must know two things:

1. How to place the center of the protractor on the vertex of the angle.
2. How to read the degrees on the protractor by moving the eyes from the vertex of the angle to the degrees of the angle along the edge.

FIGURE 6.16

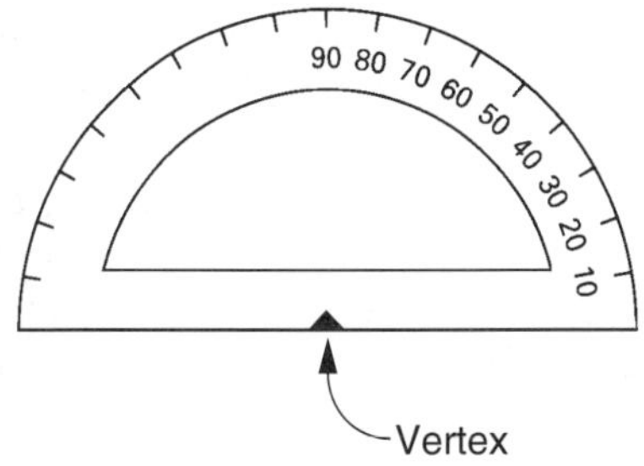

Protractor.

This is particularly important with circular protractors and those with two sets of numbers in the half-circle formation. Include measuring angles shown in various positions, not just angles with one side on a horizontal line. Angles of shapes should be measured to learn that the sum of the measures of the angles of a triangle is 180 degrees and that the angles of a quadrilateral sum to 360 degrees.

Billstein (1998) suggests making a real-world application by exploring angles used in designing airport runways. A device called a goniometer shows angles as an amount of rotation. Billstein also describes many extension activities using compasses.

A *compass* is a measurement tool that is used to make circles or portions of circles. One uses a compass by placing the spike of the compass at the center point of the circle. The measure from the spike to the pencil is the radius of the circle; it is that distance which is measured on the compass. A compass may be difficult for students to manipulate because it takes a certain amount of coordination to swirl the compass around the radial point without slippage. A purchased compass (Figure 6.17) usually has two

FIGURE 6.17

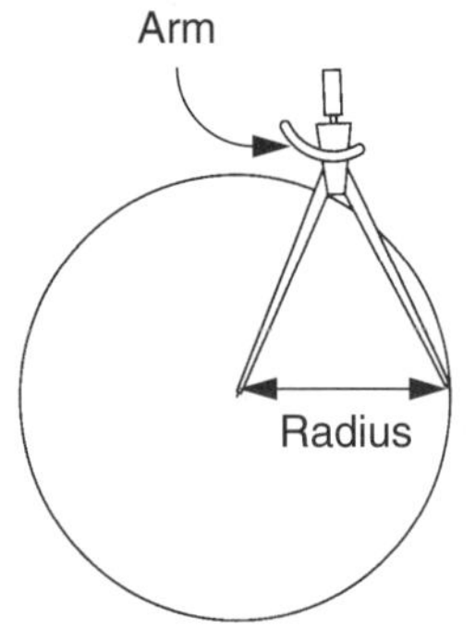

Compass for constructing circles.

measurement systems, one on either side of the arm. The metric system (in centimeters) is on one side and the standard English measurement (in inches) is on the other side.

With many geometry topics being explored in the NCTM *Principle and Standards,* the traditional focus on geometric constructions has decreased. Properties of shapes are developed through spatial skills and visual imagery. Compass, straightedge, and protractor construction tools are being reconsidered to be replaced by Mira, Logo, and geometric dot paper. Edwards, Bitter, and Hatfield (1990) provide ideas for using geometric constructions with computers.

Literature. The world of geometry abounds in many wonderful children's books. In addition to the books mentioned throughout the chapter, you should try these books for discussing shapes and properties: *The Greedy Triangle* (Burns, 1994); *Shapes, Shapes, Shapes* (Hoban, 1986); *A Cloak for the Dreamer* (Friedman, 1994); and *Color Zoo* (Ehlert, 1989). Other aspects of geometry can be investigated through angle explorations in *Angles Are Easy as Pie* (Froman, 1976) and through various types of symmetry in *What Is Symmetry?* (Emberley, 1970).

As mentioned earlier, quilts and tangrams provide enriching activities to promote geometric ideas with such books as *The Tangram Magician* (Ernst and Ernst, 1990), *The Patchwork Quilt* (Flourney, 1985), and *Sweet Clara and the Freedom Quilt* (Hopkinson, 1992). The mathematics that can be applied in art and design exists in cultural books, historical books, interior design and architecture resources, and numerous other connections.

ASSESSMENT

Field-Independent Learners

Students who process information successively (from the parts to the whole) perform geoboard activities better if the area of the polygon to be measured is partitioned into segments within the polygon and then all the segments will be added up to find the total area. The left geoboard in Figure 6.18 shows a

FIGURE 6.18

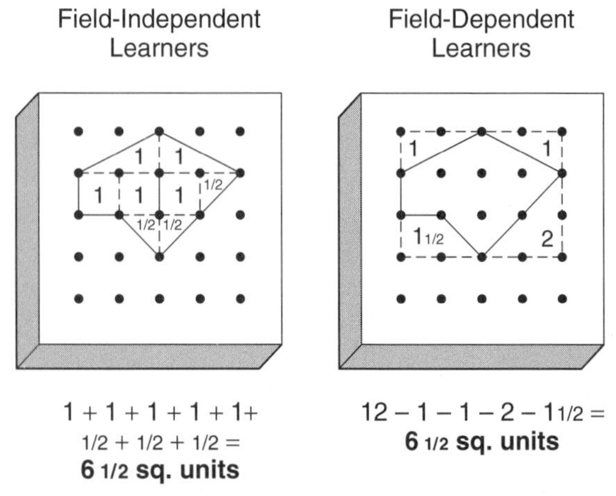

How different learners approach area with geoboards.

sample activity as a field-independent learner would perform it. The solid black line identifies the original polygon. The student uses smaller geobands to divide the figure into unit segments.

Field-Dependent Learners

Students who process information simultaneously (from the whole to the individual parts) perform geoboard activities better if the polygon to be measured is included in a whole rectangular frame from which the outer segments can be subtracted. The remaining polygon inside the solid black line is the square area measurement. The geoboard on the right of Figure 6.18 shows the action movements as a field-dependent learner would perform them.

Students with special needs may have trouble obtaining correct answers to area geoboard problems when doing the calculations one of the ways shown in Figure 6.18. Encourage them to try the other learning processing style. Frequently, the change helps correct the misconceptions. This seems to hold true for all students—not just elementary ones. The authors have watched adult learners profit from a change in learning processing style when errors occurred in geoboard activities. If the geoboard activities in this chapter seemed difficult, try doing them again, using the opposite learning/processing style.

Correcting Common Misconceptions

Angle Identification. Some students do not recognize an angle as the same if it is rotated. Students need many experiences making their own angles. Remember the video called "Shape Sort" showing such situations? There are a sizable number of middle school and high school students who do not recognize a right triangle unless the 90 degree angle is in the lower left-hand corner of a triangle.

Angle Misconceptions with Protractors. With a protractor, draw several different shapes. It is difficult to know which angle is the significant one that will make the shape when turning the protractor. The same problem occurs in Logo when a person creates a polygon because the turtle must make the exterior angle first and then make the interior angle that gives the polygon its shape.

Many interesting insights into children's mathematical thinking occur in geometric explorations. On the CD-ROM explore what children's work tells us about their mathematical understanding.

EXTENDED ACTIVITIES

Name of Activity

- What Did You Discover?
- TIMSS Assessment: Shiloh's Doghouse

PORTFOLIO

SUMMARY

The role of geometry in the elementary school curriculum is a topic of continuing debate. Research has clearly demonstrated that the responses we make to our world are influenced by our perceptions and visual images. Developing children's spatial skills and visualization abilities helps promote children's progress in mathematics. Gardner (1985) calls spatial intelligence one of the neglected areas of intelligence. He says that spatial intelligence "entails a number of loosely related capacities: the ability to recognize instances of the same element; the ability to transform or to recognize a transformation of one element into another; the capacity to conjure up a graphic likeness of spatial information" (p. 176).

Geometry relates directly to real-world experiences and should be a central topic for student investigations; however, teachers frequently omit the topic or delay it for a quick teaching lesson at the end of the year if time remains. The present move to create replacement topics to supplement or supplant textbooks has produced a rich set of geometry units. Marilyn Burns (1994), TERC (Technical Educational Research Center), *Connected Mathematics Project* (1996), and *Mathematics in Context* (1997) are just a few of these units now available. Many of the units were generated from projects funded by the National Science Foundation and represent field-tested materials. Check the chapter Bibliography for additional information. Additional chapters in this book continue the geometric approach to mathematics and extend it to other topics.

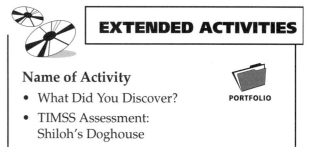

EXERCISES

For extended exercises, see the CD-ROM.

A. Memorization and Comprehension Exercises
Low-Level Thought Activities

1. Examine an elementary textbook series and list the solids covered during the first nine grades of school. Make a sketch of each one and list its properties. Write about how three-dimensional shapes extend to two-dimensional shapes.
2. Piaget's research indicates that children first have a topological view of the world rather than a Euclidean view. What does this mean to the classroom teacher and to the developmental sequence of geometric topics?
3. Explain how the geoboard can be used to teach and show the area formula for a right triangle and for a parallelogram.

B. Application and Analysis Exercises
Middle-Level Thought Activities

1. What material do you feel would be the best medium for teaching perimeter to children? Why do you prefer this material?
2. Apply this simulation as if you were the teacher: It appears that you will not complete the book this year. You need to project your end-of-year plans and discuss them with your principal. The next chapter is geometry followed by a chapter on multiplication with larger numbers. You are certain you cannot cover both chapters in the remaining time. Decide what position you will take—skip geometry or skip the last chapter on multiplication, or invent a creative solution. Defend your position as you would before your principal.
3. To reinforce mathematical connections:
   a. List five mathematical questions/problems that come from popular storybooks for children. Show how they are related to the topics of this chapter.
   b. List five ways to use the topics of this chapter when teaching lessons in reading, science, social studies, health, music, art, physical education, or language arts (writing, English grammar, poetry, and so on).

C. Synthesis and Evaluation Exercises
High-Level Thought Activities

1. Create your own lesson plan for teaching one concept using geometry. Follow these steps:
   a. Look at the NCTM *Standards.* Take a traditional grade-level textbook and compare the concepts covered and the instructional strategies for teaching geometry to the recommendations in the *Standards.* Write a paper about your observations.
   b. Use current articles from professional journals to help plan the direction of the lesson. Document your sources.
   c. Include at least one computer software program as a part of the lesson. Show how it will be integrated with the rest of the lesson.
2. Of the three types of motion geometry (translation, reflection, and rotation) which would you think to be the most difficult to teach? Design a lesson plan to teach this concept to sixth graders.
3. Design three geometry activities that incorporate multicultural linkages. Prepare assessment ideas that promote the Equity Principle.

BIBLIOGRAPHY

For an extended bibliography, see the CD-ROM.

Battista, Michael T., and Douglas H. Clements. "Geometry and Spatial Reasoning." Ed. Douglas Grouws. *Handbook of Research on Mathematics Teaching and Learning.* Reston, VA: National Council of Teachers of Mathematics, 1992. 420–464.

Bay, Jennifer M., Ann M. Bledsoe, and Robert E. Reys. "Stateing the Facts: Exploring the United States." *Mathematics Teaching in the Middle School* 4 (September 1998): 8–14.

Beaton, Albert E., Ian V. S. Smith, Michael O. Martin, Eugenio J. Gonzalez, Dana L. Kelly, and Teresa A. Smith. *Mathematics Achievement in the Middle School Years: IEA's Third International Mathematics and Science Study* (TIMSS). Chestnut Hill, MA: TIMSS International Study Center, Boston College, 1996.

Billstein, Rick. "You Are Cleared to Land." *Mathematics Teaching in the Middle Grades* 3 (May 1998): 452–456.

Bradley, Claudette. "The Four Directions Indian Beadwork Design with Logo." *Arithmetic Teacher* 39 (May 1992): 46–48.

Burger, William F., and Michael Shaughnessy. "Characterizing the van Hiele Levels of Development in Geometry."

Journal for Research in Mathematics Education 17 (January 1986): 31–48.

Burns, Marilyn. *The Math Solution: Teaching for Mastery through Problem Solving.* Sausalito, CA: Marilyn Burns Education Associates, 1984.

———. *Math By All Means.* Sausalito, CA: Math Solution Publications, 1994.

Carey, Deborah A. "The Patchwork Quilt: A Context for Problem Solving." *Arithmetic Teacher* 40 (December 1992): 199–203.

Carroll, William M. "Geometric Knowledge of Middle School Students in a Reform-based Mathematics Curriculum." *School Science and Mathematics* 98 (April 1998): 188–195.

Clements, Douglas H., and Michael T. Battista. "Geometry and Spatial Sense." Ed. Douglas A. Grouws. *Handbook of Research on Mathematics Teaching and Learning.* New York: Macmillan: 420–464.

Connected Mathematics Project. East Lansing, MI: Michigan State University, 1996.

Del Grande, John, Lorna Morrow, Douglas Clements, John Firkins, and Jeane Joyner. *Geometry and Spatial Sense.* Reston, VA: National Council of Teachers of Mathematics, 1993.

Duke, Charlotte. "Tangrams and Area." *Mathematics Teaching in the Middle School* 3 (May 1998): 485–487.

Edwards, Nancy Tanner, Gary G. Bitter, and Mary M. Hatfield. "Measurements in Geometry with Computers." *Arithmetic Teacher* 37 (February 1990): 64–67.

Forgione, Pascal D., Jr., ed. *Introduction to TIMSS: The Third International Mathematics and Science Study.* Washington, DC: U.S. Department of Education, 1997.

Fuys, David J., and Amy K. Liebov. "Geometry and Spatial Sense." Ed. Robert J. Jensen. *Research Ideas for the Classroom Early Childhood Mathematics.* Reston, VA: National Council of Teachers of Mathematics, 1993. 195–222.

Gardner, Howard. *Frames of Mind: The Theory of Multiple Intelligences.* New York: Basic Books, 1985.

Geddes, Dorothy, and Irene Fortunato. "Geometry: Research and Classroom Activities." Ed. Douglas T. Owens. *Research Ideas for the Classroom: Middle Grades Mathematics.* Reston, VA: National Council of Teachers of Mathematics, 1993. 199–222.

Harris, Jacqueline. "Using Literature to Investigate Transformations." *Teaching Children Mathematics* 4 (May 1998): 510–513.

Hart, Kathleen. "Which Comes First—Length, Area, or Volume?" *Arithmetic Teacher* 31 (May 1984): 16–18, 26–27.

Jackiw, Nicholas. *The Geometer's Sketchpad.* software. Berkeley, CA: Key Curriculum Press, 1995.

Jensen, Rosalie, and Deborah C. Spector. "Geometry Links the Two Spheres." *Arithmetic Teacher* 33 (April 1986): 13–16.

Kaiser, Barbara. "Explorations with Tessellating Polygons." *Arithmetic Teacher* 36 (December 1988): 19–24.

Kalb, Kristina Skatt. "Mathematics for the Twenty-First Century." *Teaching Children Mathematics* 1 (October 1994): 72–78.

Lamphere, Patricia. "Investigations: How Does It Look?" *Teaching Children Mathematics* (December 1994): 222–230.

Leeson, Neville J. "Improving Students' Sense of Three-Dimensional Shapes." *Teaching Children Mathematics,* 1 (September 1994): 8–11.

Mathematics in Context. Chicago: Encyclopaedia Britannica, 1997.

National Council of Teachers of Mathematics. *Curriculum and Evaluation Standards for School Mathematics.* Reston, VA: NCTM, 1989.

———. *Professional Standards for Teaching Mathematics.* Reston, VA: NCTM, 1991.

———. *Principles and Standards for School Mathematics.* Reston, VA: NCTM, 2000.

Onslow, Barry. "Pentominoes Revisited." *Arithmetic Teacher* 37 (May 1990): 5–9.

Strong, Dorothy S. (Mathematics Ed.). *Systemwide Objectives and Standards.* Vols. 1–3. Chicago: Board of Education of the City of Chicago, 1990.

Strutchens, Marilyn E., and Glendon W. Blume. "What Do Students Know about Geometry?" Eds. Patricia Ann Kenney and Edward A. Silver. *Results from the Sixth Mathematics Assessment of the National Assessment of Educational Progress.* Reston: VA: National Council of Teachers of Mathematics, 1997. 165–193.

Sunburst Communications. *Geometric Supposer.* software. Pleasantville, NY: Sunburst Communications, 1997.

Taylor, Lyn. "Exploring Geometry with the Geometer's Sketchpad." *Arithmetic Teacher* 39 (November 1992): 187–191.

Technical Educational Research Center (TERC). *Investigations in Number, Data, and Space.* Palo Alto, CA: Dale Seymour Publications, 1993.

Texas Instruments. *Cabri.* software. Dallas: TX: Texas Instruments, 1997.

Usiskin, Zalman. "Resolving the Continuing Dilemmas in School Geometry." In *Learning and Teaching Geometry, K–12,* 1987 Yearbook of the National Council of Teachers of Mathematics. Reston, VA: National Council of Teachers of Mathematics, 1987. 17–31.

Williams, Julian. "Geometry and Art." Ed. David Nelson, George Gheverghese Joseph, and Julian Williams. *Multicultural Mathematics: Teaching Mathematics from a Global Perspective.* Oxford, Eng.: Oxford University Press, 1993.

Zaslovsky, Claudia. "People Who Live in Round Houses." *Arithmetic Teacher* 37 (September 1989): 18–24.

———. "Symmetry in American Folk Art." *Arithmetic Teacher* 38 (September 1990): 6–12.

CHILDREN'S LITERATURE

Burns, Marilyn. *The Greedy Triangle.* New York: Scholastic, 1994.

Ehlert, Lois. *Color Zoo.* New York: J. B. Lippincott, 1989.

Emberley, Edward. *What Is Symmetry?* Boston: Little, Brown, 1970.

Ernst, Lisa Campbell, and Lee Ernst. *The Tangram Magician.* New York: Harry N. Abrams, 1990.

Friedman, Aileen. *A Cloak for the Dreamer.* New York: Scholastic, 1994.

Flourney, Valerie. *The Patchwork Quilt.* New York: Dial Books, 1985.

Froman, Robert. *Angles Are Easy As Pie.* New York: Crowell, 1976.

Lacapa, Michael, and Kathleen Lacapa. *Less Than Half, More Than Whole.* Flagstaff, AZ: Northland Publishing, 1994.

Tompert, Ann. *Grandfather Tang's Stories: A Tale Told with Tangrams.* New York: Crown Publishers, 1990.

Integrating Technology

Video Vignettes: Lesson Plans in Action

- *Making Tangrams*
- *Shape Sort*
- *Pizza Perimeters*

Supporting the NCTM *Principles and Standards* (2000):

- Analysis of Teaching and Learning; Teacher's Role in Discourse; Tools for Enhancing Discourse—The Teaching and Learning Principles

Computer Software Resources

...for Geometry and Spatial Sense

Internet Searches

Surfing the Internet for Geometry Topics

Use the World Wide Web (WWW) and navigate through the system, searching for new information under major headings and subheadings similar to the following:

Mathematics Education
- Geometry
  - Middle School
  - Elementary School
  - Primary
  - NSF Projects
  - Programs
- NCTM
  - Geometry

Go to The Geometry Forum at **forum.swarthmore.edu/math.topics.html**

Go to The Geometry Center at **www.geom.umn.edu.**

- *Remember...* the Web is fluid ... new topics and ways to search for topics change daily.
- Be adventurous ... think of some new things you could try.

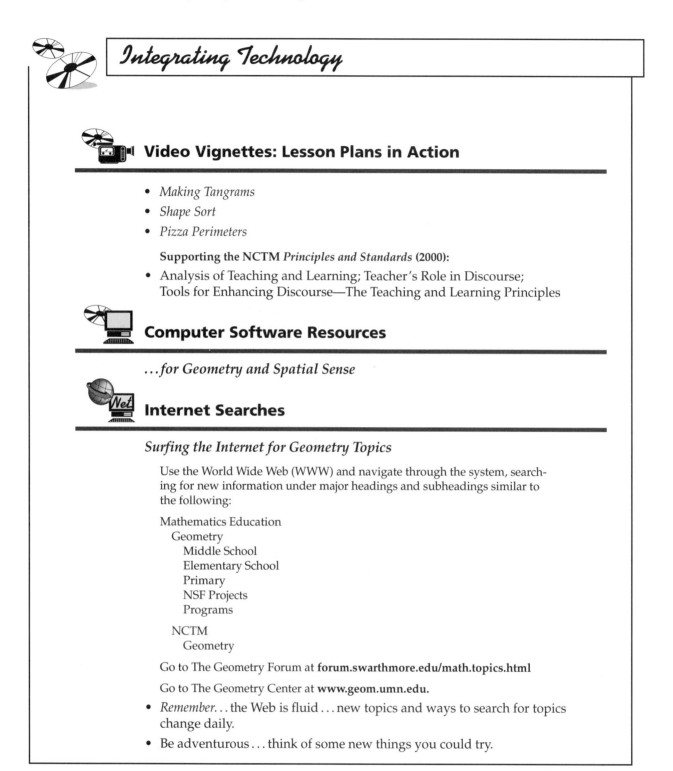

7

Measurement

Activities Index

IN THE TEXT

ON CD-ROM

In the last chapter, we developed an intuitive understanding of shapes, objects, and their relationships. Now we will explore the use of numbers and formulas to describe the world around us; in later chapters, we will use these measurement applications in problem-solving situations.

People have always measured things in the world around them. Cave dwellers judged distances by time or eye, and they compared sizes by paces or matched objects with trees, stones, or other objects common to their surroundings. There was no accuracy in that world.

As needs grew, greater accuracy was required. In order to measure clothing, weapons, and other items, rough methods of measurement were developed. Outstretched arms, heights, feet, and hands were all used for measuring. These measures differed between people and, therefore, were nonstandard. All persons had their own method of measuring. In 6000 B.C., the first known standards of measurement such as stones or feet or hands were established.

Today, measurement is used in many ways in our lives and is vital for communication. The sciences have always used measurement for communication. Most professions require measurement in some way or another. These uses vary in terms of scales, codes, numerals, and so on. For example, water hardness is measured in terms of mineral content, earthquake intensity is measured in terms of the Richter scale, and rock hardness is measured by Mohs' hardness scale. Oven and room temperatures are measured with a thermometer and may be controlled by a thermostat. Daily, people weigh themselves, cut measured material for sewing clothing, panel a room, figure the distance they have jogged, or mark off part of their yard for vegetable planting. So measurement can be different things to different people and professions.

In this book, we are emphasizing the measurement units of volume, capacity, length, mass, area, temperature, and time. Measurement procedures included are direct comparison (two and three objects), serialization, indirect comparisons, repeated measure (object used repeatedly for measurement), and select unit measures. These methods constitute the common elementary and middle school measurement curriculum.

MEASUREMENT AS A PROCESS

How Measurement Develops in the Curriculum

Measurement refers to a quality, not a quantity. In mathematics we attach qualities of measurement in order to describe them in one way with some amount of precision and accuracy independent of the particular measurement unit used. Estimation and approximate measurements need to be emphasized. "About," "close to," "nearly," "almost," and "approximately" are common terms used by children when discussing their measurements. "My finger is about 10 centimeters long," or "It is nearly one kilometer to my home." The following five measurement concepts are developed and honed in the elementary and middle school grades.

Direct Comparison. When teaching measurement we usually go through a procedure of comparison (indirect and direct), vocabulary, instrument use, and reading the instruments. Therefore, no matter what the measurement, we usually begin with direct comparisons. With children we say, "Andrea is taller than Mario"; "Maggie's chalk is longer than Juan's"; "My glass holds more than your glass." These direct comparisons are common at all levels, but especially in the primary grades. Direct comparison is done by comparing like units to one another. This process leads to such nonstandard measures as calling this book ten paper clips long or three chalkboard erasers long.

Indirect Comparison. But soon a need for communication becomes apparent, and the nonstandard measures are compared to standard measures. An example would be how many pencils long is a meter stick or how much clay is as much as one kilogram of butter. Measurement now has gone from general to specific units, and the general mechanics of measurement become apparent.

Seriation. Reading rulers, balances, scales, and containers requires some proficiency on the part of the student. Not only are numbers used, but labels of specific measure are also applied. For example, "The book is 15 cm wide," or "The coffee cup holds 250 mL." More generally, "I have a mass of 50 kg," or "I am 100 cm tall." These standard measures are now real to the student. The standard units require an awareness on the part of the student with estimation used for discussions or initial feelings. Proof and verification follow. For example, to prove that five cups of water is more than a liter of water, actual measurement can be done to prove the initial estimate. Experimentation and experience make these statements on estimation more accurate.

Frames of Reference. Therefore, students must have frames of reference for many of the standard units of measure. Specifically, the student must be able to discover that it is easier to measure a room in meters than millimeters or kilometers. The tools for measuring should have the same quality as the object being measured. Obviously, liters are not an appropriate tool for measuring distance, and grams are not an appropriate tool for measuring area.

Specific Types of Measurement. Because students now have feelings for taller than, shorter than, wider than, or bigger than, application and the language of measurement must be developed. Remember, children need as much help in building the language of measurement as they do in building the concept of counting. Once a general language of measurement has been accomplished, the language is refined to be more specific.

The types of measurement include length, mass (weight), volume, capacity, area, temperature, and time. These are the most common measurement topics in the elementary and middle school. General activities for introducing each of the concepts are essential, and numerous approaches are necessary for understanding. Therefore, building language, questioning techniques, and activities for each topic should be established.

There are two common measurement systems in the world. The United States uses the customary

Subscripts © . . . *little thoughts below the bottom line*

system and some metric, and most of the world uses the metric system exclusively. Most elementary textbooks include both systems, with each system taught separately and with no conversion of one system to the other. Consequently, the approach of this book is to treat each system independently of the other.

If you are wondering what a decameter is after reading the cartoon, you need the following refresher activity of reviewing the system of metric measurement. You may have also forgotten the standard or customary English measurement system. The customary system, often thought of as the English system until England adopted the metric system, has been the basic measurement system of the United States. People tend to forget such things as how many feet are in a mile, and so forth. This is understandable, of course, since most people do not have a real-world necessity to measure how many feet are in a mile. If you feel you need a refresher course on the customary system of measurement, it is available, along with the metric system, on the CD-ROM.

Check Your Mathematics Knowledge

- On Customary System of Measurement
- On Metric System of Measurement

. . . a refresher from mathematics content coursework . . . Lest you forget!

How the Roots of Measurement Develop in the Curriculum

Before 6000 B.C., everybody had their own method of measurement. Many were quite different from each other. There was no known standard unit of measurement. People realized a standard was needed. The first known standards of measurement were stones, feet, and hands. The ancestors of the African Americans and the ancestors of the Native Americans were the first peoples to develop systems of standard measurement.

The Teacher's Role in Cultural Awareness. The following curriculum activity outlines what children can understand and should know at different grade level points in elementary and middle school. It is up to you, the teacher, to be cognizant of these knowledge levels and present the cultural awareness that is developmentally appropriate for each age group.

Cultural Contributions

CULTURAL RELEVANCE FOR MEASUREMENT

The following material developed by the Chicago Public Schools should be shared with students at each of the appropriate grade levels.

K–3

Students should know that systems of measurement originated in ancient civilizations in response to real-life situations. For example, the annual flooding of the Nile River in Africa created a need to measure the area of triangles, rectangles, and circles. The unit of measure was the length of an early pharaoh's forearm. The 24-hour day—12 hours of day and 12 hours of night—originated in Egypt.

4–5

Students should know that systems of measurement originated in ancient civilizations in response to real-life situations. For example, the annual flooding of the Nile River in Africa created a need to measure and resurvey field boundaries after the flood. The building of the pyramids created a need to develop formulas for the volume of pyramids. The unit of measure was the cubit, the length of an early pharaoh's forearm. The 24-hour day—12 hours of day and 12 hours of night—originated in Egypt.

6–8

Students should be able to understand that systems of measurement were developed in response to the needs of real-life situations. For example, the building of the African pyramids required extremely accurate measurement to construct right angles in the base so that any error would be less than 1 part in 27,000 or 1/27,000. The unit of measure was the cubit, the length of an early pharaoh's forearm. The idea of a 24-hour day—12 hours of day and 12 hours of night—originated in Egypt. The Babylonians of

Activity Continues

Mesopotamia established the time measures of 60 seconds to 1 minute and 60 minutes to 1 hour. Native Americans, especially the Inca, Maya, and Aztec, developed a system of measures that was so accurate that they were able to lay out miles of direct highways across high mountains and rugged terrain. The Ashanti of Ghana used standard gold weights to calibrate their scales with the accuracy required by their extensive commerce (Strong, 1990).

Supporting the NCTM *Principles and Standards* (2000):

- Mathematics as Connections, Communication
- Oral Discourse of Teacher and Student; Worthwhile Mathematical Tasks—The Teaching Principle
- The Equity Principle

Creating Mathematical Connections to History. Piaget felt that tracing the order of development of mathematical concepts in history was a strong indicator of how the human brain develops its own cognitive structures. He pointed to the fact that different cultures, totally separated from one another, emerged with the remarkably similar developmental order of mathematical concepts and understandings (Piaget, 1989). This is most clearly seen in mathematics because language and customs do not get in the way of tracing a culture's ability to problem solve and reason.

Constructivists see wisdom in letting children explore mathematics like their foreparents did. They believe that if all cognitive structures develop in a similar order from stage to stage, students will move from one developmental stage to the next more effectively if asked to reconstruct the knowledge themselves (Brooks and Brooks, 1993). Therefore, activities like the following one are encouraged.

Activity 7.1

CREATING YOUR OWN NEED FOR STANDARD MEASUREMENT TOOLS

MATERIALS

- Student's own body and any piece of furniture in the classroom.

Activity Continues

DIRECTIONS

1. The following is a lesson plan dialogue created by one teacher. Plan your own dialogue lesson after reading the example.

   "We are going to measure things today the way people did long ago before the ancestors of African Americans and Native Americans thought of a better way. Let's see if we can figure out why the ancient people of Egypt and the Mayans of Central America had to come up with a better way to measure things."
2. *Ask:* "How many different ways can you measure the length and width of your desk using your body?" Have every student do this at least five different ways.
3. Compare and contrast the measurements after all students have had a chance to orally describe what they found with their measurements.
4. Then create a scenario like this one:
   "Let's say I have to go to the furniture store to replace a certain desk in the classroom that just fits in a certain spot. It has to be the exact measurements, and I cannot take it with me. I tell the store owner that the desk is the same length as Tojan's foot (take any one of the students' body measurements they have just used). Tojan cannot go with me and the store owner does not know Tojan. What could I do?"
5. Let the students problem solve a variety of solutions. Eventually someone will say you should take a paper copy of Tojan's foot so the store owner could see the correct measurement. Now it is time to do the drawing in Figure 7.1.

FIGURE 7.1

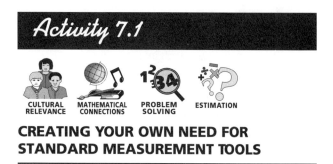

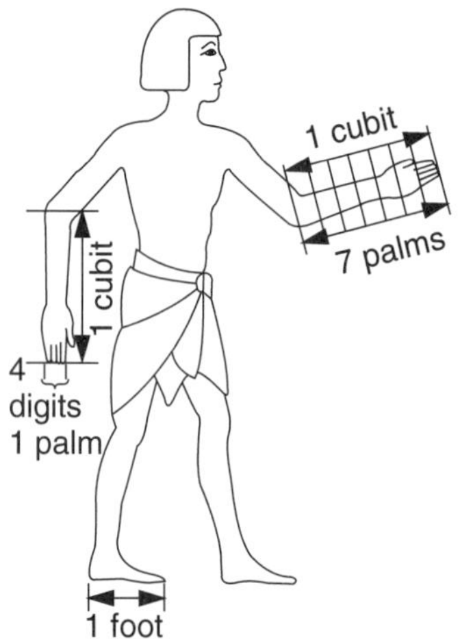

Standard ancient measurements.

Now you can explain that the students have shown that they are just as great as the ancient mathematicians were. Explain that the measurements first standardized were based on Pharaoh's body measurements because he was the famous king.

Activity Continues

6. *Now ask:* "What happened when one Pharaoh died and some other king with different body measurements came to power?" Elicit from the students' comments that the ancient people standardized even further to make a foot always the same measurement no matter what. Explain that that is how we have the name "foot" for 12 inches in our system.
7. Ask them what body parts they think an inch might have been in the old days. This is not a hard answer when the students are looking at a poster like the picture in Figure 7.1.

TEACHING STRATEGIES

Measurement concepts should build on the informal spatial understanding that children naturally have. A firm foundation in measurement concepts shows children the interconnectedness of measurement and geometry. The NCTM *Principles and Standards* (NCTM, 2000) emphasize that measurements should have real-world applications and be embedded in everyday situations. Some important components of measurement experiences are estimation and acquiring a sense of appropriate units of measure (Box 7.1). Performance on national tests indicates a lack of concentration in the area of measurement and that all students suffer from a lack of an intensive, in-depth study of measurement.

Linear Measurement

In order to teach linear measurements, activities should begin with concepts familiar to children.

Direct Comparison. Direct comparison activities on height, width, and length can be achieved with their bodies, pencils, and miscellaneous objects. Comparison of lengths, such as one object being longer, shorter, or the same as another, is essential. Comparisons should be followed by nonstandard measures such as strides, digits, palms, or paces. The children may compare their own strides with those of others in the class. Results should indicate to the children a need for a standard measure, like the cultural relevance activity at the end of the previous section. The nonstandard units can be coordinated with standard measures by discovering how many pennies long a meter stick is or how many paper clips wide a book is.

Indirect Comparison. Children eventually find that the use of some unit of measure helps them in making comparisons. Before children enter school, they begin using body parts as measuring units.

BOX 7.1 Curriculum and Evaluation Standards

Estimation

In grades K–4, the mathematics curriculum should include estimation so students can—

- Apply estimation in working with quantities, measurement, computation, and problem solving.

Measurement

In grades K–4, the mathematics curriculum should include measurement so that students can—

- Understand the attributes of length, capacity, weight, area, volume, time, temperature, and angle.
- Make and use estimates of measurement.
- Make and use measurements in problem and everyday situations.

In grades 5–8, the mathematics curriculum should include extensive concrete experiences using measurement so that students can—

- Extend their understanding of the process of measurement.
- Estimate, make, and use measurements to describe and compare phenomena.
- Select appropriate units and tools to measure to the degree of accuracy required in a particular situation.
- Understand the structure and use of systems of measurement.
- Extend their understanding of the concepts of perimeter, area, volume, angle measure, capacity, and weight and mass.
- Develop the concept of rate and other derived and indirect measurements.
- Develop formulas and procedures for determining measures to solve problems.

Source: National Council of Teachers of Mathematics, 1989, pp. 36, 51, 116.

At first children use units that are larger than the objects being compared or measured and later move to smaller units counting how many smaller units are in the object being measured. Finally, although the body is still indirectly involved, children begin using various objects as the unit of measure.

Working with parts of units is preliminary to working with standard units, such as inches, feet, and yards. The more ways in which children learn to divide nonstandard unit measurements into parts, the better prepared they will be to understand how to use standard units of measure.

After working with nonstandard units of measure, they soon find that the same type unit differs in length (people's feet differ), and consequently different people measuring the same object obtain different results. As the need to interpret and communicate measurements arises, the usefulness of these conventional standard units becomes clear. We now use a ruler marked in standard units to measure length.

Seriation. Some measurement items on the Sixth Assessment for NAEP (Kenney and Kouba, 1997) asked students to read measurements from pictorial representations of instruments such as rulers, scales, thermometers, gauges, and protractors. In general students in fourth grade had more difficulty reading instruments when the object to be measured was not aligned at the beginning of a ruler and when the scale on the instrument involved an increment other than one. Such findings are consistent with previous NAEP studies. Although scores improved greatly with ruler measurements (79 percent), by the time students were in eighth grade only 35 percent of these students obtained the correct angle measurements using a protractor. When students were asked how often they used measuring devices such as protractors, 52 percent of the eighth graders reported they had never used them!

An item on the TIMSS test asked students to approximate the length of a pencil that lay next to a ruler. The end of the pencil was resting at 3 cm and it extended beyond the centimeter ruler about a centimeter and a half. This was a multiple-choice item. Internationally, about half of the students (49 percent of the seventh graders and 52 percent of the eighth graders) were able to answer the question correctly. For U.S. students the percents answering correctly were 46 percent and 45 percent, respectively (Beaton et al., 1996). A constructed response item asked students to draw a rectangle whose length was one and one-half times the length of a given rectangle and whose width was half the width of that rectangle. A second part to the problem asked students to state the ratio of the area of the new rectangle to the area of the original rectangle. Only 24 percent of the seventh graders and 31 percent of the eighth graders were able to do the first part correctly. The second part proved even more difficult—only 6 percent of the seventh graders and 10 percent of the eighth graders were able to state a correct ratio. United States results were 11 percent and 16 percent for part one and 10 percent at both grade levels for part two (Beaton et al., 1996).

Students need to be instructed to use the ruler correctly by carefully aligning the beginning location and reading the length. First, they learn to read centimeters on the ruler. To practice this skill, the children could measure a piece of paper to find its length and width in centimeters.

Activity 7.2

PROBLEM SOLVING | ESTIMATION | MENTAL MATH

GUESSING METRIC MEASUREMENTS

DIRECTIONS

How good are you at guessing your metric measurements? For this activity you will need a meterstick and a piece of string.

PROCEDURE

1. Using string, have a partner cut a piece as long as you are tall. How does that length compare to your arm span?
2. Count how many times the string can be wrapped around your head, waist, ankles, wrist, neck, and thigh.
3. Cut a piece of string that you guess would go around your waist. Don't measure until you have cut the string. Now try it around your waist.

   How many centimeters off were you? ________ cm

   Your waist is ________ cm.
4. Repeat this activity for other parts of your body.

   Your neck = ________ cm. Answers will vary.

   Your wrist = ________ cm.

   Your thumb = ________ cm.
5. Your waist measures about ________ times your neck.

   Your waist measures about ________ times your wrist.

   Your waist measures about ________ times your thumb.

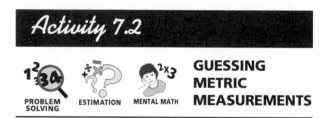

Activity Continues

6. Make a bar graph representing the different lengths of each body part.

Students need far more hands-on measurement practice than they usually receive in classrooms as noted by the assessment data reviewed in the preceding paragraphs. There is no substitute for hands-on measurement activities. Teachers are left to add additional activities from other sources since no one textbook for children includes the amount of activities needed. The NCTM Addenda Series, *Measurement in the Middle School for Grades 5–8* (Geddes, 1994) is one excellent resource. The following activity is one that is used by the authors with students as young as third grade and builds on the same ideas as the Addenda Series.

Activity 7.3

METRIC OLYMPICS

MATERIALS

- Task cards like the one in Figure 7.2

Activity Continues

- Cotton balls, straws, regular paper clips, plastic-coated paper clips, meter stick
- Clay and straight pins
- Pencil and paper

DIRECTIONS

1. Set up stations around the room for each Olympic activity: 1—Straw and Paper Clip Pole Vault; 2—Cotton Ball Shotput; 3—Straw Javelin Throw; 4—Standing Long Jump; 5—Metric Sponge Squeeze.
2. Use these words to start the activity:
   "Since the Greeks in ancient Europe, people have enjoyed the competition of the Olympics. Many people of Greek ancestry live in America today. We have their ancestors to thank for this fun activity."
3. Each student has a handout with the task cards to keep track of his or her score. An official score card is found at each of the four stations and each station has an official (student) as the recordkeeper. A child is assigned as the announcer who will do the commentary when a winner is determined. This supports speech across the curriculum. Each person keeps track of his or her own score and an awards ceremony can be planned for the winners in each category.
4. Addenda Series: *Measurement in the Middle Grades* (Geddes, 1994, p. 24) shows examples of other task cards that could be developed.

FIGURE 7.2

1. Stand at the throw line.
2. Attach a regular paper clip to the top of a straw.
3. Aim the straw, then tap the bottom to make the paper clip jump over the cross bar. Record your best measurement.
   Your best score: ____________cm (at height = ______)
   Your best score: ____________cm (at height = ______)
   Your best score: ____________cm (at height = ______)
4. Attach a plastic-coated paper clip to the top of a straw.
5. Tap the bottom of the straw aiming the paper clip over the cross bar. Did you notice a difference in the feel of the "pole?"
   If yes, which one was easiest to do? _______
   Your best score: ____________cm (at height = ______)
   Your best score: ____________cm (at height = ______)
   Your best score: ____________cm (at height = ______)
6. The official will raise the cross bar to the next level after each person on the team has had a chance to compete.
7. Do the activity again at the new height. Try this activity at three different heights.

A straw is raised and attached with straight pins to the straw poles. The base is molding clay.

Pole vault task card.

Activity Continues

Supporting the NCTM *Principles and Standards* (2000):

- Mathematics as Connections, Communication, Measurement
- Worthwhile Mathematical Tasks; Mathematics as Oral Discourse; Tools for Enhancing Discourse—The Teaching and Learning Principles

Using children's literature as an integration works well at times when more hands-on, real-world applications are needed. The literature suggestions at the end of this section (pages 156–157) give the reader many resources from which to develop more hands-on activities. Teachers can even connect books to measurement that do not have measurement as a theme. The following is a way to connect Dr. Suess's *Green Eggs and Ham* (Suess, 1963) to a centimeter activity with integration to graphing. This time it's green beans and ham.

Once there was a very small centimeter worm who was only 4 centimeters long. He heard that if a worm ate good food like vegetables and meat and a tall glass of milk, he could grow longer and longer and longer. So he'd crawl over to a dish of green beans and ham every day and gobble it all up. And do you know what happened? Each day he grew 2 centimeters longer! WOW!!! How long would he be at the end of 10 days?

Our centimeter worm learned something else too. Not only did he grow longer but he also gained weight! He was only 2 grams before he started his nutritious diet, but each day he ate his green beans and ham he would gain 3 grams. How much would he weigh at the end of 10 days?

Larger objects requiring meter measurements should then be introduced, as well as perimeter problems. An activity like the following one is an excellent time to introduce the trundle wheel to measure long lengths of more than a meter. Figure 7.3 shows how an innovative teacher can have the children make a trundle wheel out of heavy cardboard. Avino (1995) lists several clever ideas to use trundle wheels in playground activities with geometric shapes. Situations where the millimeter and kilometer would be used should also be introduced. The children should be made aware through illustration that the approximate measure depends on the unit used. As an example, one does not measure the size of a book in kilometers or the distance from Phoenix to Los Angeles in meters.

FIGURE 7.3

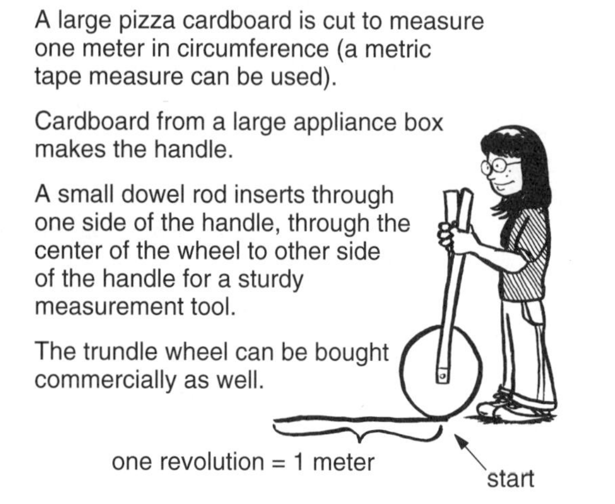

A large pizza cardboard is cut to measure one meter in circumference (a metric tape measure can be used).
Cardboard from a large appliance box makes the handle.
A small dowel rod inserts through one side of the handle, through the center of the wheel to other side of the handle for a sturdy measurement tool.
The trundle wheel can be bought commercially as well.
one revolution = 1 meter
start

Trundle wheel for large metric measurements.

Activity 7.4

ESTIMATION · MATHEMATICAL CONNECTIONS · CULTURAL RELEVANCE

ESTIMATION WITH LARGE MEASURES

DIRECTIONS

1. Have the class line up on a start line. At the signal to begin, all participants should go forward to their best estimate of a distance of 50 meters. Measure the results to determine the first three places based on those students nearest to 50 meters. Use the trundle wheel to measure.
2. Estimate other lengths using the same procedure as in number 1. Some meter lengths to use: 5 meters, 10 meters, 13 meters.
3. Metric Olympics could be planned for an entire class with activities such as a 25-meter measure, a 100-meter measure, or create a 1-kilogram clay ball.

Activity Continues

4. Have teams of students each estimate 1 hectare. Verify the estimations by measuring each other's estimate. Rank order the groups by best estimate.

Frames of Reference. Frames of reference should be established for each unit such as "The distance from the floor to my chin is 1 meter high"; "A dime is 1 millimeter thick"; "It is 1 kilometer from my home to school"; and "My little fingernail is 1 centimeter wide." Benchmarks are essential for establishing a comfortable feeling and a means of communication for distance measures.

The metric pack in Extended Activity on the CD-ROM stores typical frames of reference found in classrooms. Each child has similar packs to use in activities such as Weight with Foil Boats.

When students have gained facility with using standard units of measure, they will again begin finding discrepancies in measurements. They may even come to the conclusion that measurements can never be exact. Discussions and activities surrounding a theme of measurement accuracy are a natural. The following three activities on the CD-ROM are examples of ways to blend several topics together in a busy classroom.

EXTENDED ACTIVITIES

Name of Activity

CALCULATORS MATHEMATICAL CONNECTIONS

- Map Scales in Social Studies
- Metric Measurements
- Making a Metric Pack

Height measurement activities are also enjoyed by children, especially when they are hoping to grow daily. Rhone (1995) suggests many activities using unifix cubes and rubric assessment sheets. She has what she calls a "math author's chair" where students can sit to explain their solutions to problems for their classmates to hear. The authors suggest this idea has merit from a psychological view as well as a mathematical one. For young children and immature older students, this idea is especially appealing because it focuses attention on a particular spot in the room to which children can pay attention. Children hear fellow students answer questions from random places in the room all the time, and they may be inclined to overlook good answers as just another recitation for the teacher. This approach allows the child in the chair to take the time to develop a reasoned answer because, once in the chair, the child feels that he or she is given permission to stay longer to answer the question than a raised hand at the child's own desk would suggest.

Mass (Weight) Measurement

Mass and weight are often used interchangeably, but their meanings differ. Weight is related to the gravitational pull of the earth. It relates the action of a force (gravity, for example) on a mass. Mass remains the same regardless of location.

Children find measuring mass a more difficult concept to undertake than measuring distance. Therefore, the teaching of mass is usually accomplished through indirect comparisons, although direct comparisons are equally important.

Direct Comparison. Directly comparing trucks, cars, dolls, blocks, and miscellaneous toys by hand comparison is common. Seeing how much weight sinks a container is fun for children, especially since those activities involve water! The book, *Who Sank the Boat?* (Allen, 1982) presents an excellent anticipatory set before children make their own foil boats.

Activity 7.5

PROBLEM SOLVING MANIPULATIVES ESTIMATION MATHEMATICAL CONNECTIONS

WEIGHT WITH FOIL BOATS

MATERIALS

1. Children gather their own array of plastic toys, paper clips, and odds and ends found around the classroom.
2. Aluminum foil to make their own boats.
3. Charts and journals to record findings.
4. Metric packs—see CD-ROM.

DIRECTIONS

1. Children form their own foil boats.
2. They predict which item will sink their boat if they put items in the boat in a particular order. They then

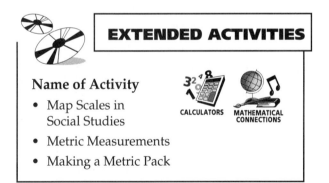

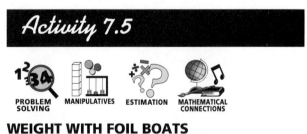

Activity Continues

change the order and predict again. Then they write journal entries to describe what happens.

FIGURE 7.4

Round #1 Order into Boat	 Mark When It Will Sink ✓ = Predict ☆ = Actual	Round #2 Order into Boat	 Mark When It Will Sink ✓ = Predict ☆ = Actual
1. 2. 3. 4. 5. 6.		1. 2. 3. 4. 5. 6.	

Journal Entry: What did you discover? Was your prediction correct?____________________________

Explain in your own words how the order and weight work together.____________________________

Chart and journal sheet for foil boat activity.

Supporting the NCTM *Principles and Standards* (2000):

- Mathematics as Problem Solving; Reasoning, Representations, Measurement
- Written Discourse by Students; Tools for Enhancing Discourse—The Teaching Principle
- The Assessment Principle

Indirect Comparison. Most comparisons are with the use of a balance, where object A is compared to the known mass piece and then object B is compared to the known mass piece. The end result is a statement that object A is more or less massive than object B and also that object A has a greater or smaller mass than the mass piece. This indirect comparison involves knowledge of a standard unit that should be introduced after nonstandard units. Some nonstandard materials that can be used in conjunction with a balance for units of mass (weight) are nails, pennies, interlocking cubes, and clay.

Activity 7.6

ESTIMATION MATHEMATICAL CONNECTIONS

FINDING MASS WITH A BALANCE IN SCIENCE

DIRECTIONS

1. Build a balance to find the mass of objects using pennies, interlocking cubes, or clay, and make comparisons to determine objects with the greater mass.

   For example: five nails have a greater mass than two pennies; or three pennies have the same mass as ten interlocking cubes.

FIGURE 7.5

Start with a plastic ruler. The cut-out parts are equidistant from each end and are measured more precisely than you can measure. This guarantees the balance will truly balance equivalent mass if cups are placed directly under the holes.

Glue wooden clothespins to plastic cups as shown. When dry, the cups will grasp the balance wherever you place them.

Drill a hole in the middle of a block of wood and screw in a wooden table leg.

Use a screw to tighten the ruler on to the table leg. Loosen the screw for easy storage. This set up costs a fraction of the price for commercial balances and will enable you to have more balances for your class.

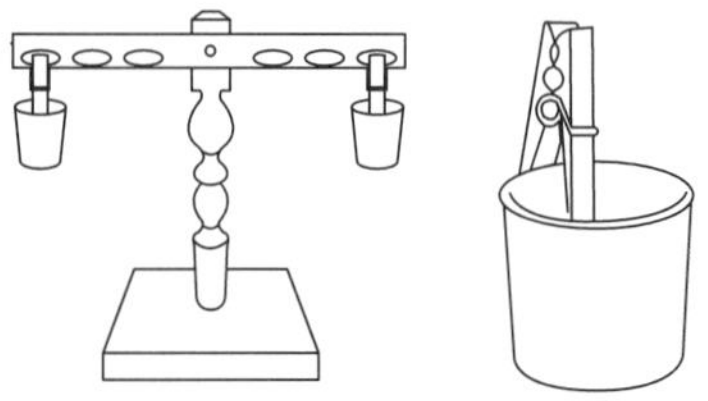

Building your own balance.

2. Estimate and record the answers before finding the actual mass.
3. Recordkeeping should indicate the status of the estimates. Hopefully, these estimates improve with experience.

Frames of Reference. After comparison of masses (weights), students will discover that a more standard measure is needed. Each measurement unit should be introduced in terms of a frame of reference. Refer to the metric pack on the CD for the frames of reference mass (weight).

A milligram has about the same mass as a drop of water. A nickel has a mass of about 5 grams. A kilogram is about the mass of this book and a tonne is used for heavy measures. As these frames of reference are developed through experimentation, ample time and instruction should be provided for students to read a balance as well as a scale. Obviously, the kilogram will mean more to students if they can record their own masses in kilograms. Smaller items, such as paper clips, nickels, and raisins can be measured in grams. The milligram and tonne are more difficult to introduce, but awareness can be realized by magazine articles, pictures, and stories indicating their use and establishing a sense of what they are.

In an attempt to improve estimation, the teacher may give statements that contain limits. Such statements might be "It has a mass of more than 1 gram but less than 5 grams," or "The student's mass is between 50 and 75 kilograms." Have several students ask which objects are about equal in mass, have the greater mass, or have the least mass.

Activity 7.7

CALCULATORS PROBLEM SOLVING

MASS WITH SILVER DOLLARS

DIRECTIONS

1. If a silver dollar has a mass of 18 grams, use a calculator to determine how much money you would have if you had a kilogram of silver dollars.
2. What would be the mass of 1000 silver dollars?
3. Use a calculator to determine how many silver dollars you are worth based on your mass.
4. Do the steps above using a nickel as the unit of measure.

The statements may be verified by actually finding each object's mass and recording it on a graph. Graph results should be discussed, and the original statements should be validated. These final procedures should help in understanding the measuring of mass.

One of the children's first encounters with the concept of mass (weight) measurement is comparing objects in their environment to see which is heavier. While the "hold-one-in-each-hand" method works well for objects that are quite different in mass (weight), more sophisticated methods must be found for objects that are quite close to the same mass (weight). Exploring and experimenting with the balance eventually leads children to an understanding of heavier and lighter in terms of the balance. An improvised teeter-totter (a plank over a brick) can provide many meaningful experiences.

The use of rubber bands will probably be the child's first experience with spring scales. Light and heavy objects should be suspended by elastic bands and their length noted. Similar experiences can be provided with springs of all kinds: fragile and strong, long and short, extension and compression.

Standard Weights for Measurement. Eventually, the need to interpret and communicate weights leads to the desire for standard weights. Many schools have sets of standard weights so that students may feel and experiment with them. Students should experience activities with the metric system as well as with the customary English system.

The standard weights are used on one side of a dual balance. Students begin to tell how much an object actually weighs in standard units—pounds or grams—depending on the system being studied at the time. Students can link to real-world mathematics by using a bathroom scale to measure things around the classroom as well as themselves. *A word to the wise:* If a teacher asks children to weigh in and keep a record of their weight, the teacher had better be prepared to do it too. It will be a sure request from the students. A teacher must be careful not to embarrass or cause humiliation to any student who may be overweight. Children in the United States are rapidly becoming overweight; so a health unit integrated with mathematics is quite possible, but dignity is the watchword of any such activity.

If the scale has both English and metric measurements on its face, one set can be covered up with masking tape if the teacher feels that the students will be too confused with two sets of measurement tools. A teacher can convert a customary scale (usually cheaper to buy) into a metric scale by using the conversion chart seen in Table 7.1. The chart is shown here solely for teachers. Children should *not* be asked to convert between scales in any activity. Learning one system at a time is enough!

Area

Area and its boundary (either perimeter or circumference) frequently confuse children. These concepts

TABLE 7.1 Make It Light...Report the Mass in Kilos

Use the bathroom scale to do this activity. Make twenty labels for the numbers 5, 10, 15, 20 . . . 90, 95, 100. Peel back the material around the window of your scale so that the window may be removed. Then, using the table below, paste the labels over the appropriate numbers.

Weight Conversion—Bathroom Scale

kg	lb	kg	lb
5	11	65	143
10	22	70	154
15	33	75	165
20	44	80	176
25	55	85	187
30	66	90	198
35	77	95	209
40	88	100	220
45	99	105	231
50	110	110	243
55	121	115	254
60	132		

For example, the 5 would be pasted on the scale at 11, the 10 at 22, the 15 at 33, and so on.

are frequently missed on state assessment tests coming in second only to volume as the concept with the greatest difficulty for students in elementary through the middle grades. On the national assessment only 37 percent of the eighth-grade students chose the correct representation for area. Students even in the twelfth grade continued to confuse area and perimeter (Kenney and Kouba, 1997). Take a look at the video vignette for an active lesson on area and perimeter.

Students will be expected to know a basic vocabulary of terms when using oral discourse to communicate ideas about area. There are many terms that label parts of shapes. Length and width are designated as the sides of rectangles. The circumference is the distance or perimeter of a circle. The diameter is the length of a straight line drawn from side to side through the center of the circle. The radius is the distance from the center to a side.

The NCTM *Standards* advocate less stress on memorizing formulas and measurement conversion equivalencies and more on estimation and setting benchmarks. Students' exploration can help derive formulas. A typical example would be if students are asked to find the area of a parallelogram when they already know how to find the area of a rectangle. As Figure 7.6 shows, one can be deduced from the other without ever memorizing a formula.

There are times when it is easier to learn a formula. Formulas involving circles seem to fall into this group. Even then exercises can be organized around the relationship between diameter and circumference rather than just memorizing a formula alone. The formula for circumference is

$$C = \pi d \qquad \text{or} \qquad C = 2\pi r$$

where d is the diameter and r is the radius. For further explorations, use the spreadsheet activities in the Integrating Technology section at the end of the chapter.

Video Vignette

Pizza Perimeters

The concept of area and perimeter confuses students, even twelfth graders. Analyze the mathematical ideas in this fourth-grade class in terms of worthwhile tasks, discourse, and learning environment.

- Use the lesson plan in Table 3.5 to help focus your thinking.
- How well do you think these students understand the distinction between the ideas of perimeter and area?

FIGURE 7.6

Deducing formulas from experience.

Activity 7.8

CALCULATORS PROBLEM SOLVING

EXPLORING CIRCUMFERENCE AND DIAMETER

PROCEDURE

1. Use your calculator for the computations. Measure the following items and find the circumference and diameter in centimeters. What patterns or relationships do you notice?

Object	C	d	$C + d$	C / d	$C - d$	$C \times d$
Soda can						
Coffee can						
Plate						
Glass						
Wastebasket						
Total =			____	____	____	____

2. Which column shows a constant relationship between circumference and diameter?
3. What is the average value of circumference divided by diameter?
4. What can you say about the ratio between circumference and diameter?

Nonstandard Units. The concept of area can be established through the use of manipulatives such as the geoboard, colored rods, or blocks. Using the geoboard, the establishment of a nonstandard square unit can lead to finding the area of numerous regions, as in Figure 7.7.

As the student constructs the square unit on each figure, there is the realization that a square unit takes up a certain amount of area regardless of the shape of the original figure. A vocabulary and a frame of reference still need to be established. Once a unit of area, such as a square, a hand, or a triangle, is established, the area of larger items like books and tables can be found.

Standard Units. However, for communication of this unit of area, a standardized unit is required. The direct comparison of which book has more area is easily accomplished without the standardized unit by placing one on top of another. As they become more nearly the same in area, measurement becomes necessary. In order to investigate which desk has the most area, newspapers, books, or bodies can all be used as measures for indirect measurement. An intriguing question might be to discover whether the round or the square table has greater area. How can this be solved? This activity leads to perimeter measure as students will probably measure the distance around. By estimating how many units will fit on each table, a specific area measure can be used to determine which has the larger area.

FIGURE 7.7

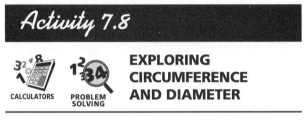

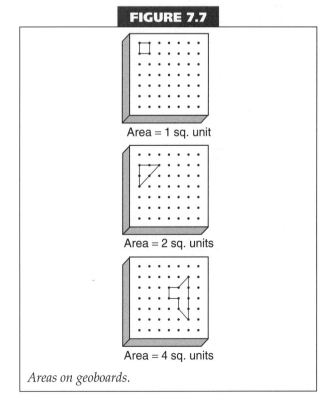

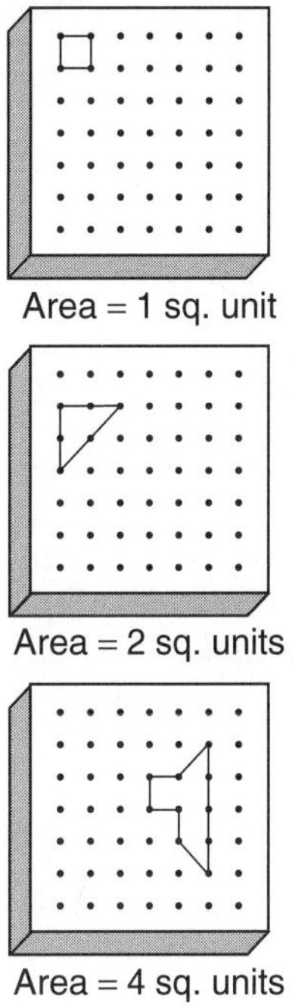

Areas on geoboards.

This activity can be reinforced by having children trace hands on squared paper and then count the number of squares covered. Estimation will be required to make whole squares.

Activity 7.9

PROBLEM SOLVING ESTIMATION MENTAL MATH

WITH CENTIMETER GRAPH PAPER

DIRECTIONS

1. Place your hand with the fingers closed on centimeter graph paper. Draw around your hand.

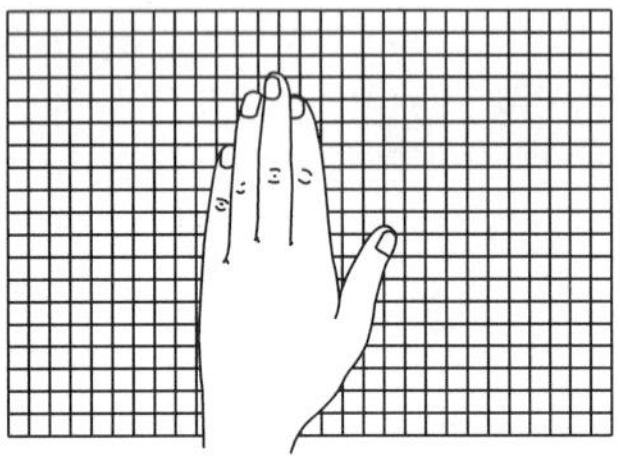

2. Guess the area of your hand in square centimeters. ______ cm^2
3. Count the square units to find the area of your hand. You should count a square if more than $\frac{1}{2}$ of it is inside the outline of your hand.
4. The area of my hand is about ______ cm^2.
5. Now draw your foot on centimeter graph paper. Try to make a better guess.
6. Guess the area of your foot in square centimeters. ______ cm^2
7. Next count the square units to find the area of your foot.
8. The area of my foot is about ______ cm^2.

Supporting the NCTM *Principles and Standards* (2000):

- Mathematics as Problem Solving, Connections, Reasoning/Patterns; Measurement
- Tools to Enhance Discourse—The Teaching Principle

Frames of Reference. Understanding the area concept can be reinforced by giving each student five tagboard squares, 5 centimeters on a side. Have each student make a design. Ask what is the area of each design. Will the area be the same for any two designs? Likewise, perimeter measures should be taken of each design. Are the perimeters of each design the same? Why or why not?

The standard unit of area for small surfaces such as a book, notebook, or desk is the square centimeter. The square meter is appropriate for determining the area of rooms in a home or school, or for finding how much carpeting is needed to cover a certain number of square meters or how much wallpaper is needed to cover a certain number of square meters. Frames of reference can be established for the square centimeter and square meter through experimentation.

Hectare is the unit used for small land measure, and the square kilometer is used for measuring large areas of land and oceans. A region of land will be needed to establish a frame of reference for the square kilometer and hectare.

One of children's first encounters with the concept of area measurement is in measuring body parts. Children have fun with activities of this nature. A similar activity is to trace around the child's body as the child lies on butcher paper. Additionally, children might want to see how many children it would take to cover a wall. When children assume different action positions (e.g., running, jumping, crouching), some interesting tracings result, offering a unique opportunity for art experiences as well.

The Use of Customary and Metric Units. The unit of area measure is a square unit, which is a square with each side equal to one unit. Although the square inch, square foot, and square yard are the most common units of area measure in the United States, most of the world uses the metric system. Hence, children should experience activities with the square meter as well as the usual standard units. The activities should lead to discovery or reinforcement of the area formula of the square (s^2), rectangle ($l \times w$) or circle (πr^2). The square unit has each side of length s, and the area formula of the square is s^2.

Remember memorization of formulas is deemphasized. Use lots of activities to "see" the formulas evolve through engaging mathematics activities. For more practice without formulas, see the activities on CD-ROM listed in the Extended Activities box on page 151.

Capacity and Volume

Capacity and volume are referred to as synonymous terms in most elementary programs. These two terms have different dictionary meanings. Volume is defined as how much space a region takes up, while capacity is how much a container will hold. Therefore, anything that can be poured is usually measured in capacity units, and the space in a room is measured in volume units.

EXTENDED ACTIVITIES

ESTIMATION PROBLEM SOLVING MANIPULATIVES

Name of Activity

- Using a Table and Square Centimeters
- Estimation with Graph Paper
- Metric Measurement with Area

In working with young children, the terms can be used interchangeably, but middle grade students will need to distinguish between them. To begin working with these units, estimating how much a jar holds or which container holds more is necessary for a grasp of the concept.

Nonstandard Units. Often children confuse the measurement of mass and capacity; therefore, containers of different sizes and shapes are needed for estimation practice. In order to make the distinction, several different size containers can be labeled, and sand or cereal can be available to fill them. Have the children estimate which container holds the most, the least, or about the same as an identified one. Next, have them verify their guesses. The children may also order the containers on the basis of how much they will hold, their heights, widths, or top circumference. Teams could be selected to perform these activities. This method gives the children a feeling of capacity depending on size and shape, not just size, as is often the case.

This activity can be followed with the question, "How much does each container hold?" The children must select a nonstandard unit to measure its capacity. They could give their answers in paper cups full, styrofoam cups full, or whatever units are selected.

Standard Units. More specific activities would be to guess which holds more than a liter, less than a liter, more than a milliliter, and so on. The answers should be proven using the standard measures of milliliter or liter. Graduated cylinders and beakers are convenient to carry out the standard measure applications. Finally, a frame of reference can be established, for example, a can of soda holds ________ mL. Familiarity with the unit has been established with the standard measure so the student would know when to use milliliters or liters. Frames of reference could be 5 mL = 1 teaspoon; ________ liters = amount of water you drink a day. Discuss what units are used to measure milk, medicine, or soda pop.

For volume measurement, the preceding procedures are appropriate, with the exception of the units. Remember, volume is the space that is occupied. The volume of the room is the number of cubic meters that will fit into the room. This includes length, width, and depth. For small measures such as the volume of a shoebox, use the cubic centimeter. Construct a cubic centimeter and have the children estimate how many will fit into a shoebox. Likewise, construct a cubic meter and have the children estimate how many cubic meters would fit into the classroom.

Apparently some people are beginning to think of questions like those in the preceding paragraphs even when they are on vacation. The park service employees at Carlsbad Caverns National Park report that one of their most interesting (and entertaining) questions from a park visitor was, "How many Ping-Pong balls would it take to fill this up?" (Online Internet, 1995). Now there's a real activity that calls for estimation and mental math!

Computing Volume. Computing the volume of the shoe box in cubic centimeters and the classroom in cubic meters using length, width, and depth (height) measurements would help establish the formula for volume as length × width × height. The estimates could then be compared with the actual computed measurements for establishing frames of reference for cubic meter and cubic centimeter. Which unit will be used for finding the volume of a basement or the volume of a dresser drawer?

Activity 7.10

MANIPULATIVES

CUBIC CENTIMETERS

DIRECTIONS

1. Construct a cubic centimeter from heavy cardboard or with any other nonporous substance.
2. Fill with 1 milliliter of water.
3. Now set up an experiment to verify that it has a mass of 1 gram.
4. Experiments can also verify equivalencies for larger units.

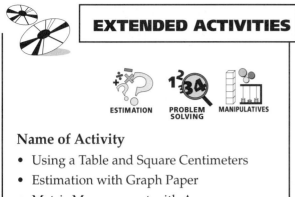

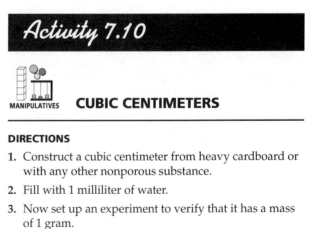

The liter and milliliter are normally used for capacity unit measures, and the cubic centimeter and cubic meter are common measurement units for volume. In the metric system, the volume, capacity, and mass measurements of water have a commonality: a cubic centimeter of pure water has a mass of one gram and a capacity of one milliliter.

Since volume and capacity are much more sophisticated concepts than either length or area, children usually gain an understanding of volume later than length or area. Children should begin their work with volume and capacity by freely playing and experimenting with pouring sand and water into containers. In so doing, they are dealing with three-dimensional space and begin establishing basic notions about it. Although they may not wonder about how many cups of sand or how much water they have for some time, they will begin to wonder which of two containers holds more or how much water they need to fill an aquarium.

Comparing Capacity and Volume. The strategy of comparing volumes and capacities by pouring water from one container to another is not easy for children to grasp. They find it difficult to believe that the quantity of the contents remains the same even though the shape of the container changes. Piaget claims that most children learn to conserve volume at about age eleven (Labinowicz, 1985). Sometimes the water or sand that fills one container does not fill another. Is the first container bigger because it is full, or is the second one bigger because more could be added to it? What if the water or sand overflows? Which container is larger then?

Children must work through these puzzling questions in their own way and in their own time before they can be expected to make comparisons and measurements with any degree of understanding. Because there are so many factors to consider, volume and capacity concepts naturally evolve later than length and area concepts. Once children have begun making volume comparison, they may begin considering how much one container holds.

When sand or water is placed in many containers, it simply runs out. After some experimentation children find that blocks or sugar cubes will better account for the space in such containers. Thus they have begun to get the idea of the cubic unit of measure.

As the need to interpret and communicate measurements arises, the need for standard units becomes apparent. Although the inch-cube, foot-cube, yard-cube and gallon are the most common units of volume measure in the United States, most of the world uses the metric system. Hence, children should experience activities with the meter-cube and liter as well as the usual standard units.

Activity 7.11

PROBLEM SOLVING ESTIMATION

COMPARING CAPACITIES

MATERIALS

- A piece of construction paper or clear acetate, scissors, tape, some beans or other dry material, and a pan

DIRECTIONS

1. Cut the construction paper or acetate in half.
2. Make a round tube by rolling one piece of the paper the long way ("hot-dog" style). Put one edge of the paper over the other and tape them together.

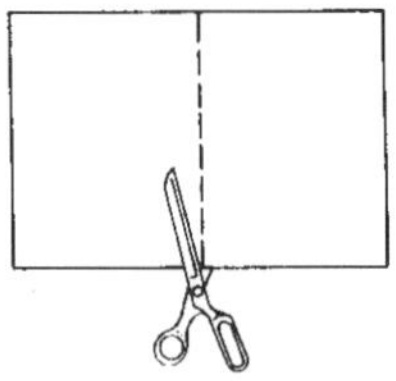

3. Make another round tube, but roll the piece of paper the other way to make a shorter, fatter tube ("hamburger" style). Put one edge of the paper over the other and tape them together.

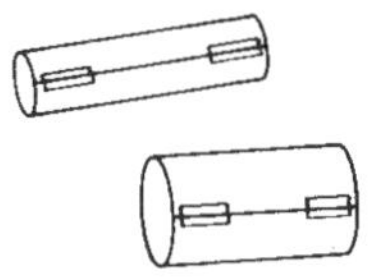

4. Place the shorter tube in the pan. Put the longer tube inside the shorter tube.

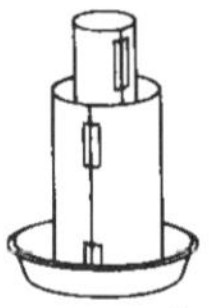

5. Use a measuring cup to fill the long tube with the dry material. Record how many cups it took to fill the long tube.

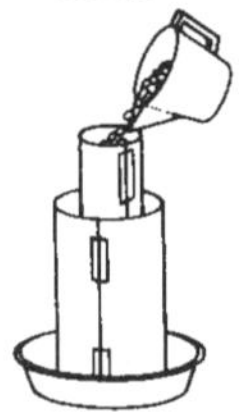

6. Mark where you think the dry material will come on the shorter tube if you pull the long tube out.

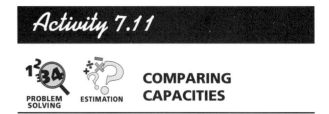

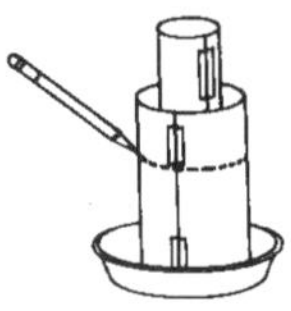

7. Now pull the long tube out. How close is your guess?
8. Since both tubes were made from the same size paper, did you expect the two tubes to hold the same amount?
9. Is the surface area the same for each tube?
10. Continue filling the shorter tube. How much more does it take to fill it?
11. In your journal, answer this question:
    How does this compare to the area and perimeter activity described in the section titled "Frames of Reference" on page 150?

Activity Continues

Supporting the NCTM *Principles and Standards* (2000):

- Mathematics as Problem Solving, Measurement
- Oral Discourse and Written Discourse of Both Teacher and Student—The Teaching Principle

Activity 7.12

MANIPULATIVES

BUILDING CUBES

DIRECTIONS

1. Use a centimeter ruler to measure the length, width, and height of a block.
2. Build larger and larger cubes using blocks.
3. Record the number of blocks on any edge and the volume for each of these larger cubes.
4. What patterns do you observe?
5. Generalize to a formula for volume of a cube.

When students have gained facility using standard units, they will begin finding discrepancies in measurements. How accurate are the measurements? Think about the degree of accuracy that is needed for real-life situations. From the activities you have performed in this chapter, deduce how precise your measurements need to be in everyday life.

EXTENDED ACTIVITIES

ESTIMATION CALCULATORS PROBLEM SOLVING

Name of Activity

- Using Volume
- Using Formulas

Time

Time is another aspect of measurement and is usually introduced with clocks and calendars. A clock measures the passage of time for each 24-hour period. Early experiences that are indirectly and unintentionally given to young children do not help them develop a clear feeling about the passage of time or the meaning of a minute or a second. For example, many adults and parents are guilty of saying phrases like "I'll be back in just a minute," or, "Just a second and I will help you." These inadvertent comments distort the child's understanding of how long a period of time is represented by the terms "minute" and "second."

Some of the children's first encounters with the concept of time measurement are general comparisons of which person or task took the least amount of time. Like other areas of measurement, since you cannot see time, you must infer it from observations of other things.

Activity 7.13

ESTIMATION PROBLEM SOLVING

SIMULTANEOUS COMPARISONS

DIRECTIONS

1. Drop two different size balls (without a push) simultaneously from the same height.
2. Which one takes the least amount of time to reach the floor? How can you tell?

Interpretation of Time. Eventually, the need to communicate and interpret time leads to the desire for standard units of time: second, minute, hour. The teacher should give children opportunities to experience 1-minute intervals to help them gain a better perception of the passing of time. To help children develop a sense of time, have them do an activity, such as counting, bouncing a ball, listening to a story, or walking about the room, for a minute. Later, have children estimate 1-minute intervals. Have them close their eyes for about how long they feel a minute lasts and when they feel a minute has elapsed, indicate with a "thumbs-up" sign. Generally, there is great variation among a group of children, which may be due to a lack of an intuitive feeling about the basic unit of time, a minute. Help children become more aware of time intervals such as 1 minute, 5 minutes, 10 minutes, and longer. This experience will clarify notions children have about the duration of time. The following activity stresses durations that go beyond 1 minute.

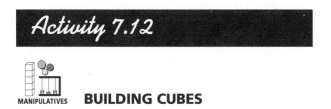

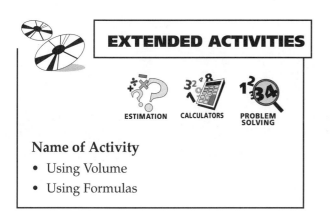

Activity 7.14

MATHEMATICAL CONNECTIONS

USE OF THE EGG TIMER IN SCIENCE

DIRECTIONS

1. Using an egg timer, record how many times you can do the following activities before the sand runs out:
   touch your toes, bounce a ball, play a chord on the piano, or hop in place.
2. Record how many seconds it takes for all the sand to run out.
3. Design a timer of your own, that is, water dripping from a can. Explain how the pioneers might have used your timer. Do this in your journal.
4. Explain to your class and your teacher how your timer works.

Understanding Passage of Time. To understand the concept of the passage of time, experiences should include activities to develop a sense of yesterday, today, and tomorrow along with the idea of the continuation of time through months. Daily calendar activities provide an excellent base. Children want to know how many more days until a special event such as a vacation, a holiday, or a school happening. With a calendar available as a reference point, the child builds some clear sense of the passage of time. The calendar shown in Figure 7.8 illustrates the many concepts included: yesterday, today, tomorrow, days of the week, days in a week, days in the current month, name of the current month, special days that month. In the primary grades, including a pattern for the days adds interest, builds an awareness of the previous month and the coming month to see the continuation of time, and reinforces previous patterning skills. During the calendar time of each school day, the teacher can include discussion about the weather and temperature, which can be excellent graphing activities (covered in Chapter 15), as well as events that will occur that day and any sharing children might want to do.

Understanding Time Sequence. Understanding time sequence is another aspect of developing an awareness of time apart from the simple reading of a clock. Have children arrange pictures of various events to indicate the order in which the events happen. For example, the pictures might include a child brushing his or her teeth, eating breakfast, just waking up, and leaving for school; another might be a child with a deflated balloon, with a large inflated balloon, the popped balloon, and the child just beginning to blow up the balloon. The task is to arrange these pictures in a logical time sequence. First experiences should involve comparing events during longer time periods such as events in their day: eat breakfast, go to school, play after school, go to bed. Many commercially made time sequence cards are available. In the classroom, many opportunities are present to discuss time sequence. For instance, the teacher might say, "First I want you to get your crayons, then color the worksheet, cut out the pictures, and put them in the collection tray."

FIGURE 7.8

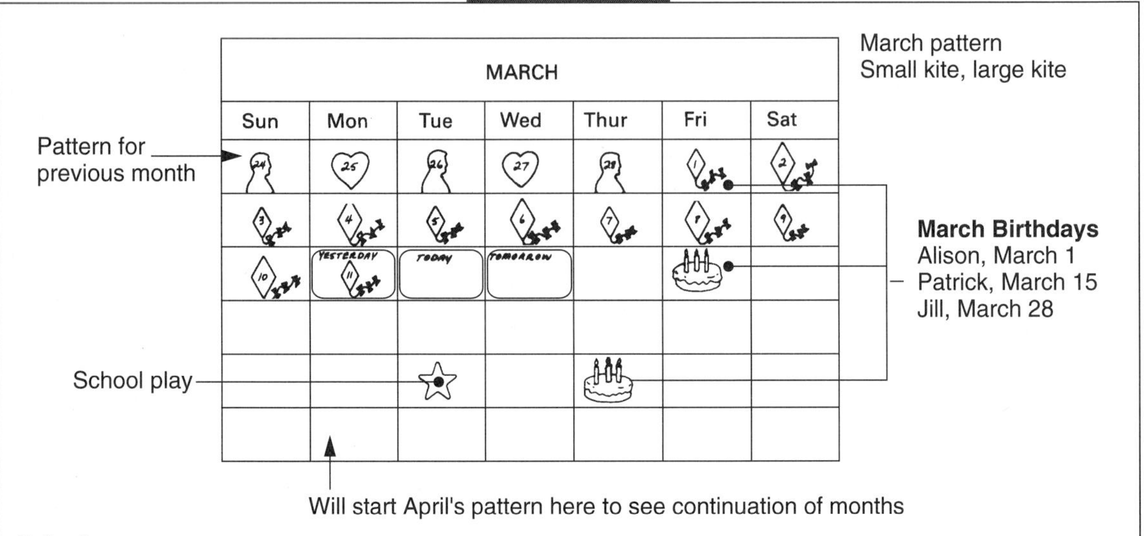

Calendar.

Children also need to develop a sense of the duration of various events and decide which event takes longer. Have children think about how long it takes to do certain things. An activity might be to look at pictures of pairs of events and decide which takes longer: brushing your teeth or taking a bath; walking to school or time spent in school; giving a dog a bath or playing a soccer game. The problem of comparing events that cannot occur simultaneously or of indicating "how long" for a single event leads children to the use of various units of time measure.

Activity 7.15

ESTIMATION PROBLEM SOLVING MANIPULATIVES

USING A PENDULUM

DIRECTIONS

1. Set up a pendulum with a string and any object attached to the end of the string.
2. Can you change the beat of a pendulum? In what way(s) can you do this?
3. Make two pendulums that swing the same. Then alter one so that it swings twice as often as the other.
4. Use the pendulum to compute how long it takes to walk the length of the room.

Once the children are ready to begin telling time, clock-reading skills can be introduced. Children must learn to read a variety of clock faces with hands that have different sizes, colors, and lengths. Some clocks have a second hand, which may add confusion. Although digital clocks are popular and easier to read initially, they do not allow children to see the relative position of the displayed time to the next hour or to the times that come before or after it.

To simplify the task of learning to tell time, one approach is to begin with only an hour-face clock. Using only an hour hand allows children to read the time as soon as the numerals 1 to 12 are recognized. The hour hand can be moved to a position a little past the hour and the child can learn to interpret this as "a little after," and when the hour hand is almost to a number the child can confidently call this "almost _________ o'clock."

When children have success with the hour hand and feel comfortable with it, the minute hand can be introduced. This process usually begins with the hour and half-hour times. The child should find the shorter hand first, read the hour, then look at the longer hand. A large wooden clock with gears is helpful for children to see the hands moving together. Allow each child many opportunities to manipulate the clock to explore its features.

When children are ready to tell time to the nearest 5 minutes (usually in second grade), a prerequisite is being able to count by fives to 60. A paper plate clock may be made for the child to practice counting by fives as each numeral on the face is touched (Figure 7.9). The teacher should emphasize that these numbers indicate minutes after on-the-hour times. To simplify the task of understanding time, we suggest that children learn only to give the minutes after the hour. This is in agreement with reading time on digital clocks and reduces teaching the concept of "minutes before the hour."

FIGURE 7.9

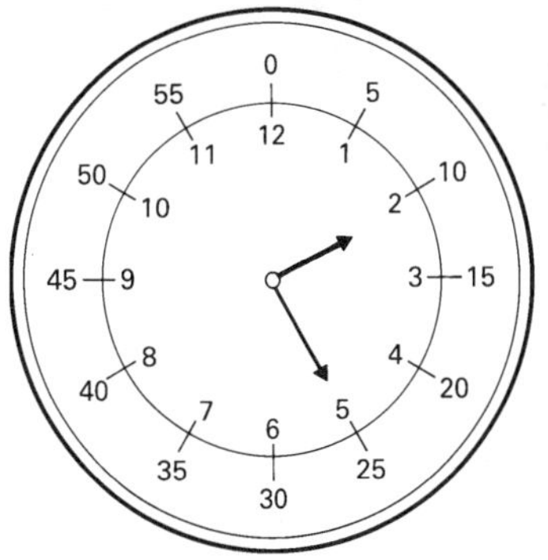

Analog clock.

Children need practice seeing how the time represented on a digital clock would look on an analog clock. They can begin with the digital time and use Logo to see the analog time. Another recommendation is to refrain from teaching the terms "quarter after," "quarter to," and "half past." These are outdated terms and add more confusion since the terms "quarter" and "half" are associated with 25 and 50 in money and now indicate 15 and 30 in time. It is better to reserve these terms for money.

Temperature

Label a thermometer with a common event for certain temperatures. This method helps the child build a frame of reference to relate the number to real events. Careful planning must be included in developing an ability for the child to read the thermometer. Introduce the concept of temperature into the curriculum with concrete experiences and establish frames of reference; for example, 32°F is the freezing point of water and 212°F is the boiling point of water, whereas in the metric system, water freezes at 0°C and boils at 100°C.

Activity 7.16

PROBLEM SOLVING MANIPULATIVES

EXPERIMENTS WITH TEMPERATURE

MATERIALS

- Thermometers with both Celsius and Fahrenheit measurements
- Ice cubes and a pan of boiling water (on a hot plate...teacher monitors this station carefully)

DIRECTIONS

Students work in pairs or small groups to do the following experiments, recording their findings in their math journals for later discussion in class:

MATH JOURNAL FOR TEMPERATURE EXPERIMENTS

	Customary System	Metric System
1. Place the thermometer under the arm for three minutes. Record temperatures.	____°F	____°C
2. Place the thermometer on an ice cube. Now in boiling water.	____°F	____°C
3. Place the thermometer on the asphalt part of the playground in the sun for four minutes.	____°F	____°C
4. Place the thermometer in the shade in the grass by the playground for four minutes.	____°F	____°C
5. Place the thermometer on your desk in the room for four minutes.	____°F	____°C

6. Think of other places to measure temperature. Check with your teacher before measuring.

Measured________________________ ____°F ____°C

Conditions ______________________________

Measured________________________ ____°F ____°C

Conditions ______________________________

Measured________________________ ____°F ____°C

Conditions ______________________________

Measured________________________ ____°F ____°C

Conditions ______________________________

Write what you learned from your observations. Be ready to share with others in class discussion:

Literature. A number of books are available to develop concepts associated with measurement. *Nine O'Clock Lullaby* (Singer, 1991) is an excellent introduction to time zones and the concept that 9:00 P.M. on the East Coast of the United States and Canada is not the same time elsewhere in the world. Each page shows what the same time on the East Coast looks like as a different time in different parts of the world. *The Grouchy Ladybug* (Carle, 1977) deals with time-lapsed ideas as well as the size of things. The ladybug finally meets her match in size and strength as the day progresses.

The following books can be used with the concepts covered in linear measurement. *How Big Is a Foot?* (Myller, 1990) develops real-world measurements around the story of a king. *Inch by Inch* (Lionni, 1960) introduces children to the cleverness of an inchworm being pursued by a hungry bird. There is even a manipulative for the children's use built into the book. Measurement activities and answers are provided. *Lengthy* (Hoff, 1964) provides an excellent introduction to length and height measurement.

EXTENDED ACTIVITIES

MANIPULATIVES CULTURAL RELEVANCE MATHEMATICAL CONNECTIONS PORTFOLIO

Name of Activity

- Social Studies and Science
- Cuisenaire Rod Clock
- TIMSS Assessment: The Bike Ramp

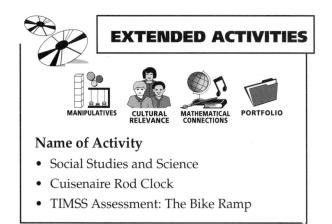

Area measurement is another popular theme in children's books. *Houses and Homes* by Ann Morris (1992) is a comprehensive book about all sorts of homes found all around the world. Each culture is celebrated for its good sense to create a home that is logically the best one for the terrain, climate, customs, and building supplies available. Measurement of the rooms in the various houses connects to the real-world experiences of the people living in such homes. One class used masking tape on the floor to show how much area was in the average African hut (a very small portion of the classroom compared with Buckingham Palace, which took up the same area as the school, parking lot, playground and the row of houses down the street combined). *Grandfather Tang's Story, a Tale Told with Tangrams* (Tompert, 1990) can be extended from its shape arrangements seen in Chapter 6 to the study of area in unit measurement with units on a standard grid used to compare the areas of different-sized tangram sets.

A wonderful book that introduces the concept of weight measurement is *Who Sank the Boat?* (Allen, 1982). General measurement ideas and those stories with more than one concept of measurement are *Mr. Archimedes' Bath* (Allen, 1980) and *Counting on Frank* (Clement, 1991), which include an introduction to the metric system, measurement problem-solving tasks, and answers to the books' adventures.

ASSESSMENT

As you can see by the six kinds of measurement we have covered in this chapter, measurement is a broad subject in elementary and middle school. Each kind of measurement could have its own rubric for assessment of what students know about the intricate workings within each measurement system. That could literally be a text in and of itself. We have chosen, instead, to concentrate on two areas where students have the most difficulty. For young elementary children, it is the concept of time. For older students, it is the concept of perimeter versus area.

Common Misconceptions of Time

Deficiencies in telling time may relate to insufficient real-life experiences reading time on a clock face. Today's child has quick access to a digital clock, which cannot give the needed exposure to telling time in a meaningful way. A child may be able to read "9:42" but will often not know that this time comes between 9:00 and 10:00. Time elapse becomes difficult to relate for the child. These children need experiences focused on constant reading of a clock face. They need to read the time every 5 minutes to actually witness the meaning of an hour and to see how the hour hand moves only a small distance during each 5-minute interval.

Because the minute hand is constantly changing position, some children have trouble seeing time elapse. When the previous minute hand remains in view as the count continues, children can see how many minutes have passed while doing an activity.

Correcting Misconceptions with the Concept of Time. Two common errors in reading time are reversing the hour hand and the minute hand and reading the actual numbers indicated rather than assigning the minute hand appropriate time values.

Reversing the Hour and Minute Hands. An example of the first error is the child reading 10:20 and 4:10, and an example of the second error is the child reading 10:20 as 10:04. See Figure 7.10.

FIGURE 7.10

Error patterns in telling time.

To remedy these problems, children should be given a progression of clock faces, each one a little more detailed than the preceding one. This procedure allows children to focus on each part of the clock independently, first working with hour-face clocks then minute-face clocks.

Reading Actual Numbers. Another aspect of understanding telling time is to relate the numbers 1 to 12 with counting by intervals of five. A flexible number line might help students to see this relationship. The following activity is provided to show a teaching aid that can be made for the children's use.

Activity 7.17

MANIPULATIVES **MAKING CLOCKS**

MATERIALS

- Paper plates
- Brad fastener
- Grosgrain ribbon or adding machine tape
- Permanent marking pen

PROCEDURE

Divide the paper plate into twelve congruent regions and label with the numbers 1 to 12 as on a clock face. Cut two clock hands from another piece of cardboard or poster board and attach in the center with a brad fastener. Take the grosgrain ribbon and stretch around the circumference of the plate. Cut the ribbon, and tape it around the plate. Mark the ribbon at each place that matches with the clock numbers. Untape the ribbon, and divide each segment into five equal regions. This will look like a flexible

Activity Continues

number line with the numbers marked in fives to 60 and with the increments by ones noted between the fives.

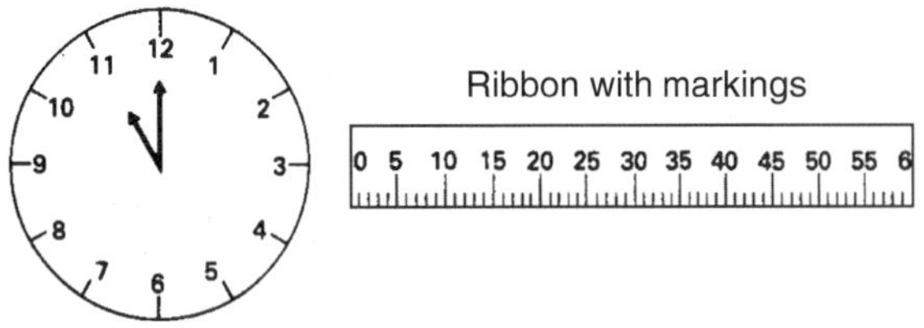

Creating a Rubric for the Assessment of Time Concepts. The following child's work gives you an excellent opportunity to start developing rubrics you can use in your own classroom to assess children with difficulties. This activity is one that shows your ability to be a true professional in today's education community. Save it for your professional portfolio for job interviews.

FIGURE 7.11

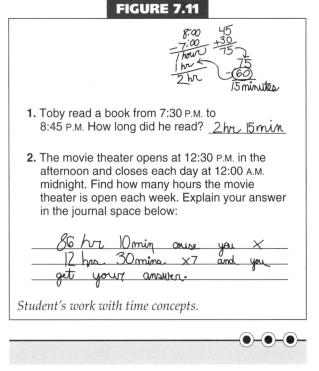

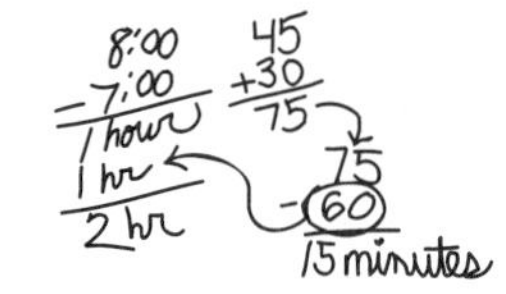

1. Toby read a book from 7:30 P.M. to 8:45 P.M. How long did he read? 2 hr 15 min

2. The movie theater opens at 12:30 P.M. in the afternoon and closes each day at 12:00 A.M. midnight. Find how many hours the movie theater is open each week. Explain your answer in the journal space below:

86 hr 10 min couse you × 12 hrs 30 mins ×7 and you get your answer.

Student's work with time concepts.

Activity 7.18

PORTFOLIO **PORTFOLIO ASSESSMENTS**

For Teacher Reflection of Students' Work in Measurement

DIRECTIONS

1. Look at this child's journal explanation in Figure 7.11. If you had to write your own rubric to score children on their understanding of time based on these problems, what would you consider prerequisite concepts?
   a. Decide what parts are crucial and what parts are just finishing touches to a true understanding of the concept.
   b. Give a numerical score to each part (more points for the important parts, less points for the less involved parts). Figure what would be the score for a person who had a perfect understanding of the concept of time as measured in the activities seen here.
   c. What would it look like as a score if the child totally misunderstood everything about the concepts of time as measured in these tasks?
2. How would this child's score measure based on your rubric? Perfect score = _______; lowest score = ______; percent this child understands _______?
3. Include the rubric in your Professional Portfolio for Job Interviews along with your analysis of each child's understanding in this activity. Other samples are on the CD.

SUMMARY

Measurement is an often overlooked topic in the elementary school. With the introduction of the metric system, our numeration system, and our monetary system, the measurement system can be taught as an integrated curriculum with each complementing the other. Measuring encourages children's active involvement in solving problems and discussing mathematics. According to the National Council of Teachers of Mathematics *Standards*, measurement is central to the curriculum because of its power to help children see that mathematics is useful in everyday situations.

The metric system uses meters, grams, and liters as the base units. Prefixes are uniform throughout the system with milli-, centi-, deci-, deca-, hecto-, and kilo- being the most common. Celsius is the unit of temperature measure. Volume is measured in cubic units and whole area is measured in square units. Students are encouraged to establish a frame of reference to get an intuitive feeling for the units.

Our customary (English) system uses inches, feet, yards, quarts, ounces, gallons, and miles as the most common units. Conversion from one unit to the next varies by unit. Fahrenheit is the unit of temperature measure. Cubic and square inches, feet, and yards are used to measure volume and capacity. The United States is one of the last five countries in the world that continues to use the customary system, although many major U.S. corporations have switched to metric measure.

In the next chapter we begin the development of the concept of number, known as number readiness. The attributes of the geometry chapter and the understanding of number, one-to-one correspondence, and counting are the emphasis of preschool and kindergarten mathematics. We have included geometry and measurement content before the chapter on number readiness so you can use the ideas to develop the understanding of number, number systems, and the use of them.

EXERCISES

For extended exercises, see the CD-ROM.

A. Memorization and Comprehension Exercises
Low-Level Thought Activities

1. Compare mass, volume, and capacity of the following

   1 liter = ______________ = ______________

2. Discuss the differences between nonstandard and standard units. Give examples of each.
3. Describe and give examples of direct and indirect measurement.
4. Obtain a copy of the mathematics objectives for your state. Are topics for metric education included? List how your state uses the metric system.

B. Application and Analysis Exercises
Middle-Level Thought Activities

1. Set up five events that take 1 minute; 1 hour.
2. Develop a classroom thermometer and have labels of similar events at various temperatures.
3. To reinforce mathematical connections:
   a. List five mathematical questions or problems that come from popular storybooks for children. Show how they are related to the topics of this chapter.
   b. List five ways to use the topics of this chapter when teaching lessons in reading, science, social studies, health, music, art, physical education, or language arts (writing, English grammar, poetry, and so on).

C. Synthesis and Evaluation Exercises
High-Level Thought Activities

1. Develop a computer- or calculator-based unit showing the relationship of the metric system, monetary system, and the base 10 numeration system.
2. Devise an original measurement project from the classroom environment that calls for determining volume.
3. Plan a metric field day or Olympics using estimation activities as found in this chapter.
4. Plan a project for family math that students can take home to complete with the family.

BIBLIOGRAPHY

For an extended bibliography, see the CD-ROM.

Avino, Diana Proto. "Playground Ponderings." *Teaching Children Mathematics* 2 (October 1995): 136.

Babbie, Earl. *Apple LOGO for Teachers.* Belmont, CA: Wadsworth, 1984.

Beaton, Albert E., Ina V. S. Mullis, Michael O. Martin, Eugenio J. Gonzalez, Dana L. Kelly, Teresa A. Smith. *Mathematics Achievement in the Middle School Years: IEA's Third International Mathematics and Science Study.* Chestnut Hill, MA: TIMSS International Study Center, Boston College, 1996.

Brooks, Jacqueline Grennon, and Martin G. Brooks. *The Case for Constructivist Classrooms.* Alexandria, VA: Association for Supervision and Curriculum Development, 1993.

Geddes, Dorothy. *Grades 5–8 Addenda Series: Measurement in the Middle Grades.* Ed. Frances R. Curcio. Reston, VA: National Council of Teachers of Mathematics, 1994.

Kenney, Patricia Ann, and Vicky L. Kouba. "What Do Students Know about Measurement?" Eds. Patricia Ann Kenney and Edward A. Silver. *Results of the Sixth Mathematics Assessment of the National Assessment of Educational Progress.* Reston, VA: National Council of Teachers of Mathematics, 1997. 141, 163.

Kouba, Vicky L., Catherine A. Brown, Thomas P. Carpenter, Mary M. Lindquist, Edward A. Silver, and Jane O. Swafford. "Results of the Fourth NAEP Assessment of Mathematics: Measurement, Geometry, Data Interpretation, Attitudes and Other Topics." *Arithmetic Teacher* 35 (May 1988): 10–16.

Labinowicz, Ed. *Learning from Children: New Beginning for Teaching Numerical Thinking, a Piagetian Approach.* Menlo Park, CA: Addison-Wesley, 1985.

Mullis, Ina V. S., John A. Dossey, Eugene H. Owen, and Gary W. Phillips. *The State of Mathematics Achievement* (Report

No. 21-ST-04). Washington, DC: Education Testing Service, 1991.

National Council of Teachers of Mathematics. *Curriculum and Evaluation Standards for School Mathematics.* Reston, VA: NCTM, 1989.

———. *Principles and Standards for School Mathematics.* Reston, VA: NCTM, 2000 (to be published).

Online Internet Communication. "Questions Asked of Park Service Employees." *Outside Magazine* (May 1995).

Piaget, Jean, perf. *Piaget on Piaget.* film. 1989.

Rhone, Lynn. "Measurement in a Primary-Grade Integrated Curriculum." *NCTM 1995 Yearbook: Connecting Mathematics across the Curriculum.* Ed. Peggy A. House. Reston, VA: National Council of Teachers of Mathematics, 1995. 124–133.

Strong, Dorothy S. (Mathematics Ed.). *Systemwide Objectives and Standards.* Vols. 1–3. Chicago: Board of Education of the City of Chicago, 1990.

———. *Mathematics Instruction Planning Manual.* Chicago: Board of Education of the City of Chicago, 1991a.

———. *Mathematics Tutor Training Manual.* Chicago: Board of Education of the City of Chicago, 1991b.

CHILDREN'S LITERATURE

Allen, Pamela. *Mr. Archimedes' Bath.* New York: Lothrop, Lee & Shepard Books, 1980.

———. *Who Sank the Boat?* New York: Coward-McCann, 1982.

Carle, Eric. *The Grouchy Ladybug.* New York: Crowell, 1977.

Clement, Rod. *Counting on Frank.* Milwaukee, WI: Gareth Stevens Publishing, 1991.

Hoff, Syd. *Lengthy.* New York: G. P. Putnam's Sons, 1964.

Lionni, Leo. *Inch by Inch.* New York: Astor-Honor, 1960.

Morris, Ann. *Houses and Homes.* New York: Lothrop, Lee & Shepard Books, 1992.

Myller, Rolf. *How Big Is a Foot?* New York: Dell Publishing, 1990.

Seuss, Dr. *Green Eggs and Ham.* New York: Random House, 1963.

Singer, Marilyn. *Nine O'Clock Lullaby.* New York: HarperCollins Children's Books, 1991.

Tompert, Ann. *Grandfather Tang's Story, A Tale Told with Tangrams.* New York: Crown Publishers, 1990.

Integrating Technology

Video Vignettes: Assessment in Action

- *Pizza Perimeter*

Supporting the NCTM *Principles and Standards* (2000):
Worthwhile Mathematical Tasks; Teacher's Role in Discourse; The Teaching Principle

Make your own assessment rubric as you follow along with students in a real classroom setting. See the last part of the Assessment section of the chapter for the introduction to this video.

Computer Software Resources

...for Measurement

Internet Searches

Surfing the Internet for Topics on Measurement

Use the World Wide Web (WWW) and navigate through the system, searching for new information under major headings and subheadings similar to the following:

Mathematics Education
  Measurement
    Area and Perimeter
    Linear
    Mass
    Weight
    Volume
    Area and Circumference
Shareware Programs
  KidCad and similar programs (for area and volume applications)
NCTM
  Measurement Issues
Children's Links
  http://www.kidlink.org
  http://pathfinder.com/pathfinder/kidstuff/kidstuff.html (WWW)

- *Remember...* the Web is fluid ... new topics and ways to search for topics change daily.
- Be adventurous ... think of some new things you could try.

Spreadsheet Activities

Name of Program

- *Metric Table Spreadsheet*
- *Calculating with a Spreadsheet*
- *Exploring Circles with Spreadsheets*

8

Number Readiness—Early Primary Mathematics

Activities Index

IN THE TEXT

ON CD-ROM

The call for curriculum reform takes into account as a basic fundamental component the need for mathematics to match the developmental needs of young children. The report, *Everybody Counts: A Report to the Nation on the Future of Mathematics Education* (National Research Council, 1989), emphasizes the importance of the construction of one's own mathematical knowledge. "Educational research offers compelling evidence that students learn mathematics well only when they construct their own mathematical understanding" (p. 58). This constructivist view of learning permeates the NCTM *Standards* in recommending a child-centered learning environment with opportunities for cooperative work, hands-on experiences, and content that is developmentally appropriate. An underlying issue is how to help children make sense of the phenomena in mathematics. The constructivist orientation guides teachers to consider more than one solution to a problem and to seek more than one reasonable interpretation. How the child views the situation is a primary goal of the teacher (von Glasersfeld, 1990).

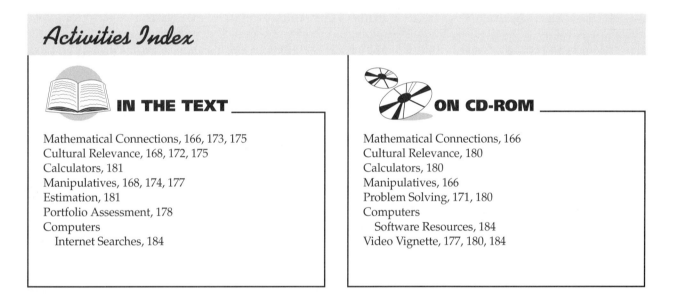

The child's environment affords rich opportunities to learn about quantities and number relationships. Examples of size, geometry, and numerals abound in storybooks, on television and in daily events in life. Children see sets of objects in the world and they watch those sets of objects increased and decreased by actions like eating, jumping rope, or bouncing a ball. Parents need to attach language to mathematical ideas and help children learn to communicate about mathematics. Research by Anderson (1997) supports the notion that parents can engage their children in activities and will find ways to mediate a range of mathematical ideas. Anderson (1998) suggests that "In informal and formal conversations with families, teachers must dispel the myth that mathematics is a school subject best left to professionals to teach" (p. 336). As early as preschool, teachers should help parents recognize the rich mathematical possibilities in commonplace environments. Parents can be reminded that storybook reading supports children's mathematical development along with early literacy.

A position statement by the National Association for the Education of Young Children (NAEYC, 1996) states, "Children need to form their own hypotheses and keep trying them through social interaction, physical manipulation, and their own thought processes" (p. 4). When a mathematics program addresses these concerns, the focus is where it should be—on the child.

In considering the child's learning of mathematics, it is useful to refer to the findings of noted psychologists and educators about children's knowledge. Ginsburg (1989) contends that children arrive at school with much informal mathematical knowledge composed of intuitions and perceptions. The successful teacher builds on this foundation of informal knowledge and relates it to the formal mathematical knowledge acquired in school. The degree to which these two types of knowledge are related and supported may determine the child's performance in mathematics.

Children must also connect conceptual knowledge and procedural knowledge. Conceptual knowledge is understanding relationships among information and connecting that information to build understanding. Procedural knowledge is composed of the symbol-representation system of mathematics and the rules, algorithms, and procedures used to solve mathematical tasks. The goal of mathematics education is to develop relationships between conceptual and procedural knowledge. Hiebert and Lindquist (1990) suggest that instruction can help children build conceptual knowledge by presenting new concepts in familiar real-life situations and with physical materials so children can connect new ideas with what they already know.

The mathematics encountered by the young child should focus on these fundamental relationships to contribute to the development of a sound knowledge base. Mathematical experiences that match the child's developmental level and stimulate the child's interest will develop the young learner's acquisition of mathematical knowledge. These suggestions are in agreement with the changes in instructional practices mentioned in the NCTM *Standards*.

Before children can use numbers with meaning, they must have a firm understanding about what numbers are and how to name them. This development period is between the ages of five and seven, and is the age span this chapter covers. Young children develop a sense of number through kinesthetic experiences. Objects need to be matched, sorted, grouped, counted, and compared. In order to best understand the importance of these activities, learning theory is discussed in terms of how children learn mathematics. Piaget's observations of young children offers great insight into their thinking and developmental stages (refer to Chapter 3).

There are some prenumber concepts that children should acquire before formal work with numbers. Teachers should be able to assess a child's readiness for number by determining what abilities the child has acquired and what perceptions the child has about the world. Prenumber concepts from Piaget's theory of cognitive development are discussed in the next section: classification, class inclusion, seriation, number conservation, and set equivalence.

A CHILD'S UNDERSTANDING OF NUMBER

For Piaget, the child actively and internally constructs knowledge by interacting with reality. Interactions with physical objects and concepts involve some personal activity and then are interpreted within the structures of logico-mathematical knowledge. As Piaget states, "In the area of logico-mathematical structures, children have real understanding only of that which they invent themselves, and each time that we try to teach them something too quickly, we keep them from reinventing it themselves" (1965, p. 21). Since Piaget's theory involves the child learning through an active role, it is known as a *Constructivist* or interactionist position (Labinowicz, 1980). Current research efforts such as Cognitively Guided Instruction (CGI) are based on the Constructivist view of learning, in which instructional activities center around children's mathematical thinking in problem-solving situations. More discussion of CGI occurs in Chapter 10.

Piaget's observations of children's knowledge of concepts reveal valuable information on understanding how children deal with mathematical concepts and offer ways to determine whether a child is ready for certain instructional topics in mathematics. The young child between the ages of five and seven is in the stage of preoperational thought. This means the child's attention is centered on a limited

BOX 8.1 Curriculum and Evaluation Standards

Number Sense and Numeration

In grades K–4 the mathematics curriculum should include whole number concepts and skills so that students can—

- Construct number meanings through real-world experiences and the use of physical materials.
- Understand our numeration system by relating counting, grouping, and place-value concepts.
- Develop number sense.
- Interpret the multiple uses of numbers encountered in the real world.

Patterns and Relationships

In grades K–4, the mathematics curriculum should include the study of patterns and relationships so that students can—

- Recognize, describe, extend, and create a wide variety of patterns.
- Represent and describe mathematical relationships.

Source: National Council of Teachers of Mathematics, 1989, pp. 38, 60.

perceptual aspect of an object or event. The child relies on perceptual evaluations in relating to the world. These are some areas of prenumber concepts that reveal how a child perceives number: classification, class inclusion, seriation, number conservation, and equivalence of sets. The child's development in terms of acquiring these skills greatly influences performance level in mathematics. Early primary teachers must have background on how to conduct interviews with children on these Piagetian tasks and how to interpret the findings in terms of curriculum considerations. Piaget's findings provide several logical ideas that influence the child's understanding of number.

Task: Classification

Classification experiences involve making decisions about certain attributes of objects and sorting them based on that classification. Attributes might include size, color, shape, thickness, texture, function, or any combinations of these.

Assessment. In Figure 8.1, a collection of three shapes in two sizes might be shown to a child. The child is asked to put the shapes into piles so that all of the objects in each pile are alike in some way. Classification is the earliest stage of logical thinking and is the foundation for graphing. The preoperational child does not determine a classification scheme but begins with one plan and changes as another feature of the material becomes obvious and important. There is no consistent thinking strategy for sorting the material. Preschool and kindergarten children sort objects first by color, as it is the most salient feature, but with maturity and experiences, sorting is done by shape and size.

FIGURE 8.1

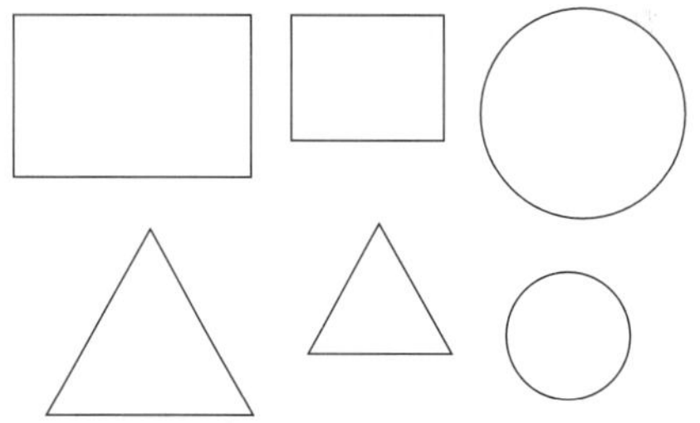

Sorting and classifying attribute blocks.

Teaching Ideas. Since classifying is a fundamental task in life and appears across the curriculum, classification needs to be encouraged through many activities. Sorting can be done with shapes, dyed pasta, bottle caps, plastic animals, items from nature (shells, seeds, pine cones, leaves, nuts), anything! The materials should be varied and interesting. Collections of fabric, pictures from magazines, junk such as old keys or nuts, bolts, screws, and buttons offer many varied opportunities for classification. Encourage children to describe and name their sets. Sorting should be done using a sorting area with a defined boundary such as a chalked circle, yarn hoops, or a sorting mat. The teacher should circulate among the children asking key questions: How are these the same? How are these different? Why does this belong in your group? What is your sorting rule? It is important to sort materials many different ways (using different sorting rules). Children need to be encouraged to use different sorting criteria and be flexible. Sorting experiences offer means to assess the children's ability to think logically, to express ideas, to apply sorting rules, and to focus their observational skills. Blindfolds can be useful to involve using other senses and ways of describing their sorting rules.

Activity 8.1

MATHEMATICAL CONNECTIONS

SORTING PROJECTS

DIRECTIONS

1. Use the list of class members' names and have the children sort the names by a given letter.
2. Say a list of short words to the students, and have them indicate all those that rhyme and those that do not rhyme.
3. In social studies, have children sort animals as farm or zoo.
4. In science, have children sort objects into those that sink and those that float or into those that a magnet attracts and those that are not attracted. Collect seeds or leaves and sort by type.

The *Sesame Street* television program has a song, "One of These Things Is Not Like the Others." In this activity, children must form mental relationships between objects to determine which one does not belong. Children can compare seasonal pictures by attributes that they have in common (are alike) and not in common (are different). For example, in February compare pictures of Lincoln and Washington or in October compare two large poster pumpkins that are different in several ways. These activities lead to more sophisticated mathematical logic in later grades such as Venn diagrams. Children need to explore relationships according to quantifiers such as "all," "some," and "none."

Associated with sorting is the idea of noting similarities and differences. This involves logical thinking. Children need a wide variety of experiences. Check the CD-ROM for activities on classification. The teacher can group children from the class into two sets—long sleeves or short sleeves; with glasses or without glasses; wearing tennis shoes or other types; shirts with logo and shirts without; or harder ones—girls with pierced ears and girls without; tennis shoes with Velcro and those with ties. This can be an exciting way to explore materials in greater detail as well as to prepare children to think logically and draw conclusions. It also leads into graphing as a visual way to describe the results. Extend classification activities to involve two or more attributes and use sorting loops to show intersecting sets.

EXTENDED ACTIVITIES

Name of Activity

- Where Does It Go?

MANIPULATIVES MATHEMATICAL CONNECTIONS

Task: Class Inclusion

A part of classification is the ability to see relationships between groups at different levels in the classification system. Grouping on the basis of class is one way to classify objects in the physical world. It is related to logical reasoning. To classify objects, their relation to other objects must be known. The idea is that all of one group can be part of another group at the same time (for example, the group of boys is part of the group of children). The Piagetian task to test class inclusion is discussed first, followed by some additional questions that prove insightful in a child's acquisition of this concept.

Assessment. Show the child a box containing twenty yellow plastic beads and seven blue plastic beads. Discuss the properties of the beads with the child—plastic, a hole through it, uneven or bumpy surface, colored. Ask, "Are there more yellow beads or more plastic beads?" The characteristic response of younger children is to answer more yellow beads. Children have problems seeing the relationship of the two classes and end up basing their responses on appearances. This mistake indicates an inability to consider the quantity of plastic beads (the larger and general class) because the answer is based on appearances and the visible, bigger set is the yellow beads.

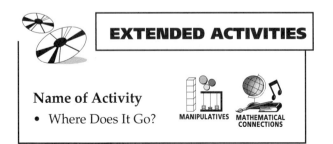

Additional experiences should include questions about children (are there more boys or more children), animals (are there more cows or more animals), fruit (are there more apples or more fruit). Suppose you give the child a collection of five plastic cows and three horses and ask, "Show me all the cows. Show me all the horses. Show me all the animals. Are there more cows or more animals?" The four- and five-year-old child answers, "More cows," as the whole group does not exist. Ask, "Than what," and the typical response is, "Than horses." The child cannot consider the whole because the two parts are horses and cows (what is seen). The child does not have the mental structures to form such classes.

Most children younger than seven have difficulty seeing that all of one group can be some or part of another group. In terms of mathematical logic, a class may be considered in terms of its parts of partial classes. Thus number can be related to logic. Piaget maintains that both class and number result from the same operational mechanism of grouping and both are needed to be understood. The young child is unable to think of one specific number in relation to other adjacent numbers; therefore, each number is approached in isolation. If the task asks the child to make a group of three blocks, followed by a task to make a group of four blocks, the young child is unable to place the two numbers and tasks into a mental relationship. This means the blocks used for the group of three will not be used to form the group of four.

Task: Number Inclusion

This mechanism is directly related to understanding the meaning of addition or number inclusion. Because addition is putting two sets together and naming it as a single number, the child who does not have the ability to place numbers into a mental relationship will have difficulty with the addition principle. The "counting on" strategy for addition (Chapter 10) holds limited meaning for the preoperational child and probably should not be attempted. For the same reasons, using fact families or the inverse principle for addition and subtraction will be of limited value to the young child.

Piaget (1965) contends that children at this stage of development are unable to have reversibility in thinking about whole to part and back to the whole again. Until these concepts are developed, which is around seven years of age (second grade), Piaget concludes: "In a word, it seems clear at this stage (stages 1 and 2) that the child is still incapable of additive composition of classes, i.e., of logical addition or subtraction" (p. 174). Therefore, although children can be taught to repeat answers to equations of basic facts, he warns that, "there is no true assimilation until the child is capable of seeing that six is a totality, containing two and four as parts, and of grouping the various combinations in additive compositions" (p. 190).

Assessment. A quick assessment can be done by asking a child to count a collection of objects. Then add two more to the group and ask how many things there are now. Many first graders will count the entire group beginning at number 1 rather than arriving at the solution by thinking of the relation of five to adjacent numbers. The unnecessary counting is a result of being unable to count on from the first set and arrive at the solution sooner.

Teaching Ideas. Children need many varied experiences of putting sets together to make the whole. They can make up number stories with counters, connecting cubes, or painted lima beans. Pattern block designs (Figure 8.2) offer opportunities to explore the class inclusion concept. Tasks, such as building a color square with Cuisenaire rods (Figure 8.3) then writing all the ways to show names for a given number, encourage children to mentally place numbers into an inclusive relationship. "Spill the Beans" activity, as well as others described under number conservation in this chapter, also foster class inclusion. Such experiences help children see that the total is constant regardless of how its parts are constructed.

FIGURE 8.2

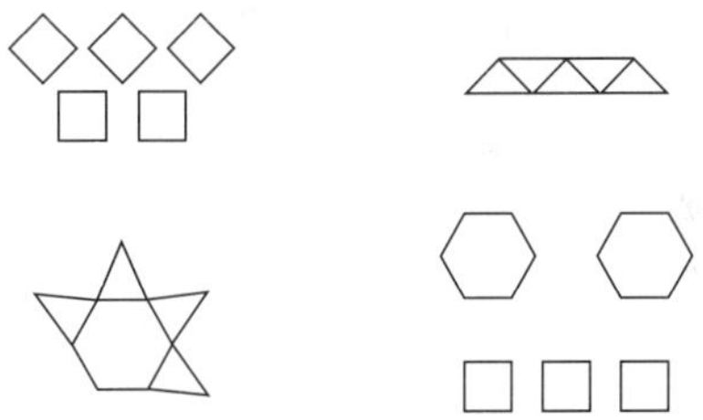

Modeling five with pattern blocks.

FIGURE 8.3

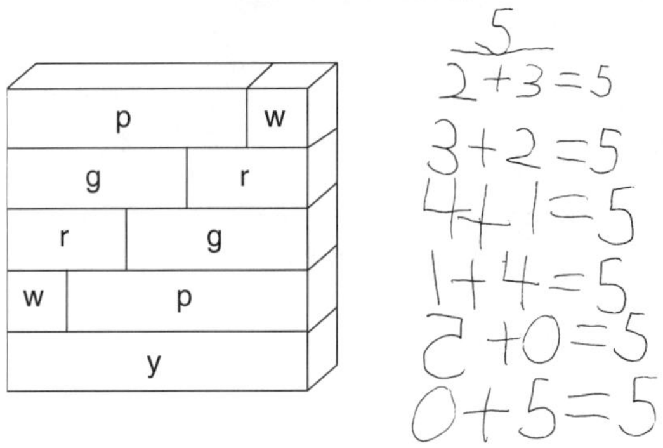

Color square for Cuisenaire rods and child's number sentences.

Activity 8.2

CULTURAL RELEVANCE

THE NUMBER FOUR

Four is an important number for many Native cultures. It symbolizes the four seasons, the four directions, Four Sacred Mountains in the Navajo Nation. Spiritual traditions often are performed in fours. The whole child is thought of in four aspects: Family, Spiritual (cultural), Education, and Self-Esteem. Indian education considers four circles of learning: Spiritual, Political, Social, and Intellectual. Find other examples in Native culture in which four plays a special number. Study other cultures to determine whether a special number is associated with any of them. Why do you think four might be chosen to be special? What about other special numbers?

Supporting the NCTM *Principles and Standards* (2000):

- Mathematics as Reasoning, Communication, Connections
- The Equity Principle

Activity 8.3

MANIPULATIVES

SPILL THE BEANS

MATERIALS

- Lima beans painted on one side, *or*
- Colored counters
- Small cup

PROCEDURE

Put a given number of beans in the cup, which represents the total or sum. Shake and spill the beans. Group those beans with the painted side showing and count for the first addend. Group the beans with the white side showing and count for the second addend. Ask children to share their number stories (or equations) with each other, such as, "4 red and 2 white makes 6." When assessment indicates some children are ready to add written symbols, have them write the accompanying number sentence when the beans are spilled.

ASSESSMENT

Watch for children who continue to count the entire set and those children who use counting-on strategies. Notice if counting by twos occurs. Think about when each child is ready to move to the connecting level and attach numbers with the action.

Activity Continues

FIGURE 8.4

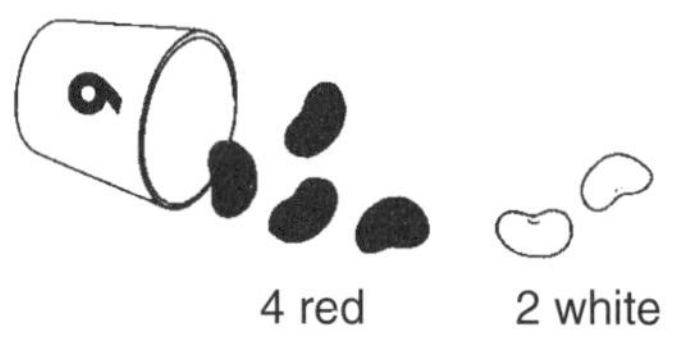

One-side-painted lima beans.

Supporting the NCTM *Principles and Standards* (2000):

- Concepts of Number and Operations
- Tools that Enhance Discourse—The Teaching Principles

Task: Seriation

The ability to seriate involves the ordering of objects and events—for example, the smallest blocks to the largest blocks. To seriate correctly, the child must make comparisons and make decisions about differences. The key to seriation is that the child understands how a single position in the series is related to both the position before and the position after it. This is similar to understanding that one object can belong to two classes at the same time, as in the class inclusion tasks. Ordering involves successive comparisons of objects so that each object or set has a unique place in the series: for example, to construct a series of ordered objects by locating the smallest object, then placing other objects in a series so that each is larger than the one before it and also smaller than the one after it. Objects may be ordered by various elements of dimension: capacity, mass, height, length, quantity.

Preoperational children have no overall plan for arranging things in a sequential order such as by length and cannot coordinate the relationships. According to Piaget, the ability to seriate is vital to the child's understanding of number. It also leads to the child's understanding of the relationship of cardinal and ordinal numbers. Children must mentally order numbers so that each one is one more than the previous number and also one less than the following number. The thinking processes necessary for seriation skills are important also in learning science, social studies, and language arts.

Assessment. To assess seriation, the child might be given a set of ten sticks or soda straws of graduated lengths and asked to arrange them from longest to shortest. The child could be given a set of pictures of graduated sizes. Since it is difficult for young children to establish a baseline for making comparisons, a ruler could be used as a straightedge or the pictures could be stood in a chalktray.

Teaching Ideas. Children could place rings on a spindle according to size relationships or they could arrange Cuisenaire rods into a staircase (Figure 8.5). (Cuisenaire rods are different colored rods in graduated lengths from 1 centimeter to 10 centimeters. Patterns for the rods are found in the Appendix and on the CD.) Classmates can be placed in order of height. A set of shapes of a given region, rectangle for example, can be made in graduated sizes from heavy poster board for the child to arrange in serial order. Ribbons or straws could be ordered from shortest to longest (or tallest). Have children think of other ways to order things such as coins by value, by size, by mass, and have them discuss their ideas. Children could order objects by a secret ordering rule and have others guess the rule.

Task: Number Conservation

Conservation of number shows how the child perceives number invariance and the degree to which the child is tied to perceptual cues. Reversibility of thought is part of this task. Can the arrangement of a constant number of objects be changed without changing the number? The ability to maintain the equivalence of sets despite their arrangement is developmental and is acquired gradually.

Place a row of eight colored chips (blue for this example) before the child. Piaget recommends at least eight objects be used for the task. Otherwise, the child might know the number perceptually without the use of logic. Beside this row, have the child form an equivalent set with chips of a different color (yellow, for example); see Figure 8.6. This task also tests the child's ability to establish one-to-one correspondence.

FIGURE 8.5

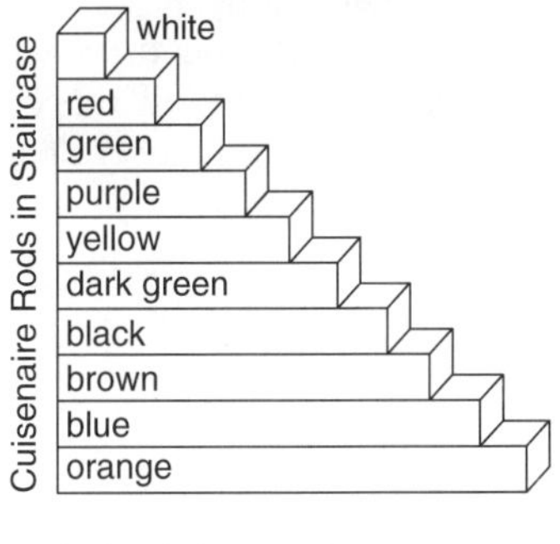

Cuisenaire rods in staircase.

FIGURE 8.6

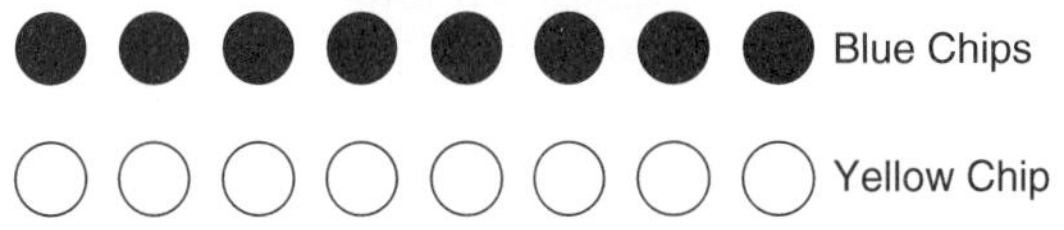

Task for number conservation.

Assessment. Point to the first row. Ask, "Are there more chips in this row or in this row (point to the second row), or are there the same number of chips?" Child responds. Ask, "How do you know that?" Child responds. Now spread out the second row of yellow chips so that the length has been extended. Ask the same question about equivalence. Ask, "Why do you think so?" Additional chips may be added to both rows, or the second row may be grouped in a stacked column or bunched together. Repeat the same questions with justification of the answers.

The child who is a nonconserver cannot maintain the equivalence of number because of changes in length that are irrelevant to number. The real issue is that the child cannot reverse the line of reasoning back to where it started. Preoperational children are so focused on the perceptual aspects of the task that a lasting equivalence or number invariance is not possible.

Conservers are not persuaded by changes in configurations or counter suggestions. They can justify their answers of "the same" by explaining that no chips were added or taken away, or that the chips could be arranged in the original position, or that the chips are spread out so the rows are longer but the number is the same.

When we relate this discussion to mathematics instruction, Piaget claims that without reversibility of thought and number conservation, the additive property cannot be understood. The child cannot understand that five will remain five if grouped as four and one, one and four, three and two, or two and three. The number in the set is still five. "Fiveness" has no meaning for the child.

Other educators or philosophers have studied Piaget's findings and have repeated his interviews and have confirmed his results. Direct instruction and schooling on conservation skills show that conservation cannot be taught with any lasting, permanent effects. Conservation abilities evolve from maturation due to experiences children have. Piagetian theory says that conservation abilities will not emerge until cognitive schemata, or the logico-mathematical structures, are in place. Number is something each human being constructs from within, and not something that is socially transmitted (Kamii, 1985).

Research (Hiebert, Carpenter, and Moser, 1982) has shown that ability to do Piagetian tasks in conservation, class inclusion, and transitivity may not be needed to solve simple addition and subtraction problems. When the same arithmetic problems were compared to a task assessing a child's information-processing ability, a small but consistent correlation was seen. However, some students scoring low on the information-processing task could solve the arithmetic problems. The findings would seem to indicate that the information-processing task and the three Piagetian tasks may not be prerequisites for applying simple strategies to solve early number facts.

Teaching Ideas. Children need experiences exploring various numbers in different arrangements. Sets must be constructed and compared by children so that lasting equivalence can be achieved no matter what the configuration. Number fans and bead cards (Figure 8.7) are teaching devices that can be used to build understanding of relationships needed for conservation. A game with painted lima beans or two-sided colored counters develops number invariance (refer back to Figure 8.4 on page 168) and allows many repetitions without boredom. Connecting cubes can be joined together to represent the same sum with various configurations and color patterns.

FIGURE 8.7

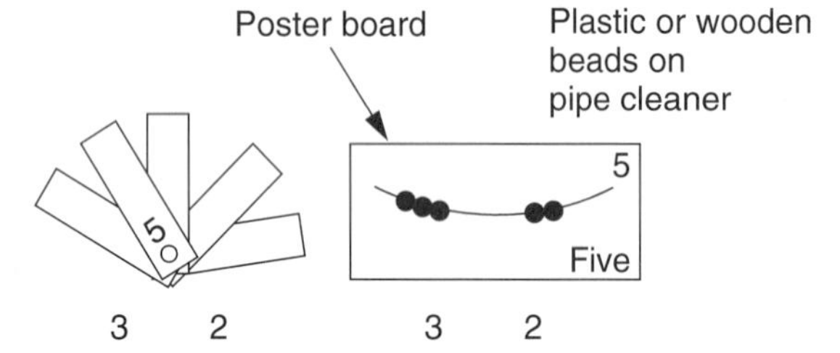

Materials for number invariance.

Mathematics Their Way (Baratta-Lorton, 1976), *Box It or Bag It Mathematics* (Burk, Snider, and Symonds, 1988), *Developing Number Concepts Using Manipulatives* (Richardson, 1998) and *Investigations in Number Data and Space* (TERC, 1998) are a few of the numerous early primary programs that promote the use of number stations and part-part-whole activities. Such activities encourage children to look for many number combinations and ways of grouping different materials for a specific number. In this way children can see different configurations and combinations which lead to number sentences related to addition and subtraction.

Kamii (1985) argues that the Piagetian class inclusion task described earlier is an indicator of children's ability to construct part-part-whole relationships. Eventually the language that accompanies such experiences should lead to encoding into writing activities (see Figure 8.17 on page 176) at the connecting level, explained in a later section in this chapter.

Task: Equivalence of Sets

A task associated with understanding number is equivalence of sets. Here the child must form an equivalent set and be able to match sets for equivalence. Perceptual cues may interfere with the young child's understanding of this aspect of number. The tasks in the following paragraphs describe how to assess set equivalence.

Assessment. Give the child a pile of lima beans. Make a set of five beans. Ask the child to make a set on a margarine lid (or any specific place to identify the set) that has the same number of beans. Ask, "Why do you think your set has the same number of beans as my set?" A child can have this understanding of one-to-one correspondence without being able to count. Another task is to make a line of counters. Below it start a second line of counters but stop before the lines are equal in number. Have the child continue the second set until it equals the numbers in the first set.

The next task tests set equivalence as well as the degree to which the child is tied to perceptions. The teacher and child each have a paper cup or small container (Figure 8.8). The child is given a group (around ten to twelve) of large lima beans or large counters. The teacher has an equivalent number of small lima beans (counters). The task is to simultaneously drop a bean into each of their cups. Because children love to race on this task, it might be advisable to say "drop" each time to keep the pace together. After all beans have been dropped into the cups ask, "Are there the same number of beans in each cup or do you have more or do I have more?" After the child responds, show the cups with the beans inside and repeat the question. The child may change the response because the size difference in the beans gives perceptual cues that may be interpreted as associated with the number. Ask for justification of each answer to gain valuable insight about how the child is thinking.

FIGURE 8.8

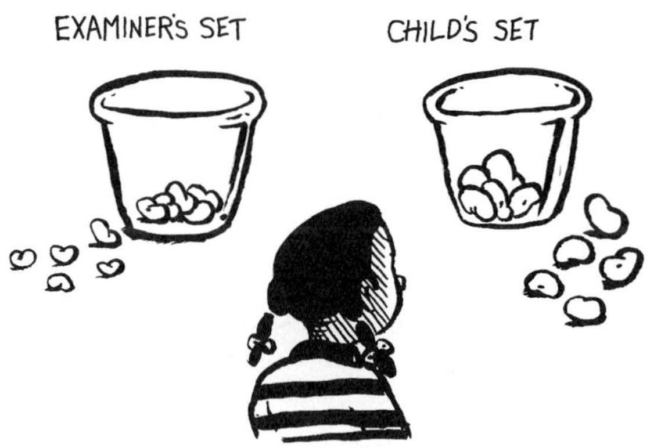

Set equivalence task.

The same thing holds true if the child is given two glasses of different sizes but the same size beads (Figure 8.9). Repeat the activity, but now the size of the container affects the child's perception of quantity even though a bead was placed simultaneously into each container.

FIGURE 8.9

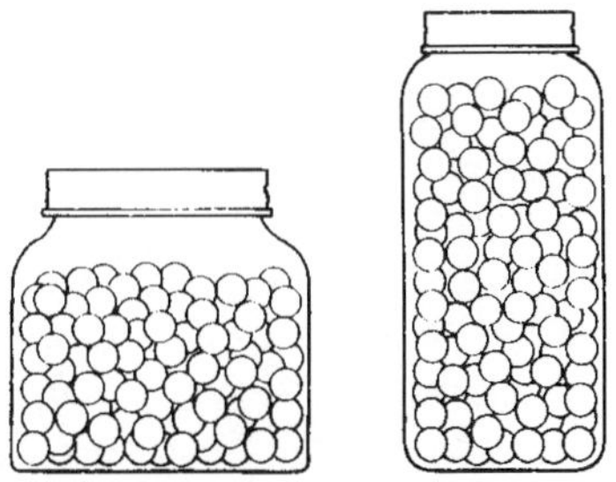

Another task for set equivalence.

Teaching Ideas. Children need practice in naming the number when given a representative set and in constructing sets of a specific amount. Have children work in pairs with junk material. Each child, taking turns, makes a set, and the other child makes a set that is equal. Use yarn to establish one-to-one matching between sets and help the child see set equivalence. Relying on counting is sometimes insufficient for the young child. In the task with the beans, it is helpful for the developmentally young child who makes decisions about number from perception to take the beans from the cups, place them in matched pairs to see equivalency, and discuss differences. Set equivalence and one-to-one matching can be done with cups and saucers, juice cans or milk cartons and straws, toy babies and bottles, jars and lids, and plastic flowers and vases (Figure 8.10).

FIGURE 8.10

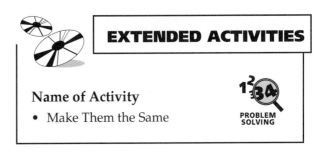

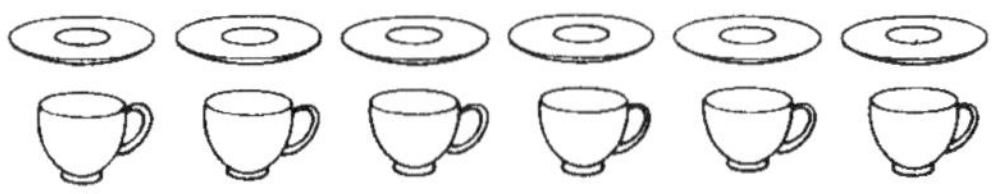

Developing set equivalence.

Implications for Curriculum

If these Piagetian ideas are applied to the learning of mathematics, there are several implications for the curriculum. First, prenumber concepts should be developed prior to introducing the child to abstract symbols. Second, teachers must develop diagnostic skills described in this chapter to assess a child's logico-mathematical knowledge and developmental level. Third, children need a learning environment that permits free exploration with concrete materials. The NCTM *Principles and Standards* (NCTM, 2000) call for learning environments in which students have opportunities to learn through active constructions with a variety of materials. Because most of these concepts are attained around the age of six or seven, the kindergarten year and a good portion of the first-grade year should be spent enjoying informal explorations with number. Some additional activities can be found on the CD-ROM.

With this knowledge of Piaget's observations and theory, compare traditional early primary classrooms. Children may lack the logical operations necessary for understanding number, yet they are introduced to basic facts, counting-on strategies, comparing numbers using greater-than or less-than symbols, missing addends, and many more concepts. Textbooks present number concepts through pictorial representations followed by abstract sym-

EXTENDED ACTIVITIES

Name of Activity

- Make Them the Same

PROBLEM SOLVING

bolism. Rather than permitting children to construct meaning about mathematics through creating and coordinating relationships, learning becomes rote memory of rules and procedures. In Piaget's words, "The true cause of failures in formal education is therefore essentially the fact that one begins with language (accompanied by drawings, fictional or narrated actions, and so forth) instead of beginning with material action" (Labinowicz, 1980, p. 167).

Assessment. Continual assessment of the child's mathematical understanding in an informal manner is an important aspect of teaching young children. From the beginning of formal schooling, educators value verbal learning and written demonstrations of understanding. Since these practices may not be consistent with performance styles of many ethnic minority groups, teachers must strive to find ways to equate learning that are compatible with other cultural groups. For African Americans, verbal and participatory learning is emphasized, whereas for Native Americans imitative learning is the norm. As young children with limited English struggle to translate their knowledge into an unfamiliar performance style plus translate to another language, teachers may conclude that the children are failing to master the concepts. According to the NCTM Equity Principle (NCTM, 2000) all students should have excellent mathematics instructional programs.

Since children are living in a society in which diversity is an ever-increasing reality, teachers must seek ways to integrate diversity into the daily program. Early primary teachers must reflect on not only the racial–ethnic composition of the class but of the classroom as well. What materials are available for children of different gender and cultural backgrounds to use and enjoy? Do the pictures, books, dolls, and stories read to the children reflect a dominate Euro-American culture? "The Challenge of Diversity" activity provides some thoughtful activities to engage children in learning mathematics.

Activity 8.4

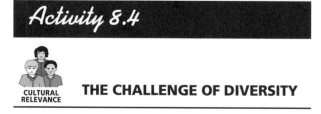

CULTURAL RELEVANCE

THE CHALLENGE OF DIVERSITY

MATERIALS

- Junk boxes
- Small chalkboards

Activity Continues

DIRECTIONS

1. To consider gender issues, have children use junk boxes that contain a wide variety of materials that would interest children from both sexes—nuts, bolts, and washers; Barbie doll accessories; keys; tools; trucks, boats, and cars; hair ribbons and barrettes; and so on. Have children use these in a free-choice situation to make up patterns, build number stories, and use for sorting.
2. To consider ethnic issues, have children work in paired groups to increase individual participation. Have them use cultural items such as Navajo beads to make patterns and develop counting and classifying skills.

Supporting the NCTM *Principles and Standards* (2000):

- Concepts of Whole Number Operations
- Tools that Enhance Discourse—The Teaching Principle
- The Equity Principle

The remainder of this chapter discusses the additional developmental needs of the young child and presents activities to match the child's thinking and to build mathematical understanding.

BUILDING THE CONCEPT OF NUMBER

Patterns

Patterns are inherent in mathematics, and the skill of recognizing patterns is valuable. Pattern recognition means identifying the repetitive nature of something. The pattern may be of a visual, auditory, or physical dimension. Discovering a pattern requires detecting differences and similarities between the elements in the pattern. Patterns should be experienced visually, auditorially, and kinesthetically. The NCTM Addenda book *Patterns* (Coburn et al., 1993) asserts that children should "be involved in recognizing, describing, extending, transferring, translating, and creating patterns" (p. 2).

Pattern should begin with an AB repetition. This means two elements will be alternated to produce the AB pattern. For example, red square, blue square, red square, blue square, or circle, square, circle, square, circle. When presenting patterns to children, it is important to include at least three repetitions. Once children have explored many varieties of this form, other simple patterns may be introduced: ABB, AAB, AABB, ABC, ABCD (Figure 8.11).

FIGURE 8.11

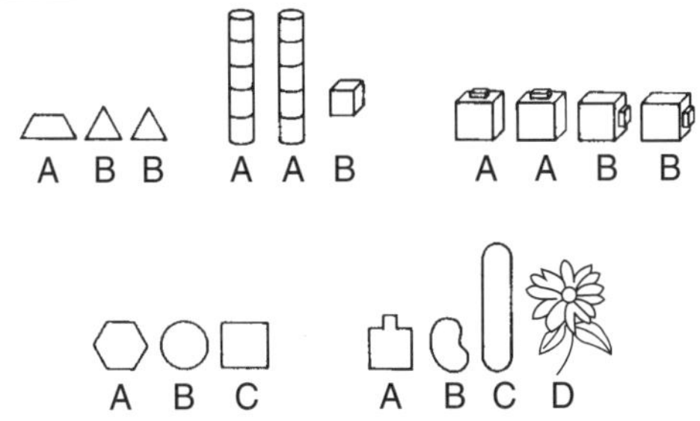

Exploring patterns.

Developing Patterning Skills. Children need to identify, analyze, copy, extend, and create many different patterns. Economopoulos (1998) suggests that comparing patterns helps children become careful observers of the structure of each pattern. As expected, patterns should be presented to children in physical ways. They can participate in forming patterns with other classmates: boy, girl; sitting, standing; hands on head, hands on hips; short pants, long pants. Body movements can be used to make patterns: snap fingers, clap hands; touch your knees, touch your toes; step, hop. Patterns may be created using some manipulatives: pattern blocks, color tiles, peg boards, connecting cubes, dyed pasta, or whatever is available.

The teacher creates a pattern such as "snap fingers, clap hands" and students can translate the pattern with the materials on hand (red circle, green circle; toothpick, macaroni). When they are comfortable with the concept of patterns, have them record their pattern by gluing construction paper shapes like the pattern blocks or connecting cubes, using stickers, or gluing the actual objects, if not intended for use again.

Activity 8.5

MATHEMATICAL CONNECTIONS

FINDING PATTERNS IN OUR LIVES

PROCEDURE

1. Take a "pattern walk" to investigate where patterns occur in our everyday lives. (social studies)
2. Listen to songs or music that has a repeated pattern. (music)

Activity Continues

3. Listen to stories that have a repeated pattern or a broken pattern. (reading)
4. Create a pattern that can be used in gym class with exercises such as hop, jump, hop, jump; touch toes, hands above head, touch toes, hands above head. (physical education)
5. Do an art project in which pattern is reflected: make strings of construction loops; string plastic or wooden beads on yarn; make a potato print pattern; paint a pattern. (art)

Number Relationships

One-to-One Correspondence. Many of life's scenarios involve establishing a one-to-one correspondence between two sets of objects, such as giving a napkin to each family member. This task is easier than counting a set and saying only one number name as each item is counted. This counting process establishes a one-to-one correspondence between the set and the counting number. Preschool children can be asked to do many household tasks to build this foundation for number: setting the table, distributing cookies to a group, getting paired with a buddy to play a game, arranging chairs at the table, and so on.

It is important that children realize that if a one-to-one correspondence exists, the items in the set can be rearranged and the matched relationship remains. Steffe and Cobb (1988) contend that children can be classified at varied levels of counting development according to their independence of perceptual and sensory cues. This aspect of one-to-one correspondence is a necessary part of Piaget's number conservation task.

More, Less, and Same. Another important consideration in early number development is the concept of comparing quantities as more, less, and same. As mentioned earlier, the young child who does not have class inclusion will not perform well on these tasks. This child does not understand relative relationships of number, namely that seven can be more (more than six) and also less (less than nine). The concept of number must be firmly established before the child is ready to make comparisons between numbers. One device that teachers have found helpful is a walk-on number line (the counting numbers beginning at zero). The child can step as the numbers are counted and relative position is sometimes easier to understand.

Activity 8.6

MANIPULATIVES

DEVELOPING MORE AND LESS

MATERIALS

- Connecting cubes
- Number cube with 0 to 6 on faces

PROCEDURE

First player rolls the cube. Get connecting cubes and make a train that long. Next player rolls and builds a train according to the number rolled. Compare trains and decide who has more (or who has less). A spinner divided into two equal regions with one-half labeled "more" and the other half labeled "less" can be used. After comparing the two trains, one child spins, and the pointer tells who is the winner (Figure 8.12).

FIGURE 8.12

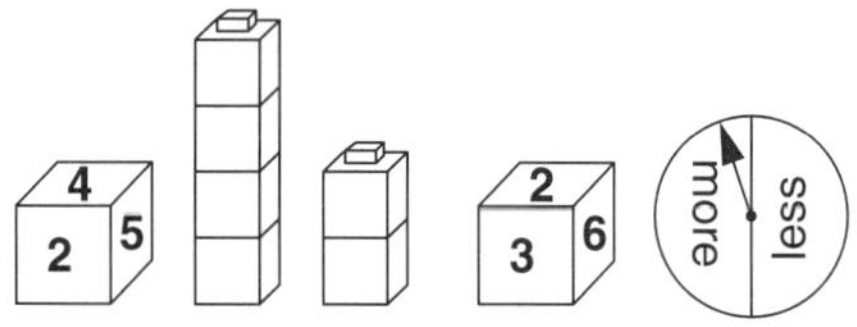

Materials to play the games.

- Connecting cubes
- More/less spinner

PROCEDURE

Each child makes a cube train out of the other's sight. They show their trains, compare them, and one child spins. The winner is the child whose train matched the spinner. *Example:* One player made a train of six; other player made a train of three. Spinner points to "less." The child with three wins.

Experiences to compare quantities are required also to build understanding. Only the concept of more, less, and same should be the focus at first, then as children develop the number relationships, how many more or less can be addressed.

Rote Counting. One of the first skills children learn in mathematics is rote counting. They count one, two, three . . . ten. Some children do this at an early age, and adults assume that the child will be a good math student. Rote counting is saying the number names in isolation without actually counting anything. It can be introduced from other children, parents, television, books, rhymes, games, and finger plays. A detailed collection of finger plays, verses, songs, and books for counting experiences can be found in *Towards a Good Beginning: Teaching Early Childhood Mathematics* (Burton, 1985).

Rote counting has no conceptual understanding of the numbers associated with it. It can be nothing more than nonsense names to some children said in a song-song fashion. But when the rote counting skill is investigated for understanding, it is obvious that the child has little or no understanding of what the number name means or represents. Rote counting is similar to learning the alphabet but having no idea of the names of the individual letters.

Research by Fuson and Hall (1983) indicates the three-and-a-half- to four-year-old group can count to thirteen on the average and the five-and-a-half- to six-year-old group can count to fifty-one on the average. Ordering the decades presented the most difficulty to the counting sequence. They conclude that young children's counting is based more on language patterns than on the structure of our number system.

Rational Counting. A more difficult counting stage is that of counting with meaning. At this point, a number meaning is assigned to the counting words. This stage develops slowly and is associated with developmental progress in the child as well as opportunities to explore the invariance or "manyness" of number. An important principle in counting is the cardinality rule, which means after counting a set, the last number name said is the quantity of that set. Another aspect of cardinality is that the order of counting the set does not matter—the result is the same.

Research by Steffe and his associates (1983) supports the relationship between the construction of the concept of number through counting and the cardinality rule. Research by Fuson and Hall (1983) indicates that even though young children can extend their conventional string of counting words, the development of number meaning comes much later. A child may know "twenty-five" in the counting sequence but may not have a number-structure meaning of two tens and five ones. After children attach an association between counting and cardinality, they are more flexible in dealing with number as quantities that can be compared, broken into parts, and seen as groups (Payne and Huinker, 1993).

Activity 8.7

CULTURAL COUNTING BOOKS

MATERIALS

- Book, *Ten Little Rabbits* (Grossman and Long, 1991)
- Writing paper and crayons

DIRECTIONS

1. Read the book to the class. Stop and ask the class to predict the next counting number.
2. Have the class discuss the rabbits' clothing and activities. Use information from the back of the book to discuss which Indian tribe is associated with each number.
3. Ask students to discuss in pairs how many rabbits there were in all. Children can use drawings or tallies to show their thinking.
4. Have them use other animals or pieces of pottery from the Native American culture to create and draw their own counting books.
5. Use other counting books to explore specific cultures such as *Count Your Way Through Mexico* (Haskins, 1989) and *Bread, Bread, Bread* (Morris, 1989). The latter author uses different breads eaten throughout the world to explore cultural diversity. *Numbers: How Do You Say It? English, French, Spanish, Italian* (Dunham, 1987) offers counting in various languages.

Many adults fail to remember how difficult and abstract the idea of number is for children to grasp. Imagine a new counting system with nonsense number names that you have to remember *in order and with meaning* and you can identify better with the frustrations of the young child.

Counting Sets. One-to-one matching is necessary for the child to be able to accurately count the number of objects or people. Textbooks have pictures of sets and the child is to circle the number name for the number of objects in the set. Other pages may show the set of objects, and the child is to write the number for the set (Figure 8.13).

Children can rote count much farther than they are able to rationally count. It proves more difficult for a child to successfully count objects in random array, whereas objects in a linear arrangement may pose no problem. Generally, the child physically touches the objects while counting and gradually will rely on visual counting. Counting does not become meaningful until about six years of age, when the child has a mental structure of number.

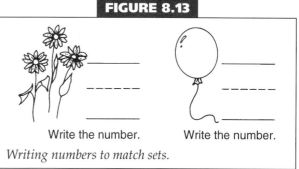

FIGURE 8.13

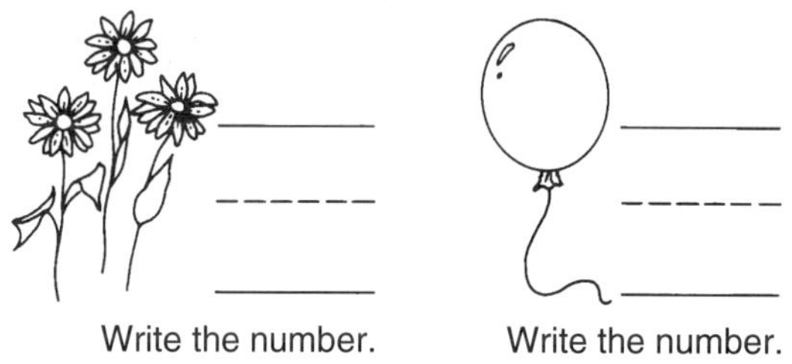

Writing numbers to match sets.

Involve the class in many counting activities to reinforce the one-to-one matching concept. Encourage children to keep records of objects by tallying. For example, have the children draw a tally for each boy that you ask to stand. Have them tally for you the number of children who are eating bag lunches. Children's first experiences with word-problem solving should involve counting and modeling. Such experiences should include a variety of problem structures (such as take-away, comparison, missing addend) as suggested by the *Standards.* More discussion about problem situations is given in Chapter 10.

Numeral-Set Association. The relation of the number in a set, the number name, and the written symbol must be well understood. An activity to develop this relationship for numbers through ten is illustrated in Figure 8.14. The child is given cards with the individual numerals 0 to 10 on them, pictures of sets from 0 to 10, and the number names. The child's task is to put appropriate cards together. The numeral-set associations should form a large part of an early primary mathematics program.

FIGURE 8.14

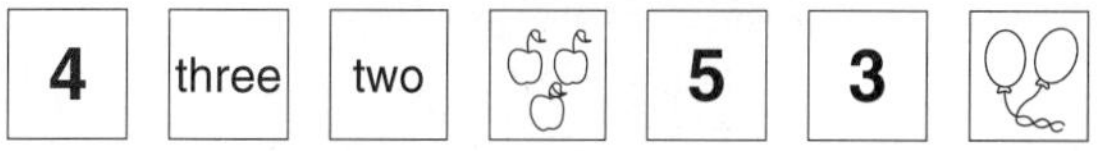

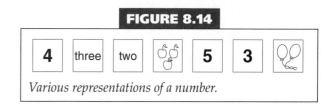

Various representations of a number.

Various arrangements of patterns for a number provide flexibility and greater transfer later. Children need to be able to recognize any sets that represent a number, regardless of the direction or composition of the members of the set. For example, 8 may be associated with each of the sets in Figure 8.15.

FIGURE 8.15

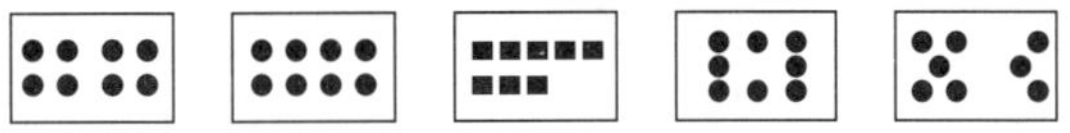

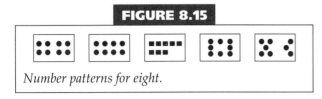

Number patterns for eight.

In addition, students can name the words as they are counted for relating reading to a math lesson. When students have a clear understanding of the numerals and their matching sets, the numeral names can be introduced. This introduction should be made when the child has constructed a set rather than according to the typical procedure followed in textbooks whenever possible. Build number charts that list the items there are "one" of in the classroom. Post the number charts and add to the lists as children discover more items. Create number charts for other numbers (Figure 8.16).

FIGURE 8.16

In our class we have . . .

One 1	Two 2	Zero 0
1 teacher	2 cabinets	0 zebras
1 flag	2 big desks	0 dogs
1 sink	2 big chairs	0 cars

Naming sets in the room.

Developing Meaning for Numbers. As children become aware that the quantity in a set they counted is named by a specific name, they begin to associate meaning to numbers. A connection must be made between the number concepts and the symbols that represent the numbers. When symbols are introduced, they hold no meaning to the child. Directed activities must be provided over a long period of time in the early primary program. Numbers should be encountered through the stages of *concrete level* (physical materials and oral naming as the counting is done), *connecting level* (with physical objects associated with the written numeral), and finally *symbolic level* (writing numerals with a meaningful visual image associated with the quantity). See Figure 8.17.

Additional books with activities to develop number concepts are *Mathematics Their Way* (Baratta-Lorton, 1976), *Mathematics Their Way: Beyond the Book: Activities and Projects from Classrooms Like Yours, Grades K–4* (Center for Innovation in Education, 1997), and books from the NCTM Addenda series such as *Number Sense and Operations* (Burton et al., 1993). Detailed explanations and pictures are provided for setting up number stations. Children freely explore numbers through a variety of materials and activities that focus on the process rather than on the answer. They construct arrangements of objects (for numbers they can count) to develop numerosity, conservation, counting skills, number sequence, and number combinations (Figure 8.18).

FIGURE 8.17

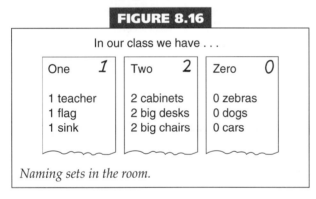

Learning stages to build set–number meaning.

The design of *Mathematics Their Way* allows for the gradual evolution of number from the intuitive concept level to the connecting level and finally to

Video Vignette

Numeral-Set Activities

In Mrs. Arroyo's first-grade class, she orally gives a number and the children are to match the quantity with numerals. As you watch this video, consider these questions:

- What informal assessments can you make about these children's counting strategies?
- Are there any numbers that they can instantly recognize without counting? Children can look at a small group of objects and know the quantity without counting the discrete items. This skill is called *subitizing*. Is there any evidence of this skill?
- What different counting strategies did you notice?
- What mathematical experiences (in terms of instructional strategies) would you suggest for these children?

the symbolic level. This developmental sequence of activities takes into account the intellectual capacities and maturation of a child. There must be a one-to-one correspondence between each number name and the objects being counted in the group for the child to truly understand the number concept being studied. The teacher's role is to provide ways to help children see the relationship between activities and the traditional mathematical symbols. The teacher must also be sensitive to know when to schedule activities at the next level by assessing when each child has acquired *real understanding* of the quantity of a given number. The assessment strategy is described in Figure 8.19.

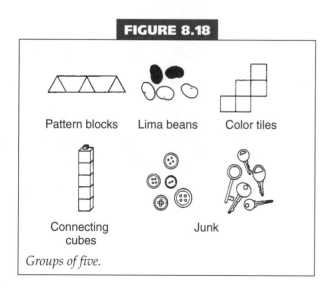

FIGURE 8.18

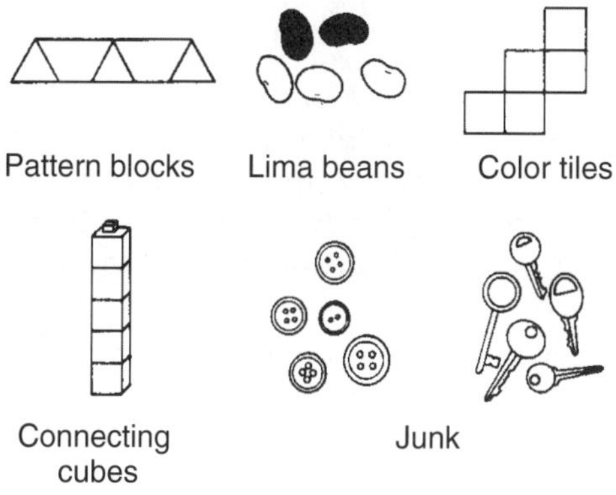

Groups of five.

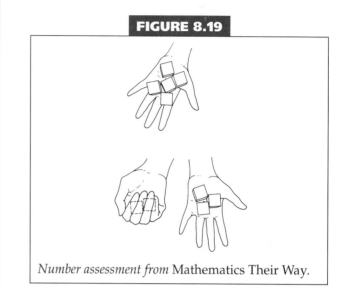

FIGURE 8.19

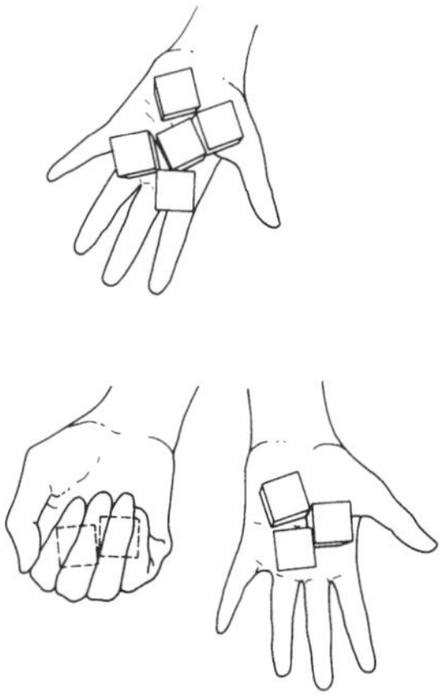

Number assessment from Mathematics Their Way.

Activity 8.8

MANIPULATIVES

ASSESSMENT OF NUMBER ACQUISITION (BARATTA-LORTON, 1976, p. 287)

Situation 1

Teacher: Count five blocks into my hand. How many blocks do I have?
Child: Five (without counting). (Shows "fiveness" and understanding of number invariance.)
Teacher: (Divides set of blocks between hands. Opens one hand and shows the blocks. [3]) I have three blocks and how many blocks are hiding in my other hand?
Child: Two. (Answers immediately without counting or guessing.)

This procedure is repeated several times with different combinations for the number. After many successful times, the child is ready to move to number six.

Situation 2

Teacher: Count five blocks into my hand. (Child performs task.)
How many blocks do I have in my hand?
Child: (Counts the blocks again.) Five.

Activity Continues

The rest of the procedure is continued and the child needs to count on or randomly guess to give the answer. This result means the child has not mastered an understanding of five and needs to have additional experiences with combinations for fives.

Literature. A number of books are available to develop concepts associated with early number readiness. Counting practice for both counting forward and counting backward are common such as *Anno's Counting Book* (Anno, 1977), *Anno's Counting House* (Anno, 1982), *The Very Hungry Caterpillar* (Carle, 1994), and *Counting on Calico* (Tildes, 1995). *Ten Black Dots* (Crews, 1986) offers an interesting way to have children establish set–symbol relationships by incorporating a given number of dots into an illustration to make a counting book to ten. *The Cheerios Counting Book* (McGrath, 1998) arranges cheerios into number patterns, shows groupings of ten and number relationships. The *M & M's Brand Counting Book* (McGrath, 1994) shows numbers to twelve and some basic operations.

Books offer experiences to help children think about classifying and sorting objects. Discussions about characteristics regarding similarities and differences promote logical reasoning. Some books to consider are: *A Children's Zoo* (Hoban, 1985); *Is It Larger? Is It Smaller?* (Hoban, 1985); *Whose Hat Is That?* (Roy, 1987). Whitin et al. (1994) describe a literature-based project using the book *How Many Snails?* (Giganti, 1988) to see classification of many attributes.

Pluckrose (1995) has written a series of books to introduce sorting activities, pattern, shape, size, and number with colorful real-world photographs (for example, *Pattern*). *The Button Box* (Reid, 1990) portrays many attributes of buttons that can extend to explorations with classification and patterns.

Activity 8.9

PORTFOLIO

PORTFOLIO ASSESSMENT

For Teacher Reflection of Student's Work in Number Readiness

- Make a collection of materials to use for assessing young children's understandings of these mathematical concepts: One-to-one correspondence, number conservation, seriation, set equivalency, class (number) inclusion, classification, patterning, and set–number association.

Activity Continues

- Design an interview protocol based on the chapter's information to assess each of the concepts mentioned above.
- Design a rubric to help define levels of verbal responses and to take into account the variety of answers.
- Prepare activities (according to the curriculum implications) for the children who have not acquired these mathematical understandings.
- Write about your assessment of the child's level of number acquisition. Collect readings about number readiness from mathematics journals to add to your portfolio.

Writing Numerals

Recognizing numerals and writing numerals involve different skills. Children are asked to match numerals to sets before writing them. The skill of associating a symbol with an amount is different from that of writing numerals. The physical skills of writing numerals include small muscle control as well as copying skills. Educators use various techniques to introduce the numerals 0 through 9. Associating a verbal sequential order with writing the numeral provides structure that helps recall. Some teachers use a color sequence for writing the numerals. The first segment is assigned a certain color, and the second segment is assigned a different color. The color sequence is the same for all the numerals. Baroody (1987) suggests having children reflect on the shapes of the numerals through verbal descriptions. He uses a "motor plan" that is practiced aloud as the children write the numerals. The motor plan describes where to begin and in which direction to proceed to form each numeral.

Teaching Ideas. Children may experience reversed numerals. Many different problems exist. Some children have certain numerals they consistently reverse and others reverse numerals when they hurry. A great number of errors are made in writing the "teens." Many first graders write "71" for "seventeen." This error is made because children write the numbers according to how they hear the number spoken. This may also be a problem later in place value understanding. Because children often write numerals before they receive formal instruction at school, teachers see many strange procedures that are difficult to stop. For example, the numeral nine is formed starting at the baseline with a straight line and the top loop added last.

To help establish the form of each numeral in the mind, teachers should provide tactile experiences accompanied with verbal structure of the sequential order of the writing. Make numerals from sandpaper or highly textured materials and have children trace the numerals. Fill a small cake pan with salt and have the child trace the numeral, shake the pan and practice again. Care should be taken to have easy-to-see models available for copying. Tracing in the air, on each other's back, and on Magic Slates or individual chalkboards provides a variety of practice activities. Furnish opportunities for writing the numerals in association with a matching set rather than in isolation.

Readiness for Operations

Once children have well-developed concepts of numbers and understand the relationships among numbers, a broader concept of number can be undertaken to include readiness for working with operations. According to the NCTM *Principles and Standards* (NCTM, 2000), beginning in preschool, all children should understand meaningful situations that lead to the four operations addition, subtraction, multiplication, and division. Building on the informal mathematical knowledge children possess when they enter school, counting activities can be directed to include joining, separating, comparing, doubling, halving, breaking sets apart, and part-part-whole. The part-part-whole relationship is fundamental to developing the concept of the four basic operations. Many parents and teachers, as well as the traditional mathematics curriculum, move children too quickly into what might be considered as the "real mathematics."

Textbook practice pages of basic facts in first grade are inappropriate for many children who are not developmentally ready for such abstractions. The child needs many experiences with number and symbols before being introduced to the signs for the operations. The child may be able to respond to questions about answers for basic facts, but often this ability is simply good recall or counting rather than solid understanding. As Dutton and Dutton (1991) assert, "In the past, for example, we have assumed that, from the beginning, children should use pencils to record or show relationships. Instead, we need to center instruction and children's activities on the development of 'thinking'—on the mental processes that children use" (p. 113).

Developing Meaning for Operations. As children develop the mental structures to deal with numbers, they can explore the operations at a concrete level. To gain understanding of the operations, children should manipulate materials and discuss and model the operations in problem-solving situations. They need to verbalize their actions and internalize the concepts before performing written work with the symbols. The same learning sequence should be followed for developing understanding about the symbols for operations that was used for developing number concepts discussed earlier in this chapter (refer back to Figure 8.17 on page 176). Activities are illustrated in Figure 8.20. After participating in and describing concrete experiences, the connecting level with symbols is modeled. When a solid understanding of the language and action is shown, the symbolic level is introduced.

FIGURE 8.20

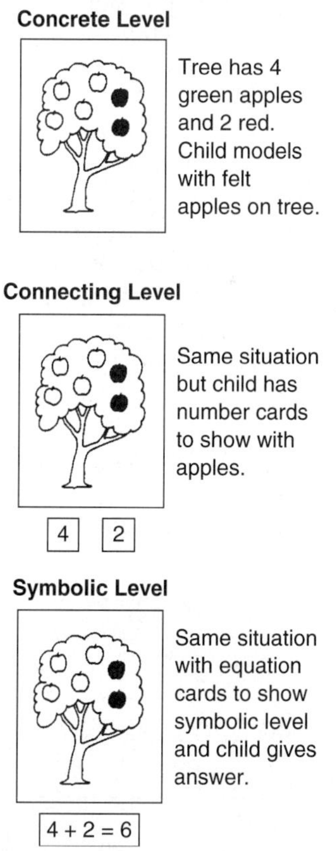

Concrete Level
Tree has 4 green apples and 2 red. Child models with felt apples on tree.
Connecting Level
Same situation but child has number cards to show with apples.
4
2
Symbolic Level
Same situation with equation cards to show symbolic level and child gives answer.
4 + 2 = 6

Learning sequence for understanding number operations.

Although the typical scope and sequence in textbooks present addition to six, subtraction to six, addition to ten, subtraction to ten, educators continue to debate whether addition and subtraction should be taught together or separately. A great deal of research has been conducted to investigate this question without any firm conclusions. Whichever approach is followed, children should be comfortable communicating about the operations orally and with objects to ensure understanding. Several activities on the CD-ROM show ways to develop understanding of operations.

Building Part-Whole Understanding. Once children are able to see relationships between numbers and connect number and set, they should begin to think in groups. The skill to quickly recognize the amount in a group without counting, called *subitizing,* becomes an important aspect of thinking in groups. Seeing the part-whole approach to groups (seeing ten as 2 fives and seven as five and two) rather than single counting by ones constitutes a valuable component for understanding addition and subtraction.

Activities to build part-whole understanding include using ten-frames (Figure 8.21). Children can place counters on the ten-frame filling the top row to five, then continuing in the bottom row to ten. In Figure 8.21, some children may see seven as "5 and 2" but other children may subitize into "4 and 3" still other children could see the number seven as "10 − 3". Action research suggests that ten-frames can be displayed to the child for one or two seconds and the 2 × 5 array helps them rapidly recognize the number (whole) as well as visually recall the two parts that form the number (Payne and Huniker, 1993). "Part-whole understanding of number provides a stronger conceptual base for addition and subtraction strategies" (p. 51). A video on the CD-ROM shows two first-grade classrooms using ten-frames in instructional settings.

FIGURE 8.21

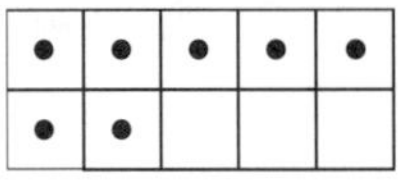

Ten-frames.

Kline (1998) offers many alternative ideas for using the "quick images" to develop mental imagery of the numbers. She suggests using the ten-frames as 5-to-10 minute warm-up activities and to ask children to describe their mental images. Kline finds ten-frames used in a horizontal fashion help her kindergarten students become fluent with teen numbers. Additional explanations and suggestions for using ten trays are provided in Chapter 10.

Video Vignette

Using Ten-Frames

Two first grade teachers are using ten-frames to help develop understanding of the power of ten.

- Watch the video of the two classrooms and compare the instructional uses of ten-frames. What do you think about the task in terms of "sound and significant mathematics?"
- Discuss your thoughts about the children's use of subitizing or counting. What can you conclude about the children's confidence with number?
- In the second sequence, what can you say about children's understandings of part-whole number relationships? Of number invariance? Of the operations being used?

Using Technology

Calculators have a place in number explorations in early primary mathematics programs. NCTM *Standards* (1989, 2000) call for appropriate and ongoing use of calculators and computers beginning in kindergarten. Some calculators can be used for counting by having the child count and push the equal (=) key to see if the counting number matches the calculator display. Counting by multiples of a number follows naturally by having the first number in the series change to reflect the counting pattern. The calculator's constant feature causes the number automatically to keep increasing or decreasing by a given amount. Counting backward is another skill that can be done on the calculator. This skill is necessary when using the "counting back" strategy for subtraction. Calculators are valuable in counting, searching for

EXTENDED ACTIVITIES

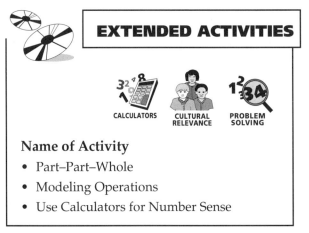

Name of Activity

- Part–Part–Whole
- Modeling Operations
- Use Calculators for Number Sense

counting patterns, and solving problems. Many computer programs are available for number recognition games, counting games, classification tasks, and exploring shapes and patterns. Check the CD-ROM programs to see listings of appropriate software and other calculator activities.

The early primary program should provide opportunities for estimation skills in various dimensions—duration of time, number, length, temperature. It should include geometry explorations with pattern blocks and geoboards, and allow explorations with numeration concepts. Each of these areas are discussed in later chapters in this text.

Activity 8.10

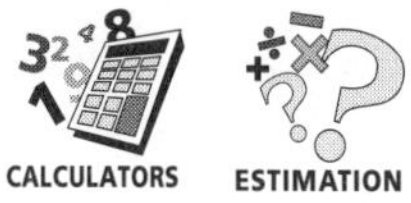

NUMBER SEQUENCE ON A CALCULATOR

MATERIALS

- Calculator

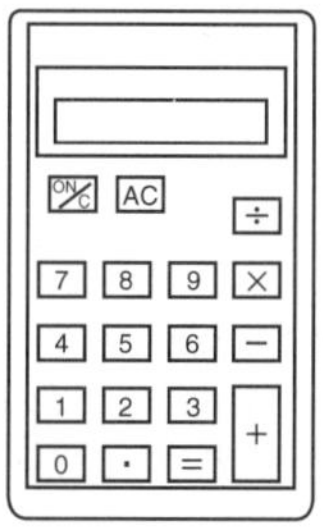

PROCEDURE

1. Count "one more" beginning at 0. Press "+" key, then "1," and "=" key. Display reads: 1. Press "=" key again (2), again (3), again (4), and continue. The calculator is counting by ones or showing "one more."

Activity Continues

2. Count "one less" beginning at 20. Start with 20. Press "–" key, then "1" key, and "=" key. Display reads: 19. Press "=" key again (18), again (17), and continue with each number showing "one less" or how to count backward.
3. Counting by other multiples is equally easy to show. Count by twos. Start with 0. Press "+," "2," and "=." Continue to press "=" to see multiples of two. Explore other operations using the same key sequence.
4. Add or subtract a constant to any number by this key sequence: To add 4, press "+," "4," "=" (display reads 4); "6," "=" (display reads 10); "2," "=" (display reads 6). To subtract a constant, begin with "–" as first input key. To incorporate *estimation,* have children make guesses about how many "=" keys it will take to reach a specific number. This relates to relative size of numbers for number sense. (Great practice for basic facts in Chapter 10.)

(*Note:* Some calculators work differently than the one described here.)

SUMMARY

The early primary curriculum for mathematics must take into account the aspects of active, direct participation by the child. The environment must be child oriented with time provided for investigations as well as for interactions with other students and the teacher. Children in early primary years should have opportunities to make sense of mathematics, to engage in active mathematics learning, and to connect mathematical language to their informal knowledge. As we keep the child's needs in mind, the primary grade experiences must be structured to nurture young children and guide them toward logical, operational thinking about the world of mathematics.

EXERCISES

For extended exercises, see the CD-ROM.

A. Memorization and Comprehension Exercises
Low-Level Thought Activities

1. Suppose there are several children in your first-grade classroom who are making number reversals. Describe the remedial activities you would use to help.
2. You are in a first-grade classroom with almost no manipulatives. The children are not understanding the meaning of subtraction. The pictures in the textbook of some birds on a limb and some birds flying away hold no meaning. What techniques would you use to help?

B. Application and Analysis Exercises
Middle-Level Thought Activities

1. Apply what you have learned to handle this parent-teacher simulation: You are using a child-oriented program with number stations, manipulative materials, and children working together and talking as they compare findings (cooperative learning), and a mother who is serving as an aide during math period challenges you that the children are "just playing" rather than "doing math." How would you respond?
2. Examine a first-grade textbook where numerals and their corresponding sets are shown. Comment about the approach used, the teaching suggestions offered in the teacher's manual, the prerequisite skills you feel are needed to complete the page successfully, and any alterations you would make in the teaching sequence.
3. Apply what you have learned in this chapter to handle the following simulation: You are a kindergarten teacher using a child-oriented program for teaching mathematics. You have some parents who are pressuring you to give their children traditional worksheets and practice dittos so they have firm evidence that mathematics is being taught. How would you respond?

C. Synthesis and Evaluation Exercises
High-Level Thought Activities

1. Devise an evaluation plan for determining whether a child can count rationally.
2. Write a proposal to your principal or supervisor describing manipulative materials with which you wish to equip your early primary classroom for teaching mathematics. Include a rationale and budget. Remember that many manipulatives can be made inexpensively. Some materials to consider are felt, various colors of plastic canvas, fun foam, sponges, strips of balsa wood, popsicle sticks, styrofoam meat containers to make Cuisenaire rods, pattern blocks, and other manipulatives mentioned in this chapter. The patterns are found in the Appendix or on the CD.
3. Read the NCTM *Curriculum and Evaluation Standards* and *Principles and Standards* (2000) with regard to the developmental aspects of early childhood education. Write a position paper concerning whether the *Standards* have addressed the mathematical needs of the young child as well as the developmental needs.

BIBLIOGRAPHY

For an extended bibliography, see the CD-ROM.

Anderson, Ann G. "Families and Mathematics: A Study of Parent-Child Interactions." *Journal for Research in Mathematics Education* 28 (July 1997): 484–511.

———. "Parents as Partners: Supporting Children's Mathematics Learning Prior to School." *Teaching Children Mathematics* 4 (February 1998): 331–337.

Baratta-Lorton, Mary. *Mathematics Their Way.* Menlo Park, CA: Addison-Wesley, 1976.

———. *Workjobs II.* Menlo Park, CA: Addison-Wesley, 1978.

Baroody, Arthur J. *Children's Mathematical Thinking: A Developmental Framework for Preschool, Primary and Special Education Teachers.* New York: Teachers College Press, Columbia University, 1987.

Burk, Donna, Allyn Snider, and Paula Symonds. *Box It or Bag It Mathematics: Teachers Resource Guide.* Salem, OR: Math Learning Center, 1988.

Burton, Grace. *Towards a Good Beginning: Teaching Early Childhood Mathematics.* Menlo Park, CA: Addison-Wesley, 1985.

Burton, Grace, M., Ann Mills, Carolyn Lennon, Cynthia Parker, Douglas Clements, John Firkins, and Jeane Joyner. *Number Sense and Operations: Addenda Series, Grades K–6.* Reston, VA: National Council of Teachers of Mathematics, 1993.

Center for Innovation in Education. *Mathematics Their Way: Beyond the Book: Activities and Projects from Classrooms Like Yours, Grades K–4.* Menlo Park, CA: Addison-Wesley, 1997.

Coburn, Terrance G. et al. *Patterns. Curriculum and Evaluation Standards for School Mathematics* Addenda Series, Grades K–6. Reston, VA: National Council of Teachers of Mathematics, 1993.

Dutton, Wilbur H., and Ann Dutton. *Mathematics Children Use and Understand: Preschool through Third Grade.* Mountain View, CA: Mayfield, 1991.

Economopoulos, Karen. "What Comes Next? The Mathematics of Pattern in Kindergarten." *Teaching Children Mathematics* 5 (December 1998): 230–233.

Fuson, Karen, and James W. Hall. "The Acquisition of Early Number Word Meanings: A Conceptual Analysis and Review." Ed. H. P. Ginsburg. *The Development of Mathematical Thinking.* New York: Academic Press, 1983.

Ginsburg, Herbert P. *Children's Arithmetic: How They Learn It and How You Teach It.* Austin: PRO-ED, 1989.

Hiebert, James, and Mary Lindquist. "Developing Mathematical Knowledge in the Young Child." Ed. Joseph N. Payne. In *Mathematics for the Young Child.* Reston, VA: NCTM, 1990. 17–36.

Hiebert, James, Thomas P. Carpenter, and James M. Moser. "Cognitive Development and Children's Solutions to Verbal Arithmetic Problems." *Journal for Research in Mathematics Education* 13 (March 1982): 83–98.

Kamii, Constance K. *Young Children Reinvent Arithmetic: Implications of Piaget's Theory.* New York: Teacher's College Press, 1985.

Kline, Kate. "Kindergarten Is More Than Counting." *Teaching Children Mathematics* 5 (October 1998): 84–87.

Labinowicz, ed. *The Piaget Primer: Thinking, Learning, Teaching.* Menlo Park, CA: Addison-Wesley, 1980.

———. *Learning from Children: New Beginnings for Teaching Numerical Thinking, A Piagetian Approach.* Menlo Park, CA: Addison-Wesley, 1985.

National Association for the Education of Young Children (NAEYC). *Developmentally Appropriate Practice in Early Childhood Programs Serving Children from Birth Through Age 8.* Washington, DC: NAEYC, 1996.

National Council of Teachers of Mathematics. *Curriculum and Evaluation Standards for School Mathematics.* Reston, VA: NCTM, 1989.

———. *Principles and Standards for School Mathematics.* Reston, VA: NCTM, 2000 (to be published).

National Research Council. *Everybody Counts: A Report to the Nation on the Future of Mathematics Education.* Washington, DC: National Academy Press, 1989.

Payne, Joseph N., and DeAnn M. Huinker. "Early Number and Numeration." Ed. Robert J. Jensen. *Research Ideas for the Classroom: Early Childhood Mathematics.* Reston, VA: NCTM, 1993. 43–70.

Piaget, Jean. *The Child's Conception of Number.* New York: Humanities Press, 1965.

Richardson, Kathy. *Developing Number Concepts Using Unifix Manipulatives.* Menlo Park, CA: Addison-Wesley, 1998.

Steffe, Leslie, and Paul Cobb. *Construction of Arithmetical Meanings and Strategies.* New York: Springer-Verlag, 1988.

Steffe, Leslie P., Ernst von Glaserfeld, J. Richards, and Paul Cobb. *Children's Counting Types: Philosophy, Theory, and Application.* New York: Praeger, 1983.

Technical Education Research Center (TERC). *Investigations in Number, Data, and Space Curriculum Series.* White Plains, NY: Dale Seymour Publications, 1998.

Von Glasersfeld, Ernst. "Abstraction, Re-presentation, and Reflection." Ed. Leslie P. Steffe. *Epistemological Foundations of Mathematical Experience.* New York: Springer-Verlag, 1990.

Whitin, David J., Heidi Mills, and Timothy O'Keefe. "Exploring Subject Areas with a Counting Book." *Teaching Children Mathematics* 1 (November 1994): 170–174.

Wirtz, Robert. *New Beginnings. A Guide to the Think, Talk, Read Math Center for Beginners.* Monterey, CA: Curriculum Development Associates, 1980.

CHILDREN'S LITERATURE

Anno, Mitsumasa. *Anno's Counting Book.* New York: Thomas Y. Crowell, 1977.

———. *Anno's Counting House.* New York: Philomel Books, 1982.

Carle, Eric. *The Very Hungry Caterpillar.* New York: Putnam, 1994.

Crews, Donald. *Ten Black Dots.* New York: Greenwillow Books, 1986.

Dunham, Meredith. *Numbers: How Do You Say It? English, French, Spanish, Italian.* New York: Lothrop, Lee and Shepard Books, 1987.

Giganti, Paul, Jr. *How Many Snails? A Counting Book.* New York: Greenwillow, 1988.

Grossman, Virginia, and Sylvia Long. *Ten Little Rabbits.* San Francisco: Chronicle Books, 1991.

Haskins, Jim. *Count Your Way Through Mexico.* Minneapolis: Carolrhoda Books, 1989.

———. *Count Your Way Through Italy.* Minneapolis: Carolrhoda Books, 1990.

Hoban, Tana. *A Children's Zoo.* New York: Greenwillow, 1985.

———. *Is It Larger? Is It Smaller?* New York: Greenwillow Books, 1985.

McGrath, Barbara Barbieri. *The M & M's Brand® Counting Book.* Watertown, MA: Charlesbridge Publishing, 1994.

———. *The Cheerios Counting Book.* New York: Scholastic, 1998.

Morris, Ann. *Bread, Bread, Bread.* New York: Lothrop, Lee and Shepard, 1989.

Pluckrose, Henry. *Pattern.* Chicago: Children's Press, 1995.

Reid, Margarette S. *The Button Box.* New York: Penguin Books, 1990.

Roy, Ron. *Whose Hat Is That?* New York: Clarion, 1987.

Tildes, Phyllis Limbacher. *Counting on Calico.* Watertown, MA: Charlesbridge Publishing, 1995.

Integrating Technology

Video Vignettes: Lesson Plans in Action

- *Numeral-Set Activities*
- *Using Ten-Frames*

Computer Software Resources

...for Early Number Readiness

Internet Searches

Surfing the Internet for Number Readiness Topics

Use the World Wide Web (WWW) and navigate through the system, searching for new information under major headings and subheadings similar to the following:

Mathematics Education
- Number Readiness
- Preschool
- Constructivists
- Early Primary Mathematics
- NCTM
  - Early Years
  - Teaching Children Mathematics

- *Remember...* the Web is fluid ... new topics and ways to search for topics change daily.
- Be adventurous ... think of some new things you could try.

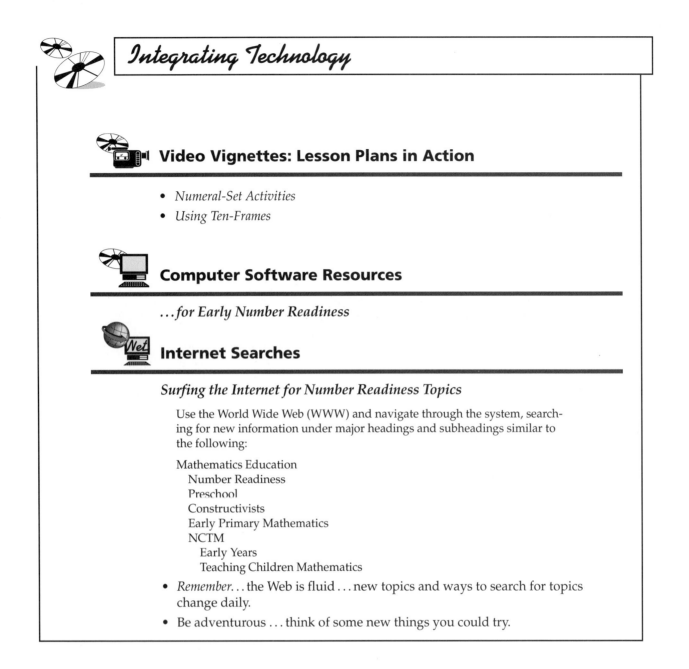

9

Numeration and Number Sense

Activities Index

IN THE TEXT

ON CD-ROM

The development of place-value understandings is an essential component of the elementary school mathematics curriculum. The part-whole understanding of number and the readiness work with addition and subtraction presented in Chapter 8 provide the conceptual base for later work with place value and larger numbers. To understand place value embodies three aspects of number: the number name (oral or written), the symbolic numeral, and the conceptual model represented with base quantities. The coordination between these three entities forms the foundation for the development of place-value concepts (Figure 9.1).

FIGURE 9.1

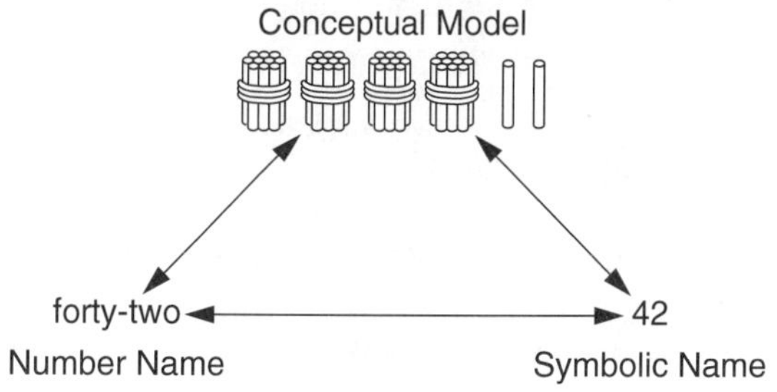

Components of place-value understanding.

Children begin to develop number meaning by counting. Counting is related to counting groups to make ten. Counting groups is different than counting individual units in a one-to-one correspondence. Children need extended experiences to be able to integrate counting patterns and construct grouping relationships. As number patterns are recognized and applied by the child, nonconventional number names often occur such as "twenty-ten" and "tenty-one."

Place-value understanding involves quantifying sets of objects by grouping by ten. Research by Steffe, Cobb, and von Glasersfeld (1988) maintains that children's place-value ideas develop from seeing numbers of a unit of one and counting by ones, to counting by groups (twos, fives, or tens), to developing notions about tens and ones that compose numbers. Kouba, Zawojewski, and Strutchens's (1997) examination of the data from the National Assessment of Educational Progress (NAEP) suggests that students at all grade levels (fourth, eighth, and twelfth) performed well on items requiring place value and rounding in familiar situations, but they had difficulty applying concepts and properties to unfamiliar situations. Students could not justify their answers or explain their reasoning. Eighth-grade students could not interpret the meaning of large numbers (22 percent answered correctly). The NCTM *Principles and Standards* (2000) call for students to develop well-understood meanings of our number system. Read through the components of the standards related to numeration in Box 9.1.

Activity 9.1

CULTURAL RELEVANCE

CHINESE NUMERATION SYSTEM

二 十 五

Asian culture has a regular system of number names. Investigate the Chinese notational system and write about the groupings, the pattern of number names, how it compares to our Hindu-Arabic system, and what limitations this system has. Explain how the abacus is associated with this number system.

BOX *9.1* Curriculum and Evaluation Standards

Number Sense and Numeration

In grades K–4, the mathematics curriculum should include whole number concepts and skills so that students can—

- Construct number meanings through real-world experiences and the use of physical materials.
- Understand our numeration system by relating counting, grouping, and place-value concepts.
- Develop number sense.
- Interpret the multiple uses of numbers encountered in the real world.

Number and Number Relationships

In grades 5–8, the mathematics curriculum should include the continued development of number and number relationships so that students can—

- Develop number sense for whole numbers, fractions, decimals, integers, and rational numbers.

Number Systems and Number Theory

In grades 5–8, the mathematics curriculum should include the study of number systems and number theory so that students can—

- Understand and appreciate the need for numbers beyond the whole numbers.
- Develop and use order relations for whole numbers, fractions, decimals, integers, and rational numbers.
- Develop and apply number theory concepts (for example, primes, factors, and multiples) in real-world and mathematical problem situations.

Source: National Council of Teachers of Mathematics, 1989, pp. 38, 87, 91.

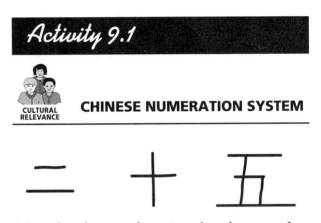

STRUCTURE OF NUMERATION SYSTEMS

Exploring the structure of a numeration system generates an appreciation and understanding of how efficiently the system operates. Numeration systems have a specific structure from which emerges place-value notations, powers, and exponents. The configuration of the base 10 system is shown in Figure 9.2. Notice that the system begins with a single basic building unit, often referred to as a *unit.* From there, each regrouping is done at ten. The models shown are known as the base 10 blocks (also referred to as place-value blocks, multibase blocks, Dienes blocks, powers of 10 blocks).

All units are single ones until the first regrouping. The configuration of the first regrouping looks like a long set of units fused together, hence, the name *long.* The 10 means one set of ten and no single units present except for those accounted for in the long.

The second type of regrouping occurs when there are ten longs (or ten groups of ten). The configuration looks like a flat with its ten longs fused together, hence the name *flat.* There are ten times ten sets of the basic building unit that can be seen in the *flat,* or one hundred pieces of the basic unit. The numeral 100 means one set in the second regrouping with no sets of ten and no single units present except for those already accounted for in the flat.

The third type of regrouping occurs when there are ten flats (or ten groups of hundreds). The configuration looks like a block with its ten flats fused together, hence the name *block.* There are ten times a hundred sets of the basic building unit that can be seen in the block, or one thousand pieces of the basic unit. Therefore, 1000 means one set in the third regrouping with no sets of hundreds, no sets of tens, and no units except for those already accounted for in the block.

Check Your Mathematics Knowledge

On Numeration and Number Sense

- Development of Numeration Systems
- Babylonian System
- Mayan System
- Roman System
- History of Hindu-Arabic System

. . . a refresher from mathematics coursework . . . Lest you forget!

FIGURE 9.2

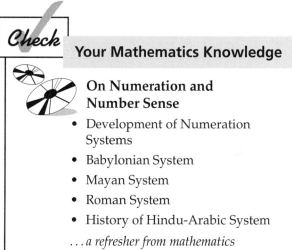

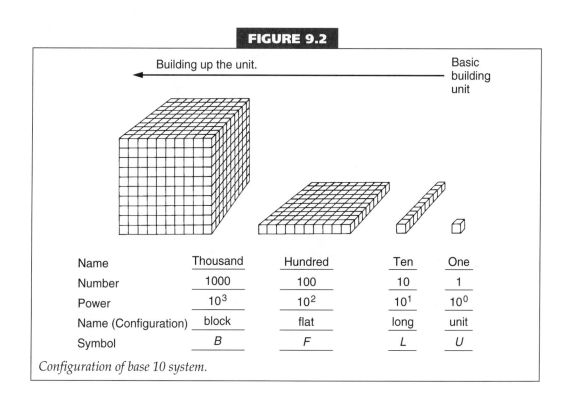

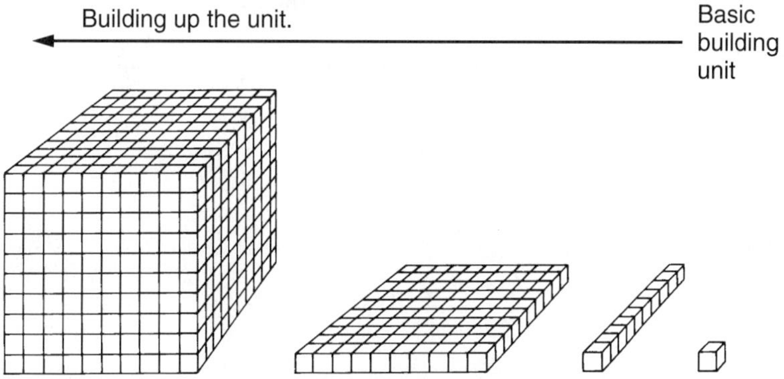

Name	Thousand	Hundred	Ten	One
Number	1000	100	10	1
Power	10^3	10^2	10^1	10^0
Name (Configuration)	block	flat	long	unit
Symbol	*B*	*F*	*L*	*U*

Configuration of base 10 system.

Subscripts©. . . *little thoughts below the bottom line*

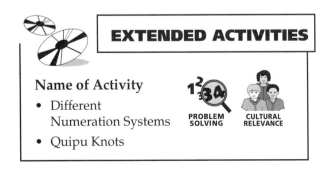

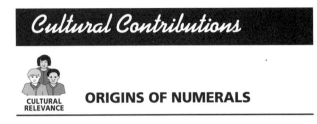

Exponents are known as powers of 10 when the base is 10. Exponents are introduced to students in the sixth or seventh grade in most textbooks. The exponent is just another way of indicating which type of regrouping is being considered. Notice that:

10^2 is read as "ten squared."

It is not by chance that the configuration for "ten squared" is in the shape of a square (the *flat*), nor is it by chance that:

10^3 is read as "ten cubed."

As Figure 9.2 shows, the shape is a cube (block). Many college students are unaware that any number that is squared or cubed becomes the shape of a square or cube when using base models. When middle grade students are first introduced to exponents, the configuration and meaning of the base 10 system (as seen in Figure 9.2) should be shown to them.

Studying the numeration systems of other cultures provides some interesting comparisons to our number system. Hughes and Anderson (1996) offer some interesting background and activities for middle grade students to explore the rich history of number systems of Native American tribes. The positional numerical system of the Mayans described by Lara-Alecio, Irby, and Morales-Aldana (1998) gives examples of representational materials and provides cultural links. Many activities can be found on the CD-ROM to explore other numeration systems for deeper understanding and appreciation of our own system.

EXTENDED ACTIVITIES

Name of Activity

- Different Numeration Systems
- Quipu Knots

PROBLEM SOLVING   CULTURAL RELEVANCE

Cultural Contributions

CULTURAL RELEVANCE

ORIGINS OF NUMERALS

Students need to know that their ancestors and the ancestors of their fellow classmates were the intelligent people who invented number systems. The Chicago Public Schools have developed a culturally relevant curriculum around the specific facts about each group. It is included here with the clarion call to use the information when planning mathematics lessons.

> *Students should know that many peoples contributed to the development of modern arithmetic and that the origins of arithmetic are international. For example, Africans were the first to use numerals. Ancient Egyptians in Africa invented a symbol for ten that replaced 10 tally marks and a symbol for one hundred that replaced 100 tally marks. The Chinese were among the first to recognize and use number patterns. The Maya in Central America used a place-value system and they used zero as a position holder hundreds of years before Europe imported modern numerals from Africa.... Modern numerals were invented by the peoples of India. That is why modern numerals are known as Hindu-Arabic numerals.* (Strong, 1990)

Decimals

Decimals are as much a part of the rational number system as are common fractions. In fact, decimals are just another name for rational numbers in the base 10 numeration system. Attention should be concentrated on the buildup of the base 10 whole number system (Figure 9.3). A new part has been added to the right. It illustrates the decomposition of the base 10 system. By extending the place-value system into smaller segments of the basic building unit and keeping the same configuration of units, we obtain the rational numbers. Notice that throughout this section, the discussion continues to key to the basic building unit, since it will be stressed in developing fractions.

FIGURE 9.3

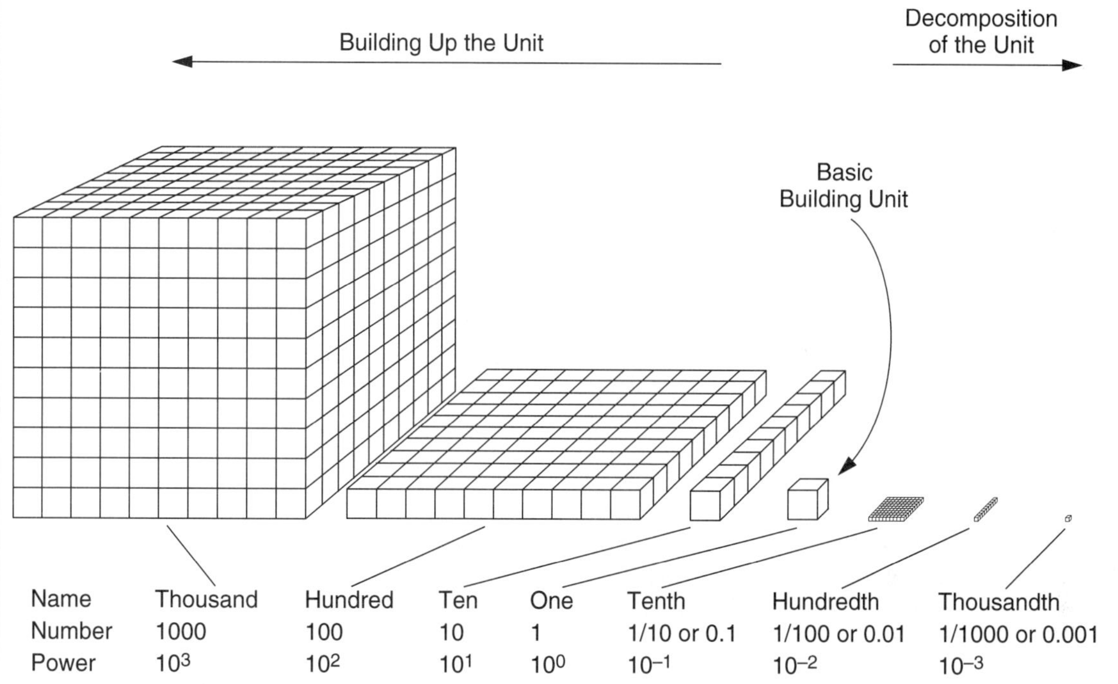

Configuration of decimal numbers related to small unit cube as the whole.

Place-value understanding in decimals requires a realization that the focal point of the place-value system is the number 1. As Sowder (1995) states, "So really 0.342 is 342 *thousandths of one.* Put another way, 0.3 is three-tenths of 1, while 3 is three ones, and 30 is three tens, or 30 ones. But by the same token that 0.3 is three-tenths of one, 3 is three-tenths of 10, 30 is three-tenths of 100 and so on up the line" (p. 21). Before moving to operations with decimal numbers, Sowder recommends postponing work with operations on decimal numbers until these place-value concepts are well developed. Wearne and Hiebert (1988) urge that if students do not have a sound understanding of place value before they learn to add and subtract decimal numbers, many errors result from flawed computational procedures that are difficult to overcome. Their research of over 700 students in grades three to nine suggests that few connections exist between students' conceptual knowledge of decimals and the symbol manipulation of rules for computation. Hiebert (1992) provides a more in-depth discussion of the research on decimal number understanding.

Just as the whole numbers are built up by groups of ten, so the fractional parts of the basic building unit can be partitioned by groups of ten. Every time we move one place to the right, the value of the digit is one-tenth as great. If the small unit cube is the whole, the configuration of the tenth is that of a flat or one-tenth of the basic building unit (Figure 9.3). The next regrouping is one-tenth of the small flat or one-hundredth of the basic building unit. It looks like a small long. The next regrouping is one-tenth of the small long or one-thousandth of the basic building unit. It looks like a little block. Notice that the three new categories of base 10 blocks fit into the same configuration as the whole number system, namely, block-long-flat, block-long-flat (reading from right to left).

However, base 10 blocks are only manufactured in units, longs, flats, and blocks. Therefore, modeling decimal numbers using base 10 blocks becomes more complicated. The unit block (tiny cube) cannot realistically be subdivided easily into tenths and hundredths as Figure 9.3 illustrates. The pieces would be too small to handle. It is important to remember that the central idea is maintaining the ten-to-one relationship. Students should investigate how the basic building unit (one whole) could be represented by various numeration blocks. What would happen if the basic unit were the large cube? What value would be given to a small cube? To the flat? How would you represent 7 tenths? 2.3? Suppose the flat represents one whole or becomes the basic building unit. What would be the value of the other base 10 blocks? Any piece can be named as the basic unit for the ones place as long as we know what represents the whole. Sowder (1997) shows other alternative number names and representations for decimals in an instructional unit on decimal numbers used in her research projects. The role of the decimal point is to show the name of the units and to separate the whole units from the parts of wholes.

A common model shown in textbooks and resource units is to name the flat or 10 × 10 cm square (formerly called the "hundreds") as the whole unit (Figure 9.4). Hence, students can model decimals through hundredths. Students study the decimal system in the upper grades when they are capable of using an object to represent more than one concept. Changing the representation of the base 10 blocks should present no problems to students when the place-value relationships are emphasized (Figure 9.5). Just as the powers of the whole numbers signify which regrouping is taking place in the buildup of the system by tens, so the negative (–) powers tell which regrouping is taking place in the decomposition of the base 10 system.

The fractional parts of the base 10 system are known as the *decimal* part of the system. "Deci" is Latin for "part of ten" or "part of a whole broken down by tens." Elementary textbooks stress the point to students by writing a decimal part of a whole with a lead zero, like this:

0.625 instead of .625

The zero in the above example reminds students that there is no whole number represented there. This text follows the same principle so that teachers can familiarize themselves with writing decimal representation in this way.

FIGURE 9.4

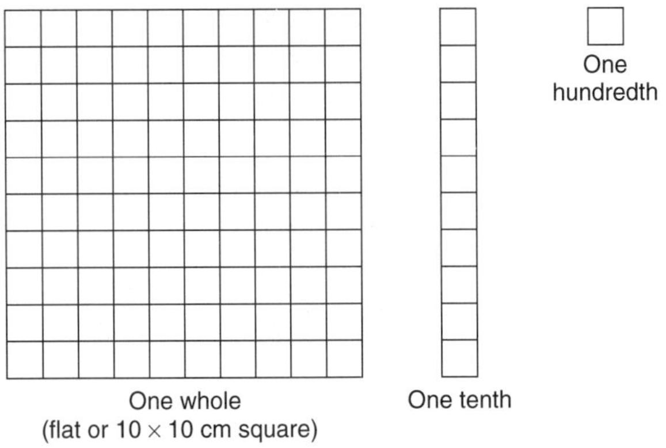

Models for decimals.

Number Bases

Multibase activities were prevalent in the upper-grade mathematics textbooks of the 1960s during the period in mathematics history known as the "New Math" era. Working with different number bases was considered quite new and revolutionary by many parents and teachers. Check the CD-ROM to see an exercise from an upper elementary textbook published in 1892 (Milne, p. 398). If the word "scale" is replaced with the word "base," it becomes apparent that different number bases have been a part of the curriculum off and on for over one hundred years.

FIGURE 9.5

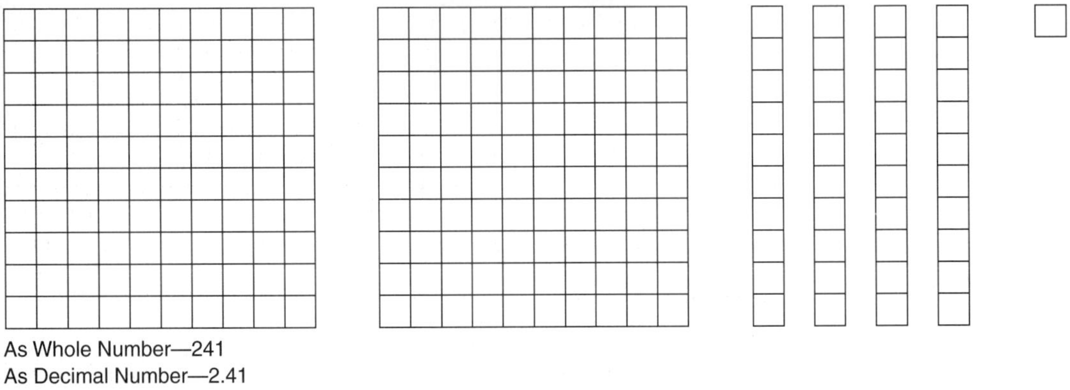

Interpreting base 10 models.

The following activities reconstruct numbers in different number bases using pictures of the multibase blocks as the manipulatives. As you go through the activities, you will be challenged to think about the groupings and relationships in much the same way that children must do as they learn the base 10 system.

Activity 9.2

PROBLEM SOLVING MANIPULATIVES

BASE 4 NUMERATION SYSTEM

DIRECTIONS

1. Sketch the configuration of the base 4 numeration system to the third regrouping.
2. Now count by units in base 4 using the number line that appears below the multibase shapes. The first four have been done for you. Label each with the corresponding numbers.

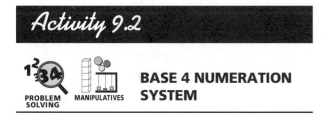

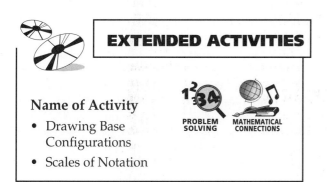

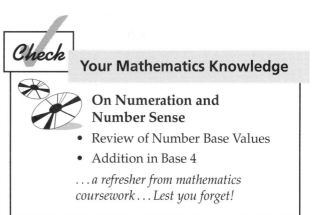

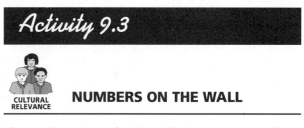

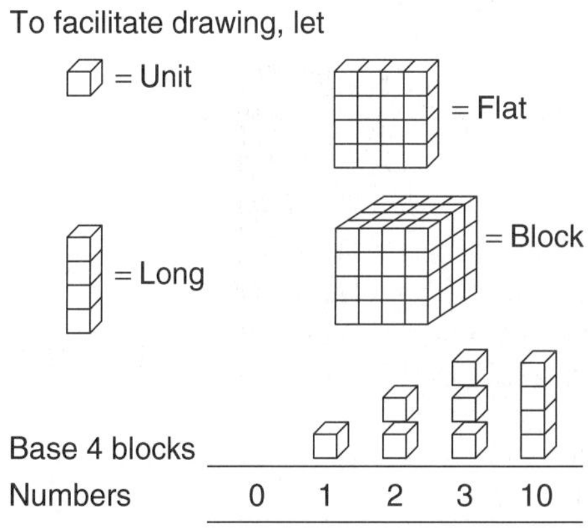

EXTENDED ACTIVITIES

Name of Activity

- Drawing Base Configurations
- Scales of Notation

PROBLEM SOLVING MATHEMATICAL CONNECTIONS

Other bases have the same configurations, and the numbers can be read as if in families or periods as well. The names *block, long,* and *flat* are used because they apply to the configurations (shapes) that appear in any number base. The family or period names can be generic too, so they can apply to any number base. Our system reads these sets of three as families or periods, and the names are consistent with the configurations (Figure 9.6).

Check Your Mathematics Knowledge

On Numeration and Number Sense

- Review of Number Base Values
- Addition in Base 4

. . . a refresher from mathematics coursework . . . Lest you forget!

Activity 9.3

CULTURAL RELEVANCE

NUMBERS ON THE WALL

The number system of early civilizations was primarily a notational system such as the Egyptians'. Investigate how we learned about other people's systems of numbers in the encyclopedia and other sources. What discovery converted the Hindu-Arabic notation into a place-value system? Explain the impact of this breakthrough finding.

Read *Talking Walls* by Margy Burns Knight (1992). How have walls been used by different cultures throughout thousands of years? Discuss how early people used walls to record important events and what role number system played.

TEACHING STRATEGIES

Instructional Sequence

There is a growing body of evidence that without direct instruction, children will invent their own strategies for adding and subtracting multidigit numbers. When this occurs, children's invented strategies are based on base 10 number concepts. For example, to add 38 and 27 using the standard algo-

FIGURE 9.6

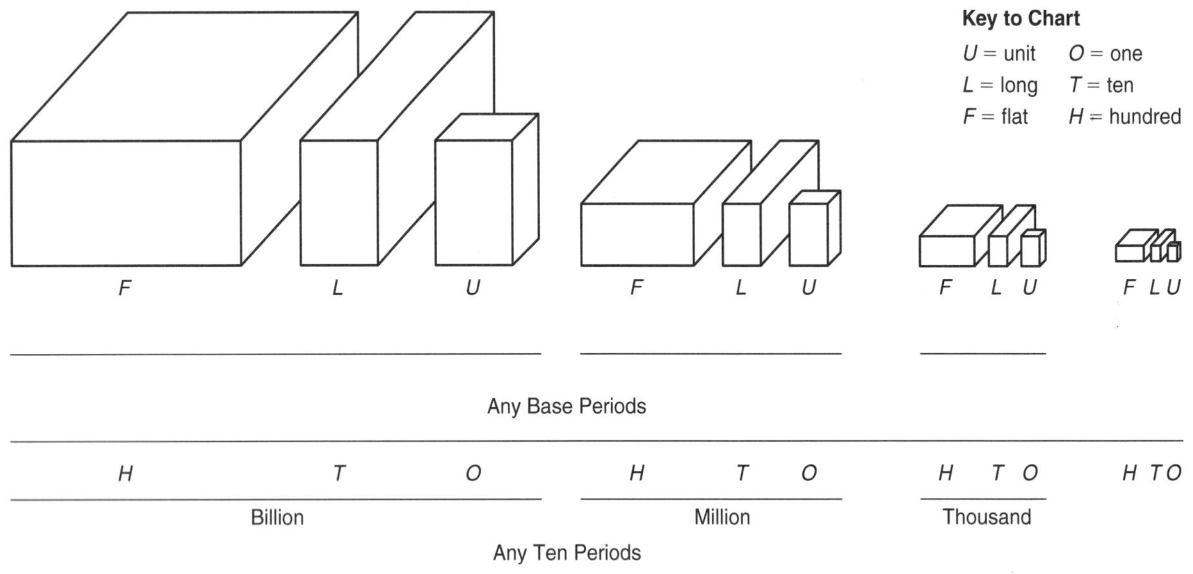

Family or period chart of the numeration system.

rithm, the numerals are aligned into columns that are added as ones and then tens. On the other hand, children's invented strategies may add the tens as 30 and 20 then the ones, or as 38 and 20, then add 7 more. Fuson et al. (1997) provide an analysis of invented strategies, and more discussion and examples appear in Chapter 11.

There is an ongoing debate about the sequence for developing base 10 concepts and children's use of invented strategies. "One perspective is that understanding multidigit procedures depends on a reasonably well-developed understanding of base-ten concepts; the other is that learning procedures for adding and subtracting multidigit numbers provides a context for motivating and supporting the development of base-ten concepts" (Carpenter et al., 1998, p. 6). Other studies (Fuson et al., 1997) suggest that invented strategies develop as children reflect upon their solutions with base 10 materials. Although initially children use various materials to represent tens and ones, as they become more comfortable with their invented procedures, their use of physical materials declines and mental calculations are done.

Whichever viewpoint you take, primary-grade teachers recognize a wide range of misconceptions that students have when working with place value. An interesting research project (Nagel and Swingen, 1998) involving students from six to thirteen years of age noticed a close link between the language used by children and the depth of their understanding of place value. Opportunities for children to act out place-value exchanges, use physical materials, and use a shared language for these processes were critical components of solid place-value understandings.

Numeration often occurs in the first few chapters of the student's textbook. Unfortunately, inadequate coverage is frequently seen, and insufficient skill maintenance is offered. Our number system is efficient with certain properties that need to be fully developed in students' minds. The first property of the system is the nature of place value.

The Nature of Place Value

Place value means that the position of a digit represents the value of the digit. In our base 10 system, there are ten digits: 0, 1, 2, 3, 4, 5, 6, 7, 8, 9. All other numbers are composed of these digits. For example, the numeral 5 looks the same in any place, but the value is different depending on the position.

Another aspect of our number system is the number's total value. *Total value* refers to the additive property of the system. This means that 358 represents the number 300 + 50 + 8 and 358 is the total value. *Expanded notation* refers to the actual value of each digit, such as 412 = 400 + 10 + 2, and *standard form* refers to writing the compact number, such as 412. During the modern math movement, heavy emphasis was placed on showing expanded forms of numbers (4 × 100) + (1 × 10) + (2 × 1), but much less time is currently devoted to this concept. Perhaps the reduced coverage on this topic in textbooks may prove to be a limitation on a child's understanding of the system. Here are some activities that focus on reinforcing this skill and developing understanding.

Activity 9.4

MENTAL MATH

FORM THE NUMBERS WITH EXPANDED NOTATION CARDS

MATERIALS

- Poster board or construction paper—three colors
- Expanded notation cards—see directions

CONSTRUCTION

1. Cut nine 3″ × 9″ rectangular strips from one color. Think of these as three 3″ × 3″ squares and in the left section write the digits 1 to 9 followed by 0 centered in each of the other square sections for *hundreds.*

4	0	0	3"

9"

6	0	3"

6"

7	3"

3"

2. Cut nine 3″ × 6″ rectangular strips from another color. Repeat the step above, only with one 0 since these are the *tens.*
3. Cut ten 3″ × 3″ squares from a third color. Write the digits 0 to 9, one per piece, centered in large form for the *ones.*

PROCEDURE

The teacher or groups of children may use these cards to form any three-digit number. The teacher or group leader says a number. The cards are selected that name that number in expanded form. Stack the cards, aligning the right edges, to see the standard numeral and separate to see the expanded form. The number can be recorded with the plus sign between each card to illustrate the additive property. To include four-digit numbers, create cards that are 3″ × 12″, and construct cards for the thousands in a similar fashion.

400 + 60 + 7 = 467

Activity 9.5

MENTAL MATH

PLACE VALUE STRIPS—AN AID TO MENTAL COMPUTATION

MATERIALS

- Felt-tip pens or any washable pens
- Laminated construction paper strips 1″ × 9″

PROCEDURE

The teacher says a three-digit number, and the students write the number on their strip in the rectangular region at the far left. After the equals sign, students place the single digit beside each appropriate place value name. In folded compact form, the strip should read 258 = 258. In unfolded, expanded form, the strip should read 258 = 2 hundreds + 5 tens + 8 ones. Various folds can be opened to expose different forms of the number, such as shown below. Such activities encourage students to be flexible in working with numbers and to see equivalent representations of numbers.

258 = 25 tens + 8 ones

258 = 258 ones

258 = 2 hundreds + 58 ones

258	=	2	hund +	5	tens +	8	ones

258	=	2	hund +	5	tens +	8	ones

258	=	2	5	8

Folded compact

Activity 9.6

MENTAL MATH

EQUAL NAMES

MATERIALS

- 48 cards—four forms for twelve numbers
  Samples:

600 = 60 tens = 600 ones = six hundred
8326 = 8000 + 300 + 20 + 6 = 83 hundreds twenty-six
= eight thousand three hundred twenty-six

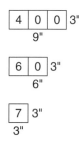

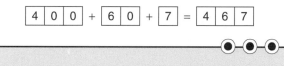

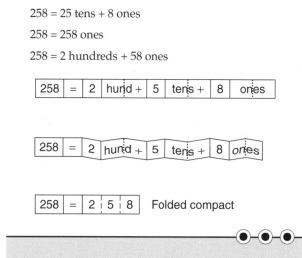

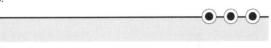

Activity Continues

PROCEDURE

Play in groups of four. Determine who goes first. Deal all cards to players. The object is to get books (total sets of four forms) of equivalent names for a number. When a book is formed, the player may lay down the cards as a set. When play begins, players may trade any cards to the player on the left. The game pauses for players to check on equivalent numbers and form books. Play continues until one player has succeeded in making all the cards into books.

Students can profit from experiences with the calculator when dealing with large multidigit numbers. A quick counting activity is to use the constant feature of the calculator and input 1 + = = =. As the student continues pushing the equals key, the counting sequence of the numbers is displayed. Students can see the changing ones column and the 0 to 9 sequence recurring.

Activity 9.7

CALCULATORS

USING CALCULATORS WITH THE EXPANDED FORM

MATERIALS

- Set of number cards
- Calculator

PROCEDURE

Read the number on the card. Express the number in expanded form (such as 3000 + 40 + 6). Enter the expanded form of the number into the calculator in any order. Did the same compact form of the number occur as the final number? This activity shows the additive property as well as the commutative property for addition.

Early Experiences. Interaction with grouping materials is the foundation for constructing understanding of place-value concepts. Young children need to physically join or group materials into sets of ten with discrete, groupable objects (such as toothpicks, straws, craft sticks, lima beans, or popcorn). In this manner, the child is responsible for forming the group rather than for trusting the trades of ten units for one ten. Some children need to continue to count and check to reassure themselves that the group represents ten. Trading is an extra step that some children may not be ready to make. It is important to sequence the use of materials according to the developmental needs of each child. Ungrouped, discrete materials should be the beginning point of investigating grouping. After initial grouping concepts are well established, proportional materials requiring trading can be introduced. Such other numeration models are discussed later in this chapter.

FIGURE 9.7

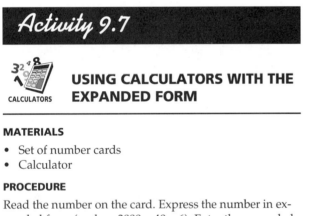

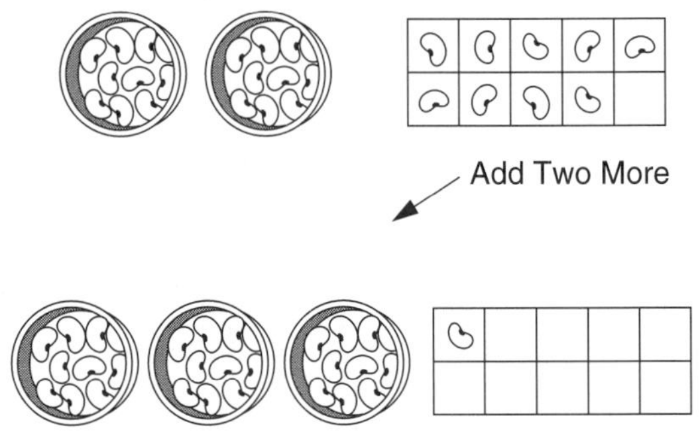

Ungrouped materials (beans and cups) with ten-frames.

Learning about number through ten-frames, also discussed in Chapter 10, is an approach that develops benchmarks of fives and tens which are helpful for numeration. The tens structure shows children how to develop numerosity rather than counting by ones (Figure 9.7). Each time the ten-frame is full, the beans are put in a portion cup to represent one ten and moved to the tens place on the place-value mat.

Play grouping games such as the "Chip Trading" Activity (see later in chapter) only using ten-frames with beans and cups. The first person who reaches 50 (or 100) is the winner. To add the connecting level to this activity, have children record the numbers on place value recording sheets from *Mathematics Their Way* (Baratta-Lorton, 1976; see Figure 9.10). Another way to add the connecting level is to have digit cards, number flips, or number tiles to model the number represented on the mat (Figure 9.8).

Numeration Models

Base 10 blocks serve as excellent models for place-value concepts, especially in establishing an under-

FIGURE 9.8

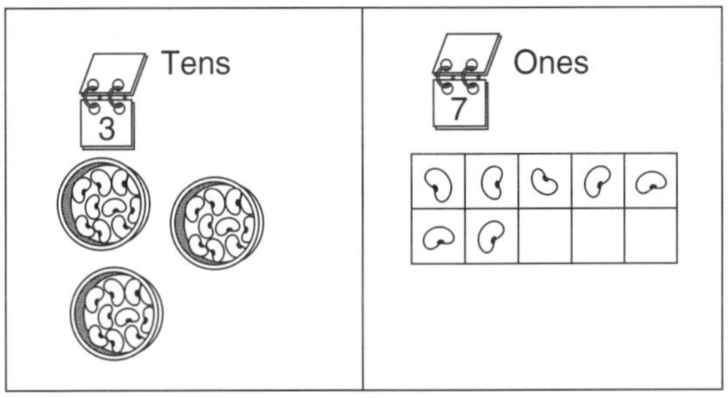

Adding the connecting level with number flip cards.

FIGURE 9.9

Proportional Models

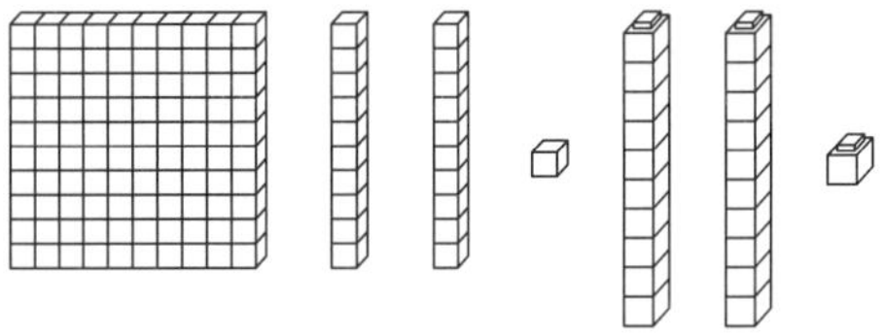

Base 10 Blocks

Purchased commercially or made out of meat trays scored with a pen or plastic canvas

Connecting Cubes

Purchased from stores to allow for perfect connections

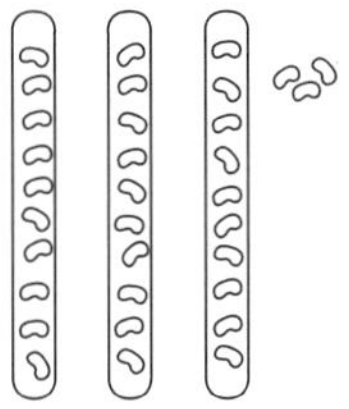

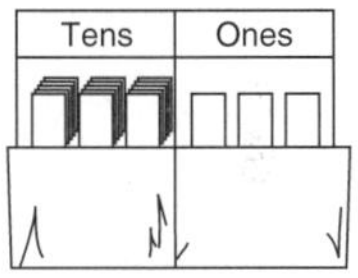

Beansticks

Tongue depressors with ten dried lima beans pasted on each stick

Pocket Chart

Tag board folded over and stapled to make a pocket, paper strips are bundled in sets of ten

Nonproportional Models

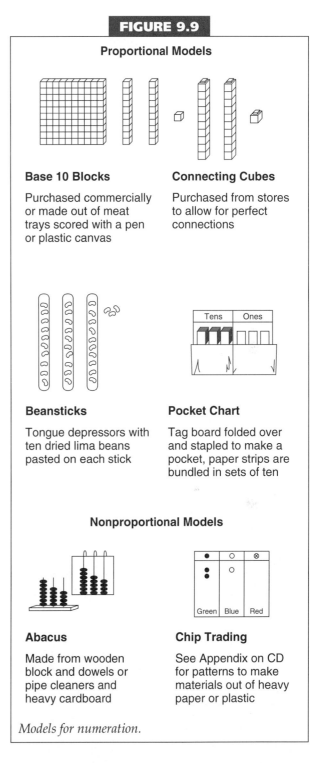

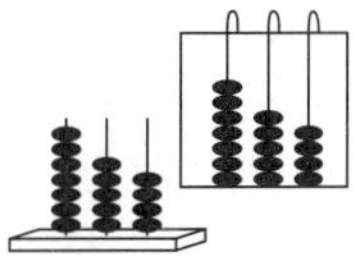

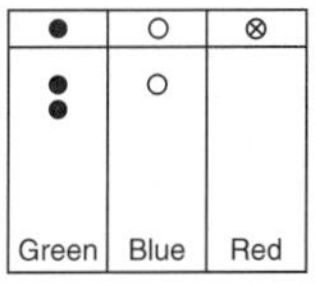

Abacus

Made from wooden block and dowels or pipe cleaners and heavy cardboard

Chip Trading

See Appendix on CD for patterns to make materials out of heavy paper or plastic

Models for numeration.

standing of ones, tens, and hundreds. Keep in mind that numbers are abstractions and children need concrete materials to construct an understanding of number and place-value notation. Interviews with children by Labinowicz (1985) provide ample evidence that many third-grade children do not relate to the thousand block because they do not conserve volume until age eleven. They focus on a surface area strategy and fail to consider the inside of the cube. Therefore, when asked how much the thousand block represents, the nonconserving child replies, "600," counting six sides of one hundred each.

Generally, the feeling is that it is important to allow children opportunities to explore the structure of other number systems by performing activities in other number bases. This is usually done in upper elementary and middle school; however, base work can be done with younger children using recording charts and counters. The emphasis should be on the trading between groups. Trading or grouping rules apply to all number bases. If the base is 4, then trades are four for one. If the base is 7, then trades are seven for one. Children may attach fear and failure to exploring patterns in base 10 because they may have been rushed to the symbolic level before real understanding of the system has occurred. Instruction with physical materials offers children a chance to investigate the patterns in our number system and internalize them.

Both proportional and nonproportional models may be used to work in other bases. When proportional models are used, the same configuration that indicates grouping occurs. Remember the repeating pattern of cube, long, flat mentioned earlier in this chapter? This pattern continues as regroupings continue. The commercial base 2 or base 4 blocks are excellent materials to show the place value concepts in other bases.

The pictures and descriptions in Figure 9.9 of place value models may help to demonstrate the differences between proportional and nonproportional models. They may also inspire ideas for appropriate teaching strategies for each one.

Activity 9.8

MENTAL MATH PROBLEM SOLVING

PLACE VALUE BINGO

MATERIALS

- Bingo boards
- Popcorn, lima beans, or any small markers
- Number list for caller

PROCEDURE

Leader or teacher is the caller who reads statements from the number list. Anyone finding that number on the board may cover it with a marker. Winner is first one with five markers in a row, column, or diagonal. The number list may be written to fit the needs of students playing the game. Here is a sample list:

The number that is one more than 34.

The number that is before 58.

The number that is ten more than 12.

A number that has three tens.

Do you see which models provide a one-to-one correspondence with the number represented and which models do not? Some models attach irrelevant attributes to the place-value positions such as size or color. Do you feel there might be problems with such models? Why?

Research (Kamii, 1986; Labinowicz, 1985) indicates that many children's understanding of place value in second through fifth grades is delayed until grouping by ten is well established. Repeated grouping experiences using multiple embodiments of materials helps internalize number ideas. To construct the ten-to-one relationship through counting and grouping materials takes more time than is typically allowed in schools.

Number Base Activities. Use various grouping intervals of threes, fives, and so on to establish the one-to-many correspondence and help children construct number meaning for smaller quantities. Throughout this section, activities to use with other number bases are included. Keep in mind that the number bases or the value of the number is not important for young children to know. Rather, it is the notion that groupings may be made in many different intervals.

Video Vignette

Numeration Games

Watch how the university professor's instruction becomes a reality in this fifth-grade classroom.

- What significant mathematical ideas are included in the exchange games described by Dr. Hatfield?
- In what ways does Mrs. Torres encourage student discourse?
- How does she promote mental calculations? When she says the boys have "very good understandings," what do you think she is informally assessing?

If base activities are done with proportional models, such as the multibase blocks described earlier in the chapter, it is clear to see that definite configurations indicate regroupings. This makes it easy for children to see the consistency between the various bases. The ability to visualize a size increase per column helps children feel comfortable with large numbers. If a nonproportional model is desired, chip-trading materials (different colored chips) work nicely. The key feature is that once trading rules have been defined, all activities follow these rules. If trades are five chips of one color for one chip of another color, base 5 is used. Trades are made for the name of the base. If trades of seven of one color for one of another color are made, then base 7 is being used. Follow these steps to see how chip trading works.

Activity 9.9

MANIPULATIVES

CHIP TRADING

MATERIALS

- Chips of three colors
- Chip-trading mat with three columns color matched to chips
- Number die

PROCEDURE

The game mat and the chips are color coded—for example, the far right column is red, the middle column is blue,

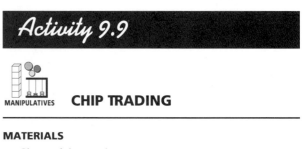

Activity Continues

and the left column is green. The trades will be five for one, so base 5 will be used. The object of the activity is to be the first player to regroup chips until a trade is made for a green chip. This means that 5 reds can be traded for 1 blue, 5 blues can be traded for 1 green and when that happens, that player wins. The focus of the activity is on making trades of five for one. Sample plays for one player follow:

Player rolls—3. Put 3 red chips in red column.

Player rolls—3. Put 3 red chips on mat. Since the total is 6, trade 5 reds for 1 blue. This leaves 1 red.

Player rolls—2. Put 2 red chips on mat. No trades.

Player rolls—4. Put 4 red chips on mat. Total is 7 red chips, so trade 5 reds for 1 blue.

Play continues until a trade of 5 blues for 1 green occurs and the player wins.

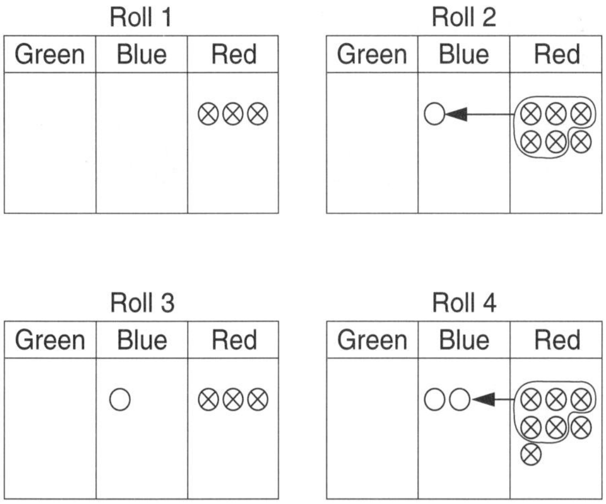

Early activities with number bases for children can be done using nonsense names for the base names. Since a four does not exist in base 4 (rather it is a 10), a nonsense name such as "frump" can be used. Therefore, the digits are 0, 1, 2, 3, and trades are made whenever there is "frump" in a group. To count, we would say, "Zero, one, two, three, frump, frumpty-one, frumpty-two, frumpty-three, frumpty-frump." Now we need to create another new name for the former term "hundred." This pattern continues.

Many educators feel that students should be comfortable with other bases and that these activities greatly enhance and strengthen base 10 ideas. As Burns (1984) asserts, to realize how our number system works, "children benefit from exploring groupings in bases other than 10 and examining the patterns that emerge. If enough time is spent with these smaller groupings, children can readily make the transfer to the patterns in base 10. In this way, base 10 evolves as part of a general structure which the children have experienced concretely" (p. 151).

Counting Activities

Counting can accompany previously described activities to help construct base 10 concepts. Thompson (1990) identifies three ways to count a set (for example, 42): Counting by ones (from one to forty-two); counting by groups of tens and singles (one, two, three, four groups of ten and one, two); and counting by tens and ones (ten, twenty, thirty, forty, forty-one, forty-two). He contends that counting by groups of tens and singles is a link between counting by ones and place value concepts. Regardless, *many* activities should involve counting to accompany the action of the grouping. As you assess children's understanding and confidence of grouping, watch for children who continue counting by ones to verify the number.

Activity 9.10

MANIPULATIVES **HANDFULS**

MATERIALS

- Beans, popcorn, connecting cubes, buttons, pasta, and so on

PROCEDURE

Child takes a handful each of several different items. Count the total number of each item by putting it into groups of tens and singles. Compare the totals and write about why handfuls are different.

ASSESSMENT

Watch for counting procedures. What do you know about the child's understanding of place value?

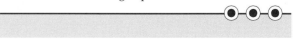

Activity 9.11

MANIPULATIVES

BEAT THE SAND!

MATERIALS

- Egg timer with sand
- Stamps and stamp pad
- Paper and markers

PROCEDURE

The timer begins and the child stamps as many times as possible before the sand is gone. Then the child counts the stamps in several different ways and shows the grouping with different markers. Have the child write about how the grouping was done.

Counting activities in base 10 are valuable for discovering the many patterns in our system as well as for understanding the number sequence. Recording the numbers on graph paper cut into three or four columns helps clarify some patterns. Study the numbers in Figure 9.10, and determine some number patterns. Can you see a rule that could be used for counting in other bases? If so, try another base and see whether the rule holds true for it.

Counting by ones, tens, hundreds, or whatever is an important activity to allow children a sense of how and when numbers change. For example, when counting by ones even with six- or seven-digit numbers, only the digit in the ones column changes or increases. Some children who have not had opportunities to explore this concept will change several digits in a large number when asked to write the number that is one more or one less.

An excellent device to illustrate this concept is an odometer. If you can secure an old one from a junkyard or used car parts shop, it will demonstrate to children how the gears work together so that when the tenths dial is at 9, one rotation will cause the tenths dial to turn to 0, and the column on the left, the ones, will increase by one. Likewise, if the tenths and ones have a 9, the next rotation will cause both 9s to become 0 and the column on the left, the tens, to increase by one. Use odometers to show patterns for decimal numbers also.

A homemade odometer can be constructed to illustrate such counting patterns, and the student can control the moving of the places. Observing such counting patterns helps solidify how the number system is structured.

FIGURE 9.10

Base 5

		4	3
		4	4
	1	0	0
	1	0	1
	1	0	2
	1	0	3
	1	0	4
	1	1	0
	1	1	1
	1	1	2
	1	1	3
	1	1	4
	1	2	0

Base 3

		0
		1
		2
	1	0
	1	1
	1	2
	2	0
	2	1
	2	2
1	0	0

Number patterns.

Activity 9.12

MATHEMATICAL CONNECTIONS

ODOMETER MATHEMATICS

MATERIALS

- Oak tag—cut in three equal strips to cover can
- Aluminum soft drink can
- Matte board or heavy cardboard
- X-acto knife

CONSTRUCTION

Cut three equal strips from oak tag to cover aluminum can. Tape strips individually to allow each to rotate independently around the can. Make an opening or "window" in the matte board that is large enough to expose one number from each strip. Cut with X-acto knife as shown and pull tabs to cover ends of can. Cut circles from oak tag to cover the ends of can and tape tabs and circles to can.

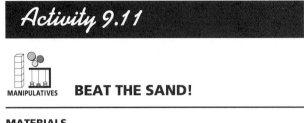

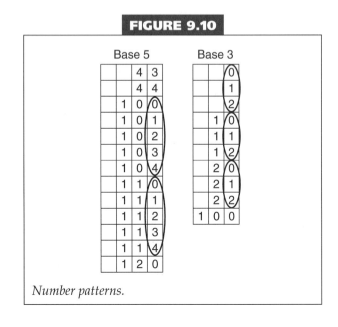

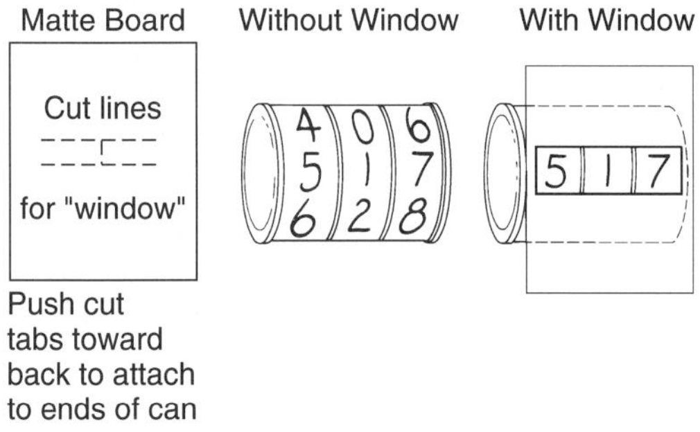

Activity Continues

PROCEDURE

The three strips (or more if using the inner roll from paper towels) can be rotated to expose the digits on the face of the odometer through the "window." Rotate each strip to show children how the digits 0 to 9 form all the numbers through 999. Some activities to do with the odometer:

1. Teacher or partner dictates a three-digit number. The student forms that number on the odometer.
2. Teacher or partner announces which counting pattern is being used (for example, adding 100 more or less). The student shows the next three numbers in that counting sequence.

Supporting the NCTM *Principles and Standards* (2000):

- Worthwhile Mathematical Tasks; Tools for Enhancing Discourse—The Teaching Principle
- The Learning Principle

Here are some additional games or activities that provide more experiences with counting patterns. Remember that numeration generally occurs at the beginning of the students' textbook, so many maintenance activities throughout the year are needed to ensure firm mastery of these concepts.

Activity 9.13

MENTAL MATH

COUNT ON FIVE—GAME 1

MATERIALS

- Number die with two sides marked as 1, 10, and 100
- Cards about 5 × 8 centimeters with a number on each card—limit size as you desire

PROCEDURE

The deck of cards is face down. Determine first player. The first player rolls the number die and draws a card from the deck. The object is to correctly name the next five consecutive numbers counting by the number face up on the number die. Next player rolls the die and draws a card to determine from which number counting will begin. *Example:* Roll is 10. Card is 47. Next five counting numbers beginning at 47 and counting by tens are 57, 67, 77, 87, 97. Play continues for

Activity Continues

designated time period as partners check one another's answers.

Activity 9.14

MENTAL MATH

COUNT ON FIVE—GAME 2

MATERIALS

- Number die with two sides marked as 2, 5, and 10
- Three decks of numeral cards, each deck with numbers for 0 to 9, that are color coded for the three counting patterns

PROCEDURE

The stacked decks are placed face down. The first player rolls the die and draws the numeral card from that particular deck. The player names the next five consecutive numbers. Second player continues in a similar manner. To distinguish the three decks (besides the color), mark the top side of the cards with the counting pattern (2, 5, or 10). *Example:* Roll 5. Card from fives deck is 165. The next five consecutive counting numbers from 165 by fives are 170, 175, 180, 185, 190.

Activity 9.15

PROBLEM SOLVING

DIGIT HUNT

MATERIALS

- Game board with numbers in each "step" of the board
- Spinner with place value names that agree with board numbers
- Spinner with numbers 0 to 9
- Game board markers

PROCEDURE

Determine who goes first by who spins the largest number. The first player spins the two spinners. The player's marker may be moved from start to the first space on the

Activity Continues

board that has that digit in the place noted on the place value spinner. Players cannot occupy the same spot. In that case, the second player to land on that spot must return to start. Players must go to the *nearest* space that has the number in the place, even if it means a move backward. The first player to reach the end (finish) is the winner.

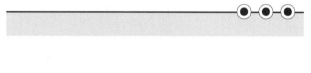

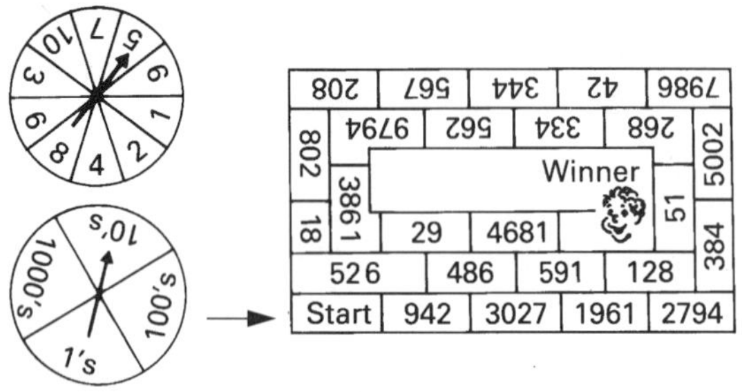

Activity Continues

Using arrow clues, the child tells his or her partner how to find the secret number. Partner tries to name the ending target number. In order to get the point, partner must write the equation to describe the moves. Reverse roles.

For example: Begin at 47. (Target is 89.)

Arrow clues: → → ↓ ↓ ↓ ↓

$47 + 1 + 1 = 49 + 10 + 10 + 10 + 10 = 89$

VARIATION

Begin with an empty hundreds chart with only 10 to 15 numbers randomly filled in. Children can pick a number and tell directional moves they would make to land on positions for other numbers on the chart. For more teaching ideas see *Math By All Means* by Marilyn Burns (1994), a Place Value Replacement Unit, grade 2.

Activity 9.16

MANIPULATIVES

HUNDREDS CHART FUN

MATERIALS

- Hundreds chart—laminated or in protective plastic sheet
- Overhead pens or washable markers

1	2	3	4	5	6	7	8	9	10
11	12	13	14	15	16	17	18	19	20
21	22	23	24	25	26	27	28	29	30
31	32	33	34	35	36	37	38	39	40
41	42	43	44	45	46	47	48	49	50
51	52	53	54	55	56	57	58	59	60
61	62	63	64	65	66	67	68	69	70
71	72	73	74	75	76	77	78	79	80
81	82	83	84	85	86	87	88	89	90
91	92	93	94	95	96	97	98	99	100

Hundreds Chart

PROCEDURE

One child picks a beginning number and names it aloud as well as picking a "secret target number."

Activity 9.17

CULTURAL RELEVANCE

YUP'IK MATHEMATICS (Alaskan Eskimos)

Yup'ik bilingual programs teach students to count to 10 using a "Western" base 10 system, but their cultural background uses a base 20 sub-base 5. The basic Yup'ik number patterns use body parts to give literal meanings to the numbers. For example, the word for six is "arvinlegen" which means "cross over" because the finger counting changes from the left hand to the right hand. To count from 11 to 20, one starts over with the left end finger and repeats the process. The Mayan system of place value is similar to Yup'ik.

Investigate how this number system works.

1. What materials, patterns, and culturally based approach to mathematics would you suggest?
2. Write a reflective paper on what difficulties might be encountered for children when a concrete contextualized counting system is formalized in the classroom.

Supporting the NCTM *Principles and Standards* (2000):

- The Equity Principle
- Number Systems; Number Representations and Relationships
- The Learning Principle

EXTENDED ACTIVITIES

PROBLEM SOLVING · CALCULATORS · MANIPULATIVES

Name of Activity

- Name the Operation
- Who Am I?
- Number Tile Fun
- Number Tile Activities
- Remove that Digit
- 100 Chart Fun

Number Sense

In addition to place-value concepts, children should develop an intuitive feel about numbers. When children have this sense for numbers, they are aware of number relationships and can make realistic estimates of computational results. The NCTM *Principles and Standards* (2000) state that children should understand multiple relationships among numbers, recognize the relative magnitude of numbers, and use benchmarks in the number system.

One way to consider number sense is through computational procedures used naturally by children. As you read Chapter 11, "Operations with Whole Numbers," think about how the children's alternative approaches to computation suggest strong intuitions about numbers. When children invent new procedures to solve problems and have flexible approaches to operations, they reflect on numbers with new meaning. Children with good number sense respond to numbers as quantities and they "tack on" or "knock off" parts as needed (Sowder and Kelin, 1993). Therefore, children with efficient, well-developed mental calculations appear to have a strong sense about number relationships. Number sense does not apply only to whole numbers, but to decimals, fractions, percents, and so on. Middle grade students should link their understanding of whole numbers to a variety of settings and other mathematics topics. Mental computation and estimation strategies are discussed in Chapter 11. You are encouraged to think about how number sense and number relationships are tied to characteristics and strategies of computational estimation as you read that chapter.

The activities suggested in this chapter are only a beginning of the multitude of experiences students should have to develop number sense. The NCTM Addenda Series has a book *Number Sense and Operations* (Burton et al., 1993), which contains many rich investigations of number sense.

Activity 9.18

MENTAL MATH

THE ANSWER IS 5. WHAT'S THE QUESTION?

Think of all the ways that you can generate problems where the answer is 5. Try to find 20 questions to pose to your friends.

For example: How much more is a dime than a nickel?
How much is one half of 10?
How much is 20 ÷ 4?
How many days in a "normal" week of school?
How many sides in a pentagon?

Activity 9.19

CULTURAL RELEVANCE

NUMBER SENSE—FROM THE RUSSIAN PERSPECTIVE

These are number sense examples that appear in Russian textbooks. Make up some grade-appropriate problems based on them.

1. If you know that 126 + 35 = 161, what is 161 – 26? Explain your thinking.
2. A two-digit number minus 10 is a one-digit number. What could the two-digit number be?
3. Count from 6 to 27 and leave out the numbers that are divisible by 3.
4. Think up a number that 8 can be subtracted from 5 times.
5. Can 20 be expressed as the sum of two even numbers? Can 21 be expressed as the sum of two odd numbers? Explain your thinking and what other number can be substituted.

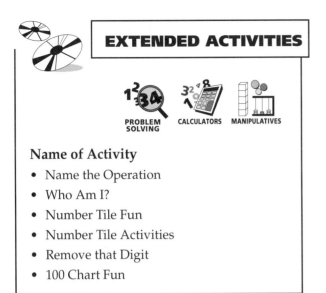

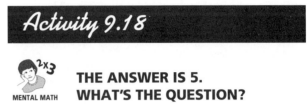

Activity 9.20

PROBLEM SOLVING MENTAL MATH

THINK ABOUT 32

1. What comes to your mind when you see or hear 32? List ten things.
2. Name ten ways to describe 32 to another person:
   32 is small compared to
   32 is almost the same as
   32 is between
   32 is about half of
3. Write ten number sentences with mixed operations that have 32 as the answer.
4. Another way to think of 32 is (2 tens and 12 ones, 1 ten and 22 ones, 32 ones)

Activity 9.21

PROBLEM SOLVING

MAKE A NUMBER

Players—small groups or entire class

MATERIALS

- Number spinner with digits 0 to 9
- Game sheets

PROCEDURE

Players take turns spinning for the 10 digits to place on the game sheets. Players must decide where to place each digit *as it is read and before* the next spin. Once the digit is placed, it cannot be changed. After all digits are placed, players read their numbers. The person(s) who is the closest to the target number *without going over* it gets a point.

Target	My Number
5	❑
10	❑
20	❑❑
50	❑❑
100	❑❑
1000	❑❑❑

Activity 9.22

ESTIMATION

HIGH-MIDDLE-LOW

Three to four players

MATERIALS

- Digit cards 0–9, one set per player

PROCEDURE

Mix digit cards and deal four cards to each player. Players arrange their cards in any order to form a four-digit number and state, "High," "Middle," or "Low." All players lay down cards and compare. Each player who was closest to being the low, middle, high number value gets a point. Shuffle and deal. First player with ten points is winner.

VARIATION

Make number cube with two faces marked 10, two faces marked 100, and two faces marked 1000. Play as above but as next step, roll the number cube and round number to the place value on the cube.

Understanding and Interpreting Large Numbers

Another aspect of number sense is the need to acquire a sense of the relative magnitude of numbers. Using manipulative models with smaller numbers will hopefully create an understanding of the trading process as well as how the powers of 10 function. Then, extending these concepts into larger numbers, using proportional and nonproportional models is essential in order to conceptualize large numbers.

It is essential for children to understand numbers from physical situations. This requires additional time, because number meanings develop gradually. Intuition about number relationships helps children decide about the reasonableness of computational answers. Understanding place value is a crucial link to acquiring number sense. As number relationships are developed, children acquire an understanding of the relative magnitude of numbers. Results from the Sixth NAEP assessment (Kouba, Zawojewski, and Strutchens, 1997) imply that students in eighth-grade have little sense of the relative magnitude of large numbers.

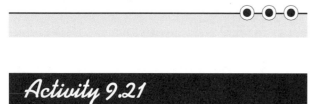

We live in a world that inundates us with large numbers. Any newspaper quickly illustrates this point: $41.2 million trade between two corporations, $3.23 million in shares traded, 2.4 billion cans of soda sold last year, $3.9 trillion national debt, to name just a few examples. Because these numbers are generally written in shortened form, a mystery is created about how much is represented by large numbers. People tend to ignore these large numbers and do not generally relate to them. Clearly, this situation is dangerous for society. If we look to most middle school textbooks for instructional techniques to interpret these numbers in standard form, we find limited coverage of this important skill. Hofstadter (1982) says we cannot have such "number numbness" or "innumeracy." People must be able to make sense of the large numbers that run their lives. Findings from numerous interviews with adults and children indicate that few people know the difference between a million and a billion (in terms of their relationship to one another) and few understand how to translate the shortened form for large numbers into standard number forms.

Activity 9.23

ESTIMATION

WHAT HAPPENS TO THE ANSWER IF...? Relative Effect of Operating on Numbers

26 + 38 = ______

What happens to the answer if...

- One is added to each addend?
- One is added to one addend?
- One is added to one addend and one is subtracted from the other addend?

4 × 12 = ______

What happens to the answer if...

- One is added to each factor?
- One is added to the first factor and one is subtracted from the other factor?
- One is added to each factor?
- One is subtracted from the first factor?

Activity 9.24

ESTIMATION

WHAT'S A MILLION LIKE? Relative Magnitude of Numbers

What's in your classroom that there could be a million of? In the school yard? What about a billion? Explain your reasoning. If you spend $10 every minute, how long would it take you to spend a thousand dollars? A million dollars? A billion dollars?

USA Today has lots of examples of statistics in the "USA Snapshots" section that uses large numbers. Find examples of large numbers in newspapers and magazines. Make a chart of the examples and write the standard number form (with all the place holders). Discuss the impact of large numbers on people and why the term "number numbness" is used regarding people's understanding of the relative magnitude of large numbers.

Design some activities that help others get an intuitive feel for these numbers. For example (September 28, 1995, p. 1B), "The federal government ran a $33.9 billion deficit in August, up 40% from August 1994. But so far this fiscal year, the budget deficit is down 18%." How much money is the difference? With some classmates, design ways to make large numbers meaningful to others and to visualize their numerical value.

Supporting the NCTM *Principles and Standards* (2000):

- Number Sense; Number Systems and Number Relationships; Reasoning, Communication, Problem Solving
- Worthwhile Mathematical Tasks—The Teaching Principle
- The Learning Principle

Activity 9.25

PROBLEM SOLVING

INTERPRETING LARGE NUMBERS

1. Ask children what is the largest number in the world and the smallest number in the world.
2. Explain the patterns in the names of the periods (families).
3. Is there such a number as a "zillion"? Why do you think this term was invented?
4. How long do you think it would take you to count to a million? A billion? A trillion?

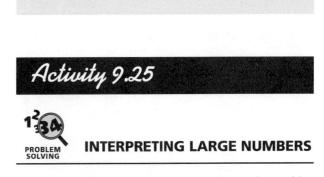

Activity Continues

5. What are some things in our environment of which we could quickly find a million? A billion?
6. Why do you think newspapers use the shortened form of large numbers?
7. Do you think you were living a million minutes ago? Figure this date to an approximate month and year. What about a million seconds ago?

Books for children by Schwartz called *How Much Is a Million?* (1985) and *If You Made a Million* (1989) provide some visualization of large numbers. Schwartz (1985) offers examples of million, billion, and trillion that children love to visualize. Other literature ideas and recommended books for numeration are given at the end of the chapter. Check the CD-ROM for additional activities to build number sense and relative magnitude of numbers. The video vignette "Whale Math" shows one teacher's imaginative lesson to develop number sense.

Reading Numbers. There are several skills involved under the term "reading numbers." Numbers literally need to be read aloud in numeral form (not given adequate time in most classrooms), read in written name form and translated into numeral form, seen in numeral form and written in name form, read in numeral form and modeled with manipulatives, and read in expanded form or exponential form and translated into standard form.

Video Vignette

Whale Math

Mrs. Shanks' multiage classroom explores relative magnitude of number using a recent field trip to Sea World.

- What techniques does Mrs. Shanks use for clarifying number meanings for her students?
- How does this lesson develop ideas about the relative magnitude of number?
- What mathematical ideas are included?
- How does Mrs. Shanks show respect for students' thinking and promote discourse?

The teen numbers seem to present many problems for some children as they hear the ones digit first and then the tens ("teen"). Many number reversals occur in the teens because on hearing "seventeen," the child writes 7 and then 1. The child might read it back to you as 17, or, given some time away from that number, the name 71 might be given to the number. It is important to have many practice opportunities for modeling the teen numbers.

A word of caution: Never read whole numbers with the word "and" between the hundreds and tens. For example, 259 is read "two hundred fifty-nine" not "two hundred *and* fifty-nine." The word "and" indicates a decimal point in the number separating the whole number from its fractional (decimal) components. We also must be careful to read numbers in complete word form and not simply the single digits. Adults often read multidigit numbers such as 34,528 as "three four five two eight" to be efficient and faster. This method is a better way to read large numbers when comparing answers or reading answers from a calculator, but it can be destructive to children who need to read, hear, and interpret numbers with place value labels. Writing checks is an application of this skill and one that students soon see a need to learn.

When reading large, multidigit numbers, it is important for students to use commas to cluster the periods together. Then it becomes a matter of grouping the digits into groups of three and reading these numbers together followed by the period name (represented by the comma). Many metric groups advocate using a space instead of a comma. However, most elementary textbooks use the comma. Each period contains a group of hundreds, tens, and ones—another pattern. The period names also follow a pattern, which is fun to explore and about which students can speculate. Study the period names and see what patterns you notice, reading from left to right:

> thousand, million, billion, trillion,
> quadrillion, quintillion, sextillion, septillion,
> octillion, nonillion, decillion, undecillion,
> duodecillion, tredecillion, quattuordecillion.

Rounding. Numeration cannot be taught without considering the importance of rounding skills. Most textbooks begin simple rounding to tens around third grade and may include rounding to hundreds. Generally, rounding is introduced with number lines (Figure 9.11) so students can see the position of the number to be rounded in relation to other numbers (multiples of 10 or 100, and so forth) depending on the place to which the number is being rounded.

FIGURE 9.11

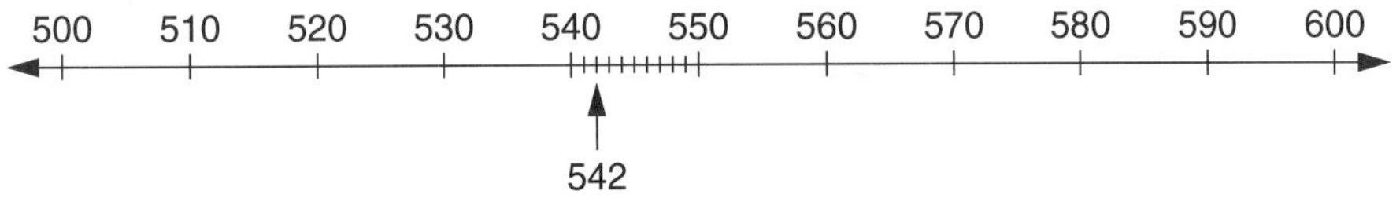

Round 542 to the nearest hundred.

Rounding on number line.

This visual aid helps children see the relative position of the numbers to each other.

Another effective activity is to give students number lines with only some reference points labeled. The task is more challenging by adding fractions or decimals. "Number Detective" from the NCTM Addenda Series (Burton et al., 1993) is an example in which students use proportional thinking and reasoning to discover the mystery number. See adaptation in Figure 9.12.

A similar activity is to have points of reference on the number line and have students place other given points (Figure 9.13). Such experiences encourage students to approach situations in a variety of ways rather than apply "rounding rules." Introducing such rules for rounding often inhibits developing a sense of number relationships.

Many times students do not see a purpose for rounding numbers because the final task is to work the problem using the actual numbers. Unfortunately, teachers often assign problems to be worked both ways—estimated by rounding and with actual numbers—and this practice causes students to believe that rounding is extra work and does not matter. Estimation is a useful, important skill for determining the reasonableness of your answer, and estimation requires an understanding of rounding. Somehow when teachers assign problems to be worked both ways, the importance of rounding and estimating is not instilled in students.

FIGURE 9.12

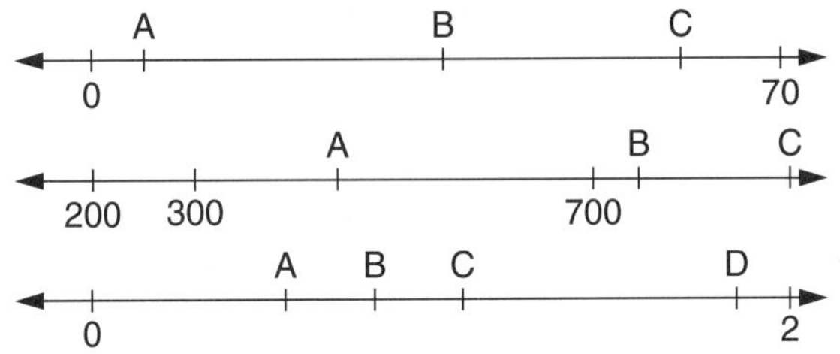

What number is it?

FIGURE 9.13

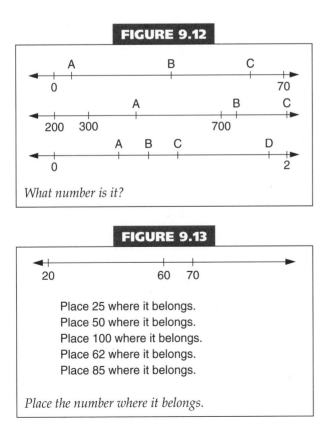

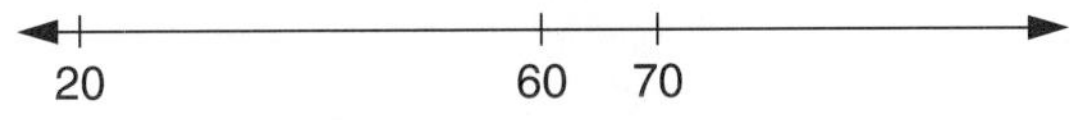

Place 25 where it belongs.
Place 50 where it belongs.
Place 100 where it belongs.
Place 62 where it belongs.
Place 85 where it belongs.

Place the number where it belongs.

Activity 9.26

ESTIMATION

ROUNDING LARGE NUMBERS

MATERIALS

- A die or number cube marked with 10 on two sides, 100 on two sides, and 1000 on two sides
- Numeral cards that include four- and five-digit numbers (or larger to match skills for desired grade level)

PROCEDURE

The students decide who begins. The first player rolls the die. The number on the face showing (10, 100, or 1000) represents the place to which the number is to be rounded. The first player draws a numeral card. This is the number being rounded. For example, roll lands on 100 and the card drawn is 4,324. The player is to round that number to the nearest 100, which is 4,300. The deck may be used over and over because the die determines the rounding place each time. The players can receive a point, token, or tally

Activity Continues

for each correct answer. The player with the most points wins. A game board can also be used. In this case, a correct answer allows the player to have a move on the board. The first player to reach the end is the winner.

Literature. Books for numeration are in two categories: counting books for numbers to ten and counting larger numbers or place value concepts. Counting books to ten are quite popular and plentiful. Check references in Chapters 8 and 10 and on the CD-ROM for this type of book. Some appealing counting books exploring number patterns, decade numbers, and other number systems are: *I Can Count to One Hundred... Can You?* (Howard, 1979); *How to Count Like a Martian* (St. John, 1975); *From One to One Hundred* (Sloat, 1991). Books with stories involving big numbers provide children with a sense of the relative magnitude of numbers. Besides the two books by David Schwartz discussed earlier, these stories fascinate children: *One Watermelon Seed* (Lottridge, 1986); *Millions of Cats* (Gag, 1928); *The Popcorn Book* (De Paola, 1978); *The King's Commissioners* (Friedman, 1994); *A Grain of Rice* (Pittman, 1986); and *The King's Chessboard* (Birch, 1988).

Decimals

As with whole numbers, reading, writing, and interpreting decimals are important skills. Opportunities should be provided for children to take oral dictation of decimals. It is important to note again that the word "and" is said for the decimal point. It separates the whole units and the parts of wholes. This is why students should read large whole numbers *without* the word "and." It can be emphasized by the following example:

Correct: 645.03—six hundred forty-five and three hundredths

Incorrect: 645.03—six hundred and forty-five and three hundredths

When learning about decimals, students should read the decimal point with the place-value terms (tenths, hundredths, thousandths) rather than as a "point" and the names of the digits. If this requirement is not stressed, students cannot acquire the place-value ideas as quickly, nor will the connection between fractions and decimals be seen as clearly. The following examples may help point out this difference.

Activity 9.27

PROBLEM SOLVING

READING DECIMAL NUMBERS

Which reading makes you understand the number better so you can write it, model it, and interpret its value?

The number	What if it were read as
378,294	"three hundred seventy-eight thousand, two hundred ninety-four"
378,294	"three seven eight two nine four"
284.325	"two hundred eighty-four point three two five"
284.325	"two hundred eighty-four and three hundred twenty-five thousandths"

Activity 9.28

MANIPULATIVES MENTAL MATH

COVER UP GAME AND ADD SOME MORE

DIRECTIONS

Start with a mixed number:

1. Begin with

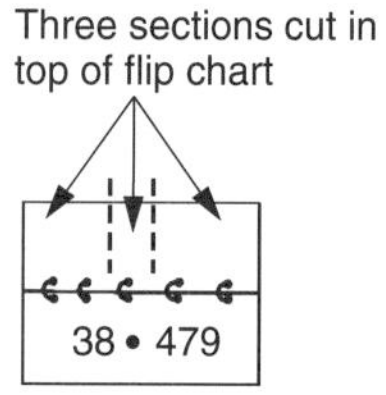

2. Cover up the decimal fraction

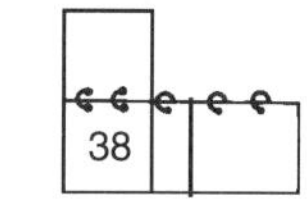

3. Read "and"

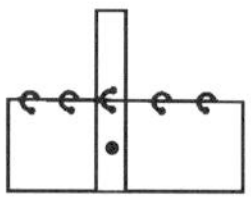

4. Read number following decimal point as if it were a whole number

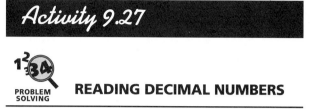

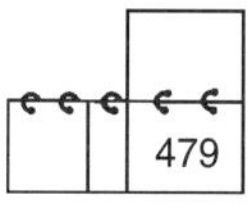

5. Read place value label of last digit "thousandths"

Activity Continues

Add the Skill of Mental Math . . .

6. As students practice reading various numbers in the sequence suggested in steps 1 to 5, have them add one more tenth, hundredth, or thousandth to the number and read it again. The procedure could continue while students are waiting in line with a few minutes to spare. They get the needed practice breaking down the parts of the mixed fraction and have a chance to practice mental math at the same time.

Supporting the NCTM *Principles and Standards* (2000):

- Worthwhile Mathematical Tasks; Students' Role in Discourse—The Teaching Principle
- Mathematics as Problem Solving, Reasoning, Communication
- Number Systems and Number Relationships

From students' earlier experiences with fractions, they should know that tenths represent a whole unit partitioned into ten equal parts. Likewise, they need to realize that 10 tenths equal the whole unit ($\frac{10}{10} = 1$). In a similar fashion, they should know that if the whole unit is partitioned into one hundred equal parts, $\frac{100}{100}$, each part is 1 out of the 100 or $\frac{1}{100}$ (one hundredth).

Representing Decimals. One of the most common and readily available models for decimals is place-value blocks (base 10 blocks). Another effective model is decimal squares made from chart or graph paper. Here, the unit square is divided into 10 equal parts (longs), and each one represents a tenth. If the unit square is divided into additional equal parts (each tenth is partitioned into 10 equal parts), the overall effect is to divide the unit square into 100 equal parts (Figure 9.14).

FIGURE 9.14

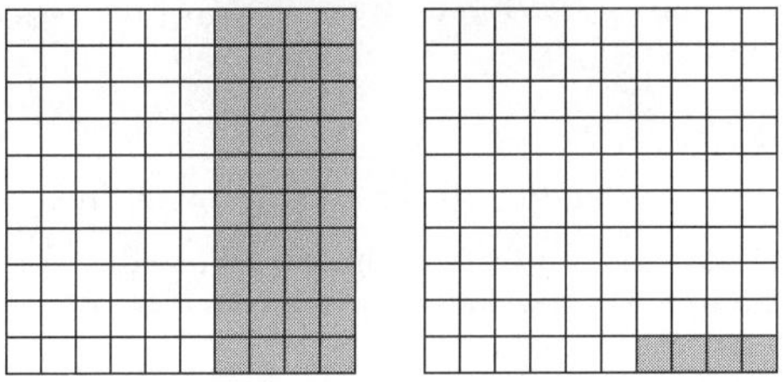

0.4 0.04

Base 10 models for decimal comparisons.

Provide opportunities for students to practice reading, writing, and representing decimals. An understanding of the place-value interpretation of decimals is a prerequisite to introducing computation with decimals. Students should identify the place-value positions of each digit as well as determine the relationships among the places, such as 10 hundredths equal 1 tenth.

Activity 9.29

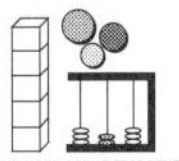

MANIPULATIVES

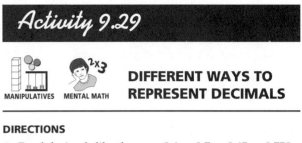

MENTAL MATH

DIFFERENT WAYS TO REPRESENT DECIMALS

DIRECTIONS

1. Read decimals like these: 0.4 0.7 0.45 0.758
2. Shade decimal squares to represent the decimals read. (See Figure 9.14.)
3. Model with flats, longs, and units as the decimals are read. (See introduction to the chapter.)
4. Connect with the pictorial level by drawing decimal squares and base 10 blocks for the examples above.
5. Use place-value grids and record each decimal.

Ones	Tenths	Hundredths	Thousandths

6. Connect with the symbolic level by writing the two ways to represent decimals—$\frac{4}{10}$ and 0.4.

Many of the games and activities mentioned earlier in this chapter for whole numbers could be easily adapted for decimal numbers. Materials for Digit Hunt and Place-Value Bingo can be created with decimal numbers; the Count on Five games can become counting games using decimals. Take a look at the CD Extended Activities and think about how these experiences can be modified to use with decimal numbers.

Comparing Decimals. Before handling operations with decimals, students need to explore and understand relationships among decimals by comparing decimals. Again, it is important to provide experiences for modeling the numbers with place-value blocks or with graph paper (decimal squares) as concrete manipulatives.

Activities for comparing decimals should embed concrete proportional materials for modeling the numbers. The quick rule of "add a zero and make the numbers have the same number of digits" presents some confusing information. Such actions are inappropriate to build a sense of the relative size of decimals. Students need to represent numbers using manipulatives to interpret which is larger: 0.7 and 0.34. Many students see the two digits in 0.34 and think this represents a greater number than 0.7. However placing 7 longs (tenths) on the flat (whole) shows 0.7 is closer to one whole than the 3 longs and 4 hundredths placed on the flat.

After introducing hundredths, the difference between four-tenths and four-hundredths must be called to the students' attention. Modeling helps focus on the size of the number and provides the visual reference needed to correctly record numbers as fractions. Confusion may occur when comparing and interpreting the numbers 0.20 and 0.02. Many opportunities with materials at the concrete and pictorial level are necessary for children to internalize the notation and values of decimals.

Activity 9.30

MANIPULATIVES

COMPARING DECIMAL NUMBERS

MATERIALS

- Deck of cards with decimal numbers
- Base 10 blocks

PROCEDURE

1. Have students in groups of two or three members.
2. Each student draws a card, reads the decimal number, and models it with blocks.
3. All students in the group compare and order the numbers from least to greatest.
4. A new set of cards is drawn and these numbers are compared in similar manner.
   Note: This activity can also be used with the big block representing the basic building unit (one whole) in order to include thousandths.

Estimation. Place-value understandings extend into estimation and building intuitions about the relative size of decimal numbers. Students need to explore estimation strategies rather than to be told rules and procedures. The 1996 NAEP results (Kouba, Zawojewski, and Strutchens, 1997) indicate that routinely worded rounding tasks resulted in higher correct responses than nonroutine tasks or in less traditional formats. For the nonroutine items fewer than one-fourth of the fourth-grade students and around half the eighth-grade students answered correctly.

Extensions of comparing activities could include locating decimal numbers on number lines to see the relative position of the numbers to each other. Look again at Figures 9.11, 9.12, and 9.13 and substitute decimal numbers. Try some of these activities to help develop benchmarks for estimation. Other games are found on the CD-ROM with Extended Activities. A game, Decimal War, on the CD may be modified by using base 10 blocks or pictorial representations of the decimal numbers.

EXTENDED ACTIVITIES

Name of Activity

- Decimal War
- Decimal Monopoly
- Links for Operations

PROBLEM SOLVING MENTAL MATH

Activity 9.31

MENTAL MATH ESTIMATION

PLACE THAT DECIMAL!

MATERIALS

- Deck of cards with decimal numbers
- Yarn, ribbon, or string with end points given such as 0 and 1 or 0.1 and 0.9

PROCEDURE

1. Determine the end points for the number line.
2. Students draw a number card and place the card on the number line where that number should be located.

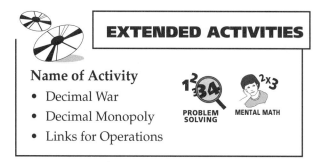

Activity 9.32

ESTIMATION **FIND A BENCHMARK**

MATERIALS

- Deck of cards with decimal numbers
- Yarn, ribbon, or string with benchmarks such as 0, 0.5, and 1

PROCEDURE

1. Each student draws a number card.
2. Place the card in relationship to being closer to 0, closer to 0.5, or closer to 1.
3. Use base 10 blocks if needed to see relationship to the whole.

ASSESSMENT

Field-Dependent Learners

Students who process information simultaneously (from the whole to the part) frequently do well with activities such as the computer spreadsheet model, in which the table changes all at once when a number is generated. They can analyze patterns from the whole table seen simultaneously. They also perform well with materials like the place-value strips because everything is already there and just needs to be folded from the expanded notation to the compact form. The base 10 blocks can be used successfully in such activities as "trading down," where the base numbers are exchanged from a large set of base 10 blocks already assembled.

Field-Independent Learners

Students who process information successively (from the parts to the whole) frequently benefit from the use of the abacus and chip trading because both materials require a detailed buildup of the place values from ones to tens to hundreds and so on. Such students may be more comfortable with the Logo computer program, which progresses from one number to the next. The base 10 blocks can be used successfully, especially in activities like "trading up," where the student builds large numbers from exchanging smaller place-value units to make larger and larger numbers from the smaller blocks.

If materials like place-value strips are used, consider pairing a field-independent learner with a field-dependent learner. It is a cooperative learning effort in which both students can learn from watching the other if they talk about what they are doing as they work.

Correcting Common Misconceptions

One common error is that children write too many zeros in the number because they are relating to the number words. For example, two hundred forty-five is written as "20045." The first three digits are recorded for the 200 and then the 45. The remediation technique to use is to ask the child to model the number with base 10 blocks. Also, additional experiences with the place value strips seen earlier in the chapter would be a valuable connecting-level experience. Special needs students need oral activities to build the language connection.

Another error is developmental in nature—when children do not conserve volume. Because children who do not conserve volume may consider the thousand block as "600," it may be wise to construct 1000 using 10 flats (hundreds blocks). Students with special needs can easily remove a layer at a time to recall there are more units inside that need to be counted. When they mistake 1000 for 600, let them count by 100s to 1000 to see that there are more blocks than 600.

Another common error in writing numerals is just the opposite problem—not using zeros as place holders in numerals where needed. In this case, because the child does not hear or read any numbers for that place value, it is simply ignored. For example, in the number "three thousand fourteen," the child would write "3,14." Again concrete models such as base 10 blocks with a place value mat or spiked abacus (Figure 9.15) help to visualize all place value positions to know where zeros are needed as place holders.

The activities on the CD-ROM offer more games and teaching strategies to help develop numeration skills and offer suggestions for special needs students.

FIGURE 9.15

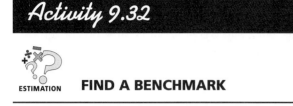

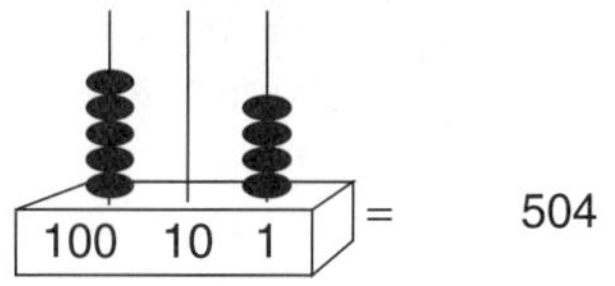

Base 10 models for decimal comparisons.

EXTENDED ACTIVITIES

Name of Activity

- Abacus Action

MANIPULATIVES

Correcting Common Misconceptions with Decimals

Nonalignment of the Decimal Points. Students are used to writing numerals from left to the right, and some students proceed to write the decimals in the same manner as in the example on the left below. Students need practice transferring decimals written in the horizontal form to the vertical form. A teaching method to mark the decimal point is as follows: Add: 235.06 + 41.25 + 9.345 = ?

	↓	Ask children to place an arrow
235.06	.	above the decimal points,
41.25	.	marking the points before
+ 9.345	+ .	writing any numerals

Annexing Zeroes. Some students see 0.500 as greater than 0.50, and 0.50 as greater than 0.5. They do not understand that annexing zeroes to the right of a decimal does *not* change the value of the decimal. Students must work with concrete manipulatives as shown in the teaching strategies section of Chapter 12. Some special needs students will need many experiences representing decimals to see numerical relationships, though other students see the pattern after a few times. Let students use the concrete materials as long as needed, using a place-value chart for decimals.

Attention to Decimal Point as Place Holder. Some students, when faced with a number like .529, totally disregard the decimal point, treating .529 as if it were a whole number. We have already stressed the importance of writing such decimals as 0.529 to emphasize that 0.529 is a part of a whole. Calculators also reinforce this approach because every decimal without a whole number is automatically recorded with the zero as a place holder whether the child enters it that way or not. Perhaps students with special needs should be encouraged to use the calculator then connect that number to place-value materials.

Name Value Confused with Place Value. Just as young children become confused with the name forty-seven and write the numeral as 407, when students learning decimals hear such name values as "eight hundredths" or "fifty-two thousandths," they write:

0.800 or 0.80	(if they remember that hundredths has only two decimal places)
0.5200 or 0.520	

Writing the numeral on a place-value chart helps if students have a folder with the rule written out to the side, as in the following example:

Rule:

1. Find the place that corresponds with the word you are saying.
2. Start writing the number there, moving from right to left.
3. Fill in any 0's you need to get to the decimal point.

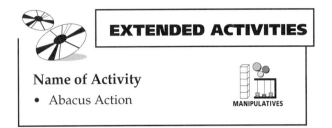

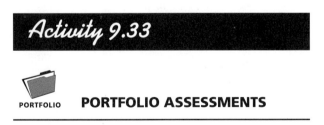

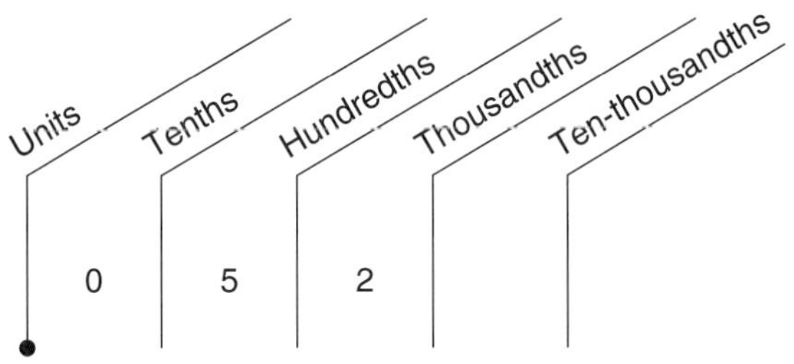

Example: "fifty-two thousandths"

Activity 9.33

PORTFOLIO **PORTFOLIO ASSESSMENTS**

For Teacher Reflection of Students' Work in Numeration and Number Sense

One important aspect of numeration and number sense is to understand the variety of equivalent forms of numbers and the multiple relationships among numbers. Look at these three examples of student's work on the next page and analyze what each child understands.

Activity Continues

Develop a rubric that you could apply to assess this aspect of numeration.

What are the next steps you would do for continuing each student's progress? What else would you like to know about each child?

Activity Continues

Supporting the NCTM *Principles and Standards* (2000):

- Worthwhile Mathematical Tasks—The Teaching Principle
- The Assessment Principle

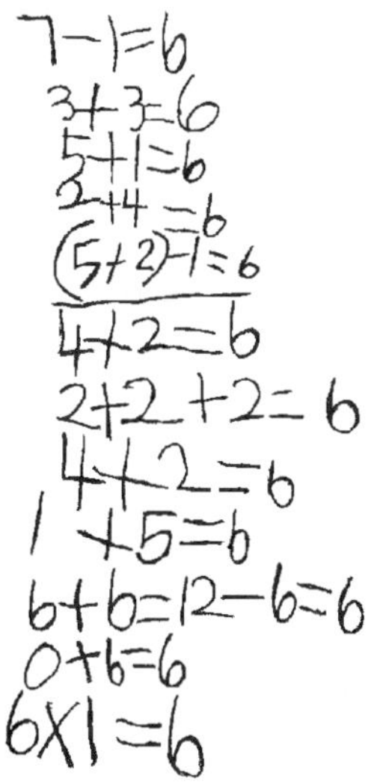

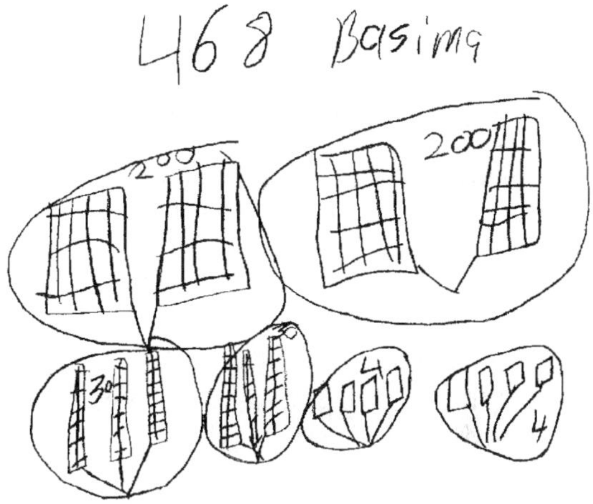

SUMMARY

For children to acquire number meanings, they must represent numbers with physical materials, explore groupings and number relationships, and extend their knowledge of whole numbers to fractions, decimals, and integers. The instructional goal is to focus on the underlying structure of the number system.

This chapter emphasized different numeration systems. The base 10 system was developed using base 10 blocks as manipulative models. Other bases were also explored. Both proportional and nonproportional models were used in the development. It is important to select models that are appropriate for the developmental needs of the children. Numeration skills and understandings are the foundation for developing algorithms and operations in Chapter 11. Chapter 10 introduces operation sense and basic facts with an emphasis on fostering number sense and problem-solving situations.

EXERCISES

For extended exercises, see the CD-ROM.

A. **Memorization and Comprehension Exercises**
Low-Level Thought Activities

1. If a child writes sixty-seven as 607, what is the child's misconception?
2. Show the difference between 0.08 and 0.80 with base 10 blocks and with graph paper.
3. Make a chart of the first thirty counting numbers in base 2, 5, and 8. Write about the patterns you see. Draw the configuration of the first four place-value positions and explain the similarities.

B. Application and Analysis Exercises
Middle-Level Thought Activities

1. Analyze what the number 214 looks like in base 3 (be careful!), in base 5, in base 9, in base 15. Draw the configuration in place-value materials.
2. Select some of the research studies on place value mentioned in this chapter. Prepare a summary of the findings and compare to suggestions in the *Standards.*
3. Search professional journals for current articles on teaching ideas for numeration. Write how these activities and teaching strategies differ from how you learned about the numeration system.

C. Synthesis and Evaluation Exercises
High-Level Thought Activities

1. Find a topic from the *NCTM Standards* from Box 9.1 that you would like to teach.
   a. Search professional journals for current articles on research findings and teaching ideas for numeration.
   b. Use current articles from the professional journals to help plan the direction of the lesson. Document your sources.
   c. Include at least one computer software program as a part of the lesson. Show how it will be integrated with the rest of the lesson.
2. Create a number line in base 7 using the multibase blocks seen in the introduction as a model.
3. Create your own number system with numeration symbols. Do it in Logo.
4. What are the unique qualities of our base 10 numeration system, and how can they be shown as the basic building blocks of many number concepts?
5. Collect ten examples of large numbers used as part of our daily exposure to very large numbers. Design a lesson to teach relative magnitude of numbers to illustrate these numbers in a real, visual way.

BIBLIOGRAPHY

For an extended bibliography, see the CD-ROM.

Baratta-Lorton, Mary. *Mathematics Their Way.* Menlo Park, CA: Addison-Wesley, 1976.

Burns, Marilyn. *The Math Solution: Teaching for Mastery through Problem Solving.* Sausalito, CA: Marilyn Burns Education Associates, 1984.

———. *Math By All Means, Place Value Grade 2.* Sausalito, CA: Marilyn Burns Education Associates, 1994.

Burton, Grace et al. *Number Sense and Operations.* Reston, VA: National Council of Teachers of Mathematics, 1993.

Carpenter, Thomas P., Megan L. Franke, Victoria R. Jocobs, Elizabeth Fennema, and Susan B. Empson. "A Longitudinal Study of Invention and Understanding in Children's Multidigit Addition and Subtraction." *Journal for Research in Mathematics Education* 29(1) (1998): 3–20.

Fuson, Karen, Diana Wearne, James C. Hiebert, Hanlie G. Murray, Pieter G. Human, Alwyn I. Olivier, Thomas P. Carpenter, and Elizabeth Fennema. "Children's Conceptual Structures for Multidigit Numbers and Methods of Multidigit Addition and Subtraction." *Journal for Research in Mathematics Education* 28(2) (1997): 130–162.

Hiebert, James. "Mathematical, Cognitive, and Instructional Analyses of Decimal Fractions." Ed. Gaea Leinhardt, Ralph Putnam, and Rosemary A. Hattrup. *Analysis of Arithmetic for Mathematics Teaching.* Hillsdale, NY: Lawrence Erlbaum Associates, 1992. 283–322.

Hofstadter, Douglas R. "Metamagical Themas: Number Numbness, or Why Innumeracy May Be Just as Dangerous as Illiteracy." *Scientific American* 246 (May 1982): 20, 24, 28, 32–34.

Hughes, Barnabas, and Kim A. Anderson. "American and Canadian Indians—Mathematical Connectors." *Mathematics Teaching in the Middle Grades* 2 (November–December 1996): 80–83.

Kamii, Constance. "Place Value: An Explanation of Its Difficulty and Educational Implications for the Primary Grades." *Journal of Research in Childhood Education* (January 1986): 75–86.

Kouba, Vicky L., Judith S. Zawojewski, and Marilyn E. Strutchens. "What Do Students Know about Numbers and Operations?" Eds. Patricia Ann Kenney and Edward A. Silver. *Results from the Sixth Mathematics Assessment of the National Assessment of Educational Progress.* Reston: VA: National Council of Teachers of Mathematics, 1997. 87–140.

Labinowicz, Ed. *Learning from Children: New Beginnings for Teaching Numerical Thinking, a Piagetian Approach.* Menlo Park, CA: Addison-Wesley, 1985.

Lara-Alecio, Rafael, Beverly J. Irby, and Leonel Morales-Aldana. "A Mathematics Lesson for the Mayan Civilization." *Teaching Children Mathematics* 5 (November 1998): 154–158.

Milne, William J. *Standard Arithmetic.* New York: American Book Co., 1892.

Nagel, Nancy G., and Cynthia Carol Swingen. "Students' Explanations of Place Value in Addition and Subtraction." *Teaching Children Mathematics* 5 (November 1998): 164–170.

National Council of Teachers of Mathematics. *Assessment Standards for School Mathematics.* Reston, VA: NCTM, 1995.

———. *Curriculum and Evaluation Standards for School Mathematics.* Reston, VA: NCTM, 1989.

———. *Principles and Standards for School Mathematics.* Reston, VA: NCTM, 2000 (to be published).

———. *Professional Standards for Teaching Mathematics.* Reston, VA: NCTM, 1991.

Payne, Joseph N., and DeAnne Huinker. "Early Number and Numeration." Ed. Robert J. Jensen. *Research Ideas for the Classroom: Early Childhood Mathematics.* Reston, VA: National Council of Teachers of Mathematics, 1993. 43–70.

Sowder, Judith T. "Instructing for Rational Number Sense." Eds. Judith T. Sowder and Bonnie P. Schappelle. *Providing a Foundation for Teaching Mathematics in the Middle Grades.* Albany, NY: State University of New York Press, 1995. 15–30.

———. "Place Value as the Key to Teaching Decimal Operations." *Teaching Children Mathematics* 3 (April 1997): 448–453.

Sowder, Judith T., and Judith Kelin. "Number Sense and Related Topics." Ed. Douglas T. Owens. *Research Ideas for the Classroom: Middle Grades Mathematics.* Reston, VA: National Council of Teachers of Mathematics, 1993. 41–57.

Steffe, Leslie P., Paul Cobb, and Ernst von Glasersfeld. *Construction of Arithmetical Meanings and Strategies.* New York: Springer-Verlag, 1988.

Strong, Dorothy S. (Mathematics ed.) *Systemwide Objectives and Standards.* Vols. 1–3. Chicago: Board of Education of the City of Chicago, 1990.

Thompson, Charles S. "Place Value and Larger Numbers." Ed. Joseph N. Payne. *Mathematics for the Young Child.* Reston, VA: National Council of Teachers of Mathematics, 1990. 89–108.

Wearne, Diana, and James Hiebert. "A Cognitive Approach to Meaningful Mathematics Instruction: Testing a Local Theory Using Decimal Numbers." *Journal of Research in Mathematics Education* 19 (November 1988): 371–384.

CHILDREN'S LITERATURE

Birch, David. *The King's Chessboard.* New York: Dial, 1988.

De Paola, Tomie. *The Popcorn Book.* New York: Holiday House, 1978.

Friedman, Aileen. *The King's Commissioners.* New York: Scholastic, 1994.

Gag, Wanda. *Millions of Cats.* New York: Coward-McCann, 1928.

Howard, Katherine. *I Can Count to One Hundred... Can You?* New York: Random House, 1979.

Knight, Margy Burns. *Talking Walls.* Gardiner, ME: Tilbury House, 1992.

Lankford, Mary D. *Dominoes Around the World.* New York: Morrow Junior Books, 1998.

Lottridge, Celia Barker. *One Watermelon Seed.* Toronto: Oxford University Press, 1986.

Pittman, Helena C. *A Grain of Rice.* New York: Hastings House, 1986.

Schwartz, David. *How Much Is a Million?* New York: Lothrop, Lee, and Shepard, 1985.

———. *If You Made a Million.* New York: Lothrop, Lee, and Shepard, 1989.

———. *G is for Googal: A Math Alphabet Book.* Berkeley, CA: Tricycle Press, 1998.

Sloat, Teri. *From One to One Hundred.* New York: Dutton Children's Books, 1991.

St. John, Glory. *How to Count Like a Martian.* New York: Henry Z. Walck, 1975.

Integrating Technology

Video Vignettes: Lesson Plans in Action

- *Numeration Games*
- *Whale Math*

Computer Software Resources

...for Numeration and Number Sense

Internet Searches

Surfing the Internet for Numeration Topics

Use the World Wide Web (WWW) and navigate through the system, searching for new information under major headings and subheadings similar to the following:

Mathematics Education
- Numeration
- Number Systems

GO to Cyberspace Middle School at **www.scri.fsu.edu.**

- Integrated Math Tools Project
- Ask Dr. Math!
- NCTM
  - Numeration
  - Number Systems

- *Remember...* the Web is fluid... new topics and ways to search for topics change daily.
- Be adventurous... think of some new things you could try.

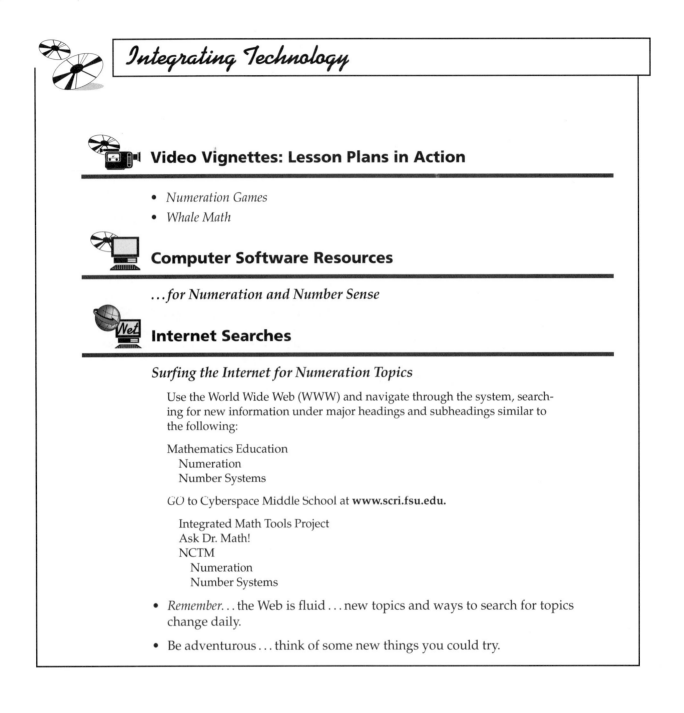

10

Operations and Number Sense

Activities Index

IN THE TEXT

ON CD-ROM

A large percentage of a child's elementary school years is spent working with the whole number system. The operations, properties, and basic facts become an important part of daily mathematics instruction. In most textbooks, children study the whole number operations in the following order: addition, subtraction, multiplication, and division. Many textbooks concentrate on addition and subtraction in first and second grade followed by multiplication and division in third grade. To keep in alignment with the NCTM *Standards* (NCTM, 1989, 2000), all four operations should be developed throughout the elementary grades as young children have intuitions that can apply to operations. A preschooler knows that when mother says to share the candies fairly with little brother that means, "one for you and one for me," so why wait until third grade to explore division concepts? Young children can relate pattern skills to skip counting—a basis for multiplication.

A variety of problem situations, beginning in kindergarten, must be developed through modeling with physical materials. Activities to develop meaning for the mathematical language and symbols should link to the children's language and informal knowledge. The relationships between operations should be investigated, as well as the various problem structures such as the missing addend, comparison, and take-away approaches to subtraction.

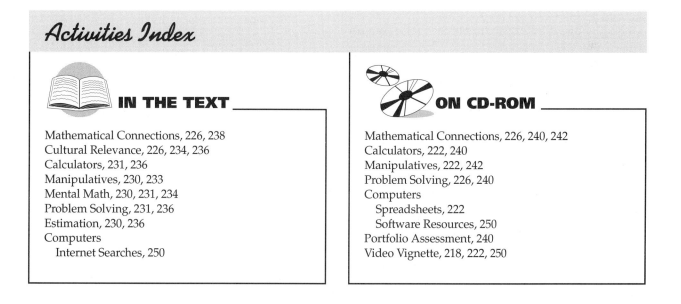

Instruction in whole number operations should be embedded in modeling and real-world problem situations. It is important to build a context for the operation and to include various problem situations for the operation. For example, to construct meaning for the operation of subtraction, teachers must include situational problems that include comparison and missing addend rather than to base word problems only on the take-away situation. Children should be modeling the operation along with the word problem. The action of the operation (joining, adding on, separating, partitioning) becomes a part of the activity. Use a story setting (the zoo, a picnic, a fish tank) to stimulate children's creation of their own word problems for understanding operations.

As students develop concepts and explore problem situations involving operations, the teacher should provide experiences to develop different meanings for operations. Mathematics learning in early grades should build an understanding of properties and relationships for each operation, develop relationships among operations, and acquire intuition about the effects of operating on a pair of numbers, such as increasing one addend and decreasing the other addend by one. Box 10.1 indicates the major components from the *Standards* (NCTM, 1989) regarding this topic.

Exploring relationships and patterns between operations helps students acquire new understandings of operations. Conceptual understanding of the operations is an important aspect of knowing mathematics and must precede basic fact mastery and computation. Concept development activities are related to the symbolic level of paper-and-pencil computation through careful bridging that connects and translates the two components. These bridging activities should encompass the oral (auditory) level, the tactile (hands-on) level, and the written (symbolic) level in both word and number form (Figure 10.1).

FIGURE 10.1

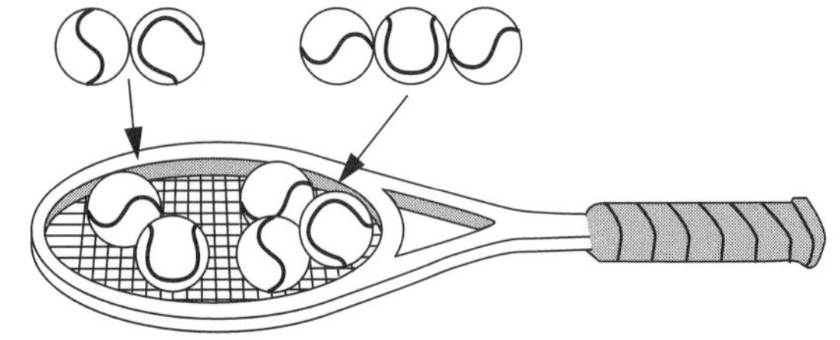

Linking models with oral and written representations.

An overview of the operations and properties appears in this section. The basic facts and how to teach them appear later under the heading Teaching Strategies.

BOX 10.1 Curriculum and Evaluation Standards

Whole Number Computation

In grades K–4, the mathematics curriculum should develop whole number computation so that students can—

- Model, explain, and develop reasonable proficiency with basic facts and algorithms.
- Use a variety of mental computation and estimation techniques.
- Use calculators in appropriate computational situations.
- Select and use computation techniques appropriate to specific problems and determine whether the results are reasonable.

Number Sense and Numeration

In grades K–4, the mathematics curriculum should include whole number concepts and skills so that students can—

- Construct number meanings through real-world experiences and the use of physical materials.
- Develop number sense.

Concepts of Whole Number Operations

In grades K–4, the mathematics curriculum should include concepts of addition, subtraction, multiplication, and division of whole numbers so that students can—

- Develop meaning for the operations by modeling and discussing a rich variety or problem situations.
- Relate the mathematical language and symbolism of operations to problem situations and informal language.
- Recognize that a wide variety of problem structures can be represented by a single operation.
- Develop operation sense.

Source: National Council of Teachers of Mathematics, 1989, pp. 38, 41, 44.

OVERVIEW OF THE OPERATIONS AND PROPERTIES

Addition

The operation known as *addition* is the process of joining things together. Sometimes two disjoint groups will be *combined,* and sometimes one part will be added to a given part in a *static* situation. Addition is the first operation introduced to children and is the easiest to understand. Even so, modeling with concrete materials and real-life examples is needed.

Combining. In this interpretation, two disjoint or separate groups are combined to form the total group. A word story might be, "Jane picked four daisies and two daffodils. How many flowers did she pick in all?"

Static. In addition problems involving static situations, there are still two distinct subsets or groups, but they are not joined. For example, "Uriah's mom has four rose bushes in the front yard and two rose bushes in the back yard. How many rose bushes does Uriah's mom have?" The rose bushes would not have to physically be together (in the modeling) to determine how many there are in the total amount. This distinction between interpretations and situations does not mean the accompanying number sentence (4 + 2 = 6) would be different. Only in modeling the word problem would there be a difference.

Both types of problems should be modeled with materials, and children should offer their own word problems to internalize the concept. Although it is not necessary for children to distinguish between the two interpretations, it is important that they encounter a wide variety of problem structures and materials to model them.

All materials that are used should represent two distinct parts (addends) that result in the whole (sum). For example, if connecting cubes are used to model the operation, four red cubes could represent the daisies or rose bushes and two yellow cubes could represent the daffodils or backyard rose bushes. The part-part-whole concept remains the same regardless of the material used—pattern blocks of two types, two-color tiles or lima beans, two types of keys or junk, and any other objects (Figure 10.2).

Concrete to Symbolic. Operation concepts can be extended in the same manner that number concepts are developed in Chapter 8 from the concrete, to the connecting, and finally to the symbolic level.

FIGURE 10.2

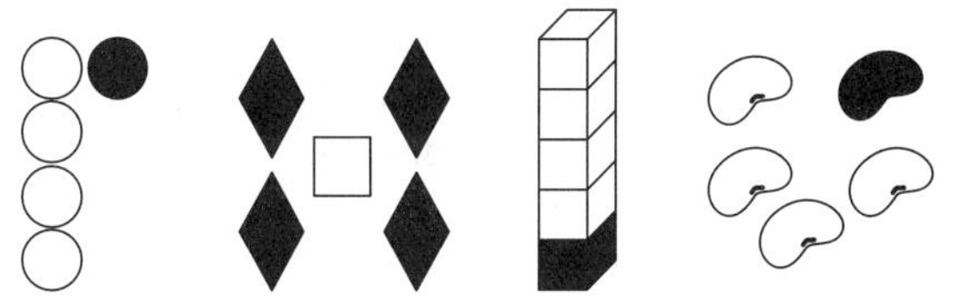

Models for addition.

After children have used different materials and variations of the part-part-whole concepts, they can share their number "stories" with other classmates. They verbalize their actions and internalize the concepts before performing written work with the symbols. Children's informal experiences with operations can be linked to the mathematical language and symbols of operations.

After participating in and describing concrete experiences, the connecting level with symbols is introduced. Activities to bridge these two levels help children relate the concrete with the symbolic. As children model with objects, the teacher writes the related number sentence on chart paper or the chalkboard. Another connecting activity is to pair children so that one child models with materials as the other child writes the number equation. Number equations written on sentence strips provide another variation. One child selects a number equation and makes up a word story while the other child constructs with models (Figure 10.3).

FIGURE 10.3

Working together in a connecting level activity.

When a solid understanding of the language and action is indicated, then and only then, are children introduced to the symbolic level. Operation meaning develops slowly through repeated exposure with numerous situational problems accompanied with modeling. The astute teacher assesses when each child is ready to make the transition from one level to the next level.

Many excellent activities and games are provided in *Mathematics Their Way* (Baratta-Lorton, 1976), *Workjobs II* (Baratta-Lorton, 1978), *Developing Number Concepts Using Manipulatives* (Richardson, 1998), *Box It or Bag It Mathematics* (Burk, Snider, and Symonds, 1988), and *Math Excursions* (Burk, Snider, and Symonds, 1992). Curriculum units developed by Marilyn Burns, TERC, Encyclopaedia Britannica, and many others offer hands-on alternative mathematics programs.

Literature. Literature provides a wealth of creative activities to incorporate the operation of addition in meaningful settings. Books, such as *Counting Wildflowers* (McMillan, 1986) and *So Many Cats* (De Regniers, 1985), engage children in interesting explorations to build familiarity with the addition operation. Use the video vignette on the CD to see a first-grade teacher using a story book to pose a problem situation.

Many children's books extend counting activities to beginning addition. An interesting approach to equivalency is in *Annie's One to Ten* (Owen, 1988) showing different combinations for addends that make ten. Other recommended books are *How Many Bears?* (Edens, 1994), *Mouse Count* (Walsh, 1991), and *How Many Feet in the Bed?* (Hamm, 1994).

Video Vignette

Dinosaur Legs

Notice how this teacher, Mrs. Boch, encourages her first graders to see many solutions to this problem.

- Compare the strategies the children used for solving this problem. Discuss the children's understanding of operations
- How did Mrs. Boch encourage her children to develop flexible thinking?
- What techniques does the teacher use to build number sense?

Properties. There are three properties that are helpful for children to understand the operation and to learn the basic facts. These properties are:

- *Identity property* (zero property)—when 0 is added to any whole number the number remains the same; the identity stays the same, $7 + 0 = 7$
- *Commutative property* (order property)—the order of the addends (parts) does not change the whole (sum); the number equation can be "turned around" and the answer is the same, $3 + 4 = 7$ and $4 + 3 = 7$
- *Associative property* (grouping property)—the addends can be combined in any grouping and the sum does not change, $(2 + 3) + 6 = 11$ or $2 + (3 + 6) = 11$

Subtraction

There are several types of problem situations that involve the operation of subtraction. Subtraction is more complex than addition. Subtraction can be defined as the inverse of addition and should be approached as a part-part-whole connection to addition. There are several types of problem situations that can be interpreted as subtraction when semantic differences in the word problem are evaluated. Fuson (1992) analyzed the problem subtypes for subtractive situations identified by research studies and found up to fifteen different structures. Research on Cognitively Guided Instruction (Carpenter, Fennema, and Franke, 1996), Conceptually Based Instruction (Hiebert and Wearne, 1993), and other such projects introducing children to a broad range of problem types improves children's problem-solving performance. Three interpretations for subtraction are covered in this book: take-away, comparison, and missing addend. All three concepts have the same subtraction equation but involve different problem situations.

Take-Away. The "*take away*" idea means that a subset of the original set is actually removed. This is probably the most easily understood and the most often applied concept of subtraction. Concrete examples are found rather easily in real-life situations, such as eating cookies, spending money, or popping balloons (Figure 10.4). A take-away word problem would be, "There were five cupcakes on the plate. Teri and Marcella each ate a cupcake. How many cupcakes were left?"

For many children, subtraction is a more difficult operation to understand, and the facts are memorized more slowly. The difficulty may be that there

FIGURE 10.4

Take-away subtraction.

are various types of subtraction (take-away, missing addend, comparison). The take-away concept is often overemphasized in the classroom to the detriment of the other two. Many teachers read the symbol for subtraction (–) as "take away" rather than minus. Minus is a word used for the sign "–," not for the concept of "take away." However, owing to the overuse of this meaning for subtraction, many young children refer to this symbol as the "take away" sign and refer to subtraction as doing "the take-aways."

Comparison. The second meaning of subtraction is *comparison.* This concept is harder for children to understand and needs many modeling experiences to develop it. The comparison concept means that two sets are modeled and compared to one another and the difference, either more than or less than, is found (Figure 10.5). The difference may be seen by a one-to-one matching as in this example: "In their lunches, four children had an apple and three children had a banana. How many more apples were there than bananas?"

FIGURE 10.5

Comparison subtraction.

Everyday examples of this may be experienced by children when comparing ages or height, comparing data on a bar graph, matching books to children in a reading group, setting the table, or getting chairs for members of a group. Comparison language of "how many more," "how many less," "how much younger," "how much heavier," accompany situational problems for this interpretation of subtraction.

Missing Addend. The third concept of subtraction is *missing addend* or *completion.* This interpretation involves the relationship of subtraction to addition as a missing part. In addition, two parts are joined to make the whole. If a part is missing and the whole is known, then how much more must be added to the part to make the whole (the target number)? Often confusion comes by being misled by the word "more" and linking addition to the two numbers rather than *adding on* to the part to make the whole (Figure 10.6). For example, "Julio knows it costs 5 cents to buy the kite, but only has 2 cents. How much more does he need to buy the kite?"

FIGURE 10.6

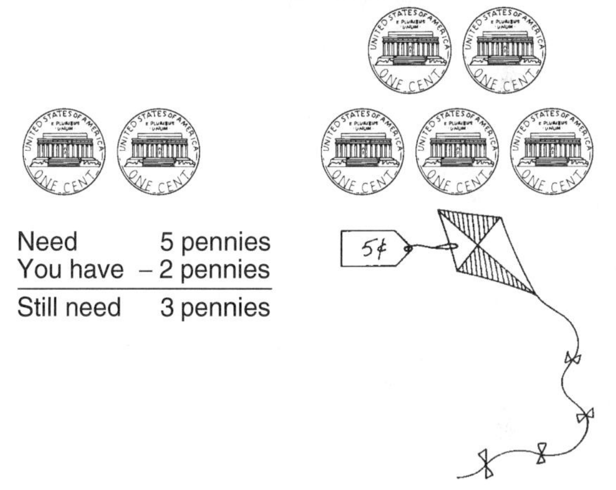

Missing addend subtraction.

This idea of finding "how many more are needed" is represented in real-world situations. Many experiences call for deciding the missing part and may be modeled as "counting on" to make the whole. The following examples ask the question of "how many more": Knowing the total cost and how much money you have, knowing the total mileage of a trip and how far you have traveled, determining the amount of change to be returned when a larger coin or bill has been given. Kamii, Lewis, and Booker (1998) suggest several games to help children focus on numerical reasoning for understanding missing-addend problems. A difficult aspect of missing addends is reversibility of the part-whole relationship, that is 3 + 2 = __ becomes 3 + __ = 5.

Literature. Numerous, entertaining books are wonderful ways to develop the operation of subtraction. Bartek (1997) shares well-known stories such as

The Three Little Pigs or nursery rhymes in a mathematics setting. A beginning list of books using take-away settings is *The Great Take-Away* (Mathews, 1980), *Five Little Monkeys Jumping on the Bed* (Christelow, 1989), *Ten Little Mice* (Dunbar, 1990), and *Roll Over!* (Gerstein, 1984). You may notice these titles sound like familiar songs by the same name. To show comparison subtraction find books on measurement that show subtraction as a comparison of lengths, weights, sizes, and so on, such as Kellogg's (1976) *Much Bigger Than Martin.*

Properties. The properties of the number system are limited since the commutative property, the associative property, and the identity property result in inequalities when working with subtraction. Older students should examine these properties to explore such relationships for the operation, for example, 7 – 3 = 4, but 3 – 7 is *not* equal to 4.

Multiplication

The conceptualization of multiplication should involve investigations of various groups, arrangements, number lines, and arrays with many types of materials. As children experience the physical models and verbalize the action with problem situations, they will be ready for the written symbols. Basically there are three different interpretations for multiplication.

Repeated Addition. Most textbooks devote primary time to combining sets of equal size or the concept of *grouping* or *repeated addition.* The aspect of multiplication that distinguishes it from addition is that for multiplication the sets must be the same size. Multiplication can be defined as repeated addition where the addends are of equal size or the addends must be the same number, for example, 3 + 3 + 3 + 3 = 12 or 4 groups of 3 are 12. Multiplication should begin as ideas about repeated addition to connect children's prior understandings of addition. Children see multiplication as counting groups of objects rather than single objects.

Learning experiences should include children describing things in real life that naturally occur in groups (eyes, tricycle wheels, packs of soda, days in a week). These groups can form problem situations when children are constructing their own word problems and modeling number sentences. Links between the language and modeling are valuable. Children need to move from a given number in a group to a given number *per* group. Another way to view multiplication word problems are rate situations such as, "Tenisha can earn $1.25 an hour babysitting her little sister. How much would she earn if she babysits for 4 hours?" Rate problems pose more difficulties because the language is not as clear as in the grouping situations (Kouba and Franklin, 1993).

Students must understand the exact wording of multiplication. For example, instead of saying "4 times 2," the teacher needs to say, "4 groups of 2." The use of the word "of" is critical because it makes the nature of multiplication (equal sets) clearer than does the word "times." This method also helps children in later elementary grades when they study multiplication of decimal and rational numbers, covered in Chapter 12 of this text. The examples in Figure 10.7 show the use of this terminology.

FIGURE 10.7

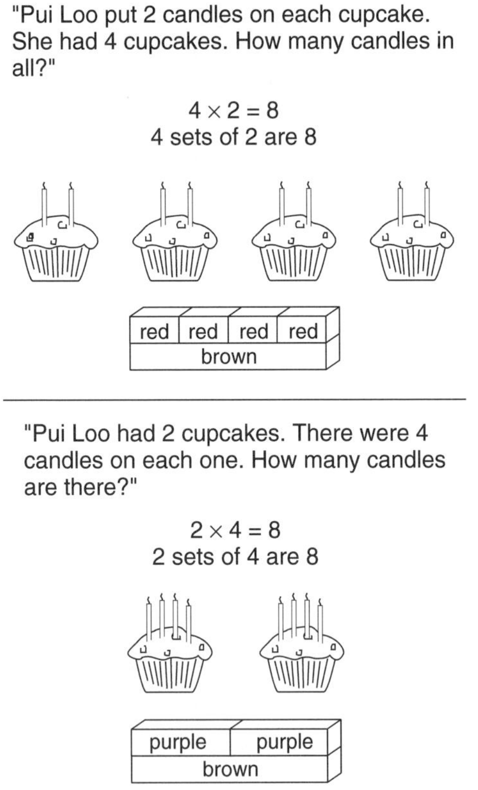

"Pui Loo put 2 candles on each cupcake. She had 4 cupcakes. How many candles in all?"
4 × 2 = 8
4 sets of 2 are 8
red
red
red
red
brown
"Pui Loo had 2 cupcakes. There were 4 candles on each one. How many candles are there?"
2 × 4 = 8
2 sets of 4 are 8
purple
purple
brown

Multiplication as repeated addition or grouping.

Activities using materials should begin in early grades to describe multiplication as repeated addition. Language becomes important in expressing number equations for multiplication. In Figure 10.8, all these groups show three groups of two. In the resulting number sentence, 3 × 2, the first number (factor) defines the number of groups and the second number (factor) defines the size of each group. Involve children in physical groupings also: Give three books to each of two children; have four children each hold up five fingers; have five children stand and decide how many eyes or toes altogether.

FIGURE 10.8

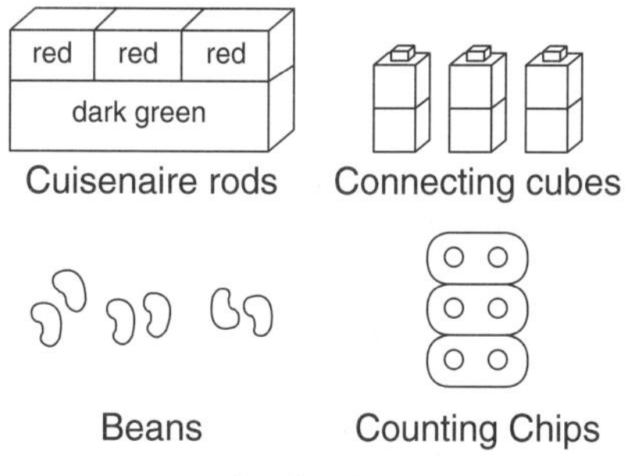

Models showing three groups of two.

Combinations. Multiplication can also be defined in terms of *combinations* or possible pairings. Other names associated with this interpretation of multiplication are *cross multiplication* or *Cartesian products.* In this sense, all elements of one set can be matched one-to-one with all the elements of another set to find the number of total possible pairs. Additional experiences and explanations are available on the CD-ROM if desired.

Real-life examples extend to selecting outfits for a trip (number of shirts matched to number of pants to produce different outfits), possible outcomes in probability experiments, or flavors of yogurt and different toppings (Figure 10.9). Every college student on a budget uses the Cartesian product in wardrobe planning! See how the clothing combines to form different outfits: "Monique is packing for a trip. She has four tops to go with a skirt, a pair of shorts, and a pair of pants. How many different outfits can she make?"

Arrays. The final interpretation of multiplication is that of an *array* model. This row-by-column problem compares to the width-times-length formula for areas of rectangular regions. The *Standards* (NCTM, 2000) call for having students build arrays showing how a product is related to its factors and seeing relationships between factor pairs. Applications to real-world situations include rows in a theater and so many seats per row, or rows in a garden and a given number of plants per row to determine the total. Children can build various numbers with color tiles or cubes and make rectangles from graph paper (Figure 10.10). Such activities offer readiness experiences for later work with factors, area, algebraic equations, and natural extensions to multidigit multiplication in Chapter 11. For example, "Mrs. Homeratha asked the children to sit in 4 rows with 3 in each row. How many children would this be?"

FIGURE 10.9

Multiplication as combinations.

FIGURE 10.10

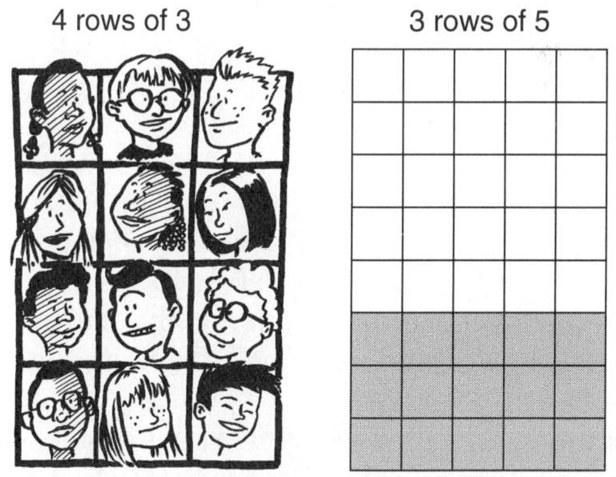

Multiplication as an array.

Perhaps it needs to be said again that all of the interpretations for an operation are written, recorded, and answered the same way. Only when situational word problems are attached to the number equation must appropriate modeling occur. When children translate word problems into number equations is when difficulty results and flexible ways to model the problem are needed.

EXTENDED ACTIVITIES

COMPUTERS MANIPULATIVES CALCULATORS

Name of Activity

- Family Game
- Facts in Color
- Calculator Capers
- Distributive Property of Multiplication over Addition Spreadsheet

Video Vignette

Cluster Problems

- Why did Mrs. Cordoba select these four equations as a "Cluster Problem"? What do you think is the purpose of this activity?
- Compare the strategies the children used for solving the problems and discuss their effectiveness.
- What mathematical thinking do you see the children using in this lesson and what meanings for multiplication do you notice?

Literature. Literature-based units for multiplication can show counting patterns, square numbers, factors and multiples, combinations, and the repeated addition concept. The list of children's books include *Anno's Multiplying Jar* (Anno and Anno, 1983), *Bunches and Bunches of Bunnies* (Mathews, 1978), *Ten Ways to Count to Ten* (Dee, 1988), *One Wide River to Cross* (Emberley, 1992), and *Socrates and the Three Little Pigs* (Mori, 1986). Children can illustrate and make up situations for their own stories about multiplication. Arrays in multiplication occur in *A Remainder of One* (Pinczes, 1995). *The King's Chessboard* (Birch, 1988), *Tops and Bottoms* (Stevens, 1995), and *Amanda Bean's Amazing Dreams* (Neuschwander, 1998) link literature to multiplication settings.

Properties. Several mathematical properties apply to multiplication. The mathematical principle called the commutative property (4×5 is the same as 5×4) relates to multiplication in the same way as it applies to addition. Although changing the order of the factors does not alter the product, when using grouping or rate problems, the roles being modeled by the factors must change. In other words, 4 groups of 5 cubes each (4×5) need to be rearranged to show the related commutative fact of 5×4, which is 5 groups with 4 cubes in each group. View the video vignette to watch children in fourth grade exploring the commutative property and how repeated addition relates to multiplication.

Practice with manipulatives helps develop understanding of the commutative property. Three other properties that relate to multiplication are described in the basic facts section of this chapter. These properties are the zero property, $0 \times 8 = 0$; the identity property, $6 \times 1 = 6$; and the distributive property $6 \times 5 = (3 \times 5) + (3 \times 5)$.

Division

Division is the mathematical operation used to separate a set into equal parts. Division is the inverse operation of multiplication—where multiplication is the operation used to combine sets of equal size into a new set. Division can be considered the opposite of multiplication or as repeated subtraction. There are two concepts of division, both of which can be easily modeled with manipulatives: partitive division and measurement division. The difference between these two situations is noted in the following table:

Measurement Division	Partitive Division
You know:	*You know:*
1. Number of objects in the original set	1. Number of objects in the original set
2. Number of objects to be in each new set	2. Number of new sets to be formed
Need to find:	*Need to find:*
3. How many new sets can be made?	3. How many objects are in each new set?

Measurement Division. *Measurement division* involves the process of taking a group of objects and separating (measuring) them into equal size groups of a specific size until all are distributed. Then the number of groups made is the answer. Here is a real-world example: "Todd has 10 marbles and wants to give 2 to each friend. How many friends will get 2 marbles?"

Figure 10.11 shows that if there are 10 marbles, and 2 are taken away each time, this can happen 5 times. This process can also be thought of as repeated subtraction, or, in equation form, as $10 \div 2 = 5$.

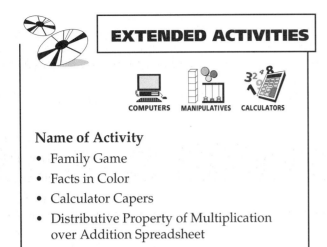

FIGURE 10.11

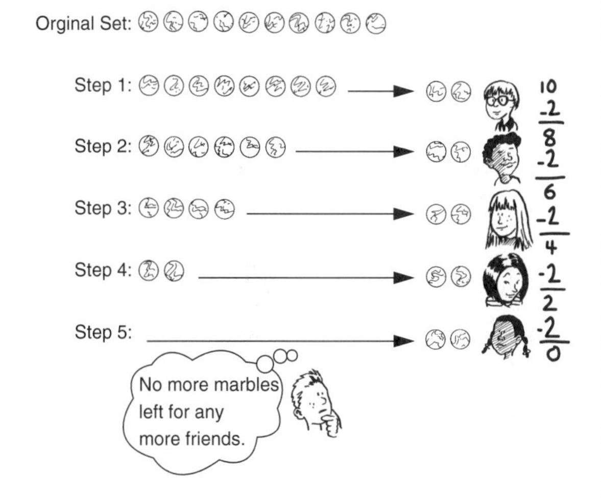

Measurement division.

FIGURE 10.12

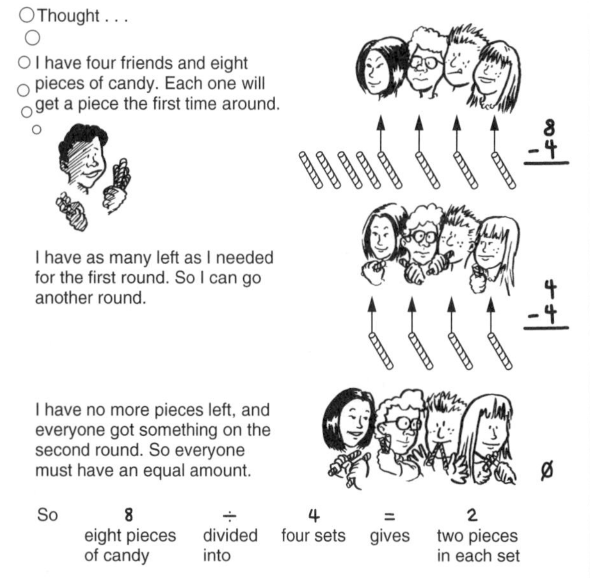

Partitive division.

Partitive Division. *Partitive division* involves the process of taking a group of objects and sharing (partitioning) them evenly into a specific number of groups until they are all gone, or none are left for another complete round. The number in each group is the answer. Dealing cards to people in a game is a common situation where partitive division is used. Here is another example of partitive division: "Enrique has 4 friends and 8 pieces of candy. He wants to give his candy away to his friends so everyone has an equal amount. How many pieces will each friend get?" (Figure 10.12).

The same equation and recording fits both division situations, 24 ÷ 4 = 6, but the modeling with objects is different. It is not important that children know the differences by name, but it is important that both types of exercises are included in building the division operation. Research (Kouba and Franklin, 1993) suggests that children use different strategies to represent measurement division problems than partitive division. These strategies should be observed, explained, and shared to help make sense of the operation. Remember that many students, even in upper elementary grades, commonly view multiplication as repeated addition and division as repeated subtraction (Figure 10.13). They need to work with a variety of problem situations and expand their views of these operations (NCTM, 2000).

A way to help you and the children remember the difference between the two types of division is by relating them in a meaningful fashion. The following is a common illustrative situation. There are 24 students in the class. You ask them to form groups by counting aloud 1–2–3–4 and then you have all the fours go into one group, the threes go to another group, and so on. This is partitive division. Another example of partitive division is when you have four children chosen as team captains and they select people to be on their team. You know the number of groups, and you are finding the size of each group. For measurement division, you would have children count aloud 1–2–3–4, and you would call that group 1. The next four children would form group 2, the next four are group 3, and continue in such a manner. Here you know the size of each group, and you are determining how many groups can be made.

Literature. *The Doorbell Rang* (Hutchins, 1986) is a delightful book exploring what effect increasing the number of groups has on the answer (the number in each group). Another book, *17 Kings and 42 Elephants* (Mahy, 1987), asks how to share the work of caring for 42 elephants and can be approached using a partitive or a measurement approach. Ask students to illustrate these stories as a means to assess their mathematical understanding and to determine if both forms of division are correctly interpreted. Division can be explored as the inverse of multiplication in books such as *The Twelve Circus Rings* (Chwast, 1993), *A Remainder of One* (Pinczes, 1995), and *One Hundred Hungry Ants* (Pinczes, 1993).

Properties. Like subtraction, the commutative and associative properties do not apply to division. The identity properties for multiplication is one

FIGURE 10.13

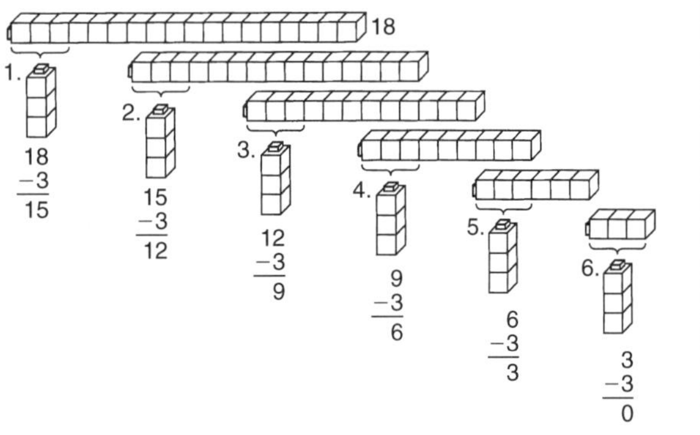

Division as repeated subtraction.

(8 × 1 = 8) and this is true for division (8 ÷ 1 = 8). The zero property in division is a special case and one that can be confusing to children. The property of division by zero says that dividing a number by zero does not compute or is undefined. Modeling and explaining this property to children is the challenge. It is not sufficient to say "dividing by zero is impossible." For example, what is the answer to 8 ÷ 0? When expressed in inverse fashion (which works with other division facts such as 8 ÷ 4 = 2 becomes 2 × 4 = 8), this would become ? × 0 = 8. Remember that any number multiplied by zero is zero, so any number used instead of the ? would produce a product of zero. Then 8 × 0 would equal 8, but that is not true. The only number that could replace 8, to make the inverse possible also, is zero. Because this does not permit computation to take place meaningfully, the situation inherently becomes "does not compute."

Children may still want to try to model examples that involve zero. As with other concepts, encourage students to make up word stories and try to model the action. Try problems with both partitive and measurement approaches to division. "How many groups of zero are in 8?" "Put 8 counters into zero groups."

Since division is the inverse of multiplication, write the related fact equations for the problem. Present the problem of 8 ÷ 0 and write the corresponding multiplication sentence that checks that problem, □ × 0 = 8. Whatever number is placed as an answer, the product is still zero. This would indicate that 0 is *not* equal to 0; therefore there is no answer to the problem and we say division by zero is undefined. If more explanation is preferred, use the CD-ROM for extra examples.

Becoming comfortable with many different problem situations for the four operations takes time. Practice with recognizing problem structures may be needed before you ask children to analyze word problems. More opportunities and examples are found on the CD-ROM.

Readiness to Learn Basic Facts

What are basic facts? Where do they come from? How many facts are there? What does it mean to *master* the basic facts? These are key questions approached in this chapter. Basic facts refer to the combinations of single-digit numbers (for addition and multiplication) and their corresponding inverse (for subtraction and division), such as, 4 + 9 = 13, 13 − 9 = 4, and 4 × 9 = 36, 36 ÷ 9 = 4. Although some textbooks and teachers continue basic facts through 12, in this book basic facts will be only numbers less than 10. There are 390 basic facts: 100 facts for addition, subtraction, and multiplication, and 90 for division. Mastery of basic facts becomes a critical issue in elementary school starting in first grade. The term "mastery" refers to the automatic recall of a basic fact combination within a 3-second time period.

Check Your Mathematics Knowledge

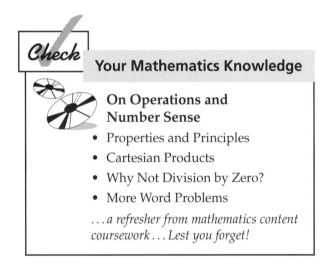

On Operations and Number Sense

- Properties and Principles
- Cartesian Products
- Why Not Division by Zero?
- More Word Problems

. . . a refresher from mathematics content coursework . . . Lest you forget!

Prerequisites. First, an understanding of the meanings of operations must be developed along with a knowledge of basic number combinations. Children might use manipulatives to discover number patterns and relationships, to model particular word problems, and to explore the joining, separating, and partitioning of groups. Second, after extensive informal experiences in varied contexts, mathematical terms and symbols can be introduced. As children acquire operation sense, a solid conceptual framework will be established on which to build the basic facts and later, the algorithms. As the

Standards (NCTM, 1989, 2000) suggest exploring numbers and operations helps children develop strategies to learn and recall basic facts. Linking the manipulation of materials to the steps of the procedures, and developing thinking patterns, teachers can foster basic fact mastery.

It is important to consider a child's readiness to learn the basic facts. Understanding these prerequisites will ensure greater success in getting children to have quick recall of the facts. Many first graders are "taught" addition and subtraction facts before they can understand them. Parents are often misled into believing that early recall of facts implies an understanding of the operation.

Piaget. Consider what Piaget tells us about children's learning and how this relates to readiness to learn basic facts. Number conservation, knowing that numbers remain the same despite various changes in configuration, is one important factor in evaluating readiness. If a child has 5 beans and forms them into a set of 3 and a set of 2, there are still 5 beans. Until a child conserves number, counting is used to name the sum rather than the child knowing the sum remains unchanged. Refer to Chapter 8 of this text for additional details about this topic.

Piaget illustrated that number is not something innately known by children. The ability to conserve number must precede the memorization of basic facts. Teachers should provide adequate time for children to internalize the invariance of number. For a child to verify the understanding of conservation, many experiences are needed with joining, separating, and comparing sets. The child who is a nonconserver will not see the relationships between families of number facts. Many of the strategies in this chapter hold little meaning for nonconservers.

The principle of class inclusion (the ability to see that all of one group can be part of another group at the same time) also deserves careful study and evaluation before beginning a program of memorizing the basic facts. Review Chapter 8 for greater details on the bead experiments. Children younger than seven have difficulty seeing the whole as being larger than its parts. The logical relationship, the inclusion relation, might not be comprehended until a child is about seven years old.

The class inclusion problem can also be a class addition problem. To solve the problem, children must consider the whole set and its parts at the same time. Children need to add the parts to obtain the whole and to be able to reverse this process (reversibility). Addition is an operation relating the parts to the whole.

$$6 + 1 = 7$$
$$2 + 5 = 7$$
$$3 + 4 = 7$$
$$5 + 2 = 7$$
$$1 + 6 = 7$$

According to Piaget, until the child understands class inclusion and reversibility of thought, basic facts are learned at a meaningless level. Teaching facts using strategies described later in this chapter may be a questionable practice. More activities to develop number meaning (described in the next section) should be included. The child who has not mastered the concept of class inclusion may not relate various number pairs with the same sum.

To understand addition as an operation, the child must be able to look at various pairs of addends and realize that the number can be expressed as the same sum. The child must also be able to realize that the sum (7) can become all these combinations. Number combinations can be developed with concrete materials such as lima beans painted red on one side, of which the child counts a given number into a small cup. The beans are spilled from the cup, and the child reads the number of painted beans as the first addend and the number of white beans as the second addend. This activity is repeated many times to build the principle of invariance of number as well as to see the possible combinations for a given sum (Figure 10.14).

FIGURE 10.14

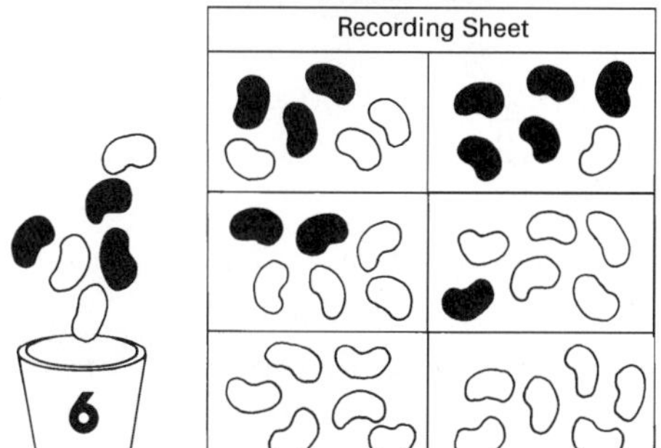

Materials to build number invariance.

Number Meaning. Another prerequisite for working with number facts is to develop meaning for the symbols. An excellent idea is to use physical objects to model number combinations in many ways. When children can successfully create and label sets, they are ready to attach the symbols to the actions.

Invite children to create number stories using concrete materials and story boards (a picture of a forest, ocean, barn, store on which the children build their stories). A source of these manipulative materials is found in Baratta-Lorton (1978). Check for additional activities for developing basic facts on the CD-ROM. Children can gain appreciation for the ways other cultures have developed the concept of number after they do their own stories as seen in "Origins of Modern Arithmetic."

Understanding the concept does not imply that facts will be mastered. Learning facts by rote does not mean understanding the operation. This sequence suggests that a solid mathematics program incorporates all three components. Meaningful problem-solving situations should accompany each step in the learning sequence. According to the *Standards*, mastery of basic facts should come after exploratory work with the operations in problem situations.

Cultural Contributions

CULTURAL RELEVANCE MATHEMATICAL CONNECTIONS

ORIGINS OF MODERN ARITHMETIC

MATERIALS

- A globe
- Pictures of ancient and modern Egypt, Central America, India

DIRECTIONS

1. Tell the children that people in ancient days did the same things with numbers that they (the children) do in arithmetic.
2. Share the following information from the Chicago mathematics teachers (Strong, 1990):

   Students should know that many peoples contributed to the development of modern arithmetic and that the origins of arithmetic are international. For example, Africans were the first to use numerals. Ancient Egyptians in Africa invented a symbol for ten that represented 10 tally marks and a symbol for one hundred that replaced 100 tally marks. The Chinese were among the first to recognize and use number patterns. The Maya in Central America used a zero as a position holder hundreds of years before Europe imported modern numerals from Africa. Modern numerals were invented by the peoples of India. That is why modern numerals are known as Hindu-Arabic numerals. (p. 38)

3. Use the globe to show where the Maya lived in Central America, and where India and Egypt are located.

Activity Continues

4. Show the pictures of the people going about their daily tasks. Talk of how they may be making up number stories about their work. Let the children pretend to live in each culture and tell a number story that could go with each picture.

Supporting the NCTM *Standards* (2000):

- Mathematics as Connections; Number Systems
- The Learning Principle
- The Equity Principle

EXTENDED ACTIVITIES

MATHEMATICAL CONNECTIONS PROBLEM SOLVING

Name of Activity

- Where in the World?
- Rummy Equations
- Contig

Thinking Strategies for the Basic Facts of Addition

The beginning step in developing basic facts is to build an understanding of the operation, discussed earlier in this chapter. Manipulatives are the important, beginning key. Children should have opportunities to represent the number equation with physical models. Teaching basic facts should center on the structure of mathematics. Simply going through the number combinations in numerical order is not enough. Research has shown that certain thinking strategies help children learn the basic facts (Baroody and Standifer, 1993; Fuson, 1992; Rathmell, 1978; Steinberg, 1985; Thornton, 1990).

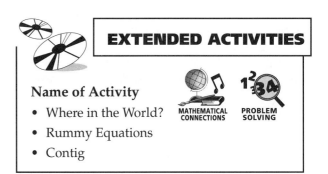

Strategy Preferences. Children should be encouraged to develop other thinking strategies or associations that may hold particular meaning for them. The fact combinations suggested in the next sections do not mean that each basic fact has one and only one category into which it is placed and by which it should be learned. Children have preferred strategies based on their individual strengths that should be identified and encouraged. Strategies should be used to foster and promote analytic thinking as well as to form clusters of facts that reduce the number of isolated facts to learn. In this way, thinking strategies are useful for students with special needs as it helps recall.

The *Standards* (NCTM, 1989, 2000) state that encouraging children to develop their own strategies enables them to understand mathematical relationships and reason. Teachers must help children build understanding by getting them to organize what they know and to disregard inefficient strategies. When children resort to using their fingers to get answers, it simply tells us that they are not ready for the symbolic level. More time should be spent at the concrete and connecting level, discussed in Chapter 8.

Addition Facts. The basic 100 addition facts (Figure 10.15) are those problems that are composed of two single-digit addends. Thus the facts include $0 + 0 = 0$ through $9 + 9 = 18$. They serve as the basis for all further addition work and need to be developed from a concrete basis of understanding to an automatic response level if they are going to be useful in computation.

FIGURE 10.15

+	0	1	2	3	4	5	6	7	8	9
0	0	1	2	3	4	5	6	7	8	9
1	1	2	3	4	5	6	7	8	9	10
2	2	3	4	5	6	7	8	9	10	11
3	3	4	5	6	7	8	9	10	11	12
4	4	5	6	7	8	9	10	11	12	13
5	5	6	7	8	9	10	11	12	13	14
6	6	7	8	9	10	11	12	13	14	15
7	7	8	9	10	11	12	13	14	15	16
8	8	9	10	11	12	13	14	15	16	17
9	9	10	11	12	13	14	15	16	17	18

100 basic addition facts.

For many children the two basic forms, horizontal $2 + 3 = 5$ and vertical,

$$\begin{array}{r} 2 \\ +\,3 \\ \hline 5 \end{array}$$

provide no real stumbling block to learning the addition facts. In teaching basic facts, both forms need to be used, and generally the horizontal form is introduced first. Children may be given help recognizing that the combinations are the same by actually writing both forms of the same fact. This should be done at the same time children are performing actions with multiple embodiments (various models).

Principles. Understanding the mathematical principles associated with each operation is important to enhance learning. An important property of addition is the *commutative principle.* Figure 10.16 shows that 45 addition facts are learned readily if the principle of commutativity is applied. The facts that are related by the commutative principle are shaded in the figure.

FIGURE 10.16

+	0	1	2	3	4	5	6	7	8	9
0		1	2	3	4	5	6	7	8	9
1	1		3	4	5	6	7	8	9	10
2	2	3		5	6	7	8	9	10	11
3	3	4	5		7	8	9	10	11	12
4	4	5	6	7		9	10	11	12	13
5	5	6	7	8	9		11	12	13	14
6	6	7	8	9	10	11		13	14	15
7	7	8	9	10	11	12	13		15	16
8	8	9	10	11	12	13	14	15		17
9	9	10	11	12	13	14	15	16	17	

Commutative property for addition.

To internalize the principle of commutativity, students need experiences with concrete materials. Figure 10.17 shows several effective manipulative devices to use. Students need to realize the power of this principle in reducing the number of facts to learn.

FIGURE 10.17

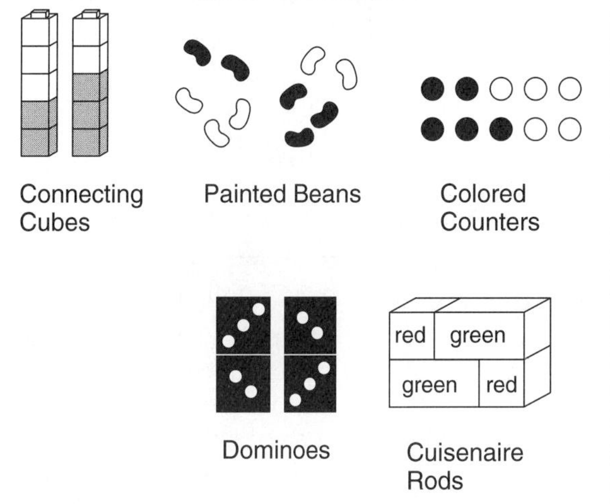

Models to show commutative property—turnaround facts.

Practice alone is not sufficient to facilitate memorizing the basic facts. Students need to increase their memorization abilities by using an organized list of the facts. This approach places the facts into categories according to the structure of mathematics and their order of difficulty. It also capitalizes on the natural thinking strategies invented by children for learning the facts. Table 10.1, the table of fact strategies, assumes that the commutative principle has been developed and continues to be emphasized. As you read the table, consider the definition and notice the systematic way the facts are related to each other. Also think about how organizing the facts in this manner reduces the number of facts to be learned and encourages retention.

The fact strategies should be shown and developed with concrete materials to ensure understanding. Many of these devices can be made inexpensively and quickly and are well worth the time. Activities with manipulatives are suggested for teaching the following fact strategies: adding one; counting on; near doubles; and bridging to ten.

Adding One. Cuisenaire rods are a good manipulative to show this principle. Have children build a staircase with the ten different colored rods. Take a white rod and "walk" it up the staircase. With each step, the children see it is one more. This procedure is shown in Figure 10.18.

FIGURE 10.18

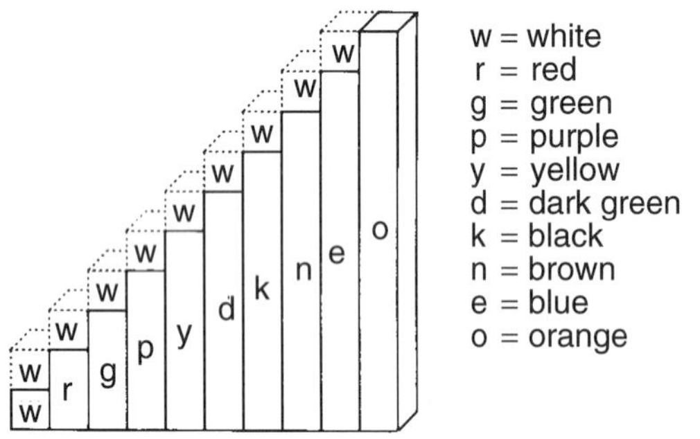

"Counting on" or "adding one more" with Cuisenaire rods.

Counting On. Much time could be spent in quick practice sessions with counting one, two, or three more than a given number. Such sessions can be done easily when children are waiting in line to wash hands, to leave for another class, or when children are lining up for recess, music, or whatever. An effective aid that can be quickly made is shown in Figure 10.19. The first addend is written to the left with the second addend being plus two or plus three. Attached as flip cards are the counting numbers the child would say to reach the sum. If the child needs this prompt, the cards can be flipped over for help. If the child wants to check the answer, it appears on the back.

FIGURE 10.19

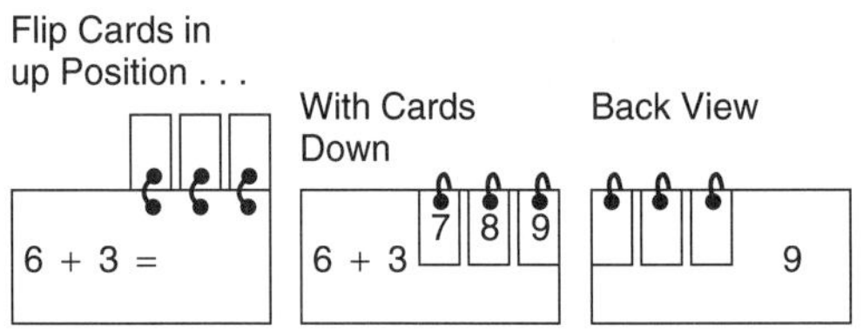

"Counting on" two or three.

A simple game is to have a deck of cards of numbers that serves as the first addend. The child rolls a die that has two faces marked with 1, two faces marked with 2, and two faces marked with 3. The die indicates the number to be added to the card drawn from the deck. If the correct sum is given, the child can move on the gameboard the number of spaces indicated on the die (Figure 10.20).

FIGURE 10.20

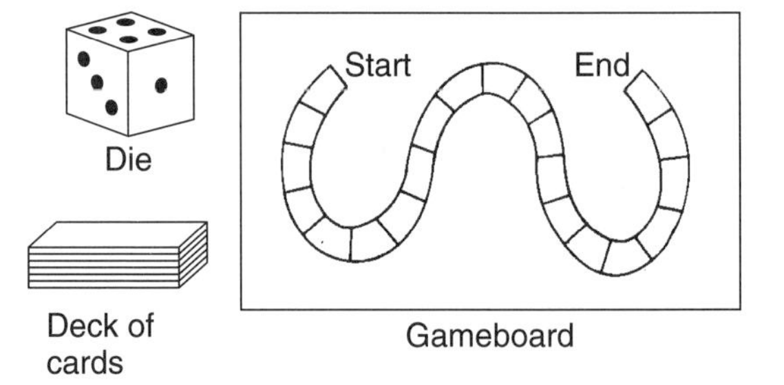

"Counting on" with game.

Near Doubles. The near-doubles strategy reinforces something a child already knows and feels comfortable with, the doubles. A teaching/practice device for near doubles is shown in Figure 10.21. We must always look for ways to build on prior knowledge to form new associations.

Bridging to 10. Many mathematics educators encourage the use of ten-frames to create mental imagery. The "Bridging to 10" activity shows teaching techniques to develop this concept. These devices may be made from egg cartons. The sides of plastic fruit baskets, plastic canvas, or chicken wire may be used to project on the overhead for whole-class discussion. Ten-frames consist of a 2 × 5 array where one side must be filled to 5 before the other side is

TABLE 10.1 Thinking Strategies for the Basic Facts of Addition

Definition

Identity Element

Adding 0 to any number does not change the number.

19 basic facts are learned.

+	0	1	2	3	4	5	6	7	8	9
0	0	1	2	3	4	5	6	7	8	9
1	1									
2	2									
3	3									
4	4									
5	5									
6	6									
7	7									
8	8									
9	9									

Adding One

Depends on understanding number seriation—adding one to any number is the same as naming the next counting number.

17 facts are learned.

+	0	1	2	3	4	5	6	7	8	9
0										
1		2	3	4	5	6	7	8	9	10
2		3								
3		4								
4		5								
5		6								
6		7								
7		8								
8		9								
9		10								

Counting On

Most effective when addend is 1, 2, or 3 more than any given number.

Involves two skills:

1. Knowing which number is greater and that counting begins here.
2. Knowing counting sequence beginning at any one-digit number.

28 additional facts are learned.

+	0	1	2	3	4	5	6	7	8	9
0										
1										
2			4	5	6	7	8	9	10	11
3			5	6	7	8	9	10	11	12
4			6	7						
5			7	8						
6			8	9						
7			9	10						
8			10	11						
9			11	12						

Definition

Doubles

Both addends are the same number.

6 facts are learned.

+	0	1	2	3	4	5	6	7	8	9
0										
1		2								
2			4							
3				6						
4					8					
5						10				
6							12			
7								14		
8									16	
9										18

Near Doubles

Use when addends are consecutive numbers.

If children know 8 + 8 = 16, then prompt them to reason that 8 + 9 is one more or 8 + 7 is one less.

10 additional facts are learned.

+	0	1	2	3	4	5	6	7	8	9
0										
1										
2				5						
3			5		7					
4				7		9				
5					9		11			
6						11		13		
7							13		15	
8								15		17
9									17	

Bridging to 10

Use when one addend is close to 10.

More difficult for children to understand because:

1. Mastery of sums to 10 must be developed first.
2. Ability to separate a number into two parts is required.
3. Must mentally keep track of changes in both addends.

16 additional facts are learned.

+	0	1	2	3	4	5	6	7	8	9
0										
1										
2										11
3									11	12
4								11	12	13
5									13	14
6										15
7					11					16
8				11	12	13				17
9			11	12	13	14	15	16	17	

Note: The blocks with numbers in the main body of the table denote new facts to be learned. The shaded part denotes facts already learned by a previous strategy. A shaded block with a number included indicates an overlap between a previously learned strategy and a new strategy.

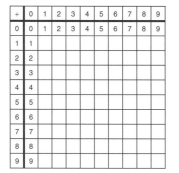

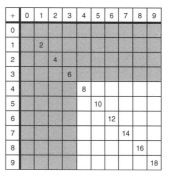

FIGURE 10.21

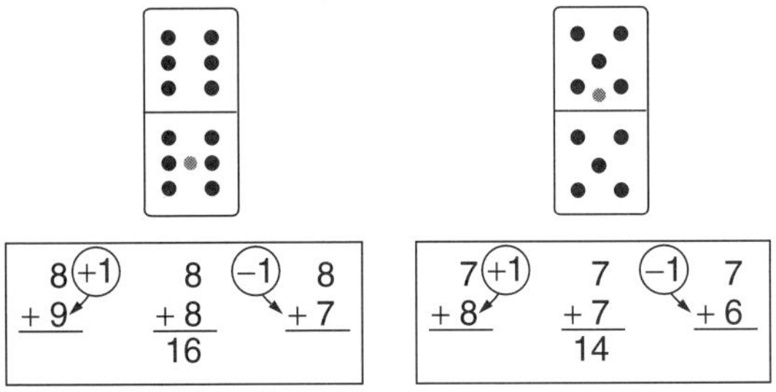

Devices to learn near doubles.

started. Counters are placed in the squares starting at the upper left and proceeding across until that row is filled. Review the video vignette, "Using Ten-Frames," in Chapter 8 if you need to refresh your memory. Number sense is developed as children predict how many more are needed to fill the row. Some children count backward from 10 while others count on to 10. This reinforces relationships between the two operations.

Activity 10.1

BRIDGING TO 10

MATERIALS

- A set of dot cards for the ten-frames
- Counters and egg cartons

DIRECTIONS

1. Teacher flashes a card to child for a second. The child puts that number of counters in the egg carton trays and says the total amount. Teacher continues in similar fashion for other numbers.
2. Teacher can also flash a dot card to the child for a second and the child tells how many more dots are needed to form 10.

Variation

MATERIALS

- Counters and egg cartons to make two ten-frames

DIRECTIONS

Teacher (or child) shows addition fact with 7, 8, or 9 as one addend. The other addend is large enough to form a sum greater than 10. A 10 is made with the first addend by adding counters from the second ten-frame.

Activity Continues

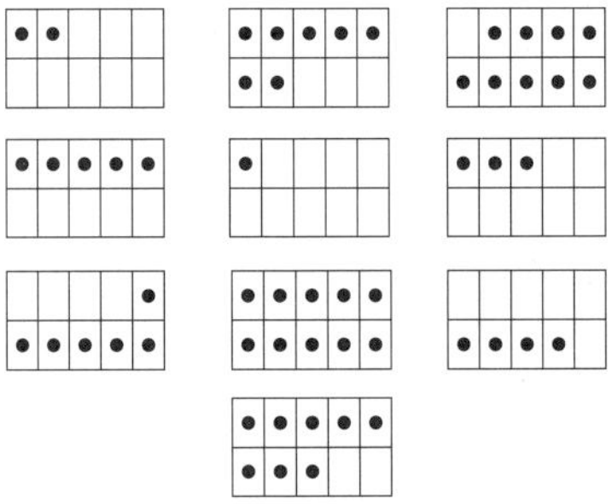

The answer appears as 10 + remaining number.

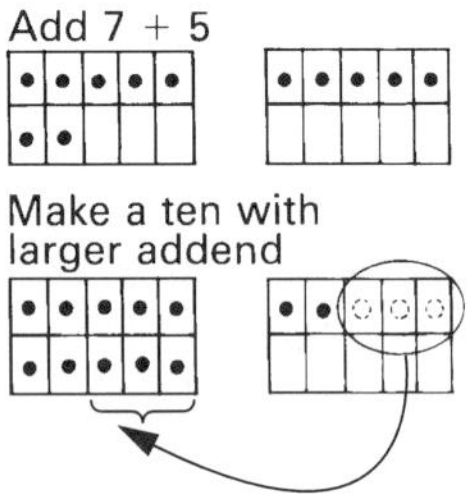

Another manipulative device to use for bridging to 10 that can be constructed easily and inexpensively is shown in Figure 10.22. It is composed of 18 plastic beads on a pipe cleaner. Ten beads are one color and eight beads are another color. When combinations are formed, the two colors indicate the two-digit number that results as the sum. The device allows for all facts through 9 + 9 (sum 18 or the total number of plastic beads) and visually indicates when a bridging to 10 occurs.

FIGURE 10.22

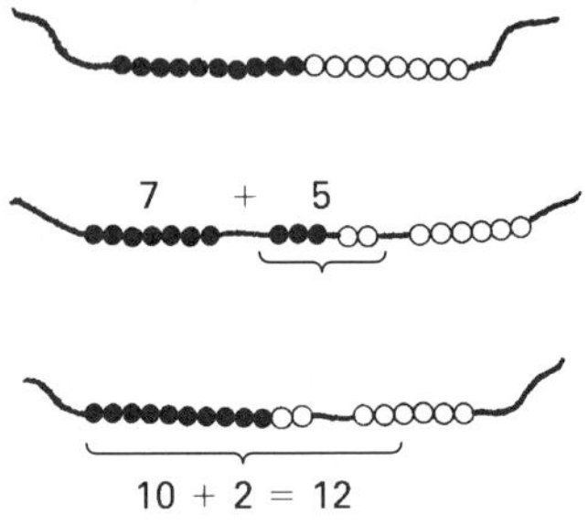

Bead cards for "bridging to 10."

Calculator activities using the constant function provide excellent experiences to help reinforce some of the strategies and relationships between the operations. Tests for commutativity, associativity, identity property, repeated addition, and repeated subtraction are only a few of the many relationships to be examined.

Activity 10.2

CALCULATORS MENTAL MATH

USING THE CALCULATOR WITH BASIC FACTS

MATERIALS

- Calculator with a constant function

DIRECTIONS

1. To practice counting on 3: push 4, push + key, push 3, push = key, new number, push = key, new number, push = key, and so on.
2. Do you see how it is storing the number each time? Try it with other numbers. (If this activity does not work on your calculator, experiment with your calculator to determine how it handles the constant function.)
3. Mentally think of what the next answer will be *before* you press the = sign. See if you were correct each time.

- This can be called mental skip counting!

Children often regard learning the 100 addition facts as an insurmountable task. When the facts are broken into groups, the task becomes manageable and reasonable to attain. When thinking strategies and fact strategies are used rather than random memorization, the facts are learned faster and retained longer.

Thinking Strategies for the Basic Facts of Subtraction

There are 100 basic subtraction facts that are formed as the inverse of addition. There appear to be two different philosophies of when subtraction facts should be introduced to children: at the same time as the related addition facts or after groups of addition facts (facts to 10 and facts to 18). Some teachers delay extensive work on subtraction facts until speed tests for addition have been mastered. Since many of the thinking strategies for subtraction are closely related to the addition facts, the authors support teaching the two operations together.

Activity 10.3

PROBLEM SOLVING MENTAL MATH

REAL-WORLD MATH—EXPLORING BASIC OPERATIONS OF SUBTRACTION

DIRECTIONS

There are three ways to think about subtraction. Study the problems and think about what equation you would use to solve each one below:

1. Mateo's teacher gave him eight pencils to sharpen and told him to make sure that each of his seventeen classmates had a sharpened pencil.
   How many more pencils will Mateo need to sharpen for the class?
2. Sedona baked fifteen cookies. If nine cookies are eaten, how many cookies are left?
3. How many more cookies did Sedona bake than were eaten?

The fact strategies for subtraction are: subtract zero; subtract the whole/almost the whole; counting back; counting on (counting up); and fact families. Keep in mind that it is critical to have children model these concepts with objects before the ideas are taught and before children are expected to use these strategies in meaningful ways. Practice with concrete manipulatives helps develop understanding and memory of these fact strategies. Fact strategies and the structure of the number system can be used to teach the facts shown in Table 10.2.

Helpful Devices. Many teachers and parents consider only flash cards although some other devices are more effective. Because missing addends is a related concept for several strategies, several teaching aids can be made to reinforce this concept. Flip cards, illustrated in Figure 10.23, enhance learning the several strategies called subtract the whole/almost the whole, counting back, and counting on. Several studies (Carpenter and Moser, 1984; Fuson, 1986; Steinberg, 1985) have shown that counting back (counting down) presents children with considerable difficulty, and research by Fuson indicates that counting up is an effective approach for first-grade children.

Analyzing the relationships between the facts of addition and subtraction helps the recall of fact families. Facts are organized into "families" to help children use a known fact to recall an unknown fact.

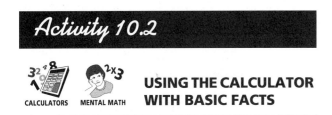

TABLE 10.2 Thinking Strategies for the Basic Facts of Subtraction

Definition

Subtract Zero

Easily learned—subtracting 0 from any number does not change the number.

10 facts learned.

–	0	1	2	3	4	5	6	7	8	9
0	0	1	2	3	4	5	6	7	8	9
1										
2										
3										
4										
5										
6										
7										
8										
9										

Subtracting the Whole/Almost the Whole

Subtracting the number from itself results in 0 left.

Almost the whole means to subtract a number that is one less than the number: 8 – 7 = 1.

18 facts learned.

–	0	1	2	3	4	5	6	7	8	9
0	0	1								
1	1	2								
2	2	3								
3	3	4								
4	4	5								
5	5	6								
6	6	7								
7	7	8								
8	8	9								
9	9	10								

Definition

Counting Back

Most effective when the number subtracted is 1, 2, or 3. Related to "counting on."

24 facts learned.

–	0	1	2	3	4	5	6	7	8	9
0										
1		2	3	4	5	6	7	8	9	10
2		3	4	5	6	7	8	9	10	11
3		4	5	6	7	8	9	10	11	12
4										
5										
6										
7										
8										
9										

Counting On

Use when 3 or less is to be subtracted. Helpful to associate with "counting on" for addition.

Missing addend approach is emphasized: 5 + ? = 8.

12 additional facts learned.

–	0	1	2	3	4	5	6	7	8	9
0										
1										
2										
3										
4		5	6	7						
5		6	7	8						
6		7	8	9						
7		8	9	10						
8		9	10	11						
9		10	11	12						

Fact Families

Emphasizes inverse operation of addition/subtraction and interrelates them.

Last 36 facts learned.

–	0	1	2	3	4	5	6	7	8	9
0										
1										
2										
3										
4					8	9	10	11	12	13
5					9	10	11	12	13	14
6					10	11	12	13	14	15
7					11	12	13	14	15	16
8					12	13	14	15	16	17
9					13	14	15	16	17	18

Note: The blocks with numbers in the main body of the table denote new facts to be learned. The shaded part denotes facts already learned by a previous strategy. A shaded block with a number included indicates an overlap between a previously learned strategy and a new strategy.

FIGURE 10.23

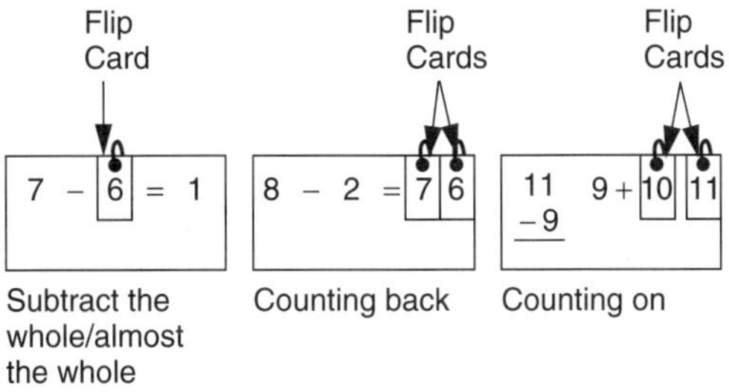

Flip cards for three subtraction fact strategies.

Fact Families. Triominoes are an effective device, made easily and inexpensively, to develop fact families (Figure 10.24). The triominoes can be color coded in clusters of facts such as: facts to 6, facts to 10, facts to 14, facts to 18. The teacher selects facts on which a child needs practice and gives that triomino to the child to write the four related equations.

FIGURE 10.24

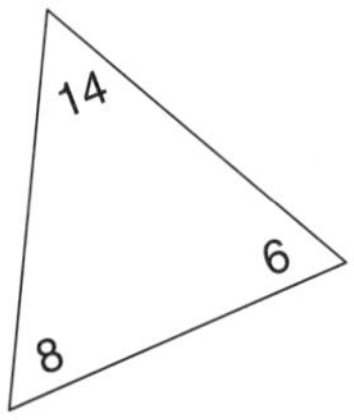

$8 + 6 = 14$
$6 + 8 = 14$
$14 - 8 = 6$
$14 - 6 = 8$

Triominoes for fact families.

When errors are noted, the teacher should ask the child to model the equation with concrete objects. This procedure will become self-correcting and a valuable learning experience. Triominoes can also be used as a practice device. If the top corner is covered, you are asking for a sum. If one of the side corners is covered, a missing addend is needed.

Using 10. The power of 10 cannot be overstated in developing thinking strategies for subtraction facts. When students master all the facts to 10 for subtraction using various strategies suggested, to subtract single-digit numbers from the teen numbers, students can think of a tens fact then add on the rest. To use this strategy for this problem, 14 − 8, the child can think of the problem as 10 − 8 which is 2, then add on the 4 from the ones place to get an answer of 6 (Figure 10.25). In this manner, all subtraction facts greater than 10 can become two-step problems—subtract from 10 then add the ones.

FIGURE 10.25

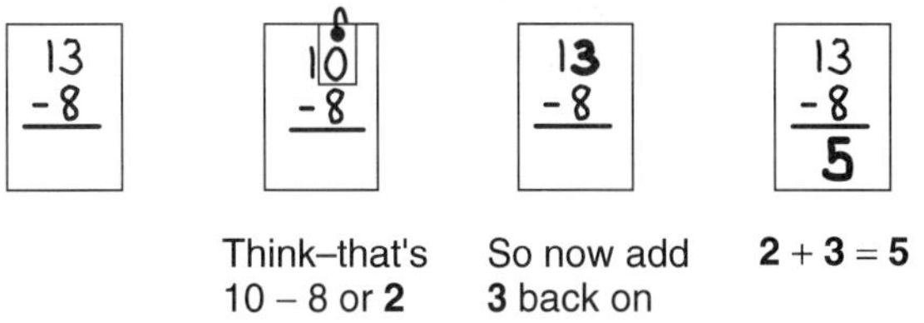

Use simpler facts to 10 then add on the 1's

Part-Whole. The important relationship between parts and wholes can be made as the four number sentences are generated with concrete modeling. If the facts related to 3, 6, and 9 are the goal, show three red counters as one set and six black counters as the second set and think of the corresponding two addition sentences for joining them and the two subtraction sentences for separating them. At the connecting level, domino dot flip cards (Figure 10.26) show the total as well as the two parts, and can alternately cover the two parts or the whole. Children can write the appropriate number sentences.

FIGURE 10.26

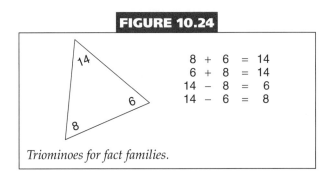

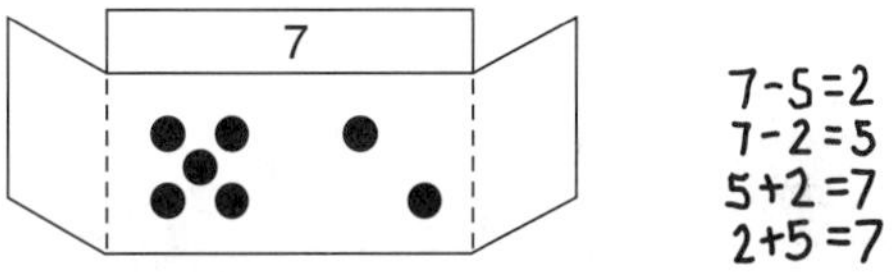

Domino dot cards for fact families show a connecting level device.

Activity 10.4

MANIPULATIVES

SUBTRACT THE WHOLE/ ALMOST THE WHOLE

MATERIALS

- Four sets of 0–9 number cards (forty in all)

DIRECTIONS

1. Have the children work in cooperative groups of two or three.
2. Shuffle the cards. Put them in a pile between two players. On alternating turns, a player draws a card from the pile. If the player can form an equation with two numbers that will give an answer with a difference

Activity Continues

of one, the player says, "UNO." The player says the number sentence (that is, 4 take away 3 is 1) and lays down the two cards, 4 and 3. Play continues until all cards have been drawn. The player with the most equations wins.

Thinking Strategies for the Basic Facts of Multiplication

Readiness activities for multiplication should begin with talking about groups of the same size and exploring counting patterns. Activities that encourage children to visualize groups along with the related languages should precede any formal use of the multiplication table or the formal word "times."

Children are eager to begin the multiplication chapter, usually included in the second-grade text. Multiplication means the world of "big kids," and young children are eager to quote products of large numbers to teacher and others.

An interesting approach for cultural awareness is offered in "Chinese Multiplication Table." Different techniques can be adopted to interpret the structure of this system and to examine the patterns.

Activity 10.5

CHINESE MULTIPLICATION TABLE

The ancestors of Asians developed a unique "one digit" table from which many patterns can be seen. This makes an intriguing problem solving puzzle for middle school.

DIRECTIONS

1. Start with a conventional multiplication table:

×	1	2	3	4	5	6	7	8	9
1	1	2	3	4	5	6	7	8	9
2	2	4	6	8	10	12	14	16	18
3	3	6	9	12	15	18	21	24	27
4	4	6	12	16	20	24	28	32	36
5	5	10	15	20	25	30	35	40	45
6	6	12	18	24	30	36	42	48	54
7	7	14	21	28	35	42	49	56	63
8	8	16	24	32	40	48	56	64	72
9	9	18	27	36	45	54	63	72	81

2. The objective is to have a table with only a one-digit number in each slot. Each digit of a two digit answer is

Activity Continues

added. For example: $27 = 2 + 7 = 9$ where 27 was, it is now 9.

3. If adding the two digits gives another two-digit number like $48 = 4 + 8 = 12$, then the 12 is added to give $12 = 1 + 2 = 3$.
4. The following table results:

×	1	2	3	4	5	6	7	8	9
1	1	2	3	4	5	6	7	8	9
2	2	4	6	8	1	3	5	7	9
3	3	6	9	3	6	9	3	6	9
4	4	8	3	7	2	6	1	5	9
5	5	1	6	2	7	3	8	4	9
6	6	3	9	6	3	9	6	3	9
7	7	5	3	1	8	6	4	2	9
8	8	7	6	5	4	3	2	1	9
9	9	9	9	9	9	9	9	9	9

5. Many patterns can be seen. See how many you can find.
6. Here are thought clues to start:
   Connect all the 8's to see a shape for 8.
   Do the same for each number.
   Many squares can be connected resulting in "reflecting" numbers, such as:

9	3	6	9
3	7	2	6
6	2	7	3
9	6	3	9

When formal drill on the basic facts is needed, the following thinking strategies should be considered. There are 100 basic multiplication facts composed from all single-digit factors. Thus the facts include $0 \times 0 = 0$ through $9 \times 9 = 81$. The resulting table is shown in Figure 10.27. As mentioned earlier, the commutative property reduces the number of facts to be learned by 45, as shown in Figure 10.28.

Strategies. Most children develop strategies for recalling the multiplication facts. Many of these strategies involve the properties of the number system and counting patterns. The fact strategies are shown in Table 10.3 with diagrams to identify which strategy is used. Remember that easier strategies should be taught first. The main fact strategies for multiplication are the identity element, zero property, skip counting, multiples of 9, and doubles.

Children should have many experiences with objects, calculators, computers, or arrays to help develop the concept for multiplication and the strate-

TABLE 10.3 Thinking Strategies for the Basic Facts of Multiplication

Definition

Identity Element

Multiplying any number by 1 results in the same number.

17 basic facts are learned.

×	0	1	2	3	4	5	6	7	8	9
0										
1		1	2	3	4	5	6	7	8	9
2		2								
3		3								
4		4								
5		5								
6		6								
7		7								
8		8								
9		9								

Zero Property

Multiplying any number by 0 results in 0 for an answer.

19 basic facts are learned.

×	0	1	2	3	4	5	6	7	8	9
0	0	0	0	0	0	0	0	0	0	0
1	0									
2	0									
3	0									
4	0									
5	0									
6	0									
7	0									
8	0									
9	0									

Definition

Multiples of 9

Many interesting patterns and relationships can be used. Finger multiplication.

9 more facts are learned.

×	0	1	2	3	4	5	6	7	8	9
0										
1										9
2										18
3										27
4										36
5										45
6										54
7										63
8										72
9		9	18	27	36	45	54	63	72	81

Doubles

The number multiplied by itself—sometimes easier facts to remember.

4 more facts are learned.

×	0	1	2	3	4	5	6	7	8	9
0										
1										
2			4							
3				9						
4					16					
5						25				
6							36			
7								49		
8									64	
9										81

Skip Counting by 2, 5, 3

Relate "twos" to doubles in addition; "fives" to counting nickels or telling time.

39 additional facts are learned.

×	0	1	2	3	4	5	6	7	8	9
0										
1			2			5				
2		2	4	6	8	10	12	14	16	18
3			6	9	12	15	18	21	24	27
4			8	12		20				
5		5	10	15	20	25	30	35	40	45
6			12	18		30				
7			14	21		35				
8			16	24		40				
9			18	27		45				

Note: The blocks with numbers in the main body of the table denote new facts to be learned. The shaded part denotes facts already learned by a previous strategy. A shaded block with a number included denotes an overlap between a previously learned strategy and a new strategy.

FIGURE 10.27

x	0	1	2	3	4	5	6	7	8	9
0	0	0	0	0	0	0	0	0	0	0
1	0	1	2	3	4	5	6	7	8	9
2	0	2	4	6	8	10	12	14	16	18
3	0	3	6	9	12	15	18	21	24	27
4	0	4	8	12	16	20	24	28	32	36
5	0	5	10	15	20	25	30	35	40	45
6	0	6	12	18	24	30	36	42	48	54
7	0	7	14	21	28	35	42	49	56	63
8	0	8	16	24	32	40	48	56	64	72
9	0	9	18	27	36	45	54	63	72	81

100 basic multiplication facts.

FIGURE 10.28

x	0	1	2	3	4	5	6	7	8	9
0		0	0	0	0	0	0	0	0	0
1	0		2	3	4	5	6	7	8	9
2	0	2		6	8	10	12	14	16	18
3	0	3	6		12	15	18	21	24	27
4	0	4	8	12		20	24	28	32	36
5	0	5	10	15	20		30	35	40	45
6	0	6	12	18	24	30		42	48	54
7	0	7	14	21	28	35	42		56	63
8	0	8	16	24	32	40	48	56		72
9	0	9	18	27	36	45	54	63	72	

Commutative property of multiplication.

gies. There are several simple computer programs that show the effect of multiplying by 1 (identity element) and multiplying by 0 (zero property). Some children like to run these programs to prove that *any* number when multiplied by 1 remains unchanged or when multiplied by 0 results in 0 for an answer. Multiplying by 0 confuses some children. They think that if you start with "something" and you multiply it by zero, you still have the "something" with which you began. In addition to serving as a way to practice, patterns and relationships of operations can be investigated.

Skip Counting. Skip counting is another major strategy that shows patterns and the structure of the number system. Calculators can provide an incentive to learn skip counting. Skip counting by two begins in most first-grade texts. Using examples in the child's world builds a visual frame of reference for these facts: two wheels on each bike, two socks in each pair, two rows in a six-pack of soda, two rows in an egg carton, two eyes on each child.

Skip counting with fives is familiar because of money (counting nickels) and time (counting 5-minute intervals). If we look at the multiples of five on a hundreds chart, a pattern quickly emerges. These activities present some ways to develop an appreciation and curiosity in children about the interesting patterns of the multiples and counting numbers.

Activity 10.6

CALCULATORS

MULTIPLICATION AS REPEATED ADDITION

The first factor names the number of groups, and the second factor names the size of each group.

Check this on your calculator:

$$48 + 48 + 48 + 48 = ?$$

Now make this into a multiplication equation:

number of groups		*size of each group*		
4	×	48	=	?

Is the answer the same? Which way requires fewer steps?

Try some others: $5 + 5 + 5 + 5 + 5 = ?$

$3 \times 9 = ?$

Write the related multiplication equation and check on your calculator:

1. $3 + 3 + 3 + 3 = ?$
2. $8 + 8 + 8 + 8 + 8 = ?$
3. $1 + 1 + 1 = ?$
4. $7 + 7 + 7 = ?$

Try this on your calculator: 8 + = = =.
What happens? Why?

Activity 10.7

PROBLEM SOLVING ESTIMATION CULTURAL RELEVANCE

FINDING MULTIPLES

Multiples of 5

MATERIALS

- Hundreds chart, paper

PROCEDURE

1. List the multiples of 5. What digits appear in the ones column? What kind of numbers are the fives facts?

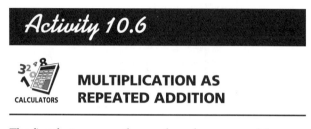

Activity Continues

1	2	3	4	5	6	7	8	9	10
11	12	13	14	15	16	17	18	19	20
21	22	23	24	25	26	27	28	29	30
31	32	33	34	35	36	37	38	39	40
41	42	43	44	45	46	47	48	49	50
51	52	53	54	55	56	57	58	59	60
61	62	63	64	65	66	67	68	69	70
71	72	73	74	75	76	77	78	79	80
81	82	83	84	85	86	87	88	89	90
91	92	93	94	95	96	97	98	99	100

Hundreds Chart

2. What pattern is found for the tens digits? Extend the chart and see if this pattern continues.
3. Add the digits together (25 = 2 + 5 = 7), (35 = 3 + 5 = 8), (45 = 4 + 5 = 9) and so on.

Multiples of 9

PROCEDURE

Circle all the multiples of 9 and look for patterns such as:

1. The tens digit in the product is 1 less than the number being multiplied by 9.

   $9 \times 4 = 36$ (3 is 1 less than 4).
2. The sum of the digits in the products is equal to 9, for example, $3 \times 9 = 27$, $2 + 7 = 9$, and $7 \times 9 = 63$, $6 + 3 = 9$.
3. The digits in the ones column decrease by 1 beginning with 9 and the digits in the tens column increase by 1 beginning with 1.
4. The numbers that are one more and one less than a multiple of consecutive numbers can be added together and form another multiple of 9.

   ....17, 18, 19....

   $17 + 19 = 36$

- Other interesting patterns of 9 are found in the culturally relevant teaching ideas in this chapter.

Multiples of 3

PROCEDURE

1. Circle the multiples of 3. What patterns do you notice?
2. Say the multiples of 3 to 30. How many multiples are in each row (decade) of the chart? List the multiples of 3. Add the digits of the two-digit numbers for each decade. What pattern do you see? ($12 \rightarrow 1 + 2 = 3$, $24 \rightarrow 2 + 4 = 6$)
3. Starting with 3, tell whether the number is odd or even. What pattern is there? What other patterns exist?

Finger Multiplication. Finding multiples of 9 is another strategy that emphasizes number patterns and relationships. Finger multiplication is a fun way to determine facts of 9. Children enjoy the "magic" of this activity as they internalize some number combinations. Use both hands with fingers spread apart. Label the fingers consecutively from 1 to 10, as indicated in Figure 10.29. Bend the "multiplier finger," that is, 4 × 9, bend the fourth finger. To read the product, count the fingers to the left of the bent finger as the tens digit (3) and the fingers to the right of the bent finger as the ones digit (6) (Figure 10.29).

FIGURE 10.29

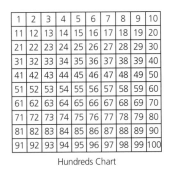

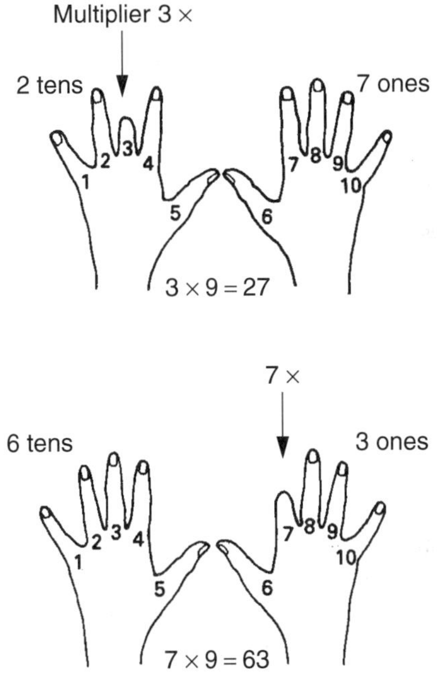

Finger multiplication for nines.

The remaining 12 facts can be learned using a variety of strategies (Figure 10.30). Since doubling is sometimes an easy mental computation task for children, it can be used to double multiples several times. The focus of this strategy is for multiples of 2, 4, 6, and 8 (to find 4×8, use 2×8 and 2×8 or think of doubling 8 twice). Figure 10.31 indicates the facts that can easily be solved by this doubling strategy.

Think: I know $3 \times 7 = 21$; since 3 is half of 6, I need to double the answer.
This will give me 6 groups of 7.

$$\text{Or} \quad \begin{array}{r} 3 \times 7 = 21 \\ +\ 3 \times 7 = \underline{21} \\ 6 \times 7 = 42 \end{array}$$

FIGURE 10.30

x	0	1	2	3	4	5	6	7	8	9
0										
1										
2										
3										
4										
5										
6										
7										
8										
9										

Remaining 12 facts to learn.

FIGURE 10.31

x	0	1	2	3	4	5	6	7	8	9
0										
1										
2										
3					12		18		24	
4				12	16	20	24	28		
5					20				40	
6				18	24			42	48	
7					28		42			
8				24		40	48		64	
9										

Facts covered by "doubling" strategy.

Activity 10.8

MATHEMATICAL CONNECTIONS

BASIC FACTS AND MUSIC

Pat, Clap, and Snap Rhythm Chant

DIRECTIONS

1. Tempo may start slowly and increase in speed quickly.
2. Adapt to all of the operations.

An example using multiplication:

Hand Movements	Words Spoken
1. Pat palms on upper part of legs two times.	"5" (with first pat) "times" (with second pat)
2. Clap hands together two times.	"3" (with first clap) "is" (with second clap)
3. Snap fingers of right hand.	"fif" (with first snap)
4. Snap fingers of left hand.	"teen" (with second snap)

Friendly Facts. The last three strategies entail using a known fact to derive an unknown fact. This approach asks students to find a friendly fact and mentally compute using addition to help. "Repeated Addition" might be a strategy to use when one factor is less than 5. The child simply changes the multiplication problem to an addition problem and solves, $4 \times 7 = 7 + 7 + 7 + 7$. "Add Another Set" uses the distributive law of multiplication and helps a child use an easier known fact to find the answer to a more difficult fact.

For 6×8, *think:* I know $5 \times 8 = 5$ groups of 8
$8 + 8 + 8 + 8 + 8 = 40$
So, $6 \times 8 = 6$ groups of 8 so add 8 more to 40

Split a Factor. This strategy encourages students to split one of the factors into two or three friendly equations of known facts. Arrays and Cuisenaire rods work effectively to visually develop this concept. Cut graph paper into a specific array, apply the distributive law to fold it into two parts (Figure 10.32). Students can write the related number equations to be certain to see the total product. Group work promotes good discussions about various ways to split the factors. One student might select the first factor and split it into several parts (for example, $7 \times 9 = [3 \times 9] + [3 \times 9] + [1 \times 9]$), while another student may select the second factor and split it apart (for example, $7 \times 9 = [7 \times 3] + [7 \times 3] + [7 \times 3]$).

Such experiences build students' confidence that if a fact is not immediately known or remembered, some strategy can be used to find the product. Using a friendly fact, or a fact that is close to the target, unknown fact is an effective way to solve difficult facts. Group work with concrete materials, arrays, and sharing among students helps motivate children to remain on task. Remember there is not a "best" way to solve these facts. Individual students will find their own preferences and should be encouraged to share them with others. Assessment should reflect these preferred strategies so each child can relate to his or her own strengths.

Thinking Strategies for the Basic Facts of Division

The final operation is division and the question is how many basic facts are there for division? Most people answer "one hundred" since that was true for the last three operations, but division has a special property that must be considered. Since division by zero cannot be done or is undefined, there are 90 basic division facts. Refer to the operation sense part

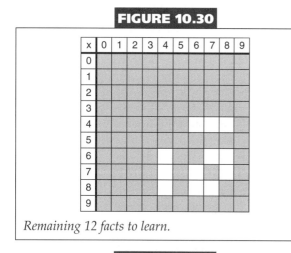

FIGURE 10.32

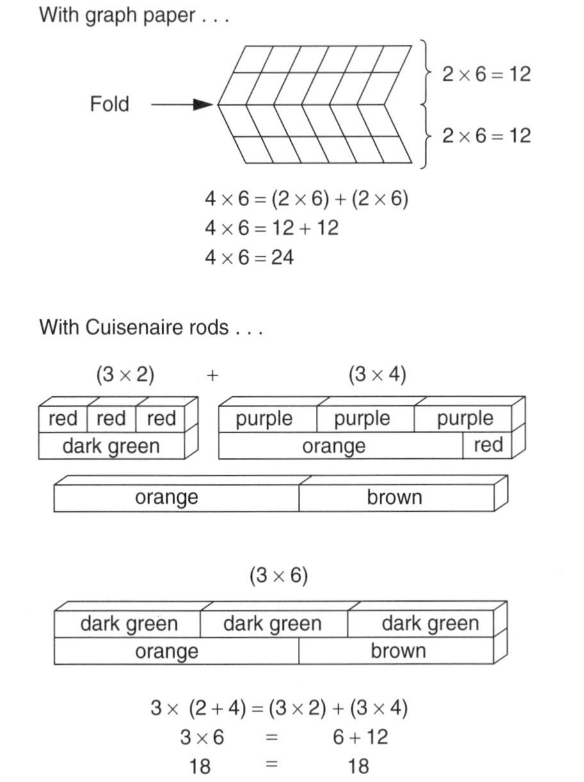

Graph paper and Cuisenaire rods show "split a factor apart" strategy.

of this chapter to refresh your thinking about why division by zero is undefined.

Missing Factor. The most useful strategy for learning division facts is to think of the problem as a missing factor and recall a related multiplication fact (28 ÷ 4 = ?; think ? × 4 = 28). This makes learning fact families for multiplication and division more important.

Triominoes are an effective device to help children practice fact families. Color coding keeps them in sets that allow for easier management. Facts can be clustered into categories, as described in the multiplication section, according to the strategies involved. When a corner of the card is covered, it means looking for the missing factor. Have children write, or say to a partner, the four related number sentences for a triomino.

$$6 \times 3 = 18$$
$$3 \times 6 = 18$$
$$18 \div 3 = 6$$
$$18 \div 6 = 3$$

The relatedness of the two operations must be emphasized and shown with concrete materials. Model the fact families with sets or arrays to establish the connection of the two operations. Figure 10.33 shows the relationship between the two operations using Cuisenaire rods as the manipulative.

FIGURE 10.33

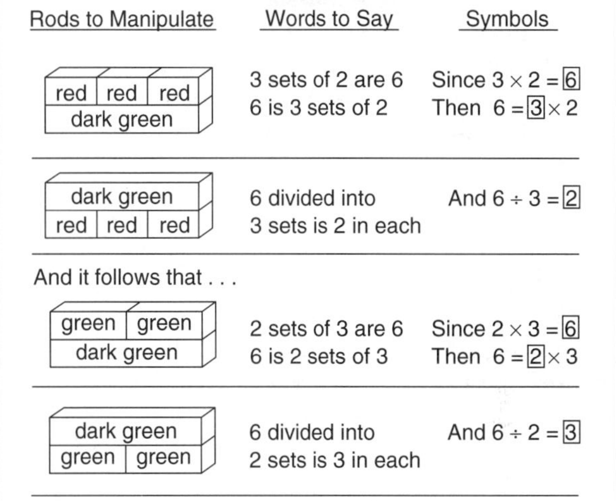

Relatedness of multiplication and division.

Mastering the Facts

If children are to be successful mastering the basic facts, the operations must be developed through multiple embodiments. Children should have opportunities for informal activities with materials to model situations involving the different operations, When drill and practice are introduced, short, frequent sessions are recommended.

Basic Facts—Pros and Cons. Many teachers, administrators, parents, and the general public believe that learning basic facts should constitute a large part of the early grades mathematics instruction. Many of these people want today's children to learn mathematics in the same manner they learned mathematics. Children do need to be proficient in basic facts to solve problems and arrive at accurate calculations. However, arithmetic computation is only one part of mathematics, and attention given to basic facts can still be directed toward thinking, reasoning, and number relationships. As children work with problem-solving situations, they will find ways to solve a wide variety of problems and will build confidence in their own abilities to understanding the operations.

The NCTM *Principles and Standards* (2000) acknowledge that a certain amount of practice is necessary to develop fluency with recalling basic facts. By fifth grade, students should have developed a number of thinking strategies to help them acquire fluency in computation. However, Burns (1996) warns against timed tests, worksheet drill, and flash cards. She contends these practices treat mathematics as isolated bits of information to memorize, do not support children's problem-solving abilities, and convey a message that rote memorization is more important than reasoning. The acquisition of single-digit basic facts is a recognized goal of the mathematics community so students in middle grades can approach mathematics full of competence and confidence.

Cluster the Facts. Facts should be leveled in terms of strategies and difficulty. Not all 100 addition facts should be studied and tested in a timed setting at the outset. Beginning speed tests with the easiest facts ensures success and a feeling of confidence. Once a satisfactory score is earned, the next level is tackled. Drill these selected new facts, then test these facts in addition to the previously learned facts. In this way, the tests gradually build until the total set of 100 addition facts is included.

Build Confidence. Teachers should make a "big deal" out of passing each test and keep individual charts and class charts. These help monitor progress and motivate children to continue mastering more facts. Encourage parents to reinforce drill at home by keeping them informed of the facts on which their child is currently working. To tell parents to "work with your child on basic facts" is almost hopeless in terms of definite results. Typically, the parents will purchase a set of flash cards and drill will be intense for only a few weeks. This approach is inappropriate because the parents are trying to practice all the facts rather than taking them in small groups that relate to thinking strategies. Both parties (parent and child) become frustrated, and soon the practice ends. Praise and positive reinforcement should be given for learning each new group of facts rather than waiting until the entire set of facts has been mastered.

Assess Mastery. An often-repeated phrase by teachers is, "Johnny doesn't know his basic facts." Presented in this negative fashion, the judgment sounds grim, but which facts and how many facts are not mastered remains unclear. It may become necessary to assess which facts are not mastered, then develop strategies to learn those facts. Two easy procedures are suggested.

EXTENDED ACTIVITIES

MATHEMATICAL CONNECTIONS · CALCULATORS · PROBLEM SOLVING · PORTFOLIO

Name of Activity

- Division by 1
- Division as Repeated Subtraction
- Basic Facts to Music
- Canister Learning Machine
- TIMSS Assessment: Aunt Bee's Bakery

Give a timed fact test for each operation with time guidelines of 3 seconds per problem (5 minutes for 100 facts and 4½ minutes for 90 facts). Ask students to work the problems row by row, answering only those facts that they know automatically without any extra thought or counting. This test should be repeated on several occasions to ensure a higher validity. Isolate the "problem facts" into clusters and work on these with many different embodiments and strategies.

Another procedure, which takes more time but seems to have more validity, is to show flash cards of facts to an individual child. In a timed sequence of no more than 3 seconds, show each fact to the child. The student must answer as quickly as possible. Correct cards are put in one pile and missed cards are put in another pile. This procedure can be repeated until you feel more assured that all the facts in the "correct pile" are known at an automatic level. Now drill and practice can begin on groups using strategies for these unknown facts as described earlier.

Practice Devices. A clever drill device is to use *glow-in-the-dark* paint to write the troublesome facts. The facts are made into a mobile. The numbers should be large enough to be seen in bed when the lights are off. This approach helps when children find it hard to sleep. The novelty is enjoyed and the facts are learned quickly (Figure 10.34). Other examples can be found on the CD.

Remember that drill activities should be varied and interesting. Many simple, inexpensive devices can be made to practice the facts. Another effective way to provide drill is with teacher-made (or commercial) games such as board games, dice games, and card games. A number of teacher-controlled microcomputer software programs are available that

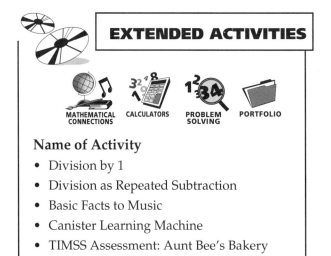

FIGURE 10.34

"Glow-in-the-dark" practice device.

provide instant reinforcement in a timed setting. Some of these are in the format of game challenges.

Audiocassette tapes with catchy songs about the facts serve as another way to help children recall the facts. Popular ones available are *I Can't Wait to Get to Math Class, Multiplication Motivation,* and *Mondo Math.* There are many activities from which a teacher may choose to help students learn the basic facts. The teacher who uses many forms of drill—calculators, games, computers, videotapes, and audiotapes—will find better attitudes and performance by students. It is the teacher who must determine which activities and strategies are suited to the needs and interests of the students.

ASSESSMENT

Field-Dependent and Field-Independent Learners

Students preferring to use field-independent processing (the parts-to-whole strategy) may understand addition and multiplication (combining parts to make the whole) better than they understand subtraction and division (moving from the whole to the detailed parts). It is just the opposite for students preferring field-dependent processing. More research is needed before definitive statements can be made. However, teachers report definite preferences with some of their students. These observations suggest that some children adopt one processing style from which they find it difficult to decenter. Both groups can learn the basic facts more efficiently and more thoroughly by applying the following teaching techniques:

- *Subtraction and Division Basic Facts: Help for the Field-Independent Learner.* When a field-independent learner is faced with subtraction and division basic facts, it may be best to look on the combinations as "missing addends" for addition and "missing factors" for multiplication. The teacher should encourage the children to ask questions like those in Figure 10.35.

FIGURE 10.35

Missing addends or missing factors help determine facts.

- *Addition and Multiplication Basic Facts: Help for the Field-Dependent Learner.* Field-dependent learners may be helped by using the idea of "subtracting as much as they can and adding as little as they can" when working with addition and multiplication. Subtracting from 10 or multiples of 10 will eliminate the largest amounts and students are left with as little as possible to add or multiply. Study the examples in Figure 10.36.

Basic Fact Tables

Basic fact tables for each operation were illustrated in this chapter. Most elementary textbooks present the table in its incomplete form and ask the children to fill it in, a task that requires successive processing, which is used by field-independent learners. The table is completed square by square in a systematic way, so number relationships develop as each number combi-

FIGURE 10.36

Multiples of 10 to determine facts.

nation is answered. The activity in the textbook may need to be modified for students preferring field-dependent approaches. They need to view the completed table before relationship patterns can be seen clearly. They become more confused by moving from row to row and column to column filling in blank squares.

It is effective to pair both learners together, allowing the field-independent learner to complete the table while the field-dependent learner watches for the overall patterns. Both learners can share what they discovered about the tables when the exercise is completed, another cooperative learning venture (Figure 10.37).

FIGURE 10.37

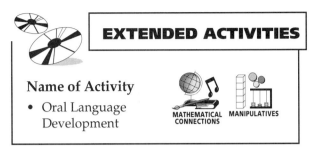

Paired learning to see patterns.

EXTENDED ACTIVITIES

Name of Activity

- Oral Language Development

MATHEMATICAL CONNECTIONS MANIPULATIVES

Correcting Common Misconceptions

Some children will still have difficulty learning basic facts. An excellent way to check understanding of the operations is to give a child physical objects and ask the child to model a number sentence. A common error is to show sets for each number but fail to perform the operation. For example:

Teacher: Displays the equation 3 + 4 = 7. "Show me what this number sentence means using these counters."

Child: The child models a set of 3 counters under the numeral "3," a set of 4 counters under the numeral "4," and a set of 7 counters under the numeral "7."

Problem: The child is merely modeling sets for the numbers rather than showing addition as the union of two discrete sets.

Remediation: Give the child many opportunities to represent the addition process in a problem-solving situation where the action of the operation is demonstrated.

Many children experience difficulties with subtraction facts over ten once the regrouping algorithm for subtraction has been learned. They apply that procedure for the two-digit numbers of the subtraction facts. When children have this problem, the teacher must show them that the regrouping yields the same number as the original number (that is, 13). Generally this error will diminish with more time given to the subtraction algorithm.

Learning-disabled children should be given facts in small chunks and speed tests in a similar fashion. Too many facts are disturbing and overwhelming to the LD child. One-minute quizzes over leveled facts work much better for children with special needs. It is suggested by Thornton and associates (1983) that a child who can write fifty digits per minute should be able to correctly write answers to thirty basic facts per minute. This five-to-three ratio may prove a useful guide in designing speed tests.

If students are having trouble going from the concrete level to the symbolic level, they may profit from the use of an individual number line placed at the top of their desks. Students can make their own from a sample. When such number lines are laminated, they have been known to last a whole school year under rugged use. If a student is growing overdependent on the number line as a crutch, it can be covered with a book and used only at the end of a session as a check. This makes an excellent connecting level technique.

Failure to understand and apply the commutative law is another area of difficulty. Here the child can work 9 + 2 by counting on, but does not readily change the order of the addends to help obtain the answer to 2 + 9. The triominoes and fact families are techniques to emphasize this concept.

Children often employ faulty reasoning when working with the basic facts. Some of the more common problems are described in the following paragraphs.

Faulty Reasoning 1

Can answer correctly	*Cannot answer correctly*
$\begin{array}{r} 9 \\ +\ 3 \\ \hline \end{array}$ or $\begin{array}{r} 7 \\ \times\ 4 \\ \hline \end{array}$	$\begin{array}{r} 3 \\ +\ 9 \\ \hline \end{array}$ or $\begin{array}{r} 4 \\ \times\ 7 \\ \hline \end{array}$
$9 + 3 =$	$3 + 9 =$
$7 \times 4 =$	$4 \times 7 =$

If this pattern is seen in a variety of basic facts, the children are likely to be "position counters"—they take whatever numeral appears in the top position or in the left position and add the numeral in the next position to it. Their count becomes confused when the larger numeral follows in the second position because there are more chances for mistakes in counting.

A teaching strategy to help remediate this problem is to develop a better understanding of the commutative principle. Even if commutativity is too difficult for early primary children to understand, they can be taught the counting-on strategy as outlined earlier in this chapter. A modified approach can be seen with multiplication. The child sees 4 × 7 as 7 taken 4 times (or 4 groups of 7) and calculates the basic fact something like this:

$$\begin{array}{r} 7 \\ +\ 7 \\ \hline 14 \end{array} \quad \text{and again} \quad \begin{array}{r} 7 \\ +\ 7 \\ \hline 14 \end{array} \quad \text{and} \quad \begin{array}{r} 14 \\ +\ 14 \\ \hline 28 \end{array}$$

When taught that the order of the numbers can be changed and the product is not affected, children can do the multiplication more quickly.

Faulty Reasoning 2

Children answer problems in the following way:

In subtraction	*In division*
$\begin{array}{r} 4 \\ -\ 1 \\ \hline 1 \end{array} \quad \begin{array}{r} 9 \\ -\ 4 \\ \hline 4 \end{array}$	$3\overline{)6}$ = 3 $6\overline{)24}$ = 6

Children who answer basic facts in this manner often do not know the basic fact in question. To obtain a simple solution, they reason, "Sometimes the answer is the same number that is taken away [the subtrahend]. Since I cannot think of an answer, I'll use the one that is already there" (in the subtrahend).

A teaching strategy is to review the fact strategy for doubles in addition. They can learn to reason that if 1 + 1 = 2 and 2 – 1 = 1, then 1 + 1 cannot equal 4 and 4 – 1 cannot equal 1. The subtrahend and the difference can only be alike in doubles. What is commonly seen in subtraction and division can also happen with addition and multiplication, but it is usually less common. Examples would be:

$$\begin{array}{r} 2 \\ +\ 8 \\ \hline 8 \end{array} \qquad \begin{array}{r} 7 \\ \times\ 5 \\ \hline 5 \end{array}$$

Faulty Reasoning 3

Children answer problems in the following way:

$$\begin{array}{r} 9 \\ -\ 1 \\ \hline 7 \end{array} \qquad \begin{array}{r} 10 \\ -\ 8 \\ \hline 1 \end{array}$$

Children may miss the correct answer by one number. As stated in the teaching strategies section of this chapter, counting-back strategies are often found to be helpful in such a situation. Sometimes mistakes like these occur because some children count rapidly and lose track of the number being removed. Sometimes children have been taught the counting-back strategy but when they try to apply it mentally, they reason that 9 – 1 = 7 by saying, "When I count back it is 9, 8, 7. If I take one away it will look like this:

Since I have 9, the one to be taken away is the 8 and that means 7 is the next number that is left."

Another reasoning pattern is to think that 10 – 8 = 1 by saying, "I'm at 10 and I need to know how many 8 is away from 10. It is 10, 9, 8. There is one number in the middle so 8 is one away from 10."

If students are struggling with keeping track of the counting when using some fact strategies, a number line can help *only if* the teacher emphasizes that the spaces between numerals are important in the counting. Many commercially prepared number lines appear like the one shown in Figure 10.38. Without augmentation, many children will use this aid incorrectly, following the misguided reasoning outlined previously.

FIGURE 10.38

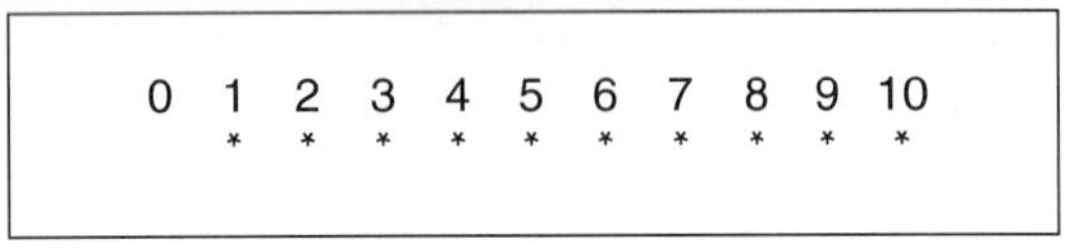

Commercially prepared number line.

Figure 10.39 shows the same number line with the curved segment between numerals to emphasize the spaces in counting. Some elementary teachers refer to the spaces as "hops" up or down the number line. A teacher may say that 10 – 1 = 9 because a person starts at the numeral 10 and hops back one space and lands on 9.

FIGURE 10.39

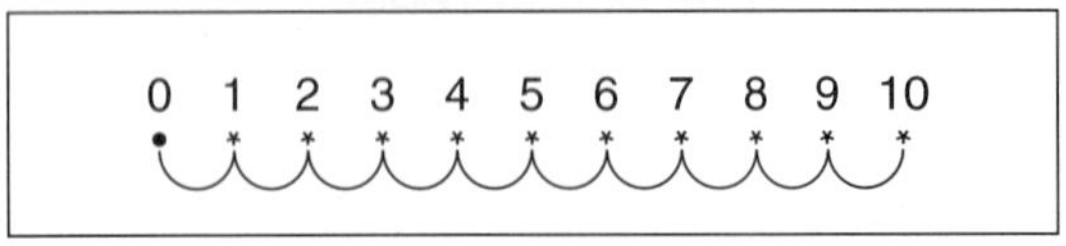

Altered number line to show spaces in counting.

Some students with special needs are just poor counters. Therefore, using any counting strategy for remediation will be unsuccessful. Such children should be encouraged to use derived fact strategies, known as DFS. The DFS have been explained earlier in this chapter. Research shows that the following ones are helpful to children needing help (Steinberg, 1985).

1. Doubles
2. Doubles + 1 and – 1
3. Doubles + 2 and – 2
4. Bridging to 10, such as:

   6 + 8 is 6 + 4 = 10 with 4 more left to add to 10 so 10 + 4 = 14

   or

   12 – 7 is 10 – 7 which is 3 with 2 left so 3 + 2 = 5

Faulty Reasoning 4

This faulty reasoning pattern belongs to the teacher rather than the children. Some teachers believe that students must move quickly from the use of concrete manipulatives to the symbolic stage where the children do worksheet after worksheet without the use of manipulatives or pictures. Children frequently give such teachers clues to their learning difficulties by their responses to basic fact problems on textbook pages or on worksheets. Figure 10.40 shows an actual worksheet of a primary child.

FIGURE 10.40

Give the missing numbers.

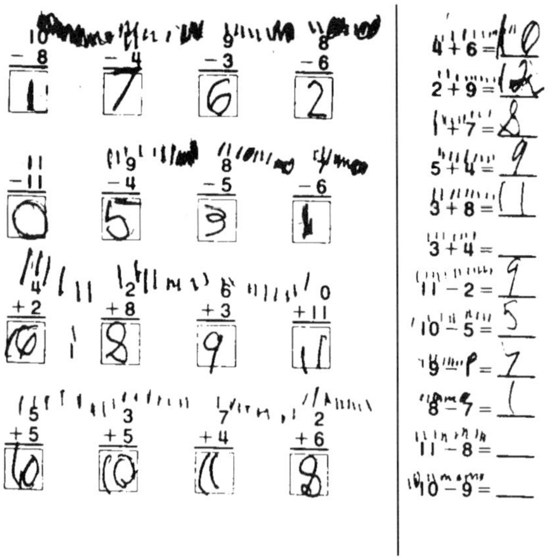

Basic facts worksheet of primary child.

The child makes very few mistakes, but it is evident that the child needs some form of concrete or semiconcrete aid to arrive at the answers. The tally marks are needed in almost every problem. The child seems to understand the property/principle of zero in addition with assurance; no tally marks are needed to check out the answers.

What should be done about this situation? More work with fact strategies and concrete materials is necessary. To demand that a child not use the tally marks would only force the child to use eye blinks, count fingers out of the teacher's view, or just guess the answer. Tally marks can help bridge the gap between concrete materials and symbolic numerals. This child needs to be encouraged to place the tally marks on a separate page where the marks can be separated for each problem, and prevent the mislearning that occurs when the child thinks the answer counted was correct.

Some children will become overdependent on the tally marks. They will need to be "weaned" from them gradually, starting with the basic facts involving adding one or taking one away. These facts can be reasoned more easily. The next step is to adopt a systematized way to introduce the teaching strategies discussed earlier in the chapter.

Teacher Assessment of Student Work: Steps in Analytic Thinking

Some people might profit from writing down their thought processes in mathematics. It can bring clarity to processes that would otherwise be easily confused. An example of such a thought process is presented here as it relates to the assessment of a child's problems in learning basic addition and subtraction facts. Excellent teaching involves the analysis of what a child understands or does not understand, and what misconceptions must be remediated.

A model outlining steps in analytic thinking is presented here so the teacher can see a way to approach the task of diagnosing a child's learning difficulties from answers a child has given to a textbook assignment. Exercises at the end of the chapter will ask the teacher to analyze the work of two other students. The analytic process applied here will be of help at the end of the chapter as well. Figure 10.41 shows the work of a first-grade student who has several misconceptions about the basic facts of subtraction.

FIGURE 10.41

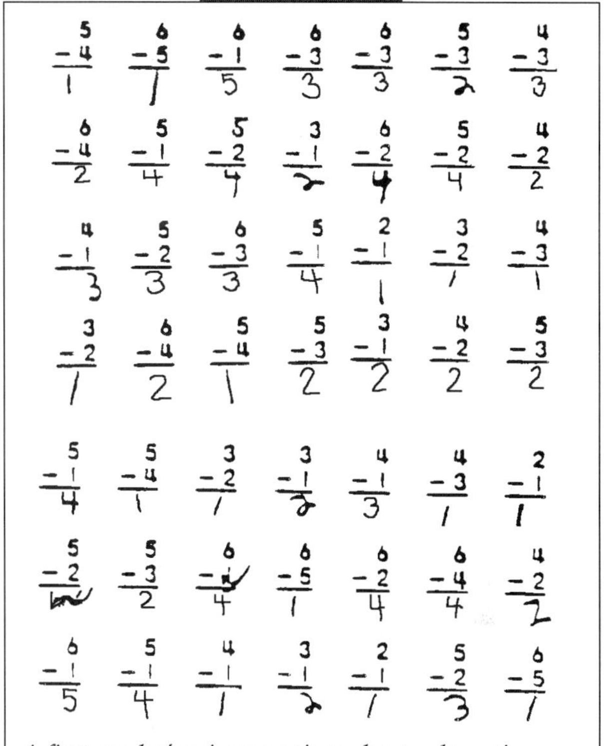

A first-grader's misconceptions about subtraction.

Steps in Analytic Thinking

1. Find the basic facts answered incorrectly (they are marked with a check).
2. Determine whether the same basic facts as those missed appear more than once on the worksheet. If so, see if the student missed the problem or answered the problem in the same way as those marked incorrect.
   a. If the same mistake is made consistently, look for patterns like those mentioned in the learning styles section of the chapter and in the assessment section.
   b. If the student sometimes answers correctly, make a chart such as the one on page 246 to analyze the answers:

      Note: This student is correct more often than not. Now a teacher must decide whether the incorrect answers were the result of sloppy work habits or a real misconception.
   c. If sloppiness is the cause, answers tend to deteriorate the further down the worksheet the student goes. Is this the case here? No.
   d. If a real misconception is the cause, further scrutiny is needed. Often all that the best teachers can do is to make an intelligent guess based on the pattern of answers. It appears that the student is doing each problem separately without seeing its connection with the other problems on the page. Hence, the student answers correctly sometimes but not other times.
3. Look for the pattern of reasoning used by the child. The most frequent pattern seen is faulty reasoning 2. The next most frequent pattern is faulty reasoning 3.

4. Refer back to the teaching strategies that help the child who makes the mistakes in faulty reasoning as listed in this section.

Basic Fact	Answered	Analysis
5 − 2	5 − 2 4	2 correct 2 incorrect —missed by one same answer
6 − 1	6 − 1 4	2 correct 1 incorrect —missed by one
6 − 4	6 − 4 4	2 correct 1 incorrect —missed by two
4 − 1	4 − 1 1	2 correct 1 incorrect —missed by two
4 − 3	4 − 3 3	2 correct 1 incorrect —missed by two

SUMMARY

One of the most talked-about elements of mathematics is the basic facts. This chapter explains the properties and operations of addition, subtraction, multiplication, and division. The properties are emphasized for effective understanding of the number system. The NCTM *Standards* provide suggestions for the curriculum. Teaching strategies for the properties are carefully introduced, including common mental arithmetic ideas (strategies) for each property. Manipulatives are included to provide adequate concrete experiences. Thinking strategies and problem solving are emphasized throughout the chapter. The assessment includes common faulty reasoning when working with basic facts. The next chapter on operations and algorithms shows how the understanding of operations and basic facts are extended to multidigit numbers.

EXERCISES

For extended exercises, see the CD-ROM.

A. Memorization and Comprehension Exercises
Low-Level Thought Activities

1. Think of another concrete material (other than Cuisenaire rods) that could show the property/principle of commutativity and associativity. Sketch those examples and explain how the principles would be taught.
2. Explain, in your own words, the difference between partitive division and measurement division. Give an example of each.
3. Explain, in your own words, why division by zero is considered "undefined" by mathematicians.

B. Application and Analysis Exercises
Middle-Level Thought Activities

1. Think of a set of triominoes to teach the division facts. Sketch some examples and explain how they could be used.
2. Pick a grade level and analyze how the basic fact strategies are presented in the textbook for that grade level. Find three word problems that could be solved by more than one strategy. Show the solutions using different strategies. Label each strategy as you use it.
3. To reinforce mathematical connections:
   a. List five mathematical questions or problems that come from popular trade books for children. Show how they are related to the topics of this chapter.
   b. List five ways to use the topics of this chapter when teaching lessons in reading, science, social studies, health, music, art, physical education, or language arts (writing, English grammar, poetry).

C. Synthesis and Evaluation Exercises
High-Level Thought Activities

1. Find a concept from the NCTM *Standards* in Box 10.1 that you would like to teach. Create (synthesize) a model lesson plan for teaching the basic facts. Evaluate how all the components can work together. Include the following components in the plan:

a. Use the current articles from the professional journals to help plan the direction of the lesson. Document your sources.
b. Include at least one computer software program as a part of the lesson. Show how it will be integrated into the lesson.
c. Develop behavioral objectives. Show how you will use these to evaluate the lesson.
d. Remember to include culturally relevant activities.

2. The multiplication table in Figure 10.42 is the work of an actual student.

FIGURE 10.42

Student's multiplication tables.

Follow the analytic thinking steps outlined in the section on diagnosing learning difficulties. Here are some questions to help you start the analytic process:
a. Does this student understand the multiplication property/principle of zero? Justify your answer.
b. Tally marks are used in some of the answers. In what section of the table do these appear? What does that tell the teacher about the set of problems that are not understood? It will be helpful to review the section on teaching strategies as it relates to the multiplication table.
c. At what point in the table does the student relate one answer (product) to the next answer (product) without regard for the multiplier and the multiplicand?
d. What pattern begins to emerge after the basic fact of 4 × 4?
e. What parts of the table does the student know well?

3. The worksheet in Figure 10.43 is another example of a student's work.

FIGURE 10.43

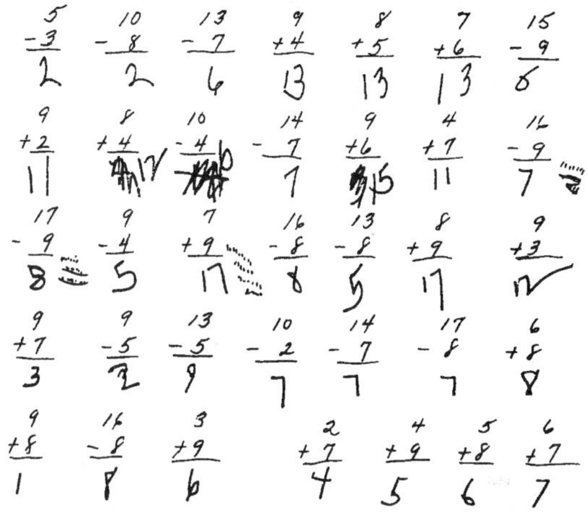

Worksheet of student.

Analyze what the student knows and what the student does not know.
a. Plan a program of remediation for the student. The questions asked in exercise C2 may be helpful here as well. Your plan should include
   (i) Analysis of the error pattern
   (ii) An evaluation of the thought processing required in the examples and the thought processing displayed by the student
   (iii) The sequential development of concrete, pictorial, and symbolic models to reteach the concept

4. Read the NCTM *Standards* regarding the issue of teaching, testing, and emphasis of basic facts. Take a position for or against this recommendation and write a position paper stating your stand and defending your position.

BIBLIOGRAPHY

For an extended bibliography, see the CD-ROM.

Baratta-Lorton, Mary. *Mathematics Their Way.* Menlo Park, CA: Addison-Wesley, 1976.

———. *Workjobs II.* Menlo Park, CA: Addison-Wesley, 1978.

Baroody, Arthur J. "Children's Difficulties in Subtraction: Some Causes and Questions." *Journal for Research in Mathematics Education* 15 (May 1984): 203–213.

———. "Mastery of the Basic Number Combinations: Internalization of Relationships or Facts?" *Journal for Research in Mathematics Education* 33 (Fall 1985): 83–98.

Baroody, Arthur J., and Dorothy J. Standifer. "Addition and Subtraction in the Primary Grades." Ed. Robert J. Jensen. *Research Ideas for the Classroom: Early Childhood Mathematics.* Reston, VA: National Council of Teachers of Mathematics, 1993. 72–102.

Bartek, Mary Marron. "Hands-on Addition and Subtraction with the Three Pigs." *Teaching Children Mathematics* 4 (October 1997): 68–71.

Burk, Donna, Allyn Snider, and Paula Symonds. *Box It or Bag It Mathematics: Teachers Resource Guide.* Salem, OR: Math Learning Center, 1988.

———. *Math Excursions I: Project-Based Mathematics for First Graders.* Portsmouth, NH: Heinemann, 1992.

Burns, Marilyn. "What I Learned from Teaching Second Grade." *Teaching Children Mathematics* 3 (November 1996): 124–127.

Carpenter, Thomas P., and James M. Moser. "The Acquisition of Addition and Subtraction Concepts in Grades One through Three." *Journal for Research in Mathematics Education* 15 (May 1984): 179–202.

Carpenter, Thomas P., Elizabeth Fennema, and Megan L. Franke. "Cognitively Guided Instruction: A Knowledge Base for Reform in Primary Mathematics Instruction." *Elementary School Journal* 97 (1996): 3–20.

Fuson, Karen C. "Teaching Children to Subtract by Counting Up." *Journal for Research in Mathematics Education* 17 (May 1986): 172–189.

———. "Research on Whole Number Addition and Subtraction." Ed. Douglas A. Grouws. *Handbook of Research on Mathematics Teaching and Learning.* New York: Macmillan, 1992. 243–275.

Hiebert, James, and Diana Wearne. "Instructional Tasks, Classroom Discourse, and Students' Learning in Second-Grade Arithmetic." *American Educational Research Journal* 30 (1993): 393–425.

I Can't Wait to Get to Math Class. J. Monroe Gleason, 1993 [audiocassette tape].

Kamii, Constance, Barbara A. Lewis and Bobbye M. Booker. "Instead of Teaching Missing Addends." *Teaching Children Mathematics* 4 (April 1998): 458–461.

Kouba, Vicky L., and Kathy Franklin. "Multiplication and Division: Sense Making and Meaning." Ed. Robert J. Jensen. *Research Ideas for the Classroom: Early Childhood Mathematics.* Reston, VA: National Council of Teachers of Mathematics, 1993. 72–102.

Multiplication Motivation. Oklahoma City, OK: Melody House. audiocassette tape. 1985.

National Council of Teachers of Mathematics. *Curriculum and Evaluation Standards for School Mathematics.* Reston, VA: NCTM, 1989.

———. *Principles and Standards for School Mathematics.* Reston, VA: NCTM, 2000 (to be published).

———. *Professional Standards for Teaching Mathematics.* Reston, VA: NCTM, 1991.

Quintero, A. H. "Children's Conceptual Understanding of Situations Involving Multiplication." *Arithmetic Teacher* 33 (January 1986): 34–37.

Rathmell, Edward C. "Using Thinking Strategies to Learn Basic Facts." In *Developing Computational Skills,* 1978 Yearbook of the National Council of Teachers of Mathematics. Reston, VA: National Council of Teachers of Mathematics, 1978. 13–38.

Richardson, Kathy. *Developing Number Concepts Using Manipulatives.* Menlo Park, CA: Addison-Wesley, 1988.

Spivack, Jonathan D., and Bradley L. Pugh. *Mondo Math, Addition Facts 1–12.* Carmichael, CA: Learning Quest. audiocassette tape. 1994.

Steinberg, Ruth M. "Instruction on Derived Facts Strategies in Addition and Subtraction." *Journal for Research in Mathematics Education* 16 (November 1985): 337–355.

Strong, Dorothy S. (Mathematics Ed.). *Systemwide Objectives and Standards.* Vols. 1–3. Chicago: Board of Education of the City of Chicago, 1990.

Thompson, Charles S., and A. Dean Hendrickson. "Verbal Addition and Subtraction Problems: Some Difficulties and Some Solutions." *Arithmetic Teacher* 33 (March 1986): 21–25.

Thornton, Carol A. "Emphasizing Thinking Strategies in Basic Fact Instruction." *Journal for Research in Mathematics Education* 9 (May 1978): 214–227.

———. "Strategies for Learning the Basic Facts." Ed. Joseph N. Payne. *Teaching and Learning Mathematics for the Young Child.* Reston, VA: National Council of Teachers of Mathematics, 1990. 133–151.

Thornton, Carol A., and Paula J. Smith. "Action Research: Strategies for Learning Subtraction Facts." *Arithmetic Teacher* 35 (April 1988): 8–12.

Thornton, Carol A., Benny F. Tucker, John A. Dossey, and Edna F. Basik. *Teaching Mathematics to Children with Special Needs.* Menlo Park, CA: Addison-Wesley, 1983.

CHILDREN'S LITERATURE

Anno, Masaichiro, and Mitsumasa Anno. *Anno's Mysterious Multiplying Jar.* New York: Philomel Books, 1983.

Birch, David. *The King's Chessboard.* New York: Dial Books for Young Readers, 1988.

Christelow, Eileen. *Five Little Monkeys Jumping on the Bed.* New York: Clarion Books, 1989.

Chwast, Seymour. *The Twelve Circus Rings.* San Diego, CA: Gulliver Books, Harcourt Brace Jovanovich, 1993.

Dee, Ruby. *Ten Ways to Count to Ten.* New York: Henry Holt, 1988.

De Regniers, Beatrice Schenk. *So Many Cats.* New York: Clarion Books, 1985.

Dunbar, Joyce. *Ten Little Mice.* New York: Harcourt Brace Jovanovich, 1990.

Edens, Cooper. *How Many Bears?* New York: Atheneum, 1994.

Emberley, Barbara. *One Wide River to Cross.* Boston: Little, Brown, 1992.

Gerstein, Mordicai. *Roll Over!* New York: Crown Publishers, 1984.

Hamm, Diane Johnston. *How Many Feet in the Bed?* New York: Simon & Schuster Books for Young Readers, 1994.

Hutchins, Pat. *The Doorbell Rang.* New York: Greenwillow Books, 1986.

Kellogg, Steven. *Much Bigger Than Martin.* New York: Dial, 1976.

Jackson, Ellen B. *Cinder Edna.* New York: Lothrop, Lee & Shepard, 1994.

Mahy, Margaret. *17 Kings and 42 Elephants.* New York: Dial Books for Young Readers, 1987.

McMillan, Bruce. *Counting Wildflowers.* New York: Lothrop, Lee & Shepard, 1986.

Mathews, Louise. *Bunches and Bunches of Bunnies.* New York: Scholastic, 1978.

———. *Bunches and Bunches of Bunnies.* New York: Scholastic, 1978.

———. *The Great Take-Away.* New York: Dodd, Mead, 1980.

Mori, Tuyosi. *Socrates and the Three Little Pigs.* New York: Philomel Books, 1986.

Owen, Annie. *Annie's One to Ten.* New York: Alfred A. Knopf, 1988.

Pinczes, Elinor J. *A Remainder of One.* New York: Houghton Mifflin, 1995.

———. *A Hundred Hungry Ants.* New York: Houghton Mifflin, 1993.

Stevens, Janet. *Tops and Bottoms.* New York: Harcourt Brace, 1995.

Walsh, Ellen Stoll. *Mouse Count.* San Diego, CA: Harcourt Brace, 1991.

Integrating Technology

Video Vignettes: Lesson Plans in Action

- *Dinosaur Legs*
- *Cluster Problems*

Computer Software Resources

. . . for Operations and Number Sense

Internet Searches

Surfing the Internet for Operations and Number Sense Topics

Use the World Wide Web (WWW) and navigate through the system, searching for new information under major headings and subheadings similar to the following:

Mathematics Education
- Basic Facts
- Addition (Facts)
- Subtraction (Facts)
- Multiplication (Facts)
- Division (Facts)
- Operations/Whole Number Operations
- Operation Sense
- Fact Strategies
- Properties
- NCTM
  - Operation Sense
  - Whole Number Operations

- *Remember. . .* the Web is fluid . . . new topics and ways to search for topics change daily.
- Be adventurous . . . think of some new things you could try.

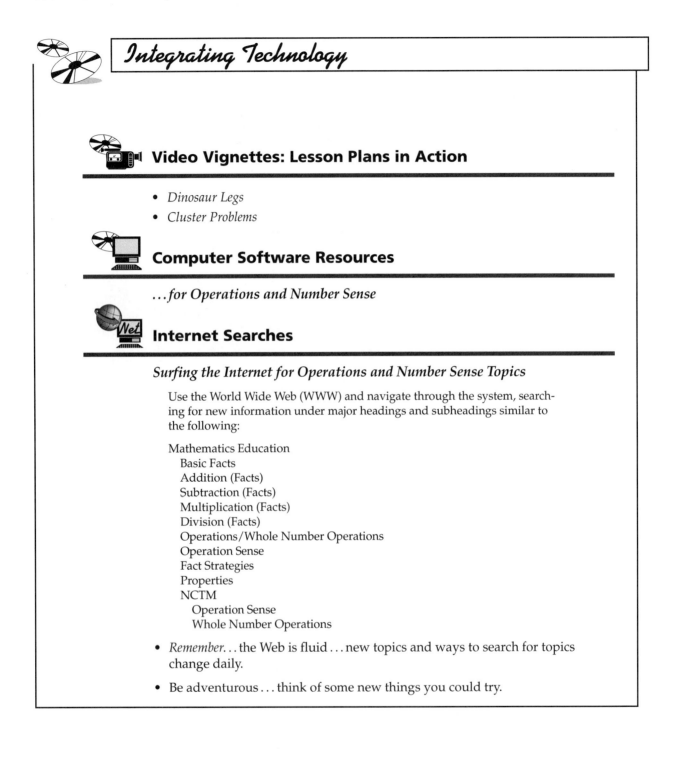

11

Operations with Whole Numbers

Activities Index

IN THE TEXT

ON CD-ROM

The basic facts and place-value concepts are applied in the computational skills required to work the algorithms. An *algorithm* is a set of rules for solving a problem, a step-by-step sequence, a method that continually repeats some basic process. This chapter covers the algorithms for the addition, subtraction, multiplication, and division of multidigit numbers. These numbers, containing two or more place values, go beyond the basic facts, which are combinations of single-digit numbers. Algorithms are efficient ways of incorporating the basic facts into larger, multidigit numbers.

THE DEVELOPMENT OF ALGORITHMIC MODELS

Elementary textbooks devote a great amount of time to the development of algorithms. Usually a textbook will present only one algorithm for each operation. It is important to remember that there is no one right way to solve a problem. In American schools, the standard algorithm is usually taught, although many educators encourage the use of a wide variety of student-invented procedures. The NCTM *Principles and Standards* (2000) maintain that children need many experiences to explore and to invent alternative strategies for doing calculations for each operation. Teaching one algorithm for an operation fails to consider the students' knowledge of place value, thinking strategies, and number relationships.

As you read this chapter, you will encounter many of the issues facing teachers in the teaching and learning of mathematics. In the United States we have maintained basically the same instructional approach to mathematics for over a hundred years. The traditional mathematics teaching emphasizes teaching procedures, especially computational procedures or algorithms. The Third International Mathematics and Science Study shows that 78 percent of the topics covered in eighth-grade mathematics curriculum in the United States are demonstrated or "taught" by the teacher and 96 percent of the time students are practicing these procedures they have been shown to do (Hiebert, 1999).

However, there are a number of alternative methods of teaching mathematics that have developed in the past decade as a consequence of the *Standards*-based mathematics reform efforts. The area of primary-grade arithmetic (learning to solve arithmetic problems involving the four basic operations) has been a focus of developing alternative approaches to mathematics teaching. Hiebert (1999) summarizes the characteristics of these programs (which will be discussed in greater detail in this chapter) as: building directly on students' entry knowledge and skills, providing for invention of alternative approaches, analyzing the various methods and approaches, and asking students to present and explain their methods. In these programs rather than the focus being on telling the students how to do the algorithms and then practice doing them, the focus is on having students acquire skills while they are solving problems and developing conceptual frameworks to understand them.

Children sometimes invent unique ways to work problems. They create their own algorithm. Teachers must be sensitive to this possibility when they give the rule "Always show your work." True, it might help decide where the error in thinking or computation occurs, but it could curtail the child's mental computations. Children are creative in adapting the techniques we teach them. Teachers can challenge children by posing problems that involve computations that they have not been formally taught how to solve. Such learning environments foster children's reasoning.

Subscripts©. . . *little thoughts below the bottom line*

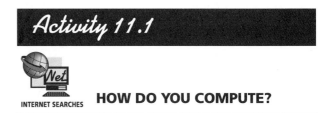

Some of these invented strategies are presented in the Activities section for each operation. The *Standards* state that it is important for children to learn the sequence of steps in the paper-and-pencil algorithms, but the meaningful development of the procedures should be emphasized.

Computation should be placed in a problem-solving environment in which students judge whether the answer can be determined by mental computation, estimation, using the calculator, or by paper-and-pencil computation. The *Standards* declare that children need to know when technology is an appropriate tool for learning mathematics. Access to calculators does not eliminate fluency with basic facts and mental calculations. Review the related *Standards* for computation in Box 11.1 to get a perspective about the role of computation.

Strong evidence (Carraher, Carraher, and Schiemann, 1985; Saxe, 1988) indicates that mathematical intuitions developed in out-of-school settings show students using mental computational methods rather than standard algorithms. Perhaps an interesting activity would be to use the Internet to communicate with students in other countries and find out how they learned to compute.

Activity 11.1

INTERNET SEARCHES

HOW DO YOU COMPUTE?

Use the Internet and explore these ideas!

Explore mental computational procedures used by school children in other countries. Try to find out the settings in which they learned to solve problems. What word problems do they associate with the algorithms?

Compare the mathematical procedures of children from rural settings to those from urban settings. What are the likes and differences of their "number sense" and perhaps street-learned strategies?

There are many algorithms that have been developed over time for each operation. Figure 11.1 on page 254 shows addition examples from an 1892 and a 1909 textbook. Examples for the other operations

BOX 11.1 Curriculum and Evaluation Standards

Whole Number Computation

In grades K–4, the mathematics curriculum should develop whole number computation so that students can—

- Model, explain, and develop reasonable proficiency with basic facts and algorithms.
- Use a variety of mental computation and estimation techniques.
- Use calculators in appropriate computational situations.
- Select and use computation techniques appropriate to specific problems and determine whether the results are reasonable.

Estimation

In grades K–4, the curriculum should include estimation so students can—

- Explore estimation strategies.
- Recognize when an estimate is appropriate.
- Determine the reasonableness of results.
- Apply estimation in working with quantities, measurement, computation, and problem solving.

Computation and Estimation

In grades 5–8, the mathematics curriculum should develop the concepts underlying computation and estimation in various contexts so that students can—

- Compute with whole numbers, fractions, decimals, integers, and rational numbers.
- Develop, analyze, and explain procedures for computation and techniques for estimation.
- Develop, analyze, and explain methods for solving proportions.
- Select and use an appropriate method for computing from among mental arithmetic, paper-and-pencil, calculator, and computer methods.
- Use computation, estimation, and proportions to solve problems.
- Use estimation to check the reasonableness of results.

Source: National Council of Teachers of Mathematics, 1989, pp. 36, 41, 94.

from textbooks ranging from 1848 to 1930 can be found on the CD-ROM.

EXTENDED ACTIVITIES

Name of Activity

PORTFOLIO MENTAL MATH

- Alternative Algorithms
- Number Sense and Mental Computation

Work with algorithms should *only* proceed when children are familiar with concepts of the operation and have a firm understanding of place value. Review Chapters 9 and 10 for help remembering teaching aspects for these topics. Exploratory experiences with the various interpretations of the operations (that is, arrays, combinations, and repeated groups for multiplication) develop meaning for discussing a variety of problem situations when using the algorithm in everyday life. Place-value concepts incorporate trading and grouping with materials to understand the base 10 numeration system—a necessary prerequisite to teach algorithms for the four operations. Students must have this basic foundation in order to build meaning for the algorithms.

Manipulative materials to teach the algorithms may be proportional or nonproportional models. Teachers must consider carefully the attributes of the models before determining which ones to use and in which sequence.

Proportional versus Nonproportional Models

Some algorithmic models are proportional in the sense that the concrete and pictorial models are based on the *structure* of the numeration system seen in Chapter 9. Every original unit in a problem is clearly seen as the unit is regrouped to a larger and larger place value.

Some algorithmic models are nonproportional in the sense that the concrete and pictorial models

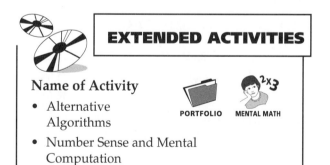

FIGURE 11.1

In Addition

From 1892

```
  $394
   476
 ₂5₁49
 $1419
```

Explanation:
Add up the columns; place number to be regrouped above the addition bar.
(Milne, *Standard Arithmetic,* p. 29.)

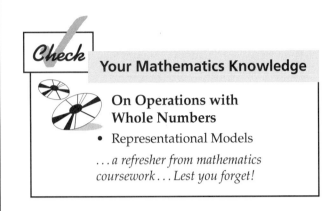

From 1909

```
 67
 86
 34
 17
17
187
```

Explanation:
Sum all units first; then sum tens and add both sums together.
(Wentworth and Smith, *Complete Arithmetic,* p. 10.)

Algorithms from the past.

do not account for every original unit as it is regrouped to larger place values. The inclusion of every original unit into the next larger place value is assumed but not clearly visible.

Examples of proportional and nonproportional models were shown in Chapter 9. They will be presented throughout this chapter to show how such models work with the regrouping of multidigit numbers.

Representational versus Nonrepresentational Models

Another way to show algorithms is through the use of representational or nonrepresentational models. *Representational models* show the regrouping strategy that occurs between powers of 10 represented by the place value of numerals. Both proportional and nonproportional models of algorithms can be representational models. If you need more examples of these models use the CD-ROM to check your mathematics knowledge.

Check Your Mathematics Knowledge

On Operations with Whole Numbers

- Representational Models

... a refresher from mathematics coursework ... Lest you forget!

You will see many different algorithms as you proceed through the chapter, some representational and some nonrepresentational. Analyze the algorithms with the knowledge that there is no one right algorithm. There are still more to be created. One of the higher-thought activities at the end of this chapter asks you to design your own algorithm for operations on multidigit numbers. There is mathematical power in the idea that any algorithm can be seen through progressively more abstract models, arriving at a correct answer no matter what model is used.

Activity 11.2

CULTURAL RELEVANCE

ALGORITHMS FROM OTHER CULTURES

- Many cultures have developed different algorithms. Look in the library for mathematics books or texts from other countries to find different examples.
- Write a pen pal in another country and ask how the four operations are done. Share your findings with your classmates.
- Use a world map and plot your class findings about cultures and algorithms. What predictions can you make about why these differences have occurred?

A special attempt has been made to choose algorithms that are quite different from one another. Some elementary and middle school students may find one algorithmic model more understandable than another. It is hoped that the teacher will see the variety of options as a way of meeting the diversified needs of students.

TEACHING STRATEGIES

The student's first experience with algorithms occurs in textbooks when the algorithms for regrouping for addition and subtraction are introduced. Students should be exposed to the concept of regrouping with concrete materials and when problem-solving situations require it. In fact, many children devise their own algorithms to solve problems with large numbers and without formal instruction in the process. Many interesting and innovative algorithms are invented by children.

The teacher's editions of textbooks offer ideas to teach the algorithms using careful sequential development. Techniques often include ideas for using concrete materials like base 10 blocks or bundles of sticks. It is important to allow time for children to become completely familiar with the algorithm at a concrete level before proceeding to the textbook's pictures (semiconcrete or pictorial level).

Remember to continue the learning sequence from the concrete level to the connecting level before jumping to the symbolic stage (check Chapter 8, Figure 8.20). Many teachers introduce algorithms with proportional materials, then after several days, give children worksheets of problems to answer, thinking they will understand. For many children, this transfer to the symbolic level does not happen. They need many extended experiences making trades with various materials and working in paired learning situations in which one student manages the materials while the other student does the symbolic recording. Students also should create word problems to accompany the computations and to provide a contextual setting.

Oral interviews with children indicate that many of them find it difficult to relate mathematical concepts to real experiences. They memorize a set of rules at a verbal level and have difficulty transferring ideas to new situations. A child who can work 42 – 18 correctly may not be able to illustrate that concept with counters, money, or concrete materials. Operations may be introduced too quickly without enough time spent on modeling, manipulating, and dramatizing the procedure. When this sequence occurs, children may not develop an "operation sense."

Changing Perspective. A large percentage of teaching time is spent on the algorithms for whole numbers. When we consider the impact and availability of calculators now, plus the increased use expected in the future, can we remain content to devote so much instructional time to the algorithms?

Many of our present-day paper-and-paper algorithms were developed over 500 years ago and yet remain a stable component of the mathematics curriculum. Perhaps we need to consider some arguments for teaching algorithms to students. Some people look to their own past experiences and say, "that's the way it's always been done." They were taught with rules and procedures and they are successful adults, so why change? Some parents, educators, and members of the general public feel that learning the basic skills of arithmetic should be teacher-directive steps for the procedures. Students need a standard routine that works for numbers and when properly executed will produce accurate computations. Time is saved when students are "given" the direct, efficient method for written calculations.

Yet, in everyday life, we *do* use alternative mental computations. Many adults think about the numbers and mentally compute in a variety of ways rather than use the standard algorithm. For example, double 38. Take a moment right now and mentally calculate this problem. Did you close your eyes and picture 38 + 38 = 8 + 8 = 16, "carry the ten" then add 3 + 3 + 1 to get 7, so 76? Or did you use some alternative strategy such as 40 + 40 = 80 – 4 = 76? Or did you say 38 + 30 = 68, then add 8 more and get 76? Many adults perform mental computations that are flexible and consider number and place-value relationships.

Some investigators contend that teaching algorithms conflicts with how children naturally approach computational situations. Madell (1985) found that on their own, children would universally begin adding from left to right. Carraher and associates (Carraher et al., 1985) studied the mathematics used by Brazilian children selling in the streets and found that children who used their own procedures made fewer errors than those using written algorithms. Some researchers (Kamii and Dominick, 1998; Narode, Board, and Davenport, 1993) conclude that once children are taught formal written algorithms, they lose conceptual knowledge and their development of numerical reasoning is hindered.

Pros and Cons of Teaching Algorithms. The NCTM 1998 yearbook, *The Teaching and Learning of Algorithms in School Mathematics* (Morrow and Kenney, 1998), presents many issues and questions regarding the question of the place of algorithms in today's mathematics curriculum. Topics include assessment of algorithms, the history of algorithms, alternative algorithms, and investigations of algorithms from addition to fractals. Carroll and Porter (1998) discuss the pros and cons of teaching specific algorithms. They list these points for teaching algorithms: written algorithms are needed for larger numbers; parents and adults see competence in computation as a measure of mathematical success; students benefit from having a range of computational options, including paper-and-pencil methods; and societal expectations make written methods for computation necessary, including a computation section on standardized tests.

The advantages of encouraging student-invented or alternative algorithms are numerous. Some of the most convincing research comes from a three-year longitudinal study (Carpenter et al., 1998) indicating that 90 percent of the students used invented strategies for adding and subtracting multidigit numbers. Moreover, "Students who used invented strategies before they learned standard algorithms demonstrated better knowledge of base-ten number concepts and were more successful in extending their knowledge to new situations than were students who initially learned standard algorithms" (p. 3).

Other mathematics educators (Burns, 1994; Kamii et al., 1993) suggest that teaching specific algorithms should be delayed in the early primary school curriculum so children can become more aware of what it means to think mathematically. The standard algorithms may be unclear to the students who learn them in meaningless ways. The notion of "ours is not to reason why, just invert and multiply" implies that these procedures will produce correct answers, so just do it! When there is a breakdown in the procedure, the child is left feeling helpless and insecure. Student-invented algorithms reflect their natural thinking and are based on their interpretations of the problem. When students develop their own procedures for solving problems, they naturally incorporate more aspects of place value and less mindless procedures such as "carry the one." When given the opportunity, students also will invent algorithms reflecting their number-sense understanding for multidigit multiplication and division. The process of inventing algorithms shows how children think about using multiples of ten to partition numbers into decades. Their understanding of place value and number sense appeared to be closely related to their invented algorithms (Baek, 1998).

Several projects designed to support children's mathematical thinking and creation of alternative strategies for problem solving provide rich frameworks for thinking about mathematics instruction. Four projects of particular interest to the authors are Cognitively Guided Instruction (Fennema et al., 1996), Conceptually Based Instruction (Hiebert and Wearne, 1993), Project IMPACT (Campbell, 1997), and Supporting Ten-Structured Thinking Project (Fuson, 1992). For a more complete discussion, Fuson et al. (1997) provide a comprehensive analysis of children's invented strategies for solving problems and describe several of the projects mentioned here.

Promoting Invented Strategies. Suppose you are interested in encouraging children to develop computational procedures or "invented" strategies. How do you make this happen? Carroll and Porter (1997) offer five suggestions: (1) Allow students time to explore their own methods and solutions; (2) have manipulatives available for modeling and to support children's thinking; (3) have children develop fact strategies along with fact knowledge; (4) present problems in context of meaningful situations; (5) encourage children to share their strategies, discuss and compare them, and learn from each other.

With a growing consensus of mathematics educators emphasizing the discovery of procedures for computation rather than memorizing traditional algorithms, you are urged to watch the video vignettes with this approach in mind. Some examples of developing children's conceptual understandings can be seen in the lesson "Understanding Multiplication" in this chapter. As you read more of this textbook, be aware of your own changing perceptions of the teaching and learning of mathematics. You might want to watch some videos again from a different lens, such as Mrs. Thomas in the "Doubling" problem in Chapter 5.

As we look at the skills and competencies needed in the workforce for the twenty-first century, the shopkeeper's computational skills play a diminished role. In the real world, computations of multidigit numbers or of several steps are handled by the ubiquitous calculator. When parents, school boards, or administrators question the decreased attention given in your classrooms to tedious, complex computations, remind them of the instructional time you have saved to spend on developing computational strategies, reasoning, probability and statistics, proportional thinking, and other topics that might otherwise not have time to be covered. Additionally, research (Bitter and Hatfield, 1992) indicates that use of calculators with middle school students did not have adverse effects on their computational abilities but did enhance their problem-solving skills, and girls felt more mathematical empowerment using the calculator.

Teaching the Addition Algorithm

The addition algorithm (addition with regrouping) should begin with proportional place-value materials such as connecting cubes, bean sticks, pocket charts, or base 10 blocks (Figure 11.2). Whatever the model, it should include some place-value boards to help children focus on a logical organizational procedure. This focus allows greater transfer from the concrete to the symbolic level.

Labinowicz (1980) has sequenced a variety of instructional materials based on their relative positions in abstraction. His sequence begins with the most concrete—lima beans in small cups. The materials are in one-to-one correspondence with the number represented. Next, he lists connecting cubes where the interlocking nature allows quick groups of ten to be formed. These materials are still in one-to-one correspondence with the number. Bean sticks or base 10 blocks are next. The groupings are fixed but the one-to-one correspondence is still present. The next level is base 10 blocks that are unscored into specific units (sometimes called Dienes blocks). With this material, the proportion of ten-to-one is shown, but the materials do not allow the child to decompose, and the one-to-one correspondence is lost (Figure 11.2).

Nonproportional materials (Figure 11.3) can also be used as instructional devices for the algorithms, but only after proportional materials have been introduced. It is important to have a sound developmental sequence because of the range in levels of representation between the various models. Labinowicz labels an abacus or chip trading as even more abstract models. Each is a nonproportional model that is representative in nature and should be presented last in the instructional sequence.

FIGURE 11.2

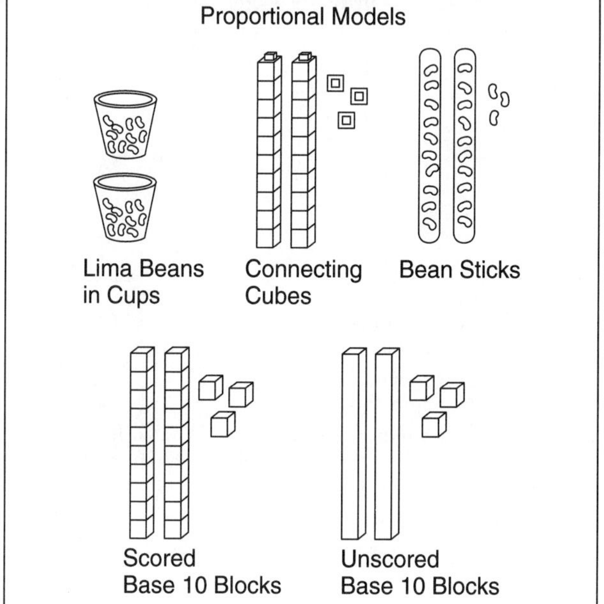

Proportional models.

FIGURE 11.3

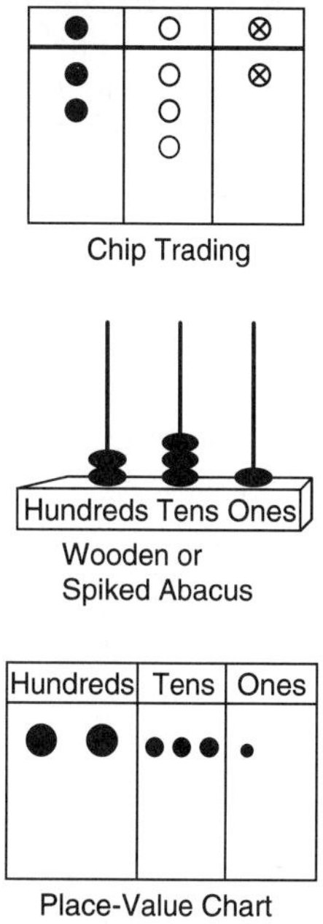

Nonproportional models.

Children are introduced to addition with two-digit numbers without regrouping in most first-grade textbooks. They are taught regrouping for addition and subtraction in second grade. The authors support teaching addition with regrouping and without regrouping together so that the mechanical aspect is replaced with thoughtful attention to the process. When word problems and situational problems accompany the presentation, children are less likely to ask, "Do I have to regroup on this one?" Manipulative materials are the key to understanding, and their use results in fewer remediation problems.

Take time now to read through the activity, "Teaching Addition with Regrouping." Can you follow the children's various thinking strategies? How would you manage a classroom of children with so many diverse approaches? Would you prefer to teach the traditional algorithm instead?

Activity 11.3

MANIPULATIVES PROBLEM SOLVING

TEACHING ADDITION WITH REGROUPING

MATERIALS

- Base 10 blocks
- Place-value mats

Situational Problem: You have collected 26 baseball cards. Your friend, Teshon, will sell you 17 baseball cards for \$4.50. If you decide to buy the cards, how many will you have then?

PROCEDURE: DIRECT INSTRUCTION APPROACH

Step 1: Place 2 tens and 6 ones on the mat in the appropriate columns.

Step 2: Place 1 ten and 7 ones on the mat.

Step 3: How many ones are there? (13) Can you make a trade of ones for tens?

Step 4: Trade 10 ones for 1 ten and place the regrouped ten in the tens place.

Step 5: Combine the tens. How many tens are there? How many in all?

Step 6: Record the steps and answer on your chalkboard. (Do this step only when the children are ready for the connecting level.)

The same teaching steps are followed if using other proportional materials. Add the connecting level to record the steps as they are being done when children are ready.

ALTERNATIVE APPROACHES

Step 1: Pose the situational problem to the children. Have materials available for those children who select to use them. Some possible approaches used by children:

Child 1: (Using mental calculations): If I have 26 and add 10 more that is 36. Then I need to add 7 more. Since 6 and 6 are 12 (that's an easy double!), I have 42, and then one more is 43.

Child 2: (Using base 10 blocks): I put the tens altogether and that makes 3 tens or 30. Then I put all the single ones in a pile and that's a lot more. I count from 6 to make ten more (from the 7 ones, the child takes 4) and that takes 4 more, so I have 40. Then I still have 3 more, so it is 43.

Child 3: (Using paper-and-pencil): I know 7 + 7 is 14, so I take one away and that leaves 13 (writes down 13). Ten and twenty is thirty (writes down 30 under the 13). Thirty and ten is forty and 3 more is 43 (draws line and writes as sum 43).

Supporting the NCTM *Principles and Standards* (2000):

- Number and Operation; Whole Number Computation; Reasoning

Activity Continues

- Tools that Enhance Discourse; Student's Role in Discourse—The Teaching and Learning Principles

Use the video vignette on the CD-ROM and watch first graders learning regrouping with addition. Analyze the teacher's approach and the child's level of understanding.

Although the foundation for the algorithm begins with two-digit numbers, children need to continue to have concrete experiences with regrouping for hundreds and thousands. At this point, many teachers claim to not have sufficient time or materials to provide direct manipulation by children with place value models. Time spent on these activities is well worth it in terms of long-range results. If a child is to truly internalize and "own" the concept, time and concrete experiences are required. Figure 11.4 shows the teaching strategy for multidigit addition.

Students can practice multidigit addition with the calculator. Since the calculator will be used by most adults to do similar problems, it helps prepare students for the adult world. Notice that the calculator worksheet has been prepared to induce interest as students work with it.

FIGURE 11.4

Situational Problem: Monday night 258 people watched the school play. Tuesday night 379 people watched the school play. How many people watched the play?

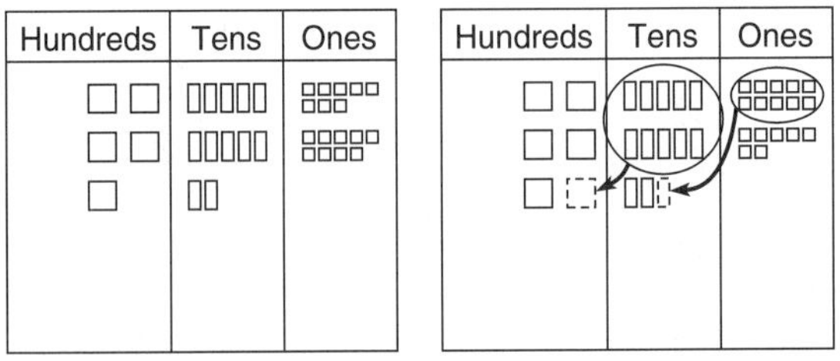

Place 258 blocks on the mat under the proper columns. Place 379 on the mat in a similar manner. Combine the pieces. Allow students to make trades when possible. The final answer shows as 637.

Add ten frames to the place value mat if you wish to show the numbers bridging to make ten of the unit. In the tens place (working from right to left), some children will see the two rows of 5 make the ten. Others will fill the 9 row in with 1 to make the ten, and still others will add 2 to the 8. Encourage them to share all their strategies (including working from left to right!).

Showing three-digit addends.

Video Vignette

Regrouping with Addition and Base 10 Blocks

Understanding Multiplication

Use these video lessons to explore the teachers' instructional styles. Compare them to the teaching approach used by Mrs. Thomas in "Doubling" in Chapter 5.

- What are the advantages and disadvantages to the direct instruction model used by the teacher in "Regrouping with Addition and Base 10 Blocks" and to the use of children's invented strategies?
- Analyze the teaching of the addition algorithm with Mrs. Arroyo and of the multiplication algorithm with Mrs. Casteneda in terms of learning environment, focus on children's understanding, and building students' empowerment and confidence in mathematics.

Activity 11.4

CALCULATORS

ADDITION PRACTICE

DIRECTIONS

Find the sums.

Add horizontally and vertically.

Use the calculator.

1)

876	+		=	1371
+		+		+
709	+		=	1341
=		=		=
	+		=	

2)

892	+		=	1292
+		+		+
641	+		=	998
=		=		=
	+		=	

Activity 11.5

MENTAL MATH

DOUBLE TROUBLE

Two to four players

MATERIALS

- Two number cubes (dice) or two with 4–9 for harder facts
- Scratch paper

DIRECTIONS

Player rolls the two cubes and either adds (or multiplies) the top faces. Play can continue with the first player as long as desired. Each individual keeps a cumulative total of all the sums or products. If the player rolls doubles, it wipes out the score for that round. Continue in a similar manner for five rounds. Winner is highest total sum for the five rounds.

Activity 11.6

PROBLEM SOLVING CALCULATORS

SPEND EXACTLY $3.55

How can you spend exactly $3.55? Can you find at least five different ways?

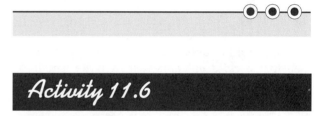

Teaching the Subtraction Algorithm

Much has been written about the subtraction algorithm and alternative algorithms to use. The most common algorithm is the decomposition method, which is traditionally the one presented in student textbooks. It can be related easily to place-value models and emphasizes the inverse relationship of addition and subtraction. There are several situations that involve different interpretations of subtraction. This chapter addresses teaching strategies for understanding the operation of subtraction using the decomposition algorithm. Although different physical situations model the subtraction operation, the standard algorithm is identical for each one.

The Decomposition Algorithm:

$$\begin{array}{r} 42 \\ -\ 17 \\ \hline 25 \end{array}$$

In ones column, we can't take 7 from 2. Regroup 4 tens as 3 tens and add 10 ones to 2 (12 ones). Now 7 from 12 is 5 and 1 ten from 3 tens is 2 tens.

Take-Away. The first kind of interpretation for subtraction is the take-away approach. It is the easiest for a child to understand and the most common one that a child encounters in real-life situations, and it is simple to represent physically. Modeling operations and algorithms with objects will allow better understanding and will prepare children to interpret the textbook pictures more clearly. The following is an example of the teaching strategies for the take-away interpretation of subtraction and alternative approaches students often take.

Activity 11.7

MANIPULATIVES PROBLEM SOLVING

TEACHING TAKE-AWAY SUBTRACTION WITH REGROUPING

MATERIALS

- Base 10 blocks
- Place-value mats

Situational Problem: Jenny had 52 cents. She bought a pencil for 27 cents. How much money does she have left?

PROCEDURE: DIRECT INSTRUCTION APPROACH

Step 1: Show 5 tens and 2 ones.

Step 2: Can you take 7 ones away from 2 ones? Regroup (trade) a ten.

Step 3: Regroup 1 ten for 10 ones. This leaves 4 tens and 12 ones.

Activity Continues

Step 4: Now take away 7 ones from 12 ones. How many are left? (5)

Step 5: Take away 2 tens from 4 tens. How many are left? (2) Answer: 25.

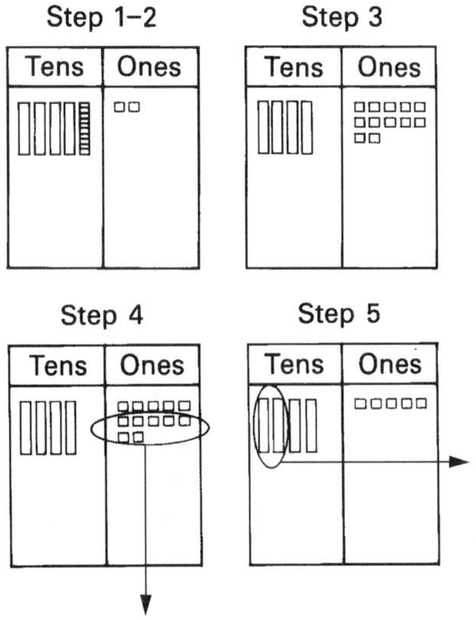

ALTERNATIVE APPROACHES

Child 1: I take 20 from 50 and leave 30 (3 tens). I can't take 7 from 2, so I take 7 from 10 which is 3. (If using blocks, trade a ten for 10 ones and remove 7.) Now I add the ones. 3 + 2 = 5 ones. Answer: 25

Child 2: (Child mentally visualizes 52.) I have 52 and I need to take 20 away. That's 30. Then I take 7 from 2 and it leaves 5 (absolute difference). I take 5 from 30 is 25. (Notice with this procedure, all computations involve facts to 10!)

Child 3:

Step 1: Show 5 tens and 2 ones with blocks.

Step 2: I can't take 7 from 2, but I can take away 2 ones. I can get a ten and take away 5 ones from it. That leaves 5 ones. (Some children will rename the ten as ten ones; others will mentally picture that step and just leave the 5 ones.). Now take 20 from 40 which is 20. Answer: 25

Supporting the NCTM *Principles and Standards* (2000):

- Number and Operation; Whole Number Computation; Mathematics as Reasoning
- Tools that Enhance Discourse; Student's Role in Discourse—The Teaching Principle
- The Learning Principle

Comparison. The second interpretation of subtraction is the comparison idea. Here a comparison is made between the two sets of numbers. Usually children do not encounter this interpretation in their textbooks until second grade. The questions for comparison involve ideas of how much more, how many more, how much less, how much older, and so on where the two sets must be compared. This is significantly more difficult for children to master. The algorithm is the same; it is a question of interpreting problem-solving situations and knowing that the subtraction operation is to be used. Many children confuse the word "more" with the idea of addition. Also in the comparison interpretation, the modeling involves making both sets and determining the difference by one-to-one matching. The teaching strategy using manipulatives follows.

Activity 11.8

MANIPULATIVES PROBLEM SOLVING

TEACHING COMPARISON SUBTRACTION WITH REGROUPING

MATERIALS

- Base 10 blocks
- Place-value mats

Situational Problem: Ramona has 52 cents. Phillip has 27 cents. How many more cents does Ramona have than Phillip?

PROCEDURE: DIRECT INSTRUCTION APPROACH

Step 1: Show 52 cents as 5 tens and 2 ones. Show 27 cents as 2 tens and 7 ones in the correct place-value positions.

Step 2: Compare the ones. You see that 7 is greater than 2. Regroup or trade a ten for 10 ones. Add these ones to the 2 ones making 12 ones. This leaves 4 tens.

Step 3: Compare 12 ones to 7 ones. Count the difference as 5 ones.

Step 4: Compare the tens: 4 tens to 2 tens—the difference is 2 tens.
Answer: 25.

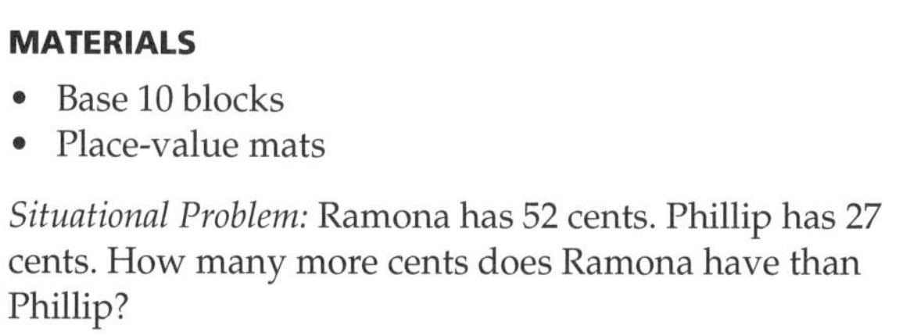

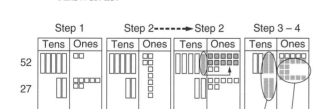

ALTERNATIVE APPROACH

Step 1: Compare the ones. They are equal as 2 ones and "cancel" each other. (May wish to remove them

Activity Continues

from the mat or leave stacked on top of each other to show they equalize.)

Step 2: Compare the 5 ones left to a ten which can be traded or regrouped as 10 ones. They are equal (cancel) at 5, which leaves 5 ones as the difference. (May remove the rest.)

Step 3: Compare the tens—4 tens to 2 tens. They are equal or cancel as 2 tens (remove from mat) and that leaves 2 tens as the difference. Answer: 25

Another alternative is to work from right to left in the same canceling procedure.

Other examples of comparison subtraction situations could be these situations: comparing the years of two people (how much older or how much younger), comparing the weight of two animals (heavier, lighter), comparing the number of minutes you exercised on Monday to the amount on Tuesday, comparing the number of students who prefer strawberry or chocolate, and so on. The comparison situations use the words "more" and "less" or the suffix "er" such as thicker, thinner; older, younger; taller, shorter; and faster, slower. On the CD under Check Your Mathematics Knowledge, there are many other situational word problems for comparison subtraction.

Missing Addend. The third interpretation for subtraction is the missing addend concept. Here the problem involves knowing what you start with or have now and knowing how many you need in all. The idea is finding how many more are needed. Writing the problem as an addition problem with a missing addend may help visualize the procedure to use to solve the problem. Using connecting cubes or base 10 blocks, the child should model the first addend and use the total as a target number. The key question becomes, How many more blocks or cubes should be added to reach the target number? This part-whole concept, or adding to a part to make the whole, appears often in measurement situations such as making change, determining how many more days until a given date, figuring how many minutes left until the play is over, and so on. Check the CD (Check your Mathematics Knowledge) for more practice on identifying problem situations as missing addend.

Activity 11.9

MANIPULATIVES PROBLEM SOLVING

TEACHING MISSING ADDEND FOR SUBTRACTION WITH REGROUPING

MATERIALS

- Number balance with tags or balance scale with blocks or centimeter cubes
- Base 10 proportional materials—base 10 blocks, connecting cubes, and so on.

Situational Problem: It is 52 miles from Phoenix to the trailhead. Consuelo drove 27 miles and bought a soda. How much further does she need to drive to reach the trailhead?

PROCEDURE: DIRECT INSTRUCTION APPROACH

Step 1: Put 52 on one side of the balance.

Step 2: Put 27 on the other side of the balance.

Step 3: Add tags or cubes to the 27 until it is balanced. How much did you add to reach 52?

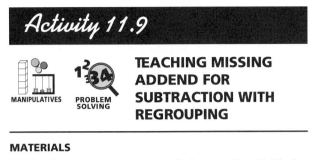

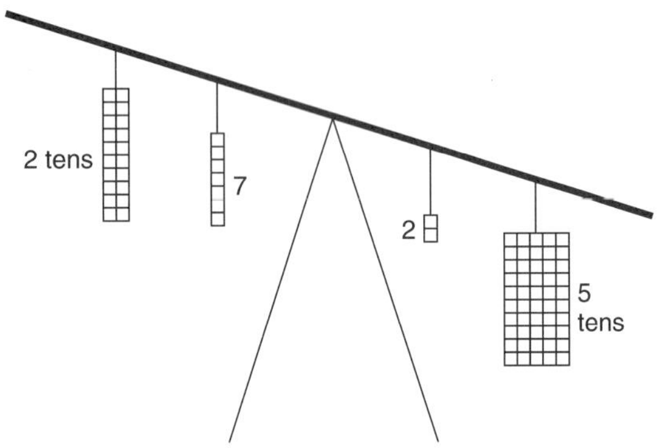

ALTERNATIVE APPROACH

Step 1: Put 27 on the place value mat (as 2 tens and 7 ones).

Step 2: *Think:* How much should I add to 27 to make 52? I can add 3, that makes 30, now add 2 more ones (32) and 2 tens (like "counting on" when making change). How much was added in all? (25)

Suggestions for Instruction. Many of the difficulties that children have with word problems requiring addition or subtraction result from the various interpretations of the operations that are possible. Explanations of addition as "putting together" and subtraction as "taking away" place limits on the operations that are inaccurate when we consider the many other situations calling for these two operations.

Zeroes pose a problem in subtraction when students need to make trades, especially when two regroupings are needed. In numbers such as 500 – 256, a common misconception is to rename the number in the hundreds place and bring over ten to the tens place *and* to the ones place (since both need help!). Another common misconception is to take the absolute difference between the two numbers, so no regrouping is done. An example is 25 – 19 = 14 because the difference between 20 and 10 is 10 and between 9 and 5 is 4. Estimation becomes a valuable way to focus attention on the reasonableness of the answer.

Teaching the Multiplication Algorithm

Before considering teaching strategies for the multiplication algorithm, a quick review of the language and mathematical concepts of multiplication is recommended. Multiplication also has several interpretations: repeated addition, a rectangular array or row-by-column, and a combination-type. It is important not to limit the children's exposure to only one approach, or they will also be limited in their abilities to decide when a problem-solving situation calls for multiplication.

Repeated Groups. Generally explorations begin with repeated addition to extend the approach most likely used by children when developing competencies for basic facts of multiplication. The repeated addition meaning of multiplication seems the easiest for students to understand and apply.

Research indicates that middle school students often have difficulty producing a pictorial representation or a word problem to accompany an equation. Instruction may be needed in the meaning of the mathematical expressions tied to drawings and manipulatives. The language of repeated addition focuses on the number of groups and size of each group. Remember from Chapter 10 the importance of using the word *of* when describing groups for multiplying? For example,

Interpretation of Multiplication:

$$4 \times 5 = 4 \text{ groups of } 5 = 5 + 5 + 5 + 5$$

To change from equation to working form:

$$4 \text{ groups of } 5 = \begin{array}{r} 5 \\ \underline{\times\, 4} \\ 20 \end{array}$$

Note: The vertical position places the 4 as the second number and still is read as 4 groups of 5.

Multiplication without regrouping usually appears in students' textbooks around the end of the third grade. This concept is easily taught and understood by children who have a reasonable proficiency with the basic facts and a firm understanding of place value. It can be modeled with base 10 blocks as shown in Figure 11.5. Expanded notation and the distributive property help teach the multiplication algorithm with regrouping by showing how the partial products can be obtained and integrated into the shortened form of the algorithm.

FIGURE 11.5

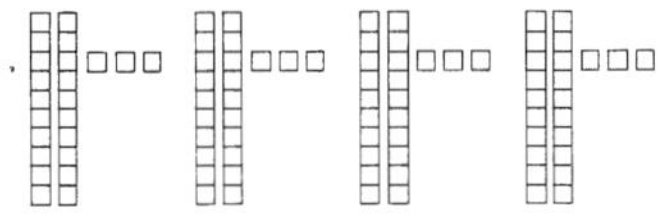

$4 \times 23 = 4$ groups of 23

Base 10 blocks for repeated addition.

When children are given opportunities to explore the repeated groups or repeated addition concept with base 10 blocks, they devise a variety of alternative approaches. Many children will combine the tens or hundreds place first, then make trades, if needed, working from left to right. Often children will record answers of partial products without the regrouping noted.

In the example 4×23, the problem can be rewritten as $(4 \times 10) + (4 \times 3)$. The teaching strategies use base 10 blocks, connecting cubes, and graph paper for arrays. Remember that all problems should be introduced in problem-solving situations and that a solid concept development with manipulatives should be established with smaller numbers because physical manipulations are difficult for larger numbers.

Partial Products

$$4 \times 23 = \begin{array}{r} 23 \\ \times\, 4 \\ \hline 12 \\ +\,80 \\ \hline 92 \end{array}$$

Expanded Notation

$$\begin{array}{rcrcl} 20 & + & 3 & & \\ \times\, 4 & & \times\, 4 & & \\ \hline 80 & + & 12 & = & 92 \end{array}$$

Multiplication requires an understanding of place-value concepts along with some mathematical terminology and properties. For a quick review of these concepts and language, you may wish to use the CD-ROM to check your mathematical background.

Activity 11.10

PROBLEM SOLVING MANIPULATIVES

MODELING MULTIPLICATION

Situational Problem: P. J. was given 4 books of tickets to sell. Each book contained 23 tickets. How many tickets had to be sold?

With Base 10 Blocks

1. Form 4 groups of 23 (2 ten sticks and 3 ones). Place on place-value mat.
2. Count ones = 12.
3. Trade 10 ones for 1 ten (base 10 blocks).
4. Count tens = 9 tens.
5. Answer: 92.

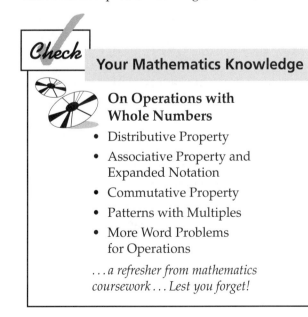

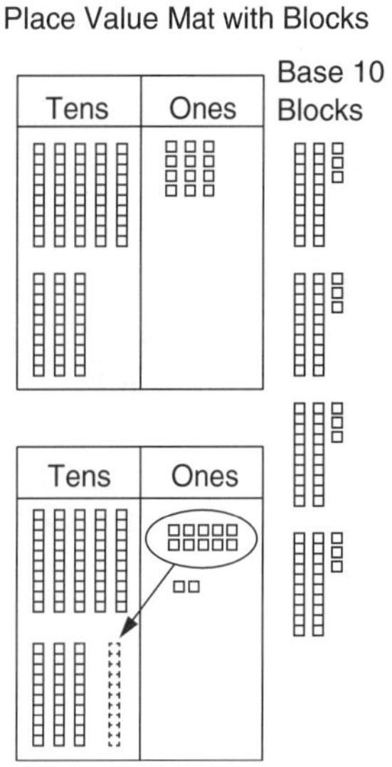

Check Your Mathematics Knowledge

On Operations with Whole Numbers

- Distributive Property
- Associative Property and Expanded Notation
- Commutative Property
- Patterns with Multiples
- More Word Problems for Operations

. . . a refresher from mathematics coursework . . . Lest you forget!

Activity Continues

With Graph Paper (Base 10 Grid Paper)

1. Cut graph paper into 4 rows down and 23 across.
2. Count ones (4 × 3 = 12); trade as 1 ten and 2 ones.
3. Count tens: 4 groups of 2 tens = 8 tens plus 1 regrouped ten = 9 tens.
4. Use expanded notation: 4 × 23 = (4 × 20) + (4 × 3)
   4 × 23 = 80 + 12
5. Show in working form.

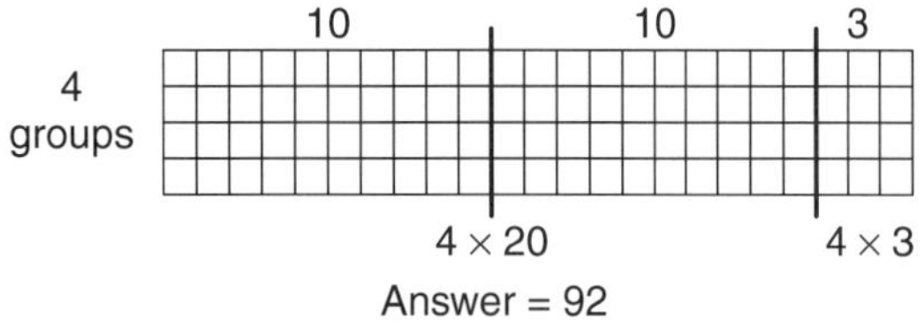

Area Model. The area model for the standard multiplication algorithm has applications for showing multiplication across many dimensions of mathematics—fractions, decimals, and algebra. The *Standards* (NCTM, 2000) proclaim that area models are helpful in visualizing numerical ideas from a geometric point of view and provide a model to see relationships between factor pairs. Area models occur again in the study of algebra and probability.

Activities such as renaming one factor in expanded notation as tens and ones and building the array formed help provide the mental visualization of what is happening with the multiplier (4 × 23 = 4 × 20 and 4 × 3). Language should accompany the modeling to help children see the connection to the repeated addition concept. In this example, 4 groups of 23 are to be made and organized into an array. Base 10 blocks can form long trains of the number being modeled, for example, 23 would be 10 + 10 + 3 ones. The next train would look the same until 4 groups of 23 are placed into the array. In this manner, the arrangement called an array is formed from the repeated groups model. Children need to determine the location of the two factors on the array—the number of *groups go down* the left side (4 groups) and the *number in the group goes across* (23 in each group). Take a look at some children using color tiles to build arrays in the video "Understanding Multiplication."

When students are ready, transfer the modeling to centimeter graph paper or base 10 grid paper (Figure 11.6). As children become comfortable with the modeling, add the recording level to build some connection from the array to the written algorithm. If students record partial products, the steps can be more readily noticed.

Video Vignette

Understanding Multiplication

Listen to these two teachers building understanding of the operation of multiplication.

- What important mathematical ideas are being enhanced in Mrs. Castenda's lesson? Discuss how you see her classroom exemplifying suggestions from the *Standards.*
- What mathematical terms and language are developed?
- How is Mr. Dillon's lesson developing a framework for these students to understand multidigit multiplication? How are these children using partial products and seeing factor pair relationships?
- How do you see these lessons connecting conceptual knowledge to procedural knowledge?

FIGURE 11.6

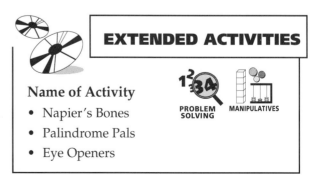

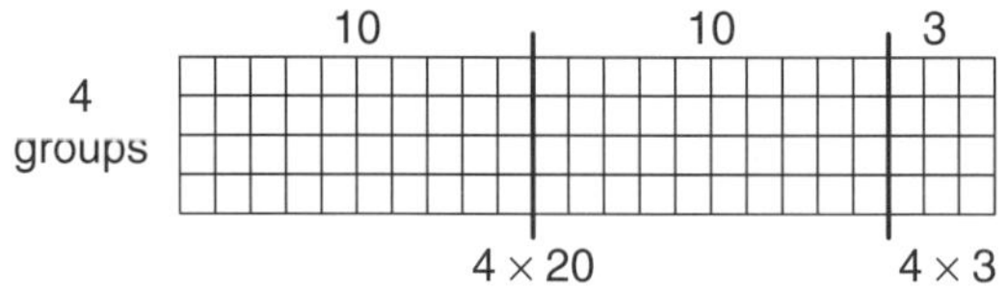

Arrays with graph paper to show the distributive property.

It makes sense to move to area models after using base 10 blocks, which become cumbersome (or perhaps not even available in sufficient numbers!) to show two-digit multipliers. Base 10 grid paper serves as an alternative to base ten blocks by allowing children to draw the outline of the problem. This is often called the "copy method" because a "copy" of the total problem is shown in a geometric area.

EXTENDED ACTIVITIES

PROBLEM SOLVING MANIPULATIVES

Name of Activity

- Napier's Bones
- Palindrome Pals
- Eye Openers

Activity 11.11

MENTAL MATH **PROVE IT**

A quick way to check multiplication problems is to "add the digits." Add until only one number remains. Try this one!

673	$6 + 7 + 3 = 16, 1 + 6 = 7$
× 236	$2 + 3 + 6 = 11, 1 + 1 = 2$
	The problem is $7 \times 2 = 14$
	and $1 + 4 = 5$

Now check all the partial products and the final product and see whether you get 5.

(Yes, $673 \times 6 = 4038 = 15 = 6$; $673 \times 30 = 20{,}190 = 12 = 3$; $673 \times 200 = 134{,}600 = 14 = 5$ and add these partial products together and get $14 = 5$. For the final product, $158{,}828 = 32 = 5$)

Try other examples and check this way.

Activity 11.12

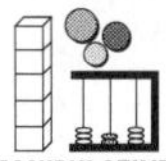

MANIPULATIVES **COPY METHOD**

The copy method can be used with the base 10 blocks and with graph paper or base 10 grid paper. The same problem will be shown using both materials.

The problem is $16 \times 24 =$ _?_

With Base 10 Blocks

Working form of the problem with partial products

	24
	× 16
6 groups of 4	24 (A)
6 groups of 20	120 (B)
10 groups of 4	40 (C)
10 groups of 20	+ 200 (D)
	384

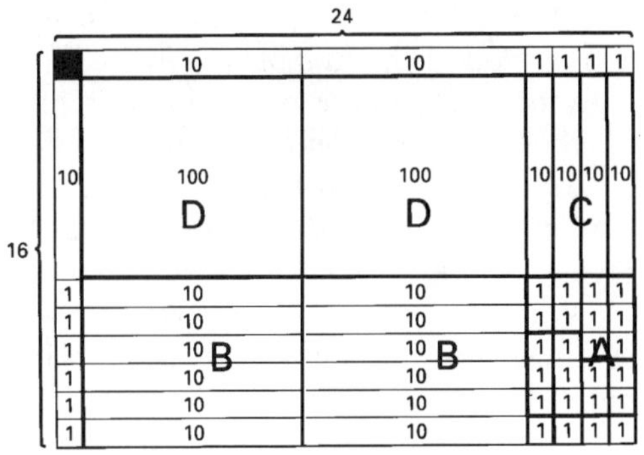

16 groups of 24

Activity Continues

Explanation with Base 10 Blocks

1. Place the 24 along the top with two sets of ten and four ones.
2. Form 16 groups on the left side. Students may see that 10 groups of 10 equal a 100 or a flat and may use two flats for D and 4 tens (longs) for C.
3. Fill in the rectangle to the right of the 16 and below the 24. All the base 10 blocks must fit in that configuration to represent the 16 groups of 24. Record the partial products.

Explanation with Graph Paper or Grid Paper

1. Mark down the left side the number of groups (16).
2. Mark across the top the size of each group (24).
3. Total = 2 hundreds + 16 tens + 24 ones = 384.

Working form of the problem with partial products

	24
	×16
6 groups of 4 ones	24 (A)
6 groups of 2 tens	120 (B)
10 groups of 4 ones	40 (C)
10 groups of 2 tens	+ 200 (D)
	384

With Graph Paper

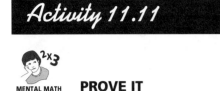

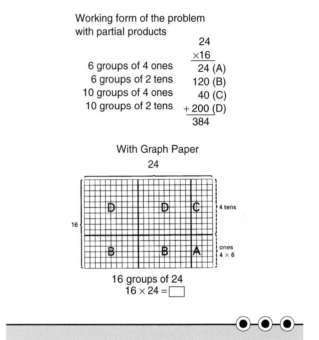

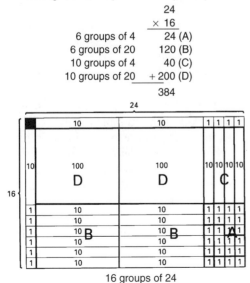

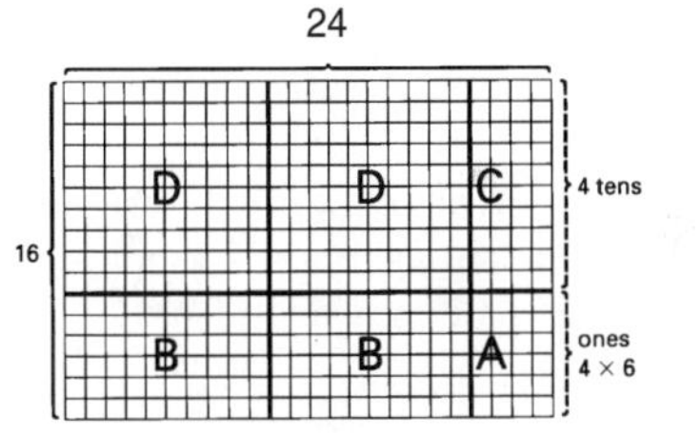

16 groups of 24
$16 \times 24 = \square$

Once children become proficient with the solution of these problems and understand the process for regrouping, they are ready to work with larger numbers in which manipulation of materials becomes too bothersome to be productive. The distributive form of the algorithm using a rectangular array can build understanding of the partial products and get a sense of the relative size of the product. Remember to evaluate whether too much instructional time is being spent on becoming proficient in multiplying large numbers, when estimation and the calculator may be more appropriate. Students might enjoy exploring how John Napier developed the lattice multiplication method. Use the activities on the CD-ROM for extension ideas.

Activity 11.13

ESTIMATION CALCULATORS **MULTIPLICATION**

The following activity can be used in a cooperative learning situation:

Estimation—Multiplication

(a game for two or more players)

HOW TO PLAY

1. Choose a number as your target.
   Circle it.

   93 556 5444 57
   212 491 649 303
   1010 237

2. Choose another number and enter it in your calculator, then enter the operation.

   Example:

   23 × _____ = (93)

   33 × 3 = 99 ← almost!

   23 × 4 = 92 ← closest

   32 × 2 = 64

3. Quick! In 5 seconds or less, enter a number that you think will produce the target number when you push the equal sign.
4. Each player tries reaching the same target number. The one who gets the closest wins one point. The first player to win 10 points wins the game.

   Display:

Enter 23					2	3
Enter ×					2	3
Estimate						4
=					9	2

Teaching the Division Algorithm

The division algorithm requires many prerequisite skills that create difficulties for children because of the numerous opportunities for error. The algorithm requires a knowledge of subtraction and multiplication algorithms, estimation skills, and an understanding of place value. Many teachers regard division of multidigit numbers as the hardest concept to teach in elementary school mathematics. A disproportionate amount of time is spent mastering this algorithm, when we consider how often adults reach for a calculator to work long division problems. Why do teachers, textbooks, competency tests, and standardized tests continue to emphasize long division? We cannot afford to spend so much instructional time on a skill that may not be necessary in this century.

However, we do not recommend that teachers stop teaching the division algorithm. Instead, the focus of instructional time should be on understanding the division algorithm using one-digit divisors with three-digit or four-digit dividends. Students should use estimation or mental calculations and use calculators for dividing large numbers that involve tedious calculations.

Using Models. In developing the algorithm, instruction should include concrete models such as base 10 blocks, connecting cubes, bean sticks, or counters and cups. Any variety of material that is available can be used. In choosing the manipulative materials to model the algorithm, remember that the actions on the materials, the language used to describe the actions, and the corresponding steps of the algorithm must be in total agreement. This is especially important in division where two different interpretations or approaches to the algorithm are possible. These result from two different situations—measurement division, which is related to successive subtraction, and partition division, which is related to fair sharing (see Chapter 10 for additional explanations about the differences). Interviews with children indicate children have difficulties in reconciling measurement and partitive division.

Once word problems or manipulatives are added to instruction, the algorithm is almost always interpreted as the partitive model (Graeber and Tanenhaus, 1993). However, the measurement concept of division lends itself for division by a rational and decimal number and therefore must not be overlooked. The suggestion is to give children opportunities to create their own arguments and explanations about the division algorithm so that instruction can be matched to the way they think.

Before the division algorithm requiring regrouping is introduced, students are exposed to division with remainders and to division of two-digit numbers where no regrouping is required. Division is the only operation in which we work from left to right, dividing the greatest place values first. Dividing by tens and multiples or powers of 10 is a skill needed for estimation as well as a way to see the effect on the size of the quotient. It is advisable to relate multiplying and dividing by multiples or powers of 10 to note relationships and patterns.

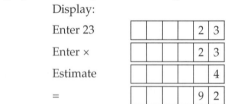

$$4 \times 6 = 24 \qquad 4 \times 60 = 240$$
$$24 \div 6 = 4 \qquad 240 \div 60 = 4$$
$$40 \times 600 = 2400 \qquad 40 \times 60 = 2400$$
$$2400 \div 600 = 40 \qquad 2400 \div 60 = 40$$

Comparing Models. Compare these two interpretations for division. Notice that the algorithm is the same but the physical manipulation and the mathematical language to explain the steps are different.

The procedure for problems with larger numbers is basically the same. It is important to select appropriate materials, some proportional and some nonproportional, that correctly model the action children need to perform with them. After a period of time working with the manipulatives, show children how to record the action symbolically to provide a connecting level between the concrete and symbolic levels. Once a problem-solving situation is involved, we must determine whether the problem calls for partition or measurement division before the action is modeled with manipulatives.

Think about different situational problems you encounter that call for measurement division rather than partitive division. More practice problems are on the CD-ROM in Check Your Mathematics Knowledge. Practice using base 10 blocks to model the problem. Compare the difference in the language used for each situation and the accompanying modeling. With measurement, the question is always how many groups can be made and the modeling is to find the number of groups to be made in each place value position (how many hundreds, how many tens, how many ones). Partitive division involves fair shares that are distributed to a given number of groups. The question is how many will each group get and the modeling is passing out blocks in each place value position. Compare the answer shown by the blocks. Can you see how they differ in Figures 11.7 and 11.8?

Whether partitive or measurement interpretation is easier for students to use in learning the division algorithm has not been determined. There is no doubt that the language of the algorithm should match the meaning of the model. Which model is being used in Figure 11.9?

Special Problems. A frequent misconception in division is the failure to record a zero as a place holder in the quotient. If a sequence of steps is followed, such as "divide–multiply–subtract–bring down," it may offer a needed structure for the child's thinking. However, the most successful way is to show the operation concretely (Figure 11.10 on page 268). When the number is smaller than the divisor and another number is to be "brought down," this

FIGURE 11.7

The Problem: 72 ÷ 6 — Model Problem

Situational Problem: 72 people. Need 6 equal teams. How many on a team?

1. Distribute the 7 tens evenly to the 6 teams.

2. Record 1 in tens column. One ten is left.

3. Break the ten into 10 ones. Add to 2; this is 12 ones.

4. Give 2 ones to each team. Record 2 in ones column.

5. So each team will have 12 players and no players are left.

Symbolic

$$\begin{array}{r} 12 \\ 6\,\overline{)72} \\ -60 \\ \hline 12 \\ -12 \\ \hline 0 \end{array}$$

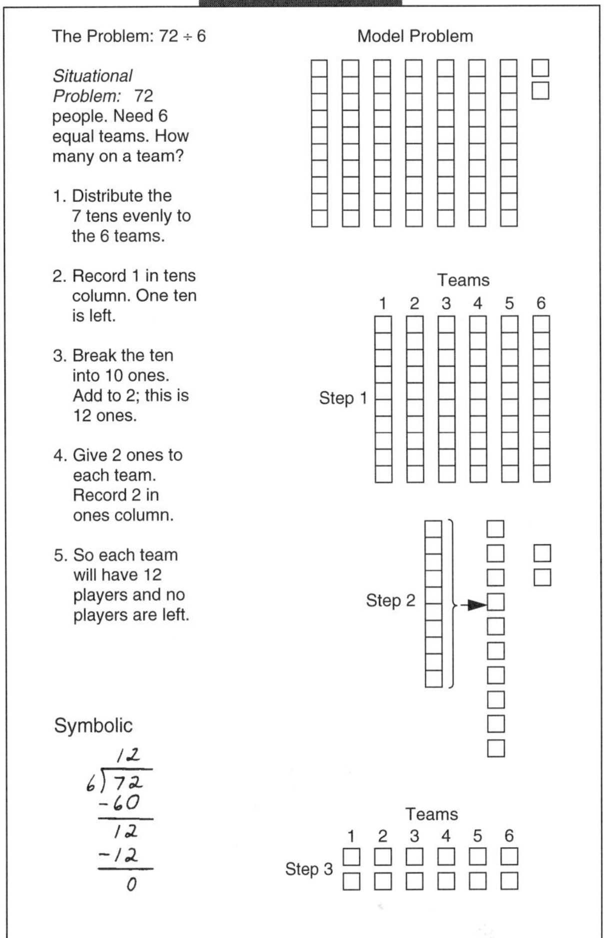

Partitive division.

division step must be recorded with a zero in the quotient. Students can use play money in denominations of thousands, hundreds, tens, and ones to add interest and variety to long division problems.

Estimating the range of a quotient helps students with the problem of using zeroes appropriately in the quotient. A quick check of an estimated quotient can be made by rounding the divisor and checking the product obtained with the dividend. If there is a large discrepancy, the student can try annexing a zero to the quotient and doing the procedure again.

	Estimate quotient	*Check and compare*	*Try again*
$21\,\overline{)422}$	$\begin{array}{r} 2 \\ 20\,\overline{)400} \end{array}$	$\begin{array}{r} 20 \\ \times 2 \\ \hline 40 \text{ not } 400 \end{array}$	$\begin{array}{r} 20 \\ \times 20 \\ \hline 400 \\ \textit{matches} \\ \textit{dividend} \\ \textit{better} \end{array}$

FIGURE 11.8

The Problem: 44 ÷ 6

Model Problem

Situational Problem: 44 people. Need 6 on each team. How many teams?

1. How many groups of 6 can you make from 44?

2. Record 7 in ones column. Two ones are left.

3. How many teams of 6 can you make? 7 with 2 people left over.

Step 1

Symbolic

$$\begin{array}{r} 7R2 \\ 6\overline{)44} \\ -42 \\ \hline 2 \end{array}$$

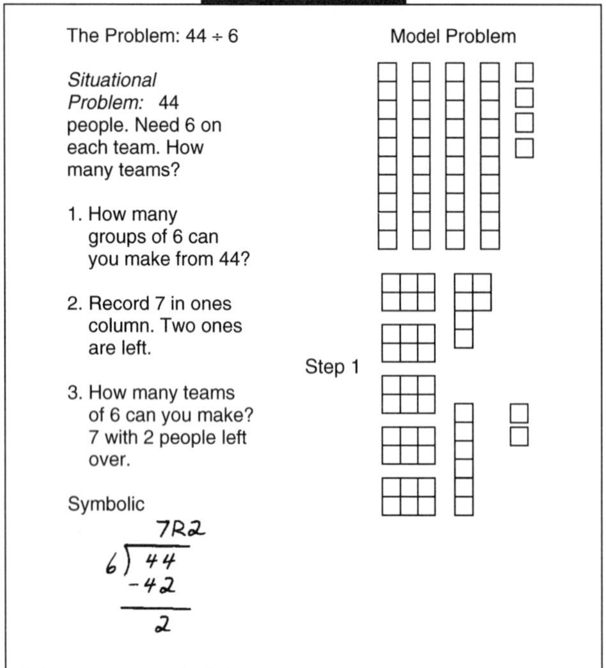

Measurement division.

FIGURE 11.9

Step 1

Hundreds	Tens	Ones

Symbolic

$$\begin{array}{r} 24 \\ 6\overline{)144} \\ -120 \\ \hline 24 \\ -24 \\ \hline 0 \end{array}$$

Step 2

Hundreds	Tens	Ones

Step 3 – 4

Hundreds	Tens	Ones

2 groups of 6 tens = 120

Step 5 – 6

Hundreds	Tens	Ones

4 groups of 6 ones = 24

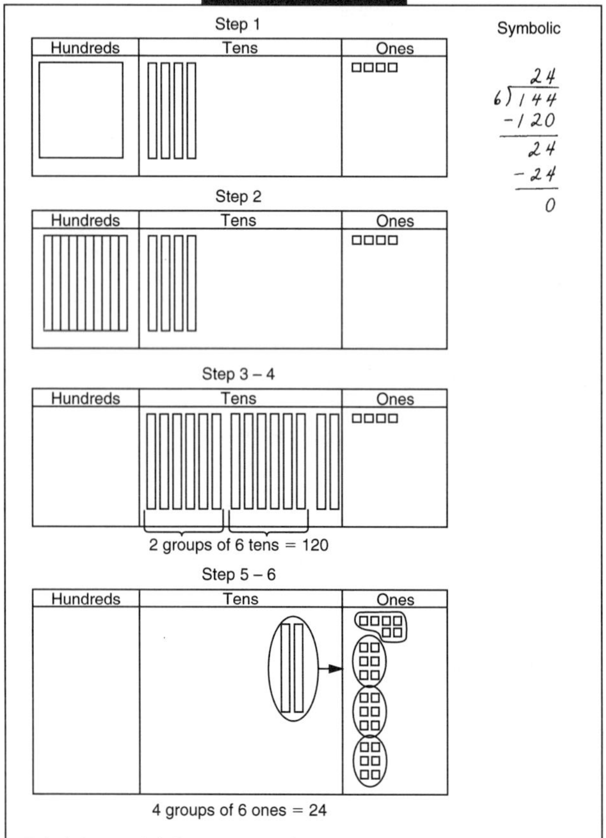

Division with larger numbers.

FIGURE 11.10

Symbolic

Hundreds	Tens	Ones

$$\begin{array}{r} 1 \\ 3\overline{)317} \\ -300 \end{array}$$

Hundreds	Tens	Ones

$$\begin{array}{r} 10 \\ 3\overline{)317} \\ -300 \\ \hline 1 \end{array}$$

$$\begin{array}{r} 10 \\ 3\overline{)317} \\ -300 \\ \hline 17 \end{array}$$

Hundreds	Tens	Ones

$$\begin{array}{r} 105R2 \\ 3\overline{)317} \\ -300 \\ \hline 17 \\ -15 \\ \hline 2 \end{array}$$

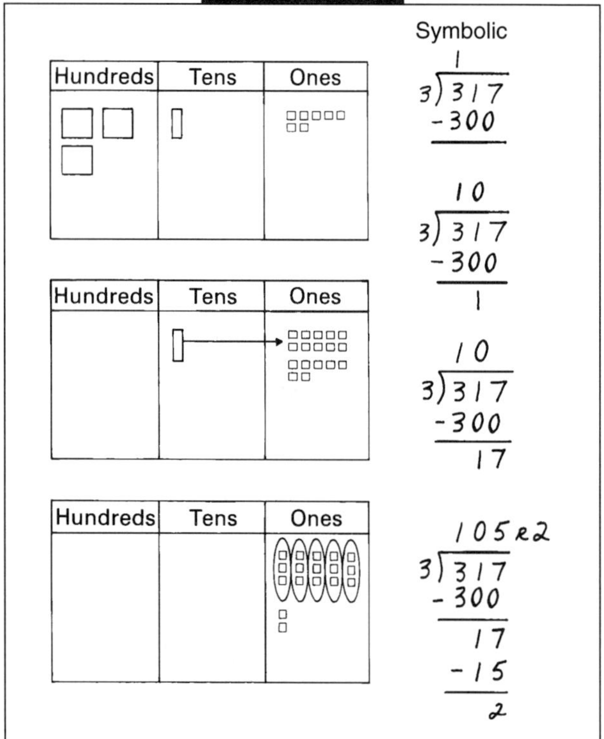

Using zeroes in the quotient.

The key to avoiding the omission of the zero in the quotient is to follow this procedure:

- Estimate the number of digits in the quotient.
- Mark those places in the quotient to remember how many digits are needed.
- Keep dividing until there are no more digits to bring down.
- Compare the remainder to be sure it is less than the divisor.
- Check the quotient by multiplying the quotient by the divisor (add remainder if needed).

The Problem: 32)6543

1. Estimate number of digits in quotient.

$$100 \times 32 = 3200$$
$$1000 \times 32 = 32,000$$

Need 6543 so quotient has three digits.

2. Mark three places in quotient.

$$\begin{array}{r} \text{-- -- --} \\ 32\overline{)6543} \end{array}$$

3. Use compatible number to estimate missing factor.

Think: $30 \times 200 = 6000$ (or $6000 \div 30 = 200$)

4. Begin dividing keeping in mind the need for three digits in quotient.
5. Use estimation and check with multiplication.

Activity 11.14

CALCULATORS

DIVISION PRACTICE WITH THE CALCULATOR

Pathways—Find the path to the END answer by dividing.

No diagonal lines allowed.

Use your calculator as needed.

Example: START

1000	2	1	10
2	4	5	5
2	5	5	5
10	2	2	1
			1

END

1) START

800	4	5	1
2	2	2	2
4	6	3	2
5	2	4	5
			1

END

2) START

19683	6	9	27
5	4	3	3
18	3	5	6
6	5	3	0.9
			9

END

Remainders. An area that causes difficulties for children is understanding how to interpret the remainders when word problems are involved. Part of the problem is that they need to reflect on the question in the word problem and label the quotient appropriately. This does not happen easily. Children work the problem and consider themselves finished with it. This is when cooperative learning experiences are valuable because students are given opportunities to verbalize the problems and to internalize meaning.

Evidence of this difficulty is shown in the following situation with fourth graders. The problem was for them to decide how many six-packs of soda should be purchased for 45 people if each person was to have one can of soda. The division posed no difficulty with an answer of 7 remainder 3. The question (how many six-packs) was answered by the students: "We need 7 of them and will have 3 left over." Three what left over—cans? people? They claimed to have 3 cans of soda 3 left over. They did not understand the need to increase the quotient. (See Figure 11.11).

FIGURE 11.11

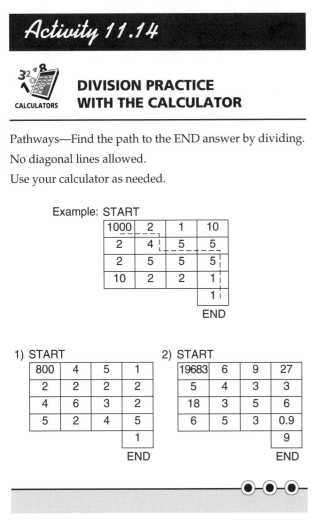

What does the remainder mean?

Activity 11.15

PROBLEM SOLVING

LEFTOVERS

Two players

MATERIALS

- Two number cubes—one labeled 1–6 and the other labeled 10–60
- Game sheets, one per player

DIRECTIONS

Players take turns rolling the number cubes. Add the numbers on the top faces and call out the number formed. Each player writes the number called next to one of the dividing numbers on the game sheet. Divide then write the remainder in the "leftover" column. Each line of the gamesheet may be used only once. After eight rolls, the leftovers are added. The player with the largest (or smallest) sum is the winner.

Activity Continues

Number Rolled	Dividing Number	Leftovers
	2	
	3	
	4	
	5	
	6	
	7	
	8	
	9	

Total Leftovers ________

Division takes a long time to master and to understand. Time spent with manipulative materials is greatly beneficial. It is more important to spend instructional time on understanding problem-solving situations and interpreting remainders than on mastering long multidigit division.

Combining the Operations

The following activities can be used when studying one operation alone or for review of the operations after all of them have been presented. Understanding the base 10 system can be enhanced as students apply what they have learned when exploring these activities. Computer activities on the CD-ROM work well with multidigit numbers. Students can create their own problems using the four operations and a calculator.

Given the opportunity, children can and will invent their own ways to solve multidigit problems. They can see a connection between their understanding of place value and basic fact strategies. In their role as assessors, teachers who encourage invented, alternative strategies to solve problems are supporting the Equity Principle *Standards* (NCTM, 2000).

Activity 11.16

MENTAL MATH **USE THOSE FOURS!**

DIRECTIONS

You must use all four 4's to create number sentences to form the numbers from 0 to 10 as the answer. You

Activity Continues

may use all four operations and may use the same operation more than once. Even exponents and decimal numbers are allowed, but not necessary. For example (but you must make your own sentence for this number too!):

0 = $4 \times 4 \div 4 - 4$

0 = ____________ 1 = ____________

2 = ____________ 3 = ____________

4 = ____________ 5 = ____________

6 = ____________ 7 = ____________

8 = ____________ 9 = ____________

10 = ____________ Make more!

Activity 11.17

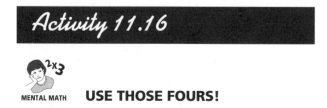

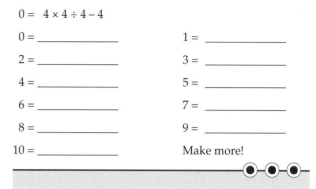

MENTAL MATH **FILL IT UP**

Two to four players

MATERIALS

- Playing Board per player
- Two regular number cubes (dice)
- Game markers (beans, clips, and so on)

DIRECTIONS

Players take turns and roll the cubes and may add, subtract, multiply, or divide the two numbers on top faces. If player gives correct answer, a marker may be placed on the number named as the answer. If player cannot make a number equation to cover a number, play goes to next player. Winner is the first player to cover all the numbers on his or her board.

0	1	2	3
4	5	6	7
8	9	10	11
12	15	16	18
20	24	25	30
36	±	×	÷

EXTENDED ACTIVITIES

COMPUTERS MENTAL MATH CALCULATORS PROBLEM SOLVING

Name of Activity

- Find the Largest and Smallest Answers
- Creating Your Own Problems
- Problem Solving with the Spreadsheet
- Powers of Ten and Division Spreadsheet
- Estimating Quotients 1 Spreadsheet
- Estimating Quotients 2 Spreadsheet

Literature. Most children's literature does not include multidigit computation, but these books provide some contextual setting for applying operations. *Building Tables on Tables: A Book about Multiplication* (Trivett, 1975) explores many grouping possibilities for the same number. *One Hundred Hungry Ants* (Pinczes, 1993) provides different ways to group 100 ants involving division. *Each Orange Had 8 Slices* (Giganti,1992) lends itself to meaningful situations to introduce repeated addition, multiplication, and division. *Alexander, Who Used to Be Rich Last Saturday* (Viorst, 1978) offers a contextual setting to use subtraction with money problems and can serve as a stimulus for writing children's own stories using larger amounts of money and more difficult subtraction problems. *Anno's Mysterious Multiplying Jar* (Anno, 1983) involves the concept of factorials, which could be used with calculators to explore large numbers.

Mental Computation

Computation can also be considered as mental computation. Mental computation involves the use of number sense, alternative algorithms, and mentally regrouping numbers into "friendly numbers." It encourages students to look at different ways to solve a problem and should be developed and rewarded. Research (Sowder and Klein, 1993) indicates that students who use mental computation appear to have a better understanding of place value, number decomposition, order of operations, and number properties.

Children need encouragement to use flexible computing strategies rather than the typical step-by-step algorithm. Devise activities that promote mental computation such as those shown here. Remember there is *no* one way to mentally compute. Children need to share their strategies and compare approaches. When teachers stress the importance of using a variety of patterns for computation, children feel encouraged to seek inventive ways to compute. When numbers are put into context with real-world settings, applications can be seen.

"I Have" is an exciting circular game that involves children in mental computation and emphasizes listening skills. The game can be varied to accommodate grade and ability levels such as including fractions, decimals, percentages, and exponents. Teachers can substitute some interesting vocabulary terms in place of a number, such as, "Add the number of degrees in a right angle," or "Divide by the number of sides on a pentagon."

Activity 11.18

MENTAL MATH **"I HAVE..."**

MATERIALS

- Prepared problem cards where one gives the answer to the next card

DIRECTIONS

Distribute the cards to the students. Have them listen carefully to each classmate read the problem card and respond if he or she has the answer card. Then read the problem on the card.

Sample Set:

I have 5, who has 3 times as much?
I have 15, who has this much plus 3?
I have 18, who has this divided by 3?
I have 6, who has half of this?
I have 3, who has this times 7 plus 2?
I have 23, who has this plus the next even number?
I have 47, who has this minus 12?
I have 35, who has this divided by 7?
I have 5—the beginning place

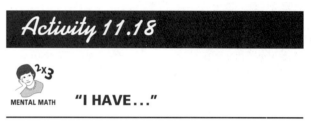

A variation of this game is to give children the number tiles 0 to 9 (or digit cards) and give a long string of mental computation and at the end say, "Show me." Children take the number tiles to form the final answer. This individual response provides a quick assessment for the teacher and involves all children in showing the answer. If you see that several children are not following the sequence, throw in a multiplication by zero and "wipe out" or start over in a subtle way. Keep the pace going about the same and remember no pencils are allowed! Try one now. How much is 3×9, $+ 5$, $\div 4$, $- 2$, square this number, $+ 4$, $\times 8$?

Activity 11.19

MENTAL MATH

MISSING NUMBERS

MATERIALS

- Digit cards or number tiles
- Calculators (optional)

DIRECTIONS

Place the digits 5 to 9 to create the problems. Check your solutions with a calculator.

Create the LARGEST ANSWER.

□□□	□□□	□□□
× □□	+ □□	− □□

□□□□ ÷ □ =

Create the SMALLEST ANSWER.

□□□	□□□	□□□
× □□	+ □□	− □□

□□□□ ÷ □ =

Compare your answers with your classmates. Were you correct? Explain your thinking and what you found out about placement of the digits for each operation. Discuss with a partner the different strategies you used for the different operations. Make up new problems using five different digits and share with a classmate. More problems are on the CD, "Find the Largest and Smallest Answers."

There are a variety of mental computation strategies including breaking numbers into parts using the distributive property, compensation, dropping common zeroes, finding compatible numbers, and annexing zeroes. The strategies vary with the operation(s) involved. Notice in these activities how the principles of the operations are used.

Activity 11.20

MENTAL MATH

USE YOUR HEAD AND LET'S COMPUTE!

Break Numbers Apart (Distributive Property)

The Hays traveled an average of 325 miles a day for 6 days. What is the total number of miles they traveled?

Think: 325×6 as $300 \times 6 + 25 \times 6$

Compensation

What is the total of items priced \$4.98 and \$7.95?

Think: \$4.98 + 2 = \$5.00 and \$7.95 + 5 = \$8.00, so \$5 + \$8 = \$13, but count back 7 = \$12.93.

Compatible Numbers

Jim has 25 cases of candy bars with 24 bars in each case. How many candy bars?

Think: $24 \times 25 = 6 \times 4 \times 25$, so $4 \times 25 = 100 \times 6 = 600$

Dropping Zeroes

Alisha needed to find the number of minutes there are in 5400 seconds.

Think: $5400 \div 60$ = Cancel the common zeroes (that's like dividing both by 10) so $540 \div 6 = 90$

Annexing Zeroes

Basima measured 34 meters on the playground. Her teacher asked her how many centimeters this would be.

Think: 34×100 means to annex or "stick on" two more zeroes or 3400

Supporting the NCTM *Principles and Standards* (2000):

- Numbers and Estimation; Relationships; Reasoning
- The Learning Principle

Estimation

Mental computation is often used for determining estimated answers. Estimation provides a "ballpark guess" about a reasonable answer. Estimation provides a check to determine if the result is reasonable. Children should develop good estimation skills for their own sake, not to simply estimate then compute a page of problems. The purpose for estimating should be rewarded rather than viewed as an extra step.

The activity "Estimation Detectives" provides a reward for being good estimators. Decisions can be made on the basis of the answers produced by estimation. Be sure you do not fall prey to the "best estimate" mentality. Often children get so locked into the "one right way" philosophy, that they will ask "who had the best estimate?" "Most students believe that the exact answer is better than an estimate, and that, in fact, estimating is just guessing" (Sowder and Wheeler, 1989). A central idea in estimating is that there are many approaches that can be used. Children need to be exposed to a variety of estimation strategies and then encouraged to think about the situation, the numbers involved, and the type of precision needed.

Activity 11.21

ESTIMATION

ESTIMATION DETECTIVES

DIRECTIONS

Look at this page of problems. Estimate the quotient for each problem. Use paper and pencil to compute the exact answer to all problems that have a two-digit quotient. Show your estimate for all the other problems.

$6\overline{)125}$	$9\overline{)1869}$	$13\overline{)117}$
$29\overline{)221}$	$42\overline{)512}$	$53\overline{)312}$
$6\overline{)685}$	$8\overline{)665}$	$24\overline{)103}$

Front-End Estimation. This strategy means to use the leading digits in the number and consider the place value position of the digits. This approach incorporates number sense and provides a quick idea of the relative size of the answer. After the initial estimate using the front-end numbers, children can consider the other numbers in the problem and adjust the estimate.

Activity 11.22

ESTIMATION

FRONT-END ESTIMATION

For addition:

$$\begin{array}{r} 961 \\ 844 \\ +\ 211 \\ \hline \end{array}$$

Think: 900 + 800 + 200 = 1900
Adjust: Since in the tens place we see 100 (6 + 4), we can adjust estimate to 2000.

Activity Continues

For subtraction:

$$\begin{array}{r} 4189 \\ -\ 2301 \\ \hline \end{array}$$

Think: 4000 – 2000 = 2000
Adjust: In tens place, we must regroup to subtract, so get closer and estimate 1800.

For multiplication:

$$\begin{array}{r} 8534 \\ \times\ \ \ 5 \\ \hline \end{array}$$

Think: 8000 × 5 = 40,000
Adjust: Multiply next digits, 500 × 5 = 2500 so estimate is around 42,500.

Compatible Numbers. This strategy uses numbers that are easy to compute because they naturally go together or are "friendly numbers." Finding numbers that make 10 or 100 aid in quicker computation. Numbers are also rounded to numbers that are easier because they are "nice numbers." For division, one way to estimate is to find the closer number of tens, hundreds, or thousands in the quotient. Students may need to look for friendly multiples that make dividing easier.

For example:

To divide 3417 by 4, *think:* 3200 ÷ 4 = 800

The same strategy is helpful to think of fractions (for example, $\frac{1}{5} \times 21$, use $\frac{1}{5} \times 20$). Compatible numbers can be mixed numbers with decimals (for example, 123.4 ÷ 3.45, use 120 ÷ 3). More of these strategies are discussed in Chapter 12.

Activity 11.23

ESTIMATION

ARE WE COMPATIBLE?

DIRECTIONS

Look for easy ways to group these numbers into Friendly Pairs to add more easily.

$$\begin{array}{r} 25 \\ 32 \\ 45 \\ +\ 74 \\ \hline \end{array} \qquad \begin{array}{r} 37 \\ 49 \\ 71 \\ 56 \\ 35 \\ +\ 69 \\ \hline \end{array} \qquad \begin{array}{r} 843 \\ 917 \\ 206 \\ 684 \\ 112 \\ +\ 388 \\ \hline \end{array}$$

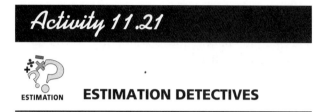

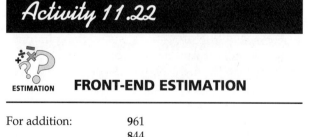

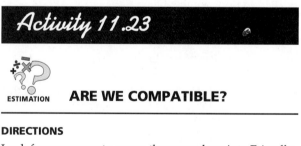

Clustering. When numbers cluster around the same amount, you can use this number and multiply by the number of addends in the group. This approach is like finding an average value for the group of numbers and then making it into a simple multiplication or repeated addition problem. It reduces the numbers with which you are working, but it is more difficult to adjust the estimate.

Estimate the total cost of these items:

$1.21 + $1.29 + $1.32 + $1.25

Since all the numbers are around $1.25, *think:*

4 × $1.25 = $5.00

Rounding. Rounding is deliberately discussed last because it is the most familiar estimation technique. The traditional rounding techniques ask students to round to a particular place-value position. When students are asked to estimate by rounding, they commonly ask "to which place?" Unfortunately this situation occurs because rounding is often done in "rounding lessons" or to check computational problems, rather than taught in a contextual setting that provides clues to this question.

Activity 11.24

ESTIMATION

TARGETING PRODUCTS

MATERIALS

- Digit cards or number tiles
- Calculators (optional)

DIRECTIONS

1. Place the digits 4 to 9 in the boxes to get a product as close to the target as possible.
2. Multiply and find out how far your answer is from the target. You get three tries for each one.

	Target
□□□□ × □ =	50,000
□□□□ × □ =	80,000
□□□□ × □ =	70,000
□□□□ × □ =	40,000
□□□□ × □□ =	40,000
□□□□ × □□ =	70,000

Compare your estimates with a partner. Whose estimate was closer to the target? Discuss your thinking strategies for digit placement.

An effective technique is to search for compatible numbers and to consider flexible rounding adjustments. For addition and subtraction, both numbers may not need to be rounded to get a good estimate. The best approach is to round numbers to reasonable values to make the computation easier. Multiplication estimation often involves rounding numbers to multiples of 10. To reduce the rounding error when multiplying, students should try to adjust the estimate by rounding one factor up and the other factor down. Experiment with numbers where you use this approach and compare it to rounding both factors up and rounding both factors down. What do you think would be a reasonable range?

ASSESSMENT

Although there are a variety of errors associated with whole number algorithms, a great many of them have to do with working with zeroes and applying place-value principles to the algorithm. Some errors are caused by difficulties with computation, such as not knowing the basic facts. Specific errors for each operation are covered, along with some remediation techniques when applicable. Generally, it can be said that most remediation involves additional experiences with concrete materials when reteaching the steps of the algorithm.

Unfortunately, most elementary mathematics methods classes do not have adequate time to cover procedures in assessment and prescriptive teaching. As a result, most teachers have had little, if any, preparation in this important dimension of teaching. How does a teacher assess learning difficulties related to mathematics? Some tests are available for diagnosing the child's achievement level or cognitive abilities, but these are generally paper-and-pencil tests that measure the symbolic level of understanding. Assessing at the concrete level is more time-consuming and difficult since it requires more interpretive skill by the teacher. Oral interviews and teacher probing are valuable assessment techniques. Teachers should observe students working individually and collectively as they communicate about mathematics. In this way, the teacher can discover the strategies used by the child to arrive at answers along with any misconceptions the child has about the algorithm and the structure of the number system. We must ensure that assessment reflects significant mathematics.

Important Aspects. The teacher should plan teaching strategies to use as many senses as possible in developing mathematical concepts. Approximately 80 percent of our sensory intake is visual, 11 percent is auditory, and 2 percent is tactile (Capps and Hatfield, 1979). Manipulative materials may provide the visual mode, but if the child is allowed to work with them, tactile as well as visual skills can be employed. Whenever possible, instruction should be based on concrete experiences that employ as many sensory modes as possible. This should be the situation for initial instruction, but it is of paramount importance during remediation.

Another important aspect of assessment is selecting appropriate materials. There are many manipulative devices the teacher may select including both proportional and nonproportional models. Which device is most appropriate depends on several aspects of the learner: maturity level, previous experiences, materials used for initial instruction, visual or perceptual problems, fine motor skills, learner's intact skills, distractibility problems, and any other special needs of the child. Preparing an instructional hierarchy that takes these issues into account is a skill that takes years to acquire. Determining the proper instructional sequence is a most difficult task. For these reasons, the teacher must carefully read each section on assessment to become an effective teacher.

Correcting Common Misconceptions

Many errors with addition and subtraction result from difficulties with regrouping. Children may not know when to regroup and will regroup when it is not necessary or will fail to regroup. As mentioned earlier, the authors advise that problems with regrouping should be introduced at the same time as problems without regrouping.

Special Needs Students. Beginners and children with special needs often benefit from using a Learning Mat (Figure 11.12) to center their attention on the materials. The mat can be a file folder, a shoebox, and so on. The important thing is that the child sees 9 holes cut so just 9 ones can fit into the slots. The tenth one is covered in black to remind the students that when all the holes are filled and this is the only one left, it is a sign that it is time to regroup. The same thing is done for tens and hundreds. If the Learning Mat is plasticized, the arrows can be drawn in crayon so that they can be changed for addition or subtraction. Ten-frames (see Chapter 10) also serve as an organizing mat to indicate when regrouping is necessary and to reduce repeated counting.

FIGURE 11.12

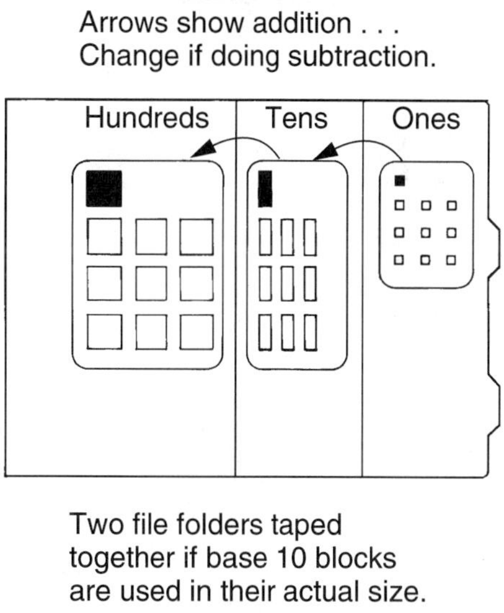
Arrows show addition . . .
Change if doing subtraction.
Hundreds
Tens
Ones
Two file folders taped
together if base 10 blocks
are used in their actual size.

Learning mat.

Common misconceptions for the algorithms of the four basic operations are presented here. Notice the suggestions of materials and approaches to use with special needs students. Study the examples and decide what error the child is making. Then work the problems given using the child's error pattern. Compare answers with those given below each example. Decide what remediation procedures you would use in each situation. In all cases, remediation involves additional experiences with place-value models so the algorithm is understood rather than just a series of memorized routines. Some additional teaching strategies are mentioned when appropriate.

Addition

Consider these problems:		*Try these using the error:*	
37	297	48	306
+ 46	+ 658	+ 29	+ 495
713	81415		
		(617)	(7911)

Error pattern: Adds by column without regrouping.

Remediation techniques: Estimate the answer and compare difference between the estimated and obtained sums. Use a closed abacus where regrouping is forced to occur because only nine chips or beads will fit in each column. Use graph paper with the rule that only one digit can be written in each section to focus attention on the need to regroup.

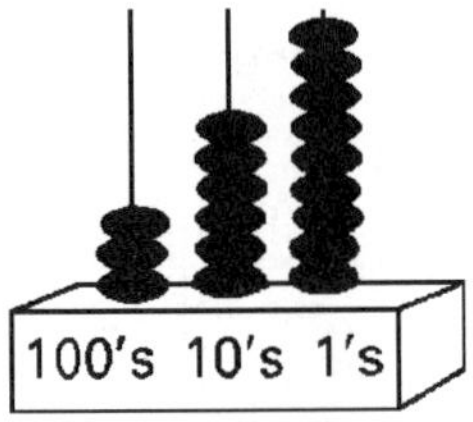

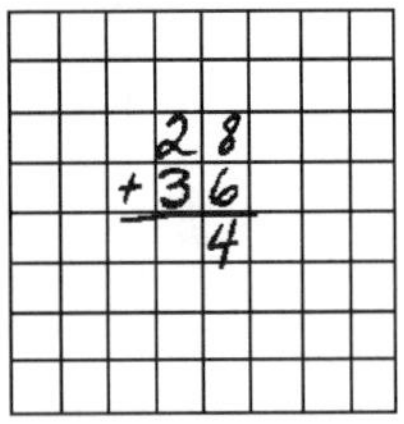

Consider these problems:		*Try these using the error:*	
28	463	346	694
+ 37	+ 358	+ 39	+ 137
515	7112	(3715)	(7212)

Error pattern: Adds from left to right.

Remediation techniques: Use a form that is placed over the problem to reveal only the ones column, then the tens, and continues in a right-to-left sequence. Also you could write "A" over the ones column, "B" over the tens column, and so on to show the sequence. Color coding works well with some children who are visually challenged.

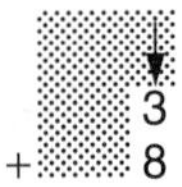


```
   ←
  CBA
  463
+ 358
```

Consider these problems:		*Try these using the error:*	
27	377	85	219
+ 35	+ 94	+ 67	+ 576
52	361	(142)	(785)

Error pattern: Fails to add the regrouped digit.

Remediation techniques: Estimating the sum will work in some cases. May need to provide a "box" at the top of the columns to the left of the ones with a large plus sign to help remind the student of this step.

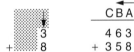

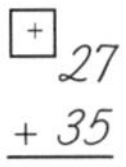

Subtraction

Consider these problems:		*Try these using the error:*	
300	56	512	309
− 198	− 29	− 258	− 98
298	33	(346)	(391)

Error pattern: Takes the smaller number from the larger without regard to position.

Remediation techniques: Estimate the answer. Have the student check using addition. In many cases, the answer is larger than the original number and makes no sense. Concrete materials can be used with a take-away model (rather than the comparison model) to show that the first number, or minuend, is modeled with the blocks or chips and the second number is removed from that set.

Consider these problems:		*Try these using the error:*	
315	746	452	315
− 138	− 159	− 189	− 96
172	551	(221)	(214)

Error pattern: Regroups all columns as ten and fails to add the previous digit.

Remediation techniques: Use concrete proportional models to review the subtraction algorithm.

Consider these problems:		*Try these using the error:*	
1 1 / 206	1 1 / 715	465	285
− 38	− 288	− 97	− 189
78	437	(378)	(96)

Error pattern: Regroups in the column farthest to the left and adds ten to each column rather than working column by column starting with the ones.

Remediation techniques: Concrete materials to reteach the steps of the algorithm. Could also use a form that allows only the column on the left to be seen at one time (as in an addition example mentioned earlier).

Consider these problems:		*Try these using the error:*	
2 16 / ~~36~~	4 12 / ~~52~~	27	98
− 14	− 36	− 19	− 26
112	16	(8)	(612)

Error pattern: Regroups all columns when regrouping is unnecessary.

Remediation techniques: This error occurs in second and third grades when the child is learning the algorithm and problems with mixed operations are included. The child continues to focus on the regrouping process and perseveres. Give mixed problems where the child is asked only if regrouping is needed. Also estimation will help alert the child to a problem in the answer.

Do you trade? Circle yes or no.

$$\begin{array}{r}26\\+12\\\hline\end{array}\ \text{Yes / No}\qquad\begin{array}{r}39\\+24\\\hline\end{array}\ \text{Yes / No}\qquad\begin{array}{r}41\\+39\\\hline\end{array}\ \text{Yes / No}$$

$$\begin{array}{r}52\\+27\\\hline\end{array}\ \text{Yes / No}\qquad\begin{array}{r}90\\+26\\\hline\end{array}\ \text{Yes / No}$$

Multiplication

Consider these problems: *Try these using the error:*

$$\begin{array}{r}37\\\times 5\\\hline 1535\end{array}\qquad\begin{array}{r}241\\\times 34\\\hline 8164\\61230\\\hline 69{,}394\end{array}\qquad\begin{array}{r}23\\\times 47\\\hline\\(9541)\end{array}\qquad\begin{array}{r}186\\\times 42\\\hline\\(453{,}852)\end{array}$$

Error pattern: Fails to regroup.

Remediation techniques: Estimation will help draw attention to the large difference in products. Use graph paper with the rule that only one digit per column can be recorded. Review the multiplication algorithm with concrete materials.

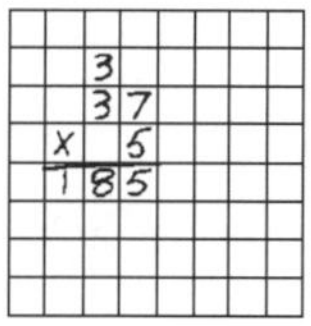

Consider these problems: *Try these using the error:*

$$\begin{array}{r}68\\\times 5\\\hline 500\end{array}\qquad\begin{array}{r}68\\\times 26\\\hline 608\\1460\\\hline 2068\end{array}\qquad\begin{array}{r}29\\\times 3\\\hline\\(127)\end{array}\qquad\begin{array}{r}52\\\times 87\\\hline\\(5284)\end{array}$$

Error pattern: Adds carried digit before multiplying the next column.

Remediation techniques: This error could be a carryover of the drill with regrouping in the addition algorithm. Estimation may help clue the student about the difference in the two products—estimated and obtained. Review of the algorithm with concrete materials may reinforce sequence of steps.

Consider these problems: *Try these using the error:*

$$\begin{array}{r}83\\\times 27\\\hline 581\\166\\\hline 747\end{array}\qquad\begin{array}{r}423\\\times 254\\\hline 1692\\2115\\846\\\hline 4653\end{array}\qquad\begin{array}{r}73\\\times 24\\\hline\\(438)\end{array}\qquad\begin{array}{r}302\\\times 58\\\hline\\(3926)\end{array}$$

Error pattern: Fails to annex a zero as a place holder when multiplying tens and hundreds.

Remediation techniques: Worksheets with these zeroes already recorded may help. Another strategy is to use a form that exposes only the column multiplied and column labels. Outlining the correct placement of steps with colored lines on graph paper helps draw attention to the sequence of the algorithm. Using concrete models is encouraged along with estimation.

$$\begin{array}{r}83\\\times 27\\\hline\end{array}$$

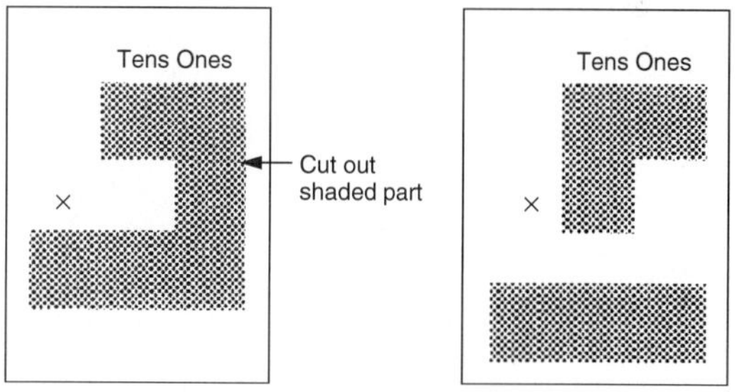

Consider these problems: *Try these using the error:*

$$\begin{array}{r}56\\\times 38\\\hline 198\end{array}\qquad\begin{array}{r}584\\\times 73\\\hline 4072\end{array}\qquad\begin{array}{r}75\\\times 29\\\hline\\(185)\end{array}\qquad\begin{array}{r}185\\\times 37\\\hline\\(575)\end{array}$$

Error pattern: Multiplies column by column like the addition and subtraction algorithm.

Remediation techniques: Use a form to help show the sequence, and use graph paper outlined with the steps. Graph paper can be color coded according to the multiplier to give visual clues. Also the distributive law will indicate the partial products and help in understanding how to complete the steps. Estimation will clue the error.

Consider these problems:		*Try these using the error:*	
265	468	327	705
× 238	× 83	× 286	× 356
2120	1404		
7950	17440	(886,622)	(60,630)
5300	31,844		
63,170			

Error pattern: Does not keep columns straight and errors occur in the adding.

Remediation techniques: Use graph paper to help keep columns in proper alignment. Can also turn notebook paper sideways which will cause the blue horizontal lines to become vertical lines to help with alignment.

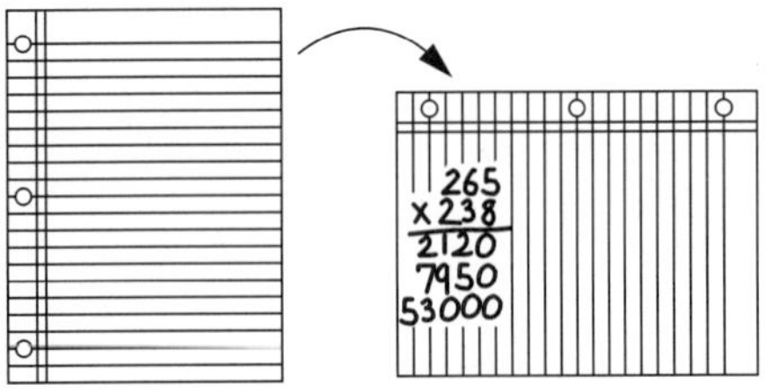

Division

Consider these problems:		*Try these using the error:*	
56 R 6	830		
9)4560	6)4818	8)5840	3)752
− 45	− 48	(73)	(25 R 2)
60	18		
− 54	− 18		
6	0		

Error pattern: Does not record zero as a place holder in the quotient when the division step cannot be done (the number is too small to be divided).

Remediation techniques: Estimation will offer the clue that there is an error. Estimating the size or range of the quotient, then marking that in the quotient with lines (two for a two-digit quotient or three for a three-digit quotient), will help draw attention to the error when it occurs. However, some children will misuse this device and will simply record a zero in the ones place to satisfy the needs of the size of the quotient. Concrete models are the best device to use as the child will see from where the zero comes.

4)352 Think → 4)320 (80 ← 2 digits) 4)352 (— —)

Consider these problems:		*Try these using the error:*	
68	19		
6)516	3)273	8)584	4)568
− 48	− 27	(37)	(241)
36	3		
− 36	− 3		
0	0		

Error pattern: Records the problem (or perhaps even works the problem) from right to left as in the other three operations.

Remediation techniques: Use play money to model the division process and visualize the algorithm. Could also use a cover form to reveal numbers in the dividend beginning with the left. Stress where the quotient will go. Estimate the quotient to determine whether it is reasonable.

Consider this problem:		*Try these using the error:*	
95 R 7	64 R 12		
4)387	9)588	6)579	8)369
− 36	− 54	(95 R 9)	(45 R 9)
27	48		
− 20	− 36		
7	12		

Error pattern: Remainder is greater than the divisor. The division was stopped too soon and is incomplete.

Remediation techniques: Stress estimation and use play money to focus on the size of the remainder.

Consider this problem:	*Try this using the error:*
15 R 3	
31)4696	16)4650
− 31	− 32
158	145
− 155	− 144
3	1
	(29 R 1)

Error pattern: Lost track of which numbers were left to "bring down."

Remediation techniques: This error happens because digits are not kept in proper alignment. Graph paper or notebook paper turned sideways offers a help for alignment.

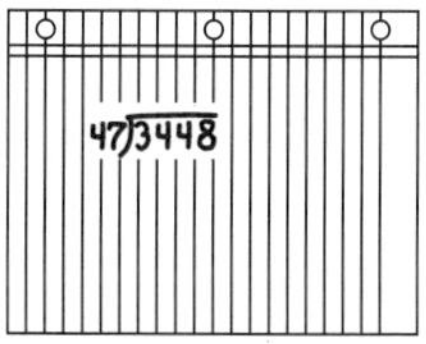

Consider these problems: Try these using the error:

$$\begin{array}{r} 862 \\ 47\overline{)3448} \\ -32 \\ \overline{24} \\ -24 \\ \overline{8} \\ -8 \\ \overline{0} \end{array}$$

$$\begin{array}{r} 3236 \; R \; 1 \\ 24\overline{)6473} \\ -6 \\ \overline{4} \\ -4 \\ \overline{7} \\ -6 \\ \overline{13} \\ -12 \\ \overline{1} \end{array}$$

$$37\overline{)9846}$$ $$43\overline{)2867}$$

$$(3282)$$ $$(716 \; R \; 3)$$

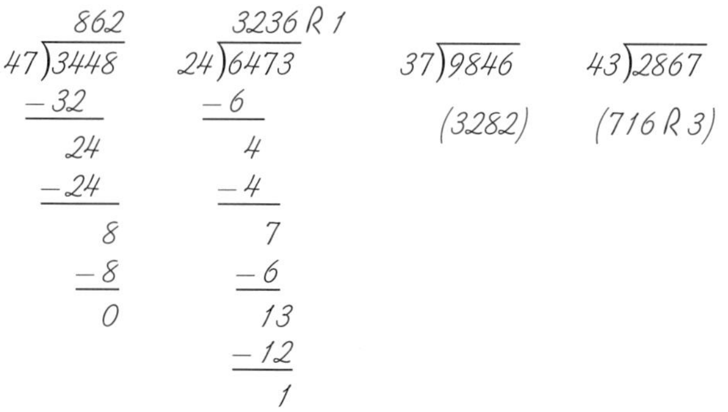

Error pattern: Uses only the first digit of the divisor to divide.

Remediation techniques: Estimate the quotient. Use graph paper to record the answer with the size of the quotient indicated. Also, checking the answer may give a clue to the error.

Field-Dependent Learners

Students who process information from the whole to the part often benefit from an organizing mat that forms an outline for placing base 10 blocks in the copy method. The copy method of multiplication and division is also helpful because the rectangular area is easily seen. The copy method of division is shown here:

The problem $21\overline{)672}$

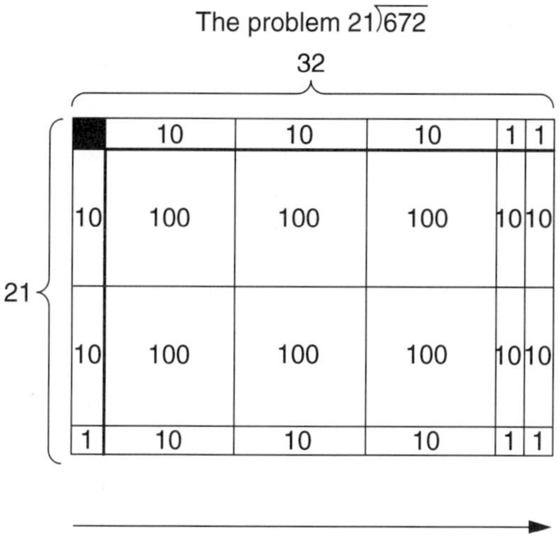

Explanation of How It Works with Base 10 Blocks:

1. The divisor, 21, is placed down the left side.

2. The dividend, 672, is represented by base 10 blocks going out to the right of the divisor to form a rectangle, showing how 672 is divided into 21 sets.

3. The quotient, 32, is represented on the top of the dark line (shown here by the dotted line above the base 10 blocks of 3 sets of ten and 2 ones). The quotient must fit exactly over the top line of the dividend. It shows how many things are in each group of the 21 groups.

4. The largest number of the base 10 blocks (in this case 6 sets of hundreds) is represented first as the dividend is modeled from left to right at the right of the dark line, then come tens and ones. The representation is just like the written numeral representation:

$$672 = 600 \; (6 \times 100)$$ six sets of 100
$$70 \; (7 \times 10)$$ seven sets of 10
$$2 \; (2 \times 1)$$ two sets of 1

5. In some examples, the dividend may need to be regrouped to smaller powers of 10 so that its configuration will fit exactly to the right of the divisor with no parts "hanging down" past the end of the divisor (as shown by the arrow in the last example).

Field-Independent Learners

Students who process information from details to the whole often benefit from the traditional algorithms that take one column at a time, find the answer, and then move on to the next column. These students are often better at performing addition and multiplication algorithms than they are at subtraction or division. Perhaps it is because both addition and multiplication are joining activities ending in the whole at the culmination of the algorithm. The important thing is to use manipulatives where exploration is possible. Work of students has been included in the exercises so that you can practice analyzing and planning instruction for typical solutions to students' difficulties.

SUMMARY

This chapter targets a redefinition of teaching and learning of algorithms for whole number computation. The challenge is to develop computation through a rich conceptual development of the operations. Rather than emphasize the rules and procedures of teaching algorithms, the teaching focus is on children's understanding of the operations. This approach highlights the role of instructional activities that support children's thinking and numerical reasoning. Teachers are called on to provide the foundation for whole numbers so students can build new ideas as they use rational and decimal numbers.

If results obtained by paper-and-pencil computations are tested as reasonable, students need skills in estimation. Estimation and mental computation play a large part in obtaining a "ballpark figure" or in simplifying the calculations. Place value and number properties are also related to understanding the algorithms. If we want children to be empowered in mathematics, more time must be spent on developing flexible thinking and conceptual understanding about the algorithms in which the emphasis is on making sense of mathematics.

The next chapter shows many numerical relationships used in fractions and decimals. Understanding problem structures for whole number operations gives the students a foundation for learning about fractions and decimal numbers.

EXERCISES

For extended exercises, see the CD-ROM.

A. **Memorization and Comprehension Exercises**
Low-Level Thought Activities

1. Explain the two types of division and give an example of each type.
2. Explain the role of estimation and rounding in the study of algorithms.
3. Explain why it is recommended that the division algorithm not be taught as a subject of drill over long periods of time.

B. **Application and Analysis Exercises**
Middle-Level Thought Activities

1. Think of an addition, multiplication, subtraction, and division algorithm modeled in this chapter. Show the same algorithm with a different manipulative material than the one used in the chapter.
2. Apply what you have learned about the copy method of multiplication and division to work a problem in division with a remainder. Try a variation of the following problem:

   21)672
   Make it 678.
   See what happens.

3. Analyze the following algorithm. It was created by a bright fourth grader. Why does it work? Try other numbers. Does it work all the time? What would tell you so?

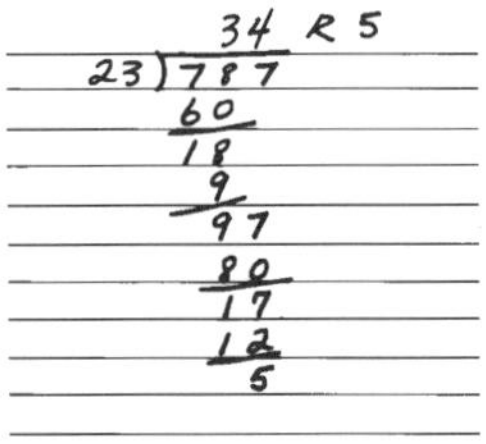

C. **Synthesis and Evaluation Exercises**
High-Level Thought Activities

1. After analyzing the student's algorithm in exercise B3, design your own algorithm. Prove that it works with several examples.
2. Find a concept from the NCTM *Standards* 2000 that you would like to teach. Search professional journals for current articles on research findings and teaching ideas with algorithms and computation.
3. Consider the importance of computational proficiency and the recommendations in the NCTM *Standards* (NCTM, 1989, 2000) that a deemphasis should be placed on tedious paper-and-pencil computation. You are a classroom teacher using textbooks that include multidigit multiplication and long division. You decide to skip that material and allow time for new topics such as number and spatial sense, relations, and functions. Some parents have challenged you. Write a position paper on how you would justify your decision.

Activity 11.25

PORTFOLIO

PORTFOLIO ASSESSMENTS

For Teacher Reflection of Students' Work with Operations on Whole Numbers

Review the student's work in Figure 11.13.

DIRECTIONS

1. Analyze the response made by this student. Create a reflective description of the error patterns you notice and the thought processing displayed by the student through the work shown.
2. Design a remediation plan to help the student overcome the misconceptions with the algorithms. Include the sequential development of concrete, pictorial, and symbolic models to reteach the concept.
3. Design a rubric that would take into account the diversity of answers while being open in your assessment.

Include the rubric in your Professional Portfolio for Job Interviews.

FIGURE 11.13

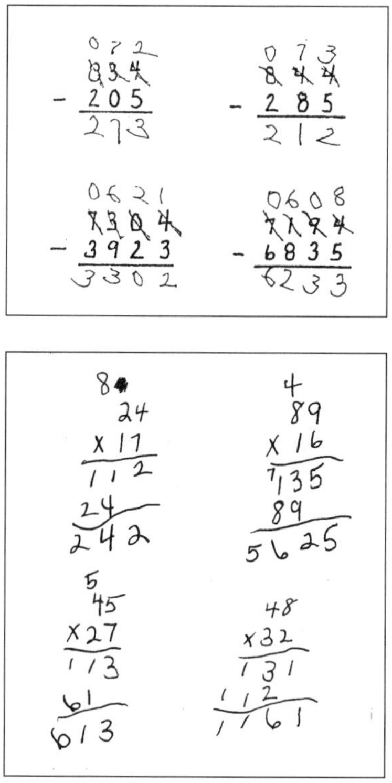

Analyze the misconception patterns.

BIBLIOGRAPHY

For an extended bibliography, see the CD-ROM.

Baek, Jae-Meen. "Children's Invented Algorithms for Multidigit Multiplication Problems." Ed. Lorna J. Morrow and Margaret J. Kenney. *The Teaching and Learning of Algorithms in School Mathematics 1998 Yearbook.* Reston, VA: National Council of Teachers of Mathematics, 1998: 151–160.

Bitter, Gary G., and Mary M. Hatfield. "Implementing Calculators in a Middle School: A Comprehensive Approach." Ed. James T. Fey and Christian R. Hirsch. *Calculators in Mathematics Education,* 1992 Yearbook of the National Council of Teachers of Mathematics. Reston, VA: National Council of Teachers of Mathematics, 1992: 200–208.

Burns, Marilyn. "Arithmetic: The Last Holdout." *Phi Delta Kappan* 75 (1994): 471–476.

Campbell, Patricia F. "Connecting Instructional Practice to Student Thinking." *Teaching Children Mathematics* 4 (October 1997): 106–110.

Campbell, Patricia F., and Martin L. Johnson, "How Primary Students Think and Learn." Ed. Iris M. Carl. *Seventy-five Years of Progress: Prospects for School Mathematics.* Reston, VA: National Council of Teachers of Mathematics, 1995. 21–42.

Capps, Lelon R., and Mary M. Hatfield. "Mathematical Concepts and Skills: Diagnosis, Prescription, and Correction of Deficiencies." Ed. Edward L. Meyen. *Instructional Planning for Exceptional Children.* Denver: Love Publishing, 1979. 279–293.

Carpenter, Thomas P., Megan L. Franke, Victoria R. Jocobs, Elizabeth Fennema, and Susan B. Empson. "A Longitudinal Study of Invention and Understanding in Children's Multidigit Addition and Subtraction." *Journal for Research in Mathematics Education* 29(1) (1998): 3–20.

Carraher, Terezinaha N., David W. Carraher, and Analucia D. Schliemann. "Mathematics in the Streets and in the Schools." *British Journal of Developmental Psychology* 3 (1985): 21–29.

Carroll, William M., and Denise Porter. "Invented Strategies Can Develop Meaningful Mathematics Procedures." *Teaching Children Mathematics 3* (March 1997). 370–374.

———. "Alternative Algorithms for Whole-Number Operations." Ed. Lorna J. Morrow and Margaret J. Kenney. *The Teaching and Learning of Algorithms in School Mathematics 1998 Yearbook.* Reston, VA: National Council of Teachers of Mathematics, 1998. 106–114.

Fennema, Elizabeth, Thomas P. Carpenter, Megan L. Franke, Linda Levi, Victoria R. Jacobs, and Susan B. Empson. "A Longitudinal Study of Learning to Use Children's Thinking in Mathematics Instruction." *Journal for Research in Mathematics Education* 27(4) (1996): 403–434.

Fuson, Karen. "Research on Whole Number Addition and Subtraction." Ed. Douglas Grouws. *Handbook of Research on Mathematics Teaching and Learning.* New York: Macmillan, 1992. 243–275.

Fuson, Karen, Diana Wearne, James C. Hiebert, Hanlie G. Murray, Pieter G. Human, Alwyn I. Olivier, Thomas P. Carpenter, and Elizabeth Fennema. "Children's Conceptual Structures for Multidigit Numbers and Methods of Multidigit Addition and Subtraction." *Journal for Research in Mathematics Education* 28(2) (1997): 130–162.

Graeber, Anna O., and Elaine Tanenhaus. "Multiplication and Division: From Whole to Rational Numbers." Ed. Douglas T. Owens. *Research Ideas for the Classroom: Middle Grades Mathematics.* New York: Macmillan Publishing Company, 1993: 99–115.

Hiebert, James. "Relationships between Research and the NCTM Standards." *Journal for Research in Mathematics Education* 30 (January 1999): 3–19.

Hiebert, James, and Diana Wearne. "Instructional Tasks, Classroom Discourse, and Students' Learning in Second-Grade Arithmetic." *American Educational Research Journal* 30 (November 1993): 393–425.

Kamii, Constance, and Ann Dominick. "The Harmful Effects of Algorithms in Grades 1–4." Ed. Lorna J. Morrow and Margaret J. Kenney. *The Teaching and Learning of Algorithms in School Mathematics 1998 Yearbook.* Reston, VA: National Council of Teachers of Mathematics, 1998. 130–140.

Kamii, Constance, Barbara A. Lewis, and Sally Jones Livingston. "Primary Arithmetic: Children Inventing Their Own Procedures." *Arithmetic Teacher* 41 (December 1993): 200–203.

Labinowicz, Ed. *The Piaget Primer: Thinking, Learning, Teaching.* Menlo Park, CA: Addison-Wesley, 1980.

Madell, Rob. "Children's Natural Processes." *Arithmetic Teacher* 32 (March 1985): 20–22.

Milne, William J. *Standard Arithmetic.* New York: American Book Company, 1892.

Morrow, Lorna J., and Margaret J. Kenney (eds.). *The Teaching and Learning of Algorithms in School Mathematics, 1998 Yearbook.* Reston, VA: NCTM, 1998.

Narode, Ronald, Jill Board, and Linda Davenport. "Algorithms Supplant Understanding: Case Studies of Primary Students' Strategies for Double-Digit Addition and Subtraction." In *Proceedings of the Fifteenth Annual Meeting, North American Chapter of the International Group for the Psychology of Mathematics Education.* Ed. Joanne Rossi Becker and Barbara J. Pence. San Jose, CA: San Jose State University, 1993: 254–260.

National Council of Teachers of Mathematics (NCTM). *Curriculum and Evaluation Standards for School Mathematics.* Reston, VA: NCTM, 1989.

———. *Principles and Standards for School Mathematics.* Reston, VA: NCTM, 2000 (to be published).

Saxe, Geoffrey B. "Candy Selling and Math Learning." *Educational Researcher* 17 (September 1988): 14–21.

Sowder, Judith T., and Judith Klein. "Number Sense and Related Topics." Ed. Douglas T. Owens. *Research Ideas for the Classroom: Middle Grades Mathematics.* New York: Macmillan, 1993. 41–57.

Sowder, Judith T., and Mary M. Wheeler. "The Development of Concepts and Strategies Used in Computational Estimation." *Journal for Research in Mathematics Education* 20 (March 1989): 130–146.

Wentworth, George, and David E. Smith. *Complete Arithmetic.* New York: Ginn, 1909.

CHILDREN'S LITERATURE

Anno, Mitsumasa. *Anno's Mysterious Multiplying Jar.* New York: Philomel Books, 1983.

Giganti, Paul, Jr. *Each Orange Had 8 Slices.* New York: Greenwillow Books, 1992.

Pinczes, Elinor J. *One Hundred Hungry Ants.* Boston: Houghton Mifflin, 1993.

Trivett, John V. *Building Tables on Tables: A Book about Multiplication.* New York: Crowell, 1975.

Viorst, Judith. *Alexander, Who Used to Be Rich Last Saturday.* New York: Atheneum, 1978.

Integrating Technology

Video Vignettes: Lesson Plans in Action

- *Regrouping with Addition and Base 10 Blocks*
- *Understanding Multiplication*

Computer Software Resources

...for Operations with Whole Numbers

Internet Searches

Surfing the Internet for Topics on Whole Number Operations or Algorithms

Use the World Wide Web (WWW) and navigate through the system, searching for new information under major headings and subheadings similar to the following:

Mathematics Education
  Algorithms
  Operations of Whole Numbers
GO to Internet Resources for the K–12 Classroom at **www.ncsa.uiuc.edu.**
GO to Ask Dr. Math at **forum.swarthmore.edu.**
Whole Numbers
  Addition
  Subtraction
  Multiplication
  Division

- *Remember*... the Web is fluid ... new topics and ways to search for topics change daily.
- Be adventurous ... think of some new things you could try.

12

Common Fractions and Decimals

Activities Index

IN THE TEXT

ON CD-ROM

This chapter provides techniques and ideas for developing meaning for fractional and decimal numbers. The central theme is how we can teach fractions and decimals so that students develop number sense and operation sense and can apply them to problem situations. This is not an easy task because rules and tricks are associated with these topics. Think about how you were taught to multiply fractions—multiply the top numbers and multiply the bottom numbers. Did the answer make sense? Probably not! Take just a minute and create a realistic word problem for $\frac{1}{3} \times \frac{5}{6}$ and for $1\frac{3}{4} \div \frac{1}{2}$.

Now think about how you were taught to multiply decimals—forget about the decimal points and just multiply like whole numbers, then count up the number of decimal points in the two factors and move over that number of places in the answer. Do such rules build a sense for the operation to enable you to create realistic word problems? A major change must occur in how we view fractions and decimals. Hopefully the activities and suggestions in this chapter will provide you with a variety of fraction and decimal interpretations and representations.

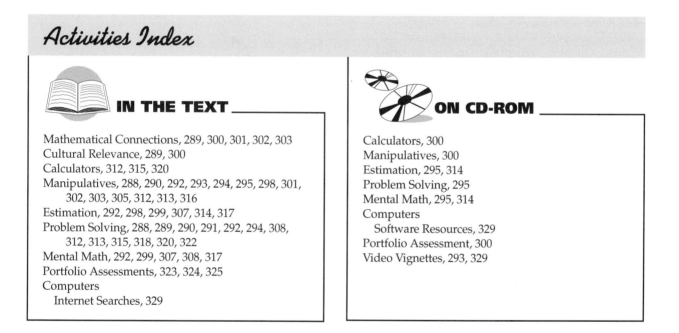

Fractions become more difficult to understand because they can be interpreted from several perspectives: part-whole of region (area model), measure, set, ratio, and division. Streefland (1993) describes the many problems students have confusing the various meanings of fractions in different contexts (scale factor, unit of measure, part-whole, ratio, and so forth). Middleton, van den Heuvel-Panhuizen, and Shew (1998) suggest that some difficulties in teaching fractions can be attributed to the extent that the differences between rational and irrational numbers are emphasized and taught as isolated topics rather than the similarities emphasized and connections strengthened.

For more background on fractions, you may check the CD-ROM for properties, definitions, and interpretations. Researchers recommend that more than one interpretation of fraction should be used and that initial instruction should begin from a part-whole perspective. The NCTM *Principles and Standards* (2000) recommend that students represent fractions in a variety of meaningful situations and that solutions should be based on students' sense of number (Box 12.1). Experience with a variety of concrete models offers a foundation for building abstract ideas. Depending on the instructional approach, different types of concrete models are used—measurement models or unit set models (Figure 12.1). Both models, as well as others, are fully discussed in the Teaching Strategies section.

FIGURE 12.1

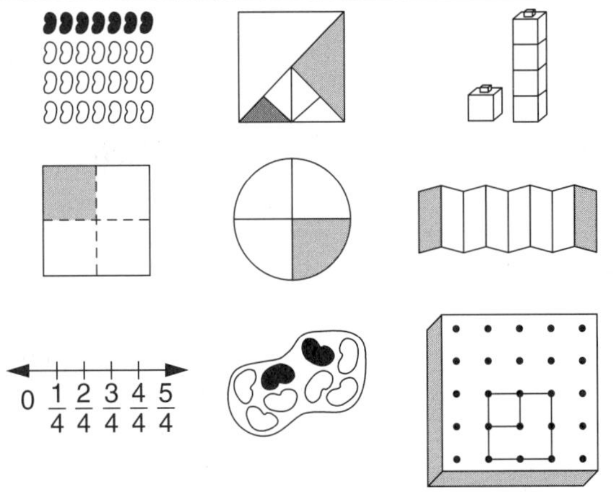

Models for fractions.

Interpretation of Fractions

Part-Whole of Region (Area Model). In this interpretation, a whole unit is subdivided into equal parts. The common circular and rectangular models play a key role. This fraction interpretation is en-

BOX 12.1 Curriculum and Evaluation Standards

Fractions and Decimals

In grades K–4, the mathematics curriculum should include fractions and decimals so that students can—

- Develop concepts of fractions, mixed numbers, and decimals.
- Develop number sense for fractions and decimals.
- Use models to relate fractions to decimals and to find equivalent fractions.
- Use models to explore operations on fractions and decimals.
- Apply fractions and decimals to problem situations.

Number and Number Relationships

In grades 5–8, the mathematics curriculum should include the continued development of number and number relationships so that students can—

- Understand, represent, and use numbers in a variety of equivalent forms (integer, fraction, decimal, percent, exponential, and scientific notation) in real-world and mathematical problem situations.
- Develop number sense for whole numbers, fractions, decimals, integers, and rational numbers.
- Investigate relationships among fractions, decimals, and percents.
- Develop and use order relations for whole numbers, fractions, decimals, integers, and rational numbers.
- Extend their understanding of whole number operations to fractions, decimals, integers, and rational numbers.
- Understand how the basic arithmetic operations are related to one another.
- Develop and apply number theory concepts (for example, primes, factors, and multiples) in real-world and mathematical problem situations.

Source: National Council of Teachers of Mathematics, 1989, pp. 57, 91.

countered often in textbooks for elementary school. Teachers may use commercial materials such as fraction pizzas that have premarked pieces. These materials are important to explore; however, teachers should also provide opportunities for students to create their own fraction materials in which the activity requires the child to assign values to the regions. Such activities link the language labels to the materials and provide meaningful contexts. Paper folding done in the activity "Cover Up" (later in the chapter) and illustrated in Figure 12.2 is a valuable experience. Children produce not only a fractional strip set to use for developing operations, but they see the result of folding congruent rectangular strips into smaller and smaller pieces.

FIGURE 12.2

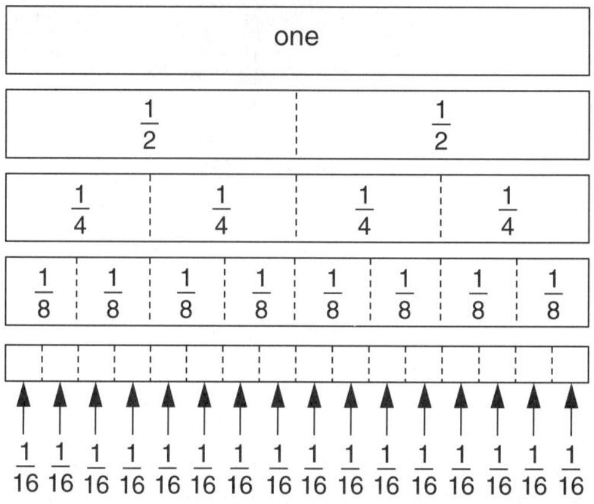

Folding rectangular strips for fractional part of region.

Measure. Fractions as a linear measure can be viewed from an area perspective or a number line model. The fraction strips mentioned earlier can be used as a measure of a given length. Cuisenaire rods can serve as a measure of one specific rod to another (Figure 12.3). Use a large piece of yarn to represent a given amount and have students subdivide it and label the points. Each of these activities represents a greater level of sophistication in the thinking required. Langford and Sarullo (1993) suggest connecting common fraction ideas to measurement ideas by using straws as a nonstandard unit of length to measure rectangular regions. Children can place segments of straws of a given unit along the edge of the region to determine fold lines.

Set. In fractional parts of a set, the whole becomes a given number of objects rather than a region (Figure 12.4). For example, there are a dozen eggs. One-fourth of them are used to make a pie. In this example, the task becomes one of partitioning the set of twelve into four equal-size sets. The whole must be seen in a different way, which is harder for children and should be done in meaningful modeling situations. Hunting (in Bezuk and Bieck, 1993) found that students partition continuous quantities (such as a

FIGURE 12.3

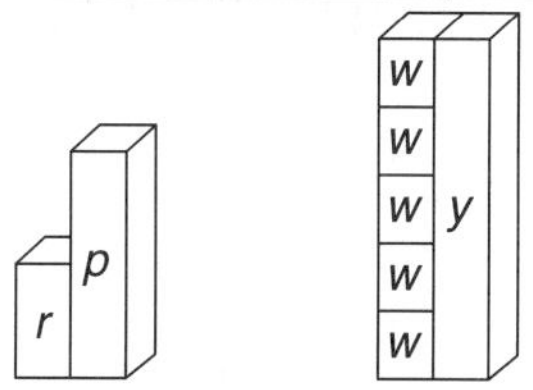

Cuisenaire rods to measure fractional parts.

FIGURE 12.4

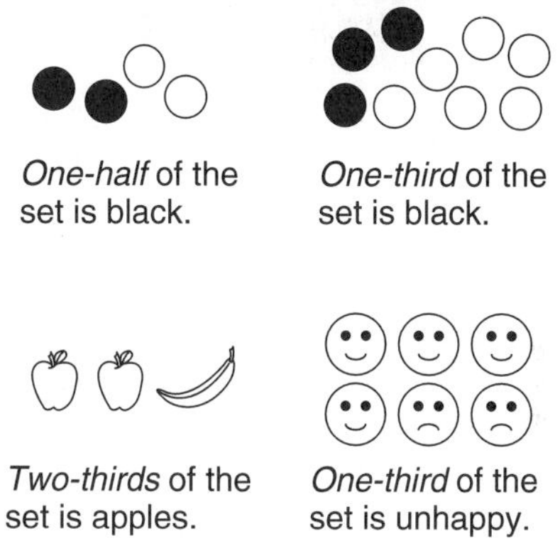

One-half of the set is black.
One-third of the set is black.
Two-thirds of the set is apples.
One-third of the set is unhappy.

Fractional part of a set.

Check Your Mathematics Knowledge

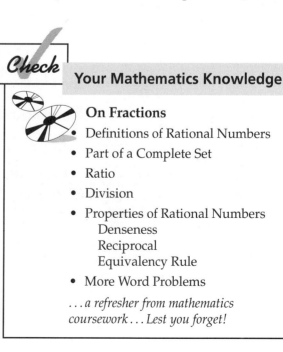

On Fractions

- Definitions of Rational Numbers
- Part of a Complete Set
- Ratio
- Division
- Properties of Rational Numbers
  - Denseness
  - Reciprocal
  - Equivalency Rule
- More Word Problems

. . . a refresher from mathematics coursework . . . Lest you forget!

region) differently from sets (or discrete quantities). He concluded that students may need an understanding of fractions as continuous quantities before understanding problems involving sets.

Ratio. A fraction such as $\frac{2}{3}$ can also represent a ratio, which means that two elements of one set are present for every three elements of another set. Students may have more difficulty with this interpretation (Figure 12.5). More aspects of the concept of ratio are addressed in Chapter 13.

FIGURE 12.5

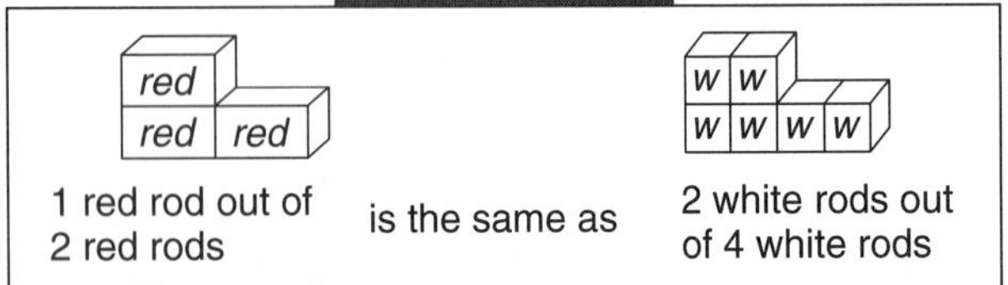
red
red red
w w
w w w w
1 red rod out of 2 red rods
is the same as
2 white rods out of 4 white rods

Fractions as ratios.

Division. Fractions denote division of one set by the other. This concept is presented after much work with fractions has taken place in the elementary school. Many elementary texts introduce this concept after decimal representations are presented because the answers will be fractional parts. Here are the equivalent forms for $\frac{10}{6}$:

$$\frac{10}{6} = 6\overline{)10} = 10 \div 6$$

TEACHING STRATEGIES: FRACTIONS

Fractions are difficult to understand for several reasons. Frequently models are not explored and used when concepts are developed. Many teachers demonstrate with pictorial models rather than concrete aids. The study of fractional numbers should begin with a variety of models and shapes. Manipulative models should be used throughout the middle school years. Unless this practice is followed, fractions will continue to be difficult to learn and internalize. Too often the rule is presented before the underlying foundation has been laid. Many terms are unclear and ambiguous such as "reduce to lowest terms." Do we really mean to make the answer smaller? What about *cancel* and what does this term imply? Operations on whole numbers and on fractional numbers are not the same. For example, multiplying whole numbers yields a product larger than either factor, while multiplying two proper fractions results in a product smaller than either factor. Proper, concise language used when teaching operations with fractions plays an important role in the correct interpretation of the numbers.

The NCTM *Principles and Standards* (NCTM, 2000) specify a deemphasis on paper-and-pencil computation with fractions. More time should be spent on creating a number sense for fractions through estimation with familiar fractions and mental computation. Oral language and concrete models are necessary components of building a conceptual understanding of fractions. In the *Standards,* it is recommended that operations with fractions and mixed numbers be limited to common fractions with simple denominators that can be visualized and correlate to simple real-world situations.

Activity 12.1

MANIPULATIVES PROBLEM SOLVING

CUISENAIRE RODS AS FRACTIONAL PARTS OF A COMPLETE SET

Find as many Cuisenaire rods that represent $\frac{1}{3}$ as you can. How can you prove that each is exactly one-third of the basic unit of wholeness?

Now find Cuisenaire rods that represent $\frac{2}{3}$.

How can you prove that each is exactly two-thirds of the basic unit of wholeness? (*Hint:* If you proved one-third, proving two-thirds should follow easily.)

Whole-to-Part Activities

Early activities with fractions should begin with the whole-part meaning of fractions. Having children divide concrete objects such as a paper, egg cartons, or scored candy bars provides direct experiences to avoid such misconceptions as wanting the "biggest half." Young children do not understand the difference between the whole and parts of a whole. An orange broken into sections means more oranges to the young child. The emphasis is on developing the concept of a whole, parts, equal-size parts, and oral names (Payne, Towsky, and Huinker, 1990).

An important, and often disregarded, consideration is to discuss what is represented by a whole. The *whole* is whatever is designated as the unit. Take a sheet of $8\frac{1}{2} \times 11$ paper. Tear it in half. Each of the two congruent regions represent one-half. Show a notepad made of half-sheets of paper. Tear off one sheet and ask if this sheet is a whole piece of paper. It is in relationship to the pad of paper, but it is one-half when compared to the former whole sheet. Do the same for a pad consisting of paper the size of one-fourth the original sheet. Again ask the preceding questions and refer to the importance of knowing what is designated as the unit. This is important in terms of understanding operations with fractions discussed later in this chapter.

Activity 12.2

MATHEMATICAL CONNECTIONS

NAME THE FRACTION—FIND THE WHOLE

MATERIALS

- Pictures of real-world objects involving equal parts
- Shapes and parts of that shape

PROCEDURE

Hold up pictures or parts of a shape. Have students name the fraction. The purpose is to show that naming the fractional part cannot be done without seeing what represents the whole except in the case of some common fractions in circular form (one-half is always thought of as a half-circle regardless of the size of the circle). Include examples of egg cartons, ten-frames, all types of area models, and tires on cars or bicycles.

Activity 12.3

MATHEMATICAL CONNECTIONS · PROBLEM SOLVING

EDIBLE FRACTIONS!

MATERIALS

- Cup of Fruit Loops, fun-size bag of M&Ms, or Skittles

PROCEDURE

1. Have students predict the number of each color in their bag or cup. Open the bag and sort into like groups.

Activity Continues

2. Make a bar graph of the data. Compare the data to predictions. Write five sentences that describe the data (for example, I have fewer orange than green).
3. Write number sentences to describe the data in terms of fractional parts, decimals, and percents (for example, red: $\frac{4}{18} = 22\% = 0.22$).
4. Combine data with entire class and make predictions on the color compositions. Discuss color preferences, how this relates to marketing. If using M&Ms discuss the addition of blue as the newest color.

Supporting the NCTM *Principles and Standards* (2000):

- Worthwhile Mathematical Tasks; Students Role in Discourse—The Teaching Principle
- Mathematics as Problem Solving; Connections; Reasoning; Representation

Fractions can be seen as parts of sets of objects. In this model, the unit represents the entire set.

Show a set of soft drinks.
How many cans are in the set? 6
Remove 2 cans. Suppose we drank 2 cans.
What part of the set did we drink? $\frac{2}{6}$
What does the 6 represent?
What does the 2 represent?
Show an egg carton with 12 eggs.
How many eggs are in the set? 12

Suppose I use 5 eggs to make a cake. Remove them.
What part of the set did I use? $\frac{5}{12}$
What does the 12 represent?
What does the 5 represent?
Repeat with connecting cubes, colored tiles, wooden cubes, and other concrete materials.

Cultural Contributions

CULTURAL RELEVANCE

ORIGINS OF FRACTIONS

It is important for students to know that fractions are not a new idea. The ancient Egyptians on the African continent invented unit fractions (numerator is one).

Cultural Contributions Continues

Grades 4–8

Students should be able to understand that systems of measurement were developed in response to the needs of real-life situations. For example, the building of the African pyramids required extremely accurate measurement to construct right angles in the base so that any error would be less than 1 part in 27,000 or $\frac{1}{27000}$. (Strong, 1990)

Activity 12.4

PROBLEM SOLVING

WHAT'S THE PART?

With Cuisenaire Rods

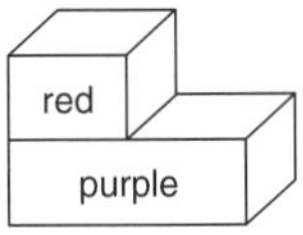

Purple is the whole, what fraction is red?

With Pattern Blocks

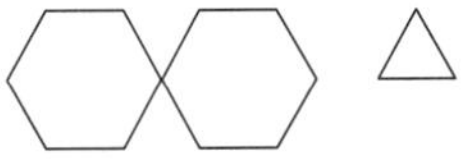

Two hexagons are the whole, what fraction is the triangle?

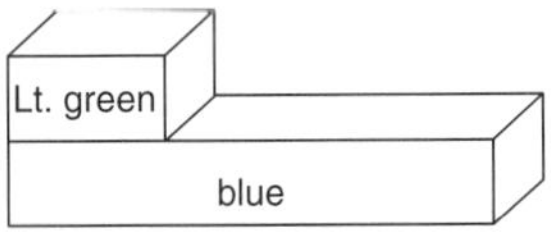

Blue is the whole, what fraction is green?

With Egg Cartons

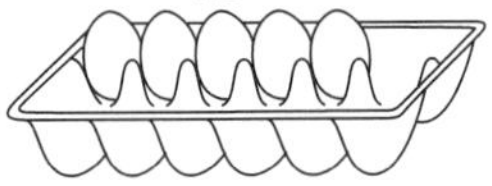

If a dozen is the whole, what fraction is this?

Have children make up their own problem cards and share with each other.

Partitioning Activities

Initial work with fractions should be based on the natural activities children experience with sharing. The sharing may be a region such as a candy bar or a set such as a bag of marbles. *Partitioning* relates to dividing parts into equal shares. In the concept development of fractions, emphasis should be on unit fractions (where the numerator is one) and on common fractions.

The region model (a circle, square, or rectangle partitioned into parts) is usually the child's introduction to work with fractions and is found in most children's elementary school textbooks. It is important not to limit the shape to the "pie shape" or circle. Various regions should be used by exploring fractions with shapes on a geoboard, with pattern blocks, Cuisenaire rods, and paper strips. Have children subdivide regions into equal-size sections. In this way, they will understand the meaning of the subdivisions (Figure 12.6).

FIGURE 12.6

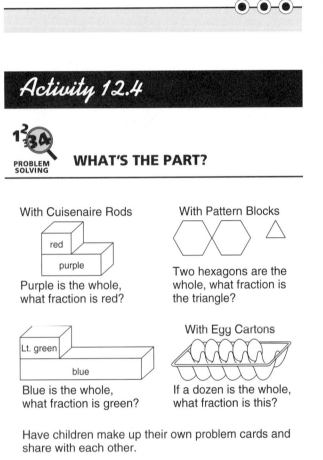

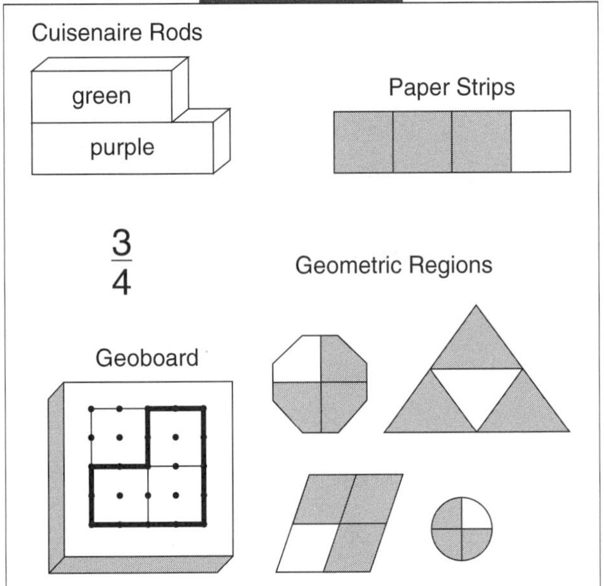

Representation of $\frac{3}{4}$.

An effective technique to develop the concept of comparing unit fractions is to take rectangular strips of construction paper, 4 × 18 inches, and fold each into various pieces. The following activity explains the procedure required to make the concrete material seen in Figure 12.2.

Use the rectangular fraction kit to compare unit fractions and to understand that the larger the denominator, the smaller the fractional size because the whole has been partitioned into more parts. A common misconception is that the larger number means more even when it appears as the denominator in a fractional number. The teacher can select three unit fractions and ask children to order from least to greatest using the fraction kit as a concrete model.

The fraction strip chart in Figure 12.7 also serves as a powerful visual tool for comparing fractions. It is made essentially the same way as the rectangular fraction strips except all the strips are pasted on a 9 × 12 piece of construction paper. Every strip can be compared with the whole unit 1, without the need to move many strips around.

FIGURE 12.7

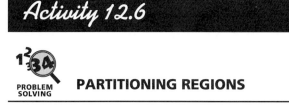

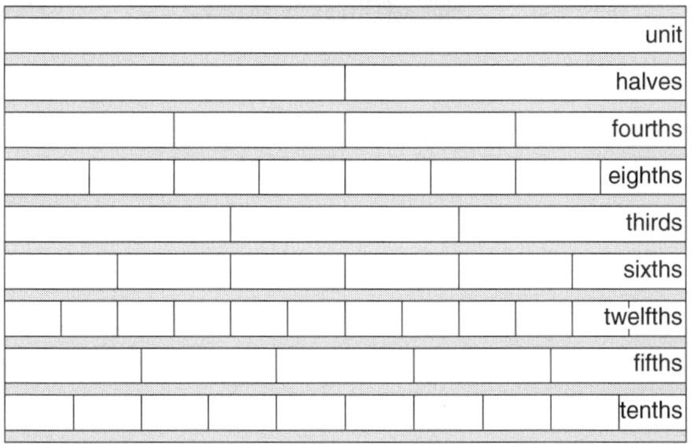

The fraction strip chart.

Activity 12.5

PROBLEM SOLVING

MAKING A RECTANGULAR FRACTION KIT

MANIPULATIVES

MATERIALS

- Five 4 × 18 inch strips of construction paper, each strip a different color
- Scissors
- Pen or pencil

PROCEDURE

1. Take one of the colored strips (indicate a specific color). Label it "one whole." Take another strip. Fold it in half lengthwise. How many equal pieces result? 2
2. Cut on the fold. What is each piece in terms of the whole (1 out of 2 or $\frac{1}{2}$). Label each piece "$\frac{1}{2}$."
3. Take a third strip. Fold in half, and fold in half again. Open it out and count how many equal pieces. 4 With older children use the language that says "$\frac{1}{2}$ of $\frac{1}{2}$" to relate to multiplication later. What is each piece in terms of the whole? ($\frac{1}{4}$) Cut on the fold. Label each piece "$\frac{1}{2}$."
4. A fourth strip is folded into 8 equal pieces and labeled as "$\frac{1}{8}$," and the fifth strip is folded into 16 equal pieces and labeled as "$\frac{1}{16}$."
5. For connecting level activities, have students write about the equivalent names for one whole, one half, etc., and the patterns they notice (more folds make smaller pieces but larger denominator).

Activity 12.6

PROBLEM SOLVING

PARTITIONING REGIONS

MATERIALS

- Pipe cleaners
- Regions—poster board shapes, attribute blocks, or whatever

PROCEDURE

Have students take a shape and use the pipe cleaners to partition it into different fractional parts. This action allows children to subdivide regions in various ways. Have them show nonexamples as well as examples.

Such activities develop flexible understandings of representing fractions. The tasks encompass a variety of concepts from equivalent fractions, use of the identity element for multiplication, multiplication as an area model, to the property of denseness.

Equivalence Activities

Equivalence is another key concept associated with fractions. Equivalence relates to the various ways that show equal shares of the same portion. Some educators believe that equivalence plays such a key role in the understanding of fractions that all work with the operations should be delayed until after the fourth grade. The NCTM *Principles and Standards* (NCTM, 2000) suggest that students should have efficient strategies to compute with fractions by the time they leave middle school. This practice would allow ample time to develop the concept of equivalence and would set the stage for later work with unlike denominators and mixed numbers. As part of equivalence, the identity element of multiplication, or property of one for multiplication, should be emphasized. The aforementioned fraction kit or fraction strip chart are ways to show how the one whole strip can be renamed, as is the problem-solving exploration activity with the fraction strip chart (Figure 12.7).

Activity 12.7

PROBLEM SOLVING

EQUIVALENT FRACTIONS: FRACTION STRIP CHART

MATERIALS

- Fraction strip chart (Figure 12.7)

PROCEDURE

For one whole—For each row, into how many pieces has the whole been partitioned? Write the name for one for each strip such as $\frac{2}{2}$, $\frac{3}{3}$, $\frac{4}{4}$. Discuss the pattern you see. What rule can you create? What other names for 1 can you name?

For one-half—Place a straightedge so that the edge is perpendicular to the mark showing $\frac{1}{2}$. Look down the rows of strips for pieces that also are equivalent to $\frac{1}{2}$ such as $\frac{2}{4}$, $\frac{3}{6}$, $\frac{5}{10}$. Make lists of all the equivalent names for $\frac{1}{2}$ and also a list of all the pieces that do not equal $\frac{1}{2}$. What patterns do you see? What kind of numbers will not be on the list of equivalent names? Repeat this procedure with all unit fractions on the chart.

Supporting the NCTM *Principles and Standards* (2000):

- Worthwhile Mathematical Tasks; Learning Environment—The Teaching Principle
- Mathematics as Problem Solving; Mathematics as Representations, Patterns

Activity 12.8

PROBLEM SOLVING MENTAL MATH

THINK ABOUT $\frac{1}{2}$

1. What comes to your mind when you see or hear $\frac{1}{2}$? List 10 things.
2. Name 10 ways to name or describe $\frac{1}{2}$. For example:

   $\frac{1}{2}$ is also 0.5

   $\frac{1}{2}$ is also $\frac{2}{4}$

   $\frac{1}{2}$ is also $\frac{50}{100}$

Activity 12.9

MANIPULATIVES

ROLLING EQUIVALENTS

MATERIALS

- Lima beans or counters
- Three dice
- Fraction strip chart (wholes, halves, thirds, fourths, fifths, sixths)

PROCEDURE

Players take turns rolling the three dice. When it is your turn, roll the dice and choose any two to make a fraction less than or equal to one using the fractions on the chart. (Roll a 2, 3, 3, and you make $\frac{2}{3}$ or $\frac{3}{3}$.) Put counters to correspond to the fraction you chose. If you chose $\frac{2}{3}$, you could put beans on 2 of the thirds or 4 beans on the sixths. The first person to fill the chart wins.

Activity 12.10

PROBLEM SOLVING ESTIMATION

FRACTION WAR

Two to four players

MATERIALS

Deck of fraction cards made as: $\frac{1}{2}$, $\frac{1}{3}$, $\frac{2}{3}$, $\frac{1}{4}$, $\frac{2}{4}$, $\frac{3}{4}$, $\frac{1}{5}$, $\frac{2}{5}$, $\frac{3}{5}$, $\frac{4}{5}$, $\frac{1}{6}$, $\frac{2}{6}$, $\frac{3}{6}$, $\frac{4}{6}$, $\frac{5}{6}$, $\frac{1}{8}$, $\frac{2}{8}$, $\frac{3}{8}$, $\frac{4}{8}$, $\frac{5}{8}$, $\frac{6}{8}$, $\frac{7}{8}$, $\frac{1}{10}$, $\frac{2}{10}$, $\frac{3}{10}$, $\frac{4}{10}$, $\frac{5}{10}$, $\frac{6}{10}$, $\frac{7}{10}$, $\frac{8}{10}$, $\frac{9}{10}$, $\frac{1}{12}$, $\frac{2}{12}$, $\frac{3}{12}$, $\frac{5}{12}$, $\frac{7}{12}$, $\frac{8}{12}$, $\frac{9}{12}$, $\frac{10}{12}$, $\frac{11}{12}$

PROCEDURE

Deal all cards face down. Each player turns up a card and the fraction of greatest value takes all the rest. Continue until all cards are used or someone has collected all the cards. If an equivalent fraction occurs, players turn up another card for rematch. Winner is the player with the most cards. May refer to fraction strip chart to handle disputes.

Many experiences are needed to internalize the concept of equivalence of fractions before the symbolic level holds meaning. The identity element for multiplication should be related to whole numbers as well as to fractional numbers.

For example:

What happens when you take any fraction and multiply it by 1?

$\frac{1}{2} \times 1 = ?$ $\frac{3}{4} \times 1 = ?$

What happens if you substitute some equivalent name for 1 and multiply a fraction by it? Will it result in the same number?

$\frac{1}{2} \times \frac{2}{2} = ?$ $\frac{3}{4} \times \frac{4}{4} = ?$

Is the outcome an equivalent name for that fraction? Why? Try several other fractions. What can you generalize from this experience?

Activity 12.11

MANIPULATIVES

FRACTIONS ON THE GEOBOARD

MATERIALS

- Geoboards and geobands
- Geoboard recording paper

PROCEDURE

Make equivalent fractions on the geoboard. Use different colored bands to partition the region. Draw on geoboard recording paper and write the equivalent fractions and why they represent the same amount. This approach helps students see the role of the whole and the parts. Encourage them to construct irregular regions and to name the fractional part represented.

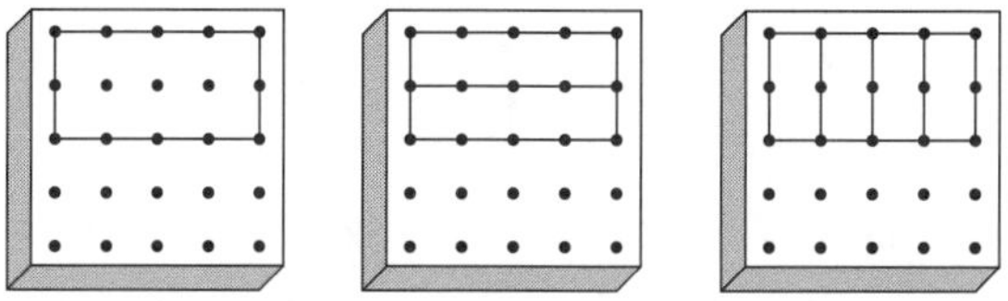

$\frac{1}{2}$ $\frac{2}{4}$ $\frac{4}{8}$

Multiple Bars. Multiple bars (Figure 12.8) offer a helpful way to show equivalent fractions. Many children are hindered with the concept development of fractions when they are not familiar with multiples. The multiple bars are cut into horizontal strips and used as explained in the following activity.

FIGURE 12.8

1	2	3	4	5	6	7	8	9	10
2	4	6	8	10	12	14	16	18	20
3	6	9	12	15	18	21	24	27	30
4	8	12	16	20	24	28	32	36	40
5	10	15	20	25	30	35	40	45	50
6	12	18	24	30	36	42	48	54	60
7	14	21	28	35	42	49	56	63	70
8	16	24	32	40	48	56	64	72	80
9	18	27	36	45	54	63	72	81	90
10	20	30	40	50	60	70	80	90	100

Multiple bars.

Multiple bars can be used to see how dividing a fraction by 1 or an equivalent name for 1 produces another equivalent name for that fraction. If the resulting fraction cannot be divided again, the fraction is said to be "expressed in lowest terms" or "expressed in simplest form." These terms are preferred by the authors because such terms are more meaningful to students than the phrase "reduced to lowest terms" and do not hold the misconception that reducing results in a reduction in the size of the region.

Video Vignette

Rectangles and Fractions

Mrs. Torres poses the task to picture a rectangle composed of color tiles with these specifications: $\frac{1}{2}$ is red, $\frac{1}{4}$ is yellow, and $\frac{1}{4}$ is green. What tiles were used in Mrs. Torres' rectangle?

- Why does Mrs. Torres direct their thinking to the chart of factors?
- What tiles do you think form Mrs. Torres' rectangle?
- In the independent activity ($\frac{1}{3}$ red and $\frac{2}{3}$ green), what probing techniques does she use when talking with Carlos about his answer?

Activity 12.12

PROBLEM SOLVING

EQUIVALENT FRACTIONS: MULTIPLE BARS

MATERIALS

- Multiple bars (Figure 12.8)

PROCEDURE

Place the 1 bar above the 8 bar to show a set of equivalent fractions for $\frac{1}{8}$. Read various equivalent names aloud. What name for 1 was used to multiply by $\frac{1}{8}$ to form $\frac{4}{32}$? ($\frac{4}{4}$) Write this number sentence:

$$\frac{1}{8} \times \frac{4}{4} = \frac{4}{32}$$

Repeat for other equivalent fractions. Place the 3 bar above the 4 bar. What fraction is formed? ($\frac{3}{4}$) Read other equivalent names for $\frac{3}{4}$. Tell what name for 1 was used to form each one.

1	2	3	4	5	6	7	8	9	10
8	16	24	32	40	48	56	64	72	80

Practice activities should not always focus on finding an equivalent fraction given the numerator or denominator. Some activities should include problems such as:

$$\frac{2}{3} \times \frac{?}{?} = \frac{12}{18}$$

What name for 1 has been multiplied by $\frac{2}{3}$?

$$\frac{12}{20} \div \frac{?}{?} = \frac{3}{5}$$

What name for 1 has $\frac{12}{20}$ been divided by?

Multiple Embodiments. We believe that multiple embodiments should always be used to help build concept development. However, in the interest of space, most of the remaining teaching strategies are covered using fraction kits made from circular or rectangular regions. Try using Cuisenaire rods, multiple bars, geoboards, and pattern blocks to teach the same strategies as modeled here with fractions. It is important to use other area models, such as rectangular and square regions. These models help children focus on the question of what is the basic unit. The widely recognizable shape of a half or fourth of a circle may give false impressions of understanding that can be detected more quickly using other shapes. You may prefer certain materials over others. Generally, students learn best when teachers feel comfortable using the materials they have chosen.

The patterns for making a circular fraction kit are on the CD-ROM. Additional equivalence activities and games are also on the CD-ROM as well as a video vignette of middle school students exploring fractions.

Many experiences are necessary in order for children to feel totally comfortable with fractional equivalencies. Activities with a variety of materials are helpful as well as playing games in a comfortable, nonthreatening environment. The following two games are from Marilyn Burns' *The Math Solution* (1984). They are to be played using the rectangular strip fraction kit described in Figure 12.2.

Activity 12.13

MANIPULATIVES

COVER UP

MATERIALS

- Rectangular fraction kit (Figure 12.2)
- Number cube marked with these sides: $\frac{1}{2}$, $\frac{1}{4}$, $\frac{1}{8}$, $\frac{1}{8}$, $\frac{1}{16}$, $\frac{1}{16}$

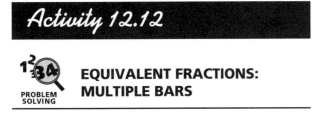

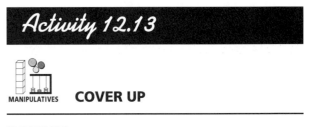

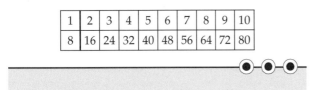

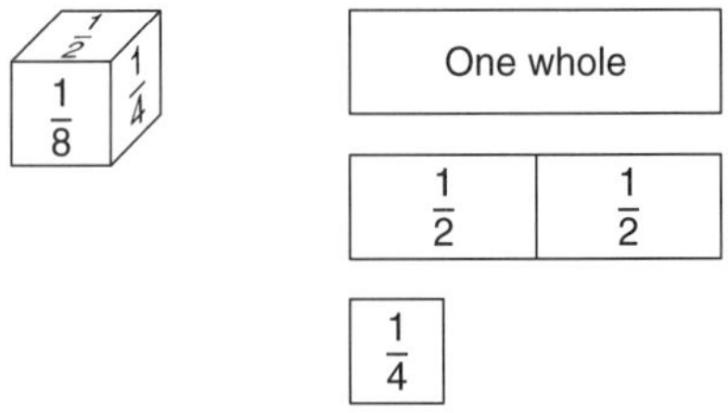

PROCEDURE

The object of the game is to be the first player to completely cover the whole strip with the other fractional pieces from the kit without overlapping.

Roll the number cube and the player rolling the least fractional number goes first. The first player rolls the number cube. This fraction tells the piece that the student puts on the whole strip. Each student builds the fractions on his or her own whole strip. If an overlap is the result, the player loses a turn and must wait until the fraction named on the number cube can be placed. For

Activity Continues

example, if the player needs only a small piece, such as an $\frac{1}{8}$ or $\frac{1}{16}$, to cover up and win, rolling a $\frac{1}{2}$ or $\frac{1}{4}$ cannot be used. The first person to cover up the entire strip wins.

$\frac{1}{2}$	$\frac{1}{4}$	$\frac{1}{8}$	$\frac{1}{8}$

Activity 12.14

MANIPULATIVES

UNCOVER

MATERIALS

- Rectangular fraction kit (Figure 12.2)
- Number cube marked with sides: $\frac{1}{2}, \frac{1}{4}, \frac{1}{8}, \frac{1}{8}, \frac{1}{16}, \frac{1}{16}$

PROCEDURE

The object of the game is to be the first player to uncover the whole strip completely. The player must roll exactly what is needed to uncover the strip in order to win. Each player has the whole strip covered with the two $\frac{1}{2}$ pieces.

$\frac{1}{2}$	$\frac{1}{2}$

Students roll the number cube, and the player rolling the least fractional number plays first. The first player rolls the number cube. The fraction on the cube tells how much the player can remove. An exchange or trade may be necessary before the fraction can be removed. This is the object behind the game as it focuses on equivalencies. For example, if a student rolls an $\frac{1}{8}$ on the first roll, one of the $\frac{1}{2}$ pieces needs to be exchanged in order to remove an $\frac{1}{8}$. Encourage students to verbalize the equivalencies exchanged.

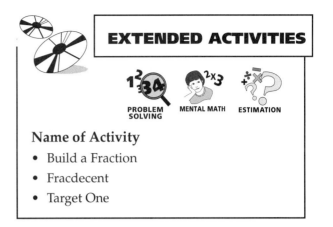

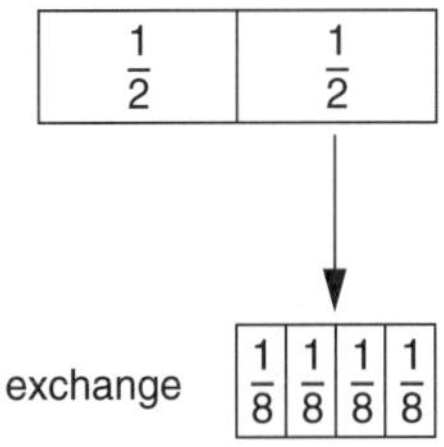

These two games help children work on equivalent fractions, estimate fractions, compare fractions, and determine relative size of fractions. After students have become familiar with these games and are ready to be introduced to the connecting level, have them record the steps on paper or small individual chalkboards as they do the action.

For example:

$\frac{1}{8}$ is rolled. On the strip, there is the $\frac{1}{4}$ piece. The problem is then $\frac{1}{4} - \frac{1}{8}$. The exchange is to trade $\frac{1}{4}$ for $\frac{2}{8}$ which is:

$$\begin{array}{r} \frac{1}{4} = \frac{2}{8} \\ -\frac{1}{8} = \frac{1}{8} \\ \hline \frac{1}{8} \end{array}$$

If the recordings are done as the exchanges are made, transfer from the concrete level to the symbolic level is much greater. These two games provide excellent readiness for addition and subtraction of unlike denominators. Check additional activities on the CD-ROM that develop multiple relationships of fractions.

Texas Instruments' fraction calculator, the Math Explorer, can simplify fractions automatically or by entering the greatest common multiple. Students can perform the four basic operations using the built-in fraction algorithm. This calculator presents many possibilities for students to test their knowledge of fractions with the power of immediate feedback. Estimation should also be included with calculator activities.

EXTENDED ACTIVITIES

PROBLEM SOLVING · MENTAL MATH · ESTIMATION

Name of Activity

- Build a Fraction
- Fracdecent
- Target One

Operations with Fractions

Exploratory fraction work should introduce the use of physical materials to solve simple real-world problems involving fractions. Many students have learned computations with fractions as procedures without developing the underlying conceptual knowledge about fractions. Since most instruction of operations with fractions occurs in the middle grades, many teachers rely on the mathematics textbook for the instruction. Dorgan (1994) investigated how textbooks covered fractions and found an average of about a third of the fifth-grade textbook devoted to fractions. She also determined that instruction in computational procedures formed the major component of the textbook approach to fractions with limited coverage of quantitative reasoning about fractions.

Although an assortment of fraction models should be used, in the interest of space the activities shown here focus primarily on the circular and rectangular fraction kits. Notice that a discussion is included at the end of this section presenting multiple embodiments. Each activity, presented here with addition and subtraction, shows the sequence with which the operations should be taught. Notice that the activities grow gradually more complex.

Addition and Subtraction

Each step in the following procedures is outlined in detail. The actions should be replicated with many examples using different materials. Manipulatives model these concepts, but all action should be accompanied with verbal descriptions, followed by the written steps, to link the algorithm with the words. There must be a link and match between what is done, said, and written. As you read, you are encouraged to model each of the examples to solidify your understanding. Remember subtraction situations with fractions must include more than take away. All problem structures (missing addend, comparison, start unknown) that you encountered for whole numbers apply to fractions. In these examples, notice the modeling that accompanies the situation.

Concept:
Adding Fractions with Like Denominators

Situational Problem:
Alfinio ran $\frac{1}{4}$ mile to Jose's house, then ran another $\frac{1}{4}$ mile to the country market. How far did he run in all?

Procedure:

The problem: $\frac{1}{4} + \frac{1}{4}$

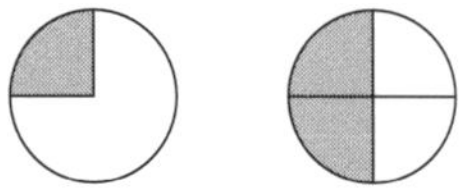

- Place a whole on the desk. Put a fourth on it.
- Add another fourth to it. How many in all?
- Record that one-fourth + one-fourth = two-fourths. Remember the numerators are added and the denominators are a label of the fractional pieces.
- Answer: $\frac{2}{4}$

Concept:
Adding Fractions with Mixed Numerals

Situational Problem:
The recipe for cookies calls for $1\frac{1}{3}$ cups of white sugar and $1\frac{1}{3}$ cups of brown sugar. How much sugar is needed?

Procedure:

The problem: $1\frac{1}{3} + 1\frac{1}{3}$

- Place two groups of one whole and one-third on the desk. Combine like units.
- Answer: $2\frac{2}{3}$

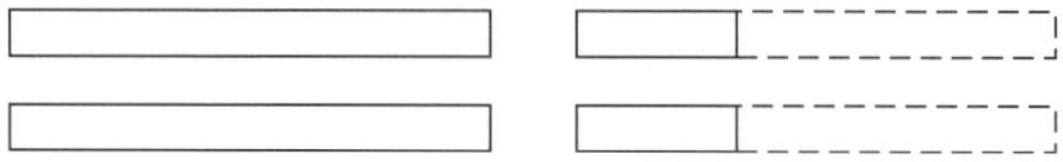

Concept:
Adding Fractions with Unlike Denominators

Situational Problem:
Lucinda practiced her flute $\frac{1}{2}$ hour in the morning and $\frac{1}{4}$ hour in the evening. What fractional part of an hour did she practice that day?

Procedure:

The problem: $\frac{1}{2} + \frac{1}{4}$

- Denominators are not the same, so the first step is to see whether one number is a multiple of the other.
- If it is, use the least common denominator. In other words, is one of the denominators a multiple of the other?
- Exchange $\frac{1}{2}$ for $\frac{2}{4}$. Record when ready for the connecting level.
- Proceed in the same manner as adding like denominators.
- Answer: $\frac{3}{4}$

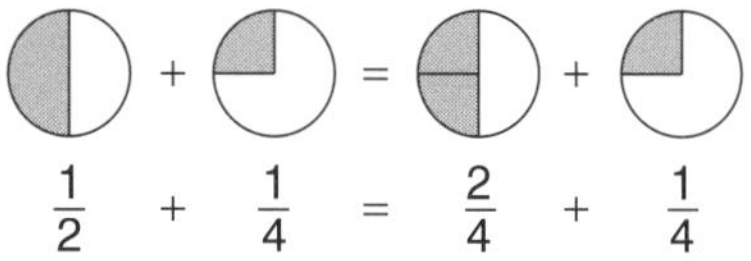

Concept:
Adding Mixed Numerals with Regrouping

Situational Problem:
Mrs. Levison's pattern for a suit says $2\frac{2}{3}$ yards are needed for the jacket and $1\frac{1}{2}$ yards are needed for the skirt. How much material should she buy to make the suit?

Procedure:

The problem: $2\frac{2}{3} + 1\frac{1}{2}$

- Form the two numbers with the fraction kit pieces.

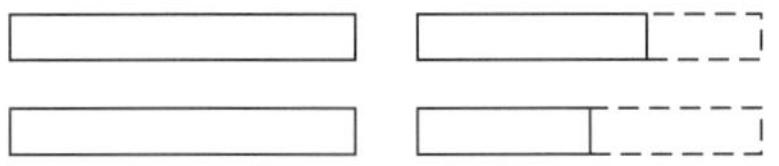

- Combine like units.

To combine the fractional units:

- Is one number a multiple of the other? (no)
- Exchange both pieces for the least common denominator (thirds and halves can become sixths). Exchange $\frac{2}{3}$ for $\frac{4}{6}$ and $\frac{1}{2}$ for $\frac{3}{6}$.
- Combine the sixths (7). Six-sixths can be regrouped as a whole with one-sixth left.
- Answer: $4\frac{1}{6}$

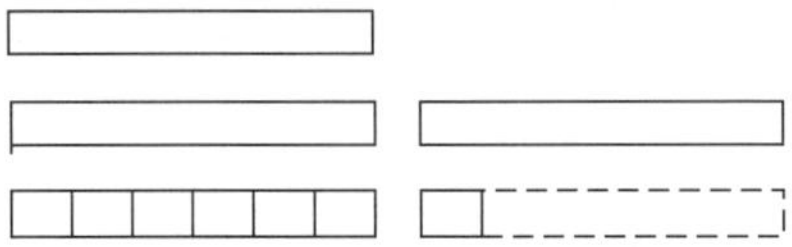

Concept:
Subtracting Fractions with Like Denominators

Situational Problem:
Janet has $\frac{3}{4}$ cup of peanut butter. She uses $\frac{1}{4}$ cup for frosting. How much peanut butter does she have left?

Procedure:

The problem: $\frac{3}{4} - \frac{1}{4}$

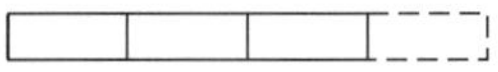

- Place three-fourths on a whole.
- To subtract one-fourth from three-fourths, simply take away the one-fourth piece.

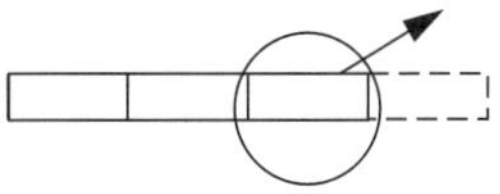

- Answer: $\frac{2}{4}$.

Concept:
Subtracting Fractions with Unlike Denominators (Take-Away Interpretation)

Situational Problem:
Mr. Nyo has $\frac{2}{3}$ gallon of gasoline. He uses $\frac{1}{4}$ gallon for his chain saw. How much gasoline does he have left?

Procedure:

The problem: $\frac{2}{3} - \frac{1}{4}$

- Place the whole piece with two-thirds on top.
- In order to subtract one-fourth, find the least common denominator. What piece can be exchanged for thirds and fourths?

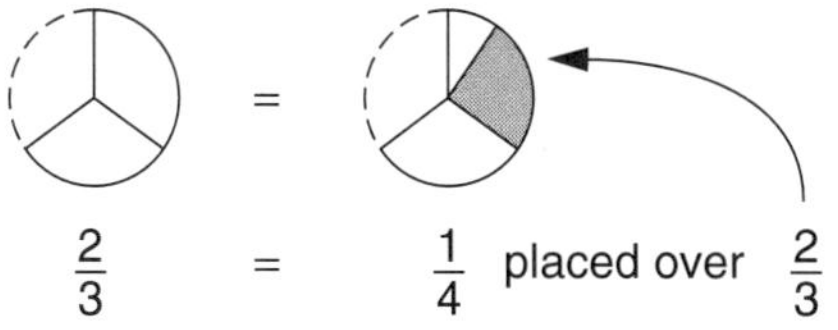

- Exchange $\frac{2}{3}$ for $\frac{8}{12}$ and $\frac{1}{4}$ for $\frac{3}{12}$.
- Now the denominators are the same, so subtract the numerators. Take away three-twelfths.

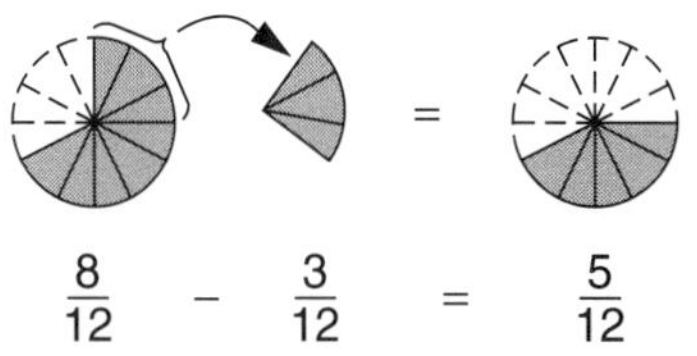

- Answer: $\frac{5}{12}$.

With subtraction, the take-away method is most commonly used; however, modeling should be done for the missing addend and comparison interpretations. Be sure that appropriate word problems accompany the modeling.

For Missing Addend Interpretation

Situational Problem:
Marcus needs $\frac{2}{3}$ cup of solvent but discovers he only has $\frac{1}{4}$ cup. He calls a friend to get some more solvent. How much more does he need?

Procedure:

The problem: $\frac{2}{3} - \frac{1}{4}$

- Begin with $\frac{1}{4}$ piece on the whole.
- How much must you add to $\frac{1}{4}$ to make $\frac{2}{3}$? (Optional—show $\frac{2}{3}$ as "target.")
- Exchange thirds and fourths for common equivalent pieces. Exchange $\frac{1}{4}$ for $\frac{3}{12}$ and $\frac{2}{3}$ for $\frac{8}{12}$.
- How much should you add to $\frac{3}{12}$ to get $\frac{8}{12}$?
- Add twelfths until you get $\frac{8}{12}$.
- Answer: $\frac{5}{12}$

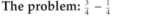

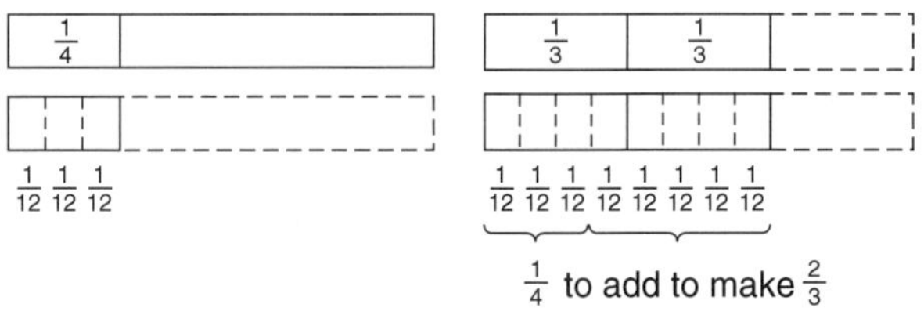

For Comparison Interpretation

Situational Problem:
The recipe for sugar cookies calls for $2\frac{1}{3}$ cups sugar. The recipe for oatmeal cookies calls for $1\frac{1}{2}$ cups sugar. How much more sugar is needed for sugar cookies?

Procedure:

The problem: $2\frac{1}{3} - 1\frac{1}{2}$

- Show the two whole pieces and the one-third piece.
- Show the one whole and one-half piece. (Remember, for comparison both numbers are modeled to be compared and the difference is found.)

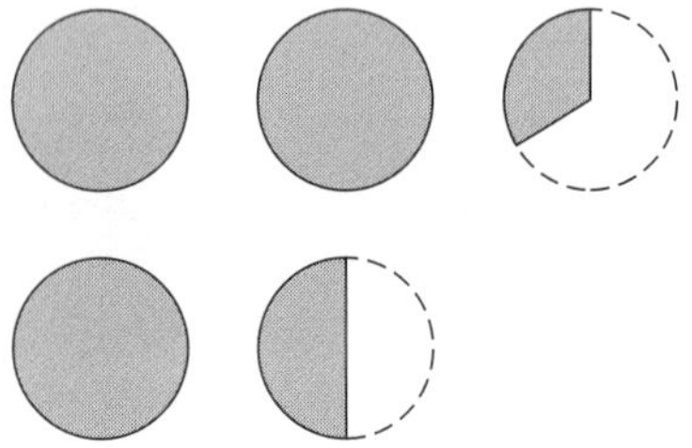

- Compare like pieces. The whole pieces "cancel" each other. Compare fractions.

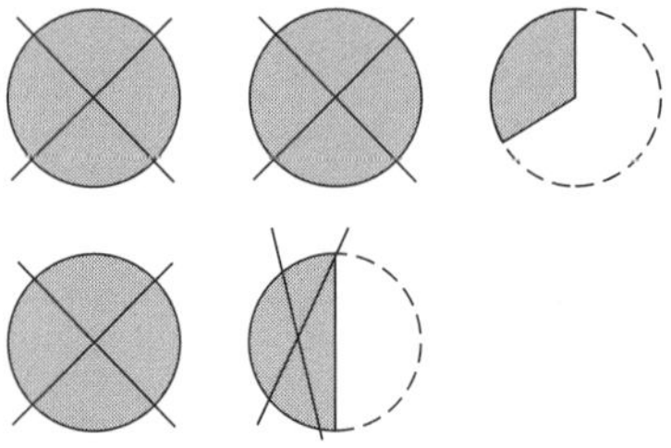

- The whole can become two halves and the halves "cancel" each other. How much is left? (one-half and one-third)
- Exchange for common denominators to give final answer. Exchange $\frac{1}{2}$ for $\frac{3}{6}$ and $\frac{1}{3}$ for $\frac{2}{6}$.
- Answer: $\frac{5}{6}$.

Activity 12.15

MANIPULATIVES

SHOWING GEOBOARD OPERATIONS

MATERIALS

- Geoboards and geobands
- Geoboard recording paper

PROCEDURE

Use geoboards to show operations of fractions. All four operations can be done on the geoboard as shown here for

Activity Continues

addition and subtraction. Have students write about their thinking and prove their answers by showing the regions. Colored bands and colored pencils help show the various parts more clearly. (Dotted lines show whole region.)

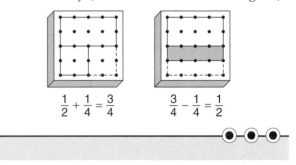

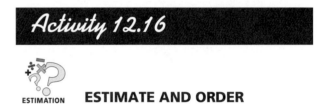

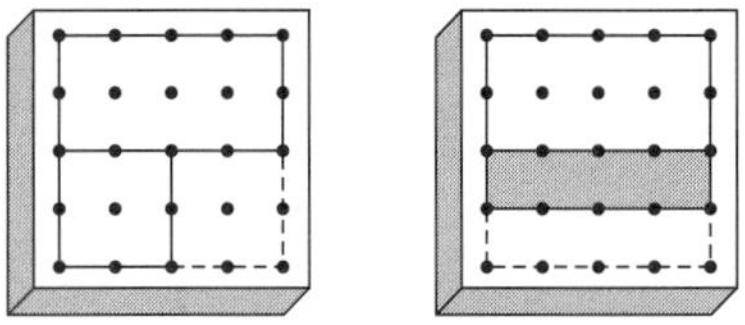

$\frac{1}{2} + \frac{1}{4} = \frac{3}{4}$ $\frac{3}{4} - \frac{1}{4} = \frac{1}{2}$

Activity 12.16

ESTIMATION

ESTIMATE AND ORDER

MATERIALS

- Forty cards with a different addition or subtraction fraction problem on each one

PROCEDURE

Shuffle the cards and deal out five cards to each player, face down. When the dealer says go, the players arrange their cards by estimating the answers so that the answers are in order from least to greatest.

Winner: The first player to order the cards correctly wins the hand. That player is the new dealer.

Supporting the NCTM *Principles and Standards* (2000):

- Number and Operation; Mathematics as Reasoning, Problem Solving
- Worthwhile Mathematical Tasks—The Teaching Principle
- The Learning Principle

Alternative Solutions. The same approach for developing alternative solutions used in Chapter 11 for whole numbers applies as well to fractions. Students who have a rich background of solving problems through multiple means will likely *not* use the step-by-step process of the traditional algorithms. They will combine the wholes first, then approach the fractions. Subtraction will create a variety of alternative solutions. For example, students might find that the natural starting point for this problem would be to break down the wholes:

One characteristic of students' thinking about fractions is their successful use of solving problems in the context of real-life scenarios. Eating pizza or pie and sharing cookies or candy bars are situations that give meaning to fraction procedures. More discussion of alternative solutions will be presented after the section in this chapter on multiplication and division.

Estimation. Estimation with fractions and mixed numbers should include some of the same strategies used for whole numbers: Using nice numbers (or compatible numbers), front-end, and rounding. Students need to establish benchmarks associated with recognizing numbers that are close to 1, $\frac{1}{2}$, or 0. This approach encourages them to consider the quantity represented by the fraction rather than get involved with the mechanics of changing to like denominators. Such activities help to emphasize that numbers in the numerator and denominator need to be compared to each other to determine their relative size. Number sense applies to fractions as much as it does to whole numbers.

Present situations in which students must estimate whether the fraction is closer to 0, to $\frac{1}{2}$, or to 1. Have students name some fractions near 0, $\frac{1}{2}$, and 1. Develop a sense of relative magnitude of a fraction, such as $\frac{3}{4}$ is large compared to $\frac{1}{3}$, about the same as $\frac{5}{8}$, and closer to 1 than to 0. It is important to establish the relationship of the numerator and denominator (that the numerator is one-half of the denominator) to help children become comfortable with this activity. They should also see that any fractional number close to 1 will have a numerator and a denominator that approach the same number. Develop activities where students must figure mentally fractional parts, such as 9 of the 20 people at the picnic were men. Was this about 0, about $\frac{1}{2}$, or about 1? If 12 of the 15 children in Mrs. Henry's class are girls, can we say over half the class is girls? Can you mentally picture a candy bar with $\frac{4}{10}$ of it cut off?

These activities are also helpful in estimating sums and differences of fractions and in giving children some checkpoint about the correctness of their answers in computational problems. You may need to write the problems on large cards to hold before the class in a limited time period or to write them on the overhead projector and control the time period to be shown. Children (and adults) have many insecurities about estimating with fractions because they have not had sufficient opportunities to practice this skill.

Activity 12.17

MENTAL MATH

ROLL AND SHOW

MATERIALS

- Fraction strip chart and two number cubes, each labeled $\frac{1}{2}$, $\frac{1}{3}$, $\frac{1}{4}$, $\frac{2}{3}$, $\frac{3}{4}$, $\frac{5}{8}$.

PROCEDURE

Player rolls the two cubes and identifies the larger fraction. The other player calls out, "Add" or "Subtract." The player must take the two numbers and perform the stated operation. The answer can then be shown and proven with the fraction strip chart.

Winner: The player with the most points when time is called.

Activity 12.18

ESTIMATION

ESTIMATION WITH FRACTIONS

PROBLEM

Look quickly at the fractional number or numbers and decide whether they are about 1, about $\frac{1}{2}$, or about 0. Determine the sum or difference.

$\frac{7}{12} + \frac{3}{6} = ?$ $\qquad$ $\frac{4}{10} + \frac{11}{10} = ?$

$\frac{2}{9} + \frac{7}{8} = ?$ $\qquad$ $\frac{9}{20} + \frac{4}{5} = ?$

$\frac{8}{9} - \frac{4}{5} = ?$ $\qquad$ $\frac{10}{9} - \frac{1}{12} = ?$

Problems can also include mixed numbers. Ask students to round to the nearest whole number and add or subtract.

$2\frac{4}{5} + 2\frac{9}{10} = ?$ $\qquad$ $3\frac{1}{9} + 8\frac{8}{10} = ?$

$7 - 2\frac{6}{7} = ?$ $\qquad$ $4\frac{8}{12} - \frac{7}{9} = ?$

Mixed Numbers. When adding and subtracting mixed numbers, students can benefit from knowing how to change a mixed number to an improper fraction. The terms *proper* and *improper fractions* are ones that may be difficult for students to remember. A *proper fraction* is one whose numerator is of a lower degree (less) than its denominator, and an *improper fraction* is one whose numerator is of a greater degree (more) or is equal to its denominator. Hence,

Proper | Improper

$$\frac{7}{12} \qquad \frac{12}{7} \quad \frac{8}{8}$$

Elementary textbooks also show students how to change improper fractions to an equivalent proper fraction. This procedure necessitates changing the improper fraction to a *mixed number,* which is a whole number and a proper fraction. Check more activities with fractions and mixed numbers on the CD-ROM.

Activity 12.19

FRACTIONS AND THE EYE OF HORUS

CULTURAL RELEVANCE · MATHEMATICAL CONNECTIONS

Zaslavsky has written books and articles on the inclusion of relevant mathematics in a multicultural context. In her study of various cultures, she noted that ancient Egyptian scribes used symbols taken from the Eye of Horus to record measurements as fractions. Give students the Eye of Horus fractions (Zaslavsky, 1993, p. 20) and have them figure a way to show in a picture the sum of all the fractions. What patterns do they notice about these unit fractions? What do these fractions tell us about the Egyptians' understanding of fractional relationships? Explain your answers. Have them investigate how other cultures use fractions.

Eyebrow		$= \frac{1}{8}$
Left Part of Eye		$= \frac{1}{2}$
Center Eye		$= \frac{1}{4}$
Right Part of Eye		$= \frac{1}{16}$
Downsweep Line		$= \frac{1}{32}$
Center Decoration		$= \frac{1}{64}$

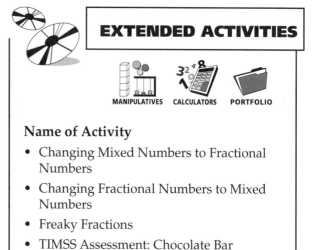

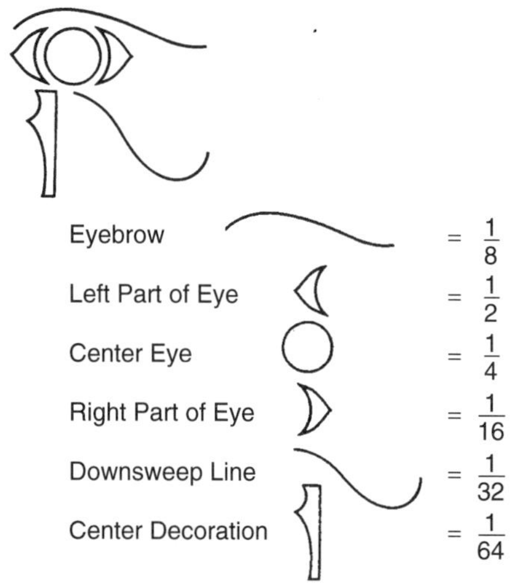

Activity Continues

Supporting the NCTM *Principles and Standards* (2000):

- Mathematics as Connections, Problem Solving; Number Relationships
- Tools to Promote Discourse; Student's Role in Discourse—The Teaching Principle
- The Equity Principle

EXTENDED ACTIVITIES

MANIPULATIVES · CALCULATORS · PORTFOLIO

Name of Activity

- Changing Mixed Numbers to Fractional Numbers
- Changing Fractional Numbers to Mixed Numbers
- Freaky Fractions
- TIMSS Assessment: Chocolate Bar

Multiplication and Division

Multiplication and division of fractions are areas that pose many difficulties for children primarily because the foundation for understanding the underlying concepts is not fully developed. The case too often is that the teacher uses the textbook examples and verbally explains them using a chalkboard or the overhead. Students are moved too quickly to the symbolic level and are given the easy-to-remember but difficult-to-comprehend rules. Errors result when students move symbols around meaninglessly as they rotely learn rules for procedures like the following:

- When multiplying fractions, multiply the numerators and the denominators.
- When dividing fractions, use the reciprocal. (Often rephrased as "Invert the second number and multiply the two numbers.")

Many teachers do not use manipulative materials in intermediate grades or the middle school. There are a limited number of materials available to model various problems. Therefore, the effectiveness of manipulatives is limited. Many examples are needed for adequate practice to solidify one's understanding of these operations with fractions.

An important aspect of multiplication is understanding the term "of" for multiplication and how it relates to whole number multiplication. It is important to build on the prior knowledge students have about whole numbers whenever possible when teaching fractions. Although there are several differences that occur with fractions and whole numbers, it is important to address them and to create bridges of understanding when desirable. The following teaching sequence is suggested:

Write this equation: $3 \times 4 = 12$

Ask students to give the mathematical language and draw the set pictures that model this equation. It says: 3 groups of 4. It means there are 4 in each group and there are 3 groups. This becomes a review of the meaning of multiplication seen in Chapter 10. If teachers use the word "of" from the beginning of multiplication, the transfer of learning will help in problems like those that follow.

Fraction × Whole Number. In problems in which a fractional number is the first factor and a whole number is the second factor, encourage students to model the action. For example, $\frac{3}{4} \times 12$ means you start with 12 and want to find out how much is $\frac{3}{4}$ of that amount (Figure 12.9). The 12 must be divided into fourths, or four groups. Then the numerator tells how many groups to consider—three groups of 3, or 9.

FIGURE 12.9

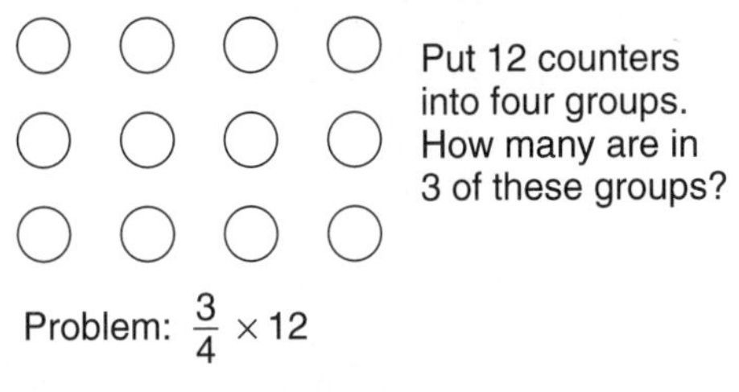

Modeling multiplication of fractions.

Include examples and experiences that are not always the "friendly numbers" that are multiples of each other. For example, have students explore and model with materials or drawings how they would solve $\frac{3}{4} \times 14$. Let them grapple with the notion of partitioning 14 into four groups. How would they subdivide the "leftovers"?

Activity 12.20

MULTIPLYING FRACTIONS—WHOLE NUMBER BY A FRACTIONAL NUMBER

MATERIALS

- Circular or rectangular fraction kits

PROCEDURE

Problem: $2 \times \frac{1}{2}$

Situational Problem: Lesley wants to double a recipe of cookies. The recipe calls for $\frac{1}{2}$ cup sugar. How much sugar will Lesley need to make 2 batches?

Take two groups of the one-half piece and place on a whole. These equal the whole.

In the problem of multiplying with a fraction, the language that accompanies the equation is that there are 2 groups of one-half.

Problem: $\frac{1}{2} \times 2$

Situational Problem: Andy's recipe calls for 2 cups flour. He wants to only use half of the recipe. How much flour will be needed?

Ask whether the commutative principle works for fractions. What is the mathematical language that accompanies this problem? It says: One-half a group of 2. What does it mean? It means there are two wholes and you take one-half of that amount. How do you model this problem? Was the answer the same? Why?

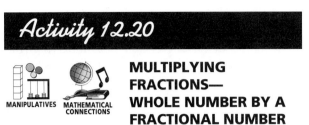

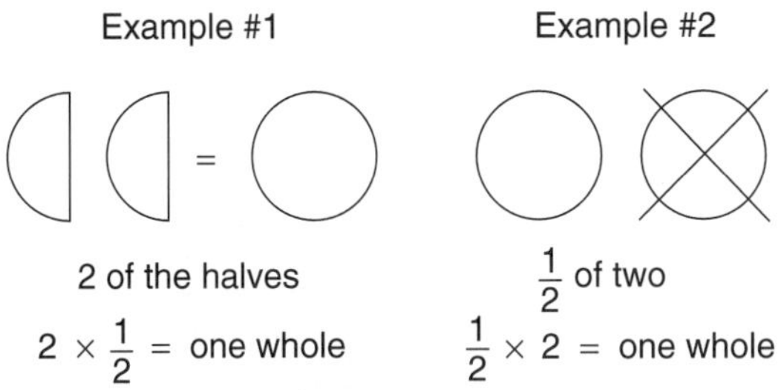

Fraction × Fraction. The next step is to multiply one fractional part by another, no longer relying on a whole number to make the concept easier to understand. Most textbooks represent this concept with an area model. Strips of paper, a modification of the area model, can substitute as a concrete model. The benefits of using an area model for multiplication include serving as a preview of models used in more advanced mathematics, including algebra and integral calculus.

Real-world situations should accompany the modeling. Practical problems should be used before introduction of the algorithm. Remember that the easy path (and commonly used one) appears to just simply give the rule, "Multiply the numerators, multiply the denominators, and get the answer." However, such instruction limits children's intuitive feel for fractions. On the other hand, modeling develops quantitative reasoning so students can estimate the size of the product, observe relationships of the factors, create real-world applications, and judge the reasonableness of their answers.

For example, the problem $\frac{3}{4} \times \frac{1}{2}$ can be modeled with geoboards, counters, drawings, and rectangular or circular regions. Students should be able to explain how the physical materials are used and to interpret the entire operation. Generally the situational problem the child creates to accompany the modeling matches the type of material used. Varying the materials becomes a powerful tool to break out of the typical mindset of formulating problems using pizza or pies. As teachers acquire more confidence in developing students' conceptual understanding of fractions, their observations can become more diagnostic in nature to determine a child's learning style as either part-to-whole or whole-to-part (Figure 12.10).

FIGURE 12.10

PROBLEM: $\frac{2}{3} \times \frac{3}{4}$

Whole-to-Part Learners

3 parts

$\frac{1}{4}$	$\frac{1}{4}$	$\frac{1}{4}$

2 parts

"To take $\frac{2}{3}$ of $\frac{3}{4}$, I need to divide the fourths into 3 parts, or thirds, and consider two of them. There are already 3 parts so two of them makes $\frac{2}{4}$."

Part-to-Whole Learners

$\frac{1}{4}$	$\frac{1}{4}$	$\frac{1}{4}$

"In order to take $\frac{2}{3}$ of $\frac{3}{4}$, each fourth needs to be divided into thirds. Then I need to take two of each third."

$\frac{1}{12}$	$\frac{1}{12}$	$\frac{1}{12}$	$\frac{1}{12}$	$\frac{1}{12}$	$\frac{1}{12}$	$\frac{1}{12}$	$\frac{1}{12}$	$\frac{1}{12}$

2 2 2

"There are 6 of these in all so that makes $\frac{1}{2}$."

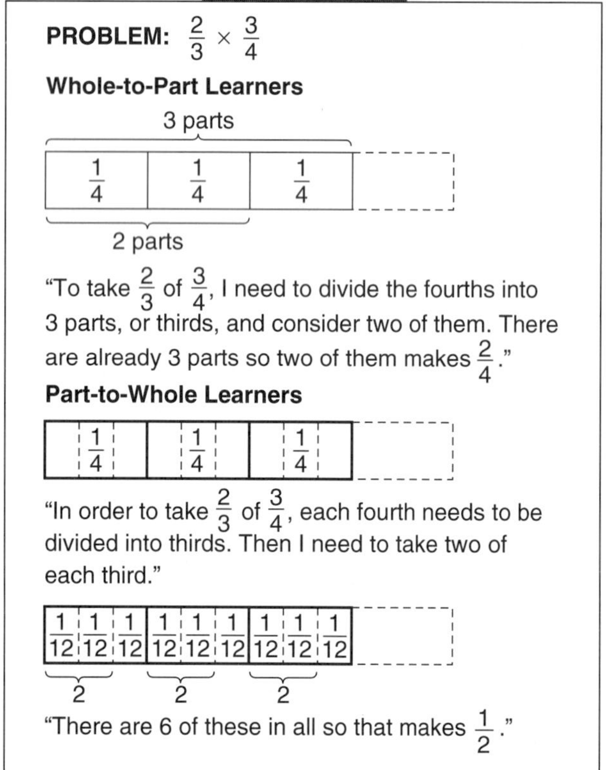

Alternative solutions show learning preference.

Activity 12.21

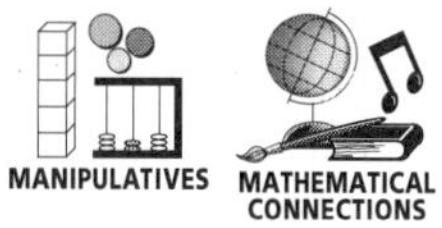

MULTIPLYING FRACTIONS— FRACTIONAL NUMBER BY A FRACTIONAL NUMBER

MANIPULATIVES MATHEMATICAL CONNECTIONS

PROCEDURE

Problem: $\frac{1}{2} \times \frac{1}{4}$

Situational Problem: Lynn's lawn mower needs $\frac{1}{4}$ pint oil to be mixed with gasoline. If only half of the mixture is made, how much oil is needed?

Do we start with halves or fourths? Remember that the second factor tells the number in the group and the first factor tells how many groups.

To model this problem, it becomes critical to have the whole piece as the representative unit. *The one-fourth is one-fourth only in relationship to the whole circular region.* To take one-half of the one-fourth, the one-fourth piece needs to be partitioned into two equal parts. What fractional piece will do this? $\frac{1}{8}$.

Place the two one-eighth pieces on the $\frac{1}{4}$. How much is half of this group? $\frac{1}{8}$.

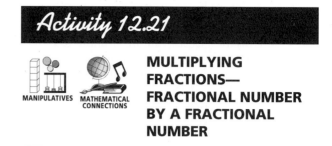

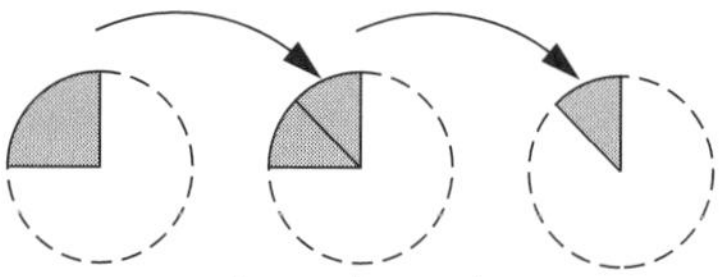

$$\frac{1}{2} \text{ of } \frac{1}{4} = \frac{1}{8}$$

Think about the answer. The one-eighth piece is one-half of the one-fourth, but it is one-eighth in relationship to the whole. Use the commutative property, and have children see the other way to consider this problem and that the answer is still the same, but the modeling is different.

It is important to provide many examples so that students become familiar with how multiplying two fractional numbers will result in a smaller amount than either of the two proper factors. Give practice estimating with fractional numbers, adapting the estimation activity seen at the end of the addition and subtraction strategies. Test the students' understanding by evaluating answers to see if the answer is reasonable. This procedure will help when numbers become too cumbersome for manipulatives to work well, and students still need to check whether their answers are in the correct range of possibilities. Multiplying two mixed numbers is an example of a cumbersome set to manipulate. The

Activity 12.22

MANIPULATIVES

UNDERSTANDING MULTIPLICATION OF FRACTIONS

MATERIALS

- Geoboards and colored geobands, recording paper
- Egg carton and lima beans or two-sided counters
- Rectangular strips

Problem: $\frac{1}{2} \times \frac{2}{3}$

PROCEDURE

1. Make a rectangle on the geoboard to represent the whole.
2. Section off to show two-thirds of the region.
3. How much is one-half of that banded region? Show with another band.
4. How would you show with egg carton and lima beans or with counters?
5. How would you show with folding paper?

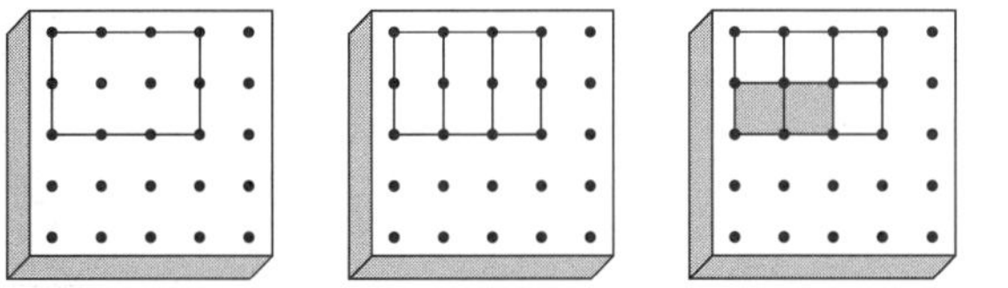

fraction kits do not work well with such problems. If sufficient prior work has been done with multiplying in ways mentioned previously, it is hoped that this process can be understood and estimations can be made to check for accuracy. Include predictions and estimations to develop quantitative understanding of fractions.

Understanding Division. Division with fractions is one of the most difficult concepts to understand. Again, it is important to relate the operation of division with whole numbers and discuss what mathematical language and models are appropriate. Consider the problem $\frac{12}{3} = 4$. What does it mean? There are 12 objects to be divided into groups of 3. The question is "How many groups of 3 are there in 12?" The answer tells you the number of groups of 3 you can get from 12. This is the measurement approach to division. You know the amount in each group and must determine the number of groups that can be made. This is the approach that will be used in division with fractional numbers. Although not every division situation (that is, division by a whole number) can be interpreted as the measurement concept of division, it fits many problems as noted in this section. Read the situational problems for the activities and think about the mathematical language. More examples of word problems are on the CD-ROM.

When students first work with division of fractions, we advocate using a common denominator approach. This keeps the operation as division rather than using the reciprocal, which converts the process into multiplication. Students are familiar with finding common denominators to add and subtract fractions, and the algorithm ties into that prior knowledge. The steps for division are the same as for addition and subtraction: find common denominators, then perform the operation (division) on the numerators.

Activity 12.23

MANIPULATIVES MATHEMATICAL CONNECTIONS

DIVISION OF FRACTIONAL NUMBERS—WHOLE NUMBER BY A FRACTION

PROCEDURE

Problem: $2 \div \frac{2}{3}$

Situational Problem: Mrs. Morozzo needs 2 cups evaporated milk for her recipe. The milk comes in cans that contain $\frac{2}{3}$ cup. How many cans of evaporated milk must she buy? How many groups of two-thirds are in two wholes?

- Begin with 2 wholes.
- The first step is the 2 wholes must be renamed or exchanged for thirds. How many thirds are there in 2? There are 6.
- How many groups of two-thirds can be formed from six thirds?
- Answer = 3. Mrs. Morozzo needs 3 cans of evaporated milk.

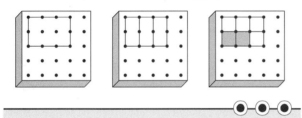

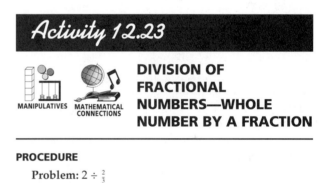

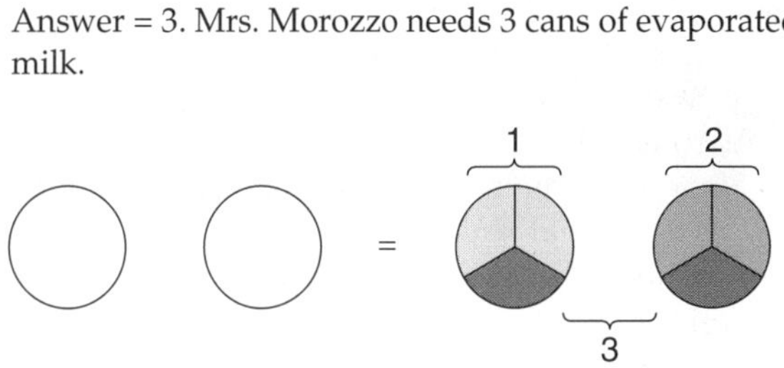

To show how the common denominator is used:

$$2 \div \frac{2}{3} = \frac{6}{3} \div \frac{2}{3} = \frac{6 \div 2}{3 \div 3} = \frac{3}{1} = 3.$$

Activity Continues

Problem: $2 \div \frac{4}{12}$

Situational Problem: Maria has 2 yards of fabric that must be cut into sections of $\frac{4}{12}$ yard each to make costume pieces. How many costumes can be made?

How many groups of four-twelfths are there in 2?

- Rename two whole pieces as twelfths.

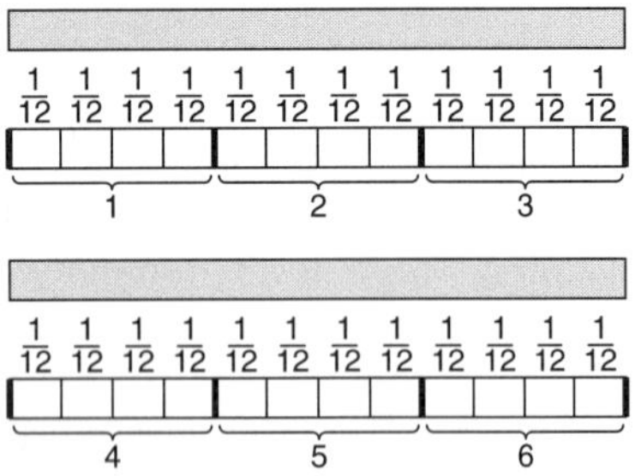

- There are 24 twelfths. Dividing them into groups of four means that 6 groups are made.
- Answer: 6.

To show the common denominator:

$$2 \div \frac{4}{12} = \frac{24}{12} \div \frac{4}{12} = \frac{24 \div 4}{12 \div 12} = \frac{6}{1} = 6$$

How many groups of four-twelfths can be made from the 24 twelfths? Look at the numerators and perform the division of $\frac{24}{4} = 6$. The answer says that there are 6 groups of 4 twelfths in 24 twelfths.

Be sure students have many experiences with this kind of problem where the division results in an equal number of groups. Have them verbalize the steps and then record the symbolic numbers and model the procedures with the fraction kit. The important thing to remember is that using the common denominator method keeps the operation of division clearly in mind rather than the traditional "invert and multiply." For most children and many teachers, the latter approach can better be interpreted as "Ours is not to reason why, simply invert and multiply." The rule is easy to learn, but students have no idea about the reasonableness of answers when problem solving.

Here are some more examples with mixed numbers as the final answer. See how the procedure works with them. Notice the relationship between the divisor and the remainder. The remainder needs to be expressed in terms of the size of the set. What part of a set or group is the remainder? Drawing on students' knowledge of whole number remainders may shed light on this new situation.

Subscripts © *. . . little thoughts below the bottom line*

Activity 12.24

MANIPULATIVES

USING THE COMMON DENOMINATOR METHOD

PROCEDURE

Problem: $2 \div \frac{3}{4}$

Situational Problem: Tenisha has 2 yards of cloth. She needs $\frac{3}{4}$ yard to cover a bar stool. How many stools can she cover? How many groups of three-fourths are there in 2?

- The first step is to rename the two wholes as fourths.
- How many are there? 8. Now the problem becomes:

$$2 \div \frac{3}{4} = \frac{8}{4} \div \frac{3}{4}$$

- How many groups of three-fourths are there in eight fourths?
- Take the eight fourths and place into groups of 3.
- There are two complete groups of 3 and a part of a group or a remainder.
- There are 2 pieces of fourths left. How many fourths make each group? 3. How many are left? 2. There are two-thirds of a complete group left. Answer is $2\frac{2}{3}$.

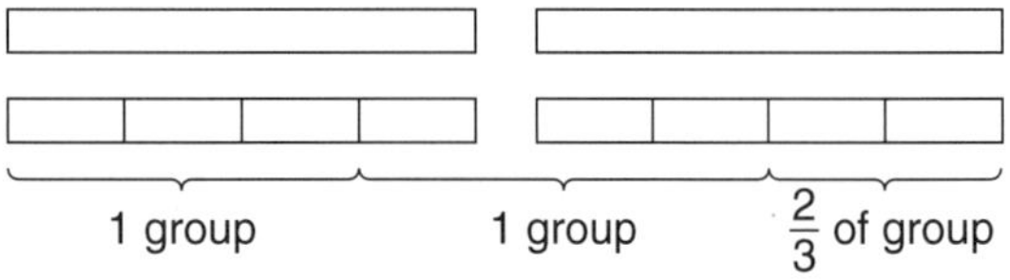

To show the common denominator:

$$2 \div \frac{3}{4} = \frac{8}{4} \div \frac{3}{4} = \frac{8 \div 3}{4 \div 4} = \frac{8 \div 3}{1} = \frac{8}{3} = 2\frac{2}{3}$$

Activity Continues

Problem: $2 \div \frac{5}{6}$

Situational Problem: The 2-foot board must be cut into segments that are $\frac{5}{6}$ foot long. How many segments can be made? What fractional part remains?

How many groups of five-sixths are there in two wholes?

- Rename the two wholes as sixths. How many groups of five-sixths are there in twelve sixths?
- Put the 12 sixths into groups of 5. There are 2 complete groups with 2 pieces left over. These are a part of the group—2 out of 5 that make a complete group.
- Answer: $2\frac{2}{5}$.

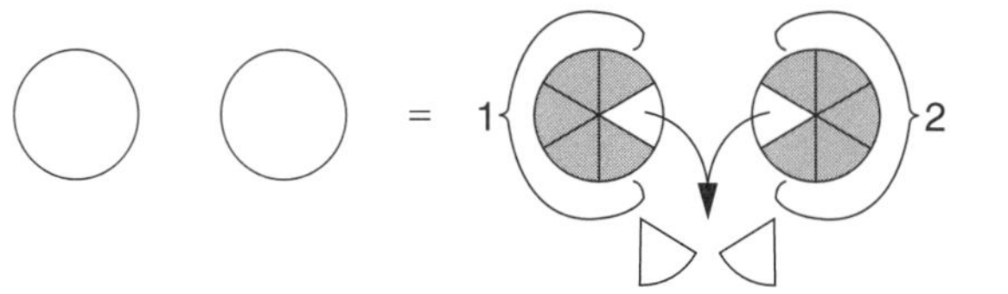

$$2 \div \frac{5}{6} \quad = \quad \frac{12}{6} = \frac{5}{6} \div 2\frac{2}{5}$$

How many $\frac{5}{6}$ are there in 2?

There are 2 sets of $\frac{5}{6}$ and

$\frac{2}{5}$ of a set.

The common denominator method can also be used with fractional numbers divided by fractional numbers. The following activities show how it can be done with the circular fraction kit. The most difficult problems to show and correctly interpret are those in which the divisor is larger than the dividend. The fraction kit can be used to model this process, and some examples are given in this text. Curcio, Sicklick, and Turkel (1987) use rectangular fraction strips to illustrate the algorithm for the division of fractions. To solidify your understanding, you may want to read and compare both approaches.

One important consideration—keep the numbers simple and within the realm of being conceptually understood. The NCTM *Standards* recommend that only common familiar fractions should be used. We must be reasonable about problem-solving situations that would require complicated fractional numbers. We cannot justify including difficult numbers that require a lot of valuable instructional time but have limited, or no, real-life application.

Activity 12.25

MANIPULATIVES

DIVISION OF FRACTIONAL NUMBERS—FRACTION BY A FRACTION

PROCEDURE

Problem: $\frac{1}{2} \div \frac{1}{4}$

Situational Problem: Mrs. Bandera has $\frac{1}{2}$ cup water. She wants to water her plants and pours $\frac{1}{4}$ cup on each plant. How many plants can she water?

- How many groups of one-fourth are there in one-half?
- Place the one-half piece on a whole.
- Rename the half as fourths.

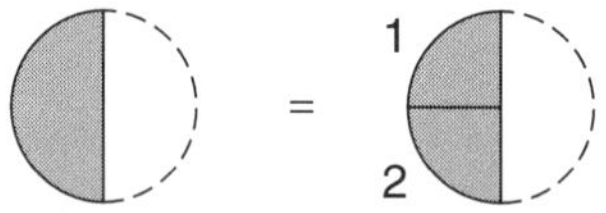

- How many groups of one-fourth can be made from two-fourths? (2)

Problem: $\frac{3}{4} \div \frac{1}{2}$

Situational Problem: Andy has $\frac{3}{4}$ pound birdseed. He knows it takes $\frac{1}{2}$ pound to fill the feeder. How many times can he fill the feeder?

How many groups of one-half can be made from three-fourths?

- First rename the one-half as fourths. How many groups of two-fourths can be made from three-fourths?
- Answer is $1\frac{1}{2}$ (one group of two-fourths can be made and one-half of a group is left).

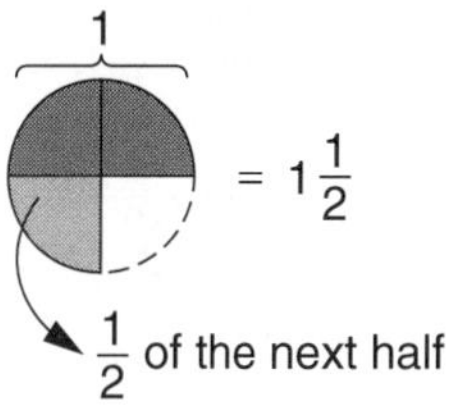

$$\frac{3}{4} \div \frac{1}{2} = \frac{3}{4} \div \frac{2}{4} = \frac{3 \div 2}{1} = \frac{3}{2} = 1\frac{1}{2}$$

Problem: $\frac{2}{3} \div \frac{3}{4}$

Situational Problem: There was $\frac{2}{3}$ yard of plywood left in Tom's garage. He knew he needed $\frac{3}{4}$ yard to complete his project. Does he have enough to complete his project? What fractional part does Tom have?

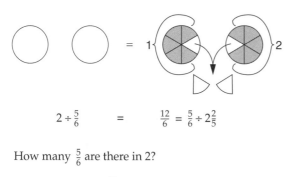

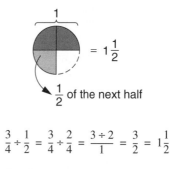

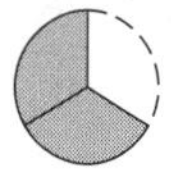

How many groups of three-fourths are in two-thirds?

Activity Continues

- Place the two-thirds on a whole. Notice that three-fourths is more than two-thirds. What fractional part is it?
- What fractional exchanges can be made for both pieces?
- Exchange $\frac{2}{3}$ for $\frac{8}{12}$ and $\frac{3}{4}$ for $\frac{9}{12}$. Compare the "whole" (nine twelfths) to the "part."
- How many groups of nine-twelfths are in eight twelfths? A whole group cannot be made. Therefore, the fractional part is $\frac{8}{9}$ of a group.

$$\frac{2}{3} \div \frac{3}{4} = \frac{8}{12} \div \frac{9}{12} = \frac{8 \div 9}{1} = \frac{8}{9}$$

In dealing with common fractions, the easier approach to use is the measurement interpretation asking how many groups can be made. Ott, Sovok, and Gibson (1991) offer many examples and situations for the partitive meaning of division of fractions. They suggest that partitive division is used in finding unit prices and averages. As you explore examples, think about how you can help students make sense of mathematics as the NCTM *Standards* recommend.

Invented Strategies. Several studies (Empson, 1995; Mack, 1990; Streefland, 1993) indicate that students possess a great deal of intuitive knowledge about fractions. Children, even in first grade, can develop meaningful procedures for solving problems involving equal sharing without explicit instruction in the standard algorithm. Middle school teachers that continue the constructivist teaching from elementary grades find that students are capable of inventing ways to add, subtract, multiply, and divide fractions without direct instruction on procedures or algorithms.

Presenting a context for understanding operations with fractions helps the students' development of understanding. Situations dealing with recipes naturally involve the concept of ratios and present opportunities for students to use familiar referents such as cups and teaspoons. Brinker (1998) presents the strategies her middle school students used to invent procedures for solving fractions and mixed-number multiplication problems. Samples of her students' thinking and their written explanations show a great deal of creative, powerful mathematical reasoning.

Many researchers are looking at the sophisticated mathematical thinking and powerful exchange of ideas that comes from children's invented solutions to fraction problems. To appreciate the constructivist's classroom and see the nature of the reasoning, we urge you to read the vignettes described by Brinker (1998), Kieren (1995), Mack (1998), and Warrington and Kamii (1998). Kieren points out that premature formalism leads to symbolic knowledge that children cannot connect to the real world and results in an inability to develop number sense and reasoning about fractions. You have heard those same warnings concerning whole number computation that is based on teaching the standard algorithm. Armstrong and Bezuk (1995) present a prototype of activities for conceptually teaching multiplication and division of fractions.

The following two examples of children's thinking come from a first-grade classroom (Empson, 1995, p. 111). The problem was:

> Seven candy bars were equally shared among three children. How much candy would each child get?

Two students' drawings show how the partitioning was done (Figure 12.11).

FIGURE 12.11

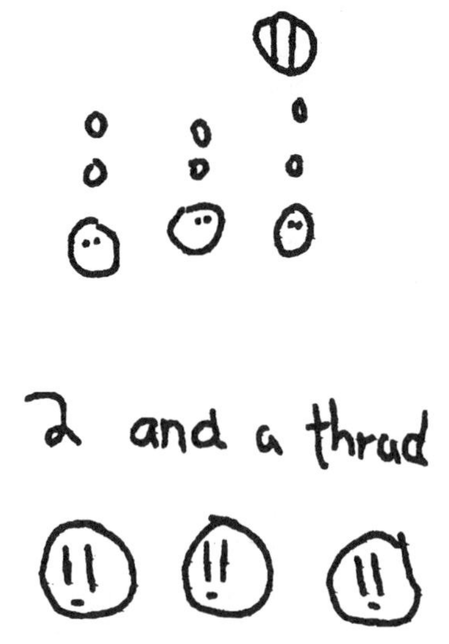

Two examples of children's sharing seven candy bars among three children by partitioning the last candy bar into thirds.

Another classroom example comes from fifth and sixth graders (Warrington, 1997) who had this problem presented to them:

> I purchased $5\frac{3}{4}$ pounds of chocolate-covered peanuts. I want to store the candy in $\frac{1}{2}$-pound bags. How many $\frac{1}{2}$-pound bags can I make?

One student responded, "You get ten bags from the five pounds because five divided by one-half is ten, and then you get another bag from the three-fourths, which makes eleven bags, and there is one-fourth of a pound left over, which makes half of a half-pound bag" (p. 393). Try this problem for yourself and think about the logical thought you might use. What aspects of equal-sharing is included? How meaningful is the answer obtained in this manner rather than the "invert and multiply" approach?

Reciprocal. When middle school students are ready to work with the reciprocal, teachers must be ready to explain why the reciprocal works. This is difficult for students to conceptualize. In the previous samples, the complete answers were always given as multiplication problems. For example:

There are two groups of one-fourth.

$$2 \times \tfrac{1}{4}$$

There are one and one-half of the two-fourths.

$$1\tfrac{1}{2} \times \tfrac{2}{4}$$

The multiplicative inverse is possible because answers to the division of fractions are inherently the inverse operation of multiplication. It was also shown that the reciprocal relationship is present, such as:

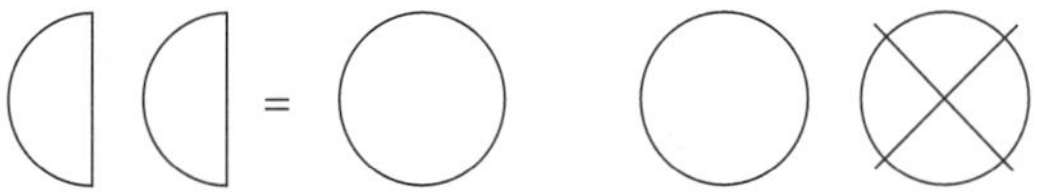

$$2 \times \frac{1}{2} = 1 \qquad \frac{1}{2} \times 2 = 1$$

Notice that each example comes back to the same basic unit of wholeness or 1. When the numerator and the denominator can be inverted and multiplied by a corresponding number in such a way as to maintain the same basic unit of wholeness, it is said that one fractional representation is in a reciprocal relationship with the other. Putting the two ideas together—(1) complete answers to division of fractions are really multiplication problems, and (2) using a reciprocal of a fraction does not change the basic unit of wholeness—one has a justification for the rule "invert and multiply." In addition, the example has shown that another property of the multiplication of fractions,

$$2 \times \frac{1}{2} \text{ and } \frac{1}{2} \times 2$$

is referred to as the commutative property.

Estimation. An important technique to help children get a sense about their answers is to encourage estimation. Experiences should be provided for students to estimate quotients. The procedure is to round each mixed number to the nearest whole number or to round fractions to more convenient numbers to allow for mental computation.

Activity 12.26

ESTIMATION

MENTAL MATH

ROUNDING MIXED NUMBERS IN DIVISION

$5\frac{3}{4} \div 2\frac{2}{3}$	Round to $6 \div 3$ so the answer is about 2.
$3\frac{1}{4} \div \frac{5}{6}$	Round to $3 \div 1$ so the answer is about 3.
$\frac{7}{8} \div \frac{1}{4}$	Round to $1 \div \frac{1}{4}$ so the answer is about 4.

Activity 12.27

ESTIMATION

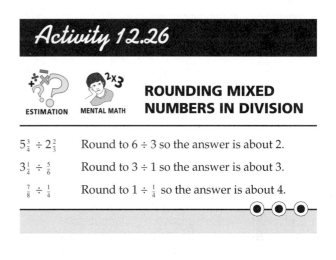

ESTIMATE AND SORT

MATERIALS

- Forty equation cards that each have a simple, common computational problem
- Playing mat or 4" × 6" note cards with the categories: *Closer to 1, Closer to $\frac{1}{2}$, Closer to 0*

PROCEDURE

Players take turns drawing a card from the deck and quickly mentally computing the answer and deciding into which category it should be placed. A time limit of 5 seconds should be allowed for each player. If the answer is correctly placed according to the other players, the card may be kept as a point card. If the answer is incorrect or not given within the time period, the card is replaced at the bottom of the deck.

Winner: The player with the most cards at the end of the playing time.

Supporting the NCTM *Principles and Standards* (2000):

- Mathematics as Reasoning; Number and Operation
- Student's Role in Discourse; Tools to Promote Discourse—The Teaching Principle
- The Mathematics Principle

Activity 12.28

MENTAL MATH PROBLEM SOLVING

FRACTION CUBE TOSS

Toss	Outcomes	Operation	Score
1	________	________	________
2	________	________	________
3	________	________	________
4	________	________	________
5	________	________	________
		Total	________

PROCEDURE

Each player tosses the cubes and records the outcomes. The player may either add, subtract, multiply, or divide the numbers in any order to get the highest possible result. One point is given for each round. The player with the greatest result wins.

Cube 1: $\frac{1}{2}$ $\frac{3}{4}$ $\frac{2}{3}$ $\frac{1}{6}$ 3 0

Cube 2: $\frac{1}{3}$ $\frac{5}{5}$ 4 $\frac{1}{4}$ $\frac{5}{6}$ $\frac{1}{2}$

Activity 12.29

MENTAL MATH

GREATEST QUOTIENT

MATERIALS

Fifty cards with the common fractions of halves through twelfths. A suggested list: $\frac{1}{2}$, $\frac{1}{3}$, $\frac{2}{3}$, $\frac{1}{4}$, $\frac{2}{4}$, $\frac{3}{4}$, $\frac{1}{5}$, $\frac{2}{5}$, $\frac{3}{5}$, $\frac{4}{5}$, $\frac{1}{6}$, $\frac{2}{6}$, $\frac{3}{6}$, $\frac{4}{6}$, $\frac{5}{6}$, $\frac{1}{8}$, $\frac{2}{8}$, $\frac{3}{8}$, $\frac{4}{8}$, $\frac{5}{8}$, $\frac{6}{8}$, $\frac{7}{8}$, $\frac{1}{9}$, $\frac{2}{9}$, $\frac{3}{9}$, $\frac{4}{9}$, $\frac{5}{9}$, $\frac{6}{9}$, $\frac{7}{9}$, $\frac{8}{9}$, $\frac{1}{10}$, $\frac{2}{10}$, $\frac{3}{10}$, $\frac{4}{10}$, $\frac{5}{10}$, $\frac{6}{10}$, $\frac{7}{10}$, $\frac{8}{10}$, $\frac{9}{10}$, $\frac{1}{12}$, $\frac{2}{12}$, $\frac{3}{12}$, $\frac{4}{12}$, $\frac{5}{12}$, $\frac{6}{12}$, $\frac{7}{12}$, $\frac{8}{12}$, $\frac{9}{12}$, $\frac{10}{12}$, $\frac{11}{12}$

PROCEDURE

Cards are spread out on the table face down. Each player takes two cards. The object of the activity is to get the greatest quotient by dividing one of the fractions by the other. Each player has the option of taking another card to improve the result or to pass. If a new card is taken, one card must be discarded so that at any one time a player has only two cards in hand. Two points are awarded to the player who has the greatest quotient with each draw of cards.

Winner: The player who first gets twenty points.

Using Other Manipulatives

A brief discussion of the teaching strategies using other manipulative materials (Figure 12.6) is presented in Tables 12.1 through 12.4 on pages 309–311 to show the power of using multiple embodiments. Always provide students with free exploration time using the various materials to help them become familiar with the relationships between the components as well as to satisfy their innate need to explore new materials. This will ensure greater participation during the instructional time.

All four operations are presented together, using the same two fractions for each of the four operations. This approach has been taken so that you can see how the same rational numbers are affected when the operations change.

Literature. Helping children develop better understandings of fractions is a task that can be enhanced through literature. Children need to see how fractions occur in real-life situations, which can be achieved through such books as *Fraction Action* (Leedy, 1994), and *Fraction Fun* (Adler, 1996). The set model of fractions can be demonstrated in *The Doorbell Rang* (Hutchins, 1986) and *Fractions Are Parts of Things* (Dennis, 1973). In the former, children must share a batch of twelve cookies. Both partitive division and fractions can be used to describe the episodes. The region or area model is portrayed in *Gator Pie* (Mathews, 1995) in which alligators determine how to cut or partition the pie into various equal parts (thirds, fourths, and so on). Some humorous complaints occur concerning equal parts, so the concept of equivalent fractions is demonstrated. *Eating Fractions* (McMillan, 1991) presents many examples of real-world pictures that show items being divided into parts. The text mentions the fraction in both written word and numbers. Equivalence is an important concept that is highlighted in *Ed Emberley's Picture Pie* (Emberley, 1984). Children can see how to cut paper into parts to make many different designs, shapes, patterns, and pictures.

Decimals

Exploratory work with decimals should be included in primary grades. The study of fractions should encompass tenths to provide a natural link to decimals and money. In most textbooks, intensive work with decimals does not begin until students have acquired skill with the manipulation of common fractions. With the increased use of calculators by students, educators may need to reconsider when to start teaching decimals. Decimals should be related to models, and the oral language should develop slowly. Early work with decimals in grades K–4

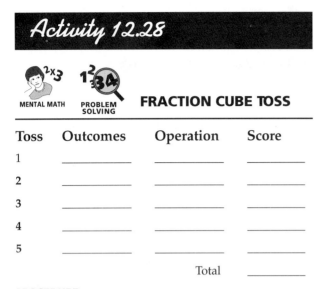

TABLE 12.1 Cuisenaire Rods—Traditional Algorithm

This method supports the way most textbooks teach the algorithm for addition and subtraction of fractions. It is the buildup of the basic unit of wholeness for one. This method finds the least common denominator without the need to find the lowest terms.

Add and Subtract: $\frac{1}{4}$ and $\frac{1}{6}$

Step 1: Represent each fraction in its original representation.

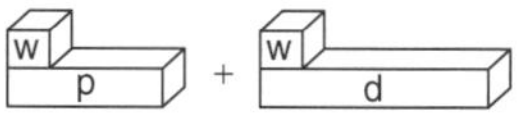

Step 2: Build up the denominator until both are the same length.

Step 3: The numerators are increased by the same respective magnitude as the denominators.

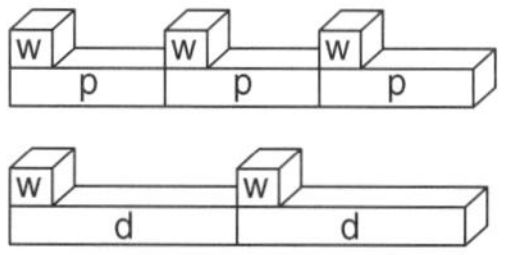

Step 4: Both numerators and denominators are represented in the equivalent rods, making an exchange for the least amount of rods to show any one number.

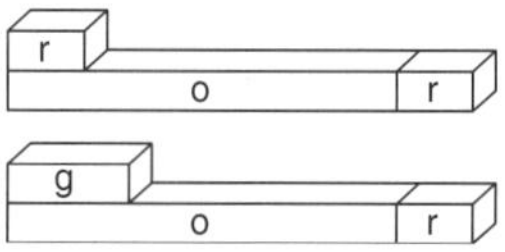

Step 5: For addition, add numerators, and represent the sum with the appropriate rod. Show the denominator as the part that stands for one. $\frac{5}{12}$.

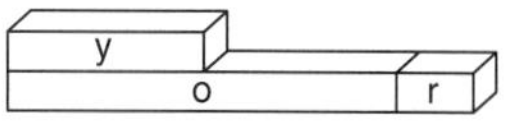

Step 6: For subtraction, compare the green rod with the red rod and show the difference, one white rod. $\frac{1}{12}$. The answer in rods is shown as follows:

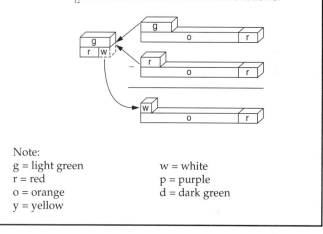

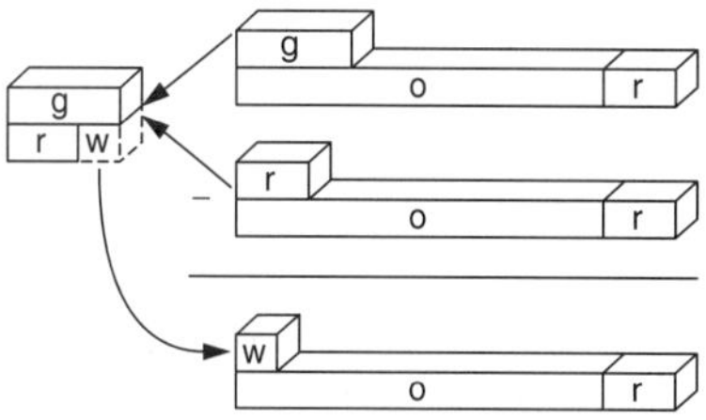

Note:
g = light green
r = red
o = orange
y = yellow
w = white
p = purple
d = dark green

should relate fractions to decimals. Building a number sense about decimals is an important goal. For example, students should recognize that 0.3 is less than $\frac{1}{2}$ because $\frac{1}{2}$ is the same amount as 0.5.

A summary of research findings (Hiebert, 1987) shows that many students, including high school students, do not realize that decimal fractions are just another way of writing common fractions and do not associate decimals as an extension of the base 10 place-value system. Researchers recommend that students have many introductory experiences with concrete materials before extensive rules are taught. The concrete materials discussed in this chapter will provide a firm background with decimals.

An analysis of the research on decimal fractions indicates there is a lack of conceptual understanding, perhaps because many students are being taught to compute with decimals before they fully grasp the basic decimal concepts. Owens and Super (1993) suggest that this situation is the result of basic decimal concepts being more difficult to teach and understand than the computational procedures along with the fact that computational algorithms are perceived by teachers to be more important or easier to teach.

There are two kinds of decimal fractions: terminating and repeating decimals. Early and middle grades deal with terminating decimals, whereas repeating decimals are taught in the sixth, seventh, and eighth grades in most mathematics texts. Students should observe the patterns that emerge when exploring terminating and repeating decimals.

Terminating Decimals. *Terminating decimals* are those that have a definite position or ending point in the base 10 number system. The point can be charted on a number line, or its position can be seen as a definite number of base 10 blocks. Common fractions can be seen as terminating decimals in the base 10 number system. An example would be $\frac{1}{2}$ (Figure 12.12).

One-half ($\frac{1}{2}$) can be seen as $\frac{5}{10}$ (0.5) or $\frac{50}{100}$ (0.50) or $\frac{500}{1000}$ (0.500). It is the same position on the number line. The only thing that is different is whether the basic unit of measure (equaling 1) is subdivided into tenths, hundredths, or thousandths.

TABLE 12.2 Pattern Blocks

Pattern blocks may be made from various colors for various shapes. The shapes have an interrelationship with each other as the drawings show below. Find all the different ways to build the yellow hexagon with different combinations of other blocks—using all the same color.

Equivalent Fractions

- If yellow hexagon = 1, what are the fractional values for other combinations?
  1 green = ? 1 blue = ? 1 red = ?
- If red trapezoid = 1, find all the fractional values of the other blocks.
  1 green = ? 1 blue = ? 1 yellow = ? 1 red = ?

  This activity can be repeated letting other blocks equal 1.
- To add or subtract with the blocks, you must decide which block to assign the value of 1. It is good to *estimate* whether your answer will be greater than or less than 1, greater than or less than $\frac{1}{2}$.

Add: $\frac{1}{2} + \frac{1}{3}$

If the yellow hexagon = 1, then the red trapezoid will be $\frac{1}{2}$, and the blue rhombus (parallelogram) will be $\frac{1}{3}$. When added together, $\frac{5}{6}$ of the yellow hexagon is covered. Answer in symbols:

$$\frac{1}{2} + \frac{1}{3} = \frac{5}{6}$$

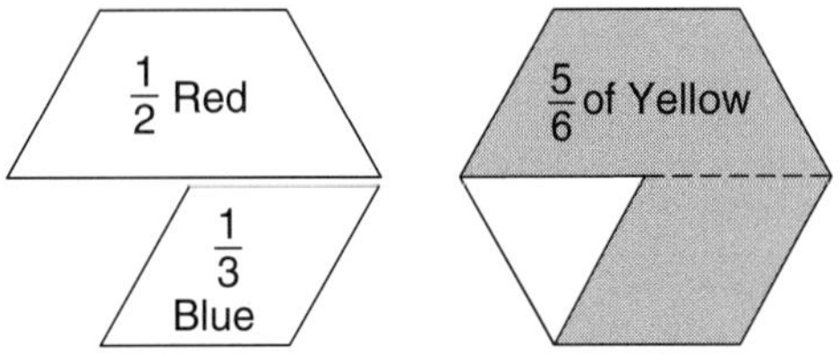

Subtract: $\frac{1}{2} - \frac{1}{3}$

If the hexagon = 1, then the blue rhombus = $\frac{1}{3}$ and the red trapezoid = $\frac{1}{2}$. The remaining part of the trapezoid is the green triangle which is $\frac{1}{6}$ of the hexagon (the whole).

Answers in symbols:

$$\frac{1}{2} - \frac{1}{3} = \frac{1}{6}$$

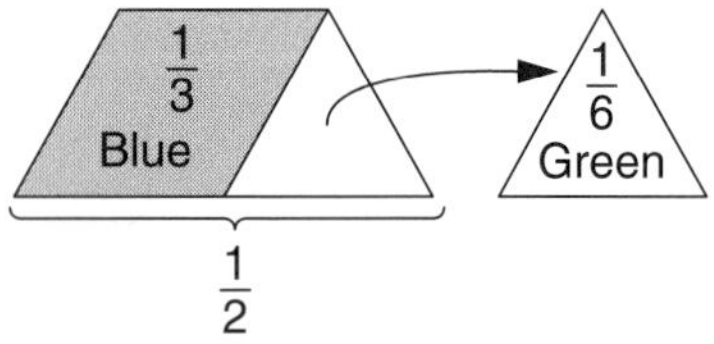

Multiply: $\frac{1}{2} \times \frac{1}{3}$

If yellow = 1, then $\frac{1}{3}$ is the blue rhombus and $\frac{1}{2}$ of $\frac{1}{3}$ is the green triangle. This is $\frac{1}{6}$ of the whole unit (yellow hexagon).

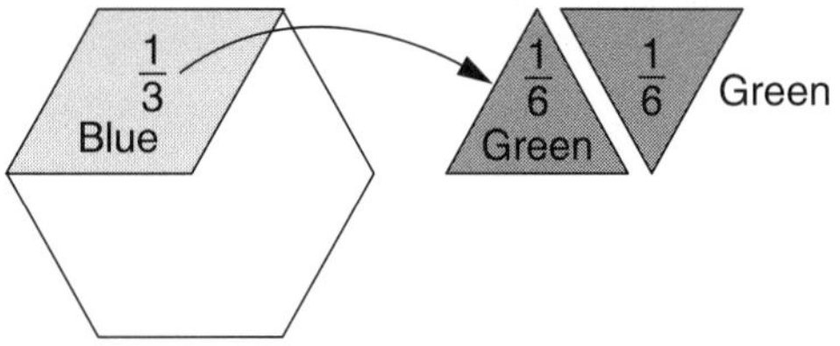

Divide: $\frac{1}{2} \div \frac{1}{3}$

If yellow = 1, then how many thirds (blue rhombus) are in the half (red trapezoid)?
Answer: There are 1 and $\frac{1}{2}$ more (green triangle) in the red trapezoid.

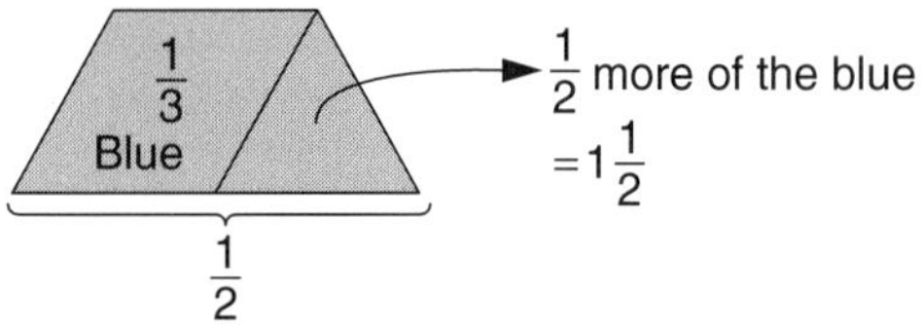

FIGURE 12.12

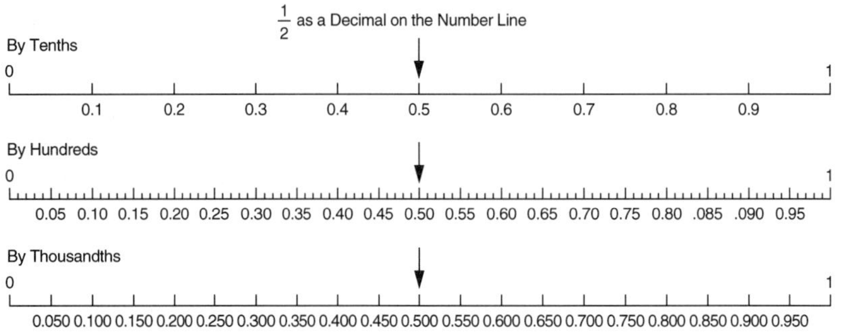

Decimal values on a number line.

TABLE 12.3 Multiple Bars

Multiple bars were first introduced in the Teaching Strategies section. Review the use of multiple bars to show equivalencies. Then do the following activities:

Add: $\frac{2}{5} + \frac{1}{3}$

Place the 2 bar above the 5 bar to form the fraction $\frac{2}{5}$ at the left of the bars. All other fractions formed across the bars are equivalent fractions to this one.

2	4	6	8	10	12	14	16	18	20
5	10	15	20	25	30	35	40	45	50

Form the second fraction with the 1 bar and the 3 bar.

1	2	3	4	5	6	7	8	9	10
3	6	9	12	15	18	21	24	27	30

Move one pair of the multiple bars until you have the same denominator lined up.

Once the denominators are alike, the operations can be performed with the numerators.

	2	4	6	8	10	12	14	16	18	20
	5	10	15	20	25	30	35	40	45	50
1	2	3	4	5	6	7	8	9	10	
3	6	9	12	15	18	21	24	27	30	

In this problem, the least common denominator is 15, and the two equivalent fractions are $\frac{2}{5} = \frac{6}{15}$ and $\frac{1}{3} = \frac{5}{15}$. The two numerators are 6 and 5 so, if these numbers are added, the result is 11 with the denominator or label of 15.

$$\frac{6}{15} + \frac{5}{15} = \frac{11}{15}$$

Subtract: $\frac{2}{5} - \frac{1}{3}$

The same procedure is used to subtract with the multiple bars, only once the numerators have been found, the operation of subtraction is performed on them.

Remember: Move one pair of the multiple bars until you have the same denominator (the least common denominator) for both fractions. Line up the bars. Now you can subtract the numerators.

$$\begin{array}{r} \frac{2}{5} = \frac{6}{15} \\ -\frac{1}{3} = \frac{5}{15} \\ \hline \frac{1}{15} \end{array}$$

TABLE 12.4 Fraction Strip Chart

Each student is given a chart like the one pictured here. The strips have already been pasted on the chart. Each student also receives loose strips of paper measuring the same as the "whole unit" shown on the chart. The whole is clearly visible at all times; therefore, a student does not lose sight of the basic unit to which all fractions must be compared.

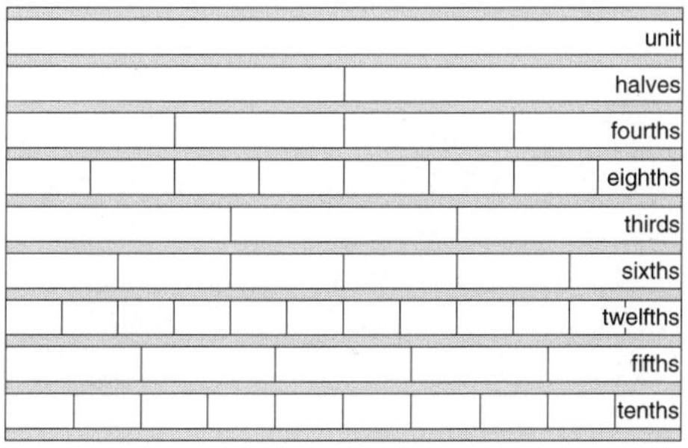

Multiply: $\frac{2}{3} \times \frac{1}{4}$

Read the problem as $\frac{2}{3}$ of $\frac{1}{4}$. Then the $\frac{1}{4}$ is found first and divided into thirds, and two of the thirds are found.

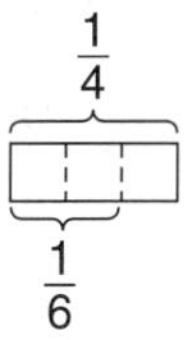

With the strip of paper at the top left edge, run the strip down until it matches an equivalent fraction, which is $\frac{1}{6}$. This way it is seen in its simplified form first.

Note one drawback: Because this method bypasses the $\frac{2}{12}$ which children would find first in the symbolic form, it makes the bridge from concrete to symbolic difficult to see.

Divide: $\frac{2}{3} \div \frac{1}{4}$

Read the problem as how many $\frac{1}{4}$'s in $\frac{2}{3}$. Find the $\frac{2}{3}$. Place a finger there and look at the $\frac{1}{4}$ strip. Compare the $\frac{2}{3}$ strip to the $\frac{1}{4}$ strip. It can be seen that there are 2 and $\frac{2}{3}$ of the $\frac{1}{4}$ strip in $\frac{2}{3}$.

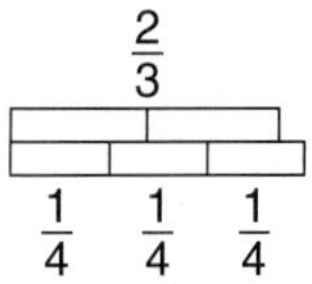

$$1 + 1 + \frac{2}{3} \text{ of the next fourth } = 2\frac{2}{3}$$

If the comparison is too difficult to do by just "eyeing" the strips, a $\frac{1}{4}$ strip may be marked from one of the loose strips and then moved down right on top of the $\frac{2}{3}$ strip for comparison.

Note: This procedure works well when the denominator of the second fraction is smaller than the denominator of the first fraction.

The same fraction, $\frac{1}{2}$, can be seen using base 10 blocks as shown in Figure 12.13. Notice that $\frac{1}{2}$ can be seen in the first regrouping of the basic building unit as $\frac{1}{2}$ of the tenths or five-tenths of the basic unit (written as 0.5). The base 10 blocks also show the markings for the next regrouping (hundredths). If divided by hundredths, there are fifty-hundredths of the basic unit (written as 0.50). If divided by thousandths (the markings are not possible on the blocks), there are five hundred–thousandths in $\frac{1}{2}$ of the basic unit (written as 0.500). It represents the same amount whether one talks of tenths, hundredths, or thousandths. There is a definite amount of blocks that can be partitioned to show the termination of the fraction $\frac{1}{2}$; hence, it is a terminating decimal.

FIGURE 12.13

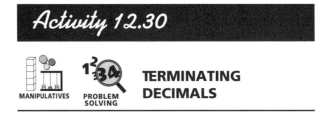

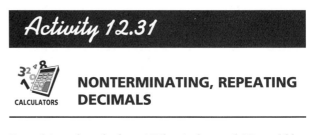

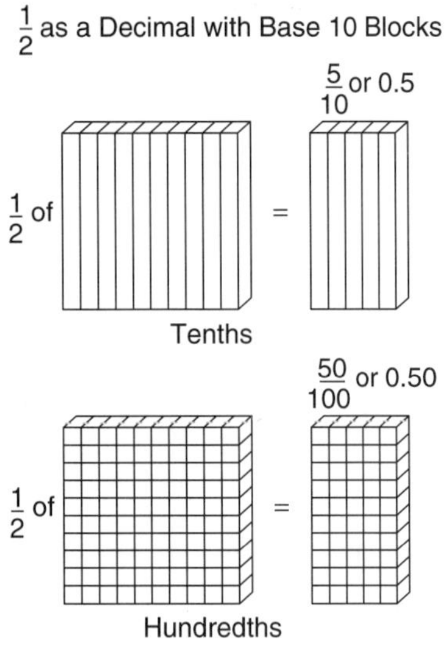

Showing equivalency with base 10 blocks.

Repeating Decimals. The existence of repeating decimals is proven in the seventh and eighth grades in most textbook series, although calculators may support an earlier introduction. A *repeating decimal* is a nonterminating decimal in which the same digit or block of digits repeats unendingly. As has been stressed numerous times previously, each new concept should be illustrated with manipulatives. The following exploration can be used with students in middle school as well as adults learning the principle for the first time.

There are some decimal fractions for which we can find no definite point on a base 10 number line and no definite amount of base 10 blocks, but we know they are there just the same. Let's use the example of $\frac{1}{3}$. Using the same base 10 decimal number line, we can divide it so that there is exactly $\frac{1}{3}$ in

Activity 12.30

MANIPULATIVES PROBLEM SOLVING

TERMINATING DECIMALS

What will happen if we try to find $\frac{1}{4}$ as a terminating decimal? Project what will happen before you test your assumptions with physical manipulatives.

1. Set up a base 10 decimal number line like the one in Figure 12.12.
2. Mark where $\frac{1}{4}$ of the basic building unit would be in tenths, hundredths, and thousandths. What did you discover?
3. Find $\frac{1}{4}$ using base 10 blocks in tenths, hundredths, and thousandths. What did you discover this time? Does it bear out what you discovered with the number line example? Is that to be expected? What will happen if we apply the same procedure to find $\frac{1}{8}$ as a terminating decimal?

Follow the same steps in reasoning as you did above.

What did you discover?

each segment of the basic building unit (see Figure 12.14). Remember that the basic building unit equals one whole.

Notice that there is no position in tenths, hundredths, or thousandths when $\frac{1}{3}$ touches a definite point; hence it does not terminate. If the number line were divided into ten-thousandths and beyond, $\frac{1}{3}$ would never meet at an exact point in the base 10 decimal system. Children can do some interesting investigations with decimals on the calculator. Let's see what they will discover when they try to divide $\frac{1}{3}$ on a calculator.

Activity 12.31

CALCULATORS

NONTERMINATING, REPEATING DECIMALS

Enter $\frac{1}{3}$ into the calculator.* What is the result? It could be recorded as:

Activity Continues

$\frac{1}{3} = 0.\overline{333333333333}$	The bar over the numbers means that it continues infinitely.
$\frac{1}{3} = 0.\overline{333333333333}$ $+\frac{1}{3} = 0.\overline{333333333333}$	Now add two more thirds to the original one.
$\frac{3}{3} = 0.\overline{999999999999}$	

Mathematicians assert that $0.\overline{999999999999}$ is equal to one whole because of examples like the one above. When a whole unit is divided by thirds nothing is taken away from or added to the basic unit; it remains intact. Therefore, $0.\overline{999999999999}$ is the nonterminating, repeating decimal for the whole number 1. It stands for one complete unit just as $\frac{3}{3}$ stands for one complete unit. This concept is a common question on college aptitude tests because it can be an easily forgotten mathematical principle.

*If the calculator has a M+ (memory plus) key, you can do the following explorations quickly by entering:

$\frac{1}{3}$ M+ M+ M+ [then press = or MT (for memory total) or MR (for memory recall)]

Linking Fractions to Decimals. Many examples of common fractions becoming decimal fractions should be modeled using base 10 blocks. Other problems to try might be $\frac{1}{2}$, $\frac{1}{5}$, and $\frac{1}{8}$. By problem solving, children can reason that if I find $\frac{1}{5}$, I can also find $\frac{3}{5}$. Children should predict the answer and then check with the blocks to make sure they were correct in their reasoning. Money provides one way to link fractions and decimals.

Children need to use base 10 blocks to work many division problems and record step-by-step actions at the symbolic level. Representations should proceed from concrete to connecting (pictorial) to symbolic. This careful sequence helps children to generalize ideas from working with models.

Activity 12.32

MANIPULATIVES PROBLEM SOLVING

DIVISION OF COMMON FRACTIONS INTO DECIMALS

DIRECTIONS

1. How would you use base 10 blocks for division using the rational number $\frac{2}{4}$?
2. What does $4\overline{)2.00}$ mean in words?

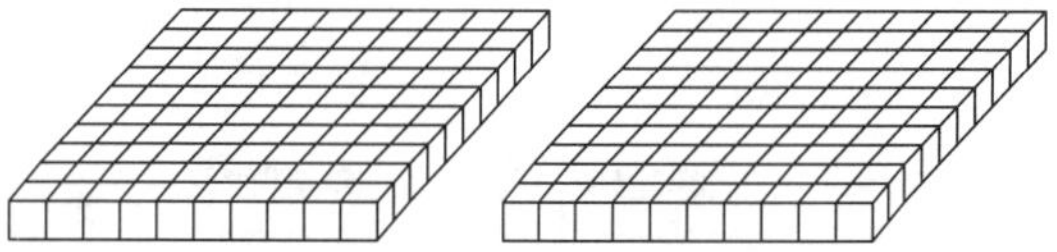

3. If you are working with the whole number 2, you will need to use 2 blocks to start your trades. Write the symbols as you regroup.
4. Now try $\frac{1}{8}$ using base 10 blocks.

FIGURE 12.14

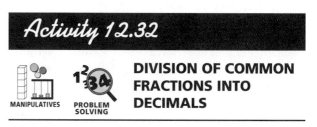

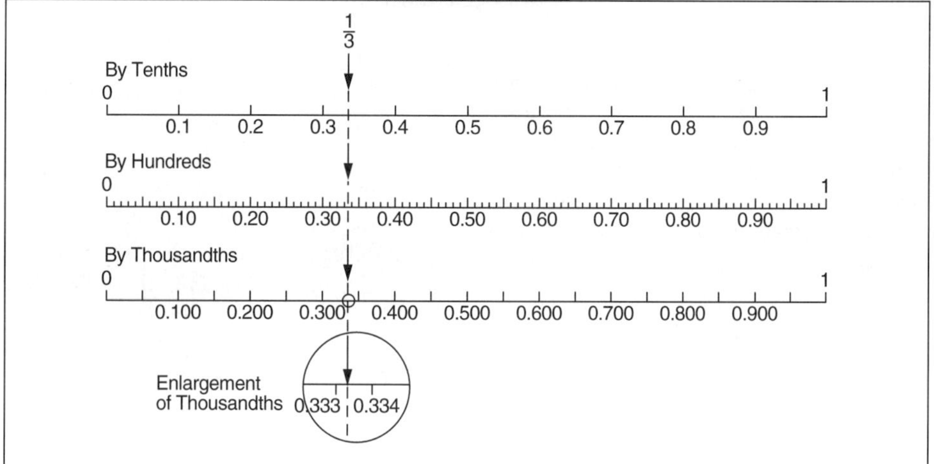

Locating $\frac{1}{3}$ on a decimal number line.

TEACHING STRATEGIES: DECIMALS

Decimals are presented as an extension of the concepts of fractions in most elementary texts. An understanding of place value and common fractions helps students learn decimal notation. Therefore, a lot of work with fractions such as $\frac{3}{10}$ proves valuable when connecting new symbolic notation (decimals) for fractions. Early exposure to decimal notation occurs in second or third grade when money concepts are developed. Pennies are related to hundredths and dimes are related to tenths. Children generally understand that pennies and dimes are parts of a dollar. Money notation found in textbooks provides experiences to count collections of dimes and pennies and to determine the total amount of money. This concrete, meaningful approach is an important bridge for learning ways to represent decimals. Though the cent sign (¢) is used with young children, decimal notation is being used in earlier grades because calculators record money transactions easily and some primary economics units include collections of more than a dollar.

Activity 12.33

ESTIMATION

LADYBUG ROUND OFF

MATERIALS

- Spinners (one for tenths, hundredths, and thousandths)

PROCEDURE

Determine which player goes first. Game *begins on tenths* spinner. Player may spin as many times as desired, recording each number spinned. When the player decides to stop, he or she adds the numbers and rounds the sum to the nearest whole number. If a player's spinner lands on a ladybug, the score for that spinner is 0 and play goes to next player. On the first player's next turn, the hundredths spinner is used and the sum of that round is found and rounded to the nearest tenth. After players have played all three spinners, they compare final sums and the highest value wins that round.

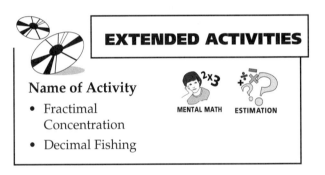

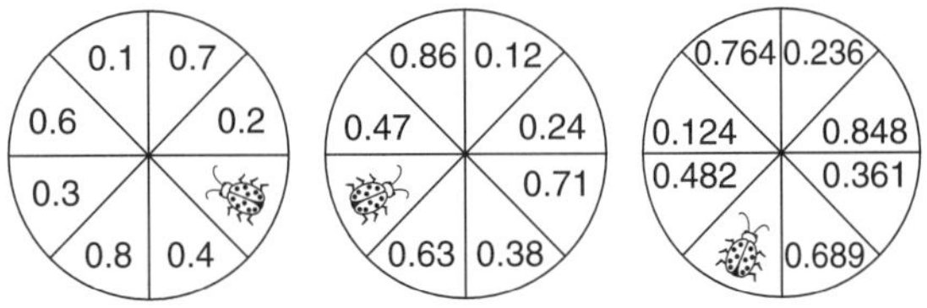

Activity Continues

Supporting the NCTM *Principles and Standards* (2000):

- Mathematics as Problem Solving; Number and Operation
- Worthwhile Mathematical Tasks; Learning Environment—The Teaching and Learning Principles

Common fractions and decimal equivalence represents an important area to develop competence and understanding. Hiebert and Wearne (1986) found that fifth-grade students had minimal understanding of the relationship between fractions and decimals. Multiple representations for a number presented conceptual difficulties for many students. Games can serve as an alternative form to practice skills and stimulate mental computations and comparisons. Check the extended activities on the CD-ROM to see how to make and use these games that focus on different names for the same number.

EXTENDED ACTIVITIES

Name of Activity

- Fractimal Concentration
- Decimal Fishing

MENTAL MATH ESTIMATION

Decimals as Money. Children enter school with a wide range of competencies in knowing the names and values of the different coins. This variation is due to the experiences they have had handling money. Often the underprivileged child has a clearer conception about money than the privileged one who has had limited opportunities to handle money.

Unfortunately, many employers comment and complain about young people's lack of competency in money skills. Although the technological advances in cash registers, calculators, and computers have altered the business scene, there is still an urgent need to better prepare students to face the demands of the job market and the world of the consumer.

Teaching money is far more effective if real coins are used. This may not be a wise practice all the time, but many activities should involve the manipulation of actual coins. Play coins should be selected carefully. Some coins are made from inexpensive plastic with pictures that do not closely resemble the actual heads and tails of real coins. The cardboard punchout coins found in the back of students' textbooks are often good representations. Have the student put these punchouts in an envelope marked with the child's name and keep the envelope in a central location for frequent use. Working in cooperative learning groups proves to be an effective method for students to practice counting coins and making change. Many commercial games and materials are available to provide practice in pretend buying and selling.

Coin recognition usually begins in kindergarten, and in first grade heavy emphasis is placed on coin recognition and counting collections of coins. "Counting on" as a method for determining change is usually introduced in third grade and continues throughout the intermediate grade textbooks.

Coin Equivalencies. One of the problems associated with learning about coins is the need to establish coin equivalencies. Textbooks do not contain sufficient pages to develop coin equivalencies, yet this is a key concept in the study of money. One successful method to use with the calendar activities (see Chapter 7) is to have children put a penny in a container for each day they are in school. After five days, the five pennies can be exchanged for a nickel. When two nickels have accumulated, they can be exchanged for a dime. Because this activity extends over an entire school year, the coin equivalencies can become well established.

Money reinforces place-value concepts because it is composed of a base 10 system. In counting numbers, exchanges of 10 individual units for a set of ten can be compared to exchanging 10 pennies for 1 dime. An important aspect of numeration is knowing how to continue a given counting sequence. This skill is needed in counting coins. The child must be able to begin a counting sequence by some value (tens) and switch to other values (fives or ones). This skill is also important in knowing how to "count on" to determine change.

The newspaper and classroom store have long been recognized as useful instructional aids to develop money concepts. The newspaper can provide comparative shopping and estimation activities, including conducting a shopping spree with a given amount of money, figuring percentage discounts on items, saving money with coupons, monthly installment buying, and discounts for cash. The classroom store offers a direct experience with buying items, paying for them, and deciding the amount of change. Children can serve as the customer or the merchant. Older children can set up and operate a school supply store to sell items such as pencils, notebooks, and school T-shirts. Purchasing imaginary stock and watching the stock market provide another valuable experience with money.

Activity 12.34

CALCULATORS PROBLEM SOLVING

PROBLEM SOLVING WITH DECIMALS

DIRECTIONS

Use a calculator and solve the following money problems.

1. Bananas \$.68/lb.

2. Cookies \$1.49 per lb.

3. What is the cost for a 3-mile taxi ride?

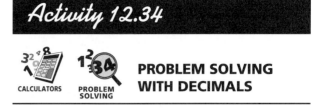

4. Using a menu from a local restaurant, plan a meal to feed each member of your class a hamburger and a soft drink. What is the total cost?
5. Using a grocery store ad from a local newspaper, create a budget for a class party.

Operations with Decimals

In teaching the four basic operations with decimals, it is important to build on prior understanding of the place value of decimals and the algorithms used with whole numbers. Because the algorithms are the same, modeling them with a variety of materials is important for special needs students and provides greater understanding and faster generalization.

Addition. Finding sums of decimal numbers should be an extension of whole number addition with the emphasis on lining up the place value associated with combining in each position or column. The following procedure should be followed when working with addition of decimals (see Figure 12.15).

1. Represent the decimals with concrete materials.
2. Estimate whether the answer will be more than one or less than 1. The same principle applies as discussed earlier with common fractions.
3. Combine like units making exchanges when necessary.
4. Record the actions and the answer in symbols.

An important task to master and remember when adding or subtracting decimal numbers is to align the decimal points so the place values are kept in mind. This is especially necessary when problems are presented in a horizontal form. Some textbooks stress the alignment of the decimal point while placing the zero in the appropriate decimal place values. The base 10 blocks seen in the introduction to this chapter show why 0.8 and 0.80 are the same amount. Working with the manipulatives makes this fact apparent to students. Pair students with special needs so one student works with the manipulative materials while the other student does the symbolic recording of the answer to incorporate a connecting level.

FIGURE 12.15

Situational Problem: You bought some black felt that was 1.75 meters long and some yellow felt that was 0.80 meters long. How much felt did you buy?

Problem: 1.75 + 0.80

1 and 75 hundredths of the next whole

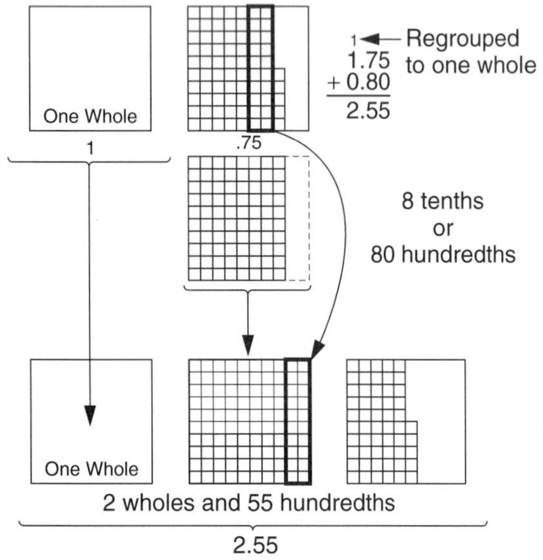

Addition of decimals.

Subtraction. The same basic principles apply to subtraction as apply to addition because one is the inverse of the other (see Figure 12.16). It is important to include the three interpretations of subtraction when working with decimals: take-away, missing addend, and comparison. Review modeling with whole number subtraction to refresh your memory. Children need to be allowed to investigate alternative solutions as they did for whole number computation.

FIGURE 12.16

Situational Problem: Rhea weighed a bag of nuts and found they were 2.32 kg. She took out 0.70 kg and weighed the nuts again. How much did she have then?

Problem: 2.32 – 0.70

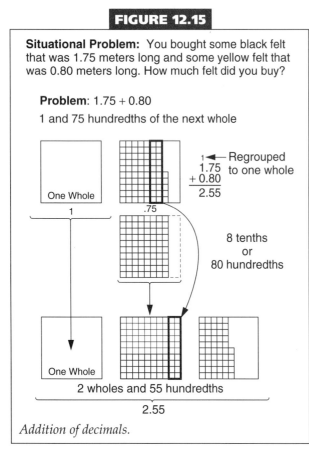

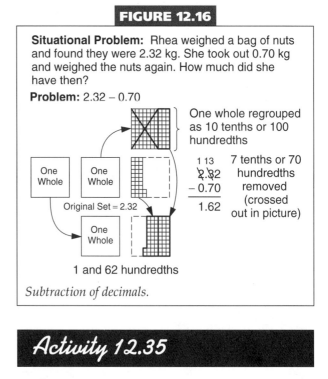

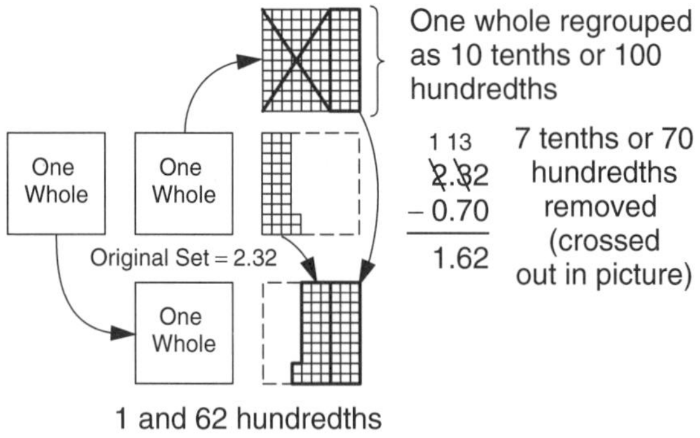

Subtraction of decimals.

Activity 12.35

MANIPULATIVES **GIVE AWAY**

MATERIALS

- Base 10 blocks (*Note:* One whole is represented by large cube.)
- Base 10 place-value mats
- Number die with 1 replaced with letter "C"

Activity Continues

- Chance cards—such as the following:
  Give away 2 tenths. Give away 3 tenths
  Give away 4 tenths. Give away 5 tenths
  (Repeat, only use word "hundredths" or "thousandths")

PROCEDURE

Players begin with one large cube on their place-value mat, which represents the value of one whole unit. Roll the die. Player with lowest number begins. Roll the die, say the number as hundredths. (If roll is 5, then player calls it 5 hundredths.) Player must "give away" or remove that amount from the playing mat. When a player rolls the "C" a chance card must be drawn.

Winner: The first player to remove or "give away" all of his or her blocks. The player must roll the exact number to give away the remaining block(s).

Students need to experience many different situational and problem structures to gain confidence in computing with decimals. Estimation strategies can be used to make the problem more manageable. Using front-end estimation and rounding to whole numbers may be appropriate to check reasonableness of answers, as indicated in the next activity.

Activity 12.36

ESTIMATION

MENTAL MATH

ROUNDING WITH DECIMALS

DIRECTIONS

Look at the problems on the left and estimate how many whole numbers will be in the answer, if any. Fill in the rest of the chart. The first two are completed as a model.

Problem	Mental Rounding	Estimated Answer
3.4 − 2.9	*Think:* 3 − 3	Less than 1
7.85 − 4.2	*Think:* 8 − 4	Around 4
11.34 − 0.895		
1.11 − 0.999		
345.25 − 245.5		
0.927 − 0.398		

Check how close you came in this activity by computing the answer.

Multiplication. Multiplication of decimals follows the same rules as multiplication of whole numbers (Chapter 11). Therefore multiplication of decimals can be modeled using the same words and patterns using the base 10 blocks as the concrete manipulatives. In Figure 12.17 the flat is the basic building unit representing one whole. The long represents tenths, and the small unit cube represents hundredths.

Products of two decimal numbers can be shown using base 10 blocks or graph paper and the copy method. Students should build an array showing the two factors with number of groups on the left (or going "down") and number in a group going "across." Each of the partial products can be shown in the same manner as with whole numbers (Figures 12.17 and 12.18).

The illustrations of a partial flat are enlarged in Figures 12.19 and 12.20. Therefore, they may appear out of proportion to you as you study these pictures compared to the others you have just seen. They may be presented to students in the same manner as strips of paper that can be folded or measured into 100 parts.

Encourage students to find patterns and to generalize the rule for the multiplication of decimals. It may seem easier and quicker to establish the rule of counting the number of decimal places for the product, but the rule is learned without meaning. Rather, teachers should ask students for place-value inter-

FIGURE 12.17

Problem: 1.4 × 2.3

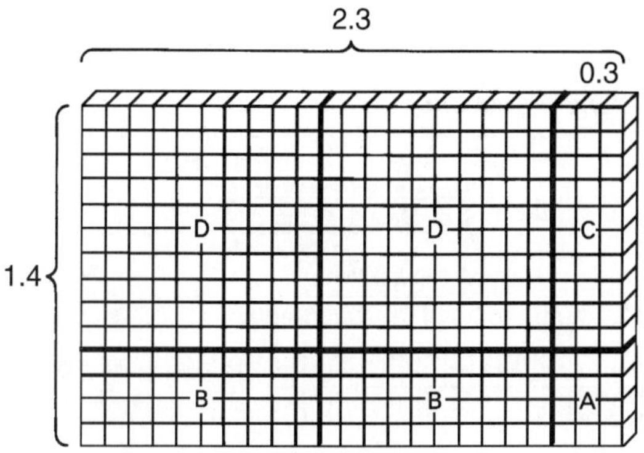

1.4 groups of 2.3

	2.3	
	× 1.4	
(A)	.12	4 tenths groups of 3 tenths
(B)	.80	4 tenths groups of 2
(C)	.30	1 group of 3 tenths
(D)	+ 2.00	1 group of 2 wholes

Multiplication of decimals.

FIGURE 12.18

2 × 0.05 = 0.10

Two groups of five-hundredths

$$\begin{array}{r} 0.05 \\ \times\ 2 \\ \hline 0.10 \end{array}$$

0.05 × 2 = 0.10

Five-hundredths of two wholes
(two has to be divided into 100 parts
and then 5 of each 100 is found)

$$\begin{array}{r} 2 \\ \times\ 0.05 \\ \hline 0.10 \end{array}$$

The answer is one-tenth.

4 × 0.2 = 0.8

Four groups of two-tenths

0.4 × 0.2 = 0.08

Four-tenths group of two-tenths

The answer is eight-hundredths.

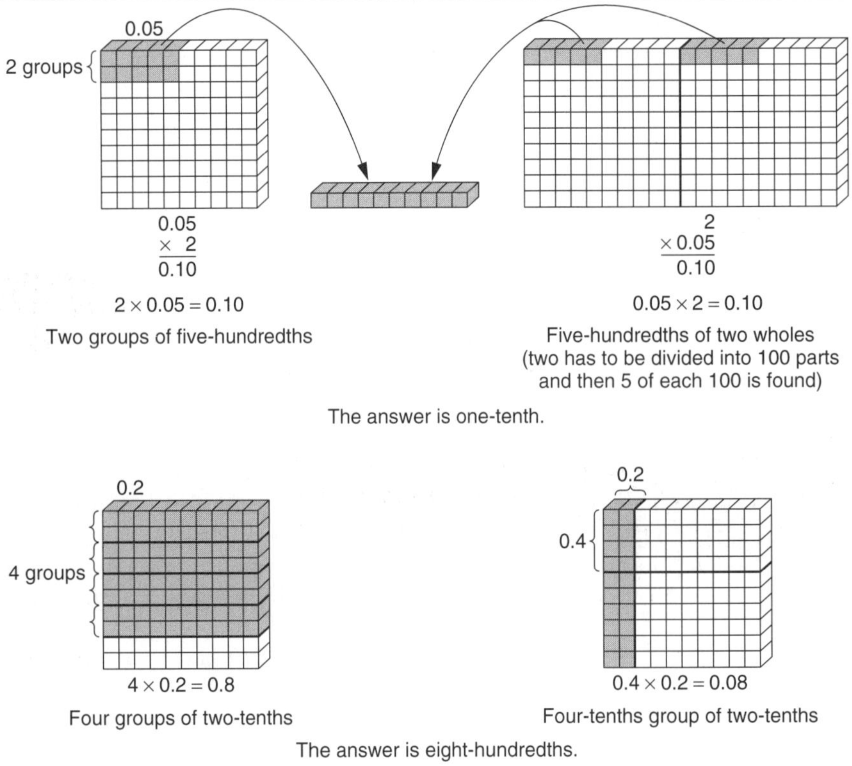

Multiplication of decimals using base 10 blocks.

FIGURE 12.19

0.2 × 0.05 = 0.01

Two-tenths of five-hundredths

0.05 × 0.2 = 0.01

Five-hundredths of two-tenths

The answer is one-hundredth.

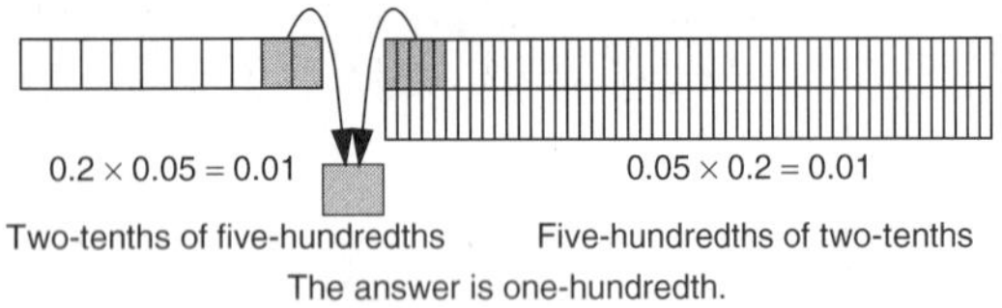

Exploring the commutative principle.

FIGURE 12.20

0.02 × 0.05 = 0.001

Two-hundredths of five-hundredths

**The answer is
one-thousandth
of the entire flat.**

0.05 × 0.02 = 0.001

Five-hundredths of two-hundredths

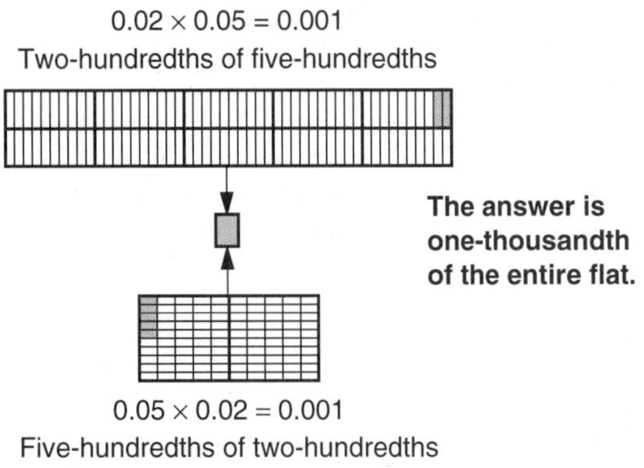

Multiplying hundredths by hundredths.

pretations and guide them in deciding on reasonable answers. Problems can be presented where the answer is given but the students' task is to determine where the decimal point should be placed in the answer.

Activity 12.37

**OBSERVATIONS OF
MULTIPLICATION WITH
BASE 10 BLOCKS**

PROBLEM
SOLVING

DIRECTIONS

1. Look at the pictorial and symbolic representations of multiplication shown in Figures 12.18, 12.19, and 12.20.

2. Fill in the chart. The first three are done as examples.

		Number of Decimal Places	
Problem	Answer	Problem	Answer
2 × 0.05	0.10	2	2
0.05 × 2	0.10	2	2
4 × 0.2	0.8	1	1

Activity Continues

3. Look for a pattern when working with decimals.
4. Generalize a rule for multiplying decimals using the pattern for clues.

Provide experiences in which students decide where the decimal point should go in a given answer. Students can use estimation to justify their answers. There should be time spent on simple calculations without a calculator; however, valuable instructional time should not be spent on tedious paper-and-pencil calculations. These can be done more readily using a calculator.

Division. Division of decimals follows the same rules as division of common fractions and whole numbers. Therefore, division of decimals may be modeled with the same words and patterns as have been used before. For example, the base 10 blocks seen in the multiplication of decimals can be used if the question is changed to represent division. Table 12.5 shows models in measurement division so you can become familiar with the language of dividing with decimals. (If needed, review Chapter 10 for discussion of the two kinds of division.)

As the decimal place values extend into the thousandths and ten thousandths, it becomes virtually impossible to do the entire problem with concrete manipulatives. The answers must be reasoned from past experiences. Estimation should be used in problem-solving situations with decimals. Students should learn to estimate answers and evaluate the reasonableness of answers. Calculators can be used to perform routine computations and should be the appropriate tool for solving division of multidigit numbers.

Suppose the problem is 1000 ÷ 0.001. Division asks the question, *"How many sets of one-thousandths (0.001) are there in 1000?"* This is a measurement interpretation of division. Manipulatives can show the beginning of the thought process. If a cube represents one whole, then a tiny cube will be one-thousandth (0.001) of the whole (Figure 12.21).

FIGURE 12.21

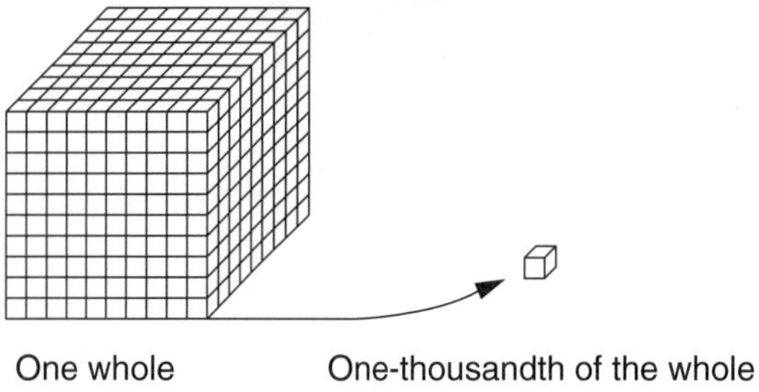

How many one-thousandths are in 1000?

TABLE 12.5 Measurement Division

Figure	In Symbols	The Questions in Division
11.17	$\begin{array}{r} 2 \\ 0.05\overline{)0.10} \end{array}$	How many sets of five-hundredths are there in 0.10? *There are two sets of 0.05 in 0.10.*
	$\begin{array}{r} 0.05 \\ 2\overline{)0.10} \end{array}$	How many sets of two are there in 0.10? *There are 5 of the hundredths (0.05) in 0.10.*
11.18	$\begin{array}{r} 0.2 \\ 0.05\overline{)0.010} \end{array}$	How many sets of five-hundredths are there in 0.01? *There are two-tenths of 0.05 in 0.01.* (The 0.2 can be seen as $\frac{1}{5}$ of 0.05 with the base 10 blocks, but since $\frac{1}{5}$ is *not* a power of ten, 0.2 is the answer.)
	$\begin{array}{r} 0.05 \\ 0.2\overline{)0.010} \end{array}$	How many sets of two-tenths are there in 0.01? *There are five of the hundredths (0.05) in 0.01.*
11.19	$\begin{array}{r} 0.02 \\ 0.05\overline{)0.0010} \end{array}$	How many sets of five-hundredths are there in 0.001? *There are two-hundredths of 0.05 in 0.001.*
	$\begin{array}{r} 0.05 \\ 0.02\overline{)0.0010} \end{array}$	How many sets of two-hundredths are there in 0.001? *There are five-hundredths of two-hundredths in 0.001.*

Now imagine that there are 1000 cubes like the one in Figure 12.21 representing the whole number of 1000. Then the same one-thousandth pictured here would make up a very, very tiny portion of the new number. So the question "How many sets of one-thousandth (0.001) are there in 1000?" would result in a very large number.

By going over the division question, students become adept at predicting whether answers to such problems will be large or small numbers. Teachers can show problems, and students can state whether the answer will be a large or small amount. This is an excellent activity to use with the every pupil response cards (EPRs) (reviewed in Chapter 3). These activities help children visualize decimals to build number sense. Special needs students need rich visualizations to make mental connections. Consider the situation of having eight-tenths and wanting to know how many groups of five-hundredths there are (Figure 12.22).

Money is a natural way to think about modeling division with decimals. When the divisor is a whole number, the partitive approach can be used. If $4.28 is to be shared among four people, the number of groups is known, and what needs to be determined is how much will be distributed to each group (Figure 12.23).

FIGURE 12.22

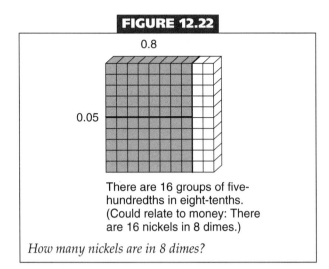

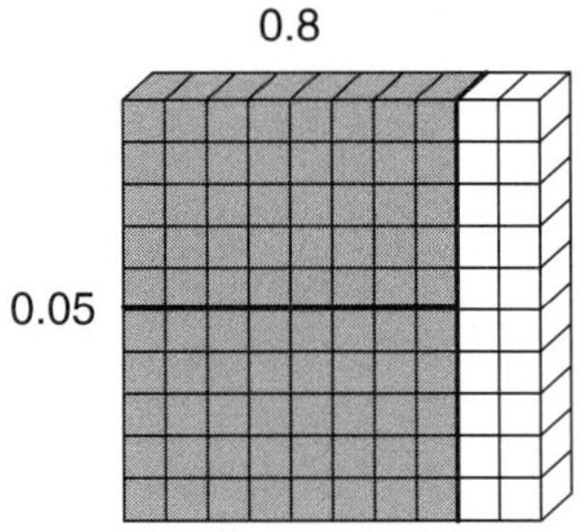

There are 16 groups of five-hundredths in eight-tenths. (Could relate to money: There are 16 nickels in 8 dimes.)

How many nickels are in 8 dimes?

After working with division of decimals, it is easy to see why many mathematics educators believe that this concept must wait to be taught until the upper elementary grades when children can visualize intellectually what is happening with minute quantities. If upper-grade students are at Piaget's concrete operational stage, there may be limited comprehension.

Activity 12.38

CALCULATORS PROBLEM SOLVING **DIVISION OF DECIMALS**

This activity promotes problem solving as well as calculator use. Find the correct pathway by dividing the first number by the second one as you trace your way to the ending numeral.

Start

1000	10	0.1	100
1000	1	0.001	0.01
0.001	1	0.01	10
100	100	10	100
			End 1

ASSESSMENT

Field-Independent Learners

Some students benefit from the gradual buildup of fractions from the parts to the corresponding whole. Materials like the fraction kits, the multiple bars, and the Cuisenaire rod algorithm for adding and subtracting fractions (explained in the earlier section on teaching strategies for fractions) are all very helpful. These materials start with one fraction, find its equivalencies, and then compare them to the whole unit before performing the mathematical operation. If students do not respond well to one of these materials or seem to forget where they are in the sequence of building to the solution, materials supporting the simultaneous thought processing of field-dependent learners should be presented.

Field-Dependent Learners

Some students benefit from having a "whole" unit constantly within sight as they work on fraction relationships. The whole and its parts are more clearly seen in materials like the fraction strip chart. Such material allows for problems to be presented by par-

FIGURE 12.23

Situational Problem: Desmond and three friends were selling used golf balls and collected \$4.28. They wanted to divide this money between them in equal amounts. How much money will each one get?

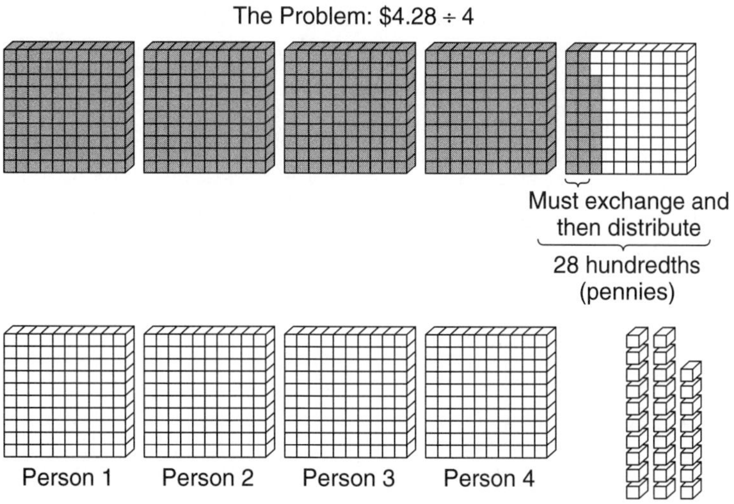

1. How many flats or one dollars will each person get?
2. How many longs or tenths (dimes) will each person get?
3. How many units or hundredths (pennies) will each person get?

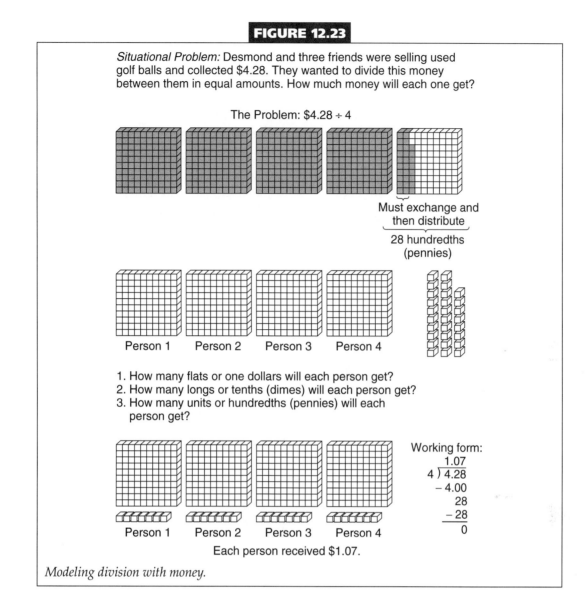

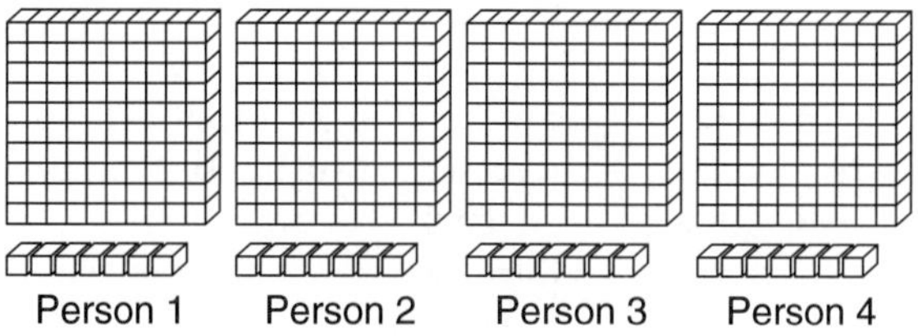

Working form:

$$\begin{array}{r} 1.07 \\ 4\,\overline{)\,4.28} \\ -\,4.00 \\ 28 \\ -\,28 \\ \hline 0 \end{array}$$

Each person received \$1.07.

Modeling division with money.

titioning from the whole to its parts. Students are not required to handle as many small pieces or make as many manipulations as they may be required to do in successive processing models.

Correcting Common Misconceptions

Adding or Subtracting Denominators as Whole Numbers. The denominator of a fraction serves as a label naming the number of parts into which the whole unit has been divided. Sometimes it is helpful for students with special needs to write the denominator in words to help focus on the numerator when teaching the symbolic level of adding and subtracting fractions. Because a common error is to add or subtract *both* the numerators and the denominators, this technique emphasizes that different parts or labels are involved, and until the parts or labels are the same, the numerators cannot be added or subtracted.

Common Errors: $\frac{2}{3} + \frac{1}{4} = \frac{3}{7}$

But: $\frac{2}{\text{thirds}} + \frac{1}{\text{fourths}} = \frac{?}{?}$

Get labels or denominators the same, then perform the operation on the numerators:

$$\frac{8}{\text{twelfths}} + \frac{3}{\text{twelfths}} = \frac{11}{\text{twelfths}}$$

Changing Mixed Numbers to Improper Fractions. Students forget the sequence of steps and which part is added or multiplied. For the mixed number $5\frac{1}{2}$, the following answers may occur when it is changed to an improper fraction:

$$\frac{5}{2} \quad \frac{1}{10} \quad \frac{6}{2} \quad \frac{6}{10} \quad \frac{8}{2}$$

Analyze what happened to obtain each answer. There are other possible variations also.

One of the most efficient means of remediation is to model the action with manipulatives using concrete or pictorial materials. More exploratory experiences are needed to build a conceptualization and visualization of the problem. The circular fraction kit works well because the student can show five circles and one-half more of the next circle. Then the student can count the number of halves to find the eleven halves.

Activity 12.39

PROBLEM SOLVING

DIAGNOSTIC HELP

The teacher asks: What did you do to $5\frac{1}{2}$ to get $\frac{11}{2}$?

Look at some more examples. Model the representation. Generalize a procedure to get these answers every time.

$$2\tfrac{3}{4} = \tfrac{11}{4}$$

$$3\tfrac{4}{10} = \tfrac{34}{10}$$

Inverting and Multiplying the Incorrect Factors. This problem occurs when the student "inverts and multiplies" the first factor instead of the second when attempting to divide one fraction by another. Some students may invert *both* fractions, thinking the rule applies to both factors.

Original Example	*Student's Work*
$\frac{1}{2} \div \frac{1}{4}$	$\frac{2}{1} \times \frac{1}{4} = \frac{1}{2}$

Switching to an entirely new algorithm is advisable. Just restating the rule may leave the student still confused. The teaching strategy for division using the circular or rectangular fraction kit would require a different setup and execution of the problem.

$$\frac{1}{2} \div \frac{1}{4} = \frac{2}{4} \div \frac{1}{4} = \frac{2 \div 1}{1} = \frac{2}{1} = 2$$

Focus the students' attention on the operation of dividing and the language of "how many groups can I get."

Multiplying and Dividing Mixed Numbers. Students know they can add or subtract the whole numbers after they have found the equivalent fractional parts. They assume logically that they can do the same when multiplying or dividing mixed numbers, yielding answers like the following:

Original Example		*Student's Answer*
$2\frac{1}{2} \times 4\frac{1}{4}$	=	$8\frac{1}{8}$

This type of problem is difficult to remediate. Some elementary textbooks insist on the change of mixed numbers to improper fractions as the first step in any addition or subtraction problem. Such texts hope that insistence on one procedure will eliminate problems with inappropriate transfer of learning later when multiplication and division of mixed numbers are taught. If students have learned different algorithms for addition and subtraction which are causing difficulties, it may be beneficial to go back to addition and subtraction, showing the improper fraction step first. After students have seen that it works with addition and subtraction, stress that the same procedure works for multiplication and division. For example:

With Addition

$$\begin{array}{rcccc} 4\frac{1}{4} & = & \frac{17}{4} & = & \frac{17}{4} \\ +2\frac{1}{2} & = & \frac{5}{2} & = & \frac{10}{4} \\ \hline & & & & \frac{27}{4} = 6\frac{3}{4} \end{array}$$

With Multiplication

$$\begin{array}{rcccc} 4\frac{1}{4} & = & \frac{17}{4} & = & \frac{17}{4} \\ \times\, 2\frac{1}{2} & = & \frac{5}{2} & = & \frac{10}{4} \\ \hline & & & & \frac{170}{16} = 10\frac{10}{16} = 10\frac{5}{8} \end{array}$$

Use the circular fraction kit to model the problem (Figure 12.24). Students should build their understanding from the mathematical representation of $2\frac{1}{2} \times 4\frac{1}{4}$. When students are involved in problem-

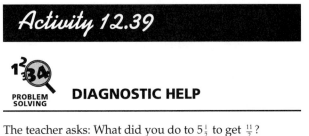

FIGURE 12.24

$2\frac{1}{2} \times 4\frac{1}{4} \longrightarrow 2\frac{1}{2}$ groups of $4\frac{1}{4}$

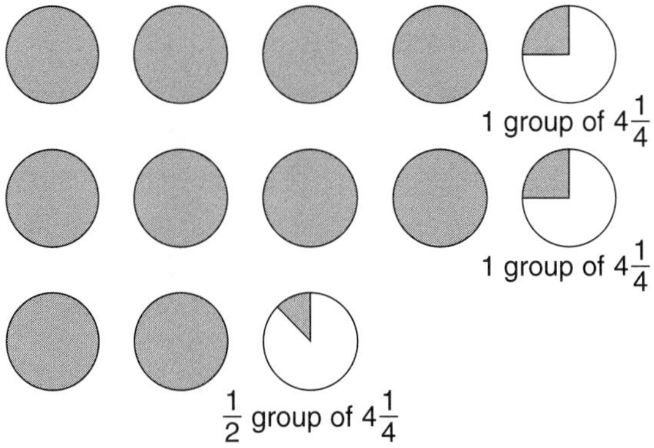

$2\frac{1}{2}$ groups of $4\frac{1}{4} = 10\frac{5}{8}$

10 wholes and $\frac{1}{4} + \frac{1}{4} + \frac{1}{8} = 10 + \frac{2}{8} + \frac{2}{8} + \frac{1}{8} = 10\frac{5}{8}$

Showing multiplication of mixed numbers.

solving experiences, they can later generalize ideas gained through models. Figure 12.24 illustrates that the problem states that $2\frac{1}{2}$ groups of $4\frac{1}{4}$ yields $10\frac{5}{8}$.

Another way to help students with multiplication of mixed numbers is to have them estimate to see if their answers are reasonable—for example:

To estimate the largest value possible:

$$2\tfrac{1}{2} \approx 3,\ 4\tfrac{1}{4} \approx 4,\ \text{so } 3 \times 4 = 12 \neq 8\tfrac{1}{8}$$

To estimate the smallest value possible:

$$2\tfrac{1}{2} \times 4 = (2 \times 4) + (\tfrac{1}{2} \times 4) = 8 + 2 = 10 \neq 8\tfrac{1}{8}$$

The answer must be between 10 and 12. The student's answer of $8\frac{1}{8}$ does not fit reasonably in the problem, and this estimation technique alerts the student to check with a different algorithm like the one shown previously or to check with manipulative materials.

Regrouping Fractions as Whole Numbers. Students frequently confuse the regrouping process of whole numbers with the regrouping process required in the subtraction of fractions.

Original Example		*Student's Work*
$5\frac{1}{4}$	=	$\not{5}4^{+1}\ \frac{2}{8} = 4\frac{12}{8}$
$-3\frac{7}{8}$		

The student regroups the 5 as 4 and 1 but "carries" the 1 over to the renamed two-eighths as if it were a whole number and not the numerator of a fraction. The student has forgotten that the whole number must be renamed as:

$$\frac{8}{8} \text{ and then added to } \frac{2}{8} \text{ to make } \frac{10}{8}$$

The strategies section stressed the need to ask, "What name is being used for one?" *constantly* as a student performs the activities. Students who forget this important step should write the question down and save it in a folder where they can refer to it as they work. Perhaps going back to concrete materials may be the next step if initial instruction did not include them.

Activity 12.40

PORTFOLIO

PORTFOLIO ASSESSMENTS

For Teacher Reflection of Students' Work with Operations on Fractions

Name Nick

Work this problem (showing all your work). $\frac{3}{4} \times \frac{1}{2} = \frac{3}{4}$

Defend your answer--how do you know it is correct?

$\frac{3}{4} \times \frac{1}{2}$

Draw or visualize how to work the problem.

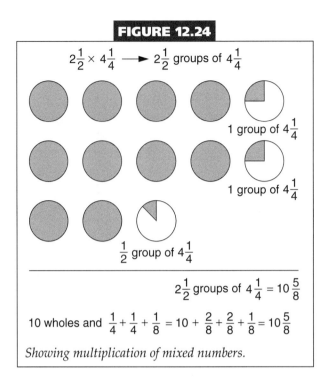

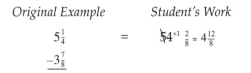

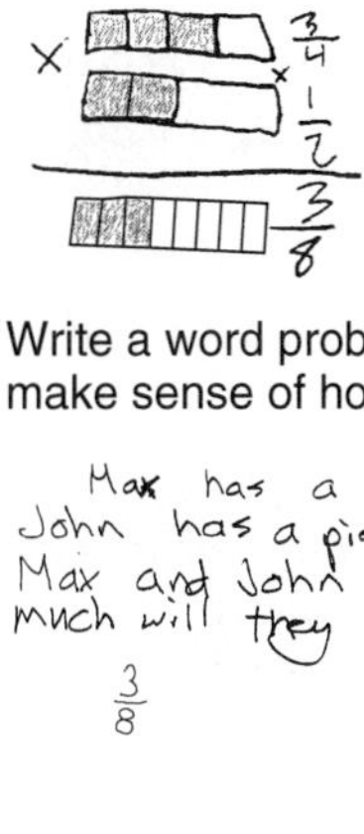

Write a word problem that will go with this problem to make sense of how to use this math in the real world.

Max has a pei; 3/4 of it is left. John has a pie; 1/2 of it is left. Max and John put it together. How much will they have?

$\frac{3}{8}$

DIRECTIONS

1. Analyze the response made by each student. Create a reflective description of what you think can be said about the student's degree of understanding of operations with fractions.

Activity Continues

2. Describe how the drawings gave clarification of each student's level of understanding. What information was gained from their drawings? Compare the various levels of understanding between the students. What NCTM *Principles and Standards* (2000) are you including in your assessments? Explain your answer.
3. Design a rubric that would take into account the diversity of answers while being open in your assessment.

   Include the rubric in your Professional Portfolio for Job Interviews.

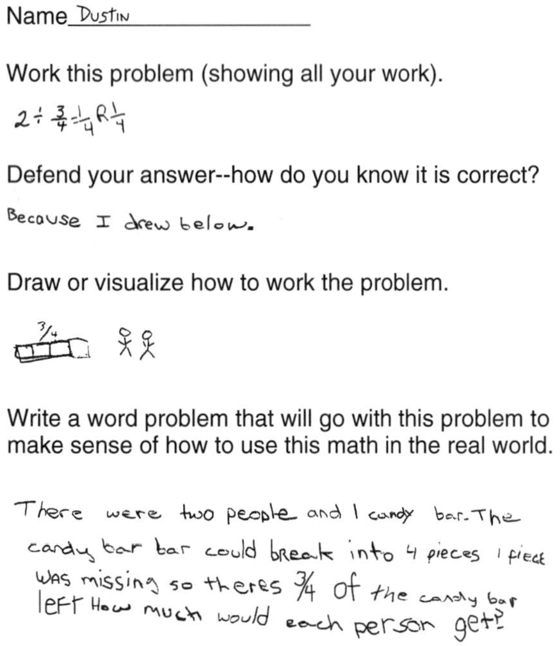
Name Dustin

Work this problem (showing all your work).

2 ÷ 3/4 = 1/4 R 1/4

Defend your answer--how do you know it is correct?

Because I drew below.

Draw or visualize how to work the problem.

Write a word problem that will go with this problem to make sense of how to use this math in the real world.

There were two people and 1 candy bar. The candy bar bar could break into 4 pieces 1 piece was missing so theres 3/4 of the candy bar left How much would each person get?

FIGURE 12.25

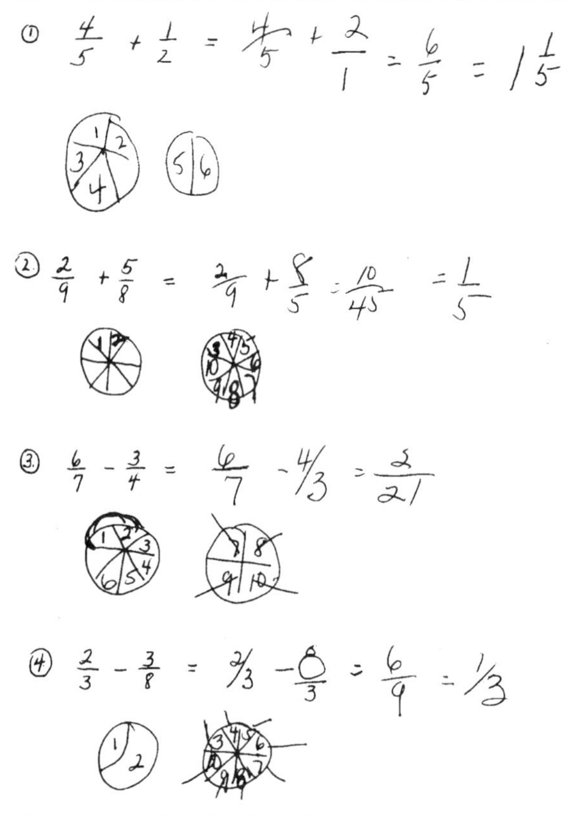

Assessment of student's work.

Activity 12.41

PORTFOLIO

ASSESSING UNDERSTANDING OF FRACTIONS

In the assessment example (Figure 12.25), to what extent do you feel this student has been exposed to concrete models? On what information do you base your decision? What conceptual understanding of operations with fractions does this student have? Think about a plan to develop meaning for operations and explain how you would instruct this child. What NCTM *Principles* (2000) will you include in your assessment?

Correcting Common Misconceptions with Decimals and Money

A common error in money skills is the inability to count collections of coins to determine how much money in all. One problem may be the lack of adequate counting skills to count by ones, fives, and tens beginning at various numbers. Children cannot shift from counting by tens to counting by fives and then to counting by ones. The hardest sequence is to start with quarters and then count by fives or tens. Figure 12.26 shows a chart to focus special needs students' attention on the visual referent. The coins on the chart have been cut and pasted from first- or second-grade workbooks and laminated onto the chart. When counting a collection of coins, children should first sort them into like coins, then begin counting with the largest value to the least value. In this manner, the child does not have to regroup numbers as often.

Another difficulty with money may be the confusion of the coins themselves. A common problem is distinguishing between a quarter and a nickel. If

FIGURE 12.26

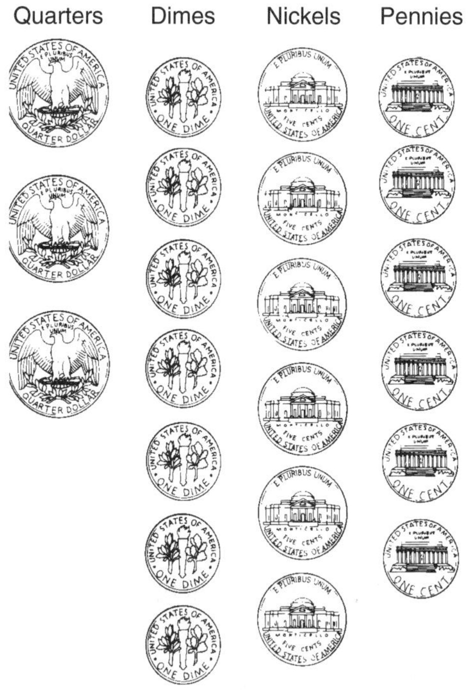

Coin counting chart.

the teacher concentrates only on size, the child is confused when the nickel is on the page without a quarter as a reference. The nickel is larger in size than the dime or penny, but is it the largest in value? Without the quarter as a reference point, it may be difficult to decide. Also, there is the issue of heads or tails—which is the easier coin for children to identify? Some educators suggest that instruction should begin with the tails of coins which have more variety on which to focus. Most teachers feel more comfortable teaching coins with the heads first because they consider this the front side of the coin.

Poor Estimation Skills in Multiplication and Division. Some students have difficulty computing with decimals because they lack a sense of place value and estimation. Therefore, these error patterns occur:

$$0.3 \times 0.3 = 0.9 \qquad 0.52\overline{)104}^{\;2}$$

They need to model such problems with manipulatives where possible, and at all times they should accompany the modeling with the oral language as shown in the Teaching Strategies part of the chapter.

This procedure helps students determine whether their answers are reasonable or not.

Activity 12.42

PORTFOLIO **PORTFOLIO ASSESSMENTS**

For Teacher Reflection of Students' Work with Multiplication of Decimals

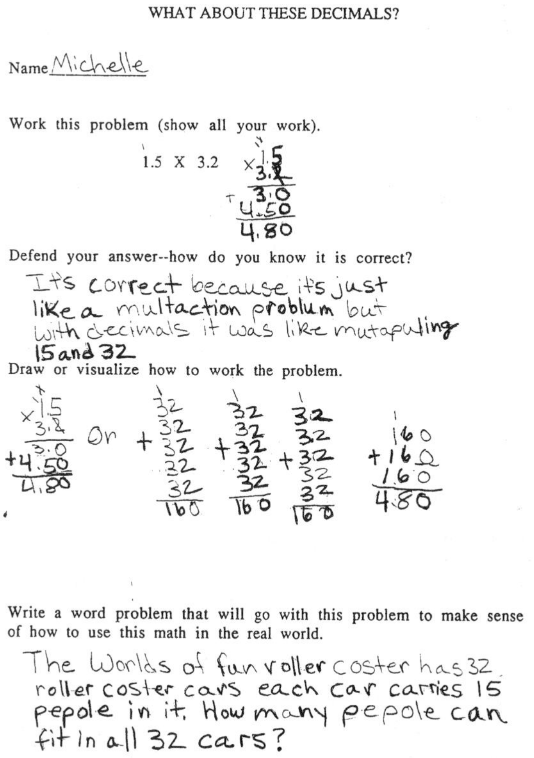
WHAT ABOUT THESE DECIMALS?

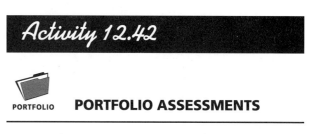

Name Michelle

Work this problem (show all your work).

1.5 X 3.2

Defend your answer--how do you know it is correct?

It's correct because it's just like a multaction problum but with decimals it was like mutapuling 15 and 32

Draw or visualize how to work the problem.

Write a word problem that will go with this problem to make sense of how to use this math in the real world.

The Worlds of fun roller coster has 32 roller coster cars each car carries 15 pepole in it. How many pepole can fit in all 32 cars?

DIRECTIONS

1. Analyze the response made by each student. Create a reflective description of what you think can be said about the student's degree of understanding of multiplication of decimals.
2. Describe how the drawings gave clarification of each student's level of understanding. What information was gained from their drawings? Compare the various levels of understanding between the students. What NCTM *Principles and Standards* (2000) are you including in your assessments? Explain your answer.
3. Design a rubric that would take into account the diversity of answers while being open in your assessment.

   Include the rubric in your Professional Portfolio for Job Interviews.

Activity Continues

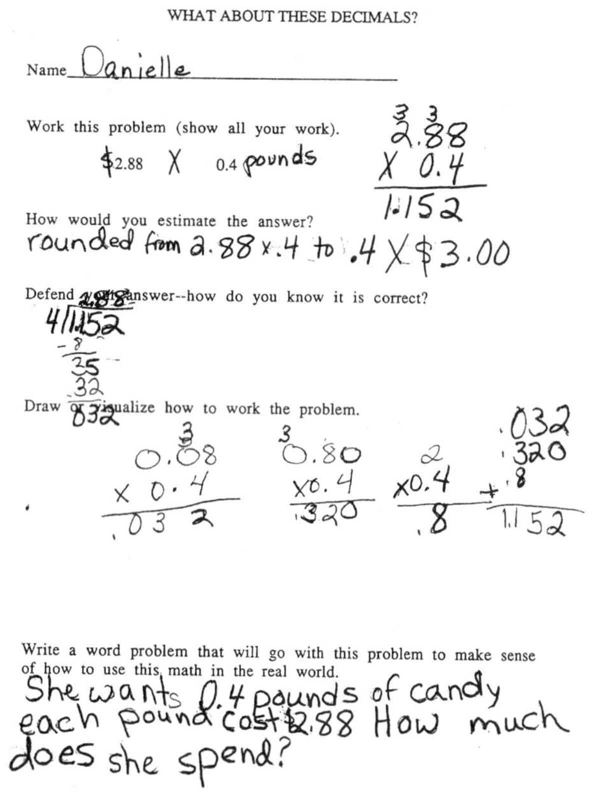

WHAT ABOUT THESE DECIMALS?

Name Danielle

Work this problem (show all your work).

$2.88 X 0.4 pounds

2.88 × 0.4 = 1.152

How would you estimate the answer?

rounded from 2.88 x .4 to .4 X $3.00

Defend your answer--how do you know it is correct?

4/1.152

Draw or visualize how to work the problem.

0.08 x 0.4 = .032 0.80 x0.4 = .320 2 x0.4 = .8 .032 + .320 + .8 = 1.152

Write a word problem that will go with this problem to make sense of how to use this math in the real world.

She wants 0.4 pounds of candy each pound cost $2.88 How much does she spend?

SUMMARY

The NCTM *Principles and Standards* (2000) suggest that students should learn fractions with understanding. How can this be accomplished? Research (Mack, 1990) suggests that students bring a great deal of informal knowledge to the classroom based on familiar situations. However, instruction with fractions and decimals often is not linked to the real world. Rules and procedures dominate the typical instruction especially with respect to teaching operations with fractions and decimals.

The NCTM *Standards* indicate that students must be helped to relate mathematics symbols to real-world situations. To help children make connections to appropriate applications, traditional instruction must change to include student-generated algorithms, working with concrete materials, and creating situational word problems to provide context and meaning. This chapter has provided activities to concentrate on developing conceptual understanding with a variety of concrete materials.

The next chapter discusses ratio, proportion, percent, and rate. Attention is given to developing the ability to see problems that can be solved with proportional reasoning.

EXERCISES

For extended exercises, see the CD-ROM.

A. Memorization and Comprehension Exercises
Low-Level Thought Activities

1. Find all the Cuisenaire rods that represent $\frac{1}{4}$. Use the fractional rods up through two orange rods as the denominator.
2. State a better terminology than "reduce to lowest terms" to help children learn mental manipulations of fractions. Explain why "reduce to lowest terms" can be a problem for children.
3. The phrase "key to the basic unit as the whole or 1" has been used repeatedly throughout the chapter. Explain why it is crucial to mention continually to children.
4. List the repeating decimals found between $\frac{1}{2}$ and $\frac{1}{10}$. Generalize a rule for finding nonterminating, repeating decimals in relation to the whole unit 1.

B. Application and Analysis Exercises
Middle-Level Thought Activities

1. Create your own pictorial example using a multiple embodiment other than the circular fraction kit to show:
   a. Whole-to-part activity
   b. A partitioning activity
   c. An equivalence activity
2. Compare the common denominator method and the reciprocal method for division of fractions. Create a new number problem (one not seen in this chapter) to show both methods. Show a pictorial model to go along with

your number problem. Practice with a model that was more difficult for you to understand as you read the chapter.

3. Look at one of the mathematics textbook series for the elementary and middle schools. Analyze how many different approaches to fractions are presented within one grade level. How many pages are devoted to concrete and pictorial models? What "extra" materials might you as a teacher need to use as supplementary work for your students?
4. Think about how you were taught to multiply and divide decimals. Write a reflective paper on how effective you feel these experiences were, including the pros and cons of this type of instruction. Compare that learning experience to what hands-on activities you did in class or as you read this chapter.

C. Synthesis and Evaluation Exercises
High-Level Thought Activities

1. Create your own lesson plan for teaching one concept using common fractions. Follow the following steps:
   a. Look at the NCTM *Standards.* Find a grade level and a concept within that grade level. Trace the previous knowledge of the concept taught in earlier grades so you will know where to begin your instruction.
   b. Use current articles from professional journals to help plan the direction of the lesson. Document your sources.
2. Prepare a lesson using a calculator that has fraction capability. In the lesson, include objectives, how to solve fraction problems using the calculator, activities, and evaluations.
3. Evaluate how teachers can use materials to develop conceptual understanding for common fractions and decimals. Which materials seem the most valuable to you? Justify your position.
4. The work of an actual student is reproduced here. Create a remediation plan to help the student overcome the misconceptions in the representation of decimals. Your plan should include the following:
   a. An analysis of the error pattern.
   b. An evaluation of the thought processing required in the examples and the thought processing displayed by the student.
   c. The sequential development of concrete, pictorial, and symbolic models to reteach the concept.

One student's written response:

Seventy-two hundredths = .720
Three tenths = .30
Eight hundredths = .800
Twenty-four thousandths = .2400

BIBLIOGRAPHY

For an extended bibliography, see the CD-ROM.

Armstrong, Barbara E., and Nadine Bezuk. "Multiplication and Division of Fractions: The Search for Meaning." Eds. Judith T. Sowder and Bonnie P. Schappelle. *Providing a Foundation for Teaching Mathematics in the Middle Grades.* Albany: State University of New York Press, 1995. 85–119.

Bezuk, Nadine S., and Marilyn Bieck. "Current Research on Rational Numbers and Common Fractions: Summary and Implications for Teachers." Ed. Douglas T. Owens. *Research Ideas for the Classroom: Middle Grades Mathematics.* Reston, VA: National Council of Teachers of Mathematics, 1993: 118–136.

Brinker, Laura. "Using Recipes and Ratio Tables to Build on Students' Understanding of Fractions." *Teaching Children Mathematics* 5 (December 1998): 218–224.

Burns, Marilyn. *The Math Solution: Teaching for Mastery through Problem Solving.* Sausalito, CA: Marilyn Burns Education Associates, 1984.

Curcio, Frances R., Francine Sicklick, and Susan B. Turkel. "Divide and Conquer: Unit Strips to the Rescue." *Arithmetic Teacher* 35 (December 1987): 6–12.

Dorgan, Karen. "What Textbooks Offer for Instruction in Fraction Concepts." *Teaching Children Mathematics* 1 (November 1994): 150–155.

Empson, Susan B. "Using Sharing Situations to Help Children Learn Fractions." *Teaching Children Mathematics* 2 (October 1995): 110–114.

Heller, Patricia M., Thomas R. Post, Merlyn Behr, and Richard Lesh. "Qualitative and Numerical Reasoning about Fractions and Rates by Seventh- and Eighth-Grade Students." *Journal for Research in Mathematics Education* 21 (November 1990): 388–402.

Hiebert, James. "Decimal Fractions." *Arithmetic Teacher* 34 (March 1987): 22–23.

Hiebert, James, and Diana Wearne. "Procedures Over Concepts: The Acquisition of Decimal Number Knowledge." Ed. James Hiebert. *Conceptual and Procedural Knowledge: The Case of Mathematics.* Hillsdale, NJ: Erlbaum, 1986: 199–223.

Kieren, Thomas E. "Creating Spaces for Learning Fractions." Eds. Judith T. Sowder and Bonnie P. Schappelle. *Providing a Foundation for Teaching Mathematics in the Middle Grades.* Albany: State University of New York Press, 1995. 31–65.

Langford, Karen, and Angela Sarullo. "Introductory Common and Decimal Fraction Concepts." Ed. Robert J. Jensen. *Research Ideas for the Classroom: Early Childhood Mathematics.* Reston, VA: National Council of Teachers of Mathematics, 1993. 223–247.

Mack, Nancy K. "Learning Fractions with Understanding: Building of Informal Knowledge." *Journal for Research in Mathematics Education* 21 (January 1990): 16–32.

———. "Building a Foundation for Understanding the Multiplication of Fractions." *Teaching Children Mathematics* 5 (September 1998): 34–38.

Middleton, James A., Marja van den Heuvel-Panhuizen, and Julia A. Shew. "Using Bare Representations for a Model for Connecting Concepts of Rational Number." *Mathematics Teaching in the Middle School* 3 (January 1998): 302–312.

National Council of Teachers of Mathematics. *Curriculum and Evaluation Standards for School Mathematics.* Reston, VA: NCTM, 1989.

———. *Principles and Standards for School Mathematics.* Reston, VA: NCTM, 2000 (to be published).

Ott, Jack M., Daniel L. Sovok, and Diana L. Gibson. "Understanding Partitive Division of Fractions." *Arithmetic Teacher* 39 (October 1991): 7–11.

Owens, Douglas T., and Douglas B. Super. "Teaching and Learning Decimal Fractions." Ed. Douglas T. Owens. *Research Ideas for the Classroom: Middle Grades Mathematics.* Reston, VA: National Council of Teachers of Mathematics, 1993. 137–158.

Payne, Joseph N. "Curricular Issues: Teaching Rational Numbers." *Arithmetic Teacher* 31 (February 1984): 14–17.

Payne, Joseph, Ann Towsky, and Deann Huinker. "Fractions and Decimals." Ed. Joseph N. Payne. *Mathematics for the Young Child.* Reston, VA: National Council of Teachers of Mathematics, 1990. 175–200.

Smith, Margaret Schwan, and Mary Kay Stein. "Selecting and Creating Mathematics Tasks: From Research to Practice." *Mathematics Teaching in the Middle School* 3 (February 1998): 344–350.

Streefland, Leen. "Fractions: A Realistic Approach." Eds. Thomas P. Carpenter, Elizabeth Fennema, and Thomas A. Romberg. Rational Numbers: An Integration of Research. Hillsdale, NJ: Lawrence Erlbaum Associates, 1993. 289–326.

Strong, Dorothy S. (Mathematics Ed.). *Systemwide Objectives and Standards.* Vols. 1–3. Chicago: Board of Education of the City of Chicago, 1990.

Warrington, Mary Ann. "How Children Think about Division with Fractions." *Mathematics Teaching in the Middle School* 2 (May 1997): 390–394.

Warrington, Mary Ann, and Constance Kamii. "Multiplication with Fractions: A Piagetian Constructivist Approach." *Mathematics Teaching in the Middle School* 3 (February 1998): 339–343.

Zaslavsky, Claudia. *Multicultural Mathematics.* New York: J. Weston Walch, 1993.

CHILDREN'S LITERATURE

Adler, David A. *Fraction Fun.* New York: Holiday House, 1996.

Dennis, Richard. *Fractions Are Parts of Things.* New York: Crowell, 1973.

Emberley, Ed. *Ed Emberley's Picture Pie: A Circle Drawing Book.* Boston: Little & Brown Publishers, 1984.

Hutchins, Pat. *The Doorbell Rang.* New York: Greenwillow, 1986.

Leedy, Loreen. *Fraction Action.* New York: Holiday House, 1994.

Mathews, Louise. *Gator Pie.* Denver, CO: Sundance, 1995.

McMillan, Bruce. *Eating Fractions.* New York: Scholastic, 1991.

Integrating Technology

Video Vignettes: Lesson Plans in Action

- *Rectangles and Fractions*

Computer Software Resources

. . . for Fractions and Decimals

Internet Searches

Surfing the Internet for Topics on Common Fractions and Decimals

Use the World Wide Web (WWW) and navigate through the system, searching for new information under major headings and subheadings similar to the following:

- Mathematics Education
  - Fractions
  - Decimals
    - NSF Projects
    - Programs
  - NCTM
    - Fractions
    - Decimals
  - NAEP Assessment Data
    - Fractions
    - Decimals

- *Remember. . .* the Web is fluid . . . new topics and ways to search for topics change daily.
- Be adventurous . . . think of some new things you could try.

13

Percent, Ratio, Proportion, and Rate

Activities Index

IN THE TEXT

ON CD-ROM

The study of ratio, proportion, percent, and rate involves largely activities for grade five through grade eight. From decimals, students proceed to the study of ratio and percent, two other focal points in the study of rational numbers. Proportion is an extension of the comparisons developed when studying ratio. Rate is another way of comparing relationships. All four concepts have many real-world applications and frequently become topics of word problems in elementary and middle school problem solving.

You may be asking, "Why are these four mathematical concepts placed together in a chapter?" Interestingly, they *are* related. Let's look at the following word problem as an example. Table 13.1 shows how rewording can change the problem from one concept to another.

The problem: "Mateo rewards himself with three bite-size candies every time he gets a hit in baseball."

All these problems have a multiplicative relationship and a constant. In this example the constant is the 3. The number of candies is three times the hits or $c = 3h$. We will see how that understanding is developed in each of the four concepts. In a school setting each concept, while related, is initially presented separately, so we present them separately in this chapter as well.

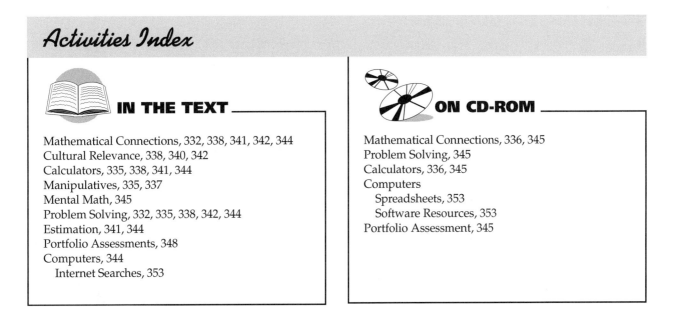

TABLE 13.1 The Questions Coming from the Situation

As a **rate** problem	Mateo eats at a rate of three candies per hit.
As a **ratio** problem	For every hit, Mateo eats three candies.
As a **proportion** problem	If Mateo eats three candies per hit, how many candies will he eat if he gets four hits?
As a **percent** problem	Of nine pieces of candy, what percent of the candy will Mateo have eaten after one hit?

TEACHING STRATEGIES

Percent

Percent means "by the hundred." Percent, when standing alone as in 32 percent, may be considered a ratio—32 parts out of 100. All percents are compared to a hundred parts or hundredths. Frequently, percent is the first ratio that students meet. Percent is usually taught right after fractions and decimals in fourth or fifth grade, but children have an intuitive sense of percent early in their school experience. This is seen in the Assessment section of this chapter when the percent work of second and third graders is reviewed.

Lembke and Reys (1994) found that fifth graders had a broad knowledge of percent in real-life situations. They found that both fifth graders and seventh graders in the study used 25 percent, 50 percent, and 100 percent as reference points (called benchmarks by Lembke and Reys) more frequently when asked to solve problems than other approaches to find percent such as a fraction, ratio, equation, drawing pictures, or trial and error. By ninth grade, the reference points were not as prevalent a choice; the idea of using an equation became the most frequent approach taken.

From Concrete to the Connecting Level. Real-world situations occur in concrete activities in informal ways before the fifth grade. Early activities encourage teachers to model wording with percents and encourage children to speak of percents following the teacher's lead (that is, oral discourse).

Money. Using money is one of children's first experiences with an intuitive sense of percent. Money is a hands-on commodity that can buy other concrete things. Children learn that 50 cents is a half of a dollar and a dollar is equivalent to 100 pennies. It also helps that 50 cents and 50 percent sound much alike in oral speech. The same can also be said for 25 percent. A delightful children's book that helps with this idea is *If You Made a Million*, by David M. Schwartz (1989). Children can be encouraged to see that they have 50 percent of a dollar when they have 50 cents, and so on.

Shapes. Early activities include subjects in which shapes and parts of shapes are used. Such activities include art where children are asked to cut a figure in half and in fourths so that they can use 50 percent of the circle and 25 percent of the circle. Notice in the following activity how a teacher can word examples so that percents can become a part of lessons in natural ways.

Check Your Mathematics Knowledge

On Percent, Ratio, Proportion, and Rate

- Definitions and Algebraic Examples
- Mental Math and Its Relationship to Percentages

. . . a refresher from mathematics content coursework . . . Lest you forget!

Activity 13.1

MATHEMATICAL CONNECTIONS · PROBLEM SOLVING

CREATING ART PROJECTS WITH PERCENT OF SHAPES

MATERIALS

- Two circles, two rectangles, two triangles, scissors
- Crayons or paint (depending on desire of teacher)
- Glue

DIRECTIONS

1. Have children cut out all the shapes.
2. Take one circle, one triangle, and one rectangle. Cut each in half, and in half again. The teacher should ask, "Show me 50 percent of the circle, . . . 25 percent of the circle." Do the same with the other shapes.

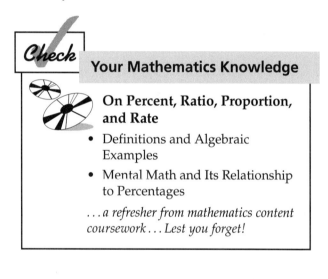

BOX 13.1 Curriculum and Evaluation Standards

Computation and Estimation

In grades 5–8, the mathematics curriculum should develop the concepts underlying computation and estimation in various contexts so that students can—

- Compute with whole numbers, fractions, decimals, integers, and rational numbers.
- Develop, analyze, and explain procedures for computation and techniques for estimation.
- Develop, analyze, and explain methods for solving proportions.
- Use computation, estimation, and proportions to solve problems.
- Use estimation to check the reasonableness of results.

Number and Number Relationships

In grades 5–8, the mathematics curriculum should include the continued development of number and number relationships so that students can—

- Understand, represent, and use numbers in a variety of equivalent forms (integer, fraction, decimal, percent, exponential, and scientific notation) in real-world and mathematical problem situations.
- Develop number sense for whole numbers, fractions, decimals, integers, and rational numbers.
- Understand and apply ratios, proportions, and percents in a wide variety of situations.
- Investigate relationships among fractions, decimals, and percents.
- Represent numerical relationships in one- and two-dimensional graphs.

Source: National Council of Teachers of Mathematics, 1989, pp. 87, 94.

Activity Continues

3. Have students create pictures (Figure 13.1) with the whole shapes and their 25 percent and 50 percent parts.
4. The children then tell each other what they have used to make each figure.
5. Teachers help children use the terminology of percent by asking such clarifying questions as:
   "What percent of the circle made the hat?"
   "What percent of the triangle made each shoe?"

FIGURE 13.1

Percent pictures by children.

Activity Continues

Supporting the NCTM *Principles and Standards* (2000):

- Mathematics as Connections; Mathematics as Communication, Representations
- Oral Discourse of Students—The Teaching Principle
- Monitoring Students' Progress; Evaluating Students' Achievement—The Assessment Principle

Tangrams can also be used to connect percents with the fractional parts. Children who have physically manipulated the tangrams in activities like those presented in Chapter 6 know which pieces are congruent to each other, and therefore, equivalent in percent to each other. Figure 13.2 is an extension of an activity developed in the NCTM Addenda Series, *Understanding Rational Numbers and Proportions* (Curcio and Bezuk, 1994). The idea has been extended in this text to show the connection to percent as a natural extension from the money concept.

Students can move from concrete figures to the connecting level of pictorial images by using interactive computer programs that allow them to construct two-dimensional figures and shade in different percentages of the picture using the many colors available in computer programs.

FIGURE 13.2

Name of Piece	Fraction of Cake	Cost	Percent of Cake	
Large triangle	$\frac{1}{4}$	\$0.25	25%	× 2
Medium triangle	$\frac{1}{8}$	\$0.12$\frac{1}{2}$	12$\frac{1}{2}$%	
Small triangle	$\frac{1}{16}$	\$0.06$\frac{1}{4}$	6$\frac{1}{4}$%	× 2
Square	$\frac{1}{8}$	\$0.12$\frac{1}{2}$	12$\frac{1}{2}$%	
Parallelogram	$\frac{1}{8}$	\$0.12$\frac{1}{2}$	12$\frac{1}{2}$%	
	$\frac{16}{16}$		100%	

Tangram Cake Total Cost \$1.00

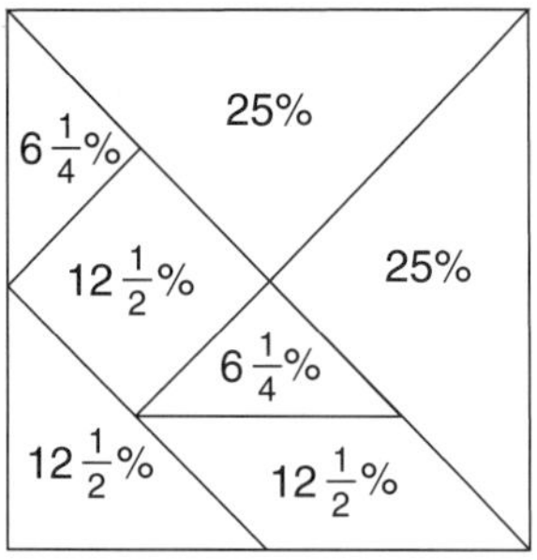

Tangram cake: 100% sold for a dollar.

From the Connecting Level to the Symbolic. By the fifth grade, students have the opportunity to work with pictorial grids of a hundred parts. The grids gradually move from a literal representation of percent to symbolic representations of different amounts that stand for whole percentages and their parts. The grids help prevent some of the problems seen in the National Assessment of Educational Progress (NAEP).

Data from the NAEP (Kouba, Zawojewski, and Strutchens, 1997) on items involving the understanding of percent, ratio, and rate was disappointing. There was improvement over the grades, but students at grade four and grade eight tended to respond to multiple-step problems by reducing them to one-step operations. On the one multiple-choice question that was the same over all three groups in the NAEP, 20 percent of the fourth graders, 36 percent of the eighth graders, and 50 percent of the twelfth graders answered it correctly. As noted throughout this chapter, it appears that more emphasis needs to be placed on understanding rather than routine procedures that do not seem to serve students well when multiple-step thinking is required.

Hundreds Grids. Hundreds grids are squares of 100 pieces. Students shade or color different parts to represent the percent of one hundred. Figure 13.3 shows an example as might appear in typical textbooks.

FIGURE 13.3

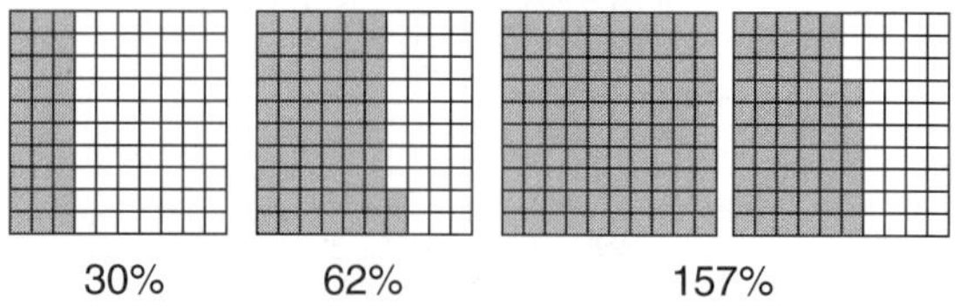

Hundred grids showing percent.

Working with the grid, students do activities where the squares take on different symbolic representations of percent. An example based on the work of Bennett and Nelson (1994, p. 23) shows how middle school students can use the grid method to solve word problems involving percentages. The Bennett-Nelson wording is used.

The Problem:

The first-year profit from a small business was \$46,500, and it increased 64 percent during the second year. What was the profit the second year?

The hundreds grid represents the first-year profit of \$46,500, and the 64 small squares in the second grid represent the percentage increase. So all 164 shaded squares represent the second-year profit. Since each small square has a value of \$46,500 ÷ 100 = \$465, the increase during the second year is 64 × \$465 = \$29,760. Thus, the second-year profit is \$46,500 + \$29,760 = \$76,260.

FIGURE 13.4

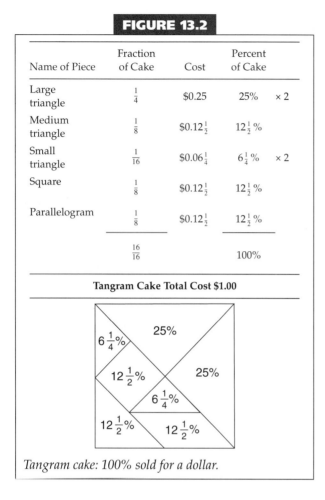

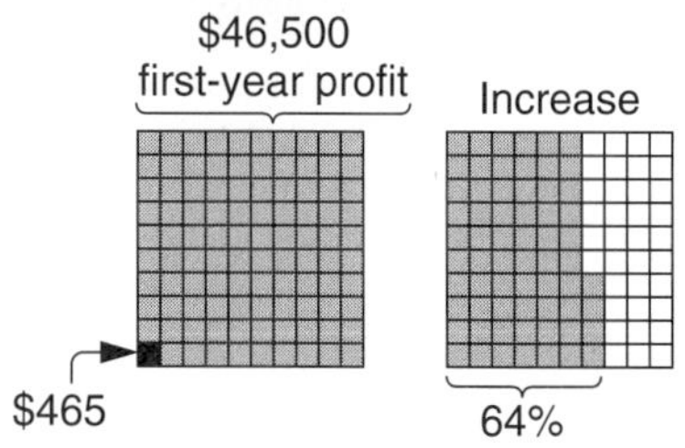

Grids showing problem solving with profit-increase problems.

A second way can also be seen with the grid. Once the $465 value of the small square is known, the total value of the 164 small squares, which is the second-year profit, is:

$$164 \times \$465 = \$76{,}260.$$

Therefore, students are given two ways to find the solution. One can be used as a check for the other. Bennett and Nelson (1994) show many more interesting ways to symbolically vary the representations in other difficult word problems with percent. Once children are familiar with the concept of increase over a two-year period, word problems can be extended to third-year profits, and so forth, as you are asked to do in the end-of-chapter exercises.

Unusual Shapes. Unusual shapes are used when divisions into parts is not so easily seen. The Assessment section shows that elementary students are not the only ones who have a difficult time showing percentages with unusual shapes. Even preservice teachers have found the task more difficult than expected. Stars are shown as the example in the following activity. This activity shows the fractional equivalent way of finding percent.

Activity 13.2

MANIPULATIVES CALCULATORS

PERCENT WITH PATTERN BLOCKS OR GRAPH PAPER

DIRECTIONS

1. Using the actual pattern blocks as models, trace around them and shade the percent of the figure indicated below each one. Be ready to use graph paper also.

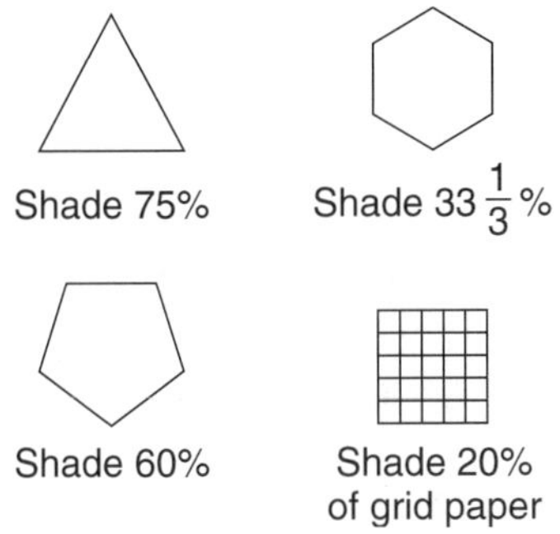

2. Trace around other pattern blocks and shade a percent of the figure. Write the percent you chose to shade or color underneath each figure.

Activity Continues

3. Do the same activity as in Step 2, using graph paper this time.
4. Check each figure to see whether it is the correct percentage by finding the common fractional equivalent. For example, in Step 1:
   If 75 percent is shaded, then $\frac{3}{4}$ of the figure (or 3 out of 4 equal sections) should be shaded.
5. Write the fractional equivalent under each percentage to show you have checked each figure.
6. Check with a calculator to see whether the fractional equivalent is the same.

Activity 13.3

PROBLEM SOLVING

EXPLAIN YOUR THINKING WITH PERCENTS (A MIDDLE SCHOOL ACTIVITY)

Estimate the size (as a percent) of each section of the circle. Explain the mathematics used to arrive at the percent of each piece of the circle.

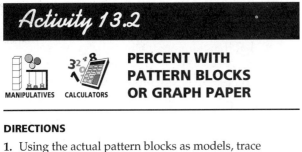

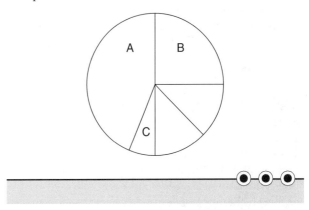

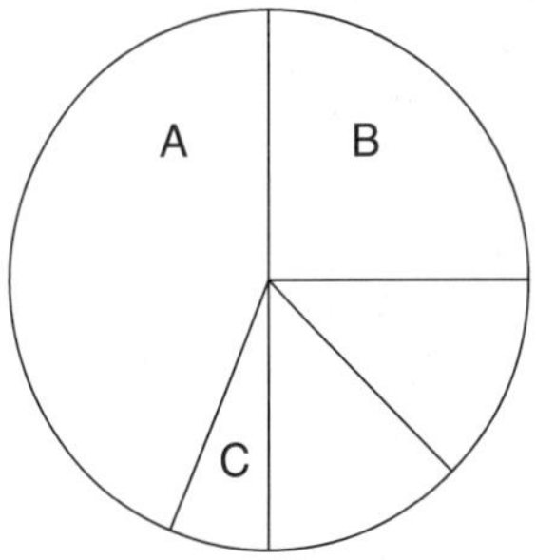

Percentages as Equations. Children do well with percent problems presented in an equation form if the numbers are kept simple so that students can visualize the answer. Figure 13.5 shows two ways the equations can be presented to children.

Real-World Mathematics. The most common use of percent in the real world is with sale items. Students need to know how to figure percents when they are buying reduced items so they have a clear

FIGURE 13.5

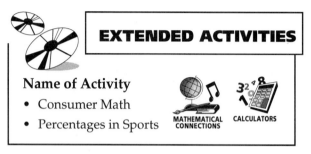

WHAT IS 50% OF 14?
50% IS HALF SO THE ANSWER IS 7.

Percents represented as equations.

understanding of the discounted price. Often a store will have a sign over a counter announcing, "20 PERCENT OFF THE TICKET PRICE." It is up to the consumer to figure out how much the item is reduced before deciding whether it is affordable at the sale price. Computer programs like the spreadsheet activity at the end of the chapter can help students analyze what steps a person must take to find percentage reductions. Additional practice can then be done on the calculator.

Children enjoy the idea of creating their own classroom stores. Many teachers integrate the study of percent with connections across the curriculum in economics. Students decide which items are to be sold at discounts by the percentage reduced on the sale price of items. Students can use (1) actual goods (penny toys, pencils, odds and ends collected by the teacher), (2) empty boxes and cans of used items, or (3) pictures from catalogs or the newspaper. Figure 13.6 shows the work of one student. This work can be adapted to computers. Students can use interactive computer programs such as Logo *Turtle Math* to write down the steps they need to remember when deciding on sale prices. By running the program and checking out some of their prices, the students discover whether their mathematical reasoning came up with the same answer as the computer program. If not, they will analyze what parts they need to redo by comparing their answers with the computer standard. This is a self-reliant way students can work with real-world situations without depending on a teacher. This takes computer use out of the drill and practice mode and into an aid to the children's own thinking.

More activities using consumer mathematics and percentages in the sports world are seen on the CD-ROM. Students who are interested in sports may enjoy setting up their own sports charts with percentage of wins to losses for their favorite professional teams or use the CD-ROM activity to keep track of their own school team's percentage of wins and losses.

EXTENDED ACTIVITIES

Name of Activity

- Consumer Math
- Percentages in Sports

MATHEMATICAL CONNECTIONS CALCULATORS

Lembke and Reys (1994) report that the most popular to least popular ways to solve percent problems by fifth and seventh graders in their study were as follows: (1) using comparisons to benchmark reference points (that is, 25 percent, 50 percent, and so forth); (2) setting up an equation (____ is a ____% of ____); (3) making a fractional equivalent; and (4) setting up a ratio. It is interesting to note that only the top quartile of students in both grades saw the ratio as a possibility to solve the problems.

Ratio

The concept of ratio is an extension from common fractions and may be written using the same symbolic notation:

$\frac{2}{5}$	The concrete manipulations are represented the same as they were in common fractions.
	Two ways to express the meaning of ratio in words are:
	two to five, *or*
2:5	For every two in one set, there are five in another set.

From Concrete to the Connecting Level. Pattern blocks and Cuisenaire rods are two of the materials children can use to express ratio (Figure 13.7). Children can start doing teacher-made activities for ratio like Activity 13.4. Using it as an example, chil-

FIGURE 13.6

Write what you will do step by step to find the sale price on items when you know the original price and what percent the item is to be reduced.

1. You put in the first price it cost.
2. Then you get the calculater to multiply the % off x .01 to get the real % and the multipuly by the first price.
3. Then you take the first price and take away the answer in #2.
4. Then you have the sale price.

A Sample Problem: You are the sales manager and you must decide what percent to take off the orginal price of your items. What price will you charge customers at the checkout counter?

Paste items and original price tags here:

Take 20 % off the sticker price.

The sale price will be $1.87 The sale price will be $14.38

1. 2.34
2. 20 x .01 x 2.34 = 0.468
3. 2.34 − 0.468 = 1.872
It's money so make it 1.87

1. $17.98
2. 20 x .01 x 17.98 = 3.596
3. 17.98 − 3.596 = 14.384
It's money so make it $14.38

Student's written journal worksheet of percent-off items.

dren can make their own activity cards. They write the answers in words (written discourse) on the back of the cards so other children can check their work after they explore the new activity cards. Two children can take turns seeing how many they can do correctly. These activities make good learning center or "extra time" activities when children find they have some free time on their hands.

FIGURE 13.7

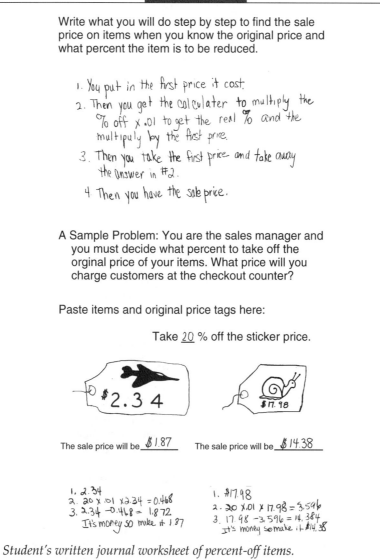

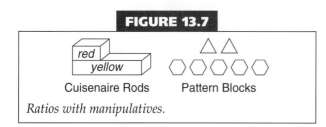

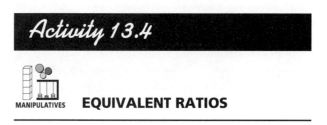

Cuisenaire Rods Pattern Blocks

Ratios with manipulatives.

Activity 13.4

MANIPULATIVES

EQUIVALENT RATIOS

DIRECTIONS

1. Using attribute blocks and pattern blocks make equivalent ratios (ratios that have the same relationship). For

Activity Continues

children, one student can start and another student can make an equivalent ratio with different attribute and pattern blocks. Which of these represent the same ratio?

Say: "For every 3 triangles there are 2 hexagons.The ratio is 3 to 2"

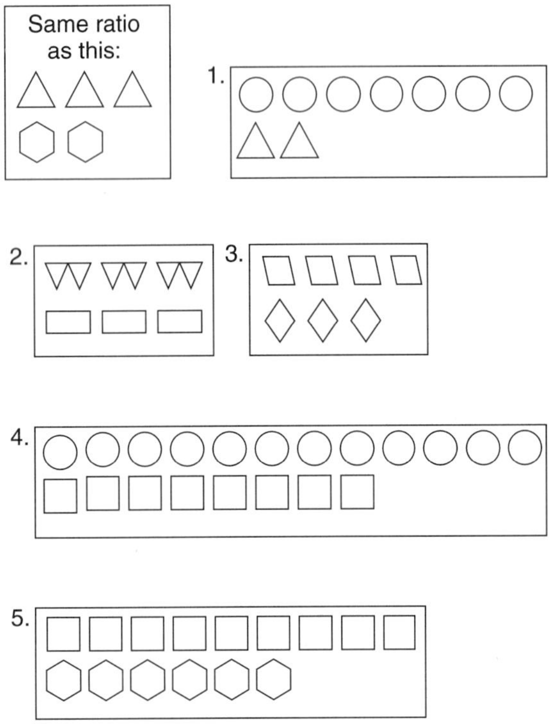

2. Continue the activity using Cuisenaire rods.
3. Think of other manipulatives that could show ratios.
4. Orally describe each ratio relationship.

Supporting the NCTM *Principles and Standards* (2000):

- Mathematics as Reasoning/Patterning; Mathematics as Communication, Representation
- Oral Discourse of Teacher and Student; Tools That Enhance Discourse—The Teaching Principle
- Mathematics Curriculum Principle...what all students need to know and do

Other activities celebrate children's literature and Native American culture. The next activity helps children see why it is important to have the right ratio of roaming area for the size of their pets. It explains why a large dog needs more room to play than does a very small dog. Children see why a walk around a neighborhood of several blocks in area becomes important to a dog or cat.

Activity 13.5

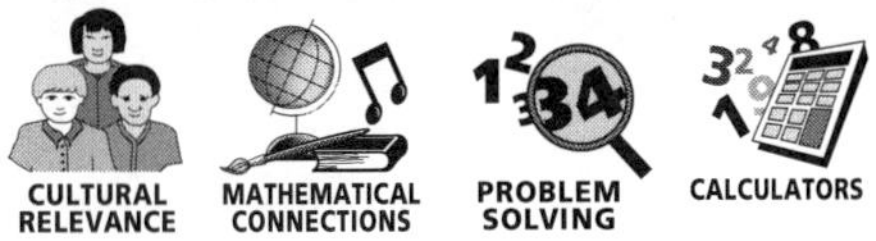

CREATING RATIOS WITH REPTILES IN NATIVE AMERICAN STORIES

MATERIALS

- "The Boy and the Rattlesnake" in *Keepers of the Animals* (Caduto and Bruchac, 1991, pp. 122–134), from the Apache Tribe in the Southwest
- Centimeter graph paper, meter sticks, newspapers, metric rulers
- Children to trace picture of lizards, snakes, turtles, salamanders, and so on, from animals, books, or encyclopedia

DIRECTIONS

1. Read the Native American story "The Boy and the Rattlesnake." Messages of story:
    - People need to use their common sense over persuasive talk.
    - Respect animals with the same respect we give humans.
    - Over 2 million reptiles are made into pets in a year's time and forced to live in a few square centimeters of cage space.

FIGURE 13.8

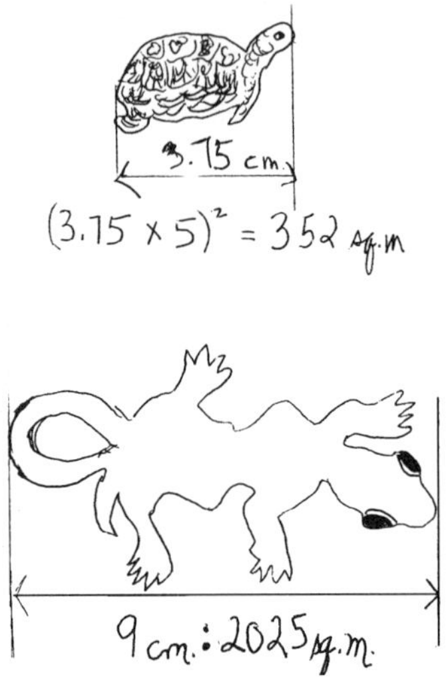

Reptile drawn by child for ratio activity.

Activity Continues

2. Reptiles need a roaming area of at least 25 square meters of space for each centimeter of their length. That's a square with the side of 5 meters for every 1 cm of reptile length.
3. How would this be expressed as a ratio?

   Take pictures of reptiles drawn by the students, have them measure the length in centimeters. Let them set up a ratio for how many square meters the reptile needs of living space.
4. With the centimeter graph paper, make a very tiny reptile and set up a ratio to its needed roaming area. There are several ways to do this—a factor-factor product model is shown here. Children can use a meter stick and newspapers taped together to measure their roaming area (Figure 13.8). Children are surprised at how large the area is for each reptile measured. One way is modeled in Figure 13.9.

FIGURE 13.9

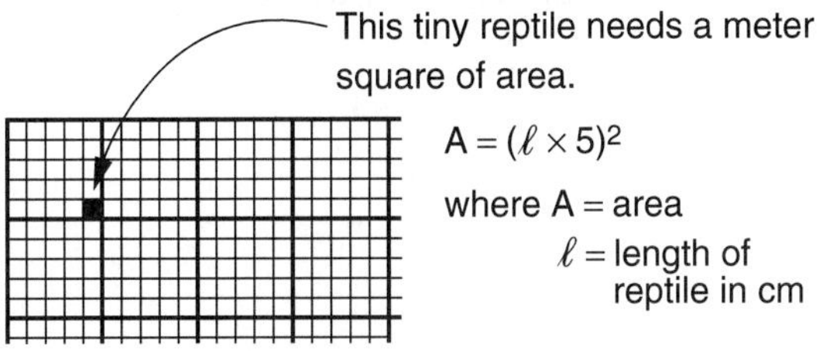

This tiny reptile needs a meter square of area.
A = (ℓ × 5)²
where A = area
ℓ = length of reptile in cm

Ratio of tiny reptile on centimeter paper.

5. Share your thoughts with others. See what area other students came up with for their reptile pictures and centimeter reptiles. (These make great bulletin boards!)

Brinker (1998) describes how ratio tables can help students plan recipe proportions. The ideas can help students get ready for assessment tests, which often expect the same mathematical modeling shown in Brinker's work.

From the Connecting Level to the Symbolic. Students can explore the several ways ratios are presented in mathematics as they become familiar with the symbolic forms of expression. The two most frequently used by students in problem solving were the part-part relationship and the factor-factor-product relationship (Barnett, Goldenstein, and Jackson, 1994). The part-part relationship was seen as the easiest method among middle schoolers as reported in research by Singer and Resnick (1992).

Part-Part Relationship. Computer programs help students move from the pictorial materials on the screen to the symbols that create the ratio. Commands like ones in Logo *Turtle Math* such as: **1part tri 4 2part pent 6** for the ratio 4:6 allow students to see that ratios are sometimes recorded symbolically as a first part to second part relationship.

Factor-Factor-Product Relationship. The previous Native American activity shows how ratio can be expressed by the part-to-part relationship and the factor-factor-product equation relationship.

The following are ratios students created using the factor-factor product relationship after reading their favorite stories from children's literature.

For every inch that Pooh Bear was round, he dug a hole twice as wide to find honey.	P = inches of Pooh; h = hole $2 \times P = h$

—developed using *Winnie the Pooh* (Milne, 1926)

For every Brachiosaurus's weight, there are 8 elephants to weigh the same amount.	w = B's weight $8 \times e = w$

—developed using *Creatures of Long Ago: Dinosaurs* (Buxton et al., 1988)

For every pup in a cup, there are three fish in a tree.	p = # of pups; f = # of fish $3 \times p = f$

—developed using *Hop on Pop* (Seuss, 1963)

The children did not seem to have trouble writing the ratios in words because the form was fairly straightforward, "for every ____ there are ____." The teachers did need to help the students see how the same relationship could be shown mathematically as an equation. The students found it easier to make a table and then work out the equation from the table. Taking the pups in the cup is the example in Table 13.2.

TABLE 13.2 Ratio Table

No. of Pups	No. of Fish
1	3
2	6
3	9

Students easily write $\_\ p = \_f$ and then they figure by trial and error where the 3 goes so that the fish are equivalent to the correct amount in the equation. As we saw in Chapter 2, just recording the variables from the language frequently results in the "variable-reversal" error. The authors have found this to be a common difficulty among all groups of students with which they have worked.

Proportions

Proportions are really equivalent ratios. The methods of finding ratios are also extended to proportions. You have already seen the start of proportional reasoning in the study of ratio as presented in the preceding section. When different values were introduced to make a new ratio, each relationship was in direct proportion to the original relationship given in the first ratio. It is a multiplicative relationship. This was seen in the Native American ratio activity when each new creature was compared to its roaming area. Each creature and its roaming area was in direct proportion to the first creature and its roaming area.

Proportional reasoning is important in applications of mathematics. The NCTM *Principles and Standards* (NCTM, 2000) states that students need to have problem situations that can be solved through proportional reasoning. Scale drawings and similar figures involve proportional reasoning.

Making a picture or representation in direct proportion to another, either larger or smaller, is called *scaling*. This idea originated on the African continent. The Logo *Turtle Math* computer language allows children to do scaling quickly. Children have the chance to work with scaling in computer simulations that resemble the way the original work was done by early Africans. They have a first-hand "feel" for multiplicative relationships after using interactive computer programs.

Cultural Contributions

CULTURAL RELEVANCE

ORIGINS OF PROPORTIONAL RELATIONSHIPS

Proportion is a concept used in real-world applications before the invention of enlargement and reduction cameras on copying machines. The following material developed by the Chicago Public Schools should be shared with students at each of the appropriate grade levels. These concepts originated on the African continent many centuries ago.

5–6

Students should know that the ancient Egyptians invented proportional scale drawings. They enlarged figures proportionally by transferring drawings from grids of smaller squares to grids of larger squares. In Egypt and Babylonia, taxation was based on proportions. A given measure of wheat was the required tax for every one hundred cattle or for every farm of a standard size.

7–8

Students should know that the ancient Egyptians invented proportional scale drawings. They enlarged figures proportionally by transferring drawings from grids of smaller squares to grids of larger squares. By 2650 B.C., Africans in ancient Egypt had invented rectangular coordinates and had used them to make scale drawings and star-clocks. (Strong, 1990)

The Part-Part Relationship in Proportions. A 12:8 ratio and a 3:2 ratio may be read as a proportion statement, "12 is to 8 as 3 is to 2." Proportions are checked the same way equivalent fractions are:

$$\frac{a}{b} = \frac{c}{d} \text{ if } ad = bc$$

$$\frac{12}{8} = \frac{3}{2} \text{ if } 12 \times 2 = 8 \times 3$$
$$24 = 24$$

It is generally called the cross-product method. However, some mathematics educators have called the setup of: $\frac{a}{b} = \frac{c}{d}$ by the term, the "rule of 3," meaning that it is easy to solve proportion problems if three of the four variables are known and only one variable is unknown. Charles and Lobato (1998) point out that expecting mastery of learning with the cross multiplication method should be delayed from grade six to grade seven to allow for more opportunities to solve proportions more informally by the "unit rate" or "factor of change" methods. *Unit rate* takes the original measure and enlarges it or decreases it by units until the desired proportion is reached. Factor of change focuses on the relationship to be maintained among factors even when a factor is changed; therefore there needs to be a corresponding change to keep the relationship constant. These are the methods presented in the next portion of this chapter.

Proportional reasoning is considered to be an important area for exploration in grades five to eight—so important, in fact, that we explore more than one approach in the remaining portion of the chapter. The next few activities show solutions in which the answers can be found by the cross-product method in the part-part relationship model.

Early Experiences with Proportion: Concrete to Connecting Level. Early experiences with proportion need to focus on things with which children are familiar and in which they have an interest. That's one reason why children enjoy activities like finding how much roaming area their own pets need as an extension of the Native American ratio activity. Children are fascinated with imagining a world in which everything they normally use could be 10 times or even a 100 times as big as they are. Remember the popularity of the movies, *Honey, I Shrunk the Kids* (1989) and *Honey, I Blew Up the Kids* (1992). Integrated units can include children's literature that emphasizes the same theme. Kliman (1993) suggests the following six children's books when working with units on proportion; the authors have added a seventh to the list:

- *Jim and the Beanstalk* by Raymond Briggs (1980)
- *Alice in Wonderland* and *Through the Looking Glass* by Lewis Carroll (1981)
- *Mouse* by Beverly Cleary and S. Ralph (1982)
- *The BFG* by Roald Dahl (1982)
- *Gulliver's Travels* by Jonathan Swift (1983)
- *Stuart Little* by E. B. White (1945)
- *Counting on Frank* by Rod Clement (1991)

Children can integrate art projects with proportion by measuring common things from their environment. Then they can enlarge the measurement dimensions by 10. These activities help children see proportion in concrete ways.

Activity 13.6

MATHEMATICAL CONNECTIONS CALCULATORS ESTIMATION

CREATING YOUR OWN WORLD 10 TIMES YOUR SIZE

MATERIALS

- Butcher paper, metric ruler, meter stick, pencil
- A set of student's choice—magic markers, crayons, paints, and so on
- Some favorite item to be measured
- Camera (optional)

DIRECTIONS

1. Estimate how large you think 10 times your item will look like. Get that much butcher paper to start the project.

Activity Continues

FIGURE 13.10

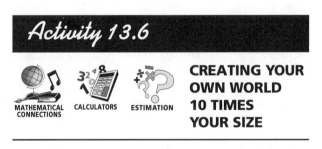

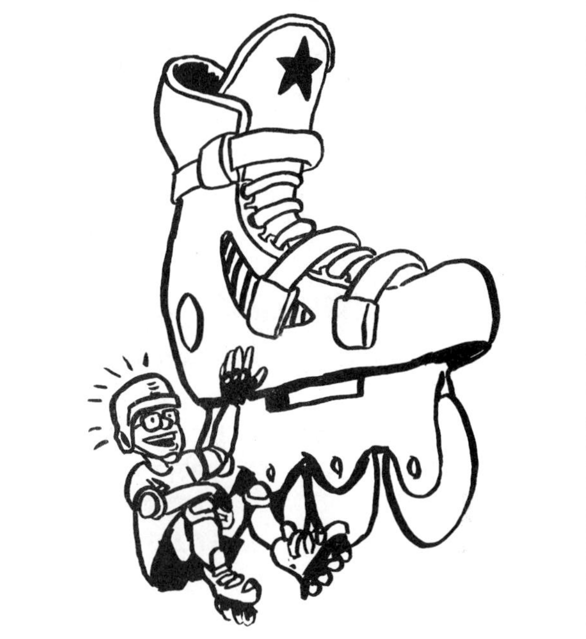

Student sitting next to his giant-sized roller blades.

2. Do the actual measurements of your item. Record them by length × width × height (for young children grades two and three, only measure length × width).
3. Make each dimension 10 times as big and record the measures on paper. Use a calculator to check whether your measures are correct if you need to do so.
4. Draw the item's magnified measures on the butcher paper.
5. Color or paint the item so it looks like the real one.
6. Write a story about your adventures if you woke up one morning to find your favorite thing was 10 times its size but you were still the same size.
7. Some teachers have even taken pictures of the student sitting next to their favorite enlarged item.

Kliman (1993) shares this story written by a student in the world of Brobdingnag. Notice how quickly it is apparent that the student understands size proportions in the story:

I was walking along one of Brod's huge sidewalks, which was like walking in a gigantic Logan Airport. Suddenly I bumped into something. It was a quarter-

full Pepsi can 4 feet 2 inches, up to my chest. Then I figured out a way to get by it, somehow, and I found myself stuck on a piece of bubble gum bigger than my foot! I was about to step and I saw a 2-foot-6-inch, 5-inch-high log. What was it? A cigarette! My, does this place have litter! (p. 319)

Another activity begins to connect the pictorial models of graphing with the concrete models of collecting and measuring actual piles of newspapers.

Activity 13.7

CULTURAL RELEVANCE MATHEMATICAL CONNECTIONS PROBLEM SOLVING

CREATING PROPORTIONS WITH NATIVE AMERICAN STORIES

MATERIALS

- "Manabozho and the Maple Trees" in *Keepers of the Earth* (Caduto and Bruchac, 1989, pp. 144–145)
- Bring in some newspapers from home to get the stack of saved newspapers started
- Yardstick for measuring height of newspapers
- Poster board for making a graph

DIRECTIONS

1. Read the Native American story "Manabozho and the Maple Trees," an Anishinabe Tribe story from the Great Lakes Region. Messages of story:
   - We must not let the trees do all our work for us. We must help save the earth and the trees too.
2. *Fact:* For every 3-foot stack of newspapers, one tree is saved.
3. Decide as a class how many trees the class would like to save. Decide how tall the stack of newspapers will need to be to save that amount of trees by recycling the paper. Set it up as a proportion:

   3 ft : 1 tree as ______ ft : ______ trees

4. Start making a graph of the proportion of trees saved to newspapers. You can use the newspapers you brought in to begin the measurement.
   - Another proportion: for every 1 foot of newspapers, you draw a third of a tree.
   - Ask the students, what could they do if there is only 1 foot of newspapers?

   1 ft : $\frac{1}{3}$ of a tree as 3 ft : 1 tree

- **Key to graph (Figure 13.11):**

Activity Continues

FIGURE 13.11

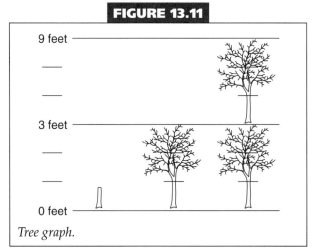

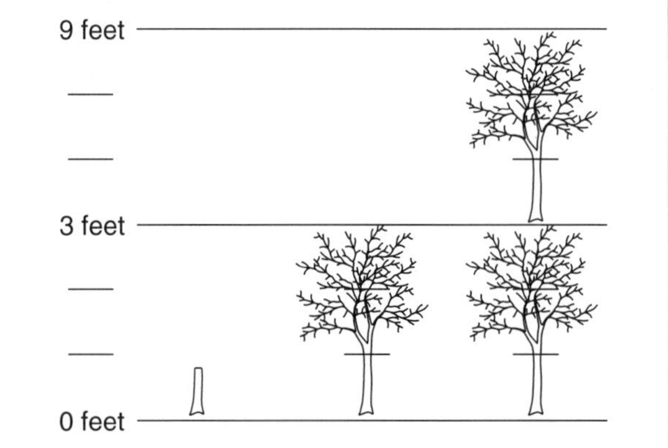

Tree graph.

5. Keep track by putting the graph up on a hall bulletin board. Ask students to talk about their project to other classes so that more newspapers can be collected.

Supporting the NCTM *Principles and Standards* (2000):

- Mathematics as Communication, Problem Solving, Connections, Representation
- Worthwhile Mathematical Tasks; Oral Discourse for Students—The Teaching Principle
- The Mathematics Curriculum Principle; Coherence

From Connecting Level to Symbolic. Proportions are the essential elements of many problem-solving activities that appear as word problems in many elementary textbooks. Typically, one ratio is given, and the next ratio is only partially finished. The problem solver must "see" the two ratios as a proportion to figure out the missing segment.

Activity 13.8

MATHEMATICAL CONNECTIONS PROBLEM SOLVING

PROPORTIONS IN ENGLISH

DIRECTIONS

1. Proportions must maintain a definite relationship among four magnitudes such that the first is in relation to the second in the same way as the third is in relation to the fourth.

Activity Continues

2. *Analogies* are really proportions with words as the magnitudes. For example:

   Oar is to rowboat as wheel is to car.

   Some standardized tests even use the mathematical symbols

   oar:rowboat = wheel:______.
3. Think of other word analogies and write them using the mathematical symbols.
4. These make great homework assignments.

Some of the most famous and infamous proportion problems from elementary and middle school texts have been the "travel" problems with the distance-to-time relationship implied. They are still seen with dread by many students and adults alike. However, one teacher found out that students actually liked travel problems if they were presented in a new way. Notice the difference:

Textbook Type	New Type
If it takes 12 seconds to go 60 miles in a rocketship, how many seconds will it take to go 55 miles?	If it takes 12 seconds for the villain to travel 60 miles to the finish line in your Nintendo game, how many seconds will it take you to win if you only need to go 55 miles to the finish line? Which one of you will win?

The Solution:

$$\frac{12}{60} = \frac{?}{55}$$

Think: Reduction

$$\frac{12 \div 12}{60 \div 12} = \frac{1}{5}$$

so

$$\frac{n \div 1}{55 \div 5}$$

so

$$n = 11 \text{ seconds}$$

Think: Cross-Multiplication

$$12 \times 55 = 60 \times n$$

$$\frac{660}{60} = \frac{60 \times n}{60}$$

$$11 = n$$

11 seconds

Labels for the proportions are important. In the preceding example, the following relationship patterns would produce valid proportions and arrive at the same answers.

Some of the new action-packed computer games lend themselves to new strategies for winning, many of which can be helped by the students' knowing

Relationship (↕)

$$\left[\frac{12 \text{ sec}}{60 \text{ min}} = \frac{N \text{ sec}}{55 \text{ min}}\right] \quad \left[\frac{60 \text{ min}}{55 \text{ min}} = \frac{12 \text{ sec}}{N \text{ sec}}\right]$$

Relationship (↔)

how fast their action figure has to move to beat out the other action figures.

Subscripts © *. . . little thoughts below the bottom line*

Other Relationship Models for Proportion. Students need to realize that the "rule of 3" in proportion problems is not the only way to explore proportion. We have already seen the use of tables and of algebraic expressions when we discussed ratios in the preceding section. Remember the "pups in the cup" example?

Another model is the use of coordinate graphs to show proportions (Figure 13.12). Middle school students should have exposure to this approach also. Taking the "pups in the cup" example, we can graph the proportion statement that "for every pup in a cup, there are three fish in the tree."

FIGURE 13.12

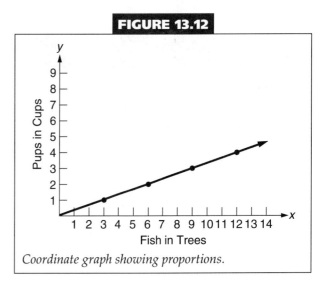

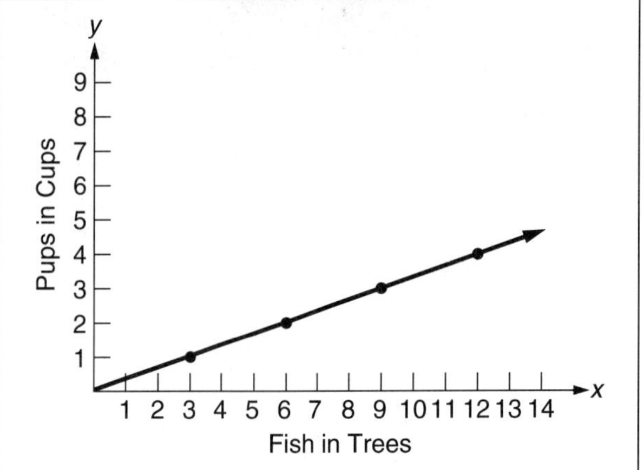

Coordinate graph showing proportions.

Activity 13.9

COMPUTERS PROBLEM SOLVING MATHEMATICAL CONNECTIONS ESTIMATION CALCULATORS

CREATING COORDINATE GRAPHS FROM OTHER PROPORTION EXAMPLES

MATERIALS

- Graph paper, pencils, or a computer coordinate graphing program or calculator

DIRECTIONS

1. Go back through this chapter and find ratio and proportion problems shown in other models.
2. Estimate what each proportion problem would look like on a coordinate graph before starting to graph each one.
3. Convert each example to the coordinate graph model.
4. Share orally with others how you set up your graphs and listen to their explanations. Compare and contrast any differences you find in your graphs.

Supporting the NCTM *Principles and Standards* (2000):

- Mathematics as Connections, Problem Solving, Communication, Representation
- Worthwhile Mathematical Tasks for Teachers—The Teaching Principle
- Monitoring Students' Progress; Evaluating Students' Achievement—The Assessment Principle

Activity 13.10

PROBLEM SOLVING CALCULATORS

MORE MIDDLE SCHOOL PROPORTIONS

1. Jo Farmer applied fertilizer to her cropland three times for the 1999 growing season. The first application, which occured in November 1998, was anhydrous ammonia (82–0–0). She applied 150 pounds per acre of material at that time. A couple of weeks before planting, Jo applied diammonium phosphate (18–46–0) at a rate of 120 pounds per acre of material.

Activity Continues

At the time of planting, Jo applied a mixed fertilizer (9–23–30) at a rate of 100 pounds per acre. What were the total pounds of actual nutrients applied per acre to Jo's cropland? (*Hint:* The analysis (82–0–0) means that Jo applied 82% active nitrogen, 0% phosphorus, and 0% potash fertilizer. The remaining 18% is a carrier that helps hold the fertilizer to the soil particles.)

2. Joe Farmer is planning for this year's planting season by trying to figure out how much chemical he will have to purchase for weed control on 350 acres of corn. Joe has had trouble with cocklebers, so this year he will apply Atrazine and Buctril.

   The Atrazine will be applied at a rate of 2.5 pounds active ingredients (ai) per acre. The Atrazine Joe uses comes in a liquid form at a rate of 1.5 pounds ai per gallon. The Atrazine costs $8.00 per gallon and is applied two weeks before planting at 2/3 the recommended rate; the final 1/3 is applied two weeks after planting.

   The Buctril is applied two weeks after planting at a rate of .25 pound ai per acre. Buctril also comes in a liquid form and the rate is 1 pound ai per gallon and costs $12.00 per gallon.

   How many gallons of both Atrazine and Buctril will Joe need and what will the total cost be?

Proportional reasoning has so many applications in the real world that Cramer and Post (1993) suggest that as much time as needed be spent with these concepts to ensure their careful development. The NCTM Addenda Series, *Understanding Rational Numbers and Proportions* (Curcio and Bezuk, 1994) shows many creative ideas to help students explore these concepts.

Rate

Rate is a term for a ratio when the ratio involves comparisons of two units uniquely different from one another. For example, 55 miles per hour is the ratio of miles to hour. Many textbooks include problems in which the ratios are expressed as rates. When the rate involves a proportion, the problem becomes more difficult. These are found frequently on standardized tests from the upper elementary grades through college entrance examinations.

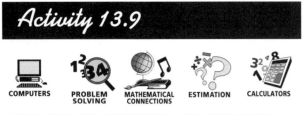

Activity 13.11

MENTAL MATH

FINDING THE RATIO IN THE RATE

DIRECTIONS

1. Think of the ratio that is implied in each of these rates:

Rate	Ratio
55 miles per hour	55 miles:1 hour
8 cans for a dollar	8:$1.00
12 eye blinks a minute	12 blinks:1 minute

2. Think of others you can add to the list.

Technically, you have already seen rate examples in the previous section when the "travel" problems were introduced. The CD-ROM activity "Rates and Proportions" provides further practice working with rates in the cross-multiplication method.

Rates can be seen in the factor-factor-product relationship of algebraic expressions. For example, for problems involving distance, rate, and time:

Let d = distance; r = rate; t = time

Three ways to set up the equation, depending on what needs to be found in the problem:

$$d = rt \qquad r = \frac{d}{t} \qquad t = \frac{d}{r}$$

Analyze the previous rate examples to determine which equation should be used. You already know what the answers should be using the other approaches, so you can reason if you were correct in your use of the equation by seeing whether your equations yield the same answers.

Middle school students have developed interesting ratio-rate problems using LEGO MINDSTORM Robotics (1998) and using radio-controlled vehicles. The students working with the radio-controlled vehicles organized a race to measure rate to the finish line depending on the length of the track. They also discovered a way to use proportional reasoning when they noticed the shadow caused by their vehicles. One middle schooler said his truck, the Intruder, was made to a scale of 1:12. He said he could figure out how long the shadow would be on a life-sized Intruder by setting up a proportion using the shadow length of the radio-controlled Intruder.

EXTENDED ACTIVITIES

CALCULATORS · MATHEMATICAL CONNECTIONS · PROBLEM SOLVING · PORTFOLIO

Name of Activity

- Proportions with Real-World Problems
- Proportions in Economics
- Finding the Height of the Flagpole
- Rates and Proportions
- Ratios with Robotics
- Emergency Medical Careers
- Response Time of Ambulances
- TIMSS Assessment: Can You Load an Airplane?

Students with Special Needs. The bright young man who created the proportional reasoning problem with the Intruder has been diagnosed with Attention Deficit Disorder (ADD). This points out once again the danger of labels. Many times engaging hands-on activities can bring out the best in all students if they are given time to think of new alternatives under stimulating conditions. Do not sell any student short. The work done with the radio-controlled vehicles and the animated robots can be seen on the CD-ROM. You can use the pictures and the activities to motivate your own students to do the same kind of activity at your school.

Percent, Ratio, Proportion, and Rate in the World of Work. Middle school is the time when students think about themselves in many occupations. As seen in Chapter 2, girls especially need a vision of the mathematics required for careers. In the CD-ROM activity "Emergency Medical Careers," middle school girls have the chance to see a female Emergency Medical Communications Officer using proportional reasoning and computers to save lives. Another series of rate and percent problems has been developed around the response time of ambulances. This problem's description comes from an ambulance company's contract with the city of Richmond, Virginia (Richmond Ambulance Authority, 1996, pp. 16–17).

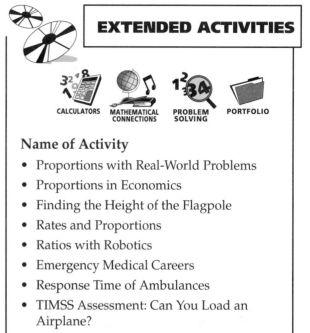

Master Contract for Paramedic Ambulance Services, July 1, 1996–2000

Categories of Emergencies		Maximum Response Time Allowed
Priority 1	Life-threatening emergency	8 min 59 sec
Priority 2	Non life-threatening emergency	12 min 59 sec
Priority 3	Urgent emergency	30 min 59 sec
Priority 4	Nonemergency	59 min 59 sec
Priority 5	Scheduled nonemergency	30 min 59 sec
Priority 6	Prescheduled nonemergency	15 min 59 sec

Response Time Performance

Response time penalties—for each priority 1, 2, 3, call not handled in the agreed on response time—contractor pays $10.00 per minute up to $250.00 per incident.

The CD-ROM contains many sample problems that can be developed around the Richmond contract with students realizing that real people actually get paid to figure out percent, rate, and ratio in the real world.

The teaching strategies in this chapter require much practice to understand fully how they apply in a variety of real-world experiences. A teacher must avoid rushing from one principle to another without adequate exploration with manipulative models. Otherwise, students will have difficulties solving problems like the preceding examples, which require an integration of all the mathematical principles studied in this chapter. The NCTM *Principles and Standards* (NCTM, 2000) states that mathematics curriculum in grades six to eight should investigate relationships between fractions, decimals, and percents. Students should understand the various representations of the same number, such as $\frac{15}{100}$, $\frac{3}{20}$, 0.15, 15%, and 15:100.

ASSESSMENT

Field-Independent and Field-Dependent Learners

Both thought-processing styles will be compared side by side to demonstrate how different students work together in cooperative learning situations.

Shaded Regions

Field-independent learners have more success finding their own fractional part from the percent given and then shading it. They should do the activity and then give it to a field-dependent learner to figure out the percent from a list of made-up answers with distractor items.

Field-dependent learners like to see the whole example and figure out the percent from there. They should explain how they get the answer for the field-independent learner because most standardized tests use this form.

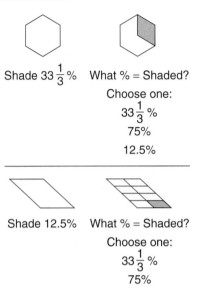

Shade $33\frac{1}{3}$% What % = Shaded?

Choose one:

$33\frac{1}{3}$%

75%

12.5%

Shade 12.5% What % = Shaded?

Choose one:

$33\frac{1}{3}$%

75%

12.5%

Spreadsheets

Observe the students as they work to see which of the actions described below are occurring, and pair students with opposite processing styles together for computer work.

Field-independent learners enjoy building the table, working from cell to cell. Creating formulas such as +a2*bl for spreadsheet programs does not seem to be a problem. They often stop after each formula and study what has happened as the number appears in each cell. They may have trouble telling all the parts of the pattern if the table is shown to them fully constructed.

Field-dependent learners are bothered with what they perceive as long, tedious work building the formula. They can often "spot" patterns more quickly and in more depth than the field-independent learner once the table is constructed.

Correcting Common Misconceptions

Many of the common misconceptions presented here are the same ones seen in the work of students with special needs. These concepts may prove challenging for all students.

Writing the Decimal with the Percent. It is common for children to hear 52 percent and write 0.52%, remembering that the number with two decimal places is "per hundredth." Reading the percent aloud with place-value labels is often all that is needed for the student to see the mistake. Fifty-two hundredths of a percent sounds much less than 52 percent.

If the problem persists, spreadsheet programs in which children can change the numbers quickly and see the results are often a good way for them to distinguish the difference because they can compare what 0.52% and 52% will give them. The use of a calculator to check percents is useful if the calculator has a % key.

Follow these steps for use with most calculators:

1. Enter 1.00 × (the percent you wish to check) = ________

   (This fixes the number in the calculator as a variable.)

   Example: 1.00 × 0.52 = 0.52 (calculator answer)

2. Press the % key. Now the number on the calculator will be treated as a percent and the resulting number is the decimal equivalent.

   Example: [press % key] results in 0.0052

3. On some calculators, a quicker way is possible. Entering 0.52 and pressing the % key will give the student a good way to see that the answer is 0.0052 instead of 0.52.

Percent of a Given Value. There are three common mistakes when calculating percent of a given value.

Forgetting the Meaning of the Term "of." Students know that a percent of an original number means it will be less than the original quantity, so they divide rather than multiply to find the percent. They reason that multiplication yields a greater number rather than a lesser number. Again, the word "of" is crucial to the problem. If this point is stressed throughout the study of multiplication from basic facts to percents, students will recognize that "of" means multiplication and that the answer is smaller than the original number, which does make sense. For example:

29% of 52

Common Error	*With "of" as Multiplication*
$0.29\overline{)52.00}$ = 179.31	52 × 0.29 = 15.08

Stopping after Percent Is Found without Further Reduction. In price-reduction problems students frequently find the percent correctly, but forget that the problem is not finished because the original price must be reduced by that percent, meaning subtraction must be used. Role-playing many shopping examples with things they enjoy buying seems to help in two-step problem-solving situations.

Thinking of Percent as Money to Be Reduced. When converting percents to decimals, the decimal reminds the student of the money that is involved in the answer. Therefore, in a price-reduction problem, 0.29 becomes $0.29 and it is reduced from the original price by subtraction. This is where estimation becomes valuable as a tool. If students have had much practice finding 10 percent of amounts, reasonable answers can be figured:

Faulty Reasoning

$$\begin{array}{r} \$52.00 \\ -\quad .29 \\ \hline \$51.71 \end{array}$$

Reasoning by Estimation

10 percent of 52 = 5.20
30 percent of 52 = 5.20 × 3 = 15.60
29 percent is slightly less than 30 percent so percent has to be a little less than 15.60 and 51.71 is nowhere close.
What will bring me closer to 15.60?

Answer: Multiplication *not* subtraction

Average and poor students will not be able to solve problems like this one unless they have had effective teachers who help them structure their thoughts.

Portfolio Assessments

Two concepts of percent are explored with students of different ages from kindergarten to adult. In the first activity students are asked to construct their own picture, building up to the whole. Then they are asked to find the percent. The second activity is a pictorial image already constructed, and the students are asked to break down the whole into its parts.

Students' Understanding of Percent: Building with Pattern Pieces. Four children worked on the task of building a picture with pattern pieces—Andrew, a kindergartner, Katelyn and Mark, both third graders, and Justin, a sixth grader.

Both Mark and Justin had expressed an interest in building a rocket ship so their paper directions were printed with their interest in mind. As you analyze how much and what each student understands about percent, it may help to know the equivalencies of the pattern pieces, shown in Table 13.3. The students' work follows the portfolio assessment activity.

TABLE 13.3 Pattern Pieces Used in Activity

Since N is the smallest piece, all the pieces will be compared to it:

V = 8N	Z = 4N
U = 2N	Y = 4N

Activity 13.12

PORTFOLIO

CREATING YOUR OWN RUBRIC FOR PERCENTS WITH MANIPULATIVES

MATERIALS

- Work of the four children (see next page):
  - Andrew, kindergarten
  - Katelyn, third grade
  - Mark, third grade
  - Justin, sixth grade

BACKGROUND TO HELP IN YOUR ANALYSIS

None of the children have had formal instruction with percents. Justin's math series is just getting ready to introduce the concept.

DIRECTIONS

Use these questions to help you start thinking about a rubric:

1. What are the positive things that you see in all the answers to the percent questions?
2. What misconceptions about percents do the children seem to have?
3. Figure out what the percents actually were and see which student came the closest. Was the student's explanation one that showed a basic understanding of percent?
4. Is there a fair scale that could be used to give a numerical score to the creative work of all children?
   If yes—what is it?
   If no—what could you substitute instead of a numerical score?

Activity Continues

5. Using some examples of rubrics presented in Chapter 4, how could you modify one or several to come up with a rubric that would assess this activity fairly?
6. What are the next steps you need to do to help all the children continue to grow?
7. Share your thoughts with others. See what your combined knowledge might be able to come up with.

Students' Understanding of Percent: Seeing Percent in Whole Figures. The next set of portfolio assessments is very interesting because it contains the work of both children and adults. The letters have been substituted for names since some of the work of the adults shows major misconceptions that may prove embarrassing. It is not the intention of the authors to make fun of any learner, but rather to show the misconceptions that occur even among intelligent, successful adults.

It should be pointed out that this activity has been a part of one of the author's final exams for the past eight years. The work of Student C and Student D represents answers seen about 25 percent of the time. All the adult students are juniors or seniors in an elementary education program. They have passed their college entrance exams with ACT scores of 21 or higher. Other pertinent information about all the students is given in the portfolio activity itself.

Activity 13.13

PORTFOLIO

ANALYZING CHILD AND ADULT KNOWLEDGE OF PERCENTS IN WHOLE FIGURES

MATERIALS

- Work of the five students (on page 350):
  - Student A, age 8—Figure 13.13
  - Student B, age 9—Figure 13.14
  - Student C, adult—Figure 13.15
  - Student D, adult—Figure 13.16
  - Student E, adult—Figure 13.17

DIRECTIONS

Use these questions to help you start thinking about the analysis:

1. How did each person attempt to break down the activity to find the percents?

Andrew made a house.

Work with Pattern Pieces

Use the pattern pieces to make something of your choice. Trace what you did on this paper, so we can have a record to remember.

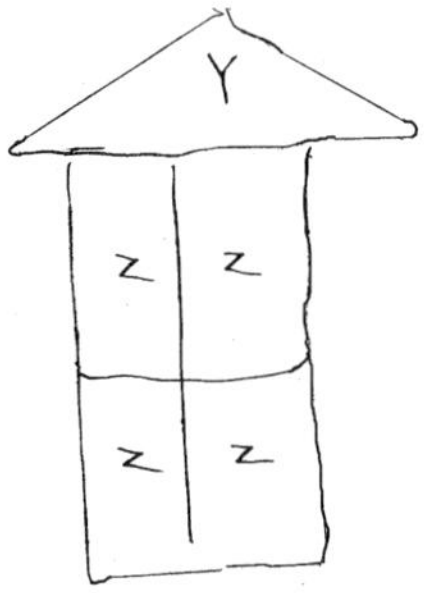

Answer these questions:

What percent of the picture is made out of "Y" pieces? 1

What percent of the picture is made out of "Z" pieces? 4

What percent of the picture is made out of "N" pieces? ______

Write how you figured out your answers:

____

____

Mark

Rocket Ship with Pattern Pieces

Draw your rocket ship with the pattern pieces like you did in class. Trace it on to this paper, showing the pieces that make up the rocket ship.

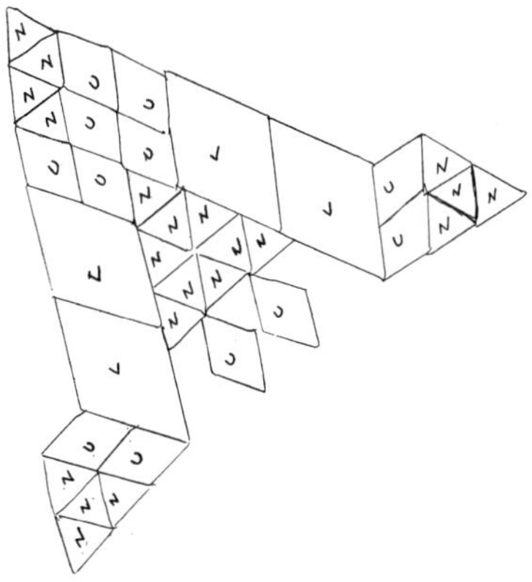

Answer these questions:

What percent of the rocket is made out of "U" pieces? 25 %

What percent of the rocket is made out of "V" pieces? 33%

What percent of the rocket is made out of "N" pieces? 16%

Write how you figured out your answers:

I counted the pieces

37	37	37
-12	- 4	-21
25	33	16

I made a chicken. Katelyn

Work with Pattern Pieces

Use the pattern pieces to make something of your choice. Trace what you did on this paper, so we can have a record to remember.

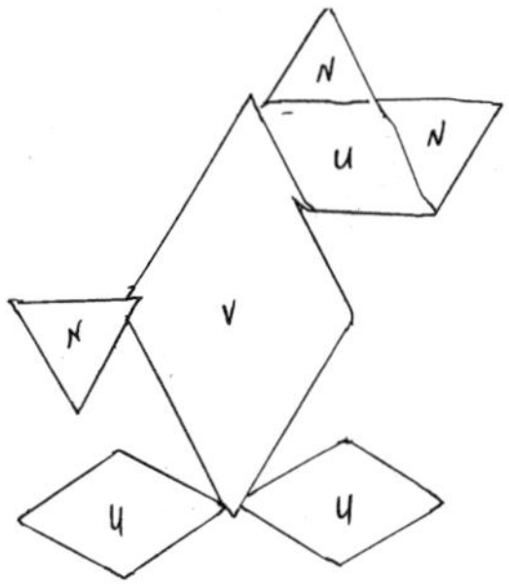

Answer these questions:

What percent of the picture is made out of "U" pieces? 40%

What percent of the picture is made out of "V" pieces? 50%

What percent of the picture is made out of "N" pieces? 10%

Write how you figured out your answers:

There are very few Ns so I said 10% and Us looked like 40% because it wasn't 50% and wasn't 10% so it was 40% and V was a big part even if there was only 1 and I said 50% and all together it makes 100% of the chicken!

Justin

Rocket Ship with Pattern Pieces

Draw your rocket ship with the pattern pieces like you did in class. Trace it on to this paper, showing the pieces that make up the rocket ship.

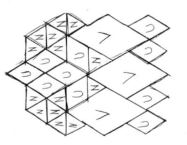

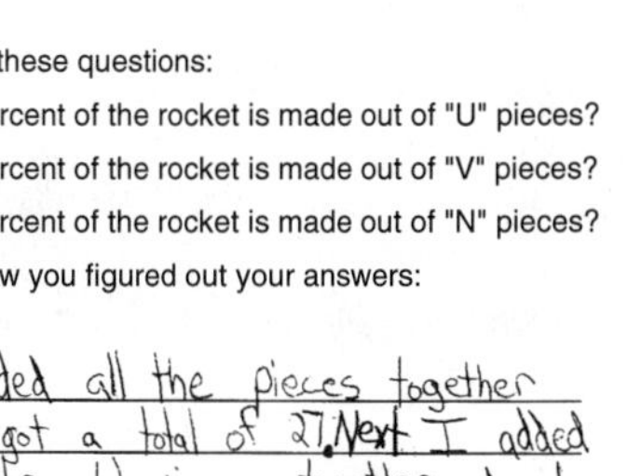

Answer these questions:

What percent of the rocket is made out of "U" pieces? 10/27

What percent of the rocket is made out of "V" pieces? 14/27

What percent of the rocket is made out of "N" pieces? 3/27

Write how you figured out your answers:

I added all the pieces together and got a total of 27. Next I added all the U pieces together and got a total of 10 and came up with a percentage of 10/27. Then I performed the same procedure with V and N.

Activity 13.13 Continues

FIGURE 13.13

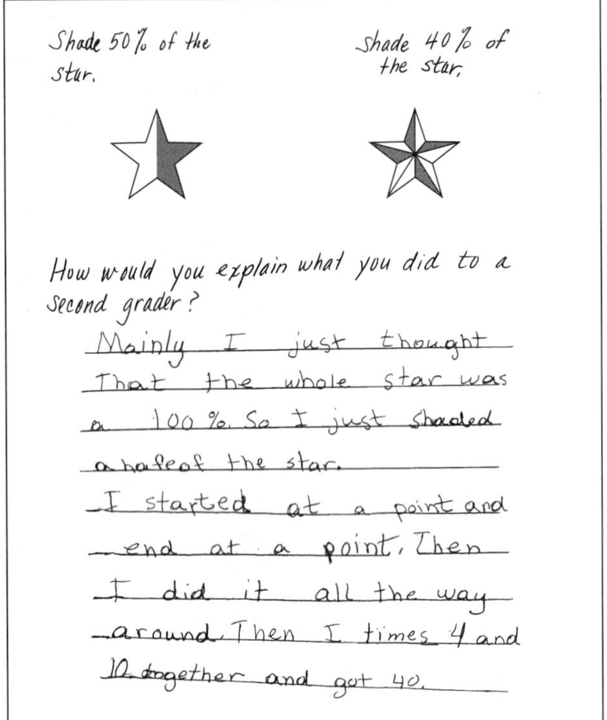
Shade 50% of the star.
Shade 40% of the star.
How would you explain what you did to a second grader?
Mainly I just thought
That the whole star was
a 100%. So I just shaded
a hafeof the star.
I started at a point and
end at a point. Then
I did it all the way
around. Then I times 4 and
10 together and got 40.

Shading percent pictures by student A, age 8.

FIGURE 13.14

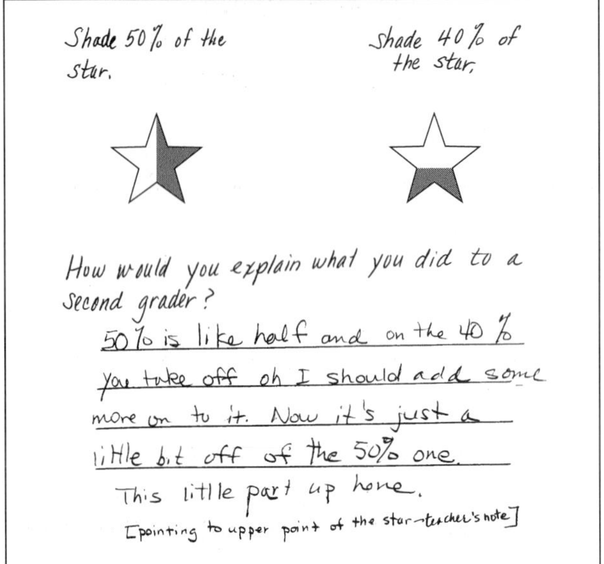
Shade 50% of the star.
Shade 40% of the star.
How would you explain what you did to a second grader?
50% is like half and on the 40%
you take off oh I should add some
more on to it. Now it's just a
little bit off of the 50% one.
This little part up here.
[pointing to upper point of the star—teacher's note]

Shading percent pictures by student B, age 9.

Activity 13.13 Continues

FIGURE 13.15

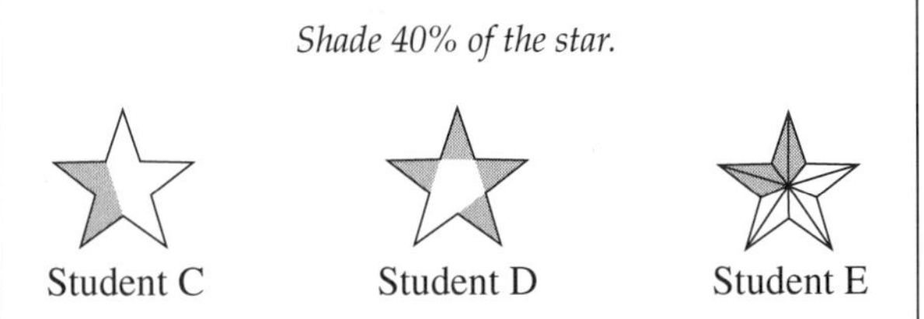
Shade 40% of the star.
Student C
Student D
Student E

Shading percent pictures by adults.

2. Which shadings showed positive understanding of percent? Did it differ with age?
3. What misconceptions about percents do the students seem to have? Did it differ with age?
4. What is noticeably missing on the task as the adults were asked to do it and the task as the elementary students were asked to do it?
5. Do you think the adult answers would improve if the task was adjusted to match the task as asked of the children? Why or why not?
6. Using some examples of rubrics presented in Chapter 4, how could you modify one or several to come up with a rubric that would assess this activity fairly?
7. What are the next steps you need to do to help all the students continue to grow?
8. Share your thoughts with others. See what your combined knowledge might be able to create.

SUMMARY

The many ideas seen in this chapter continue as Chapter 14 develops the concepts of number theory, patterns and functions, and algebra. The chapter emphasizes exploring the use of variables and applying number theory in real-life situations. This chapter's ideas are used in Chapter 15 when working statistical problems, averaging trends for graphs, and so on.

EXERCISES

For extended exercises, see the CD-ROM.

A. **Memorization and Comprehension Exercises**
Low-Level Thought Activities

1. What is the actual discount on an advertisement that reads as follows?

   All items *discounted* 50%.
   Today take an additional 30% off discount price.

2. Search the newspaper and circulars to find real-life proportion, percent, and rate problems. Set up the problems mathematically and solve.

B. **Application and Analysis Exercises**
Middle-Level Thought Activities

1. Read these proportions as one would say them in English to emphasize the mathematical meaning. Give an answer to make each proportion equivalent.

   Birds:Migration = Bears: __?__
   Snow:Snowflake = Rain: __?__
   Furnace:Heat = Air Conditioner: __?__

2. Look through elementary textbooks for word problems involving ratio, proportion, percent, and rate. What are the similarities and differences between textbook series?

3. Look at one of the mathematics textbook series for the elementary and middle schools. Analyze how many different approaches to ratio, proportion, percent, and rate are presented within one grade level. How many pages are devoted to concrete and pictorial models? What "extra" materials might you as a teacher need to use as supplementary work for your students?

4. List five ways to use the topics of this chapter when teaching lessons in reading, science, social studies, health, music, art, physical education, or language arts (writing, English grammar, poetry, and so on).

C. **Synthesis and Evaluation Exercises**
High-Level Thought Activities

1. Create your own lesson plan for teaching one concept using ratio, proportions, or percents. Follow these steps:

   a. Look at the NCTM *Principles and Standards* (2000). Find a grade level and a concept within that grade level. Trace the previous knowledge of the concept taught in earlier grades so you will know where to begin your instruction.
   b. Use current articles from professional journals to help plan the direction of the lesson. Document your sources.
   c. Include at least one computer software program as a part of the lesson. Show how it will be integrated with the rest of the lesson.
   d. Include behavioral objectives, concrete and pictorial materials, procedures, assessment rubrics, and evaluation of student mastery.
   e. Use the Chicago or TIMSS lesson plan on CD-ROM in Appendix B and include some information for culturally relevant mathematics.

2. Using the hundreds grid, make up problems like the two-year increase problem extending it to a third- and fifth-year increase. What needs to be changed and what would stay the same as the model in the chapter shows?

3. Use a geoboard to create a concrete example of a scaling problem. Set up the steps and reasoning involved to reach a solution.

4. Create a rubric for assessment of ratio and proportion problems. Do the same for proportion and rate problems.

BIBLIOGRAPHY

For an extended bibliography, see the CD-ROM.

Barnett, Carne, Donna Goldenstein, and Babette Jackson. *Research and Development of Fractions, Decimals, Ratio and Percent: Hard to Teach or Hard to Learn.* Portsmouth, NH: Heinemann, 1994.

Bennett, Albert B., Jr., and L. Ted Nelson. "A Conceptual Model for Solving Percent Problems." *Mathematics Teaching in the Middle School* 1 (April 1994): 20–25.

Brinker, Laura. "Using Recipes and Ratio Tables to Build on Students' Understanding of Fractions." *Teaching Children Mathematics* 5 (December 1998): 218–224.

Charles, Randall, and Joanne Lobato. "Ratio, Proportion & Percent." *Future Basics: Developing Numerical Power.* Monograph of the National Council of Supervisors of Mathematics (April 1998): 26–27.

Cramer, Katheen, and Thomas Post. "Making Connections: A Case for Proportionality." *Arithmetic Teacher* 40 (February 1993): 342–346.

Curcio, Frances R., and Nadine S. Bezuk. *Grades 5–8 Addenda Series: Understanding Rational Numbers and Proportions.* Ed. Frances R. Curcio. Reston, VA: National Council of Teachers of Mathematics, 1994.

Honey, I Blew Up the Kids. Dir. Joe Johnston. Perf. Rick Moranis. Burbank, CA: Walt Disney and Amblin Entertainment, 1992.

Honey, I Shrunk the Kids. Dir. Joe Johnston. Perf. Rick Moranis. Burbank, CA: Walt Disney and Amblin Entertainment, 1989.

Kliman, Marlene. "Integrating Mathematics and Literature in the Elementary Classroom." *Arithmetic Teacher* 40 (February 1993): 318–321.

Kouba, Vicky L., Judith S. Zawojewski, and Marilyn E. Strutchens. "What Do Students Know about Numbers and Operations?" *Results from the Sixth Mathematics Assessment of the National Assessment of Education Progress.* Reston, VA: National Council of Teachers of Mathematics, 1997, pp. 87–140.

Lego Group. *LEGO MINDSTORMS: Robotics Invention System.* Billund, Denmark: Lego Corp., 1998.

Lembke, Linda O., and Barbara J. Reys. "The Development of, and Interaction Between, Intuitive and School-Taught Ideas about Percent." *Journal for Research in Mathematics Education* 25 (May 1994): 237–259.

National Council of Teachers of Mathematics. *Assessment Standards for School Mathematics.* Reston, VA: NCTM, 1995.

———. *Curriculum and Evaluation Standards for School Mathematics.* Reston, VA: NCTM, 1989.

———. *Principles and Standards for School Mathematics.* Reston, VA: NCTM, 2000 (to be published).

———. *Professional Standards for Teaching Mathematics.* Reston, VA: NCTM, 1991.

Richmond Ambulance Authority. *Master Contract for Paramedic Ambulance Services. July 1, 1996–2000.* City of Richmond, VA, 1996.

Singer, Janice-Ann, and Lauren B. Resnick. "Representations of Proportional Relationships: Are Children Part-Part or Part-Whole Reasoners?" *Educational Studies in Mathematics* 23 (June 1992): 231–246.

Strong, Dorothy S. (Mathematics Ed.). *Systemwide Objectives and Standards.* Vols. 1–3. Chicago: Board of Education of the City of Chicago, 1990.

———. *Mathematics Instruction Planning Manual.* Chicago: Board of Education of the City of Chicago, 1991a.

———. *Mathematics Tutor Training Manual.* Chicago: Board of Education of the City of Chicago, 1991b.

CHILDREN'S LITERATURE

Briggs, Raymond. *Jim and the Beanstalk.* New York: Coward, McCann & Geoghegan, 1980.

Buxton, Jane H., ed. *Creatures of Long Ago: Dinosaurs.* Columbia, SC: National Geographic Society, 1988.

Caduto, Michael J., and Joseph Bruchac. *Keepers of the Earth: Native American Stories and Environmental Activities for Children.* Golden, CO: Fulcrum Publishing, 1989.

———. *Keepers of the Animals: Native American Stories and Wildlife Activities for Children.* Golden, CO: Fulcrum Publishing, 1991.

Carroll, Lewis. *Alice in Wonderland and Through the Looking Glass.* New York, NY: Putnam Publishing Group, 1981.

Cleary, Beverly, and S. Ralph. *Mouse.* New York: William Morrow, 1982.

Clement, Rod. *Counting on Frank.* Milwaukee: Gareth Stevens Publishing, 1991.

Dahl, Roald. *The BFG.* New York: Farrar, Straus and Giroux, 1982.

Milne, A. A. *Winnie-the-Pooh.* New York: E. P. Dutton, 1926.

Schwartz, David M. *If You Made a Million.* New York: Mulberry, 1989.

Seuss, Dr. *Hop on Pop.* New York: Random House, 1963.

Swift, Jonathan. *Gulliver's Travels.* New York: William Morrow, 1983.

White, E. B. *Stuart Little.* New York: Harper & Row, 1945.

Integrating Technology

Computer Spreadsheet Activity

...for Percent, Ratio, Proportion, and Rate

Computer Software Resources

...for Percent, Ratio, Proportion, and Rate

Internet Searches

Surfing the Internet for Topics on Percent, Ratio, Proportion, and Rate

Use the World Wide Web (WWW) and navigate through the system, searching for new information under major headings and subheadings similar to the following:

Mathematics Education
- Discussion Groups on Interactive Bulletin Boards

Mathematics
- Games of Proportion and Ratio
- Rate and Proportion in Middle School
- Middle School Mathematics

NCTM
- Problem Solving
- Equity Issues with Percent, Ratio, Proportion, and Rate
- Coordinate Graphs

- *Remember...* the Web is fluid ... new topics and ways to search for topics change daily.
- Be adventurous ... think of some new things you could try.

14

Number Theory, Patterns and Functions, and Algebra

Activities Index

IN THE TEXT

ON CD-ROM

Mathematicians throughout the ages have been fascinated with patterns, and many interesting relationships have been developed during the evolution of mathematics knowledge. Children are usually exposed to these ideas first with manipulatives, then with numbers beginning in Pre-K–2, extended in grades 3–5, and continuing through middle school. The units may be independent of the sequential skill development normally associated with the study of numeration, basic facts, and algorithms. Frequently textbooks use a discovery approach to simulate activities similar to those experienced by early mathematicians. Some children enjoy this approach and are challenged to find new patterns, but not all students will find patterns fascinating.

According to the NCTM *Principles and Standards* (NCTM, 2000), looking for patterns is the essence of inductive reasoning. As students explore problems with patterns, conjectures are made that must be validated. This process encourages students to develop supporting logical arguments. Cooperative learning in the TIMSS format may help students maintain concentration during the study of number theory concepts.

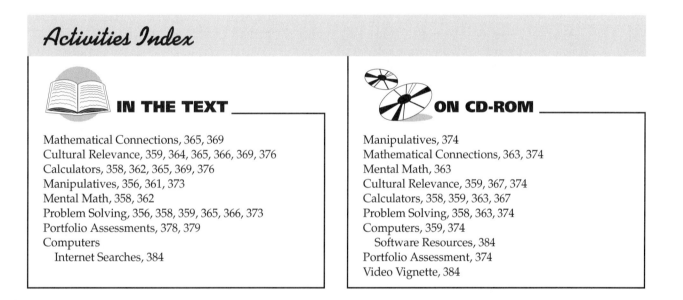

Number theory explores the relationships (patterns) between and among counting numbers and their properties. Specific definitions and properties of each concept are introduced when appropriate in the following section on teaching strategies. Beginning concepts include odd and even numbers, prime and composite numbers, greatest common factor, and least common multiple.

Patterns therefore lead to relations and functions in the middle grades. When relations and functions are generalized to variables rather than specific numbers or values, the beginning understanding of algebra is developed. Algebra takes the relations in simple arithmetic and applies the pattern as a generalization statement. Hence, $3 + 2 = 5$ becomes any number x added to any other number y yields a different distinct number z such that $x + y = z$.

The term *relations* defines the relationships seen in sets of things and seen in patterns, either within the same set or among sets. A *relation* associates the elements or patterns seen in one set to the elements or patterns seen in another set. For example, 7 *is greater than* 5 tells a relationship between 7 and 5. A *function* is a specific relation in which every element in one set is associated with only one element in another set. Using the example of 7 and 5, there are many numbers that are greater than 5, but only one number, 7, is associated with 5 if the function +2 is applied to the number 5.

There are activities in the primary grades that can be used to start children thinking about interesting patterns in numbers. A gradual progression goes from primary grade number pattern relationships to functions to generalized arithmetic (that is, algebra) by the end of middle school (Howden, 1990). The examples found in the Teaching Strategies section are meant to model this gradual transition from number patterns to algebra. Box 14.1 shows how the NCTM *Curriculum and Evaluation Standards* (1989) relate to the curriculum of elementary and middle school mathematics.

TEACHING STRATEGIES

Number Theory

Children in K–5 explore many number patterns. One of the first is the concept of even and odd numbers. Beginning work with prime and composite numbers is also a part of the early grades. Some number sequences, like the Fibonacci sequence and Pascal's triangle, can be introduced near the end of the K–5 period. The exponential ideas involved with Pascal's triangle will need to wait until the 6–8 middle school years.

Odd and Even Numbers. Children learn to tell the difference between odd and even numbers by pairing manipulative materials. A number is defined as *even* if it can be divided by two with no remainder. A number is defined as *odd* if it has a remainder of one when divided by two. Figure 14.1 shows some of the materials children can use in the primary grades to discover odd and even numbers through pairing (which is dividing a counting number by two).

From Concrete to Connecting Level. Children should be given the opportunity to draw the pictorial representations of many numbers while deciding whether the numbers are even or odd. Children will form an accurate definition of even and odd numbers if allowed to compare and contrast the paired and nonpaired sets as seen in the next activity. The numeral for each even number, *e*, can be designated on the number line. The same procedure can follow for each odd number, *o*. Children will be able to predict what larger numerals will be even or odd once the pattern is established.

	e		*e*		*e*		*e*		*e*		*e*
1	2	3	4	5	6	7	8	9	10	11	12
o		*o*		*o*		*o*		*o*		*o*	

Note that zero is considered an even number because it would fit the pattern shown on the number line.

Activity 14.1

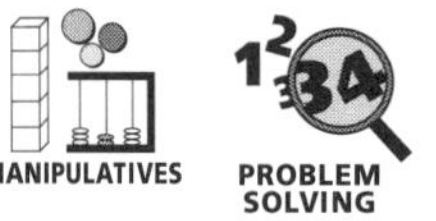

MANIPULATIVES WITH ODD AND EVEN NUMBERS

MATERIALS

- See Figure 14.1.

DIRECTIONS

1. Look at the materials shown in Figure 14.1. These are just some of the many items that can be used to show the relationship of odd numbers and even numbers.

FIGURE 14.1

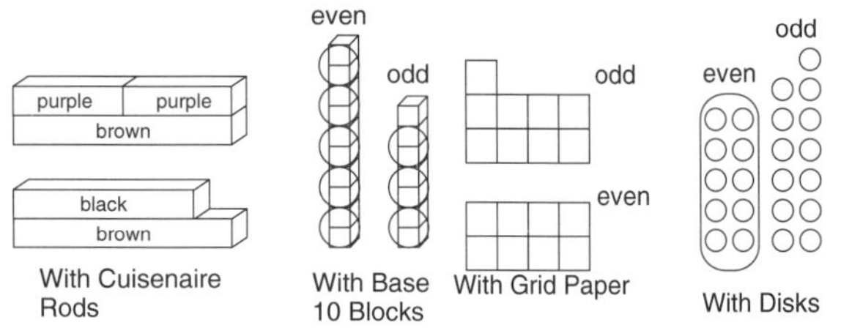

Concrete manipulatives to explore odd and even numbers.

BOX 14.1 Curriculum and Evaluation Standards

Patterns and Relationships

In grades Pre-K–5, the mathematics curriculum should include the study of patterns and relationships so that students can—

- Recognize, describe, extend, and create a wide variety of patterns.
- Represent and describe mathematical relationships.
- Explore the use of variables and open sentences to express relationships, as a precursor to algebra.

Number Systems and Number Theory

In grades 6–8, the mathematics curriculum should include the study of number systems and number theory so that students can—

- Understand and appreciate the need for numbers beyond the whole numbers.
- Develop and use order relations for whole numbers, fractions, decimals, integers, and rational numbers.
- Extend their understanding of whole number operations to fractions, decimals, integers, and rational numbers.
- Understand how the basic arithmetic operations are related to one another.
- Develop and apply number theory concepts (e.g., primes, factors, and multiples) in real-world and mathematical problem situations.

Patterns and Functions

In grades 6–8, the mathematics curriculum should include explorations of patterns and functions so that students can—

- Describe, extend, analyze, and create a wide variety of patterns.
- Describe and represent relationships with tables, graphs, and rules.
- Analyze functional relationships to explain how a change in one quantity results in a change in another.
- Use patterns and functions to represent and solve problems.

Algebra

In grades 6–8, the mathematics curriculum should include explorations of algebraic concepts and processes so that students can—

- Understand the concepts of variable, expression, and equation.
- Represent situations and number patterns with tables, graphs, verbal rules, and equations and explore the interrelationships of these representations.
- Analyze tables and graphs to identify properties and relationships.
- Develop confidence in solving linear equations using concrete, informal, and formal methods;
- Investigate inequalities and nonlinear equations formally.
- Apply algebraic methods to solve a variety of real-world and mathematical problems.

Source: National Council of Teachers of Mathematics, 1989, pp. 60, 91, 98, 102.

Activity Continues

2. Think of other manipulatives you could use to show the relationships. Draw them to share with others in a cooperative group setting.
3. Think of real-world mathematics where odd and even numbers occur.
   Example: Partitioned sections of candy boxes (even) After one person has chosen one candy (odd)
4. Prepare for oral discourse by thinking how children would be expected to explain odd and even numbers from the examples they bring to class. This could be a

Activity Continues

good homework assignment. Have them orally explain to others how the material shows odd or even concepts.

Supporting the NCTM *Principles and Standards* (2000):

- Mathematics as Reasoning; Mathematics as Problem Solving, Connections, Representations
- Oral Discourse of Teacher and Student—The Learning Principle
- Mathematics Curriculum Principle

From Connecting Level to Symbolic. Children can experiment with odd and even numbers to generalize a rule about the properties of such numbers in addition and multiplication.

Activity 14.2

CALCULATORS PROBLEM SOLVING

ADDITION WITH ODD AND EVEN NUMBERS

DIRECTIONS

1. Using a calculator, make a list of what happens when you add one even number to another even number. Do the same for odd numbers. Then combine both odd and even numbers and record the results.
2. Set up a chart like the one below. Create more examples, following the pattern as established.
3. Generalize a rule for each set.

Even + Even	Odd + Odd	Even + Odd
2 + 4 =	7 + 3 =	2 + 11 =
106 + 38 =	201 + 55 =	348 + 29 =
1346 + 2794 =	2403 + 9825 =	7374 + 5689 =

(Create some more examples of large and small numbers.)

Rule:	Rule:	Rule:
______________	______________	______________
______________	______________	______________

Students enjoy comparing charts of classmates to see whether the same rule will apply when other number combinations are used. Teachers should encourage students to see that the digit on the right of any multidigit number is the one that determines whether a number is odd or even. Students can problem solve further possibilities.

Students who enjoy problem-solving explorations like the preceding one can be challenged to find many more combinations on their own time and share them with the class.

EXTENDED ACTIVITIES

Name of Activity

- Multiplication with Odd and Even Numbers
- Odd and Even Numbers

PROBLEM SOLVING CALCULATORS

Prime and Composite Numbers. A *prime number* is an integer that is evenly divisible only by itself and one; that is, only itself and one are factors of the number. Zero and one are not considered prime numbers. A *composite number* is a number that has more than itself and one as factors. Therefore, seven is a prime number, whereas eight is a composite number.

7	8
7 × 1	8 × 1
1 × 7	1 × 8
	2 × 4
	4 × 2
	2 × 2 × 2
	etc.

Activity 14.3

MENTAL MATH

THE MYSTERY EVEN NUMBER PRIME

There is only one even number that fits the definition for a prime number. Think of many even numbers. Visualize their factors in your mind. Which factor, beside one and itself, does every even number have?

Did you think of two? The definition of an even number means that two will always be a factor of every even number. What about the two itself? Visualize the factors of two. What are they? The factors of two can only be one and itself (two). Therefore, two meets the criteria for a prime number, and it is the only even number that can be prime.

How can we know if a number is prime? The ancient Greeks had a method to find primes of a given number, and through the centuries it has become known as the Sieve of Eratosthenes.

The Sieve of Eratosthenes. More than 2000 years ago the Greek mathematician Eratosthenes created a process to help sieve (filter out) the composite numbers, leaving only the prime numbers. There are many interesting patterns to be found by using the Sieve of Eratosthenes. Teachers can lead students to discover many of the patterns on their own by asking a few leading questions such as the ones found in the problem-solving exploration that follows.

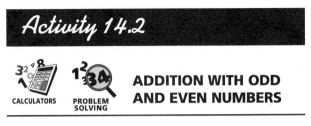

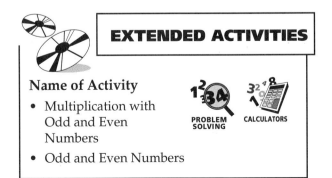

Activity 14.4

PROBLEM SOLVING | CULTURAL RELEVANCE

NUMBER PATTERNS WITH THE SIEVE OF ERATOSTHENES

DIRECTIONS

1. You are asked to use six colors on the Sieve of Eratosthenes (see chart at end of step 4) so that you can see the number patterns more easily. The colors of yellow, green, pink, light blue, red, and black are suggested, but any eye-catching colors will do.
2. On the chart in step 4, find the first prime number, which is 2, and circle it with a red marker. Now slash (/) all the multiples of 2 using the red marker. You have just eliminated all even numbers because they are composites. Note the color pattern you have just created.
3. Now find the next prime which is 3 and circle it with a green marker. Sieve (/) all the multiples of 3 using the green marker. Some numbers now have a red and green slash. You can easily see the numbers that are multiples of both 2 and 3. Note the color pattern created by the green slashes.
4. Follow the same procedure using this color code:

Primes	Color
five	= yellow
seven	= black
eleven	= pink
all others	= light blue

1	2	3	4	5	6	7	8	9	10
11	12	13	14	15	16	17	18	19	20
21	22	23	24	25	26	27	28	29	30
31	32	33	34	35	36	37	38	39	40
41	42	43	44	45	46	47	48	49	50
51	52	53	54	55	56	57	58	59	60
61	62	63	64	65	66	67	68	69	70
71	72	73	74	75	76	77	78	79	80
81	82	83	84	85	86	87	88	89	90
91	92	93	94	95	96	97	98	99	100

Questions Based on the Sieve of Eratosthenes:

1. How many of the first 100 numbers are prime?
2. Of the first 25 numbers, what percent are multiples of three numbers? Of the second 25 numbers, what percent are multiples of three numbers?
3. Would you expect this number to increase or decrease as we continue through the number system? Why?
4. The number of primes in the first 50 numbers is what fractional portion of the total primes in the first 100 numbers? What about the second 50 numbers?
5. Will the relationship found in question 4 hold for the second 100 numbers? What could be done to find out?
6. When is the first time that a multiple of 7 has not been crossed out by a multiple of a smaller prime?

Activity Continues

7. What do you notice about multiples of 11? Predict at which number the multiple of 11 will be crossed out for the first time with no smaller primes as its multiple.

A person can figure out which multidigit numbers are prime by using the Sieve of Eratosthenes. The examples on the CD-ROM are performed the way mathematicians and upper-grade students figured the problem of primes for centuries. The same process can be placed in a computer program to show what Eratosthenes and others could have done with a computer if one had been available.

You can see that a calculator can be used with large primes like the previous one. Early mathematicians used the long division algorithms to work such problems. In today's world a computer can be programmed to check on large numbers without the need to use the Sieve of Eratosthenes in the detail we have just gone through. Such a program is shown with middle school students using the computer language of Logo on the CD-ROM.

A person exposed to both methods can appreciate the power of computers. A student who has experimented with the Sieve of Eratosthenes can see the patterns and will not waste time checking numbers like 30, 125, 144, or 895. Those numbers can be noticed right away if students have been encouraged to look for easy patterns when working with the Sieve of Eratosthenes.

Fundamental Theorem of Arithmetic. One interesting feature of our number system is known as the Unique Factorization Theorem or the Fundamental

EXTENDED ACTIVITIES

COMPUTERS | CULTURAL RELEVANCE | CALCULATORS

Name of Activity

- Large Numbers with the Sieve of Eratosthenes
- Finding Prime Numbers Like the Ancient Ones Did
- Large Primes and the Computer with Middle School Students

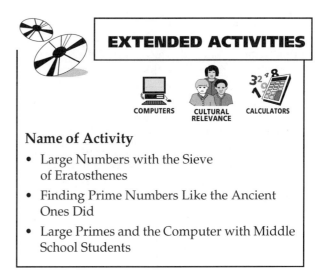

Theorem of Arithmetic. The *Fundamental Theorem of Arithmetic* states that every composite number can be expressed as a product of its primes. Applying that to what we learned about the number 201 on the CD-ROM, it can be seen that

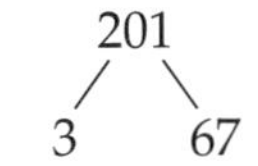

By checking the Sieve of Eratosthenes, we see that 67 is a prime, as is the familiar prime 3. Therefore, the number 201 can be expressed as 3 × 67 and will only have this one prime factorization.

Prime Factorization. Another investigation of number theory is finding the prime factorization of a number. When a composite number is divided into its primes (not including zero or one) so that only primes are present as its factors, the process is known as *prime factorization.* The following shows two methods for finding the prime factorization of the number twenty-four:

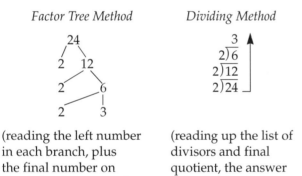

Factor Tree Method	*Dividing Method*
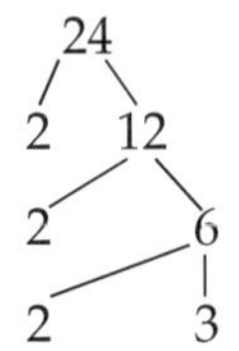	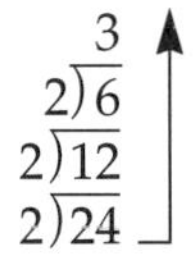
(reading the left number in each branch, plus the final number on the right, the answer is 2 × 2 × 2 × 3)	(reading up the list of divisors and final quotient, the answer is 2 × 2 × 2 × 3)

Both methods start with the smallest prime and continue its use until it is no longer a factor or divisor of the number. Then the next appropriate prime is found and the process continues until all the factors are prime numbers (factor tree method) or until the final quotient is a prime number (dividing method). Both show 2 × 2 × 2 × 3 as the prime factors of the number 24. From the associative property, we know that any arrangement of the four prime numbers will yield the unique number 24 when multiplied as factors, but it is customary to write the prime factors from least to greatest.

Least Common Multiple and Greatest Common Factor. The Least Common Multiple (LCM) and the Greatest Common Factor (GCF) can help students factor numbers efficiently. The GCF can also be called the Greatest Common Divisor, but most elementary textbooks choose the GCF terminology. The LCM and the GCF are useful when relationships between and among patterns cannot be compared until common elements are found. For instance, $\frac{1}{3}$ and $\frac{1}{4}$ need a common denominator (the LCM) before one can use the two fractions together in the operations of real-world mathematics from simple cooking and building to rocket-fuel formulas. The LCM and GCF are stressed in schools because they help find comparison relationships more quickly, enabling the efficient use of mathematics in industry and business applications.

The *least common multiple* of two counting numbers is the smallest (least) nonzero number that is a multiple of both numbers. Because every number has an infinite number of multiples, every pair of numbers has an infinite number of common multiples. The smallest of the common multiples is known as the LCM. For example, though the numbers 4 and 5 have many multiples, the least (smallest) common one is 20.

4	8	12	16	**20**	24	28	30
5	10	15	**20**	25	30	35	40

The key word is *multiple,* which implies that the resulting number will be greater than either of the two numbers. When adding and subtracting fractions, for example:

$$\tfrac{1}{3} \text{ and } \tfrac{1}{4}$$

The common denominator is 12, which is the least common multiple of 3 and 4.

The *greatest common factor* (GCF) of two counting numbers is the greatest counting number that is a factor of each of the numbers. The key word is *factor,* which implies that the resulting number will be less than either of the two numbers. The numbers 18 and 24 have several common factors (1, 2, 3, 6) and the greatest common factor is 6.

A visual way to remember the idea is to think of the placement of each in relation to a diagram. Using the numbers 8 and 12:

LCM (8, 12)	*GCF (8, 12)*
$8\overline{)\text{LCM}}$	$\text{GCF}\overline{)8}$
$12\overline{)\text{LCM}}$	$\text{GCF}\overline{)12}$

Both the LCM and GCF may be extended to more than two numbers, as seen in Figure 14.2 where the LCM and GCF of three numbers are illustrated.

Activity 14.5

MANIPULATIVES

FINDING THE LCM AND GCF WITH CUISENAIRE RODS

MATERIALS

- Cuisenaire rods.

DIRECTIONS

1. Study Figure 14.2 and see how the GCF and LCM are figured.
2. Wording to use:
   - GCF = The color *every* tower has in common. (in this example, GCF = green or 3)
   - LCM = The most of any color in the towers when taken together (in this example, red × red × yellow × green × green or 180)
3. Prepare for oral and written discourse by thinking how children would be expected to explain LCM and GCF for the examples they bring to class.
4. Think of three more numbers for which you can build prime towers with Cuisenaire rods. Figure out the LCM and GCF for the prime towers.
5. Write how you would explain this to children.

FIGURE 14.2

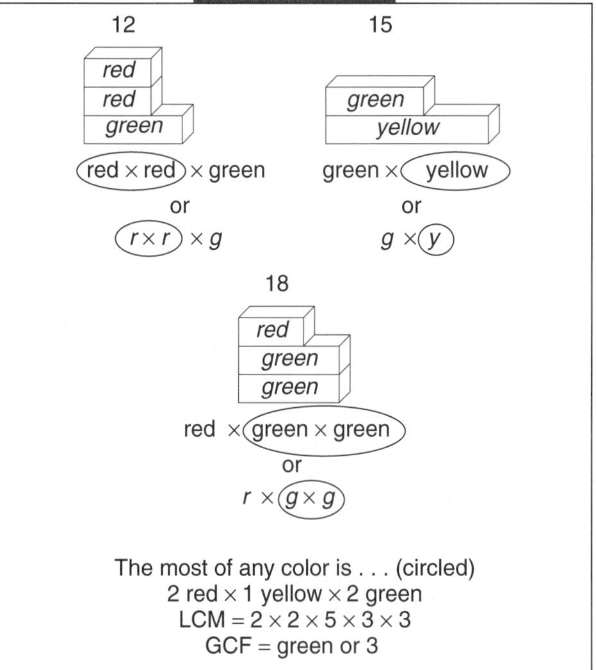

Finding LCM and GCF with Cuisenaire rods.

Supporting the NCTM *Principles and Standards* (2000):

- Mathematics as Reasoning/Patterning; Mathematics as Problem Solving, Connections, Representations

Activity Continues

- Oral Discourse; Written Discourse—The Teaching Principle
- Active Engagement with Manipulatives—The Learning Principle
- The Mathematics Curriculum Principle...what all students need to know and do

Finding the LCM and GCF of Numbers. Both the LCM and the GCF start by factoring each number to be compared into its primes (as shown in the following factor diagrams, known as factor trees). The LCM is found by looking for the number of primes used most often in each composite number. Therefore, 2 × 2 is the most twos used (seen in the number 12), whereas 3 × 3 is the most threes used (seen in the number 18). Five is used only once but it still applies because it is the most times it is used in any number. The LCM is 2 × 2 × 3 × 3 × 5 or 180. The GCF is found by looking for the greatest divisor or factor that all numbers have in common. There is only one factor common to all the numbers and that is 3. Therefore, 3 is the GCF.

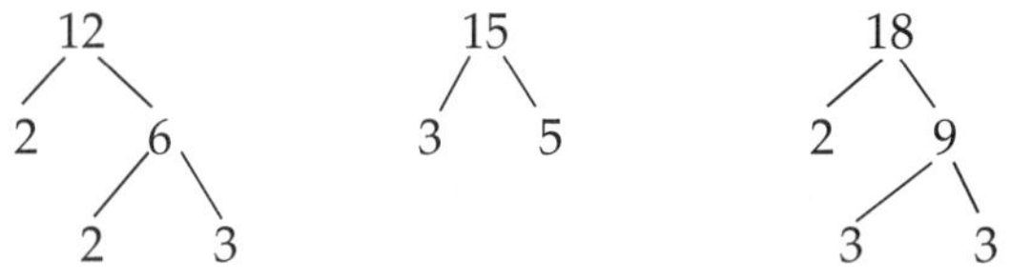

Figure 14.2 shows how the numbers 12, 15, and 18 can be factored using Cuisenaire rods. Each set of primes is made into a "prime tower" with the prime rods stacked one on top of the other. The LCM is found by asking which is the most color any prime tower uses. The answer is two reds, two greens, and one yellow, which equates with 2 × 2 × 3 × 3 × 5. The GCF is found by asking which is the largest color rod common in all three prime towers. The answer is the green rod or the numeral 3.

Venn diagrams (Figure 14.3) are another useful tool for finding the LCM, and they may appeal to students who are comfortable with set diagrams. The LCM is 30. Although 60 and 90 are also common multiples, they are not the least common multiple.

Number theory is an integral part of studying mathematics in the upper grades and middle school years. The following intermediate concepts are most often explored as sixth, seventh, and eighth grade material. Students are introduced to the concepts much as the topics are introduced here; however, time for individual exploration should be provided. These intermediate concepts are divisibility rules,

FIGURE 14.3

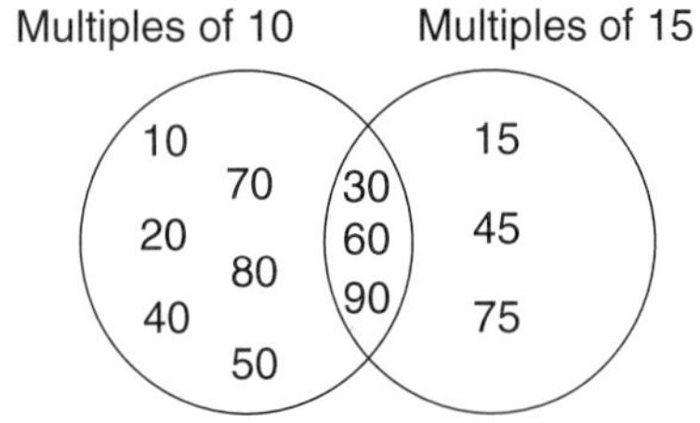

Venn diagrams with the LCM.

polygonal or figurate numbers, Pythagorean triples, Fibonacci numbers, and Pascal's triangle.

Divisibility Rules. One number is said to be *divisible* by another number if and only if the first number divides evenly into the second, leaving no remainder. Sometimes a person needs to estimate quickly whether one number will divide evenly into a greater multidigit number. Knowing some simple divisibility rules can help a person conquer the time factor on standardized achievement and aptitude tests. While other students are trying to perform laborious calculations taking up valuable time, the person who knows divisibility rules can answer more rapidly.

Divisibility rules also help economists and other professionals who have to deal with large population or demographic numbers too large to be recorded on a conventional calculator. A decision to divide the data by quarterly figures or by thirds can depend on which large number most easily divides into fourths or thirds. Divisibility rules also help children when selecting players for teams or dividing large amounts to be dispersed among many people. For example, students want eight school teams for a field day in a school with 1432 students. They know it will result in the same number of players on every team without the use of calculators or pencil-and-paper algorithms.

Divisibility rules can help find common denominators quickly. These rules were first introduced in Chapter 12. Middle school students who find number patterns interesting in and of themselves will find the explanations for the divisibility rules of interest. Those students with a mathematical inclination will want to know why divisibility tests work. The following explanations may help the teacher who finds such a question hard to answer without some study.

Divisibility by 2, 5, 10. From working with the Sieve of Eratosthenes, students can "see" patterns for the divisibility of numbers by 2, 5, and 10. They will be able to generalize that any number ending with an even number in the ones place will be divisible by 2. Any number ending with a 0 or 5 in the ones place will be divisible by 5, and any number ending with a 0 in the ones place will be divisible by 10. Other divisibility rules are not that easily seen and require more questions on the part of the teacher if rules are to be learned by students.

Divisibility by 4 and 8. Because our number system is based on regrouping at 10, the powers of 10 can help our understanding of divisibility rules. Look at the following divisibility pattern for 4:

Division by Powers of 10	*Does It Divide Evenly?*
$10^1 \div 4$	No
$10^2 \div 4$	Yes . . . and all following powers of 10 will be divided evenly also.

Rationale for the rule: Some numbers in the tens and ones place (10 to the first power) are divisible by 4, such as $4 \times 4 = 16$, $4 \times 5 = 20$. Therefore, if we look at the last two digits to the right in a multidigit number and find them divisible by 4, we know the entire number will be divisible by 4. The rule for divisibility by 4 is that *a number is divisible by 4* if and only if the last two digits of the number are divisible by 4.

Following the same reasoning, divisibility by 8 is examined on the CD-ROM. Your instructor may wish to have you explain your reasoning for the rule of divisibility by 8. The rule for divisibility by 8 is that *a number is divisible by 8* if and only if the last three digits of the number are divisible by 8.

Activity 14.6

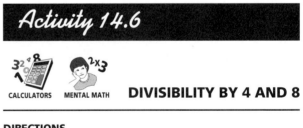

CALCULATORS MENTAL MATH

DIVISIBILITY BY 4 AND 8

DIRECTIONS

Which numbers are divisible by 4 and 8? (Students should be encouraged to fill in the right side of the chart as they work with the problems. The chart has been filled in for you.)

Problems	*Divisible by 4 or 8?*	*Explanation*
4)197,836	Yes	Because 36 is divisible by 4
8)765,872	Yes	Because 872 is divisible by 8
8)197,836	No	Because 836 is not divisible by 8

Activity Continues

Check with a calculator to see whether you were correct. Make up others and check with your calculator.

Write down what you would say to explain this to children.

Supporting the NCTM *Principles and Standards* (2000):

- Mathematics as Reasoning
- Using the Calculator—The Teaching Principle
- Using Inference—Assessment Principle

EXTENDED ACTIVITIES

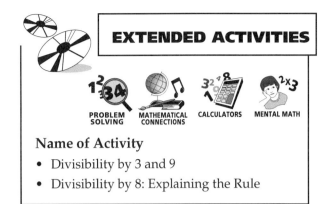

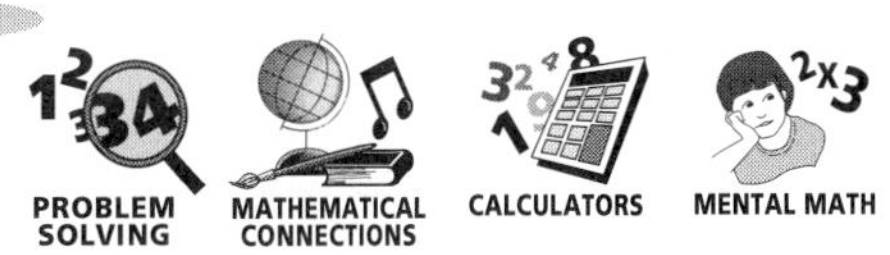

Name of Activity

- Divisibility by 3 and 9
- Divisibility by 8: Explaining the Rule

Students should also notice that any number divisible by 8 is also divisible by 4, but that not every number that is divisible by 4 will be divisible by 8. Have students discuss in cooperative learning groups why this fact is true. How does this fact relate to divisibility by 2?

Divisibility by 3 and 9. Looking once again at the powers of 10 with the division by 9:

$10^1 \div 9 = 9 + 1$	*Notice:* All these numbers have a pattern of addition along with a set of numbers that are divisible by 9.
$10^2 \div 9 = 99 + 1$	
$10^3 \div 9 = 999 + 1$	

Rationale for the rule: Any number divisible by 9 is also divisible by 3, and any number will always be divisible by 9 or 3 if and only if all the digits added together equal a number that is divisible by 9 or 3. See the CD-ROM for further explanation.

Quickly find which numbers would be divisible by 4, 8, 3, 9, or 5...

?)2537887   ?)7891302   ?)1259945

Change these numbers to make them divisible by the rest of the 4, 8, 3, 9, 5 remaining. The NAEP results (Blume and Heckman, 1997) show that 76 percent of fourth graders could answer yes/no responses to number theory questions but only 27 percent of them could give the correct written explanation to the same questions. Most chose odd and even number explanations. Only a few fourth graders gave explanations involving higher number theory concepts such as factors, multiples, and divisibility. This further supports the need for written discourse early in the mathematics curriculum.

Polygonal or Figurate Numbers. *Polygonal numbers* (also known as *figurate numbers*) are numbers that take the shape of polygons or figures. We will explore several kinds in this section. There are polygonal or figurate numbers called triangular numbers, square numbers, pentagonal numbers, hexagonal numbers, octagonal numbers, and so on. The most common are known as square numbers and take the form of a square figure. They will look like the drawings in Figure 14.4. The number pictures build as you watch the animation on the screen in Logo. Young children enjoy the animation and can predict what will happen from an intuitive sense of beginning inductive reasoning. Middle schoolers can work with the embedded pattern.

There are many possibilities for figurate (polygonal) numbers. Pythagoras, a Greek mathematician and philosopher of 2500 years ago, started a society of persons interested in many issues of that day, including clever patterns dealing with numbers. Known as the Pythagorean Society, this secret society explored many possibilities with figurate numbers. Each figurate number is found by counting the number of units used to make the original figure (polygon) and the number of equivalent units needed to produce the polygon as it grows larger. Figure 14.4 shows the configurations for the triangular, square, and pentagonal numbers as the Pythagoreans discovered them.

Square Numbers. *Perfect squares* are squares whose sides and areas are whole numbers. Figure 14.4 shows examples of perfect squares in the middle figurate numbers.

Squares can be drawn whose sides and areas are not whole numbers. For instance, a square can be drawn whose sides are 2.1×2.1, which yields a square area of 4.41, and a square with an area of 3 will yield sides whose measure is an irrational number, 1.7320508 (unending decimal). These are not considered perfect squares because the sides in both cases are not whole numbers. Therefore, a *perfect square* is a square whose sides result in a whole number with no fractional parts. An *imperfect square*

FIGURE 14.4

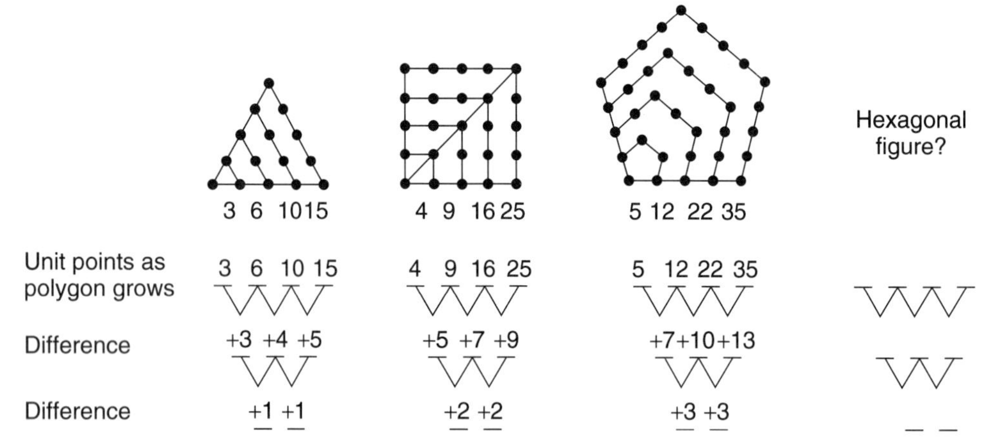

Finding the embedded pattern to generate the next figurate numbers.

is a square whose sides result in a whole number plus some fractional part.

Pythagorean Triples. Pythagoras is thought by many to have created the Pythagorean theorem, which states that

$$a^2 + b^2 = c^2$$

where a and b are legs of a right triangle and c is the hypotenuse. The hypotenuse is the side opposite the right angle.

The next activity tells the real story from history. It is one students deserve to hear.

Cultural Contributions

PYTHAGORAS AND HISTORY

CULTURAL RELEVANCE

It is enlightening for students to learn that the Babylonians on the Asian continent used the right triangle theorem 1500 years before the time of Pythagoras.

Grades 4–8

Students should know that the first concepts of congruency were developed in Africa and Asia and that cotangents and similar triangle principles were used in the building of the African pyramids. The students should examine the contributions to geometry made by peoples all over the world. For example, Eskimos build strong dome-shaped igloos in the outline of an inverted catenary. Mozambicans

Cultural Contributions Continues

build rectangular houses by using equal-length ropes as the diagonals. The Babylonians used the right triangle theorem 1500 years before the time of Pythagoras; hence, the term Pythagorean theorem *is a misnomer. Also, the modern method of using the so-called Pascal's triangle was actually invented in Asia by the Chinese and the Persians 500 years before Pascal was born.* (Strong, 1990)

A visual representation of the theorem is shown in Figure 14.5. Pythagoras found sets of three whole numbers, known as triples, that would fit this pattern. One triple given frequently as an example is the triple of 3, 4, and 5 as the sides of the right triangle (seen in Figure 14.5). If asked to find other triples, middle school students are most likely to see multiples of the 3, 4, 5 triple as possibilities.

FIGURE 14.5

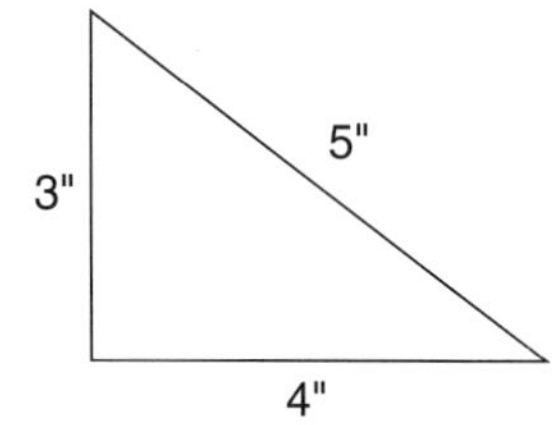

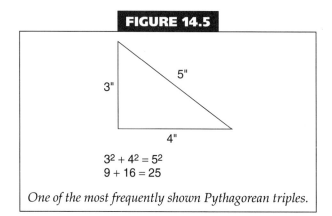

$$3^2 + 4^2 = 5^2$$
$$9 + 16 = 25$$

One of the most frequently shown Pythagorean triples.

Activity 14.7

CALCULATORS CULTURAL RELEVANCE PROBLEM SOLVING

TRIPLES

DIRECTIONS

1. Think of a pattern that might create triples from what you know about the triple 3, 4, 5.
2. Follow this theorem:

$$a^2 + b^2 = c^2$$

3. Use the calculator to see whether the triple fits the theorem.

Triples	*Theorem*
3 4 5	9 + 16 = 25
	25 = 25
6 8 10	? + ? = ?
	? = ?
? ? ?	? + ? = ?
	? = ?

4. Create four more triples, following the same pattern.
5. Generalize a rule for finding Pythagorean triples using the table you created in Step 3.

There are other ways to create Pythagorean triples. Computer programs give students an excellent chance to analyze (problem solve) other techniques.

When middle schoolers analyze embedded formulas for finding patterns (as in Figure 14.4), they see one of the uses for beginning algebra concepts, where patterns can be generalized using variables to stand for numbers.

Fibonacci Number Sequence. The Fibonacci number sequence is most often seen in the field of science but also occurs in other fields, including music, the arts, and architecture. A *Fibonacci number sequence* is defined as a sequence of numbers where any number is generated by adding the two previous numbers together. Figure 14.6 shows a diagram of the number pattern as it might occur in growing things. The numbers to the right show the number pattern as it progresses through seven cycles.

Using the model of a tree branch (Figure 14.6), Fibonacci numbers must meet the following criteria:

1. An old branch can generate a new branch only once.
2. The old branch continues to generate itself at each new level.

FIGURE 14.6

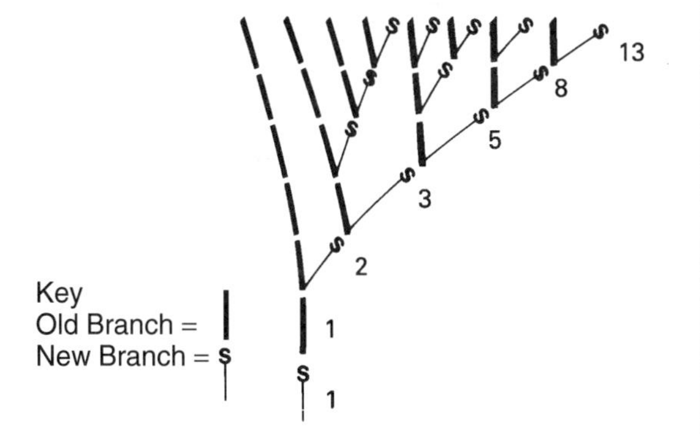

Branching model of the Fibonacci number sequence.

3. A new branch can generate itself (becoming an old branch) and a new one (at the next level of procreation).

When the number pattern becomes apparent, one can predict the number of new and old branches for endless levels yet to come. It may be easier to see the number pattern if presented horizontally with numbers only:

1 1 2 3 5 8 13 . . .

Notice that 13 is derived from adding the two numbers directly before it. Do you get 8 the same way? Do you get the other numbers the same way? Now you have established the number pattern of Fibonacci numbers.

Look at the three criteria needed in the preceding branch model. Substitute the word *variable* for the word *branch* to generalize the Fibonacci sequence to all areas. The assessment section at the end of this chapter also shows how children from grade two to grade six handle the Fibonacci sequence and how they explain what they see in the number pattern. The children's literature book, *Math Curse* (Scieszka and Smith, 1995) features the Fibonacci sequence with its humorous commentary.

Activity 14.8

MATHEMATICAL CONNECTIONS

MUSIC AND SCIENCE WITH FIBONACCI NUMBERS

DIRECTIONS

1. Because the Fibonacci sequence of numbers occurs in many fields, including music and science, students can

Activity Continues

be directed to choose a science or music topic and illustrate how the Fibonacci sequence is seen (Figure 14.7).

2. Find models in the science book and from nature.
   A hint to start: Rabbits help us see the sequence every few weeks. Think about roots and leaves of plants.
3. If students are creative, they may be able to compose their own examples of musical arrangements with the Fibonacci sequence.

FIGURE 14.7

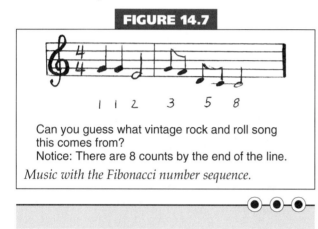

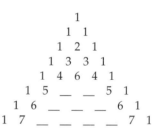

Can you guess what vintage rock and roll song this comes from?
Notice: There are 8 counts by the end of the line.

Music with the Fibonacci number sequence.

Johnson (1999) shows how the Fibonacci sequence is used in basket weaving. Good middle school lessons are included too.

Pascal's Triangle. Pascal's triangle (Figure 14.8) is a special arrangement of numbers thought to have been discovered by Blaise Pascal, a seventeenth-century mathematician. Pascal's triangle is in the configuration of a triangle with many number patterns visible as each row is added to the triangle. This arrangement of numbers relates to the number of possible outcomes in probability.

Pascal's triangle relates later to algebra and solving equations. A formal definition is left for the reader to discover during the following problem-solving activity.

It is easy to see the symmetry of Pascal's triangle. It makes an excellent bulletin board, especially if a new row is added daily, starting after the initial pattern is established at level 6.

Students find themselves anticipating what the next row will be. They should also be encouraged to look at emerging number patterns as the triangle develops. The following exploration presents the kind of questioning that will help students begin to develop problem-solving strategies using the triangle.

FIGURE 14.8

1	start
1 1	level 1
1 2 1	level 2
1 3 3 1	level 3
1 4 6 4 1	level 4
1 5 10 10 5 1	level 5
1 6 15 20 15 6 1	level 6
__ __ __ __ __ __ __ __	etc.

Pascal's triangle.

Activity 14.9

PROBLEM SOLVING · CULTURAL RELEVANCE

PASCAL'S TRIANGLE AND CULTURAL RELEVANCE

DIRECTIONS

Strong (1990) points out that the "modern method of using the so-called Pascal's triangle was actually invented in Asia by the Chinese and the Persians 500 years before Pascal was born" (p. 20). The curriculum of the Chicago Public Schools asks teachers to include this fact in the teaching of mathematics from grade 4 on.

1. This is the same as Pascal's triangle seen above. Some numbers have been removed to help you see some of the number patterns more clearly.

   1
   1 1
   1 2 1
   1 3 3 1
   1 4 6 4 1
   1 5 __ __ 5 1
   1 6 __ __ __ 6 1
   1 7 __ __ __ __ 7 1

   How many spaces will continue on the next two levels? Do you see a pattern developing?
2. The spaces give us an idea of the numbers required on each side to make the symmetry occur. By looking at the first diagram completed to level 6, we see that two tens come in the first two blank spaces after the numeral 5. Which numbers in the previous row help to produce the tens in level 5? In level 6, how were the numbers 15 and 20 chosen for that level? What numbers on the previous level helped? What will the numbers be on levels 7, 8, and 9?
3. Add the numbers horizontally on each level. What pattern do you notice? Turn the pattern into a definition of Pascal's triangle by explaining how the formula is derived.

Supporting the NCTM *Principles and Standards* (2000):

- Mathematics as Reasoning; Problem Solving, Connections, Representations

Activity Continues

- Oral Discourse; Written Discourse—The Teaching Principle
- The Equity Principle

Manouchehri and Enderson (1999) share ideas for promoting discourse using Pascal's triangle in an inquiry-oriented learning activity. They include answers by seventh graders as they worked in groups. The teachers are careful to use a form of the elaborating technique to keep the learning on task and bring out the mathematical potential of Pascal's triangle.

The patterns in number theory can be very helpful to students as they work with the number system. The unique features can help students calculate more quickly, estimate reasonable answers, perform mental computation (*mental math*), and problem solve where expanded answers can lead to new discoveries. The latter supports Bruner's idea of discovery learning as a mark of a true education.

EXTENDED ACTIVITIES

Name of Activity

- Pascal's Triangle

CALCULATORS

CULTURAL RELEVANCE

Patterns and Functions

Students who have been exposed to the properties of geometric shapes, as seen in Chapter 6, will find an easy transition to the use of functions to express relations and patterns between variables.

Activities for Pre-K–2 Grades. Even very young children can achieve an understanding of functions by looking for the pattern rule that applies to every example within a set of objects.

From Concrete to the Connecting Level. As always, the use of manipulatives is the first step in building an awareness of the functions. A box with a hole and funnel becomes the function input-output machine, as seen in Figure 14.9. The teacher puts one concrete object in the top of the function machine (in the input hole) and pulls another object out the output slot. Children are asked to reason what is happening inside the machine, what rule is being applied that tells people what will come out of the machine. Children love the mystery idea of something "special" happening inside the machine and enjoy coming up with sounds for the machine to make as well as watching the teacher model the activity.

Children can make their own machines to use in cooperative grouping. As the link to the connecting level, children are asked to make a table of input and output choices. They draw the pieces on paper as seen in the function table in Figure 14.9. First and second graders are given function relationships that only differ by one attribute. The portfolio assessment

FIGURE 14.9

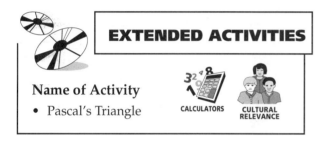

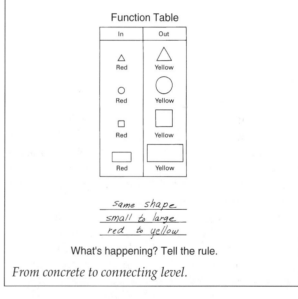

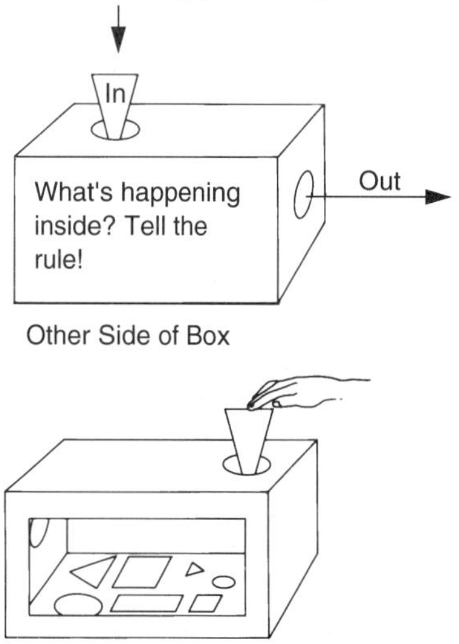

Other Side of Box

Pieces are hidden inside the box to be chosen to show the pattern relationship that develops when attribute pieces are inserted.

Students record what they see going *in* and coming *out* of the machine.

Function Table

In	Out
△ Red	△ Yellow
○ Red	○ Yellow
□ Red	□ Yellow
▭ Red	▭ Yellow

same shape
small to large
red to yellow

What's happening? Tell the rule.

From concrete to connecting level.

seen at the end of this chapter shows the typical response made by students at the end of second grade. Functions that differ by two or more changes are difficult for young children and are introduced to students in the later grades after they have proven they can reason relationships involving one attribute change.

Activities for 3–5 Grades

From Connecting Level to the Symbolic. Young children can switch from using objects to search for patterns by using facts they have learned about number combinations as seen in Figure 14.10.

FIGURE 14.10

By third grade a stylized drawing is all that is needed before students generate a function table.

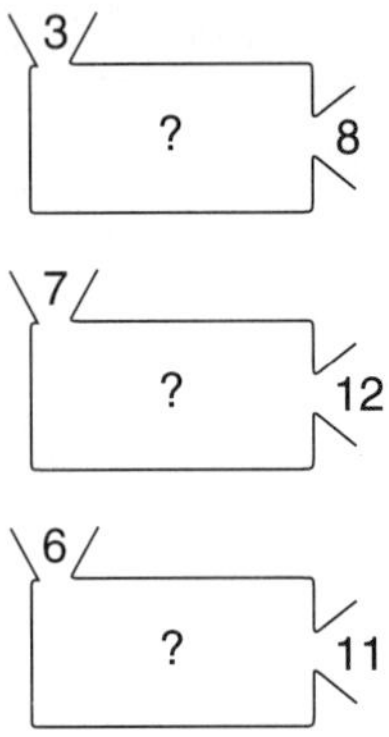

In	Out
3	8
7	12
6	11
The Rule: $x + 5$	

From connecting level to symbolic in 3–5 grades.

Willoughby (1997) and Sulzer (1998) emphasize that fourth graders can use the "$x + 5$" notation instead of saying "add 5." Sulzer also asserts that keeping the function box in the classroom all year enables fourth graders to grow in their mathematical thinking. Students create equations such as $\sqrt{x-1}+1$ and $\sqrt[3]{x-1}+1$ by the end of the year. A gradual progression of thought is included in Sulzer's article.

Activities for 6–8 Grades. Middle schoolers can handle several attribute changes at one time, as in the function table shown in Figure 14.9, which changes size and color with only shape remaining the same.

From Concrete to the Connecting Level. Many attribute changes can be introduced in the middle grades. Attribute pieces that have varying values of shape, size, color, texture, and thickness may be used. The students still use manipulatives to start their activities with multiple variables. They record their actions by drawing function tables and writing the rule as the connecting-level activity.

From Connecting Level to the Symbolic. As they gradually handle more and more attributes at the same time, teachers introduce the change from drawings to working solely on the symbolic level as in Figure 14.11.

FIGURE 14.11

Students in the higher middle school grades can find more than one solution to the function table.

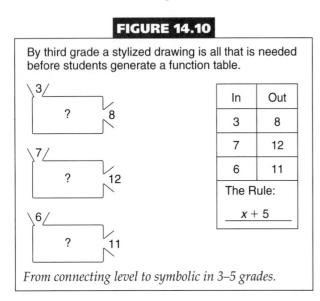

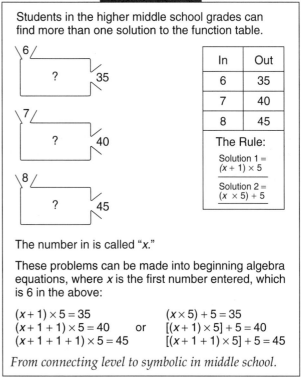

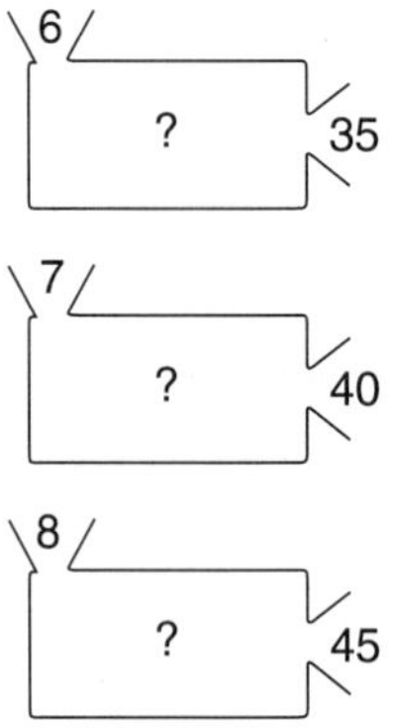

In	Out
6	35
7	40
8	45
The Rule: Solution 1 = $(x + 1) \times 5$; Solution 2 = $(x \times 5) + 5$	

The number in is called "x."

These problems can be made into beginning algebra equations, where x is the first number entered, which is 6 in the above:

$(x + 1) \times 5 = 35$ or $(x \times 5) + 5 = 35$
$(x + 1 + 1) \times 5 = 40$ or $[(x + 1) \times 5] + 5 = 40$
$(x + 1 + 1 + 1) \times 5 = 45$ or $[(x + 1 + 1) \times 5] + 5 = 45$

From connecting level to symbolic in middle school.

Middle school students are encouraged to use a variety of variables with functions and relations. Students can use the ideas to develop their own functions and their relationships in cooperative group settings. Then they can switch with other cooperative groups in the class to see whether they can detect the rules that were used in formulating the other groups' functions.

These activities lead nicely into problem solving with algebra concepts in which equations represent many different kinds of function relationships between and among variables. The development of algebraic concepts is considered in the next section.

The NCTM Addenda Series *Patterns* (Leiva, 1993) for K–6 grades provide twenty-six different lessons by grade level for work with many of the ideas presented for patterning in this chapter. The questioning skills are based on the NCTM *Curriculum and Evaluation Standards* (1989), and *Principles and Standards for School Mathematics* (2000). The activities emphasize ways of communicating and questioning during problem solving, much like the questions found in the activities of this chapter.

Teaching Integers

Many textbooks introduce integers with a number line to help students see the relationship of positive and negative numbers to each other. Moving to the right of zero results in positive numbers, and moving to the left of zero results in negative numbers. Some children's card games have a situation in which the player might lose enough points to be "in the hole." This is an opportune time to discuss negative numbers. Another situation that involves the use and interpretation of negative numbers is below-zero temperatures. It is important to encourage the correct way to read and write these numbers.

Cultural Contributions

CULTURAL RELEVANCE

THE HISTORY OF NEGATIVE NUMBERS

DIRECTIONS

1. Share with the students the knowledge that the Chinese invented negative numbers.
2. Encourage them to do the research in the school library to find out when and under what conditions the Chinese invented negative integers and who were the individuals involved (Strong, 1990).
3. Students can be encouraged to make a school bulletin board so that the rest of the school can see the contributions made by other cultures, spreading the story to other math classes as well as the whole school in general.

Teaching students the four basic operations with integers is a difficult task. Many students learn to work problems with integers by memorizing rules such as "negative times a negative is a positive." The rule may not make sense, but it produces correct answers. Physical models are seldom used as teaching devices. A number-line model has limitations, and only partial explanations.

Postman Stories. When students are introduced to addition and subtraction of integers, one simple, effective approach is to use checks (money received) and bills (money spent). Davis (1967) introduced young children to integers through the "Postman Stories" from the Madison Project. In this setting, checks represent positive numbers and bills represent negative numbers. The action of "bringing" refers to addition and the action of "taking away" refers to subtraction. When the postman brings (+) a check, this indicates adding a positive number. When the postman takes away (–) a check, the action is subtracting a positive number. In the case of bringing (+) a bill, the action would be adding a negative number. If the postman takes away a bill, the effect would be to subtract a negative number. The concept emphasizes that when a check is received, we become richer, but when a bill is received, we become poorer. Likewise, if a check must be given up (subtracted), we become poorer. Read the examples in the next activity and try to visualize the possible events that could occur in the Postman stories.

Activity 14.10

CALCULATORS MATHEMATICAL CONNECTIONS

ECONOMICS

DIRECTIONS

1. Have students act out each story or tell the end result of each story—would they be richer or poorer?
2. Have them check the result with a calculator to see how both can work together.
3. Here are the stories:

   If the postman brings(+) us a check(+) for \$3 and brings(+) another check(+) for \$5, we would have a total of \$8 or in symbols, $^{+}3 + {}^{+}5 = {}^{+}8$.

= Bank account

Balance Record	
Bills (we owe) –	Checks (we receive) +

If the postman brings(+) us a check(+) for \$6 and brings(+) a bill(–) for \$2, we would have a total of \$4 or in symbols: $^{+}6 + {}^{-}2 = {}^{+}4$.

If the postman brings(+) a bill(–) for \$5 and brings(+) another bill(–) for \$2, we would have a total of –\$7 or in symbols: $^{-}5 + {}^{-}2 = {}^{-}7$.

If the postman brings(+) a check(+) for \$3 and brings(+) a bill(–) for \$4, we would need \$1 to pay the bill, or in symbols: $^{+}3 + {}^{-}4 = {}^{-}1$.

If the postman brings(+) a check(+) for \$9 and takes away(–) a check(+) for \$2, we would be poorer in the end since the postman *takes away* a check. With symbols: $^{+}9 - {}^{+}2 = {}^{+}7$.

Activity Continues

4. *For older students (middle school age):* Create similar stories using the bank account model and buy stereos, hit CDs, cars, or items that young teenagers are looking forward to owning in the near future (if they don't have them already). The stories become relevant, and examples using checks and bills are realistic to the modern-day desire for all the luxuries.

Students need to understand that the effect of the postman taking away a check is less money. Some teachers might want to relate this event to turning a paycheck over immediately to someone to whom you owe money so you are not richer as the end result. To help clarify this situation, Davis suggests including a time factor in the imaginary story about the postman. The use of time prevents misconceptions about the mathematical equation that is appropriate for each situation.

If the postman takes away(–) a check(+) for $5 and takes away(–) another check(+) for $2, the result would be $-{}^{+}5 - {}^{+}2 = {}^{-}7$. As a result of the postman's visit, we have less money because two checks were taken away from us.

If the postman takes away(–) a bill(–) for $5 and takes away(–) a bill(–) for $2, we would be richer in the end since bills were taken away. In symbols: $-{}^{-}5 - {}^{-}2 = {}^{+}7$. Again the time factor should be emphasized. We had to give the postman bills, an action that makes us richer in the long run because we had counted on paying those bills and now we do not have to pay them. One method to help children visualize these events is to use play money. When a bill comes for $7, we set money aside to pay that amount and put the bill with it to remember it. If the postman makes an error (and errors could occur in the same amounts as bills), when we give the postman the bill, we can see the effect of making us richer.

The real challenge comes when trying to teach multiplication and division of integers with understanding. For multiplication, interpretation of the factors is a critical feature of the Postman stories. The *second* factor is the money (bill or check) and the *first* factor tells how many times the postman brings the item or takes it away. Study these examples:

${}^{+}2 \times {}^{+}3 = {}^{+}6$	The postman brings two checks for $3 each.
${}^{+}2 \times {}^{-}5 = {}^{-}10$	The postman brings two bills for $5 each.
${}^{-}3 \times {}^{+}4 = {}^{-}12$	The postman takes away three checks for $4 each. Remember—this means we are poorer when we have checks taken away.
${}^{-}2 \times {}^{-}6 = {}^{+}12$	The postman takes away two bills for $6 each. This is good. We are richer when bills are taken away.

Many educators suggest using physical models for teaching and representing integers. The positive-negative charge model has been suggested by several authors. Battista (1983) extends the model to the four operations and illustrates how the model can show properties of the system of integers. Some of the more difficult concepts are covered in "Get a Charge out of Integers" on the CD-ROM. Other children's literature books are included in the end-of-chapter bibliography.

Chang (1985) presents several models to teach addition and subtraction of integers: number line, play money (a technique that is similar to the Postman stories), and color-block technique that uses negative and positive blocks. The article outlines the teaching strategies for all three approaches in a clear, concise manner.

Students in the middle grades need concrete materials and games to reinforce concepts as much as children in lower grades. The middle grade teacher may be more reluctant to use this technique, but it has been proven effective for all grades. Games with the football field or the thermometer provide scenarios to help visualize the computation with signed numbers. Check the CD-ROM for some additional examples. Teaching operations with integers is an opportune time to challenge students to apply their prior experiences in new situations.

Beginning Algebra Concepts

Algebra is the gateway to higher mathematics. Algebra must be accessible to *all* students if we are to reach the goal of equity in mathematics. Carifio and Nasser (1995) and Lawson (1990) among others have pointed out that algebra is the entry level skill in most sciences, business, industry, and technical jobs. What makes algebra seem difficult to some people is that algebra is really two things at once. First it is a language that describes relationships and patterns between and among elements, and second it is an abstract system of its own with its own rules and definitions.

Usiskin (1992) points to algebra as a language with symbols that stand for elements of sets and operations on those symbols. He stresses three facts (p. 27) about languages that should, therefore, apply to algebra:

- It is best learned in context.
- Almost any human being can learn it.
- It is more easily learned when one is younger.

Usiskin's thoughts are keeping with the ideas of brain research seen in Chapter 3, *use it or lose it* and *the sooner the better.* That means children must start early to see how different things from their world can be seen in a relationship with other elements using letters to emphasize the relationship patterns. This is the part of algebra started in elementary school. The abstract system of knowledge with its own rules and definitions is introduced in late middle school and high school in the traditional courses known as prealgebra (grade eight) and algebra I and algebra II in high school.

Activities for K–4 Grades. Children may be taken through the degrees of abstraction from manipulatives to symbols. Cuisenaire rods lend themselves nicely to go from a pure arithmetic level with concrete manipulatives to a more abstract knowledge in symbolic notation. Figure 14.12 shows how the transition works over the grades.

FIGURE 14.12

With Concrete Rods

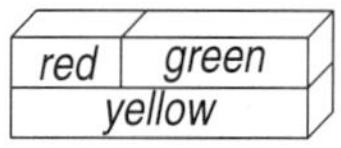

Their Symbols	Algebraic Implications
$2 + 3 = 5$	Actual whole numbers are shown.
$r + g = y$	Each letter stands for a definite rod; children see the relationship of one distinct rod to another without racing to a numerical answer.
$a + b = c$	The letters are now generalized to represent *any* number as it relates to any other unique number such that a third unique number is produced.

A gradual transition to more abstraction in elementary grades.

Children can start with one unknown variable where the relationship is the important emphasis. Connecting cubes may be used with a balance to show equations where an unknown is present. There are different bags marked *x* with various amounts of connecting cubes or rods that the children cannot see. They place each *x* bag on the balance until they get the bag that shows equivalence of sets by both sides balancing as seen in Figure 14.13. Students solve the equation first with manipulatives and then proceed to the symbolic level.

FIGURE 14.13

With a Concrete Balance and Connecting Cubes	Their Symbols	Algebraic Implications
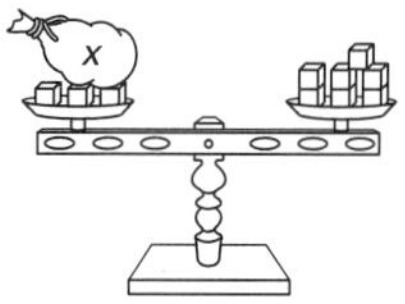	$3 + x = 7$	What must be added to 3 so the quantity is equal to 7?

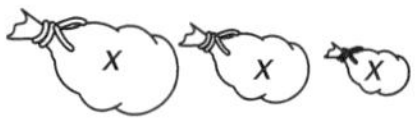

Different bags marked *x*, with different amounts. Students must find the correct amount.

Equations with one unknown in the early grades.

Note the questions asked in Figure 14.13: *What must be added to 3 so the quantity* ***is equal to*** *7?* Howden (1990) stresses the importance of that wording for teachers of young children. Teachers must *not* ask: What is added to 3 to make 7? The word *make* gives the wrong interpretation to equations as children progress up the grades. It is better to start with the proper phrases in mathematics so "un-learning" does not need to occur later in the school years. For some children imprecise language is hard to abandon later in middle school.

Using what students already know is the best starting point for any concept. If students have been exposed to the use of Cuisenaire rods in the early elementary years, their use with beginning algebra concepts will be quite natural. Teachers report that even students who have never seen the rods before become quite adept at using them if given a day to explore their use on their own. The first example uses the letter variable *y* for the yellow rod. Early algebra concepts solve for one unknown, as shown in Figure 14.14.

FIGURE 14.14

$$2y + 3 = 13$$

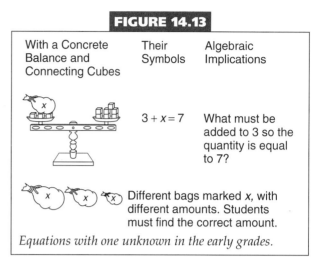

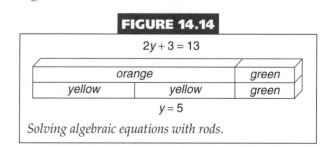

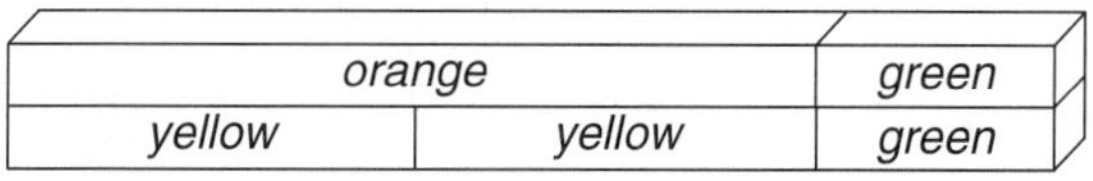

$$y = 5$$

Solving algebraic equations with rods.

Experienced rod users may translate "5" for the yellow rod too easily, and such easy solutions may inhibit the recognition of new ways of writing equations. Teachers may place an *x* for the use of *y* and set up the equation as in Figure 14.15. on page 372.

FIGURE 14.15

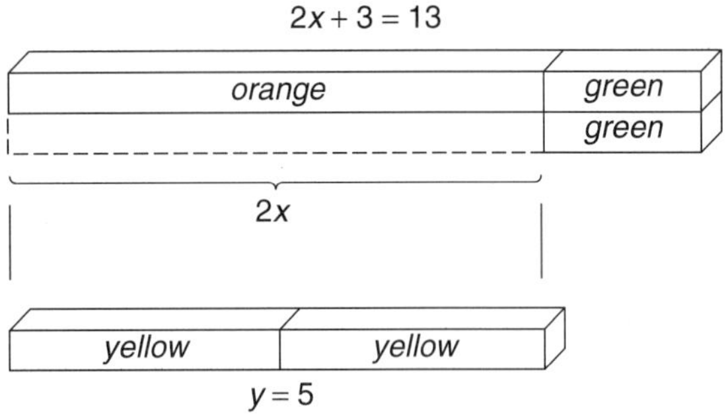

Advanced ways to use rods for experienced users.

Activities for 5–8 Grades. During the middle school years students find themselves, their hormones, lifestyles, interest, *everything,* in transition from child to teenager. It is an egocentric time when everything revolves around "what's in it for me and what will make me look good to the most peers," an "I" or "me" view of life.

Into this world, the mathematics teacher brings abstract symbols and generalizations that seem a far cry from the more interesting topics of young adolescents—cars, the opposite sex, and wearing the "right" designer labels.

Functions. To combat the egocentric nature of adolescence, teachers are choosing "real life" mathematics, the kind that would be interesting to young people. "Math in Context" and "Algebra for All" (Driscoll, Moyer, and Zawojewski, 1998) are projects that teach algebra from real-world situations. The emphasis is on solving engaging problems rather than manipulating "*x*" and "*y*" variables in row after row of algebraic equations. A sample from the "Algebra for All" project is included (Driscoll, Moyer, and Zawojewski, 1998, p. 7):

> *Look at the following table. It is a table that describes tree growth in inches per month:*
>
> | Months | 0 | 1 | 2 | 3 | 4 | 5 | 6 | — | 10 | *n* |
> |---|---|---|---|---|---|---|---|---|---|---|
> | Inches | ? | 1 | 4 | 7 | 10 | 13 | — | — | 28 | — |
>
> 1. *Write an equation that describes the growth of the tree from month to month.*
> 2. *Using the equation written in part 1, explain why in the first month the tree only grows to one inch.*
> 3. *What is the value of the height in inches at Month Zero? What is this value's meaning?*

The sixth NAEP results (Blume and Heckman, 1997) showed that 48 percent of the students in grade eight were proficient at solving for the unknowns when the equation was presented to them, but only 25 percent could generate their own equation when shown a table like the one above with parts missing. If the questions asked students to give only the next value in the table, as many as 55 percent of the grade four students and 66 percent of the grade eight students responded correctly. It is apparent that students continue to need more problem solving in the context of real world examples. They need to generate the tables, graphs, and name the variables themselves. Such tasks were part of TIMSS (Mullis, 1997), another test in which U.S. students did poorly when compared to other students around the world.

Functions that began as attribute relationships in the early grades are now extended to algebra and formula concepts. Glatzer and Lappan (1990, p. 36–37) show how Cuisenaire rods can be used to see function relationships recorded in a table and generalized to any number rod. It is adapted here as a further extension of the function table seen in the tree growth example.

Subscripts© . . . *little thoughts below the bottom line*

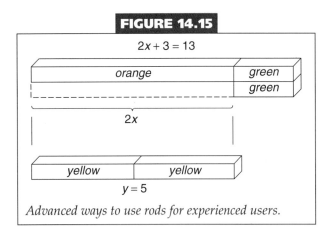

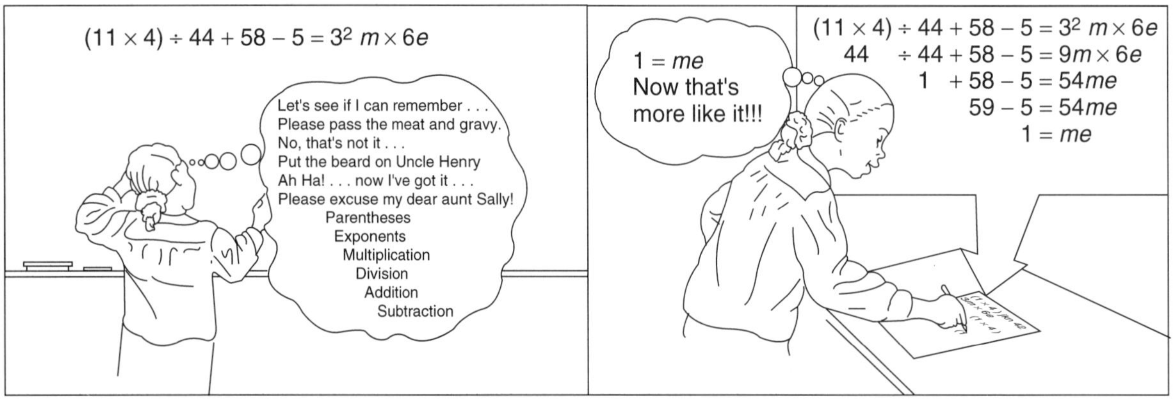

Activity 14.11

PROBLEM SOLVING MANIPULATIVES

CUISENAIRE RODS AND FUNCTION TABLES

MATERIALS

FIGURE 14.16

With the Concrete Manipulatives

Table Showing Function with Different Rod Staircases

Purple Rods (4 units in length)

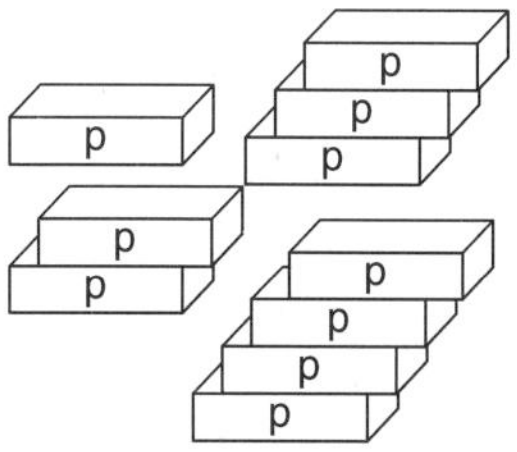

No. in Staircase	Volume	Surface Area
1	4	18
2	8	30
3	12	42
4	16	54
•	•	•
•	•	•
•	•	•
n	$4n$	$12n + 6$

Yellow Rods (5 units in length)

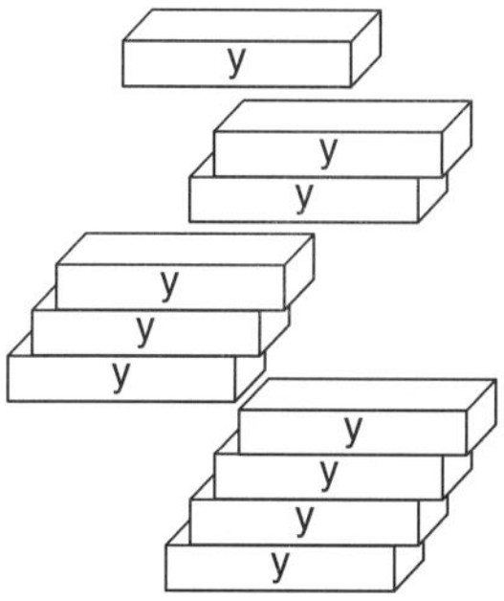

No. in Staircase	Volume	Surface Area
1	5	22
2	10	36
3	15	50
4	20	64
•	•	•
•	•	•
•	•	•
n	$5n$	$14n + 8$

Dark Green Rods (6 units in length)

You fill in the rest.

No. in Staircase	Volume	Surface Area
•	•	•
•	•	•
•	•	•

Functions with any rod staircase generalizing a formula relationship.

DIRECTIONS

1. Work in cooperative groups to problem solve what should come next in the chart.
2. Fill in the chart found in Figure 14.16. Include a sketch of the dark green rods in staircases.

Activity Continues

3. Generalize a formula for volume and a formula for surface area that will fit for any rod staircase. Listen to each other's ideas to see which formulas will work every time no matter which rod is chosen.

V = ______________

SA = ______________

Simultaneous Equations. The next activity is the same one found in Chapter 5 on Problem Solving. It, too, can be solved by tables (as in Chapter 5) or by simultaneous equations using the substitution method. One variable is defined in terms of the other, that is, by substitution. Both variables have to be substituted for each other; therefore, it requires two equations, one to find n (number of nickels) and one to find d (number of dimes). Try the next activity.

Activity 14.12

PROBLEM SOLVING

SIMULTANEOUS EQUATIONS

Jho-Ju held a yard sale and charged a dime for everything, but would accept a nickel if the buyer was a good bargainer. At the end of the day, she realized that she had sold all 20 items and taken in the grand total of $1.90. She had only dimes and nickels at the end of the day. How many of each did she have?

A start to solving:

1. Using the facts of the word problem, the two simultaneous equations can be created:

   $0.05N + 0.10D = 1.90$

   $N + D = 20$

2. Now solve for N in terms of D in both equations.
3. Then solve for D in terms of N in both equations.

The answer is provided on the CD-ROM under Jho-Ju's Problem. Also included on the CD-ROM is a TIMSS assessment task involving the topics in this chapter—a good resource as you go into the classroom.

Adolescent Literature. Any book assigned by the English teacher can be used to develop incidents in which simultaneous equations can be used. Follow the basic form shown in the preceding two examples and create word problems based on the readings of adolescents in your school. Some examples are included on the CD-ROM using the classic book, *Johnny Tremain.* Selections from the Judy Blume books can be used also.

Simultaneous equations were a part of the culture of first century B.C. in China (Nelson, 1993). Some examples show three and four unknowns, not like the easy approach of two unknowns shown to middle schoolers today. Some who enjoy the mystery quality of setting up simultaneous equations with unknowns may enjoy the activity from China.

Binomial Expressions. Manipulatives should still be used in beginning algebra so students can see how some of these strange-appearing notations are solved. Teaching-supply catalogs carry many manipulatives such as the Algeblocks to visualize equations.

Many arrangements with manipulatives will look familiar to students who have worked with such things as base 10 blocks from the second and third grade, first with whole numbers, then with decimals, and now with x as the unknown. The configurations are essentially the same. This shows a connection to action movements with algebra notation that begins to make sense out of an equation like this: $(2x + 4)(x + 4) = 2x^2 + 12x + 16$. Figure 14.17 shows how the ideas of arithmetic can blend with the concepts of algebra.

The examples given show subtle differences between functions and variables. Demana and Waits (1990) state that these subtle differences go unnoticed in most algebra curricula today and may be one of the reasons that so many students find alge-

EXTENDED ACTIVITIES

Name Of Activity

- Get a Charge out of Integers
- Jho-Ju's Problem
- Adolescent Literature with Equations in Spreadsheets
- Simultaneous Equations with Middle School Interests in Mind
- Math Dialogue with Middle School Students in Algebra for All
- Simultaneous Equations from China
- TIMSS Assessment: Earnings

FIGURE 14.17

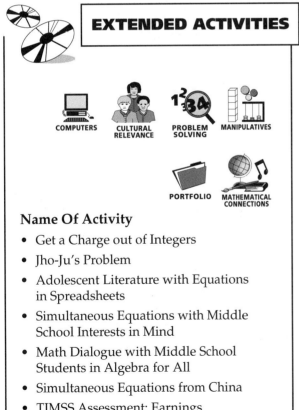

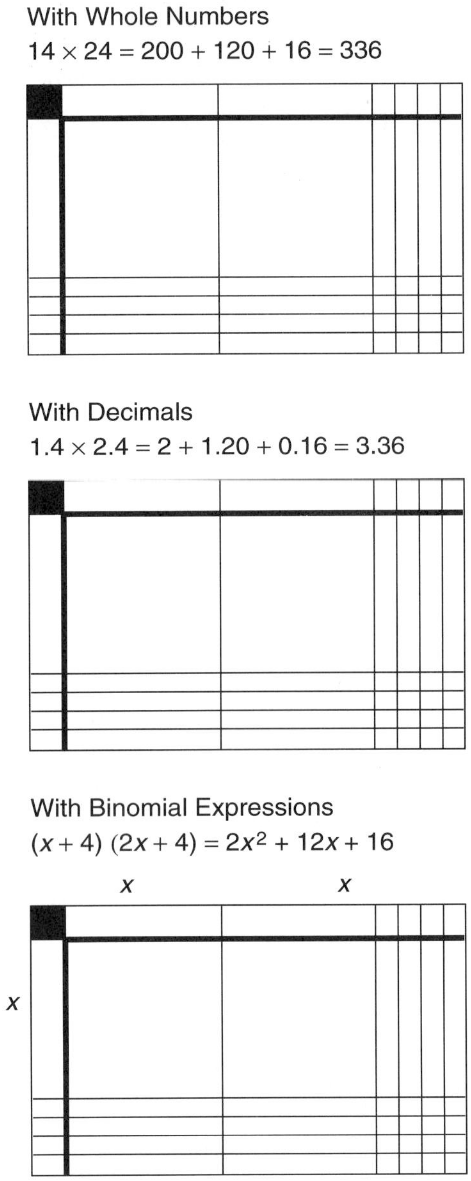

From whole number algorithms to binomial expressions.

bra difficult. Variables have different meanings and different relationships depending on the particular situation in which they are used.

- If a situation means we need to search for patterns, a **table** is a good way to focus on the functional relationship. We have just seen several examples of such functions in this chapter.
- If the situation calls for a description on a certain aspect of the relationship, a **graph** is the best to use because students can see how the effects on one changes the other.

From One Unknown to Two Unknowns in Equations and Graphs. The next step is to solve for two unknowns in the same equation. This step requires a cognitive awareness that there can be more than one pair of answers to the equation. This awareness can be proved by asking students to solve for at least three sets of the two unknown quantities, as seen in Figure 14.18.

FIGURE 14.18

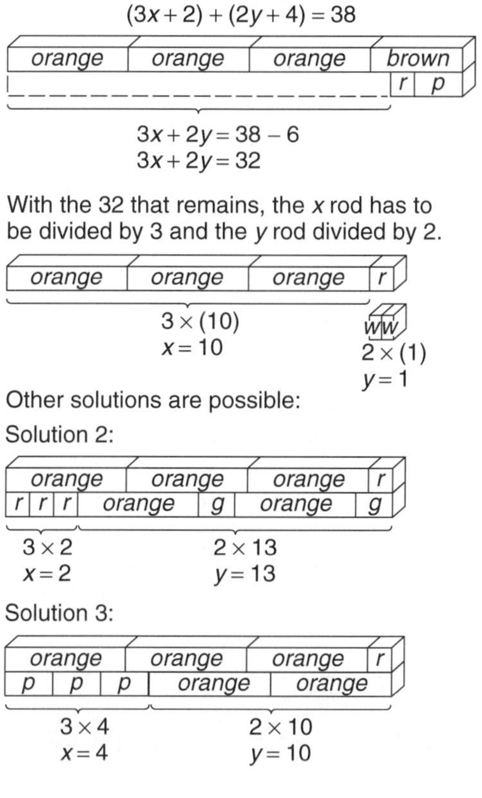

Solving two unknowns with Cuisenaire rods.

The next step is to set up a table in which the ordered pairs can be seen in a pattern of responses. If

TABLE 14.1 Variety of Intercepts

x	*y*
2	13
4	10
6	7
8	4
10	1
12	–2
14	–5

students have been working with tables from the early grades as the NCTM *Standards* advocate, the idea of a table to show the results will be easily grasped. Table 14.1 organizes the information presented in Figure 14.18 showing the variety of values assigned to *x* and *y*. Notice that negative integers are a natural part of algebra. The next step is to use the table to construct a graph showing the points and their relationship along the slope of a straight line (Figure 14.19).

FIGURE 14.19

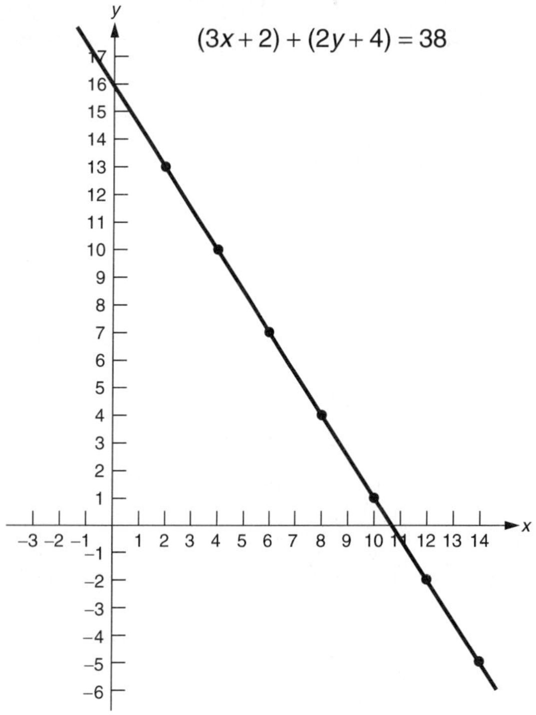

Graphing equations.

To find where the y-axis is intercepted let $x = 0$:

$$\begin{aligned} (3x + y) + 2y + 4 &= 38 \\ [3(0) + 2] + 2y + 4 &= 38 \\ (0 + 2) + 2y + 4 &= 38 \\ 2 + 2y + 4 &= 38 \\ 2y + 6 &= 38 \\ 2y &= 38 - 6 \\ 2y &= 32 \\ y &= 16 \end{aligned}$$

When the line is extended to intercept the y-axis, one can see it crosses at the number 16. This point is called the y-intercept.

To find where the line intercepts the x-axis, the equation sets y at 0:

$$\begin{aligned} (3x + 2) + [2(0) + 4] &= 38 \\ 3x + 2 + 4 &= 38 \\ 3x &= 38 - 6 \\ 3x &= 32 \\ x &= 10.66 \text{ or } 10\tfrac{2}{3} \end{aligned}$$

Notice that the x-intercept has a fractional part. Intercepts do not have to be only whole numbers.

Activity 14.13

CALCULATORS

GRAPHING CALCULATOR WITH EQUATIONS

The innovation of the graphing calculator allows students to go from the table of solutions to the graph without tediously drawing coordinates themselves. This ability makes for more immediate feedback and helps students see the mathematical connections more quickly than was ever possible before this new technology was present. Try the preceding problem with the graphing calculation.

Demana and Waits (1990) advocate that students of prealgebra and beginning algebra I classes should draw some graphs by hand before moving to graphing calculators and computers. They feel that students will understand that there are many more points on the graph than a table can generate if they draw the lines on the graph themselves. It is not so apparent when a line is quickly drawn on a graphing calculator or computer.

The twenty-first century shows the promise of new ways to use algebra with new technologies yet unseen by all of us who have gone through the traditional algebra preparation. There are many more research questions to be asked. The Internet searches will be a place to find discussion groups. Many groups are forming around the algebra issue as teachers search for better ways to ready students for this new century.

Cultural Contributions

CULTURAL RELEVANCE

ORIGINS OF ALGEBRAIC CONCEPTS

Students can begin to learn algebraic concepts from the very beginning of school. The following quotations show the culturally relevant materials that students need to know at each of the appropriate grade levels.

Grade K–3

> *Students should know that by 2650* B.C. *the Africans in ancient Egypt had invented and used scale drawings and star-clocks. The students should also know that Africans and Asians invented algebra, that the word* algebra *is Arabic in origin, and that Europe received algebra as a gift from Asia and Africa.*

Grade 4–8

> *The students should examine the Egyptian use of the distributive property. For example, ancient Egyptians multiplied 34 by 21 by multiplying 34 by (1 + 4 + 16). They used successive doubling of the product of* 1 times 34. *The Egyptians also used patterns to find the next term in a sequence such as 1, 7, 49, 343 . . . which was taken from an ancient papyrus. Students should know that the word* algebra *is Arabic in origin and that Europe received algebra as a gift from Asia and Africa.* (Strong, 1990)

ASSESSMENT

Field-Independent Learners

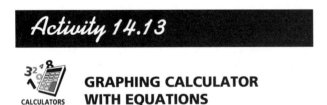

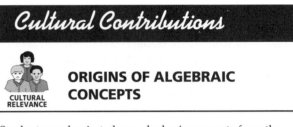

Throughout the examples in the teaching strategies section, material was presented in chart or table form so that one detail could build on another. Charts and tables, rather than diagrams, seem more helpful to students who find field-independent processing more to their liking. The step-by-step progression of the Sieve of Eratosthenes helps because primes are divided out one at a time and factors are combined in the end to see a pattern. The number pattern involved in the Fibonacci sequence may be seen more clearly if the numbers (minus the diagram) are presented in the following manner:

1 1 2 3 5 8 13 21 34 55

The diagram seems to "get in the way" of seeing the number sequence. If you found yourself confused rather than helped by the diagram, you may have been experiencing the same frustrations that successive thinkers feel at such times.

The dividing method for prime factorization is often more helpful than the stylized method of factor trees. Computer programs that develop any number pattern one step at a time may be more easily understood.

Field-Dependent Learners

Throughout the teaching strategies section, material was also presented in a diagram or stylized picture form. It is thought that such an approach may be more beneficial to the field-dependent thinker who can see patterns more easily if expressed in relationship to a whole picture or idea from the beginning. Factor trees, figurate (polygonal) numbers, Venn diagrams, graphs, and the branch drawing of the Fibonacci sequence are some of the teaching materials that can help students develop specific patterns in number theory. Logo computer programs that show the whole pattern in a drawing may prove more helpful to field-dependent learners.

Correcting Common Misconceptions

Jumping to Premature Conclusions. Frequently students will decide on an answer before the real pattern can be discerned. In their desire to find a pattern, they have been too hasty in their conclusions. A good example is the false pattern emerging from this attempt to find the solution for Pascal's triangle.

1	start
1 1	level 1
1 2 1	level 2
1 3 3 1	level 3
1 4 <u>5</u> 4 1	level 4
1 5 <u>6</u> <u>6</u> 5 1	level 5

Students who are asked to find the number pattern of Pascal's triangle after seeing only the first three levels may quite naturally jump to the wrong conclusion about the pattern. The best remediation technique is a preventive one—a teacher must anticipate the points at which a misinterpretation could easily occur and make sure that enough examples of the pattern have been given to ensure a correct analysis of the pattern. As was mentioned earlier, it is good to present at least six levels of Pascal's triangle before asking children to find the pattern involved.

Correcting Unknown Errors . . . the Reason for Oral Discourse. Some students discover the correct pattern, but a teacher may not know it because the students make careless errors that do not show what they know. In the following Fibonacci example, the student understands the pattern but might be overlooked by a teacher who was checking only the answers in the blanks. Examples like this continue to emphasize the need for the teacher and student to engage in dialogue about the pattern. The teacher must analyze the step-by-step work of each student when answers appear to be incorrect. This is where the new ideas on assessment become very important.

1 1 2 3 5 <u>8</u> <u>14</u> <u>25</u> <u>39</u> <u>64</u>

Not Seeing the Pattern. There are some special needs students who cannot see a pattern or will not search for one if it is not seen easily. Teachers must ask more probing questions in such cases. It is tempting to tell the answer rather than construct more and more decisive questions. If problem solving and self-discovery of patterns are the important components of the lesson, then probing questions and clues are the best helps a teacher can give. Notice that clues appear throughout this chapter, especially when you were asked to problem solve a pattern in number theory that could be quite difficult for the nonmathematics major. Such clues did not provide the answer but should have helped you discover a way to the solution.

Portfolio Assessments

Fibonacci Number Sequence. There are five students' work evaluated in this set of portfolio assessments. Four of the activities come from first, second, and third graders. A final journal entry was made by an eighth grader and shows the differences that occur as students mature at the end of their middle school experience.

Activity 14.14

PORTFOLIO

PORTFOLIO ASSESSMENTS

For Teacher Reflection of Students' Work in Number Patterns

DIRECTIONS

1. Analyze the responses made by the students. Consider the age and grade level of the work.
2. What likenesses do you see? What differences in reasoning do you see
   - between students of the same age and grade level?
   - between students of different ages and grade levels?
3. Two of the children chose to use Cuisenaire rods to help them figure out a pattern. Do you see a difference in their answers? Look at their sense of symmetry in the answers compared to the students who did not use rods. What is your impression of their answers? Notice that Mark drew the rods while Matthew just talked about using them.
4. Design a rubric that would take into account the diversity of answers while being fair in your assessment strategy.
   - Include the rubric in your Professional Portfolio for Job Interviews along with your analysis of each child's understanding in this activity.
   - Enjoy the student work on Fibonacci numbers seen in Figures 14.20 through 14.24.

FIGURE 14.20

Name Shawn - age 6 - first grade

The Mystery Numbers

Look at the five numbers in a row. Can you think of the three mystery numbers that would come next? Place them in the blank spaces.

1 1 2 3 5 5 6 7

Write how you figured out the answer.

because there's two ones. Then
6 becames next in the numbers.
7 comes next in numbers.

Activity Continues

FIGURE 14.21

Name Matthew - age 8 - grade 2

The Mystery Numbers

Look at the five numbers in a row. Can you think of the three mystery numbers that would come next? Place them in the blank spaces.

1 1 2 3 5 5 3 2

Write how you figured out the answer.

I Poot The Rods The
to Gether and
macht The colers

FIGURE 14.22

Name Mark - age 8 - grade 3

The Mystery Numbers

Look at the five numbers in a row. Can you think of the three mystery numbers that would come next? Place them in the blank spaces.

1 1 2 3 5 6 6 7 8 10 11

Write how you figured out the answer.

I used Cuisenaire rods.
Made stair steps and
double six.

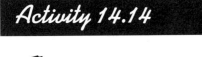

FIGURE 14.23

Name Kate - age 9 - grade 3

The Mystery Numbers

Look at the five numbers in a row. Can you think of the three mystery numbers that would come next? Place them in the blank spaces.

1 1 2 3 5 7 8 8

Write how you figured out the answer.

The skiped 4 so I skiped 6 and dubbled 8
They dubbled the fist 2 numbers so I
thougt I should dubble the end 2 numbers.

Activity Continues

FIGURE 14.24

Name Tyler -age 14 -grade 8

The Mystery Numbers

Look at the five numbers in a row. Can you think of the three mystery numbers that would come next? Place them in the blank spaces.

1 1 2 3 5 8 13 21

Write how you figured out the answer.

Just add the last two numbers each time.

It's interesting to note that all of the younger children had excellent patterns with reasonable logic to the sequences they chose. They just did not see the Fibonacci sequence. By the eighth grade, it is the first one seen and no other sequence was attempted. This particular eighth-grade class had not had a formal introduction to Fibonacci numbers, nor had Tyler heard of the sequence from any other source.

Functions—Input-Output Tables. Two students responded to this activity.

Activity 14.15

PORTFOLIO **PORTFOLIO ASSESSMENTS**

For Teacher Reflection of Students' Work on Attribute Functions

DIRECTIONS

1. Analyze the responses made by the students. Consider the age and grade level of the work.
2. What likenesses do you see? What differences in reasoning do you see? Notice there is one year and one grade level apart.

Activity Continues

Notice how many attribute changes Kate is able to handle compared to the one Greg is able to handle with only a year's developmental level apart.

Note: Piaget says that there is quite a developmental leap that occurs around the eighth to ninth year.

3. Design a rubric that would take into account the diversity of answers while being fair in your assessment strategy.
   - Include the rubric in your Professional Portfolio for Job Interviews along with your analysis of each child's understanding in this activity.
   - Enjoy the student work on attribute function tables seen in Figures 14.25 and 14.26.

Algebra. The last portfolio assessment shows the work of an eighth grader at the end of the prealgebra course. The problem is the same linear equation example shown in the algebra section of this chapter. This student did not use a graphing calculator. Rote symbol manipulation was the technique used for almost all of the prealgebra instruction. There were real-math applications shown in each section of the textbook, and students were encouraged to read them on their own as they went through the chapters. One of the most interesting comments comes when the student is asked how problems like these could be used in the real world of work. Notice the answer given by Travis. Why do you suppose he got an answer like this one?

Activity 14.16

PORTFOLIO **PORTFOLIO ASSESSMENTS**

For Teacher Reflection of Student's Work on Algebra

DIRECTIONS

1. Analyze the responses made by the student in Figure 14.27 on page 381. Consider the age and grade level of the work.
2. Consider the student's answers in light of the background information given to you about the algebra course. What can you infer about the student's experiences with algebra after reading these answers?

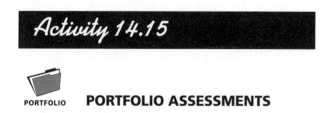

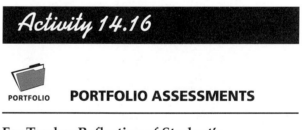

Activity Continues

FIGURE 14.25

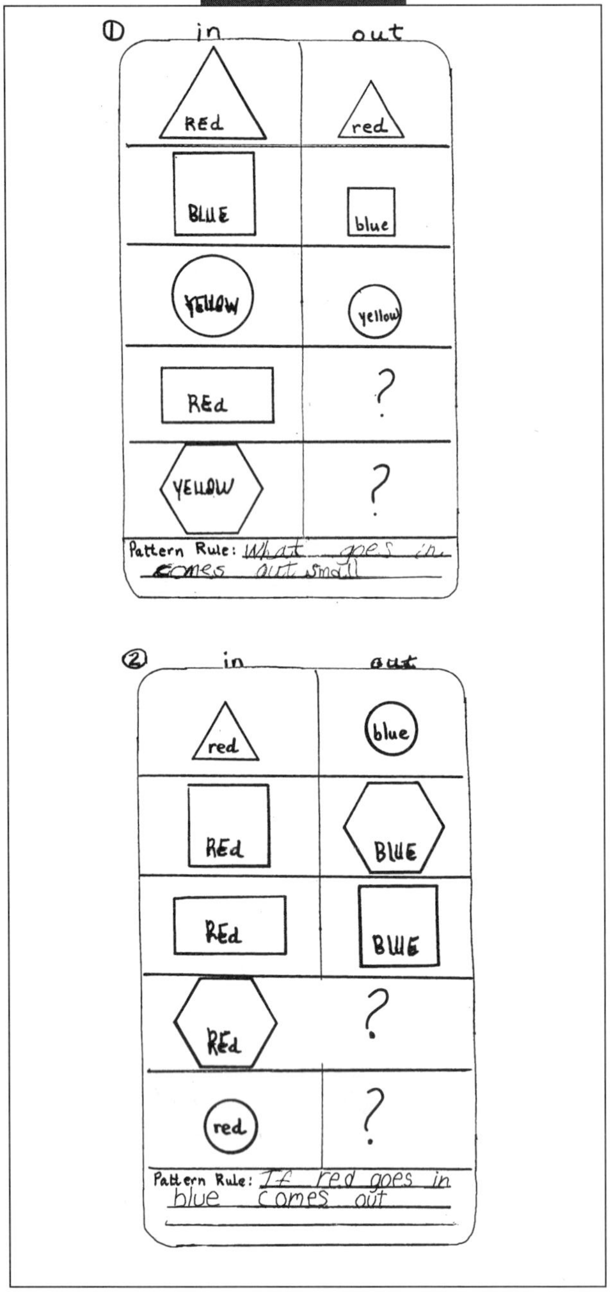

Activity Continues

FIGURE 14.26

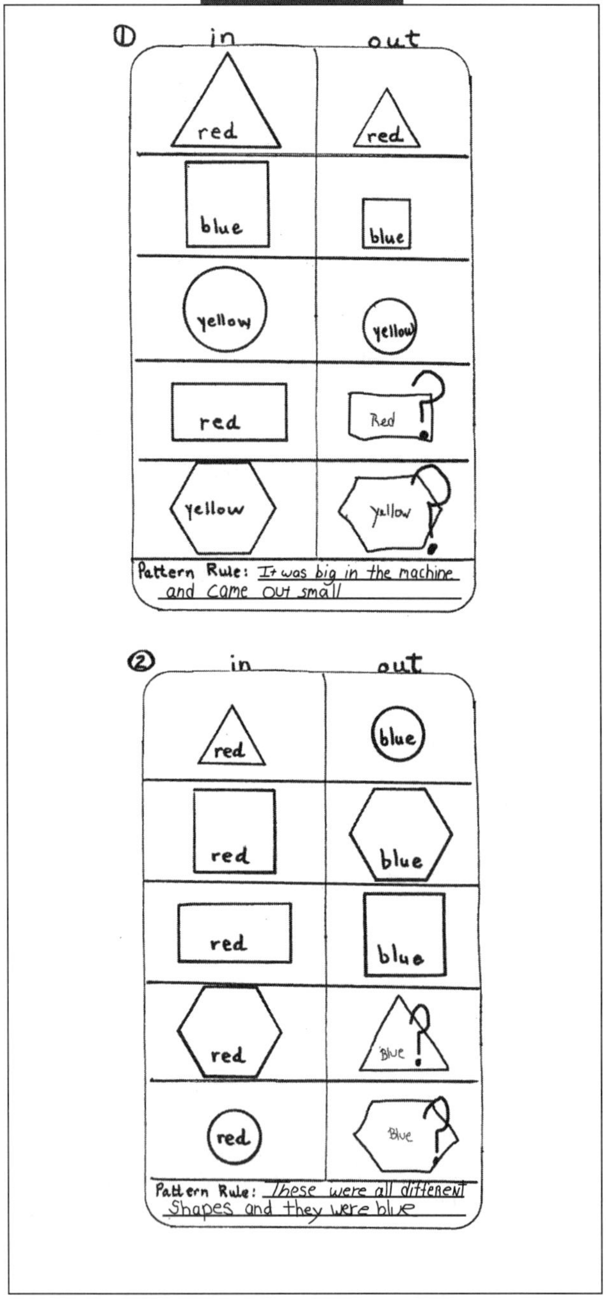

- What kind of answers would you expect if Travis had had experiences with manipulatives as well as the graph paper as shown in Activity 14.1?
- What does Travis know and not know about linear equations from his answers on this paper.

3. It may be interesting to note that this student is considered gifted by the school's testing results and was placed in an accelerated prealgebra program for the eighth grade.

4. Design a rubric that would take into account the diversity of answers while being fair in your assessment strategy.
   - Include the rubric in your Professional Portfolio for Job Interviews along with your analysis of the student's understanding in this activity.
   - Enjoy the student work on algebra seen in Figure 14.27.

Activity Continues

FIGURE 14.27

Name Travis

Complete this equation. Show how you solved it.

$(3x + 2) + (2y + 4) = 38$

$3x + 2y + 6 = 38$

$3x + 2y = 32$

$3x = 32 - 2y$

$x = 10.6 \cdot \frac{2}{3}$ $y = 1 \quad x = 10$

$32 + 2 + 2y + 4 = 38$

$38 + 2y = 38$

$y = 6$ $x = 10\frac{2}{3}$

Can you think of another way you can validate if you have solved the problem correctly? Please explain what you could do?

NO

How are the problems like these used in the real world of work?

If you have two types of one froit and you want to find out what kind, or how many of the froit in all.

What do you remember most about algebra after finishing your first year of study in algebra?

It wasn't easy remembering all the steps.

SUMMARY

This chapter discussed odd and even numbers, prime and composite numbers, and several number theories, along with patterns, functions, and beginning algebra concepts. Computer programs were provided to explore several of the theories. The Fundamental Theorem of Arithmetic, the Least Common Multiple, and the Greatest Common Factor were developed using concrete models. Divisibility rules for 2, 3, 4, 5, 8, 9, and 10 were provided. The Fibonacci number sequence and Pascal's triangle were introduced with simulations of what it might have been like to be the first mathematician to discover each pattern. It called for the use of good problem-solving skills.

The divisibility rules used in this chapter will help students find common denominators first introduced in Chapter 12 on rational numbers (common fractions). These topics are carefully developed with concrete models rather than memorized algorithms.

Children who have logical-mathematical intelligence, talked about by Gardner in Chapter 3, are frequently the students who enjoy number explorations like those found in this chapter. The students enjoy finding interesting patterns and functions with numbers. If you have students in your class who fit this description, there are many intriguing logic and pattern games that can be introduced. These children can form a cooperative group and eventually share their discoveries with the rest of the class.

Algebra is the gateway to higher mathematics and the gateway to success in most of the better job opportunities in the industrial and technological societies of today and tomorrow. We must continue to find ways to make the study of algebra more accessible and understandable to greater numbers of students in our schools.

EXERCISES

For extended exercises, see the CD-ROM.

A. Memorization and Comprehension Exercises
Low-Level Thought Activities

1. State each divisibility rule in your own words. Start each rule: "A multidigit number is divisible by ______________ if and only if ______________."

2. Test this number for divisibility by 2, 5, 10, 4, 8, 3 and 9:

$$?\overline{)946{,}872}$$

3. Change the number in exercise 2 so it is divisible by the two numbers not represented in the previous exercise.

B. Application and Analysis Exercises
Middle-Level Thought Activities

1. Find at least three more number patterns in Pascal's triangle. Explain each one.
2. Apply what you have already learned about the Sieve of Eratosthenes to decide whether 19,711 is a prime number.
3. Find divisibility rules for 6, 7, and 11.
4. Analyze the difference between the two following equations:

$$4x + y = 10 \quad \text{and} \quad 4x - y = 10$$

Predict what difference(s) will be seen if tables and graphs are constructed for both equations. Then construct two tables and their corresponding graphs to verify your predictions. Find the x- and y-intercepts for each graph. Verify the correctness by solving the equations when $x = 0$ and $y = 0$. Start each table with $x = 2$ as the first entry.

C. Synthesis and Evaluation Exercises
High-Level Thought Activities

1. Evaluate the bases between 2 and 10. In which bases is 10 an odd number? Sketch the multibase blocks in the different bases to help you. You will need to remember the definition of an odd and even number to pick the correct arrangements of multibase blocks.
2. Create two cooperative learning activities for teaching one concept in number theory. Follow these steps:
   a. Find a grade level and a number theory concept within that grade level. Trace the previous concept development of the topic taught in earlier grades so you will know where to begin your instruction.
   b. Include at least one way that the topic could be used for another academic area, supporting mathematical connections.
   c. Use current articles from professional journals to help plan the direction of the lesson. Document your sources.

   Here are some journals of note where excellent articles may be found:

   Mathematics Teacher
   Teaching Children Mathematics
   Mathematics Teaching in the Middle School

BIBLIOGRAPHY

For an extended bibliography, see the CD-ROM.

Battista, Michael T. "A Complete Model for Operations on Integers." *Arithmetic Teacher* 30 (May 1983): 26–31.

Blume, Glendon, W., and David S. Heckman. "What Do Students Know about Algebra and Functions?" Results from the Sixth Mathematics Assessment of the National Assessment of Education Progress. Reston, VA: National Council of Teachers of Mathematics, 1997.

Carifio, James, and Ramzi Nasser. "Algebra Word Problems: A Review of the Theoretical Models and Related Research Literature." Annual Meeting of the American Research Association 5–6 April 1994. *ERIC.* CD-ROM. SilverPlatter. January 1995.

Chang, Lisa. "Multiple Methods of Teaching the Addition and Subtraction of Integers." *Arithmetic Teacher* 33 (December 1985): 14–19.

Davis, Robert B. *Explorations in Mathematics: A Text for Teachers.* Palo Alto, CA: Addison-Wesley, 1967.

Demana, Franklin D., and Bert K. Waits. "Instructional Strategies and Delivery Systems." *Algebra for Everyone.* Ed. Edgar L. Edwards. Reston, VA: National Council of Teachers of Mathematics, 1990. 53–61.

Driscoll, Mark, John Moyer, and Judith S. Zawojewski. "Helping Teacher Implement Algebra for All in Milwaukee Public Schools." *Mathematics Education Leadership NCSM Journal* 2 (April 1998): 3–12.

Glatzer, David J., and Glenda Lappan. "Enhancing the Maintenance of Skills." *Algebra for Everyone.* Ed. Edgar L. Edwards. Reston, VA: National Council of Teachers of Mathematics, 1990. 34–44.

Howden, Hilde. "Prior Experiences." *Algebra for Everyone.* Ed. Edgar L. Edwards. Reston, VA: National Council of Teachers of Mathematics, 1990. 7–23.

Johnson, Art. "Now & Then: Fiber Meets Fibonacci: The Shape of Things to Come." *Mathematics Teaching in the Middle School* 4 (January 1999): 256–262.

Lawson, Dene R. "The Problem, the Issues That Speak to Change." *Algebra for Everyone.* Ed. Edgar L. Edwards. Reston, VA: National Council of Teachers of Mathematics, 1990: 1–6.

Leiva, Miriam A., ed. *Grades K–6 Addenda Series: Patterns.* Reston, VA: National Council of Teachers of Mathematics, 1993.

Lounsbury, John H., and Donald C. Clark. *Inside Grade Eight: From Apathy to Excitement.* Reston, VA: National Association of Secondary School Principals, 1990.

Manoucheri, Azita, and Mary C. Enderson. "Promoting Mathematical Discourse: Learning from Classroom Examples." *Mathematics Teaching in the Middle School* 4 (January 1999): 216–222.

Marzano, Robert J. *A Different Kind of Classroom: Teaching with Dimensions of Learning.* Alexandria, VA: Association for Supervision and Curriculum Development, 1992.

Mullis, Ina V. S. *Benchmarking to International Achievement: TIMSS as a Starting Point to Examine Student Achievement.* Washington, DC: U.S. Department of Education, 1997.

National Council of Teachers of Mathematics. *Algebra for the Twenty-first Century: Proceedings of the August 1992 Conference.* Reston, VA: NCTM, 1992.

———. *Assessment Standards for School Mathematics.* Reston, VA: NCTM, 1995.

———. *Curriculum and Evaluation Standards for School Mathematics.* Reston, VA: NCTM, 1989.

———. *Principles and Standards for School Mathematics.* Reston, VA: NCTM, 2000 (to be published).

———. *Professional Standards for Teaching Mathematics.* Reston, VA: NCTM, 1991.

Nelson, David. "Simultaneous Equations: A Numerical Approach from China." In *Multicultural Mathematics: Teaching Mathematics from a Global Perspective.* New York: Oxford University Press, 1993. 126–141.

Reese, Clyde M., Karen E. Miller, John Mazzeo, John A. Dossey. *NAEP 1996 Mathematics Report Card for the Nation and the States.* Washington, DC: National Center for Educational Statistics, 1997.

Robinson, Stephanie O., and Donald J. Dessart. "Random-Number Generators: A Mysterious Use of Algorithms." Ed. Lorna J. Morrow and Margaret J. Kenney. *The Teaching and Learning of Algorithms in School Mathematics.* 1998 Yearbook. Reston, VA: National Council of Teachers of Mathematics, 1998. 243–250.

Strong, Dorothy S. (Mathematics Ed.). *Systemwide Objectives and Standards.* Vols. 1–3. Chicago: Board of Education of the City of Chicago, 1990.

———. *Mathematics Instruction Planning Manual.* Chicago: Board of Education of the City of Chicago, 1991a.

———. *Mathematics Tutor Training Manual.* Chicago: Board of Education of the City of Chicago, 1991b.

Sulzer, James S. "The Function Box and Fourth Graders: Squares, Cubes, and Circles." *Teaching Children Mathematics* 4 (April 1998): 442–447.

Usiskin, Zalman. "Where Does Algebra Begin? Where Does Algebra End?" *Algebra for the Twenty-first Century: Proceedings of the August 1992 Conference.* Reston, VA: National Council of Teachers of Mathematics, 1992. 27–28.

Willoughby, Stephen S. "Functions from Kindergarten through Sixth Grade." *Teaching Children Mathematics* 3 (February 1997): 314–318.

CHILDREN'S LITERATURE

Adler, David A. *A Picture Book of Frederick Douglass.* New York: Holiday House, 1993.

Adler, Irving. *Integers: Positive and Negative: The Reason Why Books.* New York: John Day, 1972.

Blume, Judy. *Superfudge.* New York: E. P. Dutton, 1980.

———. *Blubber.* New York: E. P. Dutton, 1974.

———. *Otherwise Known as Sheila the Great.* New York: E. P. Dutton, 1972.

Forbes, Esther. *Johnny Tremain.* New York: Houghton, 1943.

Kelsey, Kenneth, and David King. *The Ultimate Book of Number Puzzles.* New York: Barnes and Noble, 1992.

Scieszka, Jon, and Lane Smith. *Math Curse.* New York: Viking Press, 1995.

Snape, Charles, and Heather Scott. *Puzzles, Mazes, and Numbers.* London, England: Cambridge University Press, 1995.

Solyom, Catherine, ed. *Big Block World Atlas.* Montreal: Tormont, 1997.

Integrating Technology

Video Vignettes: Lesson Plans in Action

- *The Order of Operations Song*

  This video vignette shows what a teacher and a middle school class can do together to enjoy mathematics material that would otherwise be boring to learn.

Computer Software Resources

. . . for Number Theory, Patterns and Functions, and Algebra

Internet Searches

Surfing the Internet for Topics on Number Theory, Patterns and Functions, and Algebra

Use the World Wide Web (WWW) and navigate through the system, searching for new information under major headings and subheadings similar to the following:

Mathematics Education
  Discussion Groups on Algebra
  http://www.ilstu.edu/depts/cemest/
  Interactive Bulletin Boards

Mathematics
  Logic Games
  Patterns and Relationships
  Student Internet Pals playing attribute games together

Download from **http://archives.math.utk.edu/software.html**
Look under K–12 programs
  Algebra Editor
  Algebra Graphics Program
  Algebra Plus

NCTM
  Problem Solving
  Equity Issues with Algebra
  Number Theory
  Patterns and Functions

- *Remember*. . . the Web is fluid . . . new topics and ways to search for topics change daily.
- Be adventurous . . . think of some new things you could try.

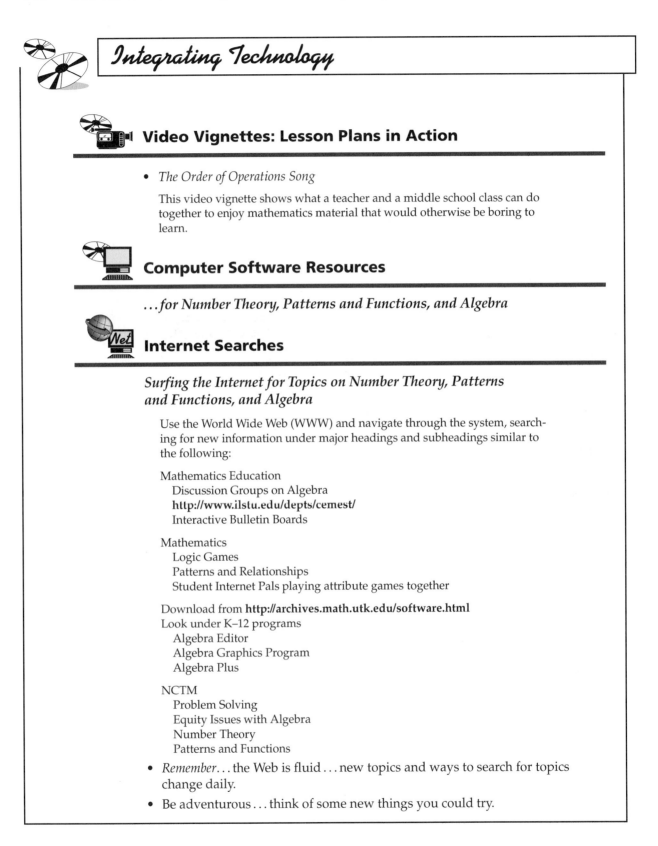

15

Data Analysis, Statistics, and Probability

Activities Index

Nowhere does the concept of "real-world mathematics" show up more predominantly than it does in the concepts of graphing, statistics, and probability. Our information society revolves around the analysis of categorized information. Information is summarized and tested for its dependability and significance in nonbiased ways that call for numerical collection of data and tests for statistical significance. Data analysis, statistics, and probability have become increasingly more important topics in the elementary and middle school curriculum.

The NCTM *Principles and Standards* (NCTM, 2000) list data analysis statistics, and probability as a part of the curriculum beginning in preschool. Students must work with data—collect it, organize and display it, analyze and interpret it—and understand how decisions are made on the basis of collected evidence. The *Standards* also call for studying probability in real-world settings (Box 15.1). Students need to investigate the notion of fairness (a natural Pre-K disposition) and chances of winning, a human interest of all ages. Because many predictions are based on probabilities, time should be allowed to make predictions based on experimental results or mathematical probability. Some items on the National Assessment of Educational Progress (Reese et al., 1997) assessed organization and interpretation of data

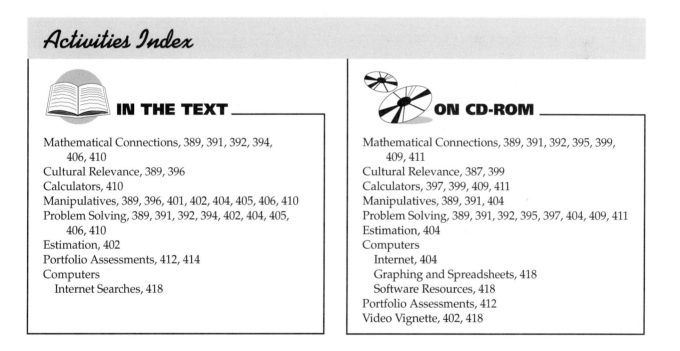

BOX 15.1 Curriculum and Evaluation Standards

Statistics and Probability

In grades K–4, the mathematics curriculum should include experiences with data analysis and probability so that students can—

- Collect, organize, and describe data.
- Construct, read, and interpret displays of data.
- Formulate and solve problems that involve collecting and analyzing data.
- Explore concepts of chance.

Statistics

In grades 5–8, the mathematics curriculum should include exploration of statistics in real-world situations so that students can—

- Systematically collect, organize, and describe data.
- Construct, read, and interpret tables, charts, and graphs.
- Make inferences and convincing arguments that are based on data analysis.
- Evaluate arguments that are based on data analysis.
- Develop an appreciation for statistical methods as powerful means for decision making.

Probability

In grades 5–8, the mathematics curriculum should include explorations of probability in real-world situations so that students can—

- Model situations by devising and carrying out experiments or simulations to determine probabilities.
- Model situations by constructing a sample space to determine probabilities.
- Appreciate the power of using a probability model by comparing experimental results with mathematical expectations.
- Make predictions that are based on experimental or theoretical probabilities.
- Develop an appreciation for the pervasive use of probability in the real world.

Source: National Council of Teachers of Mathematics, 1989, pp. 54, 105, 109.

presented in graphs and tables. The NAEP also included items about finding and using measures of central tendency. As expected, students did better on making direct readings from graphs and tables than at deciding relationships among data.

NAEP data (Zawojewski and Heckman, 1997) show gains on data analysis items. Students performed less well on the constructed-response questions than they did on the multiple choice. Bar graphs were easier for fourth graders to understand than pictographs. Half of the fourth-grade students and almost all of the eighth graders could interpret data from a graph. When asked to construct a graph from data provided, 33 percent of the fourth graders and 80 percent of the eighth graders could construct the graphs. Zawojewski and Heckman (1997) suggest that proportional reasoning may be well defined by the eighth grade, accounting for the high scores. When asked to explain their reasoning in data analysis items, only 57 percent of the eighth graders received a score of satisfactory or higher. Once again, there is evidence that written discourse is a needed part of the mathematics curriculum (Reese et al., 1997).

This chapter emphasizes the different methods of representing information as well as producing the results. *Graphing* is a common method of displaying data pictorially. *Statistics* are used to discuss data numerically. *Probability* is the mathematics used to predict outcomes.

TEACHING STRATEGIES

Data Analysis—Graphing

Graphing presents data in a concise and visual way that allows relationships in the data to be seen more easily. Students need to learn how to tally information, arrange data in a table, and display the information visually using a graph. Students can be introduced to graphing as a means of representing or organizing data early in the elementary years. Young children can make their own graphs and will benefit from collecting and organizing the information. A suggested developmental sequence for presenting graphs is generally followed in textbooks for young children.

1. Real graphs: actual objects to compare two or three groups.
2. Picture graphs: pictures or models to represent real things to compare two or three groups.

3. Real graphs: actual objects to compare four groups.
4. Picture graphs: pictures or models to compare four groups.
5. Symbolic graphs: most abstract using only symbols.

The eight kinds of graphs in Figure 15.1 are used in the elementary and middle grades, gradually proceeding from one to the other in level of difficulty—real, picture, bar, line, circle, scatter graphs. Stem and leaf and box and whisker graphs, introduced in the middle school years, will be discussed as a part of the statistics section of this chapter. As presented throughout this book, the introduction of each new concept (graph) should be from concrete to the connecting level (pictorial), to the symbolic. Figure 15.1 shows the progression of learning experiences. Please pay special note to the written descriptions under each kind of graph. It will help you plan activities for your own classroom.

When working with any graph, ask students questions about it to help focus the discussion of information available for the graph. Questions should include comparisons such as which has the most or the least, how many more or how many less, and how many in all. Students enjoy taking a survey, collecting information, and constructing opinion graphs about their classmates or school. These graphs can be displayed in the hallway and create student interest and attention. Graphing should be at least a weekly activity as it is a part of daily exposure in newspapers, magazines, and other forms of media.

Creating Real Graphs. The possibilities for topics to graph are endless and should be determined by the interests of the class.

Many articles have appeared in teacher journals and books showing clever ideas for real graphs with children. Leutzinger (1998), Bauman-Boatman, Clouthier, and Tornrose (1992), and Choate and Okey (1989) have reviewed ideas that can be used with group graphing as well as individual graphing projects. Some projects move naturally from the concrete level of real graphs to the pictorial or connecting level of picture graphs. Some of the more clever ideas suggest the use of finger puppets as a transition because they fit the description of real objects on the graph, yet they have the "look" of a picture graph.

Creating Picture Graphs. A *picture graph* represents data in the form of pictures, objects, or parts of objects as seen in Figure 15.1. Be sure not to extend the categories to four until many experiences have been provided for comparing two and three groups.

There are many examples in the professional literature of innovative activities using picture graphs. Axelson (1992) shows how picture graphs can lead naturally into the symbolic level using the real-world mathematics idea of the supermarket. She shows how journal writing can be blended into the activities after the children show the same information with a variety of graphs. Sgroi and coworkers (1995) show how children's literature can be used effectively with picture graphs. Dr. Seuss's *Green Eggs and Ham* is used as the example. Self-adhesive address labels are used to create the graphs quickly without the need to make elaborate picture materials.

Another connecting level idea is to use the actual pictures of the children in the classroom. Class pictures are usually taken at the beginning of the school year with each child receiving a sheet of small pictures. A roll of small proofs is also sent to the teacher by many photographers. These small pictures are just the size to fit on the end of a clothespin. Two ways of using the graphs appear in Figure 15.1. If the child's picture is not on the graph in the morning, the teacher knows who is absent very quickly. Children can ask comparison questions as a part of the morning math activities known as "calendar math" in many schools. For example, "How many students brought their lunch today? How many are going to buy the cold lunch choice today?... hot lunch choice today?... How many more boys than girls brought their lunch?" This last type of comparison question is frequently difficult for children in the primary grades and should be asked on a regular basis so children can see how the idea is used in a real setting that has meaning for them. Lunch choices is one of those areas where children see real meaning in mathematics!

Native Americans used the picture graph, or pictograph, in sandpaintings as ways to communicate with each other. Children in K–5 grades can

EXTENDED ACTIVITIES

Name of Activity

- Pictographs with Sandpaintings

CULTURAL RELEVANCE

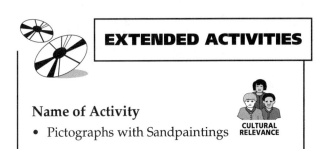

FIGURE 15.1

	Concrete	Pictorial (Connecting Level)	Symbolic
Real Graphs Form actual graphs of themselves using hair color, sex, short pants/long pants, shoes with laces or without, who eats hot lunch or bag lunch, etc. Plastic or oil cloth can make the graph magic markers or masking type.			
Transition from Real Graphs to Picture Graphs Use actual pictures of children from their small class pictures. See two ways of using the bar graphs.		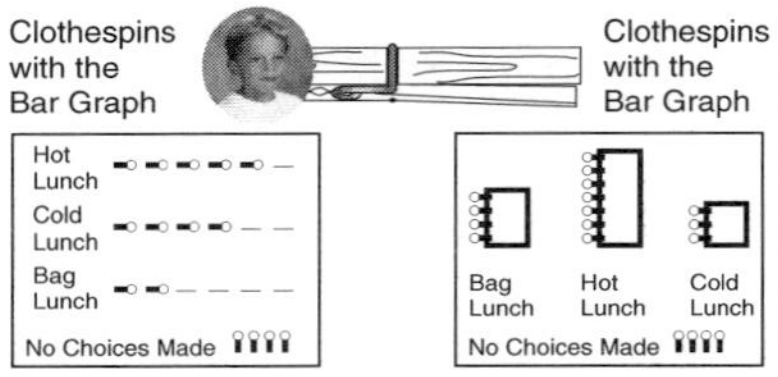 *Actual pictures of children used in two graphs.*	
Picture Graphs Cut pictures of real things to paste. Draw pictures to represent real things, or use models to stand for objects. Make the situations natural ones like the topic of how many girls are in each row in the class.		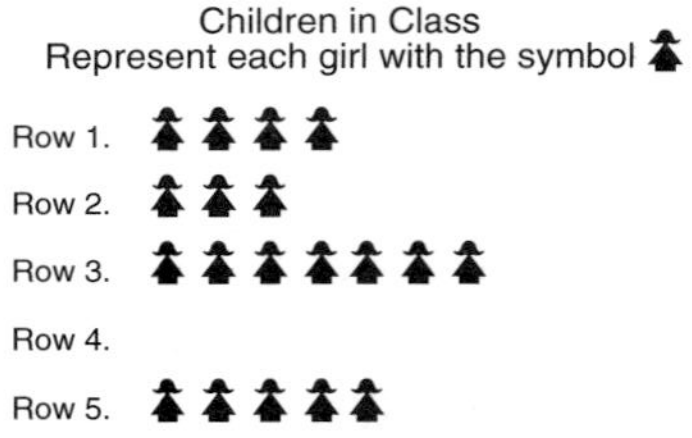 *Picture symbols of children in class.*	
Transition from Picture Graph to Symbolic Representation A symbol represents multiple units. Use when multiplication is being studied in grades 3–4. Use fractional parts only after students have shown they understand multiple units without fractional parts represented.			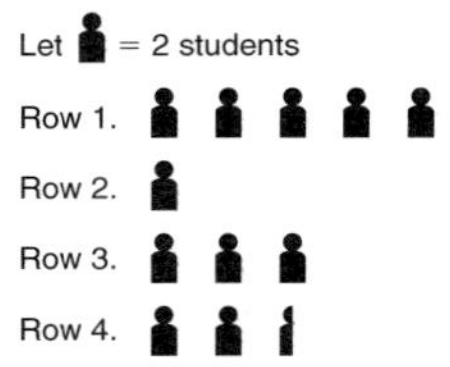 *Children in class with multiple representations.*

Developmental Sequence for Real and Picture Graphs

have fun creating their own pictographs. The following activity is an extension of ideas that originally appeared in lesson material written by Native American teachers at their annual institute at Haskell Indian University in Lawrence, Kansas (Haines, 1992). A similar activity is found on the CD-ROM.

Activity 15.1

MATHEMATICAL CONNECTIONS · CULTURAL RELEVANCE · PROBLEM SOLVING · MANIPULATIVES

NATIVE AMERICAN PICTOGRAPHS

What Teachers Need to Tell Children

"Picture graphs originated in the pictographs used by early American Indians to communicate with each other. These pictographs were of two kinds: those that represented objects and those that represented ideas." (Riley and Stonehouse, 1992, p. 70)

MATERIALS

- *From nature*—leaves, bark, stones, soil samples, and so forth, gathered from a nature walk around the school environment or brought from home as a homework assignment. Any object from their environment or picture of it can also be brought in.

DIRECTIONS

1. Students will learn the environment around them by comparing local plants, rocks, stones, other soil samples, animals, and objects from their environment.
2. Students organize their materials by categories on a picture graph. They decide how they will place the categories on the graph.
3. This can be done individually or in cooperative groups.
4. The gathering of things from nature gives the assignment a connection with science.

Supporting the NCTM *Principles and Standards* (2000):

- Mathematics as Connections; Problem Solving
- Worthwhile Mathematical Tasks—The Teaching Principle
- The Mathematics Curriculum Principle

Teachers can see why multiple units represented with one symbol seem incomprehensible to Pre-K–grade 2 children as shown in Figure 15.1. Not only does it require allowing one symbol to stand for multiple representations, but it also shows fractional parts of the symbol implying that they stand for fractional parts of the multiple representation. Pre-K–grade 2 children are literal in their interpretations of concepts and half a person does not equate well to literally minded young children!

The next two activities are found on the CD-ROM; they can be used by students in 3–5 grades to start real-world mathematics projects. Oral and written discourse can be integrated with graphing activities. Ask students what they can determine about the data from the graph. Their responses can become writings in their student journals.

EXTENDED ACTIVITIES

Name of Activity

MATHEMATICAL CONNECTIONS · PROBLEM SOLVING

- Picture Graph with School-Community Activities
- One Picture = Many Students: Making a New Picture Graph
- Native American Pictographs

Creating Bar Graphs. A *bar graph* uses discrete (separate, distinct) data on each axis. Bars represent the information by the x- and y-axes. Figure 15.2 shows the development progression of bar graphs as students proceed through the grades.

Students need experiences constructing graphs in both vertical and horizontal formats. They also need activities in which they decide the labels for the two axes. Increments should be in consecutive whole numbers; in later grades, bar graphs can have other increments such as counting by twos, fives, tens. Be sure to limit the list of choices to four or five, like the transition graph activities seen with the students' favorite academic subjects in Figure 15.2, otherwise the comparisons become too difficult. Please note written explanations in Figure 15.2.

EXTENDED ACTIVITIES

Name of Activity

PROBLEM SOLVING · MANIPULATIVES

- Bar Graphs with Favorite Sports

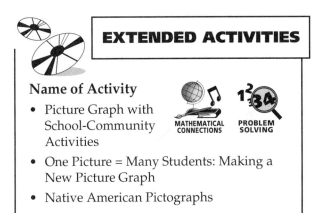

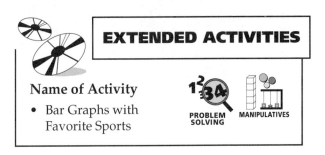

FIGURE 15.2

Levels

Kinds of Graphs	Concrete	Pictorial (Connecting Level)	Symbolic
Bar Graphs Use manipulatives such as connecting cubes. Let colored cubes represent favorite things—ice cream, toys, TV shows and so on. Transferring to graph paper becomes more abstract at the pictorial level.	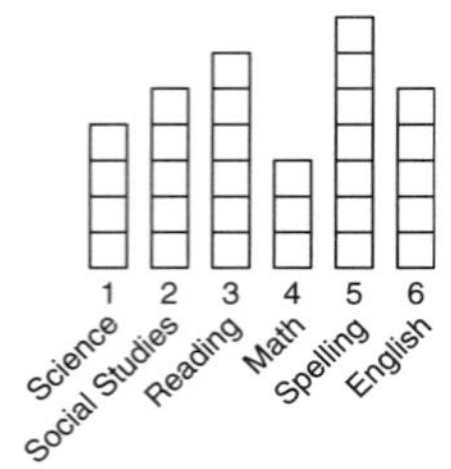	Seen two ways 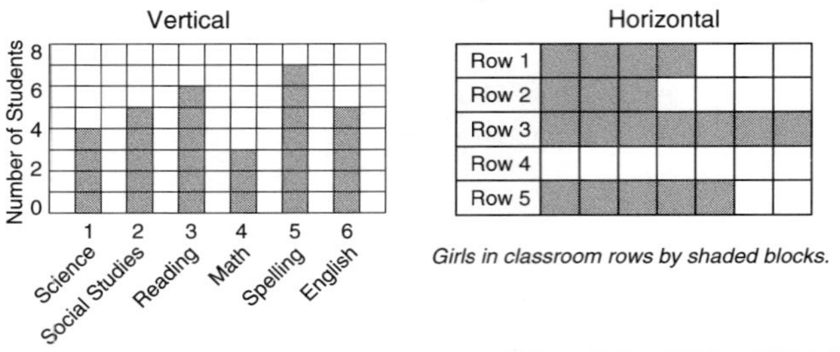 *Girls in classroom rows by shaded blocks.*	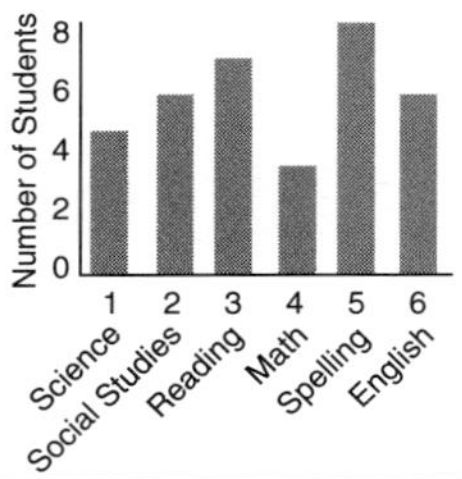
Transition from Bar Graphs to Line Graphs Students draw midpoint and connect lines over their bar graphs. Transfer to lines alone by tracing over graph as shown. This helps decrease the number of errors usually seen when students switch to line graphs.		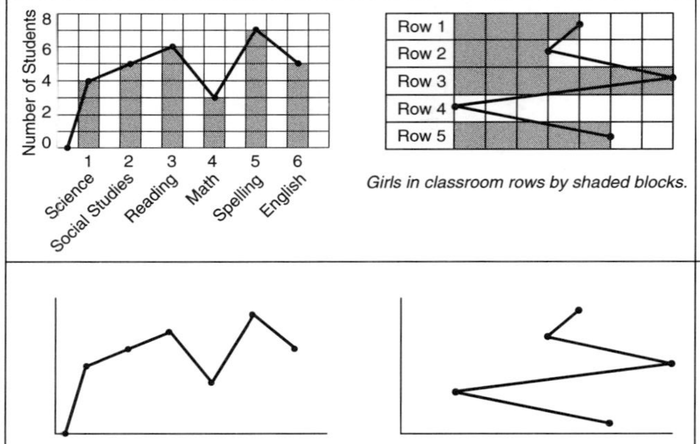	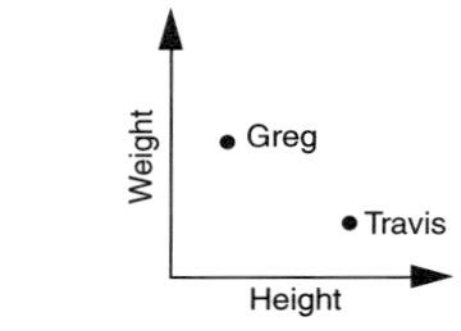 *Line graphs with messages in real-life mathematics.*
Continuous Line Graphs Toy car (Pre-K–5) and radio-controlled cars (grade 6–8) help visualize the paths of continuous graphs. Note written discourse goes along with the graphs.	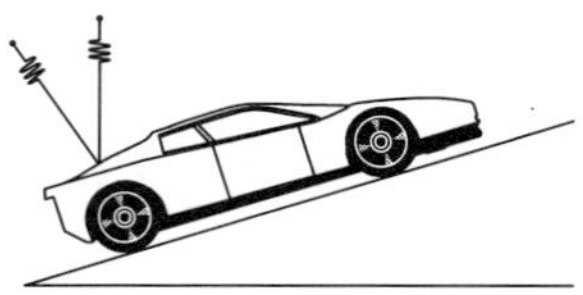	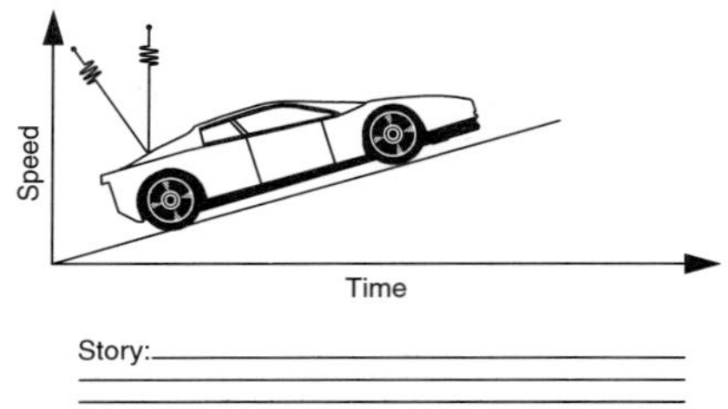	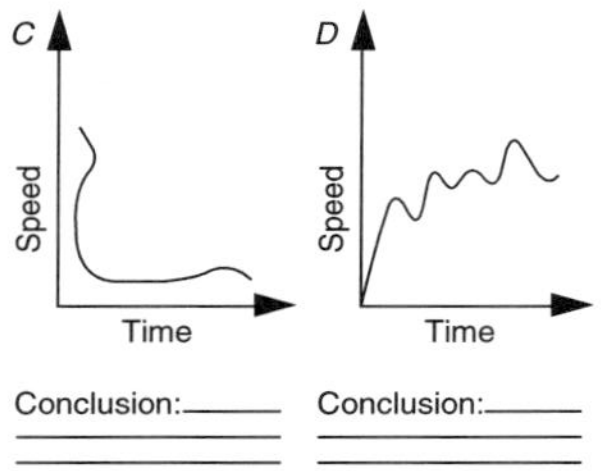

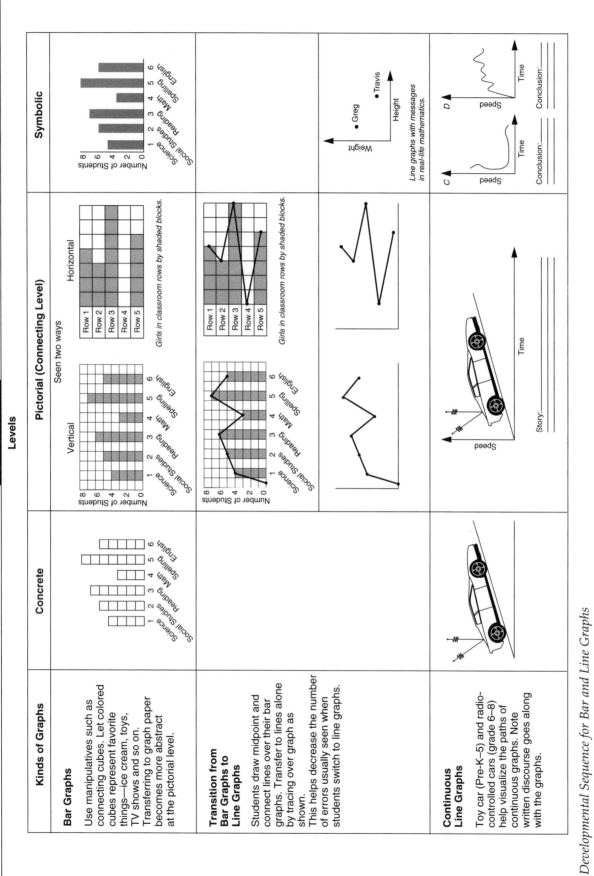

Developmental Sequence for Bar and Line Graphs

Creating Line Graphs. Our experiences indicate that upper elementary students have more problems interpreting information on a line graph than on a bar graph. It may be related to the visual interference from all lines seen simultaneously—horizontal, vertical, and broken diagonal lines. Perhaps the child does not know where to center attention. When given identical information in a bar graph and a line graph, an increased number of errors are made by children when interpreting the line graph. Creating a line graph can be done by connecting the midpoint of the top of the bars in the bar graph, as seen in the explanation in Figure 15.2.

Line Graphs with Stationary Point Values. Start with simple line graphs on the symbolic level in Figure 15.2. What information can be obtained from this line graph? The graph expresses the relationship between Greg's and Travis's height and weight. Students can write a message under the graph to explain what is happening. One message could be "Travis is taller, but Greg is heavier." This connects written discourse with data analysis.

For additional practice, the CD-ROM contains more examples for various grade levels.

EXTENDED ACTIVITIES

MATHEMATICAL CONNECTIONS PROBLEM SOLVING MANIPULATIVES

Name of Activity

- Line Graphs
- More Practice with Messages in Line Graphs
- Pre-K–2 Continuous Graphs with Cars

Continuous Line Graphs. Line graphs are often used to illustrate a continuous activity, as seen in Figure 15.2. This requires higher-level problem solving on the part of students. Young children can envision continuous graphs by working with toy cars on various kinds of inclined planes or straight raceways. The CD-ROM shows how to set up such graphs for Pre-K–2 children. Upper grade students who own radio-controlled cars can come and demonstrate their moves while children graph what they see as the "motion line" on the graph.

Activity 15.2

MATHEMATICAL CONNECTIONS PROBLEM SOLVING

PLOTTING CONTINUOUS LINE GRAPHS IN SCIENCE

DIRECTIONS

These graphs show a *continuous* activity. The first set shows the graph and asks for an interpretation. The second is open-ended for the student to create. What is the message in each graph?

1. How could you label and plot these graphs? Be sure they give the message intended. An example is presented first.

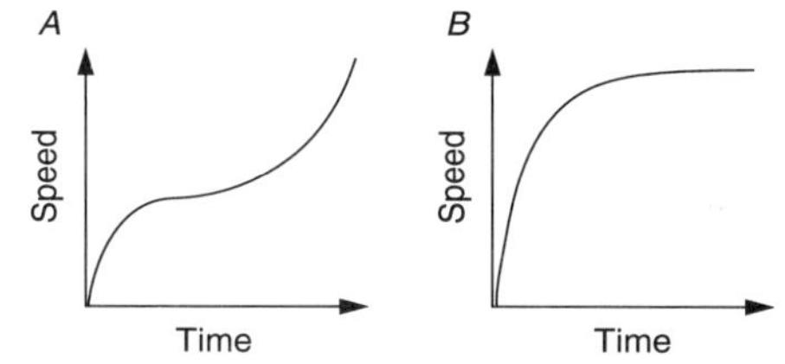

Conclusion: Conclusion:

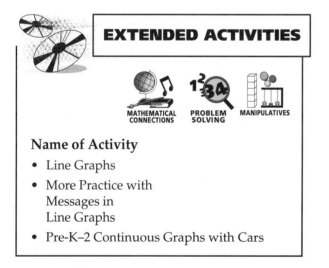

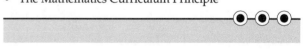

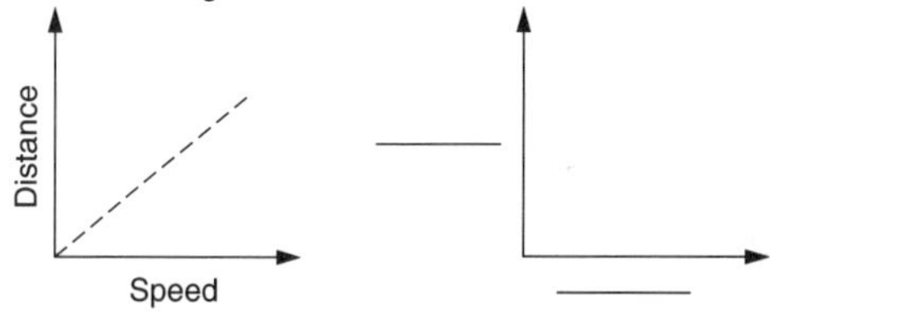

Supporting the NCTM *Principles and Standards* (2000):

- Mathematics as Connections and as Problem Solving
- Oral Discourse of Teacher and Student; Worthwhile Mathematical Tasks—The Teaching Principle
- The Mathematics Curriculum Principle

More continuous graphs have been placed on the CD-ROM. Science activities are a common setting for using graphs.

The data points are plotted and lines are drawn connecting the data points. The scale of a graph is very important. The scale used should be uniform and appropriate for the quantities to be displayed. The scale should be large enough to adequately represent the quantity being plotted. It is often necessary to use multiple units to keep the graph in reasonable proportions. Line graphs are often used because they provide a continuous representation of

EXTENDED ACTIVITIES

Name of Activity:

MATHEMATICAL CONNECTIONS PROBLEM SOLVING

- Line Graphs in Science
- More Practice with Plotting Continuous Graphs in Science
- Line Graphs with Speed and Time

data. Therefore, the scale is important to adequately reflect the data.

Graphs in the Middle School Years. By grades 5–8, middle school students can combine their knowledge of simple continuous graphs to plot more complex problems. The CD-ROM shows how middle school students can use radio-controlled cars to plot speed under different conditions, including racing times with and without various inclined planes. The CD-ROM shows the high number of excellent math problems that were generated by students when asked to make up problems involving the radio-controlled cars and the use of graphs to analyze the data collected. The pictures shown on the CD-ROM can be a motivational start for your students to create problems with radio-controlled cars as well.

Students' love of cars in the middle school years makes data collection and graphing activities more motivational even when the actual concrete items are not present as they were in the aforementioned example with the radio-controlled cars. The solution steps and the answers to the next activity appear on the CD-ROM.

Activity 15.3

MATHEMATICAL CONNECTIONS PROBLEM SOLVING

THREE CARS AND A RACE

A Hyundai, a Ford, and a Mazda enter a 10-mile race. Because the Hyundai can average only 60 miles per hour, the Ford can average 90 miles per hour, and the Mazda can average 120 miles per hour, the Hyundai is given a 2-minute head start over the Ford and a 4-minute head start over the Mazda in order to make it a fairer race. In what order do the cars finish the race?

Data Collection

Create a table showing how far each car had traveled at the end of each minute. Why are there zeros under 1 and 2 minutes for the Hyundai and under the 1, 2, 3, and 4 minutes for the Mazda?

Activity Continues

Graphing

The distance each car travels versus the time can be plotted on a coordinate graph. Graph the distance for each car (make sure you are able to distinguish the graph of each car). The first point for the Hyundai is (0, 0), for the Ford (2, 0), and for the Mazda (4, 0).

Related Equations

The distance each car travels can be represented by an equation. To write the equation representing the distance each car travels, you may use two points from your table or graph, or one point and the slope from your graph. To compare the equations, you will need to see them in slope-intercept form, $y = mx + b$. List the equations for each of the cars.

Use the data you have generated to answer the following questions. Explain how you arrived at the solution.

1. What is the order of finish?
2. If the race had been a 15-mile race, which car would have won?
3. How far will the Hyundai and the Ford have gone when the Ford catches up with the Hyundai?
4. How far will the Hyundai and the Mazda have gone when the Mazda catches up with the Hyundai?

Try your problem solving powers to do the Extended Activities, including "Buying at Super Target."

EXTENDED ACTIVITIES

Name of Activity

PROBLEM SOLVING MATHEMATICAL CONNECTIONS

- Middle School Data with Radio-Controlled Cars
- Graphs and Answers to Three Cars and a Race
- Buying at Super Target

Creating Circle Graphs. The circle or "pie" graph is used to show the relationship between a whole and its parts as shown in Figure 15.3. Note the explanations under each part of the figure.

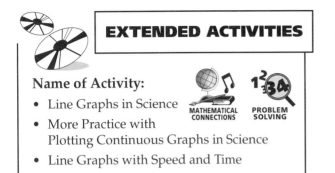

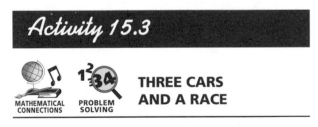

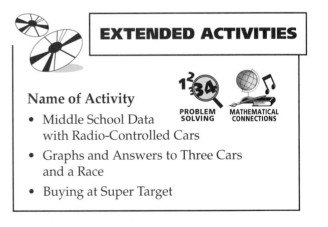

FIGURE 15.3

Concrete	Pictorial (Connecting Level)	Symbolic

Students fold circle into eight equal parts. Candies with different colored wrappers are placed on each wedge of the circle with all pieces of the same color placed together.

Real Candy Placed on Circle

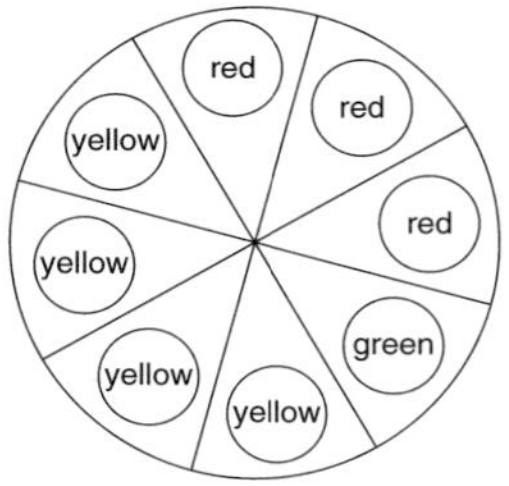

Students use crayons to color places where candy once was. Candy is now eaten, leaving the crayon colors to tell the story of what was eaten. Students ask others to look at the graph to see how much of each color was eaten.

Colors Where Candy Once Was

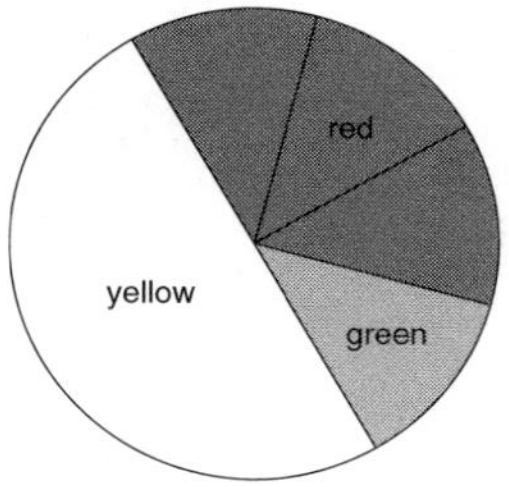

Colors Labeled as Fractional Parts

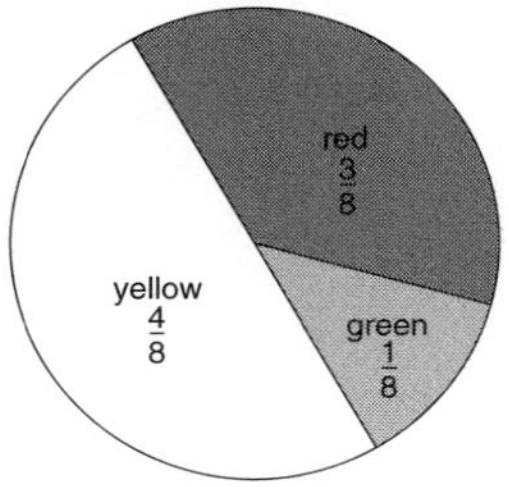

Note the subtle transition to fractional parts of the whole colored in and labeled. Activities like these can be done before children learn percents and ratios.

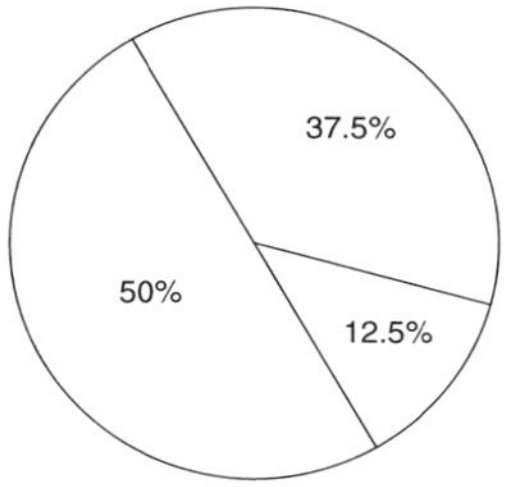

Percent graphs can be introduced after children understand the concept of percent and one ratio to another. This kind of graph is normally encountered in the fifth and sixth grade. Total degrees must equal 360°.

Note the progression from concrete to symbolic using one task to be graphed. Many activities such as these lead to the ability to analyze and create one's own graph like the one on the right. Each item is specified as a percent or portion of total—this time the total is family income. This process should be a part of upper elementary and middle school programs.

Family Budget

Food: 25%
Clothing: 20%
Shelter: 30%
Operating Expense: 10%
Auto: 10%
Other: 5%

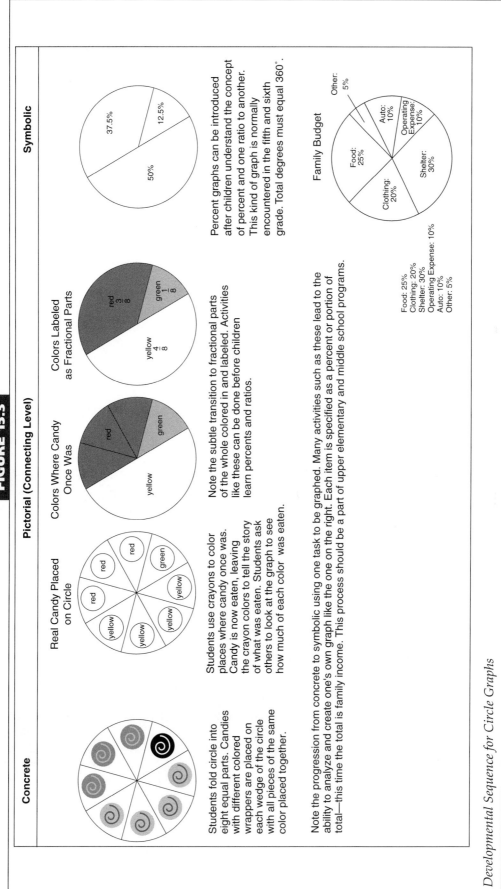

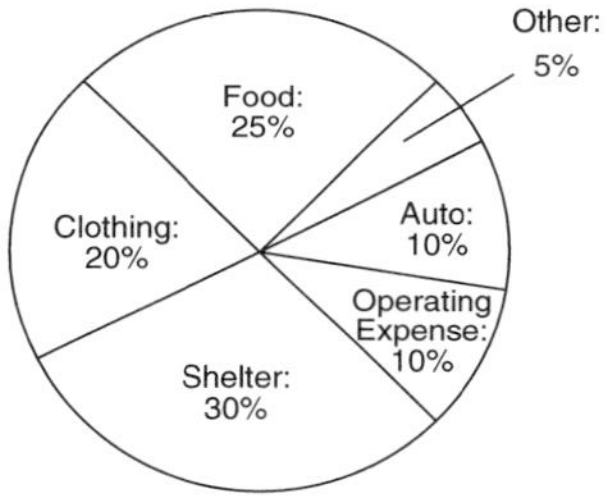

Developmental Sequence for Circle Graphs

Axelson (1992) reports that students exposed to bar, line, and circle graphs in the study of the supermarket felt that the circle graph was the best to see their data. Circle graphs define the whole and it is easy to see how each part compares to the whole. Axelson cautions that all kinds of graphs are appropriate for comparing different kinds of information. Students gain the most from graphing activities when they can decide which graph best displays the needed information. Graphing calculators can compare different graph displays quickly, enabling students to analyze differences among graphs without losing concentration in the process. It promotes higher-ordered mathematical thinking.

Creating Scatter Graphs. A *scatter graph* is the plotting of pairs of values and observing the "scatter" form they take on. Often real-world data are not "very uniform," and it is difficult to construct an accurate picture, line, bar, or circle graph. Students can plot the pairs of points and attempt to find some trend or tendency from the scatter pattern. For example, the scatter graphs in the following activity can be used to help students increase their problem-solving skills. This is usually a middle school activity.

Activity 15.4

PROBLEM SOLVING MATHEMATICAL CONNECTIONS

STORY WRITING WITH SCATTER GRAPHS

DIRECTIONS

1. Graphs I, II, and III all use the same data.
2. Label the x values and y values with identifiers.
3. Write a brief newspaper story using the data.
4. What has changed in Graph II? Does your newspaper story change from Graph I?
5. What has changed in Graph III? Does your newspaper story change from Graph I or II?

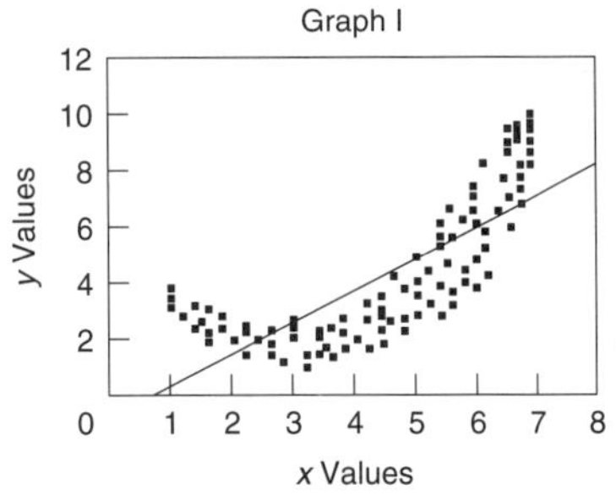

Activity Continues

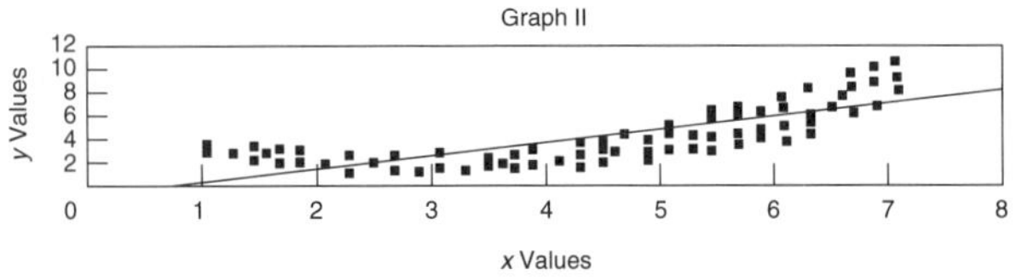

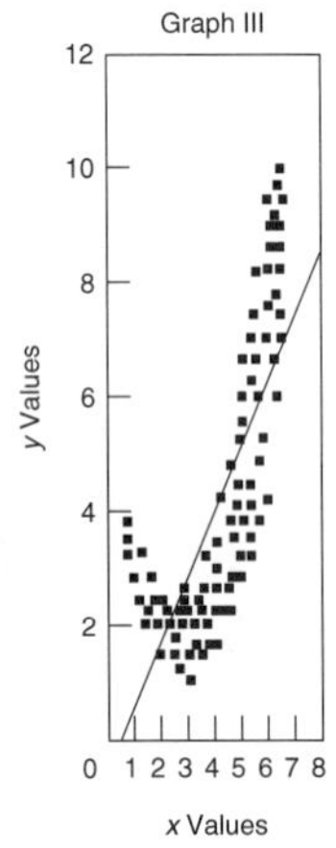

The same information can be seen by the use of different graphs. Each graph produces a different visual presentation and may convey a different perspective for the same data. Students should be encouraged to start with the graphs that seem easiest for them. Through the use of computer programs, they can see how the same information can be represented in other more difficult graphs. Computer software and the graphing calculator can greatly enhance the work of organizing and collecting data. See Graph Activities A, B, and C on the CD-ROM for graphing data that use computer graphing software or a graphing calculator. Database programs make it easy to sort data by different categories and organize it in a variety of ways. The choice of a scale to use in the graph is another important aspect of constructing a graph. Scale changes can be done easily with the computer or graphing calculator to compare different pictures of the same data. Students can make inferences, analyze the data from various perspectives, and formulate key questions.

Technology: Creating All the Graphs Together. Biehler (1994) points to the availability of technology programs as one of the reasons that innovations in presenting more intricate graphing techniques are possible at earlier and earlier grade levels.

Graphing Computer Models. It is now possible for a child to enter material to be graphed into a computer program and touch a key for each kind of graph. The graphs instantly appear, allowing the child to see how differently the material looks with each kind of graph presentation. Five of the seven graphs explored in this section are shown in the CD-ROM activity called "Graphs Compared." The graphs represent the fifth-grade scores of children on a post-test when compared with the amount of math anxiety each had before they studied a new mathematical concept with personalized mathematical problems. The scores showed that the students scored higher than would be expected for the amount of math anxiety originally experienced by the children (Habrock and Edwards, 1995). Which kinds of the graphs presented in the CD-ROM activity told the story of math anxiety best?

Other computer examples with spreadsheets and graphs are presented at the end of the chapter in the Integrating Technology section.

EXTENDED ACTIVITIES

Name of Activity

- Kinds of Graphs Compared

MATHEMATICAL CONNECTIONS | PROBLEM SOLVING

Graphing Calculator Models. Graphing calculators are being used more frequently in the high school setting at present. The graphing calculator can plot the same five graphs seen in the preceding CD-ROM activity. Perhaps it is because of the availability of many computers in the elementary and middle school labs that makes the running of data seem more accessible on a computer as opposed to the graphing calculator. If you have a graphing calculator, use the information from the scatter plot activity and the CD-ROM activity to plot the graphs. Many good analyzing questions can come from the work with new technologies.

As you can see, graphs can tell many stories, and the same data can be represented in different ways. Newspaper reporters using microcomputers and graphing programs can present data in many views. Pick up any newspaper presenting statistical data and use a computer graphing program to display the information in another way. It is important that students understand how the presentation of data can take on different forms. Each gives a unique visual presentation and yields a different impact. Check out the NCTM Addenda Series on *Dealing with Data and Chance* (Zawojewski, 1991). To be an intelligent consumer, we must be aware of how different forms of data presentation can convey different perspectives.

Statistics

The study of statistics is important in the elementary grades because society frequently organizes and expresses data numerically (statistically). Since early childhood, we have been exposed to statistics in weather predictions, newspaper ads, and test grades, and with advances in technology, additional statistical data are available. Daily living requires decisions to be made based on processing of statistical information continuously.

Students need to be aware of how statistics can be manipulated to say whatever one desires. Media experts can use statistics to mislead consumers. Reports of medical information or opinion surveys must be examined carefully before drawing conclusions. Students should be aware of how statistics shape our lives and influence our decisions. There are many misconceptions about data because key questions have not been asked: How many people were in the sample, how was the population sampled, who conducted the survey, how were the data summarized? We are inundated with statistical information and we must learn how to process this information accurately and effectively to function as knowledgeable citizens in society.

One of the first concepts of statistics encountered in daily life is that of average. The doctor tells a child "your height is about average for a six-year-old girl" or "your shoe size a little over the average for an eight-year-old boy." The teacher says, "The class average on the last test was 68," or, "You scored above the average of the class on the last exam." The *average* is a measure of central tendency of data, or an attempt to describe what is "typical" in a set of data. There are three measures that are commonly used to describe ways of viewing what is typical in a data set. They are mean, mode, and median.

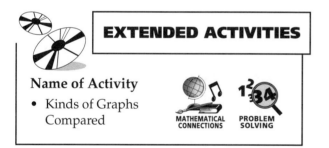

Cultural Contributions

CULTURAL RELEVANCE

CULTURAL CONTRIBUTIONS TO DATA ANALYSIS STATISTICS AND PROBABILITY

Data Analysis, statistics and probability are natural topics for which to find real-world applications. An appreciation of their usefulness can be included in the curriculum for the very young learners as well as those in upper grades. The following material developed by the Chicago Public Schools should be shared with students at each of the appropriate grade levels:

Grades K–3

Students should know that methods for collecting information and predicting outcomes were used by ancient civilizations in real-life problems. For example, in Africa, ancient Egyptian governments used measurements of the annual flood to predict the size of the harvest.

Students should know that many peoples contributed to the study of data analysis. For example, the Maya learned to predict eclipses by keeping records of the positions of the stars over the centuries. They recorded the data on charts.

Grades 4–8

Students should know that many peoples used and contributed to the study of statistics and probability. For example, the Maya learned to predict eclipses by analyzing astronomical tables that they had maintained over the centuries. The peoples of Egypt and Mesopotamia developed geometric formulas through experimentation and data analysis. Students should explore ancient methods for collecting statistics and predicting outcomes related to real-life problems. For example, in Africa, ancient Egyptians' governments prepared budgets and levied taxes based on data analysis. Measurements of the annual flood, made with a Nilometer, were used to predict the size of the harvest. (Strong, 1990)

Mean. The first measure of centeral tendency is the mean. The *mean,* or *arithmetic mean,* is most commonly used to describe the "average" of a set of data. The mean is computed by dividing the sum of the numbers by the number of members in the set. For example, if we want to know the average weight of four boys who weigh 105, 99, 110, and 90 pounds, we add 105 + 99 + 110 + 90 = 404 and divide by 4. Thus, the average weight of the four boys is 101 pounds.

From Concrete to Pictorial Connecting Level. Students should be encouraged to perform simple activities to develop an understanding of the arithmetic mean. Have students work with objects until they understand the algorithm for determining the average (arithmetic mean) of a set of data. Two examples are shown. A stylized drawing of Cuisenaire rods can be sketched much like the second example in the activity when students are ready to move to the pictorial connection level.

Activity 15.5

MANIPULATIVES

MEAN

DIRECTIONS

1. The weight of the bags of apples can be represented by objects, such as Cuisenaire rods. If the purple rod is 1 pound and the red rod is $\frac{1}{2}$ pound, the six bags of apples could be represented as follows:

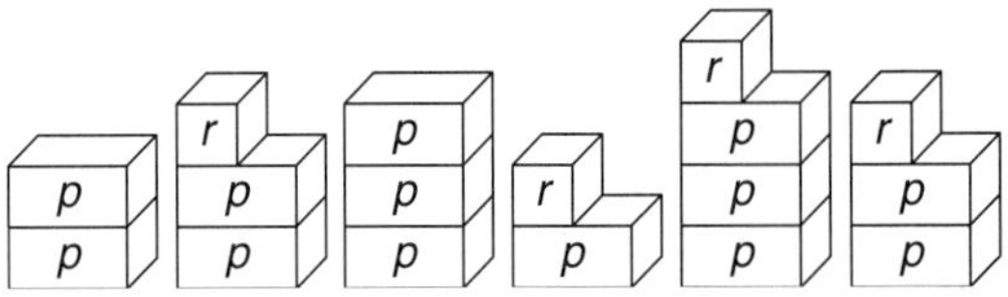

2. Rearrange the rods so there are six stacks of equal heights:

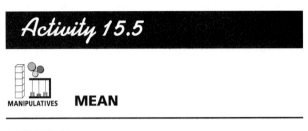

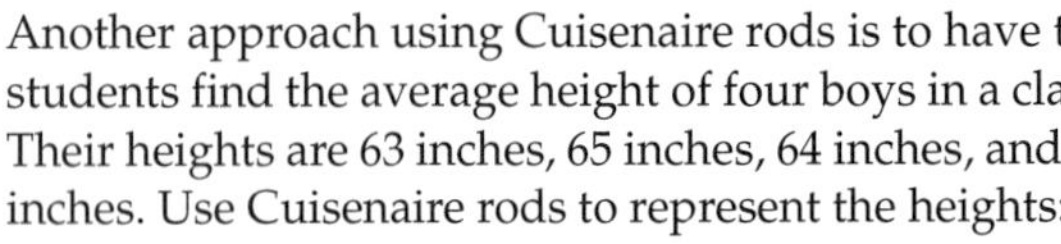

3. This is a method to discover that the arithmetic mean or average of six bags of apples weighing 2 pounds, $2\frac{1}{2}$ pounds, 3 pounds, $1\frac{1}{2}$ pounds, $3\frac{1}{2}$ pounds, and $2\frac{1}{2}$ pounds is $2\frac{1}{2}$ pounds.
4. Another approach using Cuisenaire rods is to have the students find the average height of four boys in a class. Their heights are 63 inches, 65 inches, 64 inches, and 68 inches. Use Cuisenaire rods to represent the heights:

10	10	10	10	10	10	111	
10	10	10	10	10	10	5	
10	10	10	10	10	10	1111	
10	10	10	10	10	10	5	111

5. Rearrange the rods to make each one the same length:

10	10	10	10	10	10	5
10	10	10	10	10	10	5
10	10	10	10	10	10	5
10	10	10	10	10	10	5

The average height of these four boys is 65 inches.

From Pictorial Connecting Level to Symbolic. An additional example of using pictures in the connecting level is shown on the CD-ROM. Calculators enable students to work with many numbers to find the mean on the symbolic level. An example with magic squares is found on the CD-ROM.

EXTENDED ACTIVITIES

CALCULATORS PROBLEM SOLVING

Name of Activity

- Finding the Mean: The Pictorial Level
- Finding the Mean: The Symbolic Level

Provide experiences in calculating means in practical problems using a calculator. A good source of practical problems is the daily newspaper. Class discussions could include "average rainfall," "batting average," "average speed," "stock market average," and "average points per game."

Mode. The second measure of central tendency is the mode. Because an extremely high number or an extremely low number can distort the picture of the tendency shown by the arithmetic mean, the mode is frequently used. The *mode* of a set of numbers is that number that occurs most frequently in the set. For example, the following shoe sizes were recorded for 10 pupils: 8, 7, 6, 8, 9, 6, 8, 5, 7, 8. If we put these data into a frequency table, the mode becomes more readily apparent.

Shoe Size	Number of Pupils
9	/
8	////
7	//
6	//
5	/

We can see that the most frequent score was 8; hence the mode of this set of numbers is 8.

Median. A third measure of central tendency is the median. The *median* of a set of numbers is the middle number of the set. For example, take a group of shoe sizes such as 7, 9, 3, 1, 6, 4, 10, and arrange them in order from greatest to least: 10, 9, 7, 6, 4, 3, 1. There are seven sizes. Now determine the position of the middle score. It must be the fourth score from either end; therefore, 6 is the median of this set of shoe sizes.

Here is another example, showing how to find the median of the following ages of a class:

12, 6, 7, 8, 7, 9, 10, 6, 7, 11, 12, 11

First, arrange the ages in order:

6, 6, 7, 7, 7, 8, 9, 10, 11, 11, 12, 12

How many ages are there? Twelve. Now determine the position of the middle age. It must be between the age of 8 and the age of 9. The median age is $8\frac{1}{2}$ because half of the ages are below $8\frac{1}{2}$ and half of the ages are above $8\frac{1}{2}$. Since there are an even number of ages, the median age lies halfway between the sixth and seventh age, $8\frac{1}{2}$.

Range. Another common statistical measure is the range. The *range* of a set of numbers is the difference between the highest and lowest numbers in a set. The range tells us the spread of a set of data.

Looking at one of our earlier examples of scores from a test:

Shoe Size	Number of Pupils
9	/
8	////
7	//
6	//
5	/

The range here (or spread of shoe sizes) is 9 – 5 or 4.

Here is another example with ages:

Ages	Number of Pupils
6	/
7	//
8	//
9	/
10	///
11	/
12	/

The range of ages here is 12 – 6 or 6.

Range, like the mean, is sometimes not a good measure of a distribution, because it includes the extremes and often gives a distorted picture of the data. For example, look at these two sets of numbers:

1, 1, 7, 7	mean 4; range 6
1, 4, 4, 7	mean 4; range 6

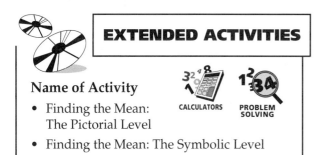

These two sets of numbers have the same mean and range, but have a very different "scatter." The mean and range in the example do not give us an accurate picture of what is happening. We do not know that the points in the second set are grouped near the mean and those in the first set are located in the extremes of the range.

Stem and Leaf Plots. In recent years, a new way of showing the median and mode of a distribution has gained popularity in the middle school curriculum. The chart at the left shows the number of things to be "plotted" from a list of data gathered. The stem and leaf plot for the same data is shown to the right:

Ages of Female Students in Math Methods Class

23	18	38	49
17	39	48	52
19	31	42	33
23	20	37	23
19			

Stem and Leaf Plot

1	8	7	9	9	
2	3	3	0	3	
3	8	9	1	3	7
4	9	8	2		
5	2				
↑	↑				
ten digits (stem)	ones digits (leaf)				

Reordered to see mode and median more easily:

Stem and Leaf Plot

1	7	8	9	9	
2	0	3	3	3	3
3	1	3	7	8	9
4	2	8	9		
5	2				

The stem and leaf plot looks like a horizontal graph of sorts, and the plot is easy to see because of its visual capabilities to explain data quickly. What can you tell from these data about the math methods class? What is the mode and median?

See what else the stem and leaf plot can do for a visual analysis when men in the math methods class are added to the stem and leaf plot.

Ages of Male Students in Math Methods Class

17	18	19	43
27	19	18	22
19			

Stem and Leaf Plot

Male							Female				
9	9	9	9	8	7	1	7	8	9	9	
				7	2	2	0	3	3	3	
						3	1	3	7	8	9
					3	4	2	8	9		
						5	2				

What can be told from the data now? What is the advantage of seeing data presented like this rather than in a normal chart formation? As you do the next activity, think about how the stem and leaf plot might have gotten its name.

The following approach is an example of the Learning Principle of the NCTM *Principles and Standards* for School Mathematics (2000). The activity emphasizes the purpose behind the stem and leaf plots used in middle school rather than calculations done without understanding what real-world examples apply.

Here is an example of another stem and leaf plot. It is similar to those found on some state assessment tests:

Stem	*Leaf*							
6	1	1	3	4	5			
7	0	2	2	5	6	7	9	9
8	4	6	7	8	8			
9	3	5	6	7	8	8	8	

What is the median?
What is the mode?

Here is an example of the kind of problem that could be solved by the stem and leaf plot above:

> In a local mall arcade, the owners and the part-time workers want to report different salary options. The owners want to report the average salaries by the mean, but the part-time workers want to report the average salaries by the median.

The stem and leaf plot represents the amount of part-time salaries report in thousands of dollars (that is, 6 | 1 = \$6100). Now the question for students becomes, "What does a stem and leaf plot do for data like that shown in the example? Why would a normal coordinate graph not work with these data? How do you suppose the stem and leaf plot got its name?" Look for the answers on the CD-ROM under "Stem and Leaf Dilemma."

Box and Whisker Plots. Like the stem and leaf plots, the box and whisker plots have gained popularity in the middle school curriculum because of their ability to show how the different ranges of data affect the distribution. Different distributions may have the same mean and mode yet represent a very different median. Think about the following report of salaries for workers in town A and town B:

Town A: 2000, 5000, 5000, 8000, 15000, 25000, 25000, 25000, 35000, 100,000
Town B: 5000, 12000, 15000, 15000, 20000, 20000, 25000, 25000, 25000, 30000

What is the mode, median, and mean of each distribution? Which "average" or measure of central tendency misrepresents the financial well-being of each town? If one takes the mean for each town, town A would appear very well off, but is it? If one compares the mode and median of both towns, they appear to be very similar towns. Comparing the two sets of information by range and differences from the median of each distribution tells the true story. That's what box and whisker plots do. See the plots for town A and town B in Figure 15.4.

FIGURE 15.4

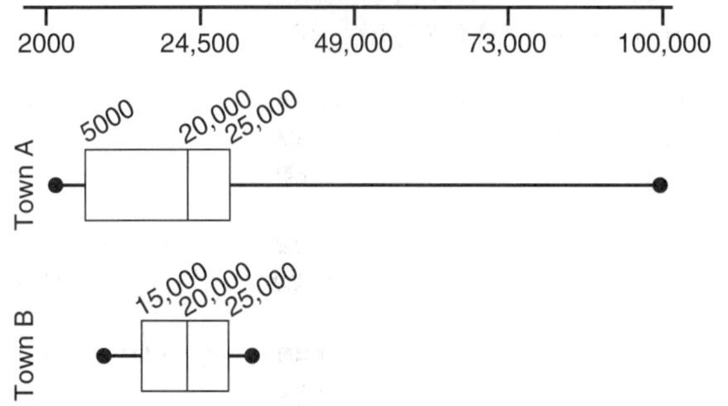

Plots for towns A and B.

A more appropriate picture of the towns can be seen. In the real world, this comparison of data matters when considering which town should receive federal funding for its less fortunate people and which may not qualify for aid. It may be easy to "eyeball" the disparity of salaries in this example, but the real-world model would have many more data points. The ability to see the disparity can get lost in the sheer volume of data.

Box and whisker plots are used when two or more sets of data need to be compared. First find the median and the quartiles (lowest 25 percent and the highest 25 percent of the data). That makes the box and the vertical line within the box show the median. Now the highest and lowest data points are marked and a line, or whisker, is drawn from the box to the highest and lowest data points. The visual image of the box and whisker can show differences in the range (whisker) and cluster of scores in the second and third quartile (the box). A graphing calculator can plot the box and whiskers configuration once you know how and why the calculations are needed.

Another middle school activity for box and whisker plots shows more data that involve variation. An example from the NCTM *Standards*, shows an application with an actual plot (Figure 15.5).

A class is divided into two large groups and then subdivided into pairs. One student in each pair estimates when one minute has passed, and the other watches the clock and records the actual time. All the students in one group concentrate on the timing task, while half the students in the second group exert constant efforts to distract their partners. The box plots show that the median times for the two groups are about the same but the times for the distracted group have greater variation. Note that in the distracted group, one data point is far enough removed from the others to be an outlier. (NCTM, 1989, p. 107)

FIGURE 15.5

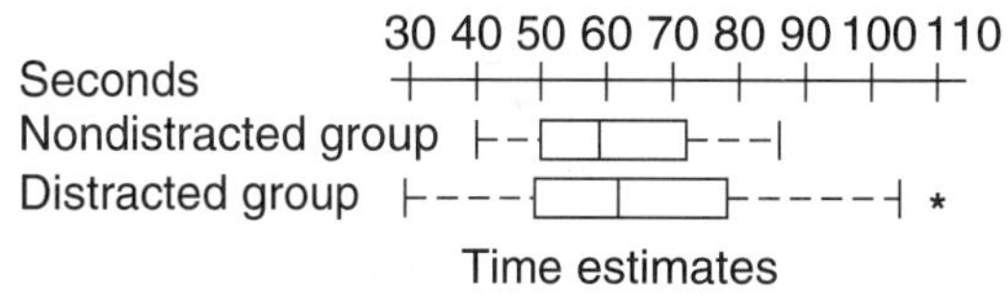

Box and whisker plot.

Putting It All Together: Statistical Information about Real-World Mathematics. The CD-ROM activity, called "Native American Lesson on Natural Resources with Statistics," shows how middle school students can learn of other cultures at the same time they are learning how to take care of the environment in real world problems. The Native American medicine wheel is used to show that the individual at the center of life is firmly connected to Mother Earth. Responsibility for the Earth and its resources is the theme of the sample statistical activity as adapted from the 1993 Summer Institute of Native American lessons on National Resources in Mathematics and Science conducted at Haskell Indian University in Lawrence, Kansas. All the lessons from K–12 are available through the U.S. Bureau of Indian Affairs (Darden et al., 1993).

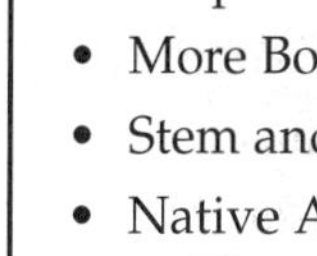

EXTENDED ACTIVITIES

Name of Activity

- Finding the Mode
- Finding the Average in Sports
- More Box and Whiskers
- Stem and Leaf Dilemma
- Native American Lesson on Natural Resources with Statistics

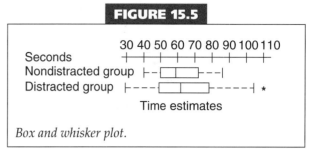

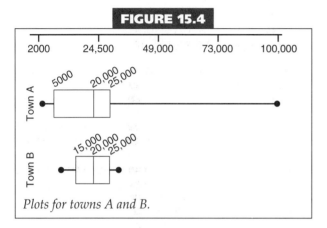

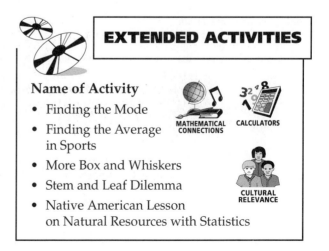

Scavo and Petraroja (1998) describe creative activities in which teachers produce real-world statistics problems of interest to students. One activity asked students to find out whether the average areas of sixth-grade rooms were larger than fifth-grade rooms. Competition among middle schoolers being what it is, sixth graders eagerly took on the project. No sixth graders want to be in smaller rooms than fifth graders.

Dean and Mayeski (1997) found that middle school math and science teachers teamed together to use the data collected and analyzed in mathematics class to solve problems students were studying in science. Other teachers use children's literature to spur interest in data collections and graphing representations. One such lesson used the book, *Visual Foolery* (DiSpezio, 1995), to learn what the average number of people would see in a variety of perceptual tasks designed to trick the eye. There are many child and adolescent books that can relate to statistics and data analysis (Thiessen, Matthias, and Smith, 1998). Some of the best are listed in the bibliography at the end of the chapter.

Following is an example of an assignment given in middle school to write a poem about a past school experience. The English teacher collected the poems and gave them to the mathematics teacher who wrote statistical problems using the poems. One such poem was:

I'll tell you of a smelly time
Where I used to go to school
When the local skunks came visiting
To break the Golden Rule.

The skunks made many tunnels
Beneath our classroom floors
Any every now and then it seemed
They knocked upon our doors.

One day I heard a frightening shout
From Collin and José
Inside the bathroom from under the tile
A skunk had come to spray.

Our principal got stinky
And our janitor did too
Before the skunks were captured
And taken to the zoo.

So when you hear your friends complain
About the bathroom smell
Remember that it would be worse
If skunks were here as well!

Greg Edwards
Swift Creek Middle School
Midlothian, VA

The mathematics teacher developed statistical problems this way:

What is the mean number of skunks at the school in a week's time using the following data? What is the mode? What is the median? What is the range?

Day 1	4 skunks
Day 2	2 skunks
Day 3	5 skunks
Day 4	6 skunks
Day 5	4 skunks
Day 6	3 skunks
Day 7	4 skunks

A teacher only needs a little creativity to have a wealth of statistical problems with real-life connections for students.

Probability

Probability is the branch of mathematics concerned with analyzing the chance that a particular event will occur. The basic purpose of probability theory is to attempt to predict the likelihood that something will or will not happen. Probability is computed on the basis of observing the number of actual outcomes and the number of possible outcomes.

$$\text{Probability of an event} = \frac{\text{Number of actual outcomes}}{\text{Total number of possible outcomes}}$$

Studying probability will help children to develop critical thinking skills and to interpret the probability that surrounds us daily. The study of chance needs to begin in an informal way in the early grades. Many students and teachers have misconceptions about the outcome of real events in life. For example, if the Watson family has three girls and is expecting a fourth child, is there an equally likely chance of having a boy or girl? Many people feel the next child "is bound to be a boy" because there are already three girls in the family. They base their predictions on their opinions about what they feel should happen (a biased reaction) rather than on fac-

Subscripts© . . . *little thoughts below the bottom line*

tual data. Statements involving probability abound in everyday situations, and it is important to make students aware of them. Students should be introduced to probability through activities with measuring uncertainty. Choice devices can be used to provide initial experiences for the study of chance—tossing a coin, rolling a die, drawing a card from a deck or a colored cube from a bag.

Students should begin by doing experiments, predicting the outcome, and recording the results. In most cases, a sample must be selected. A *sample* is a small number that represents a large group called a *population.* In most cases, it is impossible to test the total population, so a sample or samples are chosen.

A simple rubric can be selected that helps structure students' thoughts. Probability is one of those areas that appears to be less defined to a lot of students and teachers since the answers are always framed as "probables" with no exact endings ever finalized.

Rubric for Probability Problems

Begins by doing experiment	0:	Does not organize a start to the experiment
	1:	Starts experiment, but does not record results after each trial
	2:	Starts experiment, records results, but stops before enough trials are completed
	3:	Finishes experiment with results recorded with all trials completed
Predicting the outcome	0:	Does not predict an outcome
	1:	Predicts outcome only after 75 percent finish of trials
	2:	Predicts outcome after 50 percent finish of trials
	3:	Predicts outcome *before* trials begin
Checking the probability	0:	Does not compare prediction to outcomes of trials
	1:	Tells whether prediction was close, same, or far from actual outcomes of trials
	2:	Compares prediction to outcomes and explains *why* prediction was same, close, different, and so on
	3:	Explains why and projects what a general rule would be if applied to the next set of trials

Early Experiences: The Pre-K–5 Grades. Simple activities like the coin and dice toss give students in the early grades a limited number of choices from which to make predictions. Even young children can write a fraction to show how many heads they recorded out of how many total coins tossed. Charts or other recording devices need to be provided for young children. Free computer programs are available on the Internet for all grades. See Integrating Technology at the end of the chapter.

Tallies	Heads	Tails
Heads Count =	______	______
Out of Total =		
Tails Count =	______	______
Out of Total =		

As children come closer to the middle school grades, they can be encouraged to make up their own recording forms as a means of problem solving all the categories and options that need to be considered. This situation is like the real world where the boss expects the worker to come up with some form to handle the business at hand after being given a problem to solve.

Dice and Coin Tosses, Two Color Counters. From experiences like the coin toss, students can begin to predict the probability of certain events occurring. If a coin is tossed, there are two probable outcomes: heads or tails. There is an equally likely chance of it landing as a head or as a tail. If a coin is tossed 12 times, the theoretical probability is that it will land heads 6 times and tails 6 times. If one were actually to do this act, the experimental probability (actual outcome) may be quite different. Children need experiences with experimental probability.

Activity 15.6

MANIPULATIVES **COIN TOSS**

DIRECTIONS

1. A good experiment is to toss a coin 30 times and record how many heads and how many tails you get from a set number of tosses.
2. Represent the occurrences as a fraction. For example, if the outcome was 16 heads, the fraction $\frac{16}{30}$ would be the ratio of heads to the number of tosses, and $\frac{14}{30}$ would be the ratio of tails to the number of tosses.

   Heads $\frac{16}{30}$ Tails $\frac{14}{30}$

3. Record your results as a ratio.

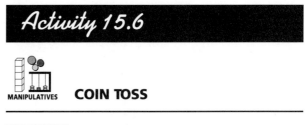

Another study of chance is tossing a die (Figure 15.6). Toss a die 100 times and record how many times each number appears. The results will indicate on the average that each number occurs about $\frac{1}{6}$ of the time. The theoretical probability of the number 4 appearing on the toss of a die is $\frac{1}{6}$. Likewise, the probability of the number 2 is $\frac{1}{6}$.

FIGURE 15.6

Probability of 4 $= \frac{1}{6}$

Probability of tossing one numeral using one die.

The following activity will let students experiment themselves.

Activity 15.7

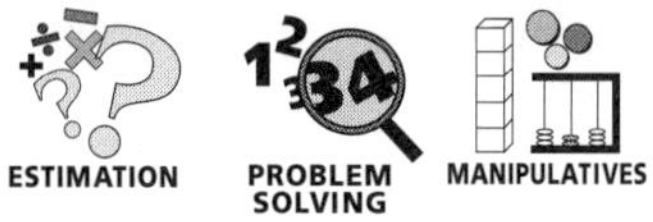

DIE TOSS

DIRECTIONS

1. Take one die and roll it 100 times. Keep a record of the number of times each number appears.

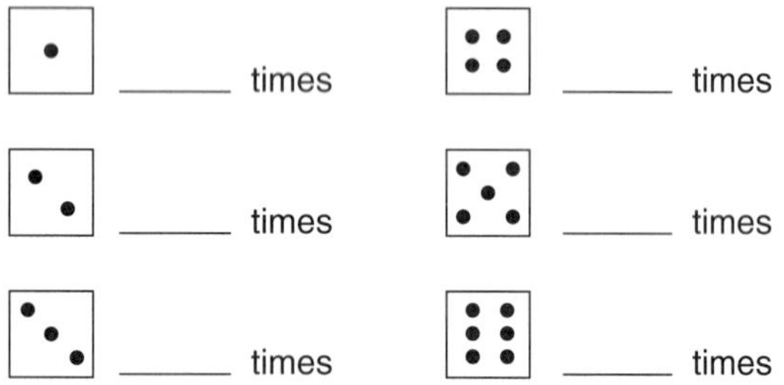

2. Divide the number of times you threw the die into the number of times your number appeared. This ratio tells you the chances of your number appearing in a certain number of trials.
3. Compare your results in the die activity to the theoretical probabilities.
4. From your record, what was the probability of a number less than 3 showing? What is the theoretical probability of this event occurring?

Activity Continues

5. What is the theoretical probability of an odd number (1, 3, 5) showing?
6. What is the theoretical probability of a prime number (2, 3, 5) showing? A multiple of 3 (3, 6) showing? A multiple of 2 (2, 4, 6) showing?

Supporting the NCTM *Principles and Standards* (2000):

- Mathematics as Problem Solving; Estimation; Probability
- Tools for Enhancing Discourse—The Teaching Principle
- The Learning Principle

Video Vignette

Graphing Probability

Ms. Bennett wants her students to discover some of the underlying concepts of probability. Notice how she uses range to show a way to list the possible combinations for two-die sums.

- At the beginning of this lesson from the children's predictions, what can be determined about her students' understanding of probability?
- Why does Ms. Bennett have the paired learning situation as the next part of her lesson? What do you think about the appropriateness of this task?
- The students' combine their data into the class chart. What do you think Ms. Bennett hoped would occur from this experience? What do their explanations about the likeliness of sums tell you about their understanding of probability?
- At the end of the lesson, what variables do her students suggest to explain the differences in the data? What follow-up activities would you suggest for students at this level of understanding?

Students should engage in many experiments to explore probability problems such as tossing a coin, tossing a die, or flipping two-colored counters until they become skillful in assigning probabilities. Freda (1998) shows how middle school students can use simulated dice programs written for the TI-82 calculator. Freda provides the calculator program and a computer version for teacher use (pp. 88–89):

FIGURE 15.7

```
option nolet
randomize
print "This is a simulation of the game that we played in
class."
do while z = 0        [Please note that this is a zero]
input prompt "How many rolls?": times
A=0
B=0
for roll= 1 to times
x=int(6*rnd)+1
y=int(6rnd)+1
c=abs(x-y)
if c=0 then A=A+1    [Change these lines to test different
if c=1 then A=A+1    versions of the game. This game
if c=2 then A=A+1    has player A winning for values of
if c=3 then B=B+1    0,1, or 2. To alter the game, change
if c=4 then B=B+1    where A=A+1 and B=B+1 and the
if c=5 then B=B+1    final two print statements.]
next roll
print "The percentage of 0,1,2 outcomes was ";100*A/
(A+B)
print "The percentage of 3,4,5 outcomes was ";100*B/
(A+B)
input prompt "Please enter 0 to try again and 1 to quit. ":z
loop
end
```

Program 1: Simulation of Dice Game Written in true BASIC

From experiments of this type with one coin or one die, the teacher should progress to experiments with two coins, colored balls, and checkers. Discussions should include notions of fairness. Have students work through these activities as they continually ask, "Is this a fair situation?"

The following two activities on the CD-ROM set up charts and tables to record tosses with more than one coin and the use of two dice at once. The tables may be printed from the CD-ROM. See *Mathematics Teaching in the Middle School* (NCTM, 1999) for a focus issue on probability.

Common Usage of Probability. A deal of playing cards provides a setting for students to work together in cooperative groups with common materials. The students use oral discourse as they make their predictions and naturally explain to each other what is happening as they participate in the actual trials. Each student should have a copy of the rubric shown earlier to remember all the parts of the activity.

FIGURE 15.8

```
Program: Diff of Dice
:ClrHome
:0 —> A
:0 —> B          [Please Note that these are zeros,
                 not letters.]
:Disp "HOW MANY ROLLS?"
:Input Z
:For (N,1,Z)
:int(rand*6)+1 —> K
:int(rand*6)+1 —> L
:abs(K-L) —> M
:If M=0          [Change this section to test different
:Then            versions. This version has Player A
:A+1 -> A        winning for values of 0,1, or 2.
:End             To alter the game, change where
:If M=1          A+1 —>A and B+1—> B and the two
                 Disp "PERCENT . . . " statements at
                 the end of the program.]
:Then
:A+1 —> A
:End
:If M=2
:Then
:A+1 —> A
:End
:If M=3
:Then
:B+1 —> B
:End
:If M=4
:Then
:B+1 —> B
:End
:If M=5
:Then
:B+1 —> B
:End
:End
:Disp "PERCENT 0, 1, 2 IS"
:Disp A*100/(A+B)
:Disp "PERCENT 3, 4, 5 IS"
:Disp B*100/(A+B)
```

Program 2: Simulation of the Dice Game Written for the TI-82 Calculator

EXTENDED ACTIVITIES

COMPUTERS MANIPULATIVES ESTIMATION PROBLEM SOLVING

Name of Activity

- Money Toss
- Creating Tables with Dice Tosses
- Probability Games on the Internet

Activity 15.8

MANIPULATIVES

PROBABILITIES WITH CARDS

DIRECTIONS

1. Place five cards with the numbers 0 through 4 on them in a cardboard box.
2. What is the probability of drawing a card with a number less than 5 on it? There are five possible outcomes, and they are all favorable; therefore, the probability of drawing a card with a number less than 5 on it is $\frac{5}{5} = 1$.
3. What is the probability of drawing a card with a number greater than 4 on it? There are five possible outcomes and none of them are favorable—the probability of this occurring is $\frac{0}{5}$ or 0.
4. If an event is sure to happen, the probability is 1. If there is no favorable outcome and an event is sure not to happen, the probability is 0.

In most experiments, we have more than one set of outcomes associated with the experiment. For example, in our previous example of tossing two coins, our probable outcomes were H–H, H–T, T–H, T–T. A pictorial way of illustrating all possibilities is with a *tree diagram.* To illustrate, use a bag containing five red and three black marbles. Draw twice with replacement (return the marble to the bag before making the second draw). What are the possible outcomes of this experiment?

You could draw a red marble first then a black marble, a red marble first and then another red marble, a black and then a red or a black and a black. We can abbreviate this as: rb, rr, br, bb.

We can represent this visually as follows (Figure 15.9). On the first draw, we can obtain either a red marble or a black marble.

FIGURE 15.9

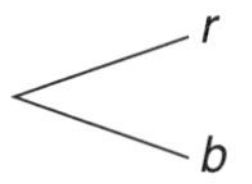

Probability of red or black on first draw.

Regardless of what occurred on the first draw, there are still two possibilities for the second draw (Figure 15.10). The tree diagram is very useful in determining possible outcomes of an experiment. We can extend our diagram to include the second draw:

FIGURE 15.10

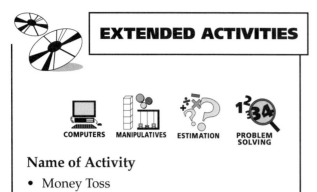

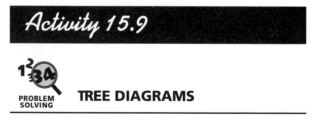

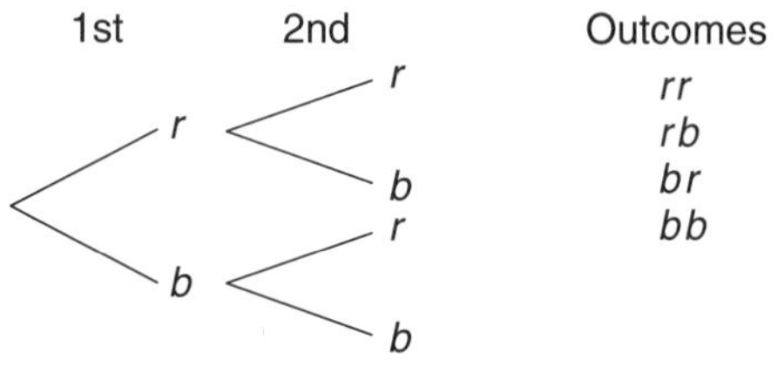

Probability of red or black extended to second draw.

Activity 15.9

PROBLEM SOLVING

TREE DIAGRAMS

DIRECTIONS

1. Draw a tree diagram illustrating the outcomes of draws from a bag containing twelve red marbles and four black marbles.
2. Marbles are drawn from the bag with replacement. Three draws are made. What are the possible outcomes?

Activity Continues

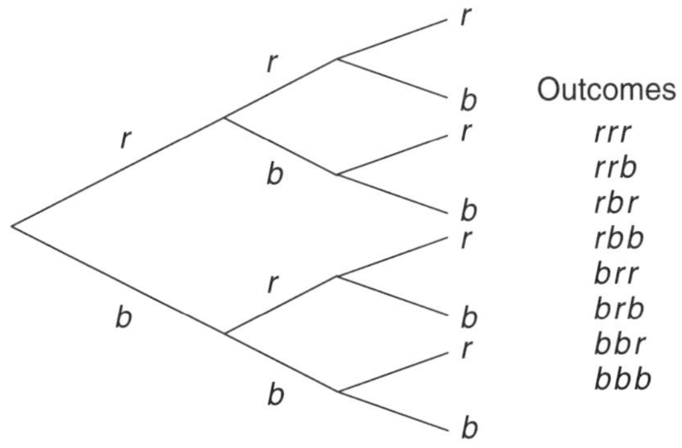

Activity 15.10

PROBLEM SOLVING MANIPULATIVES

PROBABILITY PATH

DIRECTIONS

Follow the probability path. Tossing a die five times will get you from the start position to one of the lettered boxes.

1. Toss the die. If the number on the die is odd, follow the odd path. If the number is even, follow the even path.
2. Follow the path twenty-five times. Keep a tally mark record of the box in which you finish each time. Which boxes do you end in most often? Least often?
3. What percent of the twenty-five tosses lands in each box?

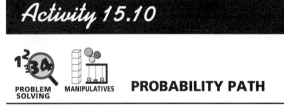

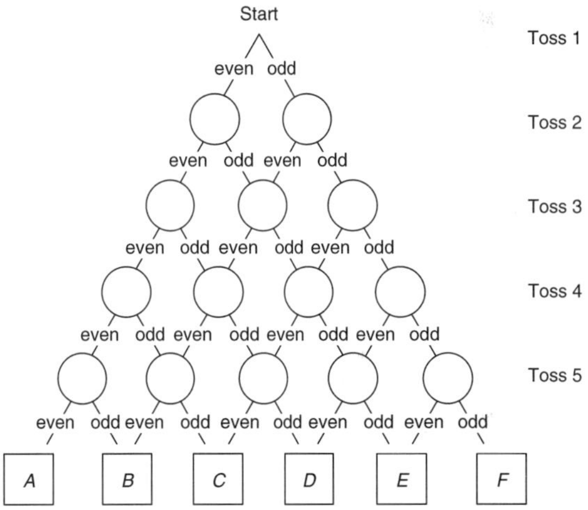

Assigning Probabilities: The 6–8 Middle School Grades. Middle school children need to approach problems in which they represent the probability of the outcome of a certain experiment in a mathematical way. For example, use a bag with twelve red marbles and four black marbles, and represent the probability that a red marble is drawn or that a black marble is drawn. Since the red marbles make up $\frac{12}{16} = \frac{3}{4}$ of the total number of marbles, $\frac{3}{4}$ can be used to represent the probability of drawing a red marble. The black marbles represent $\frac{4}{16} = \frac{1}{4}$ of the total number of marbles. Therefore, $\frac{1}{4}$ can be used to represent the probability of drawing a black marble.

In another situation, if the same bag contained four black, three green, and three red marbles, the probability of drawing a black marble would be $\frac{4}{10}$ (0.4), a green $\frac{3}{10}$ (0.3), and a red $\frac{3}{10}$ (0.3).

The probability of each outcome will be a number between 0 and 1, and the sum of all the probabilities in the experiment must equal 1. What is the probability that in the toss of a coin, "tails" will appear? $\frac{1}{2}$. What is the probability of rolling a 3 when tossing a die? $\frac{1}{6}$. Students should be allowed to perform experiments and record the results while learning to assign probabilities. Toss a die and ask how often does a 3 occur? About $\frac{1}{6}$ of the time. How often does a 2 occur? About $\frac{1}{6}$ of the time.

Experiments can be developed using dice, coins, spinners, cards, or whatever to give students experience assigning probabilities. Assigning probabilities (making selections) without bias is essential for computing the probability of events occurring. Activities using probability paths help give a sense of concreteness to a probable happening.

Identifying Different Types of Events. After working with different arrangements of probability paths, the next step is to identify different types of events. Developmentally appropriate activities for middle schoolers include the recognition that there are different types of events that can occur in the real world of mathematics. These are called events that are independent of any other event that is occurring and events that are dependent on other events that are occurring. As you can see from the following explanations, an understanding of set theory is helpful. This can be explained to middle school students without the set theory symbols for intersection and union. In those cases oral discourse of the teacher and written words on the board or overhead projector are needed at the start of developing an understanding with the manipulatives.

- **Mutually Exclusive Events (Independent Events)**

Two events are said to be *mutually exclusive* if they have no outcomes in common. For example, if x and y are mutually exclusive events with a finite (z) set of outcomes, we could represent these sets as:

If the intersection (represented by $\cap$) of the two sets is the empty set, then

$X \cap Y = 0$ (no outcomes in common)	and $P(X \cap Y) = 0$ (where P = the probability)

The addition property of two mutually exclusive events is the sum of their probabilities, which is $P(X \cup Y) = P(X) + P(Y)$. For example, if a marble is drawn at random from a bag containing four red, five black, and six green marbles, what is the probability of drawing

1. A green marble?

$$P(G) = \frac{6}{15}$$

2. A green or red marble?

$$P(G) = \frac{6}{15}$$
$$P(R) = \frac{4}{15}$$

The probability of drawing a red or a green marble can be written $P(G \cup R)$. (The symbol for "or" is $\cup$.) And, since these two events are mutually exclusive, the combined probability is

$$P(G \cup R) = \frac{6}{15} + \frac{4}{15} = \frac{10}{15} = \frac{2}{5}$$

To check our answer, compare this answer with the probability of drawing some color other than black.

$$P = 1 - \frac{5}{15} = \frac{10}{15} = \frac{2}{5}$$

Two dice are thrown. What is the probability that the sum is 5 or the sum is 7?

The possible outcomes 5 = (1,4) (2,3) (3,2) (4,1)
The possible outcomes 7 = (1,6) (6,1) (2,5) (5,2) (3,4) (4,3)

The probability of either event happening:

$$P(5 \cup 7) = \frac{4}{36} + \frac{6}{36} = \frac{10}{36} = \frac{5}{18}$$

Practice is recommended to understand the concept of mutually exclusive events. However, if students are continually reminded that mutually exclusive events are two events that have no common outcomes, they will have less difficulty with the topic.

Using the phrase "either-or" is a helpful oral discourse technique for students to reason if occurrences are mutually exclusive. The following activity shows if the pencil is *either* on the line *or* off the line. Other examples would be tossing a die that yields one choice of six numerals. You *either* get that numeral *or* you don't.

Activity 15.11

MATHEMATICAL CONNECTIONS MANIPULATIVES PROBLEM SOLVING **SCIENCE**

DIRECTIONS

1. Get a pencil and measure its length.
2. Draw parallel lines on the paper that are 1.5 times as far apart as the length of the pencil

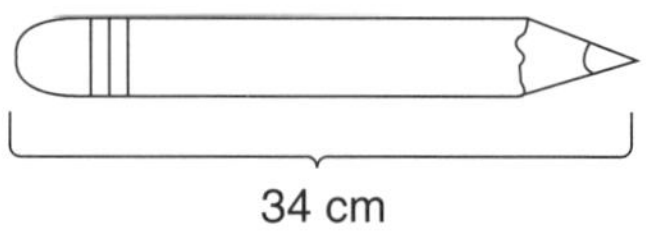

34 cm × 1.5 (distance between parallel lines)

3. Drop the pencil onto the paper from a height of about 1 meter.
4. Record on a chart, such as the one shown here, how many times the pencil touches a line or does not touch a line. Don't count it if the pencil doesn't land on the paper.

	Tally	Total
Touches a line		
Doesn't touch		

5. After a certain number of trials, such as 50, figure the probability that the pencil will touch a line when dropped. Does it make a difference whether your pencil is longer or shorter?

- **Known Conditions Imposed on Events: Conditional Probability (Dependent Events)**

In probability experiments we are often restricted by certain conditions imposed on the outcomes. How does the outcome change when a "known" is imposed on the experiment?

Suppose we throw two dice, one red and one green. If the red die shows a number that is divisible by 4, what is the probability that the total of the two dice is equal to or greater than 7? This condition that has been imposed on the experiment (the red die has a number divisible by 4) cuts down the sample or outcome.

The original sample of 36 possibilities is shown in Figure 15.11.

When the condition that the number on the red die has a number divisible by 4 is imposed, the sample reduces to 6 possibilities, and the probability of having a total greater than or equal to 7 is $\frac{4}{6} = \frac{2}{3}$ (Figure 15.12).

Probability that is *dependent* on an outcome is referred to as *conditional probability* and is represented as $P(A \mid B)$. This means the probability of A happening once B has occurred.

In the previous example, A equals the set of points representing a total dice sum of 7 or over; B equals the set of points for which the number on the red die is divisible by 4.

The symbols $A \cap B$ represent the 4 points common to A and B (7, 8, 9, 10), and the probability of B, $P(B) = \frac{6}{36} = \frac{1}{6}$. So, the probability of A occurring after B has occurred is the intersection of A and B divided by the probability of B.

The formula is as follows:

If $P(B) \neq 0$, then the conditional probability that A will occur once B has occurred is

$$P(A|B) = \frac{P(A \cap B)}{P(B)}$$

For example:

$$P(\text{sum} > 7 \mid \text{Red die divisible by 4}) = \frac{\frac{4}{36}}{\frac{6}{36}} = \frac{4}{6} = \frac{2}{3}$$

- **Independent and Dependent Events Compared**

There are certain events that are not dependent on what occurred prior to their occurrence. These events are called *independent events*. For example, if a coin is tossed, the probability of it being tails on the second toss is not dependent on what it was on the first toss. The probability of it being a tail on the second toss is $\frac{1}{2}$ regardless of whether it was a head or a tail on the first toss.

The definition for the *multiplicative property for independent events* is that the probability of independent events X and Y to occur is the product of their probability such that

FIGURE 15.11

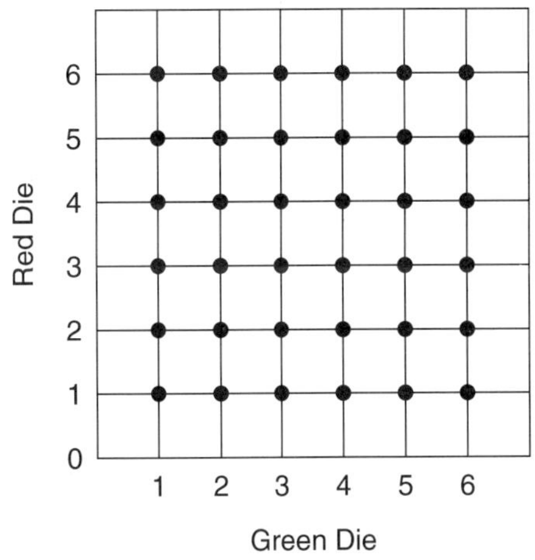

Red and green dice with all possibilities shown.

FIGURE 15.12

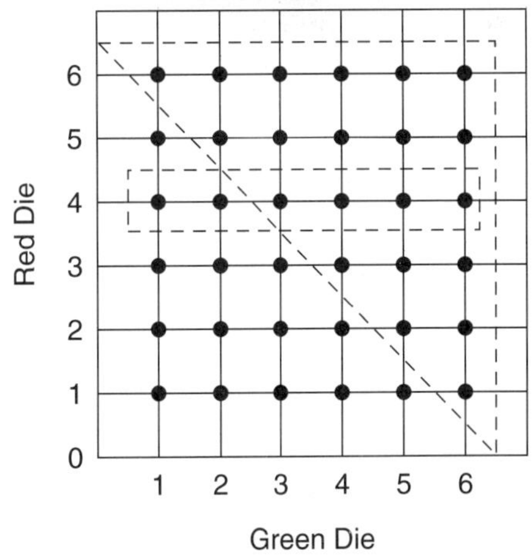

Red and green dice with conditions applied.

$$P(X \cap Y) = P(X) \times P(Y)$$

Previous bag problems, where marbles were being drawn from a bag with replacement after each draw, were examples of an independent event. Our original problem had a bag containing five red and three black marbles. Two marbles are drawn one after another, with replacement after each draw.

The probability of red on the first draw is $\frac{5}{8}$. Since the bag is restored to its original state after the drawing, the probability of drawing a red marble on the second drawing is $\frac{5}{8}$ also. A tree diagram of this experiment would look like Figure 15.13.

Repeat the same experiment without replacing the marbles. Again, make two draws, but this time do

FIGURE 15.13

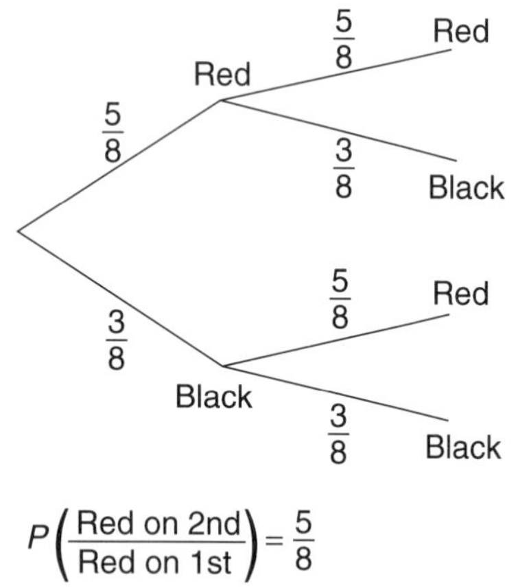

Probability of marbles with replacement after each draw.

not replace the first marble drawn. The probability of a black marble being drawn on the first draw is $\frac{3}{8}$. If the marble is drawn and not replaced, there are now seven marbles in the bag. The probability of a black marble being drawn on the second draw is $\frac{2}{7}$. A tree diagram of this experiment looks like Figure 15.14.

FIGURE 15.14

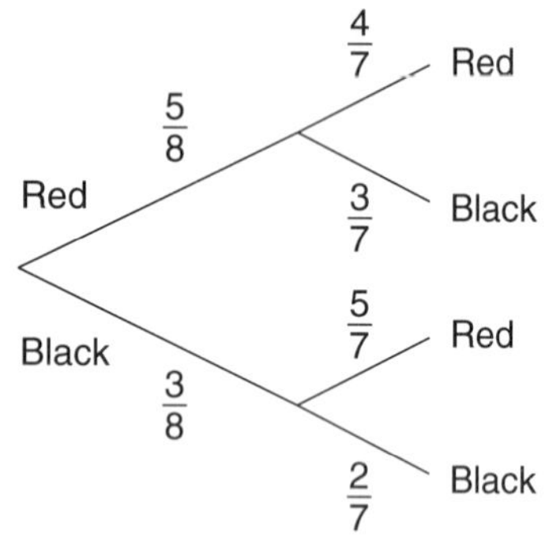

Probability of marbles without replacement after each draw.

The probability for the second draw changes because the marbles are not replaced and the content of the bag changes.

Cards, colored dice, and coins are good manipulative aids for probability experiments. Drawing diagrams and recording data can be used to develop skills in determining whether events are independent or dependent. Probability is rich with interesting problems to experiment and simulate. It provides a setting to engage middle school students in making hypotheses, testing conjectures, and justifying their conclusions. Once students have experimented, a computer can generate hundreds of simulated results.

Permutations and Combinations. Probability includes the study of permutations and combinations. These probability applications have to do with mathematically predicting the results of games and real-life situations. Before discussing permutations and combinations, the term *factorial* needs to be defined. *Factorial* is a series of multiplications of consecutive integers. For example, 6! means $6 \times 5 \times 4 \times 3 \times 2 \times 1 = 720$ and is read "six factorial."

> Factorial is used in evaluating combinations and permutations.
> Zero factorial is defined to be equal to one; that is, $0! = 1$.

Calculator keys with the factorial key [!] make it easy for middle schoolers to figure problems with permutations and combinations. Simple factorial problems like 6! shown above can be done with any calculator without the student losing track of how many times the factors are to be multiplied. No special keys are really needed when the factors are held to ten or less.

Permutations. There are many problems involving permutations. Here is one example: Suppose we wish to seat four students (Al, Beth, Cathy, and Diego) in four seats in the front of the room. How many different ways are there to seat these students?

The problem can be solved by experimenting with the actual arrangements and constructing a tree diagram following this explanation.

How many different ways are there to fill seat 1? It can be filled with

1. Al
2. Beth
3. Cathy
4. Diego

Seat 1 can be filled in four ways. When seat 1 is filled, how many ways are there to fill seat 2? If Al is in seat 1, seat 2 can be filled with

1. Beth
2. Cathy
3. Diego

There are 3 ways of filling seat 2. Suppose Beth is in the first seat, how many ways are there of filling seat 2?

1. Al
2. Cathy
3. Diego

There are three ways of filling seat 2 with seat 1 being occupied by Beth. The same is true when the first seat is filled by Cathy and when it is filled by Diego.

So there are 3 + 3 + 3 + 3 = 12 different ways of filling seats 1 and 2. They are as follows:

Al Beth → 1	Al Cathy → 1	Al Diego → 1
Cathy Al → 1	Cathy Beth → 1	Cathy Diego → 1
Beth Al → 1	Beth Cathy → 1	Beth Diego → 1
Diego Al → 1	Diego Beth → 1	Diego Cathy → 1

There are twelve ways of filling the first two seats. There now remain two different ways of filling the remaining two seats. For each way of filling the first two seats, there are a total of twenty-four ways to seat the four children in four seats. The tree diagram of this seating would look like Figure 15.15.

FIGURE 15.15

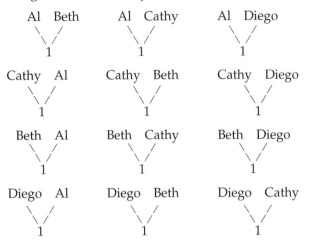

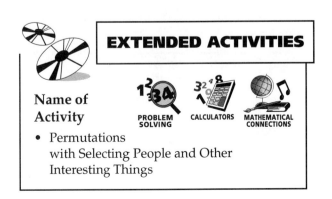

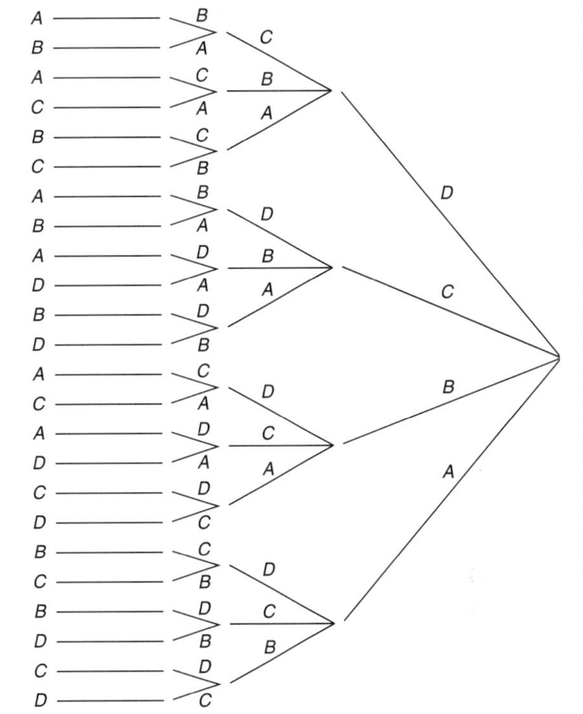

All possible ways to seat four students in four chairs.

This experiment and others like it should actually be done cooperatively with students so they can visualize the concept of ordered arrangements. Placing n objects in a particular order gives the following result:

$n = 4$: $n(n-1)(n-2)(n-3)$ ways

or $4 \times 3 \times 2 \times 1 = 24$

$n = n$: or $n! = n(n-1)(n-2)(n-3) \cdots 3, 2, 1$

The generalization of an ordered selection of x of the n objects can be done in $n(n-1)(n-2)\ldots(n-x)$ ways, which is equal to $n!/(n-x)!$ The generalized formula can be applied to the previous example as follows:

Example: 4 students
4 chairs

$$\frac{4!}{(4-4)!} = \frac{4 \times 3 \times 2 \times 1}{0!} = \frac{24}{1} = 24$$

A *permutation* of a number of objects is an ordered arrangement of those objects—that is, placing the objects in a definite order. The formula for the number of permutations is

$$_nP_x = n!/(n-x)!$$

where

x = the number of objects to be ordered

n = the original set of n objects from which x was taken

Let's do another experiment to determine the number of ways a set of letters can be ordered and then check the answer with the permutation formula.

Some middle school students may not be developmentally ready to handle the step-by-step logic of the formula developed above. The answer can be obtained if the students have a calculator with a permutation button. It would look like this on most calculators: $\boxed{nPx}$. The guidebook provided with the calculator will explain how the key can be used.

For those who want to practice with more activities, they are available on the CD-ROM.

EXTENDED ACTIVITIES

PROBLEM SOLVING CALCULATORS MATHEMATICAL CONNECTIONS

Name of Activity

- Permutations with Selecting People and Other Interesting Things

Activity 15.12

MATHEMATICAL CONNECTIONS CALCULATORS PROBLEM SOLVING

PERMUTATIONS WITH LETTERS

DIRECTIONS

1. How many three-letter arrangements can be made from the letters in the word *favorite*?

   Here the original set n contains 8 letters, and we want to order 3 of the letters, so $x = 3$.

$$_8P_3 = \frac{8!}{(8-3)!} = \frac{8!}{5!} = 8 \times 7 \times 6 = 336$$

   So there are 336 ways of combining 3 letters out of the original set, *favorite.*

2. We are having a school competition this Friday. There are 8 students entered in the broad jump. If we are going to give medals to the first 3 students, how many ways can the medals by awarded?

   For example: one way—first place to Billy, second to Jane, and third to Sam.

$$_8P_3 = \frac{8!}{(8-3)!} = \frac{8!}{5!} = 336 \text{ ways}$$

3. How many different 7-digit phone numbers can the telephone company make from the digits 0 through 9 without repeating a digit?

$$_{10}P_7 = \frac{10!}{(10-7)!} = \frac{10!}{3!} = 10 \times 9 \times 8 \times 7 \times 6 \times 5 \times 4$$

$$= 604{,}800 \text{ phone numbers}$$

4. List other situations that use the concept of permutations.

Supporting the NCTM *Principles and Standards* (2000):

- Mathematics as Problem Solving; Connections; Representations, Probability
- Tools That Enhance Discourse—The Teaching Principle
- The Learning Principle—Power to Solve New Problems

Combinations. As can be seen, permutation situations require a specific arrangement and order. Events that ignore order are called *combinations.* A solution is shown by exhausting all possibilities.

Three people form a line at the post office counter. How many different combinations are possible to be the first two in line?

Three People	*The Possibilities*
Larry	Larry, Julie
Julie	Julie, Jeff
Jeff	Jeff, Larry

Notice: Order is not important.
The total is 3.

When we want to take x number of objects from a set of n objects *without regard to order,* we are dealing with combinations instead of permutations.

The formula for combinations is as follows:

$$_nC_x = \frac{_nP_x}{x!} = \frac{n!}{x!(n-x)!}$$

Applying the formula for three objects taken two at a time gives the following results:

$$_3C_2 = \frac{3!}{2!} = \frac{3!}{2!(3-2)!}$$

$$= \frac{3 \times 2 \times 1}{2 \times 1 \times 1} = 3$$

Some calculators also have a key for combinations. It would look like this on most calculators: $\boxed{nCx}$. Following is an activity using manipulatives. Some children actually need to move the books around before using the calculator to see another way of solving the problem.

Activity 15.13

MANIPULATIVES CALCULATORS

EXPLORING COMBINATIONS

DIRECTIONS

1. Place eight different books on a table in the classroom. How many pairs of books may be selected? (Order doesn't matter.)
2. Keep a tally of the different pairs of books that are selected. Then use the formula

$$_nC_x = \frac{n!}{x!(n-x)!}$$

   to see if you get the same answer as the experiment gave.

$$_8C_2 = \frac{8!}{2!6!} = \frac{8 \times 7}{2} = \frac{56}{2} = 28 \text{ pairs}$$

For those who want to practice with more activities, they are available on CD-ROM.

EXTENDED ACTIVITIES

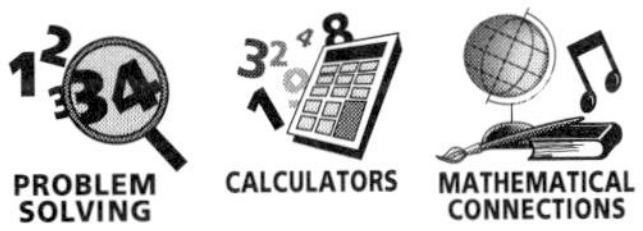

Name of Activity

- Boxes of Candy
- Combinations with Cards
- Homework Examples

Homework Possibilities. There are many ways to extend activities when students need some thought time to work out solutions. Such activities make excellent homework assignments because they do not involve the normal thought of drudgery in boring, repetitive work. The following ideas are taken from Project AIM, developed at the Teachers College of Emporia State University (Morrow and Mehring, 1993). They are meant for grades 3–8. More homework examples are on the CD-ROM.

1. Draw a spinner with at least three sections so that half the time the spinner should stop on red.
2. You have a bag with ten color tiles. There are six blue, three red, and 1 yellow. If you draw from the bag one time, predict the color you would get and why you think this would happen.
   Extension: Keep the same bag as above. Explain how you could change the bag to improve the probability of drawing a yellow.
3. You have a regular deck of playing cards containing fifty-two cards. Shuffle this deck of cards. Place face down. Draw one card at a time. Player A only keeps numbered cards that he or she draws. Player B only keeps face cards when he or she draws them. Other cards are discarded. Which player would you rather be? Explain why.

Source: Morrow and Mehring, 1993, pp. 14–15.

ASSESSMENT

Data Analysis—Graphing

The following student work demonstrates how students can interpret graphs made by others as well as those made by themselves. It is very revealing to students when they give their graphs to others who try to interpret what is happening. Rubrics that can be used by students to evaluate their own work are included.

Bar Graph Stories. The bar graph activity seen as Figure 15.16 has been used in classrooms in several different ways. Students were asked to create their own bar graphs about something they liked.

Some teachers chose to extend the activity by asking other students to use the rubric to evaluate the work of their fellow students. The rubric critique was originally created for the Project AIM grant (Morrow and Mehring, 1993) mentioned earlier in the chapter. The rubric can be used by the student-creator of the graph without the critique by another student. The different critiques and stories that accompanied this graph are seen on the CD-ROM as listed in the next activities.

Notice that Lauren takes issue with Michael's critique of her graph. Some teachers find that there can be deep hurt on the part of sensitive children when their work is critiqued by other students in a formal rubric sheet as seen on the CD-ROM. Some teachers argue that students like Lauren, even though they may be sensitive, will not forget the titles on graphs after such an evaluation by a peer. To

FIGURE 15.16

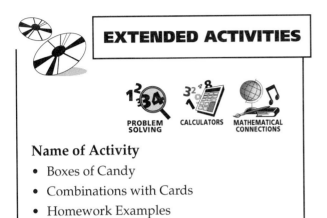

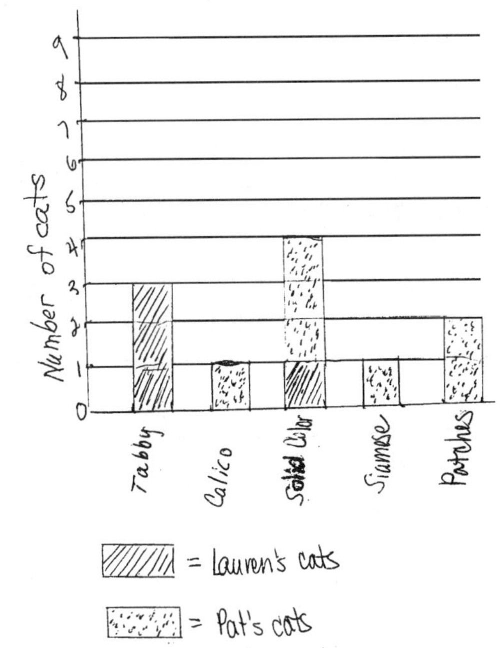

Lauren's bar graph.

use or not to use the critique sheet—it is a professional decision that each teacher must make for himself or herself with each new class in mind.

EXTENDED ACTIVITIES

Name of Activity

PORTFOLIO

- Lauren's Story... about her own graph
- Michael's Story... about Lauren's graph
- Michael's Critique... of Lauren's graph
- Lauren's Critique... of her own graph
- Bar Graph Rubric and Critique Form (Blank Rubric to Copy for Your Own Portfolio)
- TIMSS Assessment: Pasta Graphing
- TIMSS Assessment: Who's Going to Win the World Series?

Continuous Graph Stories. Figures 15.17 and 15.18 show two third graders, Kate and Mark, working on the same task. This is the first activity either one has ever worked with continuous graphs. Both have a sense of what the graph is about but each has approached the task differently. How could you make up a rubric that would give each one of them credit for what they were able to do?

Activity 15.14

PORTFOLIO

CREATING YOUR OWN RUBRIC FOR CONTINUOUS GRAPHS

MATERIALS

- Two continuous graphs by third-grade children

DIRECTIONS

- Use these questions to help you start thinking about a rubric:

1. What are the positive things that you see in both answers to the graph questions?
2. What misconceptions about the graphs do the children seem to have?
3. Is there a fair scale to use to give a numerical score to the children's creative work? If yes, what is it? If no,

Activity Continues

FIGURE 15.17

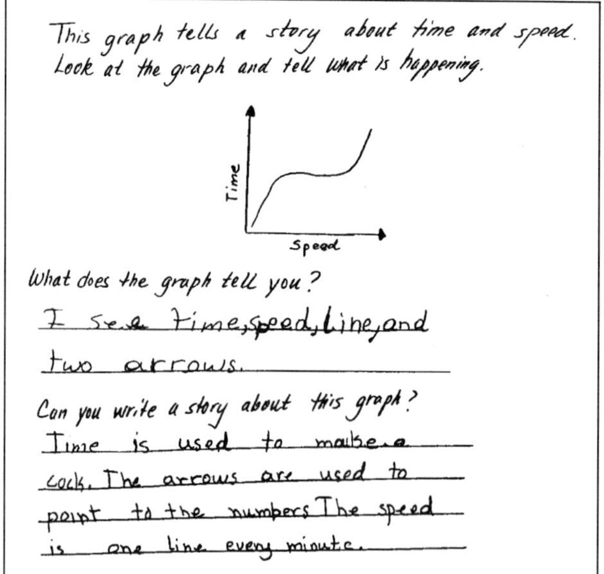
This graph tells a story about time and speed.
Look at the graph and tell what is happening.
Time
Speed
What does the graph tell you?
I see a time, speed, line, and
two arrows.
Can you write a story about this graph?
Time is used to make a
cock. The arrows are used to
point to the numbers The speed
is one line every minute.

Continuous graph interpretation by Mark.

FIGURE 15.18

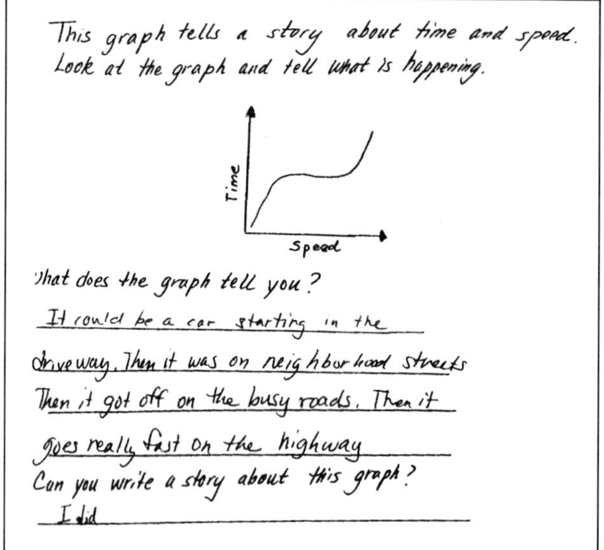
This graph tells a story about time and speed.
Look at the graph and tell what is happening.
Time
Speed
What does the graph tell you?
It could be a car starting in the
driveway. Then it was on neighborhood streets
Then it got off on the busy roads. Then it
goes really fast on the highway
Can you write a story about this graph?
I did

Continuous graph interpretation by Kate.

what could you substitute instead of a numerical score?

4. What are the next steps you need to do to help both children continue to grow?
5. Share your thoughts with others. See what your combined knowledge may be able to come up with.

Students with Special Needs. Creating one's own rubric and judging others by their own rubric may give some children with special needs a difficult time. They do better if they can start with only three data points to place on the graph with category labels that make sense easily. It should be noted; however, that the activities with radio-controlled cars for the middle school found on the CD-ROM were all ideas generated and solved by students with Attention Deficit Disorder (ADD). Their ideas flowed throughout the assignment; they were highly motivated during the lessons. It may be that students with ADD need more interesting stimuli to pay attention. Certainly the chance to "drive" a radio-controlled car is high motivation in middle school.

Averages. The concept of average is one of the most commonly used mathematics concepts in everyday circumstances. Mokros and Russell (1995) have tested children and mathematics education students to see what their understanding of averages is and how they go about finding an average. In a study with fourth graders, sixth graders, and eighth graders, they found the students see average as one of five interpretations described in Table 15.1.

Analyze the work of the following two students in Figure 15.19. Their teacher modified the worksheet of a leading math series (HBJ) to include a question at the end that became an entry in their math journals. Use Table 15.1 as a starting point to discover the understanding of averages by each of the two students.

TABLE 15.1 Mokros and Russell Study

Characteristics of the Five Predominant Approaches to Solving the Problems

Average as mode. Students with this predominant approach—

- Consistently use mode to construct a distribution or interpret an existing one.
- Lack flexibility in choosing strategies.
- Are unable to build a distribution when not allowed to use the given average as a data point.
- Use the algorithm for finding the mean infrequently or incorrectly.
- View the mode only as "the most," not as representative of the data set as a whole.
- Frequently use egocentric reasoning in their solutions.

Average as algorithm. Students with this predominant approach—

- View finding an average as carrying out the school-learned procedure for finding the arithmetic mean.
- Often exhibit a variety of useless and circular strategies that confuse total, average, and data.
- Have limited strategies for determining the reasonableness of their solutions.

Average as reasonable. Students with this predominant approach—

- View an average as a tool for making sense of the data.
- Choose an average that is representative of the data, both from a mathematical perspective and from a common-sense perspective.
- Use their real-life experiences to judge if an average is reasonable.
- May use the algorithm for finding the mean; if so, the result of the calculation is scrutinized for reasonableness.
- Believe that the mean of a particular data set is not one precise mathematical value, but an approximation that can have one of several values.

Average as midpoint. Students with this predominant approach—

- View an average as a tool for making sense of the data.
- Choose an average that is representative of the data, both from a mathematical perspective and from a common-sense perspective.
- Look for a "middle" to represent a set of data; this middle is alternately defined as the median, the middle of the x axis, or the middle of the range.
- Use symmetry when constructing a data distribution around the average. They show great fluency in constructing a data set when symmetry is allowed but have significant trouble constructing or interpreting nonsymmetrical distributions.
- Use the mean fluently as a way to "check" answers. They seem to believe the mean and middle are basically equivalent measures.

Average as mathematical point of balance. Students with this predominant approach—

- View an average as a tool for making sense of the data.
- Look for a point of balance to represent the data.
- Take into account the values of all the data points.
- Use the mean with a beginning understanding of the quantitative relationships among data, total, and average; they are able to work from a given average to data, from a given average to total, from a given total to data.
- Break problems into smaller parts and find "sub-means" as a way to solve more difficult averaging problems.

Source: Mokros and Russell, 1995, p. 26.

FIGURE 15.19

Student #1

What is the average?

365; 401; 426; 376

1568

What is the average?

3,105; 3, 110; 3010

9225

Use the table below to answer the next two questions.

Attendance at Tournament	Wed.	Thurs.	Fri.
Adults	85	92	81
Students	121	152	102

What is the average number of adults who attended the tournament each day?

258

What is the average number of students who attended the tournament each day?

375

Tell how you knew the answer to the questions.

I know we are suppozed to add all the numbers together becus they not to use any one of them by yourself.

Student #2

What is the average?

365; 401; 426; 376

What is the average?

3,105; 3, 110; 3010

Use the table below to answer the next two questions.

Attendance at Tournament	Wed.	Thurs.	Fri.
Adults	85	92	81
Students	121	152	102

What is the average number of adults who attended the tournament each day?

85

What is the average number of students who attended the tournament each day?

121

Tell how you knew the answer to the questions.

I know it's always the middle number. That's what average means. If it's got 2 middle numbers you have to use both of them to be fair.

Two students' interpretation of the average.

Activity 15.15

PORTFOLIO

CREATING YOUR OWN RUBRIC FOR AVERAGES

MATERIALS

- Two journal entries of students working with the concept of averages

DIRECTIONS

Use these questions to help you start thinking about a rubric:

Activity Continues

1. What are the positive things that you see in both answers to the averages questions?
2. What are the misconceptions about averages that the children seem to have?
3. Is there a fair scale that could be used to give a numerical score to the creative work of both children?
   If yes, what is it?
   If no, what could you substitute instead of a numerical score?
4. What are the next steps you need to do to help both children continue to grow?

Activity Continues

5. Share your thoughts with others. See what your combined knowledge may be able to produce.

Supporting the NCTM *Principles and Standards* (2000):

- Mathematics as Reasoning/Patterning; Problem Solving; Communication
- Worthwhile Mathematical Tasks—The Teaching Principle
- Monitoring Students' Progress; Evaluating Students' Achievement—The Assessment Principle

SUMMARY

Graphing, statistics, and probability are important topics in mathematics. All three topics play a significant role in a child's education, from kindergarten through grade eight. Experimentation is essential to understanding the applications and concepts of probability and statistics. Graphs can be used to illustrate information and enhance problem solving as they are applied throughout the curriculum. Many situations in real life are based on the mathematics of this chapter. Numerous professions and businesses are dependent on the basics of graphing, probability, and statistics. Technology is making the exploration and application of these topics more an integral part of our life through newspaper graphics, tables, and charts. Therefore, the mathematics curriculum needs to emphasize these topics, throughout the curriculum and especially across the curriculum.

EXERCISES

For extended exercises, see the CD-ROM.

A. Memorization and Comprehension Exercises
Low-Level Thought Activities

1. Using a microcomputer graphing program, make a circle graph from the following information:

Exam Scores	Fractional Part	Percent	Degrees
160 students passed	$\frac{160}{320}$	50	180
100 students failed	$\frac{100}{320}$	31.25	112.5
60 students didn't take the test	$\frac{60}{320}$	18.75	67.5
Total: 320 students		100	360

2. Describe an activity that will help students differentiate among mean, median, and mode.
3. Describe an activity that will help students understand the probability of a specific outcome.
4. Describe an activity that illustrates mutually exclusive events.

B. Application and Analysis Exercises
Middle-Level Thought Activities

1. In the daily newspaper, locate five instances in which the idea of statistics must be understood before the reader can interpret the material.
2. During a conference, a parent asks you: "Why should my child have to study probability?" Write an answer for the parent.

C. Synthesis and Evaluation Exercises
High-Level Thought Activities

1. Develop a lesson plan illustrating the different uses of real, picture, bar, line, circle, and scatter graphs. Include the collection of data from the class. Use a microcomputer graphing program to illustrate each type of graph using the same data. Include questions to explore labels and results.
2. Develop a computer spreadsheet gradebook to use in your classroom. The general template could be used as on the CD-ROM. Include all the information you feel is important and convenient for you to keep accurate records. Other information could include student numbers/letter grades, standard deviation, and attendance records. Provide a

printout of the final template including the results of ten student records.

3. Create your own lesson and materials to teach graphing with children's literature. Use the work of Sgroi, et al. (1995) as an example. Think of other children's books from which you can make picture graphs and other kinds of graphs.
4. Create a probability game using a different arrangement for a probability path from the one seen in this chapter. Make a rubric that would evaluate a student's learning using the probability path.

BIBLIOGRAPHY

For an extended bibliography, see the CD-ROM.

Axelson, Sharon L. "Supermarket Challenge." *Arithmetic Teacher* 40 (October 1992): 84–88.

Bauman-Boatman, Janet, Gillian R. Clouthier, and Mary Kay Tornrose. "Reviewing and Viewing Etcetera." *Arithmetic Teacher* 40 (October 1992): 128–129.

Baratta-Lorton, Mary. *Mathematics Their Way.* Menlo Park, CA: Addison-Wesley, 1976.

Biehler, Rolf. "Functional Thinking with Graphs." *Journal for Research in Mathematics Education* 25 (November 1994): 526–533.

Bohan, Harry, Beverly Irby, and Dolly Vogel. "Problem Solving: Dealing with Data in the Elementary School." *Teaching Children Mathematics* 1 (January 1995): 256–260.

Choate, Laura Duncan, and JoAnn King Okey. *Graphing Primer, Grades K–2.* Palo Alto, CA: Dale Seymour Publications, 1989.

Darden, Phyllis, Ivadene Dhority, Grover Parsons, Steve Poppe, Reggie Rowland, and Rae F. Thompson. "Science/Math—Seventh & Eighth Grade." *Natural Resources in Mathematics and Science: Summer 1993.* Washington, DC: U.S. Bureau of Indian Affairs, 1993.

Dean, Ceri B., and Fran E. Mayeski. "Targeting Professional Development at Student Success." *Education Issues in the Heartland.* (Fall 1997): 23–29.

Freda, Andrew. "Roll the Dice—An Introduction to Probability." *Mathematics Teaching in the Middle School* 4 (October 1998): 85–89.

Habrock, Tanya, and Nancy Tanner Edwards. "Manipulatives or Personalized Math Problems: Which Is Better for Students-at-Risk?" Address. Central Regional Conference of the National Council of Teachers of Mathematics, Springfield, MO, 13 October 1995.

Haines, Joyce E., ed. *Culturally-Based Mathematics and Science Curriculum 1992.* Washington, DC: U.S. Bureau of Indian Affairs, 1992.

Kinneavy, Kevin. "The Pond: Doing Research Together." *Mathematics Teaching in the Middle School* 1 (March–April 1996): 696–702.

Leutzinger, Larry, Ed. *Mathematics in the Middle.* Reston, VA: National Council of Teachers of Mathematics, 1998.

Martin, Carol L., Becky Young Bear, Georgie Riley, John Wray, Vera M. Freeman, and Mary Stonehouse. "Math—Kindergarten Bar and Picture Graphs." *Culturally-Based Mathematics and Science Curriculum 1992.* Ed. Joyce E. Haines. Washington, DC: U.S. Bureau of Indian Affairs, 1992.

Mokros, Jan, and Susan Jo Russell. "Children's Concepts of Average and Representativeness." *Journal for Research in Mathematics Education* 26 (January 1995): 20–39.

Morrow, Jean, and Tes Mehring, ed. *Project A.I.M.: Assessment Activities and Rubrics for Mathematics.* Emporia, KS: The Teachers College, Emporia State University, 1993.

National Council of Teachers of Mathematics. *Curriculum and Evaluation Standards for School Mathematics.* Reston, VA: NCTM, 1989.

———. *Principles and Standards for School Mathematics.* Reston, VA: NCTM, 2000 (to be published).

———. *Mathematics Teaching in the Middle School.* Focus issue on Probability. 4 (May 1999): 493–557.

Reese, Clyde M., Karen E. Miller, John Mazzeo, and John A. Dossey. *NAEP 1996 Mathematics Report Card for the Nation and the States.* Washington, DC: National Center for Educational Statistics, 1997.

Riley, Georgie, and Mary Stonehouse. "Math—Kindergarten Bar and Picture Graphs." *Culturally-Based Mathematics and Science Curriculum 1992.* Ed. Joyce E. Haines. Washington, DC: U.S. Bureau of Indian Affairs, 1992.

Robinson, Stephanie O., and Donald J. Dessart. "Random-Number Generators: A Mysterious Use of Algorithms." Ed. Lorna J. Morrow and Margaret J. Kenney, *The Teaching and Learning of Algorithms in Scholl Mathematics.* 1998 Yearbook. Reston, VA: National Council of Teachers of Mathematics, 1998. 243–250.

Scavo, Thomas R., and Bryon Petraroja. "Adventures in Statistics" *Teaching Children Mathematics* 4 (March 1998): 394–400.

Sgroi, Laura A., Nancy Gropper, Mary Tom Kilker, Nancy M. Rambusch, and Barbara Semonite. "Assessing Young Children's Mathematical Understandings." *Teaching Children Mathematics* 1 (January 1995): 275–277.

Strong, Dorothy S. (Mathematics Ed.). *Systemwide Objectives and Standards.* Vols. 1–3. Chicago: Board of Education of the City of Chicago, 1990.

———. *Mathematics Instruction Planning Manual.* Chicago: Board of Education of the City of Chicago, 1991a.

———. *Mathematics Tutor Training Manual.* Chicago: Board of Education of the City of Chicago, 1991b.

Zawojewski, Judith S., ed. *Grades 5–8 Addenda Series: Dealing with Data and Chance.* Reston, VA: National Council of Teachers of Mathematics, 1991.

Zawojewski, Judith S., and David S. Heckman. "What Do Students Know about Data Analysis, Statistics, and Probability?" Results from the Sixth Mathematics Assessment of the National Assessment of Education Progress. Reston, VA: National Council of Teachers of Mathematics, 1997.

CHILDREN'S LITERATURE

Ash, Russell. *Incredible Comparisons.* New York: Dorling Kindersley, 1996.

Burns, Marilyn. *I Hate Mathematics Book.* Boston: Little, Brown, 1975.

———. *Math for Smarty Pants.* Boston: Little, Brown, 1982.

Clement, Rod. *Counting on Frank.* Milwaukee: Gareth Stevens Children's Books, 1991.

Cushman, Jean. *Do You Wanna Bet? Your Chance to Find Out about Probability.* New York: Clarion Books, 1991.

DiSpezio, Michael. *Visual Foolery.* Montreal: Tormont, 1995.

Morgan, Rowland. *In the Next Three Seconds.* New York: Lodestar Books, 1997.

Scieszka, Jon. *Math Curse.* New York: Viking, 1995.

Snape, Charles, and Heather Scott. *Puzzles, Mazes and Numbers.* London, England: Cambridge University Press, 1995.

Seuss, Dr. *Green Eggs and Ham.* New York: Random House, 1987.

Thiessen, Diane, Margaret Matthias, and Jacquelin Smith. *The Wonderful World of Mathematics.* 2nd ed. Reston, VA: National Council of Teachers of Mathematics, 1998.

Time Life for Children Staff. *From Head to Toe: Body Math.* Alexandria, VA: Time-Life for Children, 1993.

———. *The Mystery of Sunken Treasure: Sea Math.* Alexandria, VA: Time-Life for Children, 1993.

———. *Play Ball: Sports Math.* Alexandria, VA: Time-Life for Children, 1993.

Walpole, Brenda. *Speed.* Milwaukee: Gareth Stevens, 1995.

Integrating Technology

Video Vignette: Lesson Plans in Action

- *Graphing Possibility*

Extended Graphing Activities

- Name of Program: *Reading/Alphabet with Circle Graphs*
- Name of Program: *Circle Graphs*
- Name of Program: *Comparing Different Types of Graphs*
- Name of Program: *Spreadsheet for Graphing Activities*

Computer Software Resources

. . . for Graphing, Statistics, and Probability

Internet Searches

Surfing the Internet for Topics on Graphing, Statistics, and Probability

Use the World Wide Web (WWW) and navigate through the system, searching for new information under major headings and subheadings similar to the following:

Mathematics Education
  Discussion Groups on Graphing, Statistics, and Probability
  Discussion Groups on Use of the Graphing Calculator
  Interactive Bulletin Boards
Mathematics
  Graphing
  Probability
  Statistics
  Graphing Calculator
  Student Internet Pals playing probability games together
NCTM
  Problems Solving with Graphs, Statistics, Probability

- *Remember*. . . the Web is fluid . . . new topics and ways to search for topics change daily.
- Be adventurous . . . think of some new things you could try.

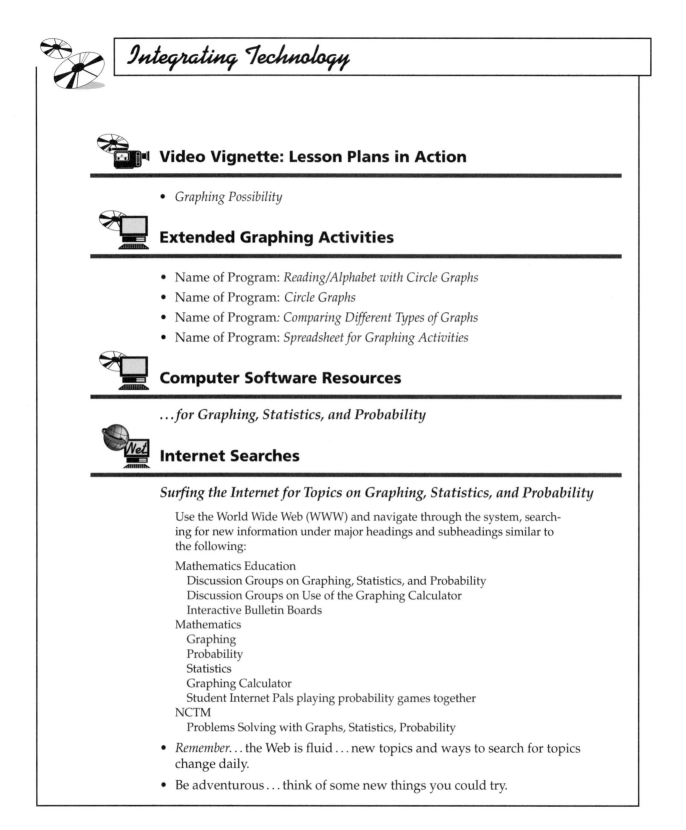

Appendix
Paper Models and Patterns

(Reduced size—full size in color on CD-ROM)

PAPER PATTERN BLOCKS

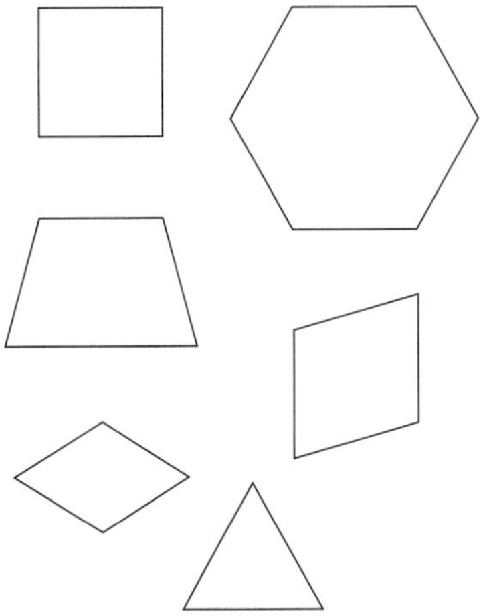

TANGRAM

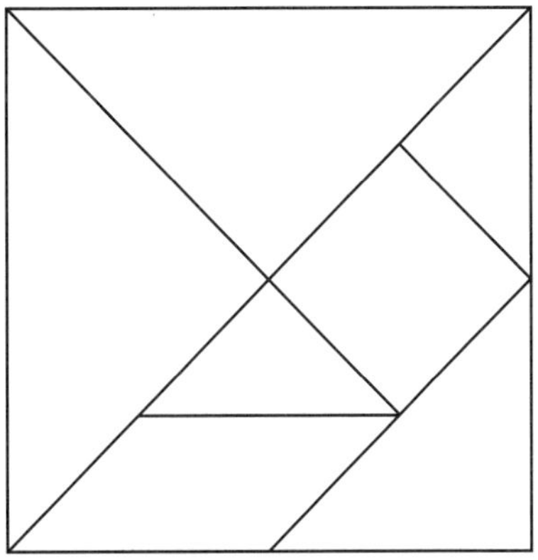

CIRCULAR FRACTION KIT

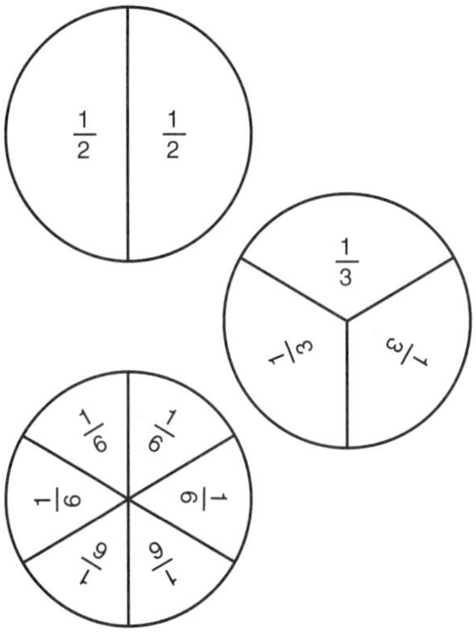

GEOBOARD RECORDING PAPER

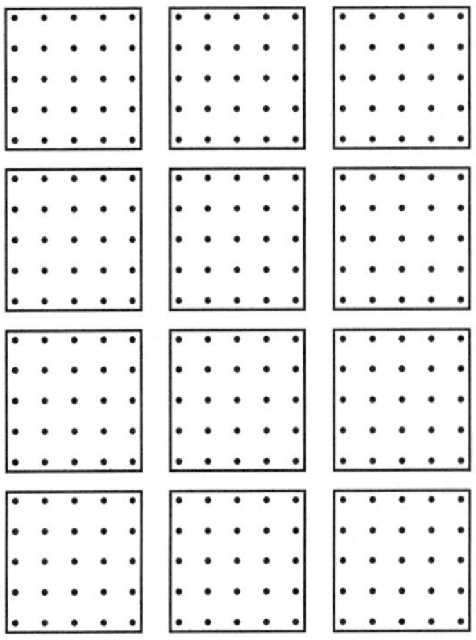

ISOMETRIC DOT PAPER

CENTIMETER GRID PAPER

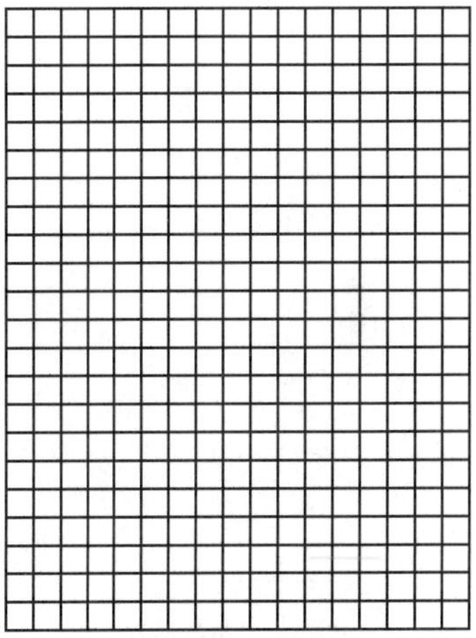

FRACTION BARS

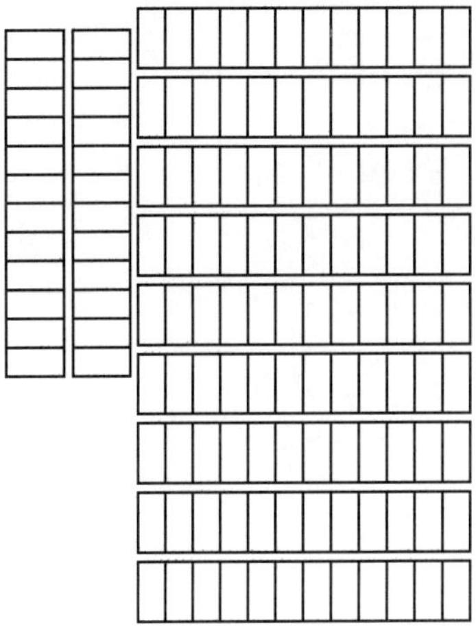

BASE 10 BLOCKS

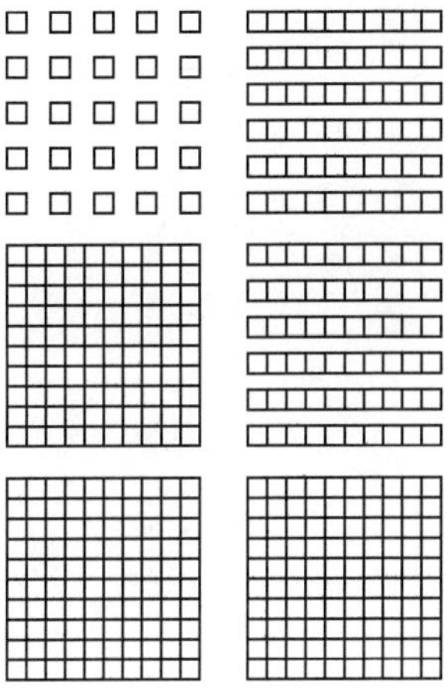

PENTOMINOES

CHIP TRADING MAT

Red	Green	Blue	Yellow

CHIP TRADING CHIPS

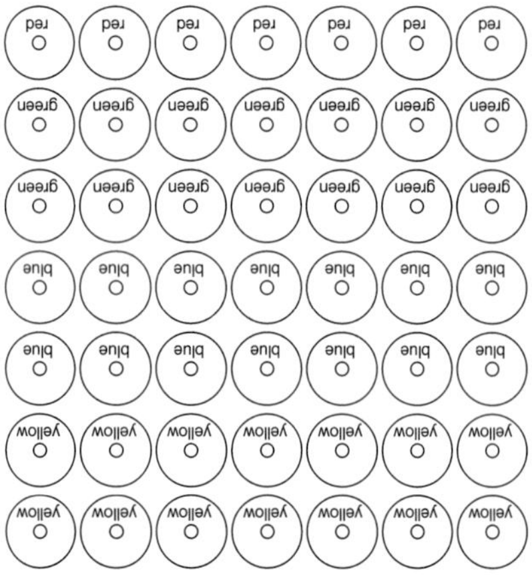

RECTANGULAR GEOBOARD TEMPLATE

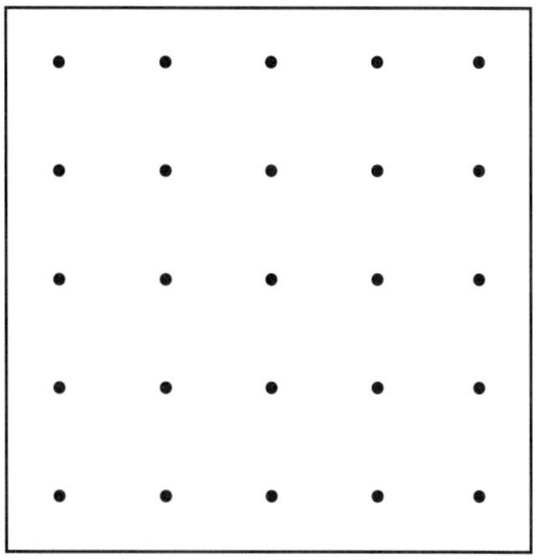

REGULAR POLYHEDRA

Cube (6 faces)

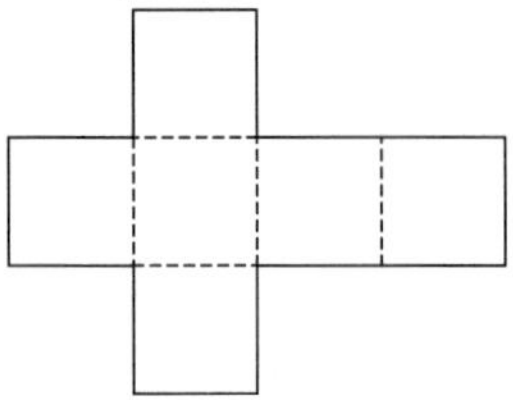

Octahedron (8 faces)

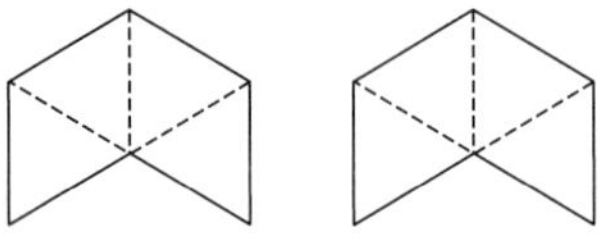

Tetrahedron (4 faces)

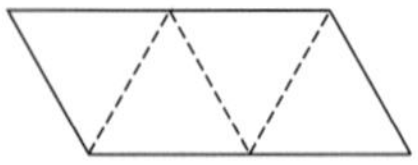

PRISM, PYRAMID, AND CYLINDER

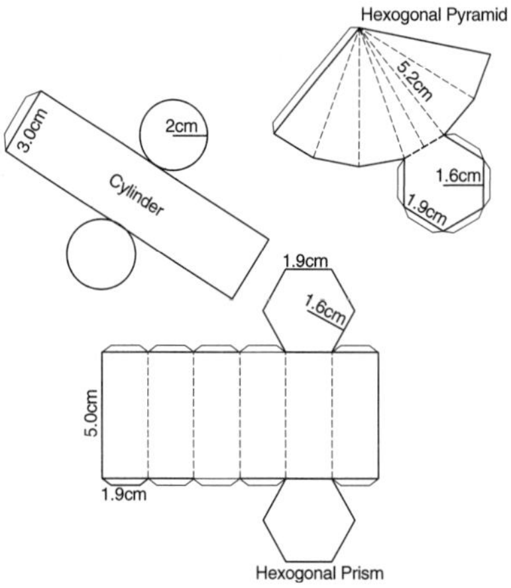

COMPASS

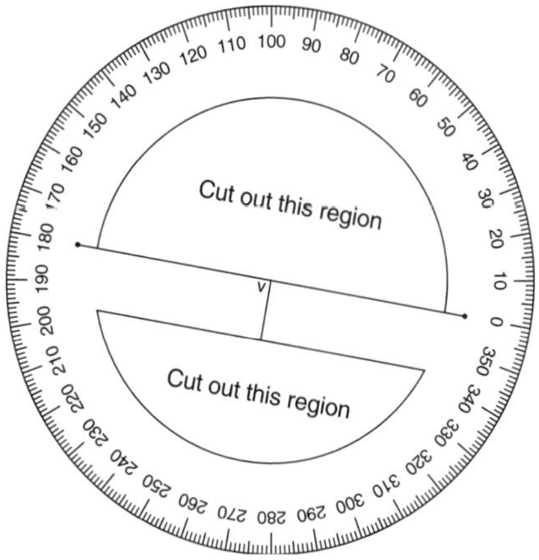

CUISENAIRE RODS

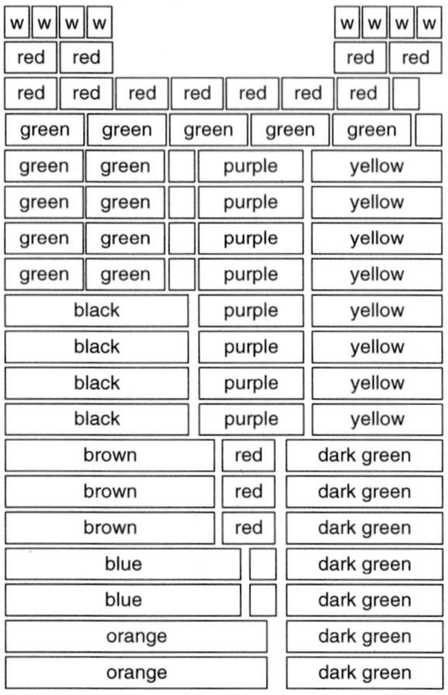

ATTRIBUTE PIECES

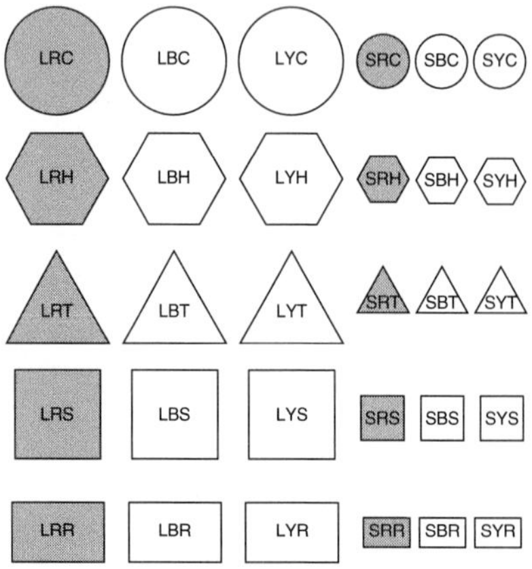

Index

Credits

Excerpts reprinted with permission from *Curriculum and Evaluation Standards for School Mathematics,* copyright 1989 by the National Council of Teachers of Mathematics. All rights reserved.

Excerpts reprinted with permission from *Professional Standards for Teaching Mathematics,* copyright 1991 by the National Council of Teachers of Mathematics. All rights reserved.

Excerpts reprinted with permission from *Assessment Standards for School Mathematics,* copyright 1995 by the National Council of Teachers of Mathematics. All rights reserved.

Excerpts reprinted with permission from *Principles and Standards for School Mathematics,* copyright 2000 (to be published) by the National Council of Teachers of Mathematics. All rights reserved.

Taxman game reprinted with permission from *Measuring Up: Prototypes for Mathematics Assessment.* Copyright © 1993 by the National Academy of Sciences. Courtesy of the National Academy Press, Washington, D.C.

Figure 12.11 adapted with permission from *Teaching Children Mathematics,* copyright 1995 by the National Council of Teachers of Mathematics. All rights reserved.

Emergency Medical Careers Activity on CD-ROM (Chapter 13), photos and excerpts reprinted courtesy of David P. Edwards, Clinical & Research Director, Richmond Ambulance Authority.

Figures 15.7 and 15.8 reprinted with permission from *Mathematics Teaching in the Middle School,* copyright 1998 by the National Council of Teachers of Mathematics. All rights reserved.